STATE IMMUNITY

Selected Materials and Commentary

State Immunity

Selected Materials and Commentary

ANDREW DICKINSON

RAE LINDSAY

JAMES P LOONAM

With a foreword by
Sir Robert Jennings, QC
*Formerly Whewell Professor of International
Law at Cambridge, and formerly Judge and
President of the International Court of Justice
in The Hague*

OXFORD
UNIVERSITY PRESS

OXFORD
UNIVERSITY PRESS

Great Clarendon Street, Oxford OX2 6DP

Oxford University Press is a department of the University of Oxford.
It furthers the University's objective of excellence in research, scholarship,
and education by publishing worldwide in

Oxford New York

Auckland Bangkok Buenos Aires Cape Town Chennai
Dar es Salaam Delhi Hong Kong Istanbul Karachi Kolkata
Kuala Lumpur Madrid Melbourne Mexico City Mumbai Nairobi
São Paulo Shanghai Taipei Tokyo Toronto

Oxford is a registered trade mark of Oxford University Press
in the UK and in certain other countries

Published in the United States
by Oxford University Press Inc., New York

British Library Cataloguing in Publication Data

Data available

Library of Congress Cataloging in Publication Data

Data available

ISBN 0–19–924326–3

1 3 5 7 9 10 8 6 4 2

Typeset by Newgen Imaging Systems (P) Ltd., Chennai, India
Printed in Great Britain
on acid-free paper by Biddles Ltd., King's Lynn

Foreword

by Sir Robert Jennings, QC

This is a felicitously new kind of law book: a collection of international and national legal materials in this often controversial area, with detailed commentary on the legal position in two leading jurisdictions. It is primarily for practitioners but will also interest academics. It seeks to satisfy a need for a clear and easily usable source and guide to the legal source materials needed for dealing with a class of legal problem which, if by no means new, is now very much commoner and more important in practice than ever before; that is to say, questions that consist of rules of international law that, for their effectiveness, have to be incorporated also in domestic systems of law where they are intended to be operated. Faced with a case or problem of this sort, practitioners have therefore to consult not only rules of public international law but also the corresponding rules of domestic legislation as well as decided cases of one or perhaps more domestic systems, and probably also rules of private international law. This is not so much, therefore, a "grey" area of law as an often very extensive area of highly complex and technical law combining different rules from different legal provenances. It is an area in which it is easy to fall into error unless all the relevant materials are brought together at the outset for a common consideration and assessment. A prime example of such an area is state immunity.

It would, moreover, be mistaken to assume that, because they derive from a common source in public international law, the ultimately applicable rules of law must be the same for all jurisdictions. There will inevitably be differences, not only because of differences between public laws of different jurisdictions but also because of differences, often subtle, of drafting methods and of legal cultures. The practical situation is therefore that for a particular case or problem, to know the public international law is only a beginning; and the differences of the meaning and effect of each international law rule as it is applied in different state jurisdictions can make differences of outcome in particular cases. In short, one normally has to consult the whole body of public international, municipal and private international laws. It is no longer possible or permissible in actual practice in this now very common kind of situation to be the old-fashioned straight and specialized public international law expert.

This situation demands a new approach to the exposition and explanation of this law. Happily, the kind of aid needed to lead one to the broad expanses of knowledge necessary for coping with this kind of situation is exemplified by the present work. Its plan is to set out the texts of principal international instruments as well as the corresponding domestic legislation in the United Kingdom or in the United States as the case might be (although at the end of this volume legislative materials from Australia, Canada, Pakistan, Singapore and South Africa are also usefully reproduced). The work also, reproduces other essential preparatory work for key international materials such as the Final Report of the International Law Commission and the European Convention on State Immunity.

In the case of the United Kingdom and the United States' legislation, following each section is what the authors call a "commentary". This might be a little open to misunderstanding. It is not, in the main, a commentary in the sense of the editors expressing their opinions. Instead, the commentary consists of pithy statements of the essential secondary sources needed for an understanding of the legislative provisions being dealt with. For example, the commentary gives references to any relevant case decisions with perhaps a brief description of the points on which the case should be consulted. It also, where relevant, indicates other sources such as, for example (in the case of the UK) for statutes, pertinent passages from Hansard, or the official "Explanatory Notes" provided when the draft Bill was presented to Parliament. The commentary even gives important negative information such as a comment on one section to the effect that there have been no cases involving that provision to date: a short comment but one which potentially might be a great saver of anxious and tedious searches.

As the authors explain, the endeavour has been to provide a pretty complete though brief statement of the factual materials that might be needed for the full study and understanding of the legal position at the time of writing of the texts of each instrument, whether international or domestic, that is the subject of this valuable kind of commentary: a factual statement of essential raw materials and where to find them.

In this valuable endeavour the authors have succeeded admirably. This volume amply provides the kind of basic research that a practising lawyer faced with a case or brief would need at the outset to do or have done. Each commentary has subheadings that make it easier to find one's way about (headings such as "Legislative history" and "Application"). The commentary is not a guide to the literature on these matters; that can be found in other reference series. All three authors have themselves considerable experience of working on state immunity cases in their own offices of Clifford Chance in London and New York, so they know very well from their own experience what is needed.

Those who find themselves involved in a state immunity case are now very fortunate to be able to have in convenient book form this kind of highly skilled and specialized work. One may say with assurance that, now that this publication is available, any practising lawyer, whether solicitor, attorney, counsel, judge or arbitrator, who is faced with a state immunity case yet fails to consult this splendid book fails to do so at his or her peril.

But this is much more than a working text for practitioners. It is remarkable how much more clearly the law on this important subject stands out when the core domestic and international texts are assembled, and illuminated by a commentary identifying the most relevant consideration and analysis of those texts. A "collection" it may be; but one which will assist scholars and practitioners to understand the limits and application of state immunity in two major common law jurisdictions. There is much that is similar between the two legal systems; but there are interesting divergences barely noticed by other writers. In the United States, immunity and jurisdiction are treated as indivisible; indeed, the courts seem also to treat immunity as a defence. In England, all three occupy distinct places in legal proceedings. Unless these important differences are understood, lawyers and diplomats may misconceive the role which immunity will continue to play in international relations between states.

RYJ

Cambridge, January 2004

Preface

The past 30 years have seen important legal developments in relation to the immunities and privileges enjoyed by the subjects of international law, not least the enactment in several jurisdictions of detailed legislation on these issues and important decisions of international and domestic courts. At the heart of these developments, claims by States and other persons acting under their authority to immunities and privileges before courts and tribunals are a continuing source of controversy (as evidenced, for example, by the decisions in the *Pinochet* and *Al-Adsani* cases, discussed in the commentary on the UK State Immunity Act 1978).

The idea of collecting together a volume of international materials on state immunity was first mooted in 2000, at a time when Clifford Chance was heavily involved in preparing for the International Law Association's 69th international conference in London. That an apparently straightforward exercise has taken some three years to come to maturity is due in part to the developments already noted, but is principally attributable to the editors' professional and family commitments. We are extremely grateful to our commissioning editor, John Louth, and his team for their patience and support.

Andrew Dickinson was principally responsible for collecting and arranging the materials in Parts 1, 2 and 5. He also prepared the commentary on the UK State Immunity Act 1978 in Part 4. James Loonam, with Rae Lindsay and a team of contributors at Clifford Chance in New York, was responsible for the United States' law materials and commentary in Part 3.

We are grateful to those in London, New York and elsewhere who have been involved in putting together this volume and offered guidance and support, including: Jeremy P Carver CBE, Laura Leibfreid, Ryan T Trainer, Bill Burke-White, Kerry McGrath, Laura Uberti, David L Cook, Clifford Bloomfield, Christina Taber-Kewene, Joan Papke, Christopher Land, Sujeet Mehta, Paxton J Marshall, Thomas Filardo, Christopher O'Rourke, Brian Lavin, Catherine Koh, Chrys Carey, Thomas Thornhill, Ariane West-Pernica, Amber Wessels, Victoria Dickerson, Carmel Weitzmann, Carl Jenkins, Maria Dolan, Katherine Gammon, Joanne Slater, Louize Green, Juliet Goy, Tomas Cerdan, Edu Prim and Pablo Cavallero.

Andrew Dickinson
James P Loonam
Rae Lindsay

November 2003

The Authors

Andrew Dickinson is a consultant to Clifford Chance LLP, having been a solicitor at the firm from 1997 to 2003. Andrew read law at St Edmund Hall, Oxford (MA, BCL). His main area of specialism is private international law, and he has published several articles in this field. He is a visiting fellow in private international law at the British Institute of International and Comparative Law. In his practice as a solicitor, he has regularly advised both state and non-state clients as to the immunities and privileges enjoyed by foreign sovereign states and other international legal persons. He is married to Ann Marie and they have a one-year old son, Jonathan.

Rae Lindsay is a partner in Clifford Chance LLP specializing in public and private international law. She is currently based in the New York office of Clifford Chance, having previously practised with the firm in London for 14 years. During her career with Clifford Chance, she has represented a number of states in litigation involving issues of state and/or diplomatic immunity, and has advised a variety of clients on many areas of the law relating to the privileges and immunities of international legal persons. She is a member of the International Law Association's Committee on the Accountability of International Organisations.

James P Loonam is an associate at the New York office of Clifford Chance US LLP. James is a member of the Litigation and Dispute Resolution department and he specializes in matters of international law. He graduated with Honours from the University of Connecticut, School of Law, where he was a member of the Connecticut Law Review.

Acknowledgements

Crown Copyright material is reproduced under Class Licence Number C01P0000148 with the permission of HMSO and the Queen's Printer for Scotland.

The European Convention on State Immunity (Convention, Additional Protocol, Explanatory Reports on the Convention and Additional Protocol, Reservations and Declarations) © Council of Europe is reproduced by kind permission of the Council of Europe.

The International Law Commission Final Draft Articles and Commentary on Jurisdictional Immunities of States and their Property (1991), the Report of the Ad Hoc Committee on Jurisdictional Immunities of States and Their Property (24–28 February 2003), and extracts from the Rome Statute of the International Criminal Court (Rome, 17 July 1998) are reproduced by kind permission of the United Nations. The United Nations is the author of the original material.

The International Law Association Revised Draft Articles for a Convention on State Immunity (Buenos Aires, 14–20 August 1994) are reproduced by kind permission of the International Law Association.

The Resolution of the Institut de Droit International on Contemporary Problems Concerning the Immunity of States in Relation to Questions of Jurisdiction and Enforcement (Basle, 2 September 1991) and L'Institut de Droit International: Resolution on Immunities from Jurisdiction and Execution of Heads of State and of Government in International Law (2001) are reproduced by kind permission of L'Institut de Droit International.

All Australian legislation herein is reproduced by permission but does not purport to be the official or authorised version. It is subject to Commonwealth of Australia copyright. The Australian *Copyright Act 1968* permits certain reproduction and publication of Commonwealth legislation and judgements. In particular, section 182A of the Act enables a complete copy to be made by or on behalf of a particular person. For reproduction or publication beyond that permitted by the Act, permission should be sought in writing. Requests should be addressed to Commonwealth Copyright Administration, Australian Government Department of Communications, Information Technology and the Arts, GPO Box 2154, Canberra ACT 2601, Australia or posted at http://www.dcita.gov.au/cca.

The Foreign States Immunities Act, No. 87 of 1981 as amended by the Foreign States Immunities Amendment Act, no. 48 of 1985, and the Foreign

States Immunities Amendment Act, No. 48 of 1985 are reproduced under the South African Government Printer's Copyright Authority No. 11175 dated 12 January 2004.

Every effort has been made to contact the owners of Copyright legislation reproduced in this book. We would be pleased to rectify any omissions in any reprinting or new edition of this work.

Table of Contents

PART 3 UNITED STATES OF AMERICA

PART 4 UNITED KINGDOM

PART 5 OTHER NATIONAL LEGISLATION

Table of Cases

Tables of Legislation and Other Materials

National Legislation

Argentina

Australia

Canada

People's Republic of China

Singapore

South Africa

United Kingdom

United States

USSR

Table of Abbreviations

1961 Vienna Convention	Vienna Convention on Diplomatic Relations 1961 (Cmnd 1368)
1963 Vienna Convention	Vienna Convention on Consular Relations 1963 (Cmnd 2113)
1978 Act	UK State Immunity Act 1978
AC	Appeal Cases (Law Reports)
All ER	All England Law Reports
BCLC	Butterworths Company Law Cases
Brussels Convention	Convention for the Unification of Certain Rules Concerning the Immunity of State-owned Ships (Brussels, 10 April 1926) (Cmnd 5672) and Additional Protocol (Brussels, 24 May 1934) (Cmnd 5673)
BYIL	British Yearbook of International Law
CA	Court of Appeal
Ch	Chancery (Law Reports)
Civil Procedure Rules	Civil Procedure Rules (SI 1998/3132, as amended)
Cm	Command Papers 1986–
Cmd	Command Papers 1919–1956
Cmnd	Command Papers 1957–1986
Comm	Commercial Court, Queen's Bench Division, High Court of England and Wales
Denza	Eileen Denza, *Diplomatic Law—Commentary on the Vienna Convention on Diplomatic Relations* (2nd edn, Oxford, 1998)
Dicey and Morris	Sir Lawrence Collins and others (ed.), *Dicey and Morris, The Conflict of Laws* (13th edn, London, 2000)
DLR	Dominion Law Reports (Canada)
EAT	Employment Appeals Tribunal
ECHR	European Convention on Human Rights
ECtHR	European Court of Human Rights
European Convention	European Convention on State Immunity (Basle, 16 May 1972) (Cmnd 5081; ETS No. 74).

EWHL, EWCA, EWHC	Neutral citations to English cases after 2001 (High Court after 2002)[1]
Explanatory Report	Explanatory Report to the European Convention on State Immunity
F 2d, 3d	Federal Reporter 2d, 3d Series
F Supp	Federal Supplement
FCO	Foreign and Commonwealth Office (UK)
Fox	Hazel Fox QC, *The Law of State Immunity* (Oxford, 2002)
FSIA	US Foreign Sovereign Immunities Act 1976 (28 U.S.C. §§ 1330, 1441(d), 1391(f) and 1602–1611)
HL	House of Lords
ICLQ	International and Comparative Law Quarterly
ICJ	International Court of Justice
ICR	Industrial Court Reports
ILA	International Law Association
ILC	International Law Commission
ILR	International Law Reports
ILRM	Irish Law Reports Monthly
IR	Irish Reports
Lee	Luke T Lee, *Consular Law and Practice* (Oxford, 1991)
Lewis	Charles J Lewis, *State and Diplomatic Immunity* (3rd edn, Oxford, 1990)
LNTS	League of Nations Treaty Series
Oppenheim	Sir Robert Jennings QC and Sir Arthur Watts KCMG QC (ed.), *Oppenheim's International Law* (9th edn, 1992)
PC	Privy Council
QB	Queen's Bench (Law Reports)
SI	Statutory Instrument
UK	United Kingdom of Great Britain and Northern Ireland
UN	United Nations
US	United States
YBILC	Yearbook of the International Law Commission

---

[1] If no other report cited, cases are unreported.

PART 1
TREATIES

Convention for the Unification of Certain Rules Concerning the   **1.001**
Immunity of State-owned Ships (Brussels, 10 April 1926)
and Additional Protocol (Brussels, 24 May 1934)[1]

[Convention: Translation of the original French text][2]

The President of the German Reich, His Majesty the King of the Belgians, the President of the Republic of Brazil, the President of the Republic of Chile, His Majesty the King of Denmark and Iceland, His Majesty the King of Spain, the Head of the Estonian State, the President of the French Republic, His Majesty the King of the United Kingdom of Great Britain, Ireland and the British Dominions beyond the Seas, Emperor of India, His Serene Highness the Regent of the Kingdom of Hungary, His Majesty the King of Italy, His Majesty the Emperor of Japan, the President of the Republic of Latvia, the President of the Republic of Mexico, His Majesty the King of Norway, Her Majesty the Queen of the Netherlands, the President of the Republic of Poland, the President of the Portuguese Republic, His Majesty the King of Romania, His Majesty the King of the Serbs, Croats and Slovenes, and His Majesty the King of Sweden.

Recognising the desirability of establishing by common agreement certain uniform rules concerning the immunity of State-owned ships, have decided to

---

[1] Referred to collectively below as the "Brussels Convention". Convention: Cmnd 5672; 176 LNTS 199. Protocol: Cmnd 5673; 176 LNTS 215. See Sucharitkul, *State Immunities and Trading Activities in International Law* (London, 1959), 92–100; Hudson, *International Legislation* (Washington, 1931–1949), vol iii, at 1837; Oppenheim, vol 1, para 565, esp. fn 13.

See also Convention on the High Seas (Geneva, 1958) (Cmnd 1929), Art 8 (immunity of warships), Art 9 (immunity of ships on government non-commercial service), Art 11 (jurisdiction in respect of collisions); Convention on the Territorial Sea and the Contiguous Zone (Geneva, 1958) (Cmnd 2511), Arts 14–17 (right of innocent passage), Arts 18–20 (rules applicable to merchant ships), Arts 21–22 (rules applicable to government ships other than warships), Art 23 (rule applicable to warships); United Nations Convention on the Law of the Sea (Montego Bay, 1982) (Cmnd 8941), Arts 17–26 (right of innocent passage), Arts 27–28 (rules applicable to merchant ships and government ships operated for commercial purposes), Arts 29–32 (rules applicable to warships and other government ships operated for non-commercial purposes), Art 95 (immunity of warships on the high seas), Art 96 (immunity of ships used only on government non-commercial service), Art 97 (penal jurisdiction in matters of collision or any other incident of navigation), Art 236 (state immunity-protection of marine environment). See generally Oppenheim, vol 1, paras 560–565.   [2] Source: Cmnd 5672 (HMSO).

conclude a convention to this effect and have designated as their plenipotentiaries, viz:

[List of plenipotentiaries omitted]

Who, having been duly authorised for this purpose, have agreed as follows:

1.002   Article 1

Sea-going ships owned or operated by States, cargoes owned by them, and cargoes and passengers carried on State-owned ships, as well as the States which own or operate such ships and own such cargoes shall be subject, as regards claims in respect of the operation of such ships or in respect of the carriage of such cargoes, to the same rules of liability and the same obligations as those applicable in the case of privately-owned ships, cargoes and equipment.

1.003   Article 2

As regards such liabilities and obligations, the rules relating to the jurisdiction of the Courts, rights of action and procedure shall be the same as for merchant ships belonging to private owners and for private cargoes and their owners.

1.004   Article 3

(1) The provisions of the two preceding Articles shall not apply to ships of war, State-owned yachts, patrol vessels, hospital ships, fleet auxiliaries, supply ships and other vessels owned or operated by a State and employed exclusively at the time when the cause of action arises on Government and non-commercial service, and such ships shall not be subject to seizure, arrest or detention by any legal process, nor to any proceedings *in rem*.

Nevertheless, claimants shall have the right to proceed before the appropriate Courts of the State which owns or operates the ship in the following cases:

   (i) claims in respect of collision or other accidents of navigation;
  (ii) claims in respect of salvage or in the nature of salvage and in respect of general average;
 (iii) claims in respect of repairs, supplies or other contracts relating to the ship;

and the State shall not be entitled to rely upon any immunity as a defence.

(2) The same rules shall apply to State-owned cargoes carried on board any of the above-mentioned ships.

(3) State-owned cargoes carried on board merchant ships for Government and non-commercial purposes shall not be subject to seizure, arrest or detention by any legal process nor to any proceedings *in rem*.

Nevertheless, claims in respect of collisions and nautical accidents, claims in respect of salvage or in the nature of salvage and in respect of general average, as well as claims in respect of contracts relating to such cargoes, may be brought before the Court which has jurisdiction in virtue of Article 2.

Article 4   1.005

States shall be entitled to rely on all defences, prescriptions and limitations of liability available to privately-owned ships and their owners.

Any necessary adaptation or modification of provisions relating to such defences, prescriptions and limitations of liability for the purpose of making them applicable to ships of war or to the State-owned ships specified in Article 3 shall form the subject of a special Convention to be concluded hereafter. In the meantime, the measures necessary for this purpose may be effected by national legislation in conformity with the spirit and principles of this Convention.

Article 5   1.006

If in any proceedings to which Article 3 applies there is, in the opinion of the Court, a doubt on the question of the Government and non-commercial character of the ship or the cargo, a certificate signed by the diplomatic representative of the contracting State to which the ship or the cargo belongs, communicated to the Court through the Government of the State before whose Courts and Tribunals the case is pending, shall be conclusive evidence that the ship or the cargo falls within the terms of Article 3, but only for the purpose of obtaining the discharge of any seizure, arrest or detention effected by judicial process.

Article 6   1.007

The provisions of the present Convention shall be applied in each contracting State, but without any obligation to extend the benefit thereof to non-contracting States and their nationals, and with the right in making any such extension to impose a condition of reciprocity.

Nothing in the present Convention shall be held to prevent a contracting State from prescribing by its own laws the rights of its national before its own Courts.

Article 7   1.008

In time of war each contracting State reserves to itself the right of suspending the application of the present Convention by a declaration notified to the other contracting States, to the effect that neither ships owned or operated by that State, nor cargoes owned by it shall be subject to any arrest, seizure or detention by a foreign Court of law. But the claimant shall have the right to take proceedings before the appropriate Court in accordance with Articles 2 and 3.

1.009 **Article 8**

Nothing in the present Convention shall prejudice the right of the contracting States to take any measures necessitated by the rights and duties of neutrality.

1.010 **Article 9**

After the expiration of a period of not more than two years from the date on which the Convention is signed, the Belgian Government shall communicate with the Governments of the high contracting parties which have declared themselves ready to ratify it with a view to deciding whether it shall be put into force. Ratifications shall be deposited at Brussels at a date which shall be fixed by agreement between the said Governments. The first deposit of ratifications shall be recorded in a *procès-verbal* signed by the representatives of the States which are parties to it and by the Belgian Minister for Foreign Affairs.

Each subsequent deposit of ratifications shall be made by means of a written notification addressed to the Belgian Government and accompanied by the instrument of ratification.

A duly certified copy of the *procès-verbal* relating to the first deposit of ratifications and the notifications mentioned in the preceding paragraph, as well as the instruments of ratification which accompanied them, shall be sent forthwith by the Belgian Government through the diplomatic channel to the States which have signed the present Convention, or which have acceded to it. In the cases contemplated in the preceding paragraph the Belgian Government shall state at the same time the date on which it received the notification.

1.011 **Article 10**

Non-signatory States may accede to the present Convention whether or not they were represented at the International Conference at Brussels.

A State which desires to accede shall notify its intention in writing to the Belgian Government, and shall at the same time transmit to that Government the document of accession which shall be deposited in the archives of the Belgian Government.

The Belgian Government shall transmit immediately to all the States which have signed or acceded to the Convention a duly certified copy of the notification and of the instrument of accession, stating the date on which it received the notification.

1.012 **Article 11**

The high contracting parties may at the time of signature, deposit of ratification or accession, declare that their acceptance of the present Convention does not apply to any one or more of the self-governing Dominions, colonies, possessions, protectorates or overseas territories under their sovereignty or authority. They may subsequently accede separately in the name of any of such self-governing Dominions, colonies, possessions, protectorates or overseas territories excluded in their original declaration. They may also in accordance with its provisions denounce the present Convention separately in respect of each or any of such self-governing Dominions, colonies, possessions, protectorates or overseas territories under their sovereignty or authority.

Article 12   1.013

In the case of States which have taken part in the first deposit of ratifications, the present Convention shall take effect one year after the date of the *procès-verbal* of that deposit. As regards the States which ratify the Convention subsequently, or which accede to it, and also in cases in which the Convention is subsequently put into force in accordance with Article 11, it shall take effect six months after the notifications mentioned in Article 9, paragraph 2, and in Article 10, paragraph 2, have been received by the Belgian Government.

Article 13   1.014

In the event of one of the contracting States wishing to denounce the present Convention, the denunciation shall be notified in writing to the Belgian Government, which shall immediately communicate a duly certified copy thereof to all the other States, at the same time informing them of the date on which it was received. The denunciation shall operate only in respect of the State which has made the notification and be effective one year after the notification has reached the Belgian Government.

Article 14   1.015

Each Contracting State shall have the right to call for a new Conference for the purpose of considering possible amendments to the present Convention.

Any State which proposes to exercise this right shall notify its intention one year in advance to the other States through the Belgian Government, which will assume the duty of summoning the Conference.

Done at Brussels, in a single copy, the 10th April, 1926

[List of signatories omitted]

[Additional Protocol: Translation of the original French text][3]   1.016

The Governments signatory to the International Convention for the Unification of certain Rules concerning the Immunity of State-owned Ships, recognising the

---

[3] Source: Cmnd 5673 (HMSO).

necessity of making clearer certain provisions of the Convention, have appointed the undersigned plenipotentiaries, who, having communicated their respective full powers found in good and due form, have agreed as follows:

1.017   I.

Whereas it has been doubted whether, and to what extent, the expression "exploités par lui"[4] in article 3 of the Convention extends or could be construed as extending to ships chartered by a State, whether for time or voyage, it is hereby declared for the purpose of removing such doubts, as follows:

> "Ships on charter to a State, whether for time or voyage, while exclusively engaged on governmental and non-commercial service, and cargoes carried therein, shall not be subject to any arrest, seizure or detention whatsoever, but this immunity shall not prejudice in any other respect any rights or remedies accruing to the parties concerned. A certificate given by a diplomatic representative of the State concerned in manner provided by article 5 of the Convention shall be conclusive evidence of the nature of the service on which the ship is engaged."

1.018   II.

For the purpose of the exception provided by article 3, paragraph 1, it is understood that the ownership or operation of a ship acquired or operated by a State at the time when steps by way of seizure, arrest or detention are taken has the same legal consequences as ownership or operation at the time when the cause of action arises.

That article may accordingly be invoked by States in favour of ships belonging to or operated by them at the time when steps are taken by way of seizure, arrest or detention, if the ships are engaged exclusively in Government and non-commercial service.

1.019   III.

It is understood that nothing in the provisions of article 5 of the Convention prevents Governments interested from themselves appearing before the Court in which the legal proceedings are pending in accordance with the procedure prescribed by the national law, and producing to it the certificate contemplated by the said article.

1.020   IV.

Inasmuch as the Convention in no respect affects the rights and obligations of belligerents and neutrals, article 7 does not in any way prejudice the jurisdiction of duly constituted Prize Courts.

---

[4] The words "appartenant à un État ou exploités par lui" appear in the English translation of the Convention as "owned or operated by a State" (see 1.004 above).

V.

1.021

It is agreed that nothing contained in the provisions of article 2 of the Convention shall limit or affect in any way the application of rules of procedure prescribed by national law with regard to proceedings to which the State is a Party.

VI.

1.022

Where any question of the furnishing of evidence or production of documents arises and the Government concerned is of opinion that the furnishing of such evidence or the production of such documents would be detrimental to its national interests, the said Government may decline to furnish such evidence or to produce such documents by pleading the necessity of safeguarding national interests.

In faith whereof the undersigned duly authorised by their Governments have signed the present supplementary protocol which shall be considered as forming an integral part of the Convention of the 10th April, 1926, to which it relates.

Done at Brussels, the 24th May, 1934, in a single copy, which shall remain in the archives of the Belgian Government.

[List of signatories omitted]

Signatures, Accessions and Ratifications[5]

1.023

[State (*original signatory); Date of accession or ratification; Date of entry into force]

Argentina; 19.04.1961; 19.10.1961
Belgium*; 08.01.1936; 08.01.1937
Brazil*; 08.01.1936; 08.01.1937
Chile*; 08.01.1936; 08.01.1937
Cyprus; 19.07.1988;19.01.1989
Denmark*; 16.11.1950; 16.05.1951
Egypt[6]; 17.2.1960;17.8.1960
Estonia*; 08.01.1936; 08.01.1937
France*; 27.07.1955; 27.01.1956
Germany*[7]; 27.06.1936; 08.01.1937
Greece; 19.05.1951;19.11.1951
Hungary*; 08.01.1936; 08.01.1937
Italy*; 27.01.1937; 27.07.1937

---

[5] As at 2003 (Source: Belgian Ministry of Foreign Affairs—http://www.diplomatie.be/fr/word/treaties/i6.doc). [6] By the accession of the United Arab Republic.
[7] Convention reinstated as from 1.11.1953 between, on the one hand, the German Federal Republic and, on the other hand, the Allied Powers except Hungary, Poland and Romania.

Libya[8]; 27.01.1937; 27.07.1937
Luxembourg; 18.02.1991;18.08.1991
Madagascar[9]; 27.07.1955; 27.01.1956
Mexico*[10]; – ; –
Netherlands*[11]; 08.07.1936; 08.01.1967
Norway*; 25.04.1939; 25.10.1939
Poland*[12]; 08.01.1936; 08.01.1937
Portugal*; 27.06.1938; 27.12.1938
Romania[13]; 04.08.1937; 04.02.1938
Somalia[14]; 27.01.1937; 27.07.1937
Spain*[15]; – ; –
Surinam[16]; 08.07.1936; 08.01.1937
Sweden*; 01.07.1938; 01.01.1939
Switzerland; 28.05.1954; 28.11.1954
Syria[17]; 17.02.1960;17.08.1960
Turkey; 04.07.1955; 04.01.1956
United Kingdom*[18]; 03.07.1979; 03.01.1980
Uruguay; 15.09.1970;15.03.1971
Yugoslavia*[19]; – ; –
Zaire; 17.07.1967;17.01.1968

1.024   **Declarations and Reservations of the United Kingdom**

(1) *Reservations*

We reserve the right to apply Article 1 of the Convention to any claim in respect of a ship which falls within the Admiralty jurisdiction of Our courts, or of Our Courts in any territory in respect of which We are party to the Convention.

---

[8] By the ratification of Italy.
[9] By the ratification of France, conforming to Art 11. Confirmation of the Malagasy Republic registered on 13.07.1965.   [10] Mexico has signed but not ratified the Convention and Protocol.
[11] By a *note verbale* received on 03.01.1986, the Kingdom of the Netherlands notified that the Convention and Protocol should apply to the Kingdom in Europe, the Netherlands Antilles and Aruba effective from 1.01.1986.
[12] Convention denounced on 17.03.1952, effective from 17.03.1953. New ratification on 16.07.1976, effective from 16.01.1977. Excludes the Free Port of Danzig.
[13] Convention denounced on 21.09.1959, effective from 21.09.1960.
[14] By the ratification of Italy for Italian Somalia.
[15] Spain has signed but not ratified the Convention and Protocol.
[16] By the ratification of the Netherlands.
[17] By the accession of the United Arab Republic, confirmed by Syrian Arab Republic on 8.10.1962.
[18] The United Kingdom has since ratified the treaty in respect of Bailiwick of Guernsey, Bailiwick of Jersey and the Isle of Man; 17.11.1987; 19.05.1988. See Reservations and Declaration below.
[19] Convention signed by the Kingdom of Serbs, Croats and Slovenes. Protocol signed by Yugoslavia. Yugoslavia has not ratified the Convention and Protocol. For international and UK practice on the succession by the Federal Republic of Yugoslavia, Bosnia Her, Croatia, Macedonia and Slovenia to treaties entered into by the former Socialist Federal Republic of Yugoslavia, see Aust, *Modern Treaty Law and Practice* (Cambridge, 2000), 315–317.

We reserve the right, with respect to Article 2 of the Convention, to apply in proceedings concerning another High Contracting Party or ship of another High Contracting Party the rules of procedure set out in Chapter II of the European Convention on State Immunity, signed at Basle on the Sixteenth day of May in the Year of Our Lord One thousand Nine hundred and Seventy-two.

In order to give effect to the terms of any international agreement with a non-Contracting State, We reserve the right to make special provision

(a) as regards the delay or arrest of a ship or cargo belonging to such a State, and

(b) to prohibit seizure of or execution against such a ship or cargo.

(2) *Declaration (see Art. 11 of la Convention)*

The Convention and the Protocol are not applicable to the following territories: Bailiwick of Guernsey, Bailiwick of Jersey, Isle of Man,[20] Bermuda, British Territory of the Indian Ocean, Gibraltar.

---

[20] The United Kingdom has since ratified the Convention in respect of Guernsey, Jersey and the Isle of Man (see fn 18 above).

1.025 European Convention on State Immunity[21],
Additional Protocol and Explanatory Reports

European Convention on State Immunity

Preamble

The member States of the Council of Europe, signatory hereto,

Considering that the aim of the Council of Europe is to achieve a greater unity between its Members;

Taking into account the fact that there is in international law a tendency to restrict the cases in which a State may claim immunity before foreign courts;

Desiring to establish in their mutual relations common rules relating to the scope of the immunity of one State from the jurisdiction of the courts of another State, and designed to ensure compliance with judgments given against another State;

Considering that the adoption of such rules will tend to advance the work of harmonisation undertaken by the member States of the Council of Europe in the legal field.

Have agreed as follows:

CHAPTER I

Immunity from jurisdiction

1.026 **Article 1**

1. A Contracting State which institutes or intervenes in proceedings before a court of another Contracting State submits, for the purpose of those proceedings, to the jurisdiction of the courts of that State.

2. Such a Contracting State cannot claim immunity from the jurisdiction of the courts of the other Contracting State in respect of any counterclaim:

   (a) arising out of the legal relationship or the facts on which the principal claim is based;

   (b) if, according to the provisions of this Convention, it would not have been entitled to invoke immunity in respect of that counterclaim had separate proceedings been brought against it in those courts.

3. A Contracting State which makes a counterclaim in proceedings before a court of another Contracting State submits to the jurisdiction of the courts

---

[21] Referred to below as the "European Convention". Basle, 16 May 1972; Cmnd 5081; ETS No 74. See Sinclair (1973) 22 ICLQ 254 and the other materials cited by Oppenheim, vol 1, 343, fn 8.

of that State with respect not only to the counterclaim but also to the principal claim.

Article 2   1.027

A Contracting State cannot claim immunity from the jurisdiction of a court of another Contracting State if it has undertaken to submit to the jurisdiction of that court either:

(a) by international agreement;
(b) by an express term contained in a contract in writing; or
(c) by an express consent given after a dispute between the parties has arisen.

Article 3   1.028

1. A Contracting State cannot claim immunity from the jurisdiction of a court of another Contracting State if, before claiming immunity, it takes any step in the proceedings relating to the merits. However, if the State satisfies the court that it could not have acquired knowledge of facts on which a claim to immunity can be based until after it has taken such a step, it can claim immunity based on these facts if it does so at the earliest possible moment.

2. A Contracting State is not deemed to have waived immunity if it appears before a court of another Contracting State in order to assert immunity.

Article 4   1.029

1. Subject to the provisions of Article 5, a Contracting State cannot claim immunity from the jurisdiction of the courts of another Contracting State if the proceedings relate to an obligation of the State, which, by virtue of a contract, falls to be discharged in the territory of the State of the forum.

2. Paragraph 1 shall not apply:
   (a) in the case of a contract concluded between States;
   (b) if the parties to the contract have otherwise agreed in writing;
   (c) if the State is party to a contract concluded on its territory and the obligation of the State is governed by its administrative law.

Article 5   1.030

1. A Contracting State cannot claim immunity from the jurisdiction of a court of another Contracting State if the proceedings relate to a contract of employment between the State and an individual where the work has to be performed on the territory of the State of the forum.

2. Paragraph 1 shall not apply where:
   (a) the individual is a national of the employing State at the time when the proceedings are brought;

(b) at the time when the contract was entered into the individual was neither a national of the State of the forum nor habitually resident in that State; or

(c) the parties to the contract have otherwise agreed in writing, unless, in accordance with the law of the State of the forum, the courts of that State have exclusive jurisdiction by reason of the subject-matter.

3. Where the work is done for an office, agency or other establishment referred to in Article 7, paragraphs 2 (a) and (b) of the present Article apply only if, at the time the contract was entered into, the individual had his habitual residence in the Contracting State which employs him.

1.031   Article 6

1. A Contracting State cannot claim immunity from the jurisdiction of a court of another Contracting State if it participates with one or more private persons in a company, association or other legal entity having its seat, registered office or principal place of business on the territory of the State of the forum, and the proceedings concern the relationship, in matters arising out of that participation, between the State on the one hand and the entity or any other participant on the other hand.

2. Paragraph 1 shall not apply if it is otherwise agreed in writing.

1.032   Article 7

1. A Contracting State cannot claim immunity from the jurisdiction of a court of another Contracting State if it has on the territory of the State of the forum an office, agency or other establishment through which it engages, in the same manner as a private person, in an industrial, commercial or financial activity, and the proceedings relate to that activity of the office, agency or establishment.

2. Paragraph 1 shall not apply if all the parties to the dispute are States, or if the parties have otherwise agreed in writing.

1.033   Article 8

A Contracting State cannot claim immunity from the jurisdiction of a court of another Contracting State if the proceedings relate:

(a) to a patent, industrial design, trade-mark, service mark or other similar right which, in the State of the forum, has been applied for, registered or deposited or is otherwise protected, and in respect of which the State is the applicant or owner;

(b) to an alleged infringement by it, in the territory of the State of the forum, of such a right belonging to a third person and protected in that State;

(c) to an alleged infringement by it, in the territory of the State of the forum, of copyright belonging to a third person and protected in that State;

(d) to the right to use a trade name in the State of the forum.

Article 9 1.034

A Contracting State cannot claim immunity from the jurisdiction of a court of another Contracting State if the proceedings relate to:

(a) its rights or interests in, or its use or possession of, immovable property; or

(b) its obligations arising out of its rights or interests in, or use or possession of, immovable property

and the property is situated in the territory of the State of the forum.

Article 10 1.035

A Contracting State cannot claim immunity from the jurisdiction of a court of another Contracting State if the proceedings relate to a right in movable or immovable property arising by way of succession, gift or *bona vacantia*.

Article 11 1.036

A Contracting State cannot claim immunity from the jurisdiction of a court of another Contracting State in proceedings which relate to redress for injury to the person or damage to tangible property, if the facts which occasioned the injury or damage occurred in the territory of the State of the forum, and if the author of the injury or damage was present in that territory at the time when those facts occurred.

Article 12 1.037

1. Where a Contracting State has agreed in writing to submit to arbitration a dispute which has arisen or may arise out of a civil or commercial matter, that State may not claim immunity from the jurisdiction of a court of another Contracting State on the territory or according to the law of which the arbitration has taken or will take place in respect of any proceedings relating to:

    (a) the validity or interpretation of the arbitration agreement;
    (b) the arbitration procedure;
    (c) the setting aside of the award,

    unless the arbitration agreement otherwise provides.

2. Paragraph 1 shall not apply to an arbitration agreement between States.

1.038 Article 13

Paragraph 1 of Article 1 shall not apply where a Contracting State asserts, in proceedings pending before a court of another Contracting State to which it is not a party, that it has a right or interest in property which is the subject-matter of the proceedings, and the circumstances are such that it would have been entitled to immunity if the proceedings had been brought against it.

1.039 Article 14

Nothing in this Convention shall be interpreted as preventing a court of a Contracting State from administering or supervising or arranging for the administration of property, such as trust property or the estate of a bankrupt, solely on account of the fact that another Contracting State has a right or interest in the property.

1.040 Article 15

A Contracting State shall be entitled to immunity from the jurisdiction of the courts of another Contracting State if the proceedings do not fall within Articles 1 to 14; the court shall decline to entertain such proceedings even if the State does not appear.

CHAPTER II

Procedural rules

1.041 Article 16

1. In proceedings against a Contracting State in a court of another Contracting State, the following rules shall apply.

2. The competent authorities of the State of the forum shall transmit

 —the original or a copy of the document by which the proceedings are instituted;

 —a copy of any judgment given by default against a State which was defendant in the proceedings,

 through the diplomatic channel to the Ministry of Foreign Affairs of the defendant State, for onward transmission, where appropriate, to the competent authority. These documents shall be accompanied, if necessary, by a translation into the official language, or one of the official languages, of the defendant State.

3. Service of the documents referred to in paragraph 2 is deemed to have been effected by their receipt by the Ministry of Foreign Affairs.

4. The time-limits within which the State must enter an appearance or appeal against any judgment given by default shall begin to run two months after the

date on which the document by which the proceedings were instituted or the copy of the judgment is received by the Ministry of Foreign Affairs.

5. If it rests with the court to prescribe the time-limits for entering an appearance or for appealing against a judgment given by default, the court shall allow the State not less than two months after the date on which the document by which the proceedings are instituted or the copy of the judgment is received by the Ministry of Foreign Affairs.

6. A Contracting State which appears in the proceedings is deemed to have waived any objection to the method of service.

7. If the Contracting State has not appeared, judgment by default may be given against it only if it is established that the document by which the proceedings were instituted has been transmitted in conformity with paragraph 2, and that the time-limits for entering an appearance provided for in paragraphs 4 and 5 have been observed.

Article 17 1.042

No security, bond or deposit, however described, which could not have been required in the State of the forum of a national of that State or a person domiciled or resident there, shall be required of a Contracting State to guarantee the payment of judicial costs or expenses. A State which is a claimant in the courts of another Contracting State shall pay any judicial costs or expenses for which it may become liable.

Article 18 1.043

A court before which proceedings to which a Contracting State is a Contracting State may not be subjected to any measure of coercion, or any penalty, by reason of its failure or refusal to disclose any documents or other evidence. However the court may draw any conclusion it thinks fit from such failure or refusal.

Article 19 1.044

1. A court before which proceedings to which a Contracting State is a party are instituted shall, at the request of one of the parties or, if its national law so permits, of its own motion, decline to proceed with the case or shall stay the proceedings if other proceedings between the same parties, based on the same facts and having the same purpose:
   (a) are pending before a court of that Contracting State and were the first to be instituted; or
   (b) are pending before a court of any other Contracting State, were the first to be instituted and may result in a judgment to which the State

party to the proceedings must give effect by virtue of Article 20 or Article 25.

2. Any Contracting State whose law gives the courts a discretion to decline to proceed with a case or to stay the proceedings in cases where proceedings between the same parties, based on the same facts and having the same purpose, are pending before a court of another Contracting State, may, by notification addressed to the Secretary General of the Council of Europe, declare that its courts shall not be bound by the provisions of paragraph 1.

CHAPTER III

Effect of Judgment

1.045 Article 20

1. A Contracting State shall give effect to a judgment given against it by a court of another Contracting State:

   (a) if, in accordance with the provisions of Articles 1 to 13, the State could not claim immunity from jurisdiction; and

   (b) if the judgment cannot or can no longer be set aside if obtained by default, or if it is not or is no longer subject to appeal or any other form of ordinary review or to annulment.

2. Nevertheless, a Contracting State is not obliged to give effect to such a judgment in any case:

   (a) where it would be manifestly contrary to public policy in that State to do so, or where, in the circumstances, either party had no adequate opportunity fairly to present his case;

   (b) where proceedings between the same parties, based on the same facts and having the same purpose:

      (i) are pending before a court of that State and were the first to be instituted;

      (ii) are pending before a court of another Contracting State, were the first to be instituted and may result in a judgment to which the State party to the proceedings must give effect under the terms of this Convention;

   (c) where the result of the judgment is inconsistent with the result of another judgment given between the same parties:

      (i) by a court of the Contracting State, if the proceedings before that court were the first to be instituted or if the other judgment has been given before the judgment satisfied the conditions specified in paragraph 1(b); or

(ii) by a court of another Contracting State where the other judgment is the first to satisfy the requirements laid down in the present Convention;

(d) where the provisions of Article 16 have not been observed and the State has not entered an appearance or has not appealed against a judgment by default.

3. In addition, in the cases provided for in Article 10, a Contracting State is not obliged to give effect to the judgment:

(a) if the courts of the State of the forum would not have been entitled to assume jurisdiction had they applied, mutatis mutandis, the rules of jurisdiction (other than those mentioned in the Annex to the present Convention) which operate in the State against which judgment is given; or

(b) if the court, by applying a law other than that which would have been applied in accordance with the rules of private international law of that State, has reached a result different from that which would have been reached by applying the law determined by those rules.

However, a Contracting State may not rely upon the grounds of refusal specified in sub-paragraphs (a) and (b) above if it is bound by an agreement with the State of the forum on the recognition and enforcement of judgments and the judgment fulfils the requirement of that agreement as regards jurisdiction and, where appropriate, the law applied.

Article 21   1.046

1. Where a judgment has been given against a Contracting State and that State does not give effect thereto, the party which seeks to invoke the judgment shall be entitled to have determined by the competent court of that State the question whether effect should be given to the judgment in accordance with Article 20. Proceedings may also be brought before this court by the State against which judgment has been given, if its law so permits.

2. Save in so far as may be necessary for the application of Article 20, the competent court of the State in question may not review the merits of the judgment.

3. Where proceedings are instituted before a court of a State in accordance with paragraph 1:

(a) the parties shall be given an opportunity to be heard in the proceedings;

(b) documents produced by the party seeking to invoke the judgment shall not be subject to legalisation or any other like formality;

(c) no security, bond or deposit, however described, shall be required of the party invoking the judgment by reason of his nationality, domicile or residence;

(d) the party invoking the judgment shall be entitled to legal aid under conditions no less favourable than those applicable to nationals of the State who are domiciled and resident therein.

4. Each Contracting State shall, when depositing its instrument of ratification, acceptance or accession, designate the court or courts referred to in paragraph 1, and inform the Secretary General of the Council of Europe thereof.

1.047   Article 22

1. A Contracting State shall give effect to a settlement to which it is a party and which has been made before a court of another Contracting State in the course of the proceedings; the provisions of Article 20 do not apply to such a settlement.

2. If the State does not give effect to the settlement, the procedure provided for in Article 21 may be used.

1.048   Article 23

No measures of execution or preventive measures against the property of a Contracting State may be taken in the territory of another Contracting State except where and to the extent that the State has expressly consented thereto in writing in any particular case.

CHAPTER IV

Optional provisions

1.049   Article 24

1. Notwithstanding the provisions of Article 15, any State may, when signing this Convention or depositing its instrument of ratification, acceptance or accession, or at any later date, by notification addressed to the Secretary General of the Council of Europe, declare that, in cases not falling within Articles 1 to 13, its courts shall be entitled to entertain proceedings against another Contracting State to the extent that its courts are entitled to entertain proceedings against States not party to the present Convention. Such a declaration shall be without prejudice to the immunity from jurisdiction which foreign States enjoy in respect of acts performed in the exercise of sovereign authority (*acta jure imperii*).

2. The courts of a State which has made the declaration provided for in paragraph 1 shall not however be entitled to entertain such proceedings against another Contracting State if their jurisdiction could have been based solely on one or more of the grounds mentioned in the Annex to the present Convention,

unless that other Contracting State has taken a step in the proceedings relating to the merits without first challenging the jurisdiction of the court.

3. The provisions of Chapter II apply to proceedings instituted against a Contracting State in accordance with the present article.

4. The declaration made under paragraph 1 may be withdrawn by notification addressed to the Secretary General of the Council of Europe. The withdrawal shall take effect three months after the date of its receipt, but this shall not affect proceedings instituted before the date on which the withdrawal becomes effective.

Article 25 1.050

1. Any Contracting State which has made a declaration under Article 24 shall, in cases not falling within Articles 1 to 13, give effect to a judgment given by a court of another Contracting State which has made a like declaration:
   (a) if the conditions prescribed in paragraph 1(b) of Article 20 have been fulfilled; and
   (b) if the court is considered to have jurisdiction in accordance with the following paragraphs.

2. However, the Contracting State is not obliged to give effect to such a judgment:
   (a) if there is a ground for refusal as provided for in paragraph 2 of Article 20; or
   (b) if the provisions of paragraph 2 of Article 24 have not been observed.

3. Subject to the provisions of paragraph 4, a court of a Contracting State shall be considered to have jurisdiction for the purpose of paragraph 1(b):
   (a) if its jurisdiction is recognised in accordance with the provisions of an agreement to which the State of the forum and the other Contracting State are Parties;
   (b) where there is no agreement between the two States concerning the recognition and enforcement of judgments in civil matters, if the courts of the State of the forum would have been entitled to assume jurisdiction had they applied, mutatis mutandis, the rules of jurisdiction (other than those mentioned in the Annex to the present Convention) which operate in the State against which the judgment was given. This provision does not apply to questions arising out of contracts.

4. The Contracting States having made the declaration provided for in Article 24 may, by means of a supplementary agreement to this Convention, determine the circumstances in which their courts shall be considered to have jurisdiction for the purposes of paragraph 1(b) of this Article.

5. If the Contracting State does not give effect to the judgment, the procedure provided for in Article 21 may be used.

1.051 Article 26

Notwithstanding the provisions of Article 23, a judgment rendered against a Contracting State in proceedings relating to an industrial or commercial activity, in which the State is engaged in the same manner as a private person, may be enforced in the State of the forum against property of the State against which judgment has been given, used exclusively in connection with such an activity, if:

(a) both the State of the forum and the State against which the judgment has been given have made declarations under Article 24;

(b) the proceedings which resulted in the judgment fell within Articles 1 to 13 or were instituted in accordance with paragraphs 1 and 2 of Article 24; and

(c) the judgment satisfies the requirements laid down in paragraph 1(b) of Article 20.

CHAPTER V

General provisions

1.052 Article 27

1. For the purposes of the present Convention, the expression "Contracting State" shall not include any legal entity of a Contracting State which is distinct therefrom and is capable of suing or being sued, even if that entity has been entrusted with public functions.

2. Proceedings may be instituted against any entity referred to in paragraph 1 before the courts of another Contracting State in the same manner as against a private person; however, the courts may not entertain proceedings in respect of acts performed by the entity in the exercise of sovereign authority (*acta jure imperii*).

3. Proceedings may in any event be instituted against any such entity before those courts if, in corresponding circumstances, the courts would have had jurisdiction if the proceedings had been instituted against a Contracting State.

1.053 Article 28

1. Without prejudice to the provisions of Article 27, the constituent States of a Federal State do not enjoy immunity.

2. However, a Federal State Party to the present Convention may, by notification addressed to the Secretary General of the Council of Europe, declare that its constituent States may invoke the provisions of the Convention applicable to Contracting States, and have the same obligations.

3. Where a Federal State has made a declaration in accordance with paragraph 2, service of documents on a constituent State of a Federation shall be made on the Ministry of Foreign Affairs of the Federal State, in conformity with Article 16.

4. The Federal State alone is competent to make the declarations, notifications and communications provided for in the present Convention, and the Federal State alone may be party to proceedings pursuant to Article 34.

Article 29   1.054

The present Convention shall not apply to proceedings concerning:

(a) social security;
(b) damage or injury in nuclear matters;
(c) customs duties, taxes or penalties.

Article 30   1.055

The present Convention shall not apply to proceedings in respect of claims relating to the operation of seagoing vessels owned or operated by a Contracting State or to the carriage of cargoes and of passengers by such vessels or to the carriage of cargoes owned by a Contracting State and carried on board merchant vessels.

Article 31   1.056

Nothing in this Convention shall affect any immunities or privileges enjoyed by a Contracting State in respect of anything done or omitted to be done by, or in relation to, its armed forces when on the territory of another Contracting State.

Article 32   1.057

Nothing in the present Convention shall affect privileges and immunities relating to the exercise of the functions of diplomatic missions and consular posts and of persons connected with them.

Article 33   1.058

Nothing in the present Convention shall affect existing or future international agreements in special fields which relate to matters dealt with in the present Convention.

Article 34   1.059

1. Any dispute which might arise between two or more Contracting States concerning the interpretation or application of the present Convention shall be submitted to the International Court of Justice on the application of one of the parties to the dispute or by special agreement unless the parties agree on a different method of peaceful settlement of the dispute.

2. However, proceedings may not be instituted before the International Court of Justice which relate to:

(a) a dispute concerning a question arising in proceedings instituted against a Contracting State before a court of another Contracting State, before the court has given a judgment which fulfils the condition provided for in paragraph 1(b) of Article 20;

(b) a dispute concerning a question arising in proceedings instituted before a court of a Contracting State in accordance with paragraph 1 of Article 21, before the court has rendered a final decision in such proceedings.

1.060 **Article 35**

1. The present Convention shall apply only to proceedings introduced after its entry into force.

2. When a State has become party to this Convention after it has entered into force, the Convention shall apply only to proceedings introduced after it has entered into force with respect to that State.

3. Nothing in this Convention shall apply to proceedings arising out of, or judgments based on, acts, omissions or facts prior to the date on which the present Convention is opened for signature.

CHAPTER VI

Final provisions

1.061 **Article 36**

1. The present Convention shall be open to signature by the member States of the Council of Europe. It shall be subject to ratification or acceptance. Instruments of ratification or acceptance shall be deposited with the Secretary General of the Council of Europe.

2. The Convention shall enter into force three months after the date of the deposit of the third instrument of ratification or acceptance.[22]

3. In respect of a signatory State ratifying or accepting subsequently, the Convention shall enter into force three months after the date of the deposit of its instrument of ratification or acceptance.

1.062 **Article 37**

1. After the entry into force of the present Convention, the Committee of Ministers of the Council of Europe may, by a decision taken by a unanimous

---

[22] The Convention entered into force on 11 June 1976.

vote of the members casting a vote, invite any non-member State to accede thereto.

2. Such accession shall be effected by depositing with the Secretary General of the Council of Europe an instrument of accession which shall take effect three months after the date of its deposit.

3. However, if a State having already acceded to the Convention notifies the Secretary General of the Council of Europe of its objection to the accession of another non-member State, before the entry into force of this accession, the Convention shall not apply to the relations between these two States.

Article 38   1.063

1. Any State may, at the time of signature or when depositing its instrument of ratification, acceptance or accession, specify the territory or territories to which the present Convention shall apply.

2. Any State may, when depositing its instrument of ratification, acceptance or accession or at any later date, by declaration addressed to the Secretary General of the Council of Europe, extend this Convention to any other territory or territories specified in the declaration and for whose international relations it is responsible or on whose behalf it is authorised to give undertakings.

3. Any declaration made in pursuance of the preceding paragraph may, in respect of any territory mentioned in such declaration, be withdrawn according to the procedure laid down in Article 40 of this Convention.

Article 39   1.064

No reservation is permitted to the present Convention.

Article 40   1.065

1. Any Contracting State may, in so far as it is concerned, denounce this Convention by means of a notification addressed to the Secretary General of the Council of Europe.

2. Such denunciation shall take effect six months after the date of receipt by the Secretary General of such notification. This Convention shall, however, continue to apply to proceedings introduced before the date on which the denunciation takes effect, and to judgments given in such proceedings.

Article 41   1.066

The Secretary General of the Council of Europe shall notify the member States of the Council of Europe and any State which has acceded to this Convention of:

(a) any signature;
(b) any deposit of an instrument of ratification, acceptance or accession;

(c) any date of entry into force of this Convention in accordance with Articles 36 and 37 thereof;

(d) any notification received in pursuance of the provisions of paragraph 2 of Article 19;

(e) any communication received in pursuance of the provisions of paragraph 4 of Article 21;

(f) any notification received in pursuance of the provisions of paragraph 1 of Article 24;

(g) the withdrawal of any notification made in pursuance of the provisions of paragraph 4 of Article 24;

(h) any notification received in pursuance of the provisions of paragraph 2 of Article 28;

(i) any notification received in pursuance of the provisions of paragraph 3 of Article 37;

(j) any declaration received in pursuance of the provisions of Article 38;

(k) any notification received in pursuance of the provisions of Article 40 and the date on which denunciation takes effect.

In witness whereof the undersigned, being duly authorised thereto, have signed this Convention.

Done at Basle, this 16th day of May 1972, in English and French, both texts being equally authoritative, in a single copy which shall remain deposited in the archives of the Council of Europe. The Secretary General of the Council of Europe shall transmit certified copies to each of the signatory and acceding States.

[List of signatories omitted]

1.067 Annex

The grounds of jurisdiction referred to in paragraph 3, sub-paragraph (a), of Article 20, paragraph 2 of Article 24 and paragraph 3, sub-paragraph (b), of Article 25 are the following:

(a) the presence in the territory of the State of the forum of property belonging to the defendant, or the seizure by the plaintiff of property situated there, unless

—the action is brought to assert proprietary or possessory rights in that property, or arises from another issue relating to such property; or

—the property constitutes the security for a debt which is the subject-matter of the action;

(b) the nationality of the plaintiff;

(c) the domicile, habitual residence or ordinary residence of the plaintiff within the territory of the State of the forum unless the assumption of jurisdiction on such a ground is permitted by way of an exception made on account of the particular subject-matter of a class of contracts;

(d) the fact that the defendant carried on business within the territory of the State of the forum, unless the action arises from that business;

(e) a unilateral specification of the forum by the plaintiff, particularly in an invoice.

A legal person shall be considered to have its domicile or habitual residence where it has its seat, registered office or principal place of business.

Signatures and Ratifications[23]   **1.068**

[State; Date of signature (*signatory to Additional Protocol;† ratified Additional Protocol); Date of ratification; Date of entry into force]

Austria*†[24];16.05.1972; 10.07.1974; 11.06.1976
Belgium*†[25]; 16.05.1972; 27.10.1975; 11.06.1976
Cyprus*†; 15.12.1975; 10.03.1976; 11.06.1976
Germany*[26]; 16.05.1972; 15.05.1990; 16.08.1990
Luxembourg*†[27]; 16.05.1972; 11.12.1986; 12.03.1987
Netherlands*†[28]; 16.05.1972; 21.02.1985; 22.05.1985
Portugal; 10.05.1979; – ; – ;
Switzerland*†[29]; 16.05.1972; 06.07.1982; 07.10.1980
United Kingdom[30]; 16.05.1972; 03.07.1979 ; 04.10.1979

Declarations[31]   **1.069**

Austria

On depositing its instrument of ratification the Republic of Austria declared:

according to Article 28 para. 2 of the European Convention on State Immunity that its constituent States Burgenland, Carinthia, Lower Austria, Upper Austria, Salzburg, Styria, Tyrol, Vorarlberg and Vienna may invoke the provisions of the European Convention on State Immunity applicable to Contracting States, and have the same obligations.

---

[23] As at 17 October 2003 (Source: Council of Europe Treaty Office —http://conventions/coe.int).
[24] For texts of declarations see below.   [25] For texts of declarations see below.
[26] For texts of declarations see below.   [27] For texts of declarations see below.
[28] For texts of declarations see below.   [29] For texts of declarations see below.
[30] The United Kingdom ratified on behalf of the United Kingdom of Great Britain and Northern Ireland, Belize, British Antarctic Territory, British Virgin Islands, Cayman Islands, Falkland Islands and Dependencies, Gilbert Islands, Hong Kong, Montserrat, Pitcairn, Henderson, Ducie and Oeno Islands, Saint Helena and Dependencies, Turks and Caicos Islands, United Kingdom Sovereign Base Areas of Akrotiri and Dhekelia in the Island of Cyprus. The United Kingdom has since extended its ratification of the Convention to Guernsey, Jersey and the Isle of Man. See declarations below.
[31] As at 17 October 2003 (Source: Council of Europe Treaty Office—http://conventions/coe.int).

On 17 December 1976 the Federal President signed the following declaration:

> In compliance with paragraph 4 of Article 21 of the European Convention on State Immunity, the Republic of Austria declares that it designates the Vienna Regional Civil Court (*Landesgericht für Zivilrechtssachen Wien*) as solely competent to determine whether the Republic of Austria shall give effect, in accordance with Article 20 of the above-mentioned Convention to any judgment given by a court of another Contracting State.

Belgium

On depositing its instrument of ratification the Kingdom of Belgium declared:

> [Translation]
> In accordance with Article 21, the Belgian Government designates the "Tribunal de première instance" for determining the question whether the Belgian State should give effect to a foreign judgment.
>
> With reference to Article 24, the Belgian Government declares that, in cases not falling within Articles 1 to 13, its courts shall be entitled to entertain proceedings against another Contracting State to the extent that its courts are entitled to entertain proceedings against States not Party to the present Convention. Such a declaration shall be without prejudice to the immunity from jurisdiction which foreign States enjoy in respect of acts performed in the exercise of sovereign authority (*acta jure imperii*).

Declaration contained in a letter from the Minister of Foreign Affairs of Belgium, dated 4 September 2003, transmitted by the Permanent Representative of Belgium and registered at the Secretariat General on 23 September 2003:

> In accordance with Article 28, paragraph 2 of the Convention, the Kingdom of Belgium declares that the French Community, the Flemish Community and the German-speaking Community as well as the Walloon Region, the Flemish Region and the Brussels-Capital Region may invoke the provisions of the European Convention on State Immunity applicable to Contracting States, and have the same obligations.

Germany

Declarations contained in two letters from the Permanent Representative, dated 15 May 1990, handed to the Secretary General at the time of deposit of the instrument of ratification:

> I have the honour to declare on behalf of the Federal Republic of Germany that the Convention shall also apply to Land Berlin with effect from the date on which it enters into force for the Federal Republic of Germany.
>
> I have the honour to make the following declarations on behalf of the Federal Republic of Germany:
>
> Paragraph 4 of Article 21:
>
> The question whether effect should be given by the Federal Republic of Germany or a Land to a judgment rendered by a court of another

Contracting State in accordance with Article 20 or Article 25 or to a settlement in accordance with Article 22 of the Convention is determined by the competent Regional Court (Landgericht) in whose administrative district the Federal Government has its seat.

Article 24:

The Federal Republic of Germany declares in accordance with paragraph 1 of Article 24 of the Convention that, in cases not falling within Articles 1 to 13, its courts are entitled to entertain proceedings against another Contracting State to the extent that its courts are entitled to entertain proceedings against States not Party to the Convention. Such a declaration is without prejudice to the immunity from jurisdiction which foreign States enjoy in respect of acts performed in the exercise of sovereign authority (*acta jure imperii*).

Paragraph 2 of Article 28:

The Federal Republic of Germany declares in accordance with paragraph 2 of Article 28 of the Convention that the Länder of Baden-Württemberg, Bavaria, Berlin, Bremen, Hamburg, Hesse, Lower Saxony, North-Rhine/Westphalia, Rhineland-Palatinate, Saarland and Schleswig-Holstein may invoke the provisions of the Convention applicable to Contracting States and have the same obligations.

Declaration contained in a letter from the Permanent Representative, dated 3 June 1992, registered at the Secretariat General on 5 June 1992:

The Federal Republic of Germany hereby amends its declaration relating to Article 28 para. 2 of the Convention to the effect that all constituent states (Laender) of the Federal Republic of Germany, namely Baden-Württemberg, Bavaria, Berlin, Brandenburg, Bremen, Hamburg, Hesse, Mecklenburg-Western Pomerania, Lower Saxony, North-Rhine/Westphalia, Rhineland-Palatina, Saarland, Saxony, Saxony-Anhalt, Schleswig-Holstein and Thuringia shall be able to invoke the provisions of the Convention applying to the Contracting States and shall have the same duties as the latter.

Luxembourg

Declarations made at the time of deposit of the instrument of ratification:

1. The competent Court, under Article 21 of the Convention, to determine the question whether effect should be given to a judgment delivered in pursuance of Article 20, is the Court of Appeal of Luxembourg, judging in accordance with the procedure of civil appeals, as for summary and urgent matters. Its decision is subject to appeal to the Supreme Court in compliance with the ordinary rules in civil matters.

2. In accordance with Article 24 of the Convention, the Courts of Luxembourg are entitled, in cases falling outside Articles 1 to 13 of the Convention, to entertain proceedings against another Contracting State to the extent to which its Courts are entitled to entertain such proceedings against States not Party to the Convention.

Netherlands

Declarations made at the time of deposit of the instrument of acceptance:

> I have the honour, with reference to Article 24, first paragraph, of the
> European Convention on State Immunity, to declare, on behalf of the
> Kingdom of the Netherlands that in cases not falling within Articles 1 to 13,
> its courts shall be entitled to entertain proceedings against another
> Contracting State to the extent that its courts are entitled to entertain
> proceedings against States not Party to the present Convention.
>
>   The district court (*Arrondissementsrechtbank*) of The Hague has been
> designated as the competent court referred to in Article 21, first paragraph,
> of the Convention.

Declaration contained in the instrument of acceptance, deposited on 21 February
1985:

> The Kingdom of the Netherlands accepts the said Convention and
> Protocol for the Kingdom in Europe.

Switzerland

Declaration contained in a letter from the Permanent Representative of
Switzerland, dated 6 July 1982, handed to the Secretary General at the time of
deposit of the instrument of ratification:

> I have the honour to declare on behalf of the Swiss Federal Council and in
> accordance with Article 24 of the Convention, that in cases not falling
> within Articles 1 to 13, the Swiss courts shall be entitled to entertain pro-
> ceedings against another Contracting State to the extent that its courts are
> entitled to entertain proceedings against States not Party to the present
> Convention.

United Kingdom

On depositing its instrument of ratification the United Kingdom declared by
letter from its Permanent Representative dated 2 July 1979:

> (a) In pursuance of the provisions of paragraph 1 of Article 24 thereof,
>   the United Kingdom hereby declare that, in cases not falling within
>   Article 1 to 13, their courts and the courts of any territory in respect of
>   which they are a Party to the Convention shall be entitled to entertain
>   proceedings against another Contracting State so the extent that these
>   courts are entitled to entertain proceedings against States not Party to
>   the present Convention. This declaration is without prejudice to the
>   immunity from jurisdiction which foreign States enjoy in respect of
>   acts performed in the exercise of sovereign authority (*acta jure imperii*).
>
> (b) In pursuance of the provisions of paragraph 2 of Article 19, the
>   United Kingdom hereby declare that their courts, and the courts of

any territory in respect of which they are a Party to the Convention, shall not be bound by the provisions of paragraph 1 of that Article,

(c) In pursuance of the provisions of paragraph 4 of Article 21, the United Kingdom hereby designate as competent courts:

in England and Wales—the High Court of Justice;
in Scotland—the Court of Session;
in Northern Ireland—the Supreme Court of Judicature;
and in any other territory in respect of which they are a Party to the Convention—the Supreme Court of the territory concerned.

The question whether effect is to be given so a judgment in accordance with paragraph 1 of Article 21 may however also be justiciable in other civil courts in the exercise of their normal jurisdiction.

I also have the honour to inform you that simultaneously an instrument of ratification of the International Convention for the Unification of certain Rules concerning the Immunity of State-owned Ships, done at Brussels on 10 April, 1926, and of the protocol supplementary thereto, done at Brussels on 24 May, 1934, is being deposited with the Government of the Kingdom of Belgium. This instrument of ratification, signed by Her Majesty The Queen in respect of the United Kingdom of Great Britain and Northern Ireland, contains the following reservations:

"We reserve the right to apply Article 1 of the Convention to any claim in respect of a ship which falls within the Admiralty jurisdiction of Our courts, or of Our courts in any territory in respect of which We are party to the Convention.

We reserve the right, with respect to Article 2 of the Convention, to apply in proceedings concerning another High Contracting Party or ship of another High Contracting Party the rules of procedure set out in Chapter II of the European Convention on State Immunity, signed at Basle on the Sixteenth day of May, in the Year of Our Lord One thousand Nine hundred and Seventy-two.

In order to give effect to the terms of any international agreement with a non-Contracting State, We reserve the right to make special provision

(a) as regards the delay or arrest of a ship or cargo belonging to such a State, and
(b) to prohibit seizure of or execution against such a ship or cargo."

Declarations contained in a letter from the Permanent Representative of the United Kingdom dated 25 November 1987, registered at the Secretariat General on 27 November 1987:

I have the honour to refer to the European Convention on State Immunity, done at Basle on 16 May 1972, which the Government of the United Kingdom of Great Britain and Northern Ireland ratified on 3 July 1979. In accordance with Article 38, paragraph 2, thereof, I hereby declare, on behalf of the Government of the United Kingdom, that the said Convention shall extend to Guernsey, Jersey and the Isle of Man.

I have the further honour to state that the notifications made to your predecessor in paragraph 1.a and b of Mr Cape's letter of 2 July 1979[32] in connection with the said Convention shall apply equally to Guernsey, Jersey and the Isle of Man as territories in respect of which the United Kingdom is a Party to the said Convention.

In addition, in pursuance of the provisions of paragraph 4 of Article 21 of the said Convention, the United Kingdom designate as competent courts:
In Guernsey:

— in the Island of Guernsey: the Royal Court of Guernsey;
— in the Island of Alderney: the Court of Alderney;
— in the Island of Sark: the Court of the Seneschal;

In Jersey:- the Royal Court of Jersey;
In the Isle of Man:- the High Court of Justice of the Isle of Man.

The question whether effect is to be given to a judgment in accordance with paragraph 1 of Article 21 may however also be justiciable in other civil courts in the exercise of their normal jurisdiction.

I further have the honour to inform you that the United Kingdom is also acceding, separately in the name of Guernsey, Jersey and the Isle of Man, to the International Convention for the Unification of certain Rules concerning the Immunity of State-owned Ships, done at Brussels on 10 April 1926, and of the protocol supplementary thereto, done at Brussels on 24 May 1934, subject to the same reservations as are referred to in paragraph 2 of Mr Cape's aforementioned letter.

---

[32] See above.

Additional Protocol to the European Convention on State Immunity[33]   **1.070**

The member States of the Council of Europe, signatory to the present Protocol, Having taken note of the European Convention on State Immunity—hereinafter referred to as "the Convention"—and in particular Articles 21 and 34 thereof;

Desiring to develop the work of harmonisation in the field covered by the Convention by the addition of provisions concerning a European procedure for the settlement of disputes,

Have agreed as follows:

PART I

Article 1   **1.071**

1. Where a judgment has been given against a State Party to the Convention and that State does not give effect thereto, the party which seeks to invoke the judgment shall be entitled to have determined the question whether effect should be given to the judgment in conformity with Article 20 or Article 25 of the Convention, by Instituting proceedings before either:

   (a) the competent court of that State in application of Article 21 of the Convention; or

   (b) the European Tribunal constituted in conformity with the provisions of Part III of the present Protocol, provided that that State is a Party to the present Protocol and has not made the declaration referred to in Part IV thereof.

   The choice between these two possibilities shall be final.

2. If the State intends to institute proceedings before its court in accordance with the provisions of paragraph 1 of Article 21 of the Convention, it must give notice of its intention to do so to the party in whose favour the judgment has been given; the State may thereafter institute such proceedings only if the party has not, within three months of receiving notice, instituted proceedings before the European Tribunal. Once this period has elapsed, the party in whose favour the judgment has been given may no longer institute proceedings before the European Tribunal.

3. Save in so far as may be necessary for the application of Articles 20 and 25 of the Convention, the European Tribunal may not review the merits of the judgment.

---

[33] ETS No 74A. The Additional Protocol entered into force on 22 May 1985.

PART II

1.072   Article 2

1. Any dispute which might arise between two or more States Parties to the present Protocol concerning the interpretation or application of the Convention shall be submitted, on the application of one of the parties to the dispute or by special agreement, to the European Tribunal constituted in conformity with the provisions of Part III of the present Protocol. The States Parties to the present Protocol undertake not to submit such a dispute to a different mode of settlement.

2. If the dispute concerns a question arising in proceedings instituted before a court of one State Party to the Convention against another State Party to the Convention, or a question arising in proceedings instituted before a court of a State Party to the Convention in accordance with Article 21 of the Convention, it may not be referred to the European Tribunal until the court has given a final decision in such proceedings.

3. Proceedings may not be instituted before the European Tribunal which relate to a dispute concerning a judgment which it has already determined or is required to determine by virtue of Part I of this Protocol.

1.073   Article 3

Nothing in the present Protocol shall be interpreted as preventing the European Tribunal from determining any dispute which might arise between two or more States Parties to the Convention concerning the interpretation or application thereof and which might be submitted to it by special agreement, even if these States, or any of them, are not Parties to the present Protocol.

PART III

1.074   Article 4

1. There shall be established a European Tribunal in matters of State Immunity to determine cases brought before it in conformity with the provisions of Parts I and II of the present Protocol.

2. The European Tribunal shall consist of the members of the European Court of Human Rights and, in respect of each non-member State of the Council of Europe which has acceded to the present Protocol, a person possessing the qualifications required of members of that Court designated, with the agreement of the Committee of Ministers of the Council of Europe, by the government of that State for a period of nine years.

3. The President of the European Tribunal shall be the President of the European Court of Human Rights.

Article 5

1.075

1. Where proceedings are instituted before the European Tribunal in accordance with the provisions of Part I of the present Protocol, the European Tribunal shall consist of a Chamber composed of seven members. There shall sit as ex officio members of the Chamber the member of the European Tribunal who is a national of the State against which the judgment has been given and the member of the European Tribunal who is a national of the State of the forum, or, should there be no such member in one or the other case, a person designated by the government of the State concerned to sit in the capacity of a member of the Chamber. The names of the other five members shall be chosen by lot by the President of the European Tribunal in the presence of the Registrar.

2. Where proceedings are instituted before the European Tribunal in accordance with the provisions of Part II of the present Protocol, the Chamber shall be constituted in the manner provided for in the preceding paragraph. However, there shall sit as ex officio members of the Chamber the members of the European Tribunal who are nationals of the States parties to the dispute or, should there be no such member, a person designated by the government of the State concerned to sit in the capacity of a member of the Chamber.

3. Where a case pending before a Chamber raises a serious question affecting the interpretation of the Convention or of the present Protocol, the Chamber may, at any time, relinquish jurisdiction in favour of the European Tribunal meeting in plenary session. The relinquishment of jurisdiction shall be obligatory where the resolution of such question might have a result inconsistent with a judgment previously delivered by a Chamber or by the European Tribunal meeting in plenary session. The relinquishment of jurisdiction shall be final. Reasons need not be given for the decision to relinquish jurisdiction.

Article 6

1.076

1. The European Tribunal shall decide any disputes as to whether the Tribunal has jurisdiction.

2. The hearings of the European Tribunal shall be public unless the Tribunal in exceptional circumstances decides otherwise.

3. The judgments of the European Tribunal, taken by a majority of the members present, are to be delivered in public session. Reasons shall be given for the judgment of the European Tribunal. If the judgment does not represent in whole or in part the unanimous opinion of the European Tribunal, any member shall be entitled to deliver a separate opinion.

4. The judgments of the European Tribunal shall be final and binding upon the parties.

1.077   Article 7

   1. The European Tribunal shall draw up its own rules and fix its own procedure.

   2. The Registry of the European Tribunal shall be provided by the Registrar of the European Court of Human Rights.

1.078   Article 8

   1. The operating costs of the European Tribunal shall be borne by the Council of Europe. States non-members of the Council of Europe having acceded to the present Protocol shall contribute thereto in a manner to be decided by the Committee of Ministers after agreement with these States.

   2. The members of the European Tribunal shall receive for each day of duty a compensation to be determined by the Committee of Ministers.

PART IV

1.079   Article 9

   1. Any State may, by notification addressed to the Secretary General of the Council of Europe at the moment of its signature of the present Protocol, or of the deposit of its instrument of ratification, acceptance or accession thereto, declare that it will only be bound by Parts II to V of the present Protocol.

   2. Such a notification may be withdrawn at any time.

PART V

1.080   Article 10

   1. The present Protocol shall be open to signature by the member States of the Council of Europe which have signed the Convention. It shall be subject to ratification or acceptance. Instruments of ratification or acceptance shall be deposited with the Secretary General of the Council of Europe.

   2. The present Protocol shall enter into force three months after the date of the deposit of the fifth instrument of ratification or acceptance.

   3. In respect of a signatory State ratifying or accepting subsequently, the Protocol shall enter into force three months after the date of the deposit of its instrument of ratification or acceptance.

   4. A member State of the Council of Europe may not ratify or accept the present Protocol without having ratified or accepted the Convention.

1.081   Article 11

   1. A State which has acceded to the Convention may accede to the present Protocol after the Protocol has entered into force.

2. Such accession shall be effected by depositing with the Secretary General of the Council of Europe an instrument of accession which shall take effect three months after the date of its deposit.

Article 12 1.082

No reservation is permitted to the present Protocol.

Article 13 1.083

1. Any Contracting State may, in so far as it is concerned, denounce the present Protocol by means of a notification addressed to the Secretary General of the Council of Europe.

2. Such denunciation shall take effect six months after the date of receipt by the Secretary General of such notification. The Protocol shall, however, continue to apply to proceedings introduced in conformity with the provisions of the Protocol before the date on which such denunciation takes effect.

3. Denunciation of the Convention shall automatically entail denunciation of the present Protocol.

Article 14 1.084

The Secretary General of the Council of Europe shall notify the member States of the Council and any State which has acceded to the Convention of:

(a) any signature of the present Protocol;
(b) any deposit of an instrument of ratification, acceptance or accession;
(c) any date of entry into force of the present Protocol in accordance with Articles 10 and 11 thereof;
(d) any notification received in pursuance of the provisions of Part IV and any withdrawal of any such notification;
(e) any notification received in pursuance of the provisions of Article 13 and the date on which such denunciation takes effect.

In witness whereof the undersigned, being duly authorised thereto, have signed the present Protocol.

[List of signatories omitted]

Done at Basle, this 16th day of May 1972, in English and French, both texts being equally authoritative, in a single copy which shall remain deposited in the archives of the Council of Europe. The Secretary General of the Council of Europe shall transmit certified copies to each of the signatory and acceding States.

1.085 Resolution (72) 2 of the Committee of Ministers of the Council of Europe adopted at the 206th Meeting of the Ministers' Deputies on 18 January 1972;

The Committee of Ministers of the Council of Europe, having taken note of the text of the European Convention on State Immunity;

Considering that one of the aims of this Convention is to ensure compliance with judgments given against a State,

Recommends the governments of those member States which shall become Parties to this Convention to establish, for the purpose of Article 21 of the Convention, a procedure which shall be as expeditious and simple as possible.

1.086   **Signatures and Ratifications**

[State; Date of signature; Date of ratification; Date of entry into force]

Austria; 16.05.1972; 10.07.1974; 22.05.1985
Belgium; 16.05.1972; 27.10.1975; 22.05.1985
Cyprus; 15.12.1975; 10.03.1976; 22.05.1985
Germany; 16.05.1972; – ; -
Luxembourg; 16.05.1972; 11.12.1986; 12.03.1987
Netherlands; 16.05.1972; 21.02.1985; 22.05.1985
Portugal; 10.05.1979; – ; –
Switzerland; 16.05.1972; 16.07.1982; 22.05.1985

1.087   **Declarations**

Netherlands

Declaration made at the time of deposit of instrument of acceptance:

The Kingdom of the Netherlands accepts the said Convention and Protocol for the Kingdom in Europe.

1.088   **Explanatory Report on the European Convention on State Immunity**

I. The European Convention on State Immunity and its Additional Protocol, drawn up within the Council of Europe by a committee of governmental experts under the authority of the European Committee on Legal Co-operation (CCJ), were opened to signature by the member States of the Council on 16 May 1972, at Basle, on the occasion of the VIIth Conference of European Ministers of Justice.

II. The text of the explanatory reports prepared by the committee of experts and submitted to the Committee of Ministers of the Council of Europe, as amended by the CCJ, do not constitute instruments providing an authoritative interpretation of the text of the Convention and of its Additional Protocol, although they might be of such a nature as to facilitate the application of the provisions therein contained.

Introduction

1. "State immunity" is a concept of international law, which has developed out of the principle *par in parem non habet imperium*, by virtue of which one State is not, subject to the jurisdiction of another State.

2. For many years State immunity has occupied the attention of eminent jurists. It is also the object of abundant case law. The development of international relations and the increasing intervention of States in spheres belonging to private law have posed the problem still more acutely by increasing the number of disputes opposing individuals and foreign States.

There are, at present, two theories, that of absolute State immunity which is the logical consequence of the principle stated above and that of relative State immunity which is tending to predominate on account of the requirement of modern conditions. According to this latter theory, the State enjoys immunity for acts *iure imperii* but not for acts *iure gestionis*, that is to say when it acts in the same way as a private person in relations governed by private law. This divergence of opinion causes difficulties in international relations. States whose courts and administrative authorities apply the theory of absolute State immunity are led to call for the same treatment abroad.

3. There have been several attempts on the international level to solve these difficulties.

The first was the draft International Regulations on the jurisdiction of Courts in proceedings against sovereign States or Heads of foreign States, which were the subject of a resolution of the plenary Assembly of the Institute of International Law on 11 September 1891. On 30 April 1954, the Institute adopted new resolutions on the immunity of foreign States from jurisdiction and execution (*Annuaire de l'Institut de Droit International*, Vol. 45 (II) (1954), pp. 293–294).

On 10 April 1926 the International Convention for the Unification of Certain Rules relating to the Immunity of State-owned Vessels was opened for signature in Brussels. This Convention is in force between a number of States and is, so far, the only attempt at international unification in the field of State immunity which has proved successful in practice. On 24 May 1934 a Protocol was added to the Convention.

Also worthy of mention are: a comprehensive draft prepared by Harvard University in 1932 (Harvard Research in International Law: "Competence of Courts in regard to Foreign States", *American Journal of International Law* 26 (1932), Suppl. pp. 453 et seq.); studies by the International Law Association in 1952 (International Law Association, Report on the 45th Conference 1952, pp. VI et seq.) and a resolution adopted by the International Bar Association at its meeting in Salzburg in July 1960.

The League of Nations, and, more recently, the United Nations International Law Commission, have also included the problem of State immunity in their work programme but without reaching positive conclusions.

In addition, the Afro-Asian Legal Consultative Committee has recently considered the question of State immunity.

4. By resolution (63) 29, of 13 December 1963, the Committee of Ministers of the Council of Europe included the subject of State immunity in the Council of Europe Inter-governmental Work Programme.

5. At the third Conference of European Ministers of Justice in Dublin in May 1964, the Austrian delegation submitted a detailed report on the problem connected with the concept of State immunity and in particular on the advisability and prospects of Council of Europe action in this field. This report was largely based on the article "Zur Frage der Staatenimmunität" ("Observations on the question of State immunity") by K. Herndl, *Juristische Blätter*, 1962, pp. 15 et seq. Shortly after the publication of this article, an important decision of the German Federal Constitutional Court of 30 April 1963 (*Entscheidungen des Bundesverfassungsgerichts*, Vol. 16, pp. 27 et seq.; see also *Neue Juristische Wochenschrift*, 1963, p. 1732 et seq.) adopted the principle of relative State immunity.

This report dealt not only with jurisdictional immunity but also with immunity from execution. The question of whether it is possible to proceed to measures of execution against the property of foreign States is controversial. In certain States, such execution is prohibited while in others it is permitted, and in yet others it depends on authorisation. In the two latter cases, it cannot however take place against the property of a foreign State which is used for public purposes and it is sometimes difficult to distinguish such property from that which is used for private purposes. The report therefore recommended that execution should not be levied against the property of foreign States, but that an attempt should be made to reach an international agreement whereby States would comply voluntarily with judgments given against them.

In Resolution No. 4, the third Conference of European Ministers of Justice recommended that the European Committee on Legal Co-operation (CCJ), a sub-committee of the CCJ, or a committee of experts, should be instructed to make a study of the problems of State immunity. The Committee of Ministers accepted this recommendation.

6. A committee of experts, which met on a number of occasions during the years 1965 to 1970, has drawn up a draft European Convention on State immunity. If this Convention is ratified by the requisite number of States, it will be the first international Convention of a general nature in the field of State immunity, the Brussels Convention of 1926 being concerned only with State-owned vessels.

General comments

7. By limiting the number of cases in which States can invoke jurisdictional immunity, the Convention is consistent with the trend taking place in the case-law and legal writings in the majority of countries.

The Convention requires each Contracting State to give effect to judgments rendered against it by the courts of another Contracting State. It is in particular for this reason that it operates only between the Contracting States on the basis of the special confidence subsisting among the Members of the Council of Europe. The Convention confers no rights on non-Contracting States; in particular, it leaves open all questions as to the exercise of jurisdiction against non-Contracting States in Contracting States, and vice versa.

8. The Convention applies only to the jurisdiction of courts, whether judicial or administrative. It does not deal with the treatment of Contracting States by the administrative authorities or other Contracting States.

9. Consideration was given to the question whether the Convention could not have been confined to immunity from jurisdiction, by simply determining the cases in which a State could not invoke immunity. It was argued in support of this proposition that such a Convention would represent in itself a considerable step forward compared with the present situation, and that difficulties concerning execution of judgments given on the basis of the Convention would not be so great that they could not in due course be overcome by the application of the provisions of treaties on the recognition and enforcement of foreign judgments; the result would then be an identical regime applicable to States and private persons.

This approach did not, however, commend itself. For States which already draw the distinction between acts *iure gestionis* and acts *iure imperii*, the drawing-up of a catalogue of cases in which the State could not invoke immunity would have represented no advance over the present situation.

Moreover, it must be acknowledged that difficulties concerning immunity from execution are at least as great as those arising in connection with immunity from jurisdiction. Recourse to treaties on the recognition and enforcement of foreign judgments, in so far as those treaties might be applicable to judgments given against States, did not seem adequate to meet these difficulties. There is as yet no extensive network of bilateral and multilateral agreements between member States of the Council of Europe. Furthermore, there are deep-seated differences between national laws, which would be keenly felt in the absence of treaties according reciprocity of treatment. A harmonisation of the laws of the member States of the Council of Europe would not therefore have been achieved.

Finally, the absence of any provision relating to problems of immunity from execution would have left unresolved the question whether execution can be

levied in the State of the forum against the property of the State against which
a judgment had been given in application of the Convention. Uncertainty on this
point would have made it more difficult for some States to accept the Convention.

10. The broad lines of the Convention are:

(1) The cases in which immunity from jurisdiction is not granted to a Con-
     tracting State are listed in Chapter I. The list of cases incorporates a series of
     connecting links, which are designed to prevent proceedings being insti-
     tuted against a State in the courts of another State where the dispute is not
     sufficiently closely related to the territory of the State of the forum to justify
     the exercise of jurisdiction by a court in that State. These links are also nec-
     essary to establish bases of jurisdiction which would be accepted when the
     foreign judgment comes to be submitted for recognition and enforcement
     (see No. 3). The connecting links do not themselves confer jurisdiction on
     the courts of Contracting States. Only such jurisdiction can be exercised as
     is already provided for by national legislation or international agreements.

(2) Immunity from jurisdiction must be granted in all cases which are not
     included in the list (Article 15).

(3) A Contracting State must give effect to judgments rendered against it in
     cases where it cannot claim immunity under Articles 1 to 13. In order to
     ensure that this obligation is effectively discharged, judicial safeguards are
     provided in Article 21. These judicial safeguards have been inserted
     because Article 23 prohibits execution being levied in one Contracting
     State against the property of another Contracting State.

(4) Chapter 4 of the Convention contains an optional system. If the States
     make use of the faculty provided for in Article 24, they may declare that
     their courts are entitled to entertain proceedings against another Con-
     tracting State to the extent that they are so entitled against States not party
     to this Convention. The obligation to give effect to judgments rendered in
     cases not falling within Articles 1–13, exists only as between States which
     have made this declaration (Article 25). Moreover, these States accept an
     exception to the general rule which prohibits execution against the prop-
     erty of a foreign State (Article 26).

(5) Entities established by a Contracting State do not enjoy immunity. How-
     ever, the possibility remains that the courts of a Contracting State might be
     required not to entertain certain proceedings brought against such entities
     (see Article 27).

11. In addition to these fundamental provisions, the Convention contains
rules on other important questions connected with the participation of foreign

States in court proceedings, which have often led to difficulties in practice. These rules relate in particular to the service of judicial documents on foreign States, the exemption of foreign States from having to provide security for costs, and the prohibition of penalties against a State which, being a party to proceedings, refuses to produce evidence.

Title and preamble   1.091

12. The Convention does not cover the problem of immunity in proceedings before administrative authorities of another State. On the other hand, it includes provisions on matters other than immunity, which arise in judicial proceedings to which a State is a party: for example, service of process on a State. It also lays upon States the duty to give effect to certain judgments. Since immunity is the central theme, the title of the Convention for reasons of brevity and descriptiveness refers to that alone.

13. The introductory and final recitals of the preamble follow the same lines as other Council of Europe conventions in the legal field. The preamble also mentions particular reasons for the conclusion of this Convention, and stresses that its aim is to resolve problems of immunity solely in the relations between Contracting States which are Members of the Council of Europe (as to the possibility of accession by non-member States of the Council of Europe, see Article 37).

CHAPTER 1

Article 1   1.092

14. A State which of its own will institutes legal proceedings as claimant or intervening party may not subsequently invoke immunity. It is obliged, like any other party, to respect the rules of procedure of the national law of the court to which the case has been referred. This principle is modified to some extent by Article 18 which is based on the British concept of "Crown Privilege".

15. Submission to the jurisdiction of another State extends to proceedings before appeal courts. It also covers the case where a court decides, on account of its own lack of competence, to refer the matter to another court in the same State.
Such submission does not, however, extend to proceedings concerning the enforcement of a judgment given against the State.

16. The word "intervenes" does not include cases of compulsory intervention provided for in the law of certain States, except where the State participates actively in the proceedings without invoking its immunity.

17. By advancing claims in bankruptcy or similar proceedings, the State assumes the role of a claimant and, as such, submits to the jurisdiction of the

courts of the State where the proceedings were instituted; it is subject to this jurisdiction even where, for procedural reasons, the role of the parties is reversed. That might be the case, for example, if the debt claimed by the State is contested by another creditor or by the trustee in bankruptcy.

18. Paragraph 2 deals with a counterclaim brought either against a State which is the claimant in the proceedings or, if the rules of procedure in force in the State of the forum so permit, against a State which intervenes in the proceedings. The wording of the connecting link in sub-paragraph (a) is based on Article 11 (2) of the Hague Convention of 1 February 1971 on the Recognition and Enforcement of Foreign Judgments in Civil and Commercial Matters.

The provision contained in sub-paragraph (b) provides that the State which institutes proceedings or intervenes cannot claim immunity in respect of a counterclaim if it could not have claimed immunity had these proceedings been instituted against it as a principal claim. The position of the State, in the case of a similar counterclaim, must not be different from that which would result from proceedings brought against it on the basis of Articles 2 to 13.

19. Paragraph 3 concerns the defendant State which brings a counterclaim. In this case, the submission to the jurisdiction of the courts of the State of the forum operates not only in relation to the counterclaim but also to the principal claim.

20. Article 3, paragraph 2, and Article 13 contain a limitation on the possible application of Article 1, paragraph 1.

1.093 Article 2

21. This article concerns cases in which a Contracting State has expressly undertaken to submit to the jurisdiction of a foreign court. It applies to submission to the jurisdiction of a specific court, as well as to submission to the jurisdiction of any of the courts in a specified State to which the dispute may, in this case, be referred as the court which is competent *ratione materiae* and *ratione loci*.

22. Any person or body empowered to conclude written contracts in the name of the State is also deemed to have the authority to submit that State to the jurisdiction of a foreign court, in the case of disputes arising from such contract.

23. The use of the term "contract in writing" in Article 2, sub-paragraph (b), is meant not only to exclude contracts concluded orally, but also any implication of a tacit submission for instance as a result of the acceptance by the State of a clause waiving immunity, inserted by the other party in an invoice.

24. For the purposes of this article, a specification that the law of a particular State is to be applied, does not by itself imply submission to the jurisdiction of the courts of that State.

Article 3 1.094

25. This article determines the extent to which a State's conduct in proceedings amounts or does not amount to a waiver of immunity. The form of a waiver is not determined by the Convention. The term "if it appears" also covers the State as intervening party.

Article 4 1.095

26. In principle, immunity should not be granted to a State with respect to any contracts it has concluded. The article compensates to a certain degree for the relatively narrow scope of Article 7 (see below).

According to the procedural law of some States, the jurisdiction of a court depends on the place where the disputed contractual obligation arose or where it was discharged or falls to be discharged. Other States do not recognise this basis of jurisdiction or do so only in special circumstances. The connecting link in Article 4 therefore represents a compromise.

27. Where a contract imposes several obligations, immunity cannot be invoked in the courts of the State where the particular obligation which is the subject of the dispute falls to be discharged.

28. The contract need not be in writing if an oral contract is valid under the applicable law. The requirement that the obligation must be discharged in the territory of the State of the forum is not to be regarded as unsatisfied merely because the defendant claims that the obligation has already been discharged.

29. The Convention is intended to improve the legal position of individuals in their relations with States. It is not concerned with the protection of one State against another (paragraph 2, sub-paragraph (a)).

There is no reason in principle for disregarding the express intention of the parties to a contract. The words "have agreed otherwise" in paragraph 2, sub-paragraph (b), can refer to different possibilities. The parties may agree that the State should be entitled to immunity or that some court other than that of the place of performance should have jurisdiction, or that the dispute should be submitted to arbitration. The parties may also simply agree that Article 4 (1) of the Convention shall not apply.

By virtue of sub-paragraph (c), the State may invoke its immunity if two conditions are fulfilled, that is to say, if the contract has been concluded on its territory and if the obligation of the State is governed by the administrative law of that State. The fulfilment of these two conditions is intended to ensure that Article 4 should not have too broad a scope by including contracts concluded by a State in the exercise of its sovereign powers, for example contracts relating to scholarships or subsidies.

1.096   Article 5

30. This article concerns contracts of employment. A distinction has been drawn between contracts of employment and other contracts (Article 4) because in certain circumstances it may be justifiable to accord immunity to a defendant State under a contract of employment particularly when the employee is a national of the employing State (see paragraph 2, sub-paragraph (a)). The same is true when the employee is a national neither of the State for whom he works, nor of the State where he works, and where the contract of employment was not concluded on the territory of the latter State-namely where the employee is a foreign worker who has not been locally recruited (see paragraph 2, sub-paragraph (b)). In both cases the links between the employee and the employing State (in whose courts the employee may always bring proceedings), are generally closer than those between the employee and the State of the forum.

The article uses the expression "contract of employment" (in French: *contrat de travail*). This expression is to be understood in a wide sense, comprising the contracts with manual workers as well as contracts with other employees.

Paragraph 2, sub-paragraph (c) enables a Contracting State to invoke immunity where the contract of employment contains a clause in writing providing for the settlement of disputes by a court other than that of the State of the forum, for example a court of the employing State or an arbitral tribunal. But such a clause would not have the effect of making the employing State immune from the jurisdiction of the State of the forum where that State's law on employment confers exclusive jurisdiction on its own courts. Jurisdiction is not exclusive for this purpose if resort may be had to arbitration.

Article 5 also covers contracts between an individual and a State for work to be done as an employee of an office, agency or other establishment referred to in Article 7. But the grant of immunity to the employing State as provided in paragraph 2, sub-paragraphs (a) and (b) can only be justified where the individual has his habitual residence in the territory of that State at the time of the conclusion of the contract (paragraph 3). "Habitual residence" is to be understood as a question of fact.

As regards contracts of employment with diplomatic missions or consular posts, Article 32 shall also be taken into account.

1.097   Article 6

31. This article concerns the participation of a State in companies, associations or other legal entities whether or not they are endowed with legal personality. Whether these entities are profit-making or not is immaterial. The expression "participates" indicates that the article is concerned with the rights and obligations of members of the company, association or other legal entity as such.

The article is, therefore, not concerned with the State as a creditor or debtor of such entities. International organisations are excluded from the application of the article. On the other hand, all entities recognised by municipal law, even "public law" entities, are included. Instances of a State participating in a "public law" entity of another State will, admittedly, be rare.

In the phrase "with one or more private persons", the term "private persons" is intended to cover legal entities as well as natural persons.

Moreover, while it is necessary that at least one private person participates in the entity, nothing prevents one or more "public law" entities participating therein also.

32. The entity in which the State participates must have certain links with the territory of the State of the forum. Paragraph 1 mentions several alternative criteria which are generally accepted. The seat is normally the place from which the entity is directed: the registered office is generally the place where the entity is formally constituted or incorporated; and the principal place of business means the place where the major part of its business is conducted.

33. With regard to paragraph 2, the reader is referred to the commentary on Article 4, paragraph 2, sub-paragraph (b) (paragraph 29 above).

34. The expression "if it is otherwise agreed" in paragraph 2 should be interpreted broadly. It applies not only to contracts between members or between a member and an entity, but also to terms in the constitution of the entity, even though the instrument establishing the constitution may not be considered as a contract in all States.

Article 7   1.098

35. This article covers the principal activities of a State *iure gestionis*. Had the Convention dealt simply with questions of jurisdictional immunity, it might have been possible to frame the article in more general terms so as to extend it to cover all cases where a State engages in industrial, commercial or financial activities having a territorial connection with the State of the forum. As the Convention requires States to give effect to judgments rendered against them, it was necessary to insert a connecting link to found the jurisdiction of the courts of the State of the forum, namely the presence on the territory of this State of an office, agency or other establishment of the foreign State. This limitation is counter-balanced by the broad terms of Article 4: most industrial, commercial or financial activities carried on by a State on the territory of another State where it has no office, agency or establishment would probably give rise to contractual obligations which are dealt with by Article 4.

36. The concept of establishment is to be understood as one of fact. This connecting link is in line with the provisions on jurisdiction contained in various agreements on the enforcement of judgments (see Article 10 (2) of the

Hague Convention of 11 February 1971 on the Recognition and Enforcement of Foreign Judgments in Civil and Commercial Matters).

37. The expression "in the same manner as a private person" (*more privatorum*) is to be construed in the abstract. In particular, the fact that the law of the State of the forum or that of the defendant State would prohibit private persons from exercising the relevant activity, would permit only certain categories of persons to do so, or would contain special rules governing the exercise of that activity by the State, is to be left out of account. If, for example, a State undertaking not having a legal personality distinct from that of the State, embarks on a commercial activity on the territory of another State where it has an agency, the courts of that State may entertain proceedings against the undertaking even if (unlike a private person) it was under no obligation to be listed in the trade register.

38. The connecting links provided for in paragraph 1 need not exist at the time when the proceedings are instituted. A link must however have existed at the time when the act which gave rise to the dispute occurred.

39. Consideration was given to the question whether the connecting links would not have the effect of excluding loans issued abroad from the application of Article 7. However it appeared on investigation that in respect of such loans, States normally submit to the jurisdiction of the courts of the State of issue. In that event Article 2 (b) will apply, and the debtor State will not be able to invoke immunity. Under Article 4 (1) t is also subject to the jurisdiction of any other State on whose territory it has undertaken to refund the capital or pay the interest.

With regard to paragraph 2, the reader is again referred to the first two paragraphs of the commentary on Article 4 (2), sub-paragraphs (a) and (b) (paragraph 29 above).

1.099 Article 8

40. This provision has been drafted so as to cover all cases where a State is involved in a dispute relating to one of the rights mentioned in sub-paragraphs (a) to (d), provided there is an adequate connection with the State of the forum.

The expression "other similar right" (sub-paragraph (a)) applies to any other rights of the same nature as those expressly mentioned, which may be applied for, registered or deposited.

Proceedings relating to the rights of an employee in his invention may, depending upon the circumstances and the law which is applicable, fall within the scope of Article 5 or Article 8.

41. Sub-paragraphs (b) and (c) provide an instance of the Convention not allowing immunity from claims relating to tortious acts of foreign States (see the commentary to Article 11).

42. Reference is made in sub-paragraph (d) to a "trade name" in order to avoid any doubt as to the inclusion of such names in the general list in sub-paragraph (a). The term "right to the use of a trade mark" is to be interpreted in a broad sense to attract all possible forms of protection. This provision applies in particular to disputes relating to the registration of a trade name.

Article 9 1.100

43. This article provides that there shall be no immunity in proceedings concerning the rights and obligations of a State in, or in connection with, immovable property situated in the territory of the State of the forum. It should be read in conjunction with Article 32.

Under certain legal systems possession is not strictly speaking a right in the sense attributed to that term. For this reason express reference is made to it in sub-paragraphs (a) and (b) of this article.

44. The expressions "rights", "use" and "possession" must be interpreted broadly. Article 9 covers inter alia:

(1) proceedings against States concerning their rights in immovable property in the State of the forum;
(2) proceedings relating to mortgages whether the foreign State is mortgagor or mortgagee;
(3) proceedings relating to nuisance;
(4) proceedings arising from the unauthorised (permanent or temporary) use of immovable property including actions in trespass, whether an injunction is claimed or damages or both;
(5) proceedings concerning rights to the use of immovable property in the State of the forum, for example, actions to establish the existence or non-existence of a lease or tenancy agreement, or for possession or eviction;
(6) proceedings relating to payments due from a State for the use of immovable property, or of a part thereof, in the State of the forum, with the exception of dues or taxes (see Article 29, sub-paragraph (c));
(7) proceedings relating to the liabilities of a State as the owner or occupier of immovable property in the State of the forum (for example accidents caused by the dilapidated state of the building, *actio de electis vel effusis*).

Article 10 1.101

45. According to this article immunity may not be claimed in disputes relating to rights arising by way of succession, gift or *bona vacantia*.

However, it has not been possible to provide for connecting links. In virtually no other sphere of private international law are there such differences between legal systems as there are in determining the competent jurisdiction or the applicable law. Some States regard the domicile of the deceased as the determining factor, whereas others recognise only the competence of the authorities of the State of which the deceased was a national, and apply the law of that State. Moreover, at least in regard to any immovable property forming part of the estate, the State in which that property is situated is often considered to have exclusive jurisdiction.

In consequence a special system has had to be set up concerning the obligations of a State to give effect to a judgment rendered against it (see Article 20(3)).

46. A State's right to the undisposed goods of a deceased person is in certain legal systems considered a right of succession, in others a right of forfeiture of goods without ownership (*bona vacantia*). Separate mention was made of *bona vacantia* to cover the latter concept.

1.102   Article 11

47. This article has been drafted on the lines of Article 10 (4) of the Hague Convention of 1 February 1971 on the Recognition and Enforcement of Foreign Judgments in Civil and Commercial Matters.

48. Where there has been injury to the person or damage to property, the rule of non-immunity applies equally to any concomitant claims for non-material damage resulting from the same acts, provided of course that a claim for such damage lies under the applicable law (e.g. in respect of *pretium doloris*). Where there has been no physical injury and no damage to tangible property, the article does not apply. This is the case, for example, as regards unfair competition (subject to the applicability of other articles of the Convention, such as Article 7) or defamation.

49. The author of the damage must have been on the territory of the State of the forum at the time the damage was caused: this requirement does not apply, however, to the person whose liability is in issue. For example, when a vehicle belonging to a State is involved in a traffic accident, then, provided the driver of the vehicle was present, the State as owner or possessor of the vehicle may be sued, even though the plaintiff does not seek to establish the personal liability of the driver.

1.103   Article 12

50. A party to an arbitration agreement may in certain cases be required to appear before a national court. The most important are those mentioned in paragraph 1(a) to (c) of this Article. Sub-paragraph (b) is mainly concerned with measures to initiate the arbitration (appointment of arbitrators), but also covers other instances of judicial control over arbitration procedures known to certain national systems (for example decisions concerning a challenge to the arbitrator).

51. It should be made clear that proceedings concerned with the enforcement of arbitral awards are outside the scope of the Convention and governed by domestic law and any international convention which may be applicable: Article 20 does not therefore apply.

52. The written requirement has been provided for because of the importance of the agreement of a State to arbitration. This may lead to some slight deviation from the practice followed under other international agreements on arbitration.

53. It could be questioned whether decisions to which Article 12 applies are of such a nature that a foreign State can be required to give effect to them under Article 20. For they are not judgments ordering performance or payment, but declaratory judgments on matters of fact or law or merely procedural directions. The foreign State is nevertheless bound to give effect to them. The State may not, for instance, institute proceedings before its own courts in respect of a dispute if the validity of an arbitration agreement covering that dispute has been judicially confirmed.

Article 13 — 1.104

54. This article introduces an exception to Article 1, paragraph 1. It concerns the special case in which a State intervenes in proceedings to which it is not a party in order to invoke its immunity. In common law countries, a judicial decision can sometimes affect third parties; such is the case, for example, with actions *in rem*. By permitting a State to claim immunity in such cases notwithstanding the provisions of Article 1, paragraph 1, Article 13 gives States a chance to safeguard their rights or interests in the property which is the subject of the dispute.

Article 14 — 1.105

55. This provision is intended to prevent State immunity from obstructing the legal administration of property. Apart from the administration of the estate of a bankrupt or a trust, there are other cases of the judicial administration of property such as the administration of the estates of deceased persons and, in many countries, arrangements and compositions with creditors. The rule in Article 14 applies whether the court administers the property itself or merely arranges for, or supervises, the administration. Consequently, the fact that a foreign State claims a right or interest in a part of the property of the estate will not prevent the court from administering or supervising the administration of the property, including that part of it over which the State claims a right or interest.

Article 15 — 1.106

56. The Convention represents a compromise between the doctrines of absolute and relative State immunity. A State cannot claim immunity in cases

falling under Articles 1 to 14. On the other hand, it is entitled to immunity in respect of all other acts even those which are according to the doctrine of relative State immunity, *acta iure gestionis*.

This rule is, however, subject to qualification (see paragraph 96 below).

The Convention relates only to immunity or non-immunity from the jurisdiction of the courts of another Contracting State. Article 15 cannot therefore be invoked as a ground for claiming immunity from proceedings which are not of a judicial character.

57. A foreign State's immunity from jurisdiction must be recognised *ex officio* where that State does not appear and the proceedings do not fall within Articles 1 to 14.

CHAPTER II

1.107 **Article 16**

58. Difficulties often occur in connection with the service of writs in proceedings against States. The rules concerning the representation of States in judicial proceedings are frequently complex, and vary from State to State. The plaintiff, and even the court may not know on whom a writ issued against a State should be served.

The authorities of the defendant State are also faced with problems. In the time allowed to parties to enter an appearance, which is frequently very short, the competent authority in the defendant State must be identified and informed and the necessary consultations held.

Article 16 safeguards the interests of both parties by providing that transmission of the most important documents to the Foreign Ministry of the defendant State constitutes effective service and by ensuring adequate time-limits.

This article implies that it is the State as such which is sued; the question whether, according to national law, it is represented by one of its organs, falls outside the scope of the Convention. Moreover, this article is not concerned with determining which authorities are competent to represent the State in proceedings brought against it.

The terminology used in the French text, *signification ou notification* takes account of the methods provided for the service of judicial documents in different legal systems, as does the Hague Convention of 15 November 1965 concerning *La signification et la notification à l'étranger des actes judiciaires et extrajudiciaires en matière civile ou commerciale*.

59. It was originally thought that provision should be made for documents instituting proceedings to be transmitted to the Foreign Ministry of the defendant State through the diplomatic channels of that State. Although this practice will probably be adopted in the large majority of cases, the article does

not specifically mention diplomatic channels, as relations between member States of the Council of Europe are not always conducted through these channels.

60. Paragraph 2 contains the rules for transmitting documents by which proceedings are instituted and copies of judgments by default; it thus applies to what may be considered the two most important cases from the point of view of safeguarding the defendant. The Foreign Ministry is obliged to accept writs served on it even if it believes that the proceedings brought against the State are unjustified, that the court is not competent to entertain the proceedings, or that the defendant State may claim immunity. On the other hand, by accepting the documents, the defendant State in no way renounces its right to invoke its grounds of defence or to claim immunity.

The Foreign Ministry is not obliged to accept process directed against a legal entity which is distinct from the State and is capable of suing or being sued (see Article 27).

The procedural concepts referred to in Article 16 (in particular "the document by which the proceedings are instituted" and "judgment by default") are to be given the meaning they have in the *lex fori*, as it does not at present seem possible to reach unification of practice or even common definitions on this point. Consequently the applicability of Article 16 to documents relating to the introduction of appeals also depends on the *lex fori*.

61. When transmitting a document instituting proceedings to the Foreign Ministry, the diplomatic mission of the State of the forum should ensure that it provides the information necessary to enable the authority which is competent to represent the defendant State to be identified. If necessary, the diplomatic mission may be asked to give additional information.

62. The translation which must accompany the documents referred to in paragraph 2 is solely for purposes of information. The Convention does not require the translator to have any special qualifications or that the accuracy of the translation be confirmed by a duly authorised person.

As a result of the absence of any provision in the Convention on the subject, no legalisation or like formality is required either for the documents transmitted or for the letters of transmission.

63. Paragraph 3, which constitutes an innovation for most judicial systems takes account of the interests both of the plaintiff and of the defendant State. It safeguards the Plaintiff's interests by facilitating determination of the date on which service is deemed to have been effected. It safeguards the defendant State's rights by protecting it from any form of service which is deemed to have been effected by a fiction, such as service on the *parquet*, and from time-limits which begin to run from the date on which the document is posted.

64. The time-limits allowed to parties for the entering of an appearance or for bringing appeals vary from one State to another. Paragraph 4 might have been drafted so as to extend by two months the time-limits provided by the national law but that would have necessitated the incorporation in each legal system of special time-limits when the defendant is a Contracting State. It therefore seemed more convenient simply to postpone by two months the date from which time begins to run. This two month period should be sufficient to permit the Foreign Ministry to give notice to the competent authority in its own State and for the necessary consultations to take place in that State.

65. Paragraph 5 takes account of the situation in certain legal systems, in particular Scandinavian systems.

66. Paragraph 6 refers only to the method of service of the document by which the proceedings are instituted. It does not prevent a State from appearing, in accordance with the procedure in force in the State of the forum, in order to claim that it had not been allowed the time for entering an appearance provided for in paragraphs 4 and 5.

This paragraph also applies when the foreign State participates in the proceedings only in order to assert its immunity.

67. Paragraphs 6 and 7 are particularly important when interpreted in conjunction with Article 20 (2) (d) (see paragraph 82 below).

1.108   Article 17

68. Under Article 17 of the Hague Convention of 1 March 1954 relating to civil procedure, only nationals of Contracting States are exempt from the obligation to provide security for costs. The authorities indicate that this exemption covers legal persons and commercial companies. Whether it would include the foreign State as plaintiff is doubtful. Article 17 of the present Convention is based on Article 17 of the 1954 Hague Convention. It was thought unnecessary to confine the article to foreign States which are plaintiffs or intervening parties, since, at any rate under the law of the States which took part in the drafting of the Convention, a defendant is not required to provide security for costs.

69. By contrast, the second sentence requiring a foreign State to pay costs, applies only to a State as plaintiff or intervening party. The second sentence differs from Articles 18 and 19 of the 1954 Hague Convention in that it does not provide for the enforcement of decisions on the payment of costs but rather imposes an obligation on the foreign State to pay the costs and expenses which the court or other competent authority of the State of the forum has ordered it to pay. Article 20, paragraphs (2) and (3), cannot be invoked as grounds for a refusal to pay costs. Moreover the obligation to pay is not subject to the control procedure provided for in Article 21 (see below). On the other hand, Article 23 and, where is applies, Article 26 do apply to orders for costs against a State.

Article 18 1.109

70. In some States, penalties may be imposed on a party which fails or refuses to comply with a court order to produce evidence (contempt of court). Article 18 provides that these penalties may not be imposed on States. However, the court retains whatever discretion it may have under its own law to draw the appropriate conclusions from a State's failure or refusal to comply.

71. The refusal of a State to produce evidence is generally based on a desire not to divulge secrets, more especially for reasons of national security. The Convention does not require a State to give reasons for its refusal.

Article 19 1.110

72. This article deals with pending proceedings. Proceedings based on the same facts should not be brought against a State in different courts. The introductory sentence follows the pattern of numerous agreements on the recognition and enforcement of foreign judgments, for example, Article 20 of the Hague Convention of 1 February 1971 which has been mentioned above. A choice is given to the court between discontinuing or staying the proceedings, in accordance with the *lex fori*, which must however permit one or the other. The duration of the stay is also determined by the *lex fori*. However, where sub-paragraph (b) applies, proceedings may not be resumed until it is reasonably certain that the proceedings which were the first to be instituted will not result in a decision to which the State must give effect in accordance with Article 20.

73. Article 19, paragraph 1 does not prevent the court also taking account of pending proceedings in cases and on conditions other than those mentioned therein where the lex fori so provides.

74. The principal object of paragraph 1, sub-paragraph (a) is to prevent subsequent applications to the court of another Contracting State by a person who fears that he may not be successful in the proceedings he has already instituted against a State before one of its own courts. Sub-paragraph (b) prevents a defendant State from instituting proceedings before its own courts (for example, for a declaratory judgment) in order to be able to invoke Article 20 (2) (b), or (c), and to evade its obligation to give effect to a foreign judgment.

75. Paragraph 2 of Article 19 permits derogation from the obligations contained in this article.

CHAPTER III

Article 20 1.111

76. The structure of the Convention consists of a list of cases where immunity cannot be granted and a general provision (Article 15) specifying that immunity shall be granted in all other cases. This is supplemented by an obligation

imposed on foreign States to give effect to judgments rendered against them: this is the object of Article 20.

The expression "give effect" does not necessarily imply the making of a payment or, indeed, any transfer of property. It may signify an obligation to accept a state of affairs determined by a declaratory judgment. The State must submit to the judgment in good faith: this may even involve acquiescence in the dismissal of an action instituted in a foreign country and consequently refraining from instituting further proceedings based on the same facts before one of its own courts or before a court of a third State.

The Convention is concerned only with the obligation of a State to give effect to a judgment. Judgments given in favour of States against private persons will continue to be governed by the ordinary rules (the national law, or international Conventions on recognition and enforcement of judgments).

The Convention deliberately abstains from providing any machinery of recognition or enforcement since the primary obligation of the State is to give effect to the judgment. Moreover, enforcement against the property of a foreign State is considered by some States to be contrary to international law while in others it is governed by special rules of a restrictive nature. The system established under the Convention safeguards as effectively as possible the rights of the person in whose favour judgment has been given.

77. Article 20, paragraph 1 (a) makes reference not only to Articles 1 to 12, but also to Article 13, which supplements Article 1. On the other hand, it does not refer to Article 14 which (in order to cover a situation which can arise in some countries) is intended purely to permit a court to administer property even when a Contracting State claims a right in that property; here the State does not submit to the jurisdiction so as to be obliged to give effect to the judgment.

78. The conditions laid down in paragraph 1 (a) require no comment. The terms used in paragraph 1 (b) take account of the fact that forms of appeal or review vary from State to State.

79. In some States, both the authorities and the case-law distinguish between international and domestic *ordre public*. Paragraph 2 (a) uses the term in the narrower of the two senses, i.e. international *ordre public*.

The concept of *ordre public* has no exact equivalent in English, the term "public policy" being insufficiently comprehensive. The expression "either party had no adequate opportunity fairly to present his case" has been added to the English text to take account of the procedural aspect of the concept of *ordre public*. This expression is based on the wording of Article 5 (1) of the Hague Convention of 1 February 1971 on the Recognition and Enforcement of Foreign Judgments in Civil and Commercial Matters. The inclusion of the word "manifestly" is intended to underline the exceptional nature of cases where objections can be raised on grounds of *ordre public*. On this point, the draft follows certain recent conventions of the Hague Conference on Private International Law (e.g. the above-mentioned provision of the Hague Convention of 1 February 1971).

80. Paragraph 2 (b), which makes the existence of pending proceedings a ground for a refusal to give effect to the judgment, corresponds to Article 19. Where a judgment has been given by a court of first instance, but is not yet final, the law of some States regards the case as still pending; in other States such a judgment has the effect that the proceedings are no longer considered to be pending. In the latter group of States, recognition of the foreign judgment would be refused on account of the judgment being now *res judicata*. For the application of the Convention, this doctrinal difference has little practical effect, since paragraph (b) and (c) make both *lis pendens* and *res judicata* grounds for refusing to give effect to a judgment.

It will often be difficult to foresee whether proceedings first instituted before a court of another Contracting State will result in a decision to which a State will be obliged to give effect. Under the terms of sub-paragraph (b)(ii), it is sufficient that such a decision may result.

81. Paragraph 2 (c), which makes the existence of another (conflicting) decision a reason for not giving effect to the judgment, is drafted in wider terms than the provision dealing with pending proceedings. Here it is not a question of proceedings instituted on the same grounds and having the same purposes. It is sufficient that the judgment should have been given between the same parties and that its effect (and not its *ratio decidendi*) is inconsistent with those of the other judgment. It is not necessary for the purposes of paragraph 2 (c)(i) that the judgment should have become final.

It has not been possible to specify in sub-paragraph (c)(i) conditions as to the sequence of events which will completely exclude the possibility that a foreign defendant State may subsequently bring proceedings before its own courts in order to obtain an "inconsistent" judgment. The respect due to the judgment of a national court requires that it should be maintained at least where it had already been given at the time when the foreign judgment became final, even if the proceedings were instituted after those which resulted in the foreign judgment. On this point it is Article 19 which is designed to forestall abuses by preventing a judgment being given by a court of the State which is a party to the earlier proceedings.

82. The reason for refusal given in sub-paragraph (d) is common form in enforcement treaties: due rights to establish a defence must have been accorded in the State of origin. The sub-paragraph is worded in such a way that it does not require a State which has not entered an appearance or appealed against a

judgment by default to offer any explanations. It is sufficient to establish that the provisions of Article 16 have not been observed.

83. Brief reference has already been made, in the comments on Article 10 (succession, *bona vacantia*, gifts) to the need to specify special grounds for refusing to give effect to judgments relating to the matters referred to in that article (see paragraph 45 above). In addition to the grounds of refusal set out in paragraphs 1 and 2, two extra grounds have been added for these cases by paragraph 3: one relating to the jurisdiction of the court, and the other the applicable law.

Under sub-paragraph (a), a State is not required to give effect to a judgment where the courts of the State of the forum would not have had jurisdiction if (hypothetically) they had applied the jurisdictional rules in force in the State against which judgment has been given. The expression *mutatis mutandis* serves to underline that, in the hypothesis that the courts of the State of the forum would have applied the jurisdictional rules of the State against which judgment has been given, the assumption must equally be made that these rules are applied not to the State against which judgment has been given but to the State of the forum. An exception is made for the case where in the circumstances jurisdiction could only have been based on an "exorbitant" ground. Rules of jurisdiction based on "exorbitant" grounds are excepted from the jurisdictional rules so to be applied.

The rule in sub-paragraph (b) is taken from the Hague Convention of 1 February 1971 (see Article 7, paragraph 2). A "different result" is meant to be one which is different in substance from that which would have been reached by the courts of the State which is called upon to give effect to the judgment.

The final sub-paragraph of paragraph 3 provides for the eventuality of the State of the forum and the State against which the judgment has been given being parties to a treaty on the recognition and enforcement of judgments. In that event a State must give effect to the judgment if it conforms with the treaty's requirements both as to jurisdiction and as to applicable law.

1.112   Article 21

84. It is to be assumed that Contracting States will fulfil the obligations which they have undertaken by virtue of Article 20 (see also Article 25) without any need for a control procedure. But as one of the major objects of the Convention is to protect the position of a private person who is engaged in litigation against a State, it was thought unavoidable to have some such procedure.

Paragraph 1 of Article 21 gives anyone who wishes to enforce a judgment given in his favour against a State a possibility of instituting proceedings before a court of that State. This procedure derives from the classical concept of the *exequatur* granted to a foreign judgment by the courts of the State in which execution is sought.

85. The competent national court of the defendant State before which proceedings have been instituted pursuant to paragraph 1 must decide whether the State is obliged to give effect to the foreign judgment. The issue may be brought before the court by any person on whom the judgment confers rights. Whether the State may also institute proceedings before this court to obtain a decision declaring that it is not bound to give effect to a foreign judgment, is left to be determined by the law of that State.

No time-limit has been laid down within which proceedings must be instituted before the competent national court. Under the Convention the duty to give effect to a judgment arises as soon as it is final and capable of execution in the State of the forum, there being no need for the successful party to institute any proceedings for its enforcement before an authority of the defendant State. At this stage, therefore, no special means of communication are provided for between the successful party and the defendant State.

Paragraph 2 simply states a rule which is to be found—expressly or impliedly—in treaties concerning the recognition and enforcement of foreign judgments.

86. Paragraph 3 is designed to grant the best possible facilities to parties who, in accordance with paragraph 1, institute proceedings before the competent court of the State against which a judgment has been given.

87. The Convention does not specify which documents have to be produced by an applicant, for this depends on the relevant rules of procedure. The same is true of the need to provide translations. In any event, any documents which have to be produced are exempt from legalisation (paragraph 3 (b)). "Any other like formality" refers particularly to the certification provided for by the Hague Convention of 5 October 1961 Abolishing the Requirement of Legalisation for Foreign Public Documents.

88. Paragraph 3 (c) is worded in terms similar to those of the first sentence of Article 17.

89. Some conventions provide that a party who has received free legal aid before the court which gave the judgment is also entitled to it as of right for any enforcement proceedings. However, the circumstances in which legal aid is granted depend on the standard of living and average income in each State, as well as on the expense of litigation. The automatic grant of legal aid would, therefore, in some circumstances have had the effect that persons seeking to enforce a foreign judgment would have received aid under more favourable conditions than those applicable to any other persons. It thus seemed preferable, in sub-paragraph (d), to treat foreign applicants in the same way as nationals. The wording takes account of the fact that in some member States

of the Council of Europe entitlement to legal aid depends on nationality and in others on domicile or residence.

90. Paragraph 4 (which should be read with Article 41(e)) is designed to assist persons who decide to institute proceedings before the competent court of the defendant State.

1.113   Article 22

91. In some member States of the Council of Europe, proceedings frequently end in a judicial settlement which can be enforced like judgments. Article 22 requires Contracting States to give effect to judicial settlements even where, according to the applicable rules of procedure, such a settlement would not be enforceable. The conditions laid down in Article 20, whether positive or negative, do not apply to judicial settlements. A party, which has entered into a settlement with a foreign State, should be entitled to establish his rights in the same way as a party which has obtained a judgment (Article 21). Similarly, the rule prohibiting measures of execution applies to judicial settlements (Article 23; see however Article 26).

1.114   Article 23

92. In some States the rule which prohibits execution against the property of a foreign State is regarded as a rule of international law; in other States, execution against the property of a foreign State is considered permissible under strictly defined conditions. As already explained it is one of the objectives of the present Convention to protect the rights of individuals. The Convention system therefore represents a compromise in that it combines an obligation on States to give effect to judgments (the obligation being controlled by judicial safeguards) with a rule permitting no execution. For States having made the declaration referred to in Article 24, see paragraph 100 below.

93. The term "preventive measures" in Article 23 extends only to such measures as may be taken with a view to eventual execution.

94. The last part of the sentence enables a State to waive immunity from execution. Waivers of this kind, subject to specified limits, are frequently found in the case of State loans.

95. Article 23 applies only to execution of judgments given in pursuance of the Convention: arbitral awards do not, for example, fall within the scope of the article.

CHAPTER IV

1.115   Article 24

96. Certain States which at present apply rules of qualified State immunity considered that Article 15, which provides that immunity must be accorded to

States in all cases other than those falling within Articles 1 to 13, was too rigid either because some acts *iure gestionis* fall outside the cases covered by these articles, or because the connecting links prescribed in these articles do not correspond with rules of jurisdictional competence applied in those States. Article 24 permits States to derogate from the provisions of Article 15.

Pursuant to paragraph 1, Contracting States have the option of declaring, by notification to the Secretary General of the Council of Europe, that their courts are to be entitled to entertain proceedings against other Contracting States to the extent that they may entertain such proceedings against third States; for this purpose, treaties concluded with third States which relate to problems of immunity, should not be taken into account. In other words, the regime applied by the courts of a State which has made the declaration will not be affected by the Convention, and can even continue to develop along its own lines.

The declaration addressed to the Secretary General of the Council of Europe will not affect the immunity from jurisdiction enjoyed by foreign States in respect of acts done in the exercise of sovereign authority (*acta iure imperii*).

The consequences of the declaration are set out in Articles 25 and 26.

97. However, the courts may not entertain proceedings with in the "grey zone" (i.e. the matters not covered by Articles 1 to 13 which are subjected to jurisdiction in relations with non-Contracting States) if their jurisdiction can be based solely on an "exorbitant" ground of jurisdiction (paragraph 2: for further details, see the Annex).

98. Paragraph 1 does not refer to Article 14, which provides that nothing in the Convention is to prevent a court from administering property solely on account of the fact that a foreign State has a right or interest in the property. It is never necessary to apply Article 24 to reach results which Article 14 enables one to achieve. In similar fashion, Articles 25 and 26 do not apply to judgments concerning the administration of such property.

Article 25   1.116

99. A State which makes a declaration under Article 24 opts for a system according to which its courts may exercise jurisdiction, even as against Contracting States, in cases other than those provided in Articles 1 to 13, that is to say in the "grey zone" (cf. paragraphs 96 and 97 above). Article 25 sets out the conditions under which States which have made the declaration must give effect to "grey zone" judgments given against them.

100. Apart from Article 10, for which special rules are laid down in paragraph 3 of Article 20, and Article 13 which is merely an exception to Article 1, Articles 1 to 13 all contain territorial connecting links. It was not possible to provide such connecting links in Article 25 since disputes falling within the "grey zone" are too diverse to admit of classification.

101. It would not, however, be appropriate to require States to give effect to judgments irrespective of any justification for the assumption of jurisdiction by the State of the forum.

Paragraph 3, sub-paragraphs (a) and (b) set out the circumstances in which this jurisdiction must be considered as sufficiently well-founded to justify acceptance of the obligation to give effect to the judgment.

Sub-paragraph (a) deals with the case where there is a treaty between the State of the forum and the defendant State which provides for the mutual recognition of certain grounds of jurisdiction. This might involve either express treaty provisions conferring jurisdiction either with a view to recognition and execution of the resulting judgments ("double treaty", "direct jurisdiction") or for other purposes; or it might involve simply certain jurisdictional conditions which must be fulfilled before there is any obligation to recognise or execute the judgment ("simple treaty", "indirect jurisdiction"). It is only fair that any ground of jurisdiction which States have undertaken mutually to recognise, irrespective of who is the defendant, should also be recognised for the purposes of Article 25.

Sub-paragraph (b) applies where there is no agreement on recognition and enforcement between the State of the forum and the defendant State which covers the whole civil and commercial field or at least a large part of it.

It is narrower in scope than sub-paragraph (a) because it applies irrespective of treaties which establish jurisdiction for purposes other than recognition and enforcement of judgments; in fact such agreements always relate to a limited field and should not therefore adversely affect the operation of this supplementary rule. Where there is no relevant agreement, the Convention provides that the jurisdiction of the courts of the State of the forum must be recognised whenever those courts would have had jurisdiction over the dispute which was the subject of the judgment had they applied *mutatis mutandis* the jurisdictional rules of the defendant State. There is, however, a further condition that in applying this test, the court of the defendant State need not take into account any rules of jurisdiction set out in the Annex. This exception seems all the more justified in that these rules are not in any event accepted as a basis of jurisdiction under Article 24, paragraph 2.

For the meaning of the term *mutatis mutandis*, which in this context might give rise to difficulty, the reader is referred to the explanation given in paragraph 83 above.

102. Moreover, always given the assurance of a general agreement on recognition and execution, it was decided, in view of the fact that in relation to contracts no satisfactory connecting link could be found, to exempt in paragraph 3 (b) *in fine*, States from the obligation to give effect to judgments in cases relating to a

contract. Naturally, this does not apply where the contract is to be discharged in the State of the forum, in which case Article 4 applies.

103. Paragraph 4 draws attention to a possibility which is also covered more generally by Article 33. This may be of assistance to States which are authorised under their constitution to conclude an agreement of this kind without submitting it for parliamentary approval.

Article 26 1.117

104. This article introduces for the purposes of the optional regime provided for in Article 24, an exception to the rule in Article 23 (which forbids the levying of execution against the property of a foreign State): execution may be levied in the State of the forum against any property of a foreign State used exclusively in connection with an industrial or commercial activity, provided that the proceedings relate exclusively to such an activity of the State, and that both the States have made the declaration provided for in Article 24.

105. Article 26 only applies to proceedings concerning industrial or commercial activities in which the State engages "in the same manner as a private person". This expression has the same meaning here as in Article 7 (see commentary under paragraph 37 above). The article is based on the principle that a State should, in respect of its activities *iure gestionis* in the industrial and commercial field, be placed so far as possible on the same footing as a private person.

106. Where Article 26 permits execution against the property of a foreign State in the State of the forum conservatory measures may also be taken against such property with a view to ensuring eventual execution of the judgment (see paragraph 93 above).

CHAPTER V

Article 27 1.118

107. In practice, proceedings are frequently brought by an individual, not, strictly speaking, against a State itself, but against a legal entity established under the authority of the State and exercising public functions. As an important consequence of paragraph 1 provisions of the Convention which lay down special rules for proceedings to which one of the parties is a State (Articles 16–19), those dealing with the obligation to comply with a judgment or a settlement (Articles 20–22), and those prohibiting execution in the territory of the State of the forum (Article 23), do not apply to such entities.

108. For the purpose of defining these entities, the criterion of legal personality alone is not adequate, for even a State authority may have legal

personality without constituting an entity distinct from the State. On the other hand, it was considered that a dual test comprising (1) distinct existence separate and apart from the executive organs of the State and (2) capacity to sue or be sued, i.e. the ability to assume the role of either plaintiff or defendant in court proceedings, could provide a satisfactory means of identifying those legal entities in Contracting States which should not be treated as the State.

109. The entities referred to in Article 27 may be, *inter alia*, political subdivisions (subject to the federal clause in Article 28) or State agencies, such as national banks or railway administrations.

Paragraph 2 is worded in such a way that where an entity is authorised to exercise public functions in the State of the forum an action may be brought against it provided the proceedings do not relate to acts performed by the entity in the exercise of sovereign authority (*acta iure imperii*). Paragraph 3 provides that an entity may not enjoy more favourable treatment than a Contracting State.

The overall effect of Article 27 is to deny to entities, when they are not exercising public functions, any right to treatment different from that accorded to a private person.

1.119 Article 28

110. The constituent States of a federal State exercise in their own right a large number of functions which in unitary States are performed either by the central authority itself or by authorities answerable to it. This being so, the question arises whether these constituent States should be able to claim immunity *ratione personae*, or at least *ratione materiae*, when proceedings are brought against them in a foreign court.

Paragraph 1 lays down the principle that a federal State may not enjoy immunity *ratione personae*.

However, for the reasons stated, a federal State may make a declaration to the effect that for the purposes of the Convention, a constituent State of the federation is to have the same rights and to be subject to the same obligations as a Contracting State.

The declaration must be notified by the federal State to the Secretary General of the Council of Europe. The effect of the declaration is that the provisions of the Convention on immunity and non-immunity from jurisdiction, on immunity from execution and on the effects of judgments given against a State, become applicable in proceedings instituted against a constituent State of the federation before the courts of a foreign State.

111. For the sake of simplicity and to avoid uncertainty, the Ministry of Foreign Affairs of the federal State is empowered to receive the documents

mentioned in Article 16, even in the case of proceedings brought against its constituent States.

All declarations, notifications and communications which Contracting States may make or are required to make under the terms of the Convention will be made by the federal State.

112. Where a federal State does not make the declaration provided for in Article 28, paragraph 2, its constituent States are considered as being entities in the sense of Article 27.

Article 29   1.120

113. This article excludes certain matters from the field of application of the Convention. The Convention is essentially concerned with "private law" disputes between individuals and States.

In some countries social security forms part of public law, in others part of private law, in still others it falls somewhere between the two; and finally, there are States in which no distinction is made between public and private law. In the absence of an express exclusion a question might have arisen whether or not disputes concerning social security would fall within Articles 4 and 7.

Damage and injury in nuclear matters have been excluded so as to render Article 11 inapplicable. Other conventions deal with nuclear damage.

Customs duties, taxes, penalties and fines have been excluded because in some countries they do not fall exclusively under public law or because the dividing line between public and private law is ill-defined or non-existent. Article 9 in particular might otherwise have been applicable.

114. It should be stressed that these same matters are also excluded from the field of application of the Hague Convention of 1 February 1971 on the Recognition and Enforcement of Foreign Judgments in Civil and Commercial Matters (Article 1, paragraph 2 nos. 6 and 7, and paragraph 3).

The exclusion of these matters from the field of application of the present Convention does not by any means imply that, by an argument *a contrario* based on Article 15, the courts of Contracting States are to have jurisdiction to deal with disputes which might arise in these fields or that judgments given in these fields can be enforced in the State of the forum against property of a foreign State. It means only that, since the provisions of the Convention may not be invoked, recourse must be had to general rules of law.

Article 30   1.121

115. The purpose of this article is to exclude matters covered by the Brussels Convention of 10 April 1926 for the Unification of certain Rules concerning the Immunity of State-owned Vessels, and the Protocol of 24 May 1934. These instruments are in force between a fairly large number of member States

of the Council of Europe. The expressions used in Article 30 should be interpreted in accordance with the interpretation generally given to them in these two instruments.

1.122 **Article 31**

116. The Convention is not intended to govern situations which may arise in the event of armed conflict; nor can it be invoked to resolve problems which may arise between allied States as a result of the stationing of forces. These problems are generally dealt with by special agreements (cf. Article 33).

Article 31 likewise excludes any questions of immunity from jurisdiction which may arise as a result of visits by the naval forces of a foreign State.

It prevents the Convention being interpreted as having any influence upon these matters.

1.123 **Article 32**

117. Diplomatic and consular immunities and privileges are already governed by rules of international law, notably those contained in the Vienna Conventions of 18 April 1961 and 24 April 1963, and in bilateral agreements. The considerations which underlie these privileges and immunities are different from those underlying the present Convention. The Convention cannot prejudice diplomatic and consular immunities, directly or indirectly. It is clear from Article 32—and this is confirmed by Article 33—that in the event of conflict between the present Convention and the instruments mentioned above, the provisions of the latter shall prevail.

1.124 **Article 33**

118. The authors of the Convention considered in detail the relationship between the Convention and the bilateral or multilateral treaties on the jurisdiction of courts, and the recognition and enforcement of judgments. There is one point to be made at the outset: in the event of proceedings instituted by a State against a private person or of a judgment given in favour of a State against such a person, it is these treaties which will apply and the Convention in no way derogates from them.

As regards proceedings instituted or judgments given against a State, the Position becomes more difficult. In some treaties the rules relating to jurisdiction differ from the connecting links set out in the present Convention: the conditions for the recognition and enforcement of judgments contained in these treaties may be different from those laid down in Articles 20 and 25 (for example, as regards the finality of the foreign judgment); and, lastly, according to these treaties, judgments may be recognised and enforced without regard to the nationality or other personal characteristics of the defendant.

The authors of the Convention take the view that, as between the Contracting Parties, the Convention prevails over enforcement treaties, by virtue of the rule *lex specialis derogat generali*.

119. By virtue of the same principle, Article 16 of the Convention derogates from the provisions of other treaties on the service of judicial documents. But two or more Contracting States may adopt a different scheme from that laid down in Article 16.

120. Among the international agreements which remain unaffected by the Convention by virtue of Article 33 are agreements dealing specifically (i.e. otherwise than in a general manner) with State immunity as well as the rules to be applied where a State is party to proceedings and enforcement of judgments by States (cf. Article 7 of the European Convention on Compulsory Insurance against Civil Liability of Motor Vehicles of 20 April 1959). Similarly unaffected are agreements which, whether on a temporary or a permanent basis, remove from the jurisdiction of the courts particular claims against certain States or groups of States (e.g. Article 5 of the London Agreement on German External Debts of 27 February 1953 and Article 3 of Chapter 6 and Article 1 of Chapter 9 of the Convention on the Settlement of Matters arising out of the War and the Occupation, amended text of 23 October 1954).

Article 34   1.125

121. Under this article, the International Court of Justice has jurisdiction in respect of disputes between Contracting States on the interpretation or application of the Convention.

122. By virtue of paragraph 2 no dispute pending before a national court, whether relating to proceedings on the merits of the case between a private individual and a State (sub-paragraph (a)), or proceedings to establish the obligation to give effect to a judgment (sub-paragraph (b)), may be submitted to the ICJ before the national court has given its final decision (cf. Article 29 of the European Convention for the Peaceful Settlement of Disputes, of 29 April 1957).

Article 35   1.126

123. The application of the Convention to proceedings already instituted at the time of its entry into force would have necessitated complex transitional arrangements, and might have given rise to difficulties for any parties who had acted on the basis of the situation existing in the State of the forum at the time when the proceedings were instituted. Paragraph 3 excludes from the field of application of the Convention disputes relating to events in the too distant past.

CHAPTER VI

1.127 **Articles 36–41**

124. These articles contain the final clauses which are customary in conventions of a legal character concluded under the auspices of the Council of Europe. The Convention is semi-open in character. The clause on the accession of non-member States of the Council of Europe follows a number of precedents. Paragraph 3 of Article 37 seeks to safeguard the rights of acceding States by allowing them not to apply the provisions of the Convention in their relations with a State which subsequently accedes.

1.128 **Annex**

125. This Annex to which reference is made in Article 20, paragraph 3, sub-paragraph (a), Article 24, paragraph 2 and Article 25, paragraph 3, sub-paragraph (b) (see above), is based largely on points 4 and 5 of the Additional Protocol to the Hague Convention on the Recognition and Enforcement of Foreign Judgments in Civil and Commercial Matters of the same date.

However, the Annex does not contain a provision equivalent to point 4 (e) of that Protocol (service of a writ on the defendant during his temporary presence in the State of the forum) since these cases are of no practical interest for the purposes of the Convention.

1.129 **Resolution (72) 2 of the Committee of Ministers of the Council of Europe**

126. A unification of the procedure which is to be followed in cases to which Article 21 applies would have gone beyond the aims of the present Convention. Even the elaboration of very general rules would have encountered great difficulty due to the diversity in the systems of legal organisation of the member States.

What is indispensable, in the interest of the party who seeks to invoke the judgment, is that the proceedings be as simple and expeditious as possible.

It will be for each State Party to the Convention to determine the best means for it to implement the recommendation contained in the resolution.

1.130 **Explanatory Report on the Additional Protocol to the European Convention on State Immunity**

General comments

1. The Additional Protocol to the European Convention on State Immunity establishes on two distinct levels particular European procedures for the settlement of disputes arising from the application of the Convention. First, Part I

provides for the institution of international proceedings for the benefit of the party in whose favour judgment has been given against a Contracting State within the framework of the Convention. Secondly, Part II confers jurisdiction in relation to inter-State disputes on a European Tribunal instead of the International Court of Justice as provided for in Article 34 of the Convention.

In order to ensure uniform decisions for all disputes relating to the interpretation and application of the Convention, both kinds of proceedings—those instituted on the application of an individual and those relating to inter-State disputes—will be heard by one and the same judicial organ, namely the European Tribunal set up under the Protocol and constituted as described in Part III thereof.

2. The Additional Protocol is optional in character; it applies only to those States parties to the Convention which have ratified, accepted or acceded to it. Furthermore, while the jurisdiction of the European Tribunal to determine inter-State disputes is compulsory for each Party to the Protocol and in relations between them, any Party to the Protocol has the option to exclude individual petitions from the jurisdiction of the Tribunal by notifying the Secretary General of the Council of Europe (Part IV).

PART I

Article 1   1.131

3. This article, in providing for the institution of European proceedings by private persons against a State party to the Convention does not preclude the application of the provisions of Article 21 of the Convention whereby the party in whose favour a judgment has been given and the State against which the judgment has been given are entitled to have determined by the competent court in that State the question whether effect shall be given to the judgment. However, as a further measure of protection for the private individual opposing a State in civil proceedings, a concern which is a major feature of the Convention, Article 1, paragraph 1, gives the person seeking to invoke a judgment rendered against a State the choice between two procedures: proceedings pursuant to Article 21 of the Convention, or proceedings before the European Tribunal, whichever may appear most suitable. Cases may be submitted to the European Tribunal by any person upon whom the judgment confers rights.

Article 1, paragraph 3, of the Protocol does no more than restate a rule already contained, either explicitly or implicitly, in treaties relating to the recognition and enforcement of foreign judgments.

4. Paragraph 2 of Article 1 deals with the case where the State itself intends to institute proceedings before its own court in accordance with Article 21, paragraph 1, of the Convention. The obligation to give notice and the time-limit stipulated in this paragraph are designed to prevent a State, which has accepted

generally the jurisdiction of the European Tribunal, from denying to the individual the opportunity of bringing the dispute before that Tribunal by initiating a kind of pre-emptive action before its own national courts.

5. Apart from the three months' time-limit specified in paragraph 2, within which the individual must act if he so wishes, no time-limit is set for the institution of proceedings before the competent national court or the European Tribunal. Under the terms of the Convention, the obligation to give effect to the judgment exists as soon as the latter becomes final and enforceable in the State of the forum, and there is no need for the party in whose favour judgment has been given to submit a request to an official authority of the defendant State.

6. It must be emphasised that the State against which judgment is given cannot bring proceedings against the individual before the European Tribunal. If it could, the State might exploit this possibility to exert pressure on the individual (bearing in mind the possible costs) to waive his claim or accept an unfavourable settlement.

7. Subject to the provisions of Article 10, paragraph 3, of the Protocol, concerning its entry into force, every Party to the Protocol which has not made the declaration provided for in Part IV accepts the jurisdiction of the Tribunal as described in Part 1. Jurisdiction under Part I can be exercised even where only one Party to the Protocol has accepted it, since there is no provision for reciprocity in this respect.

Nothing in the Protocol prevents the Parties making provision for a means of settlement other than recourse to the European Tribunal; in the event of an objection being made against effect being given to the judgment, the dispute could, for example, be submitted to arbitration.

PART II

1.132 Article 2

8. This article establishes, in relations between the Parties to the Protocol, the jurisdiction of the European Tribunal to deal with inter-State disputes concerning the interpretation or application of the Convention. This jurisdiction is compulsory, since disputes may be submitted to the Tribunal not only by special agreement but also on the unilateral application of one of the Parties to the dispute.

9. The last sentence of paragraph 1 requires the Parties to the Protocol not to submit a dispute concerning the Convention to a mode of settlement other than the jurisdiction of the European Tribunal, which should ensure uniformity of decisions.

Its most important consequence, however, is that Article 34 of the Convention concerning the jurisdiction of the International Court of Justice, does not apply as between Parties to the Protocol.

10. Paragraph 2 makes it impossible to submit to the European Tribunal a dispute concerning a question pending before a national court, before a final decision has been rendered on that question (cf. Article 29 of the European Convention for the Peaceful Settlement of Disputes of 29 April 1957) whether the proceedings concern the merits of a case between a private individual and a State or have been instituted to establish an obligation to give effect to judgment.

Paragraph 3 ensures that the same case cannot be brought twice before the European Tribunal, first as a dispute between a private person and the State, and secondly as a dispute between two Contracting States. In any event, the decision of the European Tribunal is final: neither it nor any other international or national body can then be asked to determine the dispute.

Article 3   1.133

11. Under general international law, any international court is deemed competent to decide disputes submitted by special agreement by States which have not previously recognised its jurisdiction, provided the case submitted lies within the general scope of the judicial functions entrusted to it. Article 3 confirms this rule in respect of disputes concerning the interpretation or application of the Convention which might arise between Contracting States not all of which are Parties to the Protocol.

PART III   1.134

12. The rules governing the constitution and operation of the European Tribunal are designed to ensure the effectiveness of its jurisdiction, while at the same time keeping the procedure as simple and inexpensive as possible. It cannot be foreseen whether frequent recourse will be had to the Additional Protocol. On the other hand, it seemed advisable to link this new legal body fairly closely to the Council of Europe's judicial organ, the European Court of Human Rights, which has already proved its worth. But it was not possible simply to entrust that Court with the tasks which the European Tribunal will have to discharge, principally because the semi-open character of the Convention (cf. Article 37 of the Convention) may entail the participation of judges nominated by non-member States of the Council of Europe.

13. The Protocol does not deal with the question of languages, nor with cases where more than two Contracting States are involved in proceedings.

These and other matters will be dealt with by the Rules of Procedure mentioned in Article 7, paragraph 1, of the Protocol.

1.135 PART IV

14. Under Article 9, a Party to the Protocol may refuse to recognise the jurisdiction of the European Tribunal in respect of proceedings instituted by private persons in accordance with the provisions of Part I. The notification to this effect must be communicated not later than the date of ratification or acceptance of the Protocol or accession thereto.

1.136 PART V

15. The final clauses contained in Articles 10 to 14 of the Protocol follow the pattern of final clauses in conventions and agreements drawn up within the Council of Europe. Special mention should however be made of a basic underlying principle. The Protocol may not be signed by a State which has not signed the Convention nor may it be ratified or accepted by a State which has not already ratified or accepted the Convention; again no State may accede to it unless it has acceded to the Convention in accordance with the provisions laid down in the final clauses of the latter.

The number of ratifications needed for the Protocol to enter into force has been set at five—a higher number than that required for the entry into force of the Convention. There is of course no point in setting up a European Tribunal unless a sufficient number of cases can be expected to be brought before it.

Statute of the International Criminal Court
(Rome, 17 July 1998) (Extract)[34]

PART 2. JURISDICTION, ADMISSIBILITY AND APPLICABLE LAW

Article 5   1.138

Crimes within the jurisdiction of the Court

1. The jurisdiction of the Court shall be limited to the most serious crimes of concern to the international community as a whole. The Court has jurisdiction in accordance with this Statute with respect to the following crimes:

   (a) The crime of genocide;
   (b) Crimes against humanity;
   (c) War crimes;
   (d) The crime of aggression.

2. The Court shall exercise jurisdiction over the crime of aggression once a provision is adopted in accordance with articles 121 and 123 defining the crime and setting out the conditions under which the Court shall exercise jurisdiction with respect to this crime. Such a provision shall be consistent with the relevant provisions of the Charter of the United Nations.

Article 6   1.139

Genocide

For the purpose of this Statute, "genocide" means any of the following acts committed with intent to destroy, in whole or in part, a national, ethnical, racial or religious group, as such:

(a) Killing members of the group;
(b) Causing serious bodily or mental harm to members of the group;
(c) Deliberately inflicting on the group conditions of life calculated to bring about its physical destruction in whole or in part;
(d) Imposing measures intended to prevent births within the group;
(e) Forcibly transferring children of the group to another group.

---

[34] As corrected by the *procès-verbaux* of 10 November 1998 and 12 July 1999. For the entire text of the statute and supporting materials (including a list of signatures, ratifications, accessions, declarations and reservations) see http://www.un.org/law/icc. As at 1 July 2002 (the date on which the statute entered into force) there had been 78 ratifications/accessions. As at 17 October 2003, there were 92 participants. For a history of the proposals for the creation of an international criminal court, see the Final Act of the United Nations Diplomatic Conference of Plenipotentiaries on the Establishment of an international Criminal Court (17 June 1998) (U.N. Doc.A/CONF.183.10*) (http://www.un.org/law/icc/statute/finalfra.htm).

1.140 Article 7

Crimes against humanity

1. For the purpose of this Statute, "crime against humanity" means any of the following acts when committed as part of a widespread or systematic attack directed against any civilian population, with knowledge of the attack:

    (a) Murder;
    (b) Extermination;
    (c) Enslavement;
    (d) Deportation or forcible transfer of population;
    (e) Imprisonment or other severe deprivation of physical liberty in violation of fundamental rules of international law;
    (f) Torture;
    (g) Rape, sexual slavery, enforced prostitution, forced pregnancy, enforced sterilization, or any other form of sexual violence of comparable gravity;
    (h) Persecution against any identifiable group or collectivity on political, racial, national, ethnic, cultural, religious, gender as defined in paragraph 3, or other grounds that are universally recognized as impermissible under international law, in connection with any act referred to in this paragraph or any crime within the jurisdiction of the Court;
    (i) Enforced disappearance of persons;
    (j) The crime of apartheid;
    (k) Other inhumane acts of a similar character intentionally causing great suffering, or serious injury to body or to mental or physical health.

2. For the purpose of paragraph 1:

    (a) "Attack directed against any civilian population" means a course of conduct involving the multiple commission of acts referred to in paragraph 1 against any civilian population, pursuant to or in furtherance of a State or organizational policy to commit such attack;
    (b) "Extermination" includes the intentional infliction of conditions of life, *inter alia* the deprivation of access to food and medicine, calculated to bring about the destruction of part of a population;
    (c) "Enslavement" means the exercise of any or all of the powers attaching to the right of ownership over a person and includes the exercise of such power in the course of trafficking in persons, in particular women and children;
    (d) "Deportation or forcible transfer of population" means forced displacement of the persons concerned by expulsion or other coercive acts from the area in which they are lawfully present, without grounds permitted under international law;

(e) "Torture" means the intentional infliction of severe pain or suffering, whether physical or mental, upon a person in the custody or under the control of the accused; except that torture shall not include pain or suffering arising only from, inherent in or incidental to, lawful sanctions;

(f) "Forced pregnancy" means the unlawful confinement of a woman forcibly made pregnant, with the intent of affecting the ethnic composition of any population or carrying out other grave violations of international law. This definition shall not in any way be interpreted as affecting national laws relating to pregnancy;

(g) "Persecution" means the intentional and severe deprivation of fundamental rights contrary to international law by reason of the identity of the group or collectivity;

(h) "The crime of apartheid" means inhumane acts of a character similar to those referred to in paragraph 1, committed in the context of an institutionalized regime of systematic oppression and domination by one racial group over any other racial group or groups and committed with the intention of maintaining that regime;

(i) "Enforced disappearance of persons" means the arrest, detention or abduction of persons by, or with the authorization, support or acquiescence of, a State or a political organization, followed by a refusal to acknowledge that deprivation of freedom or to give information on the fate or whereabouts of those persons, with the intention of removing them from the protection of the law for a prolonged period of time.

3. For the purpose of this Statute, it is understood that the term "gender" refers to the two sexes, male and female, within the context of society. The term "gender" does not indicate any meaning different from the above.

Article 8   1.141

War crimes

1. The Court shall have jurisdiction in respect of war crimes in particular when committed as part of a plan or policy or as part of a large-scale commission of such crimes.

2. For the purpose of this Statute, "war crimes" means:

(a) Grave breaches of the Geneva Conventions of 12 August 1949, namely, any of the following acts against persons or property protected under the provisions of the relevant Geneva Convention:

   (i) Wilful killing;

   (ii) Torture or inhuman treatment, including biological experiments;

    (iii) Wilfully causing great suffering, or serious injury to body or health;

    (iv) Extensive destruction and appropriation of property, not justified by military necessity and carried out unlawfully and wantonly;

    (v) Compelling a prisoner of war or other protected person to serve in the forces of a hostile Power;

    (vi) Wilfully depriving a prisoner of war or other protected person of the rights of fair and regular trial;

    (vii) Unlawful deportation or transfer or unlawful confinement;

    (viii) Taking of hostages.

(b) Other serious violations of the laws and customs applicable in international armed conflict, within the established framework of international law, namely, any of the following acts:

    (i) Intentionally directing attacks against the civilian population as such or against individual civilians not taking direct part in hostilities;

    (ii) Intentionally directing attacks against civilian objects, that is, objects which are not military objectives;

    (iii) Intentionally directing attacks against personnel, installations, material, units or vehicles involved in a humanitarian assistance or peacekeeping mission in accordance with the Charter of the United Nations, as long as they are entitled to the protection given to civilians or civilian objects under the international law of armed conflict;

    (iv) Intentionally launching an attack in the knowledge that such attack will cause incidental loss of life or injury to civilians or damage to civilian objects or widespread, long-term and severe damage to the natural environment which would be clearly excessive in relation to the concrete and direct overall military advantage anticipated;

    (v) Attacking or bombarding, by whatever means, towns, villages, dwellings or buildings which are undefended and which are not military objectives;

    (vi) Killing or wounding a combatant who, having laid down his arms or having no longer means of defence, has surrendered at discretion;

    (vii) Making improper use of a flag of truce, of the flag or of the military insignia and uniform of the enemy or of the United Nations, as well as of the distinctive emblems of the Geneva Conventions, resulting in death or serious personal injury;

    (viii) The transfer, directly or indirectly, by the Occupying Power of parts of its own civilian population into the territory it occupies, or the deportation or transfer of all or parts of the population of the occupied territory within or outside this territory;

(ix) Intentionally directing attacks against buildings dedicated to religion, education, art, science or charitable purposes, historic monuments, hospitals and places where the sick and wounded are collected, provided they are not military objectives;

(x) Subjecting persons who are in the power of an adverse party to physical mutilation or to medical or scientific experiments of any kind which are neither justified by the medical, dental or hospital treatment of the person concerned nor carried out in his or her interest, and which cause death to or seriously endanger the health of such person or persons;

(xi) Killing or wounding treacherously individuals belonging to the hostile nation or army;

(xii) Declaring that no quarter will be given;

(xiii) Destroying or seizing the enemy's property unless such destruction or seizure be imperatively demanded by the necessities of war;

(xiv) Declaring abolished, suspended or inadmissible in a court of law the rights and actions of the nationals of the hostile party;

(xv) Compelling the nationals of the hostile party to take part in the operations of war directed against their own country, even if they were in the belligerent's service before the commencement of the war;

(xvi) Pillaging a town or place, even when taken by assault;

(xvii) Employing poison or poisoned weapons;

(xviii) Employing asphyxiating, poisonous or other gases, and all analogous liquids, materials or devices;

(xix) Employing bullets which expand or flatten easily in the human body, such as bullets with a hard envelope which does not entirely cover the core or is pierced with incisions;

(xx) Employing weapons, projectiles and material and methods of warfare which are of a nature to cause superfluous injury or unnecessary suffering or which are inherently indiscriminate in violation of the international law of armed conflict, provided that such weapons, projectiles and material and methods of warfare are the subject of a comprehensive prohibition and are included in an annex to this Statute, by an amendment in accordance with the relevant provisions set forth in articles 121 and 123;

(xxi) Committing outrages upon personal dignity, in particular humiliating and degrading treatment;

(xxii) Committing rape, sexual slavery, enforced prostitution, forced pregnancy, as defined in article 7, paragraph 2 (f), enforced sterilization, or any other form of sexual violence also constituting a grave breach of the Geneva Conventions;

(xxiii) Utilizing the presence of a civilian or other protected person to render certain points, areas or military forces immune from military operations;

(xxiv) Intentionally directing attacks against buildings, material, medical units and transport, and personnel using the distinctive emblems of the Geneva Conventions in conformity with international law;

(xxv) Intentionally using starvation of civilians as a method of warfare by depriving them of objects indispensable to their survival, including wilfully impeding relief supplies as provided for under the Geneva Conventions;

(xxvi) Conscripting or enlisting children under the age of fifteen years into the national armed forces or using them to participate actively in hostilities.

(c) In the case of an armed conflict not of an international character, serious violations of article 3 common to the four Geneva Conventions of 12 August 1949, namely, any of the following acts committed against persons taking no active part in the hostilities, including members of armed forces who have laid down their arms and those placed *hors de combat* by sickness, wounds, detention or any other cause:

(i) Violence to life and person, in particular murder of all kinds, mutilation, cruel treatment and torture;

(ii) Committing outrages upon personal dignity, in particular humiliating and degrading treatment;

(iii) Taking of hostages;

(iv) The passing of sentences and the carrying out of executions without previous judgement pronounced by a regularly constituted court, affording all judicial guarantees which are generally recognized as indispensable.

(d) Paragraph 2 (c) applies to armed conflicts not of an international character and thus does not apply to situations of internal disturbances and tensions, such as riots, isolated and sporadic acts of violence or other acts of a similar nature.

(e) Other serious violations of the laws and customs applicable in armed conflicts not of an international character, within the established framework of international law, namely, any of the following acts:

- (i) Intentionally directing attacks against the civilian population as such or against individual civilians not taking direct part in hostilities;
- (ii) Intentionally directing attacks against buildings, material, medical units and transport, and personnel using the distinctive emblems of the Geneva Conventions in conformity with international law;
- (iii) Intentionally directing attacks against personnel, installations, material, units or vehicles involved in a humanitarian assistance or peacekeeping mission in accordance with the Charter of the United Nations, as long as they are entitled to the protection given to civilians or civilian objects under the international law of armed conflict;
- (iv) Intentionally directing attacks against buildings dedicated to religion, education, art, science or charitable purposes, historic monuments, hospitals and places where the sick and wounded are collected, provided they are not military objectives;
- (v) Pillaging a town or place, even when taken by assault;
- (vi) Committing rape, sexual slavery, enforced prostitution, forced pregnancy, as defined in article 7, paragraph 2 (f), enforced sterilization, and any other form of sexual violence also constituting a serious violation of article 3 common to the four Geneva Conventions;
- (vii) Conscripting or enlisting children under the age of fifteen years into armed forces or groups or using them to participate actively in hostilities;
- (viii) Ordering the displacement of the civilian population for reasons related to the conflict, unless the security of the civilians involved or imperative military reasons so demand;
- (ix) Killing or wounding treacherously a combatant adversary;
- (x) Declaring that no quarter will be given;
- (xi) Subjecting persons who are in the power of another party to the conflict to physical mutilation or to medical or scientific experiments of any kind which are neither justified by the medical, dental or hospital treatment of the person concerned nor carried out in his or her interest, and which cause death to or seriously endanger the health of such person or persons;
- (xii) Destroying or seizing the property of an adversary unless such destruction or seizure be imperatively demanded by the necessities of the conflict;

(f) Paragraph 2 (e) applies to armed conflicts not of an international character and thus does not apply to situations of internal disturbances and tensions, such as riots, isolated and sporadic acts of violence or other acts of a similar nature. It applies to armed conflicts that take place in the territory of a State when there is protracted armed conflict between governmental authorities and organized armed groups or between such groups.

3. Nothing in paragraph 2(c) and (e) shall affect the responsibility of a Government to maintain or re-establish law and order in the State or to defend the unity and territorial integrity of the State, by all legitimate means.

1.142   Article 9

Elements of Crimes

1. Elements of Crimes shall assist the Court in the interpretation and application of articles 6, 7 and 8. They shall be adopted by a two-thirds majority of the members of the Assembly of States Parties.

2. Amendments to the Elements of Crimes may be proposed by:

   (a) Any State Party;
   (b) The judges acting by an absolute majority;
   (c) The Prosecutor.

   Such amendments shall be adopted by a two-thirds majority of the members of the Assembly of States Parties.

3. The Elements of Crimes and amendments thereto shall be consistent with this Statute.

1.143   Article 10

Nothing in this Part shall be interpreted as limiting or prejudicing in any way existing or developing rules of international law for purposes other than this Statute.

1.144   Article 11

Jurisdiction ratione temporis

1. The Court has jurisdiction only with respect to crimes committed after the entry into force of this Statute.

2. If a State becomes a Party to this Statute after its entry into force, the Court may exercise its jurisdiction only with respect to crimes committed after the entry into force of this Statute for that State, unless that State has made a declaration under article 12, paragraph 3.

1.145   Article 12

Preconditions to the exercise of jurisdiction

1. A State which becomes a Party to this Statute thereby accepts the jurisdiction of the Court with respect to the crimes referred to in article 5.

2. In the case of article 13, paragraph (a) or (c), the Court may exercise its jurisdiction if one or more of the following States are Parties to this Statute or have accepted the jurisdiction of the Court in accordance with paragraph 3:

   (a) The State on the territory of which the conduct in question occurred or, if the crime was committed on board a vessel or aircraft, the State of registration of that vessel or aircraft;

   (b) The State of which the person accused of the crime is a national.

3. If the acceptance of a State which is not a Party to this Statute is required under paragraph 2, that State may, by declaration lodged with the Registrar, accept the exercise of jurisdiction by the Court with respect to the crime in question. The accepting State shall cooperate with the Court without any delay or exception in accordance with Part 9.

Article 13   1.146

Exercise of jurisdiction

The Court may exercise its jurisdiction with respect to a crime referred to in article 5 in accordance with the provisions of this Statute if:

(a) A situation in which one or more of such crimes appears to have been committed is referred to the Prosecutor by a State Party in accordance with article 14;

(b) A situation in which one or more of such crimes appears to have been committed is referred to the Prosecutor by the Security Council acting under Chapter VII of the Charter of the United Nations; or

(c) The Prosecutor has initiated an investigation in respect of such a crime in accordance with article 15.

…

Article 27   1.147

Irrelevance of official capacity

1. This Statute shall apply equally to all persons without any distinction based on official capacity. In particular, official capacity as a Head of State or Government, a member of a Government or parliament, an elected representative or a government official shall in no case exempt a person from criminal responsibility under this Statute, nor shall it, in and of itself, constitute a ground for reduction of sentence.

2. Immunities or special procedural rules which may attach to the official capacity of a person, whether under national or international law, shall not bar the Court from exercising its jurisdiction over such a person.

…

1.148 Article 98

Cooperation with respect to waiver of immunity and consent to surrender

1. The Court may not proceed with a request for surrender or assistance which would require the requested State to act inconsistently with its obligations under international law with respect to the State or diplomatic immunity of a person or property of a third State, unless the Court can first obtain the cooperation of that third State for the waiver of the immunity.

2. The Court may not proceed with a request for surrender which would require the requested State to act inconsistently with its obligations under international agreements pursuant to which the consent of a sending State is required to surrender a person of that State to the Court, unless the Court can first obtain the cooperation of the sending State for the giving of consent for the surrender.

PART 2
OTHER INTERNATIONAL
MATERIALS

ILC Final Draft Articles and Commentary on Jurisdictional Immunities of States and their Property (1991)[1]

2.001

PART I

Introduction

Scope of the present articles

Article 1

2.002

The present articles apply to the immunity of a State and its property from the jurisdiction of the courts of another State

Commentary[2]

2.003

(1) The purpose of the present articles is to formulate rules of international law on the topic of jurisdictional immunities of States and their property.

(2) Article 1 indicates the subject matter to which the articles should apply. In any given situation in which the question of State immunity may arise, a few basic notions or concepts appear to be inevitable. In the first place, the main character of the present draft articles is "jurisdictional immunities". The expression "jurisdictional immunities" in this context is used not only in relation to the right of sovereign States to exemption from the exercise of the power to adjudicate, normally assumed by the judiciary or magistrate within a legal system of the territorial State, but also in relation to the non-exercise of all other administrative and executive powers, by whatever measures or procedures and by whatever authorities of the territorial State, in relation to a judicial proceeding. The concept therefore covers the

[1] YBILC (43rd session), Vol II, Pt 2, 13. For history of the proposals and selected bibliography, see Watts, *The International Law Commission 1949–1998*, Vol III (Oxford, 1999), 1999–2005. See also http://www.un.org/law/ilc/guide/gfra.htm. An Ad Hoc Committee on Jurisdictional Immunities of States and their Properties was established by the General Assembly in its resolution 55/150 of 12 December 2000. The Committee's final report, dated 28 February 2003, is reproduced at 2.048 to 2.077 below. See http://www.un.org/law/jurisdictionalimmunities.

[2] The notes 24–186 in the official commentary to Arts 1–22 below are taken from the Yearbook of the International Law Commission and reproduced at the end of this section.

entire judicial process, from the initiation or institution of proceedings, service of writs, investigation, examination, trial, orders which can constitute provisional or interim measures, to decisions rendering various instances of judgements and execution of the judgements thus rendered or their suspension and further exemption. It should be stated further that the scope of the articles covers not only the question of immunities of a State from adjudication before the court of another State but also that of immunity of a State in respect of property from measures of constraint, such as attachment and execution in connection with a proceeding before a court of another State, as provided in part IV. Secondly, the existence of two independent sovereign States is a prerequisite to the question of jurisdictional immunities, namely, a foreign State and a State of the forum. The draft articles generally refer to "a State" and "another State" but it has been found useful to use "foreign State" and "State of the forum" in certain articles for the sake of clarity. A definition of the term "State" for the purpose of the present articles is found in article 2.

(3) The phrase "of the courts" in the present text is designed to confirm the understanding that the scope of the current topic is confined primarily to immunity from the jurisdiction "of the courts" of States. A definition of the term "court" is found in article 2.

Use of terms

2.004 **Article 2**

1. For the purposes of the present articles:
    (a) "court" means any organ of a State, however named, entitled to exercise judicial functions;
    (b) "State" means:
        (i)   the State and its various organs of government;
        (ii) constituent units of a federal State;
        (iii) political subdivisions of the State which are entitled to perform acts in the exercise of the sovereign authority of the State;
        (iv) agencies or instrumentalities of the State and other entities, to the extent that they are entitled to perform acts in the exercise of the sovereign authority of the State;
        (v)   representatives of the State acting in that capacity;
    (c) "commercial transaction" means:
        (i)   any commercial contract or transaction for the sale of goods or supply of services;
        (ii) any contract for a loan or other transaction of a financial nature, including any obligation of guarantee or of indemnity in respect of any such loan or transaction;

    (iii) any other contract or transaction of a commercial, industrial, trading or professional nature, but not including a contract of employment of persons.

2. In determining whether a contract or transaction is a "commercial transaction" under paragraph 1 (c), reference should be made primarily to the nature of the contract or transaction, but its purpose should also be taken into account if, in the practice of the State which is a party to it, that purpose is relevant to determining the non-commercial character of the contract or transaction.

3. The provisions of paragraphs 1 and 2 regarding the use of terms in the present articles are without prejudice to the use of those terms or to the meanings which may be given to them in other international instruments or in the internal law of any State.

Commentary

Paragraph 1

(1) The present article combines original articles 2 and 3 provisionally adopted on first reading, taking into account the suggestion which was proposed and supported by members of the Commission as well as delegations in the Sixth Committee.

Paragraph 1 (a)

(2) A definition of the term "court" was deemed necessary in connection with article 1. In the context of the present articles, any organ of a State empowered to exercise judicial functions is a court, regardless of the level and whatever nomenclature is used. Although the draft articles do not define the term "proceeding", it should be understood that they do not cover criminal proceedings.

(3) With regard to the term "judicial functions", it should be noted that such functions vary under different constitutional and legal systems. For this reason, the Commission decided not to include a definition of the term "judicial functions" in the present article. The scope of judicial functions, however, should be understood to cover such functions whether exercised by courts or by administrative organs. Judicial functions may be exercised in connection with a legal proceeding at different stages, prior to the institution or during the development of a legal proceeding, or at the final stage of enforcement of judgements. Such judicial functions may include adjudication of litigation or dispute settlement, determination of questions of law and of fact, order of interim and enforcement measures at all stages of legal proceedings and such other administrative and executive functions as are normally exercised by, or under, the judicial authorities of a State in connection with, in the course of, or pursuant to, a legal proceeding. Although judicial functions are determined by the internal organizational structure of each State, the term does not, for the purposes of the present articles, cover the administration of justice in all its aspects which, at least

under certain legal systems, might include other functions related to the appointment of judges.

(4) It should be noted also that this definition may, under different constitutional and legal systems, cover the exercise of the power to order or adopt enforcement measures (sometimes called "quasi-judicial functions") by specific administrative organs of the State.

Paragraph 1 (b)

(5) In view of different jurisprudential approaches to the meaning of "State" in the context of jurisdictional immunities, it was considered useful to spell out the special meaning of the term for the purposes of the present articles. The general terms used in describing "State" should not imply that the provision is an open-ended formula. The term "State" should be understood in the light of its object and purpose, namely to identify those entities or persons entitled to invoke the immunity of the State where a State can claim immunity and also to identify certain subdivisions or instrumentalities of a State that are entitled to invoke immunity when performing acts in the exercise of sovereign authority. Accordingly, in the context of the present articles, the expression "State" should be understood as comprehending all types or categories of entities and individuals so identified which may benefit from the protection of State immunity.

Paragraph 1 (b) (i)

(6) The first category includes the State itself, acting in its own name and through its various organs of government, however designated, such as the sovereign or head of State, the head of government, the central government, various ministries and departments of government, ministerial or sub-ministerial departments, offices or bureaux, as well as subordinate organs and missions representing the State, including diplomatic missions and consular posts, permanent missions and delegations. The use of the expression "various organs of government" is intended to include all branches of government and is not limited to the executive branch only.

(7) The expression "State" includes fully sovereign and independent foreign States, and also, by extension, entities that are sometimes not really foreign and at other times not fully independent or only partially sovereign.[24] Certainly the cloak of State immunity covers all foreign States regardless of their form of government, whether a kingdom, empire or republic, a federal union, a confederation of States or otherwise.[25]

(8) A sovereign or a head of State, in his public capacity as a principal organ of a State, is also entitled to immunity to the same extent as the State itself, on the ground that the crown, the reigning monarch, the sovereign head of State or indeed a head of State may be equated with the central Government.

(9) A State is generally represented by the Government in most, if not all, of its international relations and transactions. Therefore a proceeding against the Government eo nomine is not distinguishable from a direct action against the State.[26]

State practice has long recognized the practical effect of a suit against a foreign Government as identical with a proceeding against the State.[27]

(10) Just as the State is represented by its Government, which is identified with it for most practical purposes, the Government is often composed of State organs and departments or ministries that act on its behalf. Such organs of State and departments of government can be, and are often, constituted as separate legal entities within the internal legal system of the State. Lacking as they do international legal personality as a sovereign entity, they could nevertheless represent the State or act on behalf of the central Government of the State, which they in fact constitute integral parts thereof. Such State organs or departments of government comprise the various ministries of a Government,[28] including the armed forces,[29] the subordinate divisions or departments within each ministry, such as embassies,[30] special missions[31] and consular posts[32] and offices, commissions, or councils[33] which need not form part of any ministry but are themselves autonomous State organs answerable to the central Government or to one of its departments, or administered by the central Government. Other principal organs of the State such as the legislature and the judiciary of a foreign State would be equally identifiable with the State itself if an action were or could be instituted against them in respect of their public or official acts.

Paragraph 1 (b) (ii)

(11) The second category covers the constituent units of a federal State. Constituent units of a federal State are regarded as a State for purposes of the present draft articles. No special provision for federal States appeared in the text of original article 3, paragraph 1, containing the definition of "State" as provisionally adopted on first reading. The Commission, taking into account the views expressed by some members of the Commission as well as Governments, agreed to introduce this provision on second reading. In some federal systems, constituent units are distinguishable from the political subdivisions referred to in paragraph 1 (b) (iii) in the sense that these units are, for historical or other reasons, to be accorded the same immunities as those of the State, without the additional requirement that they perform acts in the exercise of the sovereign authority of the State. Paragraph 1 (b) (ii) was introduced with this particular situation in mind. However, State practice has not been uniform on this question.[34] In some other federal systems they are not distinguishable from political subdivisions, as they are accorded the jurisdictional immunities of the federal State only to the extent that they perform acts in the exercise of "sovereign authority". This uncertain status of constituent units of a State is preserved by the European Convention on State Immunity and Additional Protocol, 1972.[35] Therefore, it depends upon the constitutional practice or historical background of a particular federal State whether its constituent units are treated as a State under this paragraph or under paragraph 1 (b) (iii) below.

Paragraph 1 (b) (iii)

(12) The third category covers subdivisions of a State which are entitled, under internal law, to perform acts in the exercise of the sovereign authority of the State.

The corresponding term for "sovereign authority" used in the French text is prérogatives de la puissance publique. The Commission discussed at length whether in the English text "sovereign authority" or "governmental authority" should be used and has come to the conclusion that "sovereign authority" seems to be, in this case, the nearest equivalent to prérogatives de la puissance publique.[36] Some members, on the other hand, expressed the view that the term "sovereign authority" was normally associated with the international personality of the State, in accordance with international law, which was not the subject of the paragraph. Consequently it was held that "governmental authority" was a better English translation of the French expression la puissance publique. Autonomous regions of a State which are entitled, under internal law, to perform acts in the exercise of sovereign authority may also invoke sovereign immunity under this category.

(13) Whatever the status of subdivisions of a State, there is nothing to preclude the possibility of such entities being constituted or authorized under internal law to act as organs of the central Government or as State agencies performing sovereign acts of the foreign State.[37] It is not difficult to envisage circumstances in which such subdivisions may in fact be exercising sovereign authority assigned to them by the State. There are cases where, dictated by expediency, the courts have refrained from entertaining suits against such autonomous entities, holding them to be an integral part of the foreign Government.[38]

Paragraph 1 (b) (iv)

(14) The fourth category embraces the agencies or instrumentalities of the State and other entities, including private entities, but only to the extent that they are entitled to perform acts in the exercise of prérogative de la puissance publique. Beyond or outside the sphere of acts performed by them in the exercise of the sovereign authority of the State, they do not enjoy any jurisdictional immunity. Thus, in the case of an agency or instrumentality or other entity which is entitled to perform acts in the exercise of sovereign authority as well as acts of a private nature, immunity may be invoked only in respect of the acts performed in the exercise of sovereign authority.

(15) The reference to "other entities" has been added on second reading and is intended to cover non-governmental entities when in exceptional cases endowed with governmental authority. It takes into account the practice which was resorted to relatively often after the Second World War and still exists, to some extent, in recent times, in which a State entrusts a private entity with certain governmental authority to perform acts in the exercise of the sovereign authority of the State. Examples may be found in the practice of certain commercial banks which are entrusted by a Government to deal also with import and export licensing which is

exclusively within governmental powers. Therefore, when private entities perform such governmental functions, to that extent, they should be considered a "State" for the purposes of the present articles. One member, however, expressed doubts as to whether the examples cited were common enough to warrant the inclusion of the reference. Another member noted that in the present context the term prérogative de la puissance publique clearly means "government authority".[39] The concept of "agencies or instrumentalities of the State or other entities" could theoretically include State enterprises or other entities established by the State performing commercial transactions. For the purpose of the present articles, however, such State enterprises or other entities are presumed not to be entitled to perform governmental functions, and accordingly, as a rule, are not entitled to invoke immunity from jurisdiction of the courts of another State (see art. 10, para. 3).

(16) There is in practice no hard-and-fast line to be drawn between agencies or instrumentalities of a State and departments of government. The expression "agencies or instrumentalities"[40] indicates the interchangeability of the two terms.[41] Proceedings against an agency of a foreign Government[42] or an instrumentality of a foreign State, whether or not incorporated as a separate entity, could be considered to be a proceeding against the foreign State, particularly when the cause of action relates to the activities conducted by the agency or instrumentality of a State in the exercise of sovereign authority of that State.[43]

Paragraph 1 (b) (v)

(17) The fifth and last category of beneficiaries of State immunity encompasses all the natural persons who are authorized to represent the State in all its manifestations, as comprehended in the first four categories mentioned in paragraphs 1 (b) (i) to (iv). Thus, sovereigns and heads of State in their public capacity would be included under this category as well as in the first category, being in the broader sense organs of the Government of the State. Other representatives include heads of Government, heads of ministerial departments, ambassadors, heads of mission, diplomatic agents and consular officers, in their representative capacity.[44] The reference at the end of paragraph 1 (b) (v) to "in that capacity" is intended to clarify that such immunities are accorded to their representative capacity ratione materiae.

(18) It is to be observed that, in actual practice, proceedings may be instituted, not only against the government departments or offices concerned, but also against their directors or permanent representatives in their official capacities.[45] Actions against such representatives or agents of a foreign Government in respect of their official acts are essentially proceedings against the State they represent. The foreign State, acting through its representatives, is immune ratione materiae. Such immunities characterized as ratione materiae are accorded for the benefit of the State and are not in any way affected by the change or termination of the official functions of the representatives concerned. Thus, no action will be successfully brought against a former

representative of a foreign State in respect of an act performed by him in his official capacity. State immunity survives the termination of the mission or the office of the representative concerned. This is so because the immunity in question not only belongs to the State, but is also based on the sovereign nature or official character of the activities, being immunity ratione materiae.[46]

(19) Of all the immunities enjoyed by representatives of Government and State agents, two types of beneficiaries of State immunities deserve special attention, namely, the immunities of personal sovereigns and those of ambassadors and diplomatic agents.[47] *Apart from immunities ratione materiae by reason of the activities or the official functions of representatives, personal sovereigns and ambassadors are entitled, to some extent in their own right, to immunities ratione personae in respect of their persons or activities that are personal to them and unconnected with official functions. The immunities ratione personae, unlike immunities ratione materiae which continue to survive after the termination of the official functions, will no longer be operative once the public offices are vacated or terminated. All activities of the sovereigns and ambassadors which do not relate to their official functions are subject to review by the local jurisdiction, once the sovereigns or ambassadors have relinquished their posts.*[48] *Indeed, even such immunities inure not to the personal benefit of sovereigns and ambassadors but to the benefit of the States they represent, to enable them to fulfil their representative functions or for the effective performance of their official duties.*[49] *This proposition is further reflected, in the case of diplomatic agents, in the rule that diplomatic immunities can only be waived by an authorized representative of the sending State and with proper governmental authorization.*[50]

Paragraph 1 (c)

(20) The expression "commercial transaction" calls for a definition in order to list the types of contracts or transactions which are intended to fall within its scope. The term "commercial contract", which was adopted on first reading for the original draft article 2, paragraph 1, subparagraph (b), was replaced by the term "commercial transaction" in response to the preference for that change expressed by some members of the Commission and some delegations in the Sixth Committee.[51] *As will be discussed below, the term "transaction" is generally understood to have a wider meaning than the term "contract", including non-contractual activities such as business negotiations. The term "transaction" presents, however, some difficulties of translation into other official languages, owing to the existence of different terminologies in use in different legal systems. It is to be observed that "commercial transaction", as referred to in paragraph 2 (a) of article 10, namely, transactions between States and those on a government-to-government basis, are excluded from the application of paragraph 1 of that article. For such transactions, State immunity subsists and continues to apply. Some members considered that the use of the term "commercial" in the definition should be avoided as being tautological and circular.*

The Commission considered this question in some detail on second reading and sought an alternative wording which would eliminate the term "commercial" at least in paragraph 1 (c) (i) and (iii), but was unable to find an appropriate formulation. In the view of one member, profit-making was the most important criterion for the determination of the commercial character of a contract or transaction, and should have been incorporated in the definition of "commercial transaction".

(21) For the purposes of the draft articles, the expression "commercial transaction" covers three categories of transactions. In the first place, it covers all kinds of commercial contracts or transactions for the sale of goods or supply of services.

(22) Secondly, the expression "commercial transaction" covers inter alia a contract for a loan or other transaction of a financial nature, such as commercial loans or credits or bonds floated in the money market of another State. A State is often required not only to raise a loan in its own name, but sometimes also to provide a guarantee or surety for one of its national enterprises in regard to a purchase, say, of civil or commercial aircraft, which is in turn financed by foreign banks or a consortium of financial institutions. Such an undertaking may be given by a State in the form of a contract of guarantee embodying an obligation of guarantee for the repayment or settlement of the loan taken by one of its enterprises and to make payment in the event of default by the co-contractor, or an obligation of indemnity to be paid for the loss incurred by a party to the principal contract for a loan or a transaction of a financial nature. The difference between an obligation of guarantee and one of indemnity may consist in the relative directness or readiness of available remedies in relation to non-performance or non-fulfilment of contractual obligations by one of the original parties to the principal contract. An obligation of indemnity could also be described in terms of willingness or readiness to reimburse one of the original parties for the expense or losses incurred as a result of the failure of another party to honour its contractual commitments with or without consequential right of subrogation. The Commission reworded the text of subparagraph (ii) slightly on second reading to take account of the fact that an obligation of guarantee could exist not only in the case of a loan, but also in other agreements of a financial nature. The same thing applies to indemnity as well. The Commission therefore combined the reference to the obligation of guarantee and that to the obligation of indemnity so that they apply both to the contracts for a loan and to other agreements of a financial nature.

(23) Thirdly, the expression "commercial transaction" also covers other types of contracts or transactions of a commercial, industrial, trading or professional nature, thus taking in a wide variety of fields of State activities, especially manufacturing, and possibly investment, as well as other transactions. "Contracts of employment" are excluded from this definition since they form the subject of a separate rule, as will emerge from the examination of draft article 11.

(24) Examples of the various types of transactions categorized as commercial transactions are abundant, as illustrated in the commentary to article 10.[52]

Paragraph 2

(25) In order to provide guidance for determining whether a contract or transaction is a "commercial transaction" under paragraph 1 (c), two tests are suggested to be applied successively. In the first place, reference should be made primarily to the nature of the contract or transaction. If it is established that it is non-commercial or governmental in nature, there would be no necessity to enquire further as to its purpose.

(26) However, if, after the application of the "nature" test, the contract or transaction appears to be commercial, then it is open to the defendant State to contest this finding by reference to the purpose of the contract or transaction if, in its practice, that purpose is relevant to determining the non-commercial character of the contract or transaction. This two-pronged approach, which provides for the consideration not only of the nature, but in some instances also of the purpose of the contract or transaction, is designed to provide an adequate safeguard and protection for developing countries, especially in their endeavours to promote national economic development. Defendant States should be given an opportunity to prove that, in their practice, a given contract or transaction should be treated as non-commercial because its purpose is clearly public and supported by raison d'état, such as the procurement of food supplies to feed a population, relieve a famine situation or revitalize a vulnerable area, or supply medicaments to combat a spreading epidemic, provided that it is the practice of that State to conclude such contracts or transactions for such public ends. It should be noted, however, that it is the competent court, and not the defendant State, which determines in each case the commercial or non-commercial character of a contract or transaction taking into account the practice of the defendant States. Some delegations in the Sixth Committee as well as members of the Commission stated that they would have preferred to exclude the reference to the purpose test which, in their view, was liable to subjective interpretation.

(27) Controversies have loomed large in the practice of States, as can be seen from the survey of State practice contained in the commentary to article 10. Paragraph 2 of article 2 is aimed at reducing unnecessary controversies arising from the application of a single test, such as the nature of the contract or transaction, which is initially a useful test, but not by any means a conclusive one in all cases. This provision is therefore designed to provide a supplementary standard for determining, in certain cases, whether a particular contract or transaction is "commercial" or "non-commercial". The "purpose" test should not therefore be disregarded totally.[53] A balanced approach is thus ensured by the possibility of reference, as appropriate, to the criterion of the purpose, as well as that of the nature, of the contract or transaction.[54]

(28) What is said above applies equally to a contract for the sale of goods or the supply of services or to other types of commercial transactions as defined in article 2, paragraph 1 (c). For instance, a contract of loan to make such a purchase or a contract of guarantee for such a loan could be non-commercial in character, having regard

ultimately also to the public purpose for which the contract of purchase was concluded. For example, a contract of guarantee for a loan to purchase food supplies to relieve famine would usually be non-commercial in character because of its presumably public purpose.

Paragraph 3

(29) Paragraph 3 is designed to confine the use of terms in paragraphs 1 and 2, namely "court", "State" and "commercial transaction", to the context of jurisdictional immunities of States and their property. Clearly, these terms may have different meanings in other international instruments, such as multilateral conventions or bilateral agreements, or in the internal law of any State in respect of other legal relationships. It is thus a signal to States which ratify or accede or adhere to the present articles that they may do so without having to amend their internal law regarding other matters, because the three terms used have been given specific meaning in the current context only. These definitions are without prejudice to other meanings already given or to be given to these terms in the internal law of States or in international instruments. It should be observed nevertheless that for the States parties to the present articles, the meanings ascribed to those terms by article 2, paragraphs 1 and 2, would have to be followed in all questions relating to jurisdictional immunities of States and their property under the present articles.

(30) Although paragraph 3 confines itself to the terms defined in paragraphs 1 and 2, it applies also to other expressions used in the present draft articles but which are not specifically defined. This understanding is necessary in order to maintain the autonomous character of the articles.

Privileges and immunities not affected by the present articles

Article 3   2.006

1. The present articles are without prejudice to the privileges and immunities enjoyed by a State under international law in relation to the exercise of the functions of:

   (a) its diplomatic missions, consular posts, special missions, missions to international organizations, or delegations to organs of international organizations or to international conferences; and

   (b) persons connected with them.

2. The present articles are likewise without prejudice to privileges and immunities accorded under international law to Heads of State *ratione personae*.

Commentary   2.007

(1) Article 3 was originally conceived as a signpost to preclude the possibility of overlapping between the present articles and certain existing conventions dealing with the status, privileges, immunities and facilities of specific categories of representatives

of Governments. It was originally drafted as a one-paragraph article concerning existing regimes of diplomatic and consular immunities which should continue to apply unaffected by the present articles. Historically, diplomatic immunities under customary international law were the first to be considered ripe for codification, as indeed they have been in the Vienna Convention on Diplomatic Relations, 1961, and in the various bilateral consular agreements. Another classic example of immunities enjoyed under customary international law is furnished by the immunity of sovereigns or other heads of State. A provision indicating that the present draft articles are without prejudice to these immunities appears as paragraph 2 of article 3. Both paragraphs are intended to preserve the privileges and immunities already accorded to specific entities and persons by virtue of existing general international law and more fully by relevant international conventions in force, which remain unaffected by the present articles. In order to conform to this understanding and to align the text of paragraph 1 to that of paragraph 2, the phrase "under international law" has been added to the text of paragraph 1 as adopted provisionally on first reading.

Paragraph 1

(2) Paragraph 1, in its original version, contained specific references to the various international instruments with varying degrees of adherence and ratification. Mention was made of the following missions and persons representing States:

- *(i) diplomatic missions under the Vienna Convention on Diplomatic Relations of 1961;*
- *(ii) consular missions under the Vienna Convention on Consular Relations of 1963;*
- *(iii) special missions under the Convention on Special Missions of 1969;*
- *(iv) representation of States under the Vienna Convention on the Representation of States in Their Relations with International Organizations of a Universal Character of 1975;*
- *(v) permanent missions or delegations and observer delegations of States to international organizations or their organs in general;*[55]
- *(vi) internationally protected persons under the Convention on the Prevention and Punishment of Crimes against Internationally Protected Persons, including Diplomatic Agents of 1973.*

(3) Article 3 has since been revised and is now appropriately entitled, "Privileges and immunities not affected by the present articles". A general reference is preferred without any specific enumeration of missions governed by existing international instruments whose status in multilateral relations is far from uniform. Paragraph 1 deals with the following two categories:

- *(i) diplomatic, consular or special missions as well as missions to international organizations or delegations to organs of international organizations or to international conferences;*
- *(ii) persons connected with such missions.*

The extent of privileges and immunities enjoyed by a State in relation to the exercise of the functions of the entities referred to in subparagraph 1 (a) is determined by the provisions of the relevant international conventions referred to in paragraph (2) above, where applicable, or by general international law. The Commission had, in this connection, added the words "under international law" after the words "enjoyed by a State". This addition established the necessary parallel between paragraphs 1 and 2. The expression "persons connected with them [missions]" is to be construed similarly.

(4) The expressions "missions" and "delegations" also include permanent observer missions and observer delegations within the meaning of the Vienna Convention on Representation of States of 1975.

(5) The article is intended to leave existing special regimes unaffected, especially with regard to persons connected with the missions listed. Their immunities may also be regarded, in the ultimate analysis, as State immunity, since the immunities enjoyed by them belong to the State and can be waived at any time by the State or States concerned.

Paragraph 2

(6) Paragraph 2 is designed to include an express reference to the immunities extended under existing international law to foreign sovereigns or other heads of State in their private capacities, ratione personae. Jurisdictional immunities of States in respect of sovereigns or other heads of State acting as State organs or State representatives are dealt with under article 2. Article 2, paragraph 1 (b) (i) and (v) covers the various organs of the Government of a State and State representatives, including heads of State, irrespective of the systems of government. The reservation of article 3, paragraph 2, therefore refers exclusively to the private acts or personal immunities and privileges recognized and accorded in the practice of States, without any suggestion that their status should in any way be affected by the present articles. The existing customary law is left untouched.[56]

(7) The present draft articles do not prejudge the extent of immunities granted by States to foreign sovereigns or other heads of State, their families or household staff which may also, in practice, cover other members of their entourage. Similarly, the present articles do not prejudge the extent of immunities granted by States to heads of Government and ministers for foreign affairs. Those persons are, however, not expressly included in paragraph 2, since it would be difficult to prepare an exhaustive list, and any enumeration of such persons would moreover raise the issues of the basis and of the extent of the jurisdictional immunity exercised by such persons. A proposal was made at one stage to add, after "heads of State" in paragraph 2, "heads of government and ministers for foreign affairs", but was not accepted by the Commission.

Non-retroactivity of the present articles

2.008 Article 4

Without prejudice to the application of any rules set forth in the present articles to which jurisdictional immunities of States and their property are subject under international law independently of the present articles, the articles shall not apply to any question of jurisdictional immunities of States or their property arising in a proceeding instituted against a State before a court of another State prior to the entry into force of the present articles for the States concerned.

2.009 *Commentary*

(1) Under article 28 of the Vienna Convention on the Law of Treaties, non-retroactivity is the rule in the absence of any provision in the articles to the contrary. The question arises nevertheless as regards the nature and extent of the non-retroactive effect of the application of the present articles. It is necessary to determine a precise point in time at which the articles would apply as between the States which have accepted their provisions. The Commission has decided to select a time which is relatively precise, namely, that the principle of non-retroactivity applies to proceedings instituted prior to the entry into force of the articles as between the States concerned.

(2) Thus, as between the States concerned, the present articles are applicable in respect of proceedings instituted before a court after their entry into force. Article 4 therefore does not purport to touch upon the question of non-retroactivity in other contexts, such as diplomatic negotiations concerning the question of whether a State has violated its obligations under international law to accord jurisdictional immunity to another State in accordance with the rules of international law. This article, by providing specifically for non-retroactivity in respect of a proceeding before a court, does not in any way affect the general rule of non-retroactivity under article 28 of the Vienna Convention on the Law of Treaties. The present draft articles are without prejudice to the application of other rules to which jurisdictional immunities of States and their property are subject under international law, independently of the present articles. Nor are they intended to prejudice current or future developments of international law in this area or in any other related areas not covered by them.

PART II GENERAL PRINCIPLES

State immunity

2.010 Article 5

A State enjoys immunity, in respect of itself and its property, from the jurisdiction of the courts of another State subject to the provisions of the present articles.

Commentary

(1) Article 5 as provisionally adopted at the thirty-second session of the Commission (then article 6) contained a commentary with an extensive survey of State judicial, executive and legislative practice.[57] *The commentary is still generally applicable, except for the passages dealing with the formula adopted then and the two-pronged approach to the formulation of immunity as conferring a right and also as imposing a duty. The second prong is now fully covered in article 6 (Modalities for giving effect to State immunity).*

(2) The formulation of article 5, which expresses the main principle of State immunity, has been difficult, as it is a delicate matter. Legal theories abound as to the exact nature and basis of immunity. There is common agreement that for acts performed in the exercise of the prérogatives de la puissance publique or "sovereign authority of the State", there is undisputed immunity. Beyond or around the hard core of immunity, there appears to be a grey area in which opinions and existing case law and, indeed, legislation still vary. Some of these indicate that immunity constitutes an exception to the principle of territorial sovereignty of the State of the forum and as such should be substantiated in each case. Others refer to State immunity as a general rule or general principle of international law. This rule is not absolute in any event since even the most unqualified of all the theories of immunity admits one important exception, namely, consent, which also forms the basis for other principles of international law. Others still adhere to the theory that the rule of State immunity is a unitary rule and is inherently subject to existing limitations. Both immunity and non-immunity are part of the same rule. In other words, immunity exists together with its innate qualifications and limitations.

(3) In formulating the text of article 5, the Commission has considered all the relevant doctrines as well as treaties, case law and national legislation, and was able to adopt a compromise formula stating a basic principle of immunity qualified by the provisions of the present articles incorporating those specifying the types of proceedings in which State immunity cannot be invoked. The text adopted on first reading contained square brackets specifying that State immunity was also subject to "the relevant rules of general international law". The purpose of that phrase had been to stress that the present articles did not prevent the development of international law and that, consequently, the immunities guaranteed to States were subject both to present articles and to general international law. This passage had given rise to a number of views, some in favour of its retention and others against. Some members who spoke against retention expressed the view that the retention of the phrase might entail the danger of allowing unilateral interpretation of the draft articles to the extent that exceptions to State immunities could be unduly widened. The Commission finally decided to delete it on second reading for it was considered that any immunity or exception to immunity accorded under the present articles would have

no effect on general international law and would not prejudice the future develop-ment of State practice. If the articles became a convention, they would be applicable only as between the States which became parties to it. Article 5 is also to be under-stood as the statement of the principle of State immunity forming the basis of the present draft articles and does not prejudge the question of the extent to which the articles, including article 5, should be regarded as codifying the rules of existing international law.

Modalities for giving effect to State immunity

2.012　**Article 6**

1. A State shall give effect to State immunity under article 5 by refraining from exercising jurisdiction in a proceeding before its courts against another State and to that end shall ensure that its courts determine on their own ini-tiative that the immunity of that other State under article 5 is respected.

2. A proceeding before a court of a State shall be considered to have been insti-tuted against another State if that other State:

    (a) is named as a party to that proceeding; or

    (b) is not named as a party to the proceeding but the proceeding in effect seeks to affect the property, rights, interests or activities of that other State.

2.013　*Commentary*

Paragraph 1

(1) In article 6, paragraph 1, an attempt is made to identify the content of the obliga-tion to give effect to State immunity and the modalities for giving effect to that obligation. The rule of State immunity may be viewed from the standpoint of the State giving or granting jurisdictional immunity, in which case a separate and com-plementary article is warranted.[58] *Emphasis is placed, therefore, not so much on the sovereignty of the State claiming immunity, but more precisely on the independence and sovereignty of the State which is required by international law to recognize and accord jurisdictional immunity to another State. Of course, the obligation to give effect to State immunity stated in article 6 applies only to those situations in which the State claiming immunity is entitled thereto under the present draft articles. Since immunity, under article 5, is expressly from the "jurisdiction of another State", there is a clear and unmistakable presupposition of the existence of "jurisdic-tion" of that other State over the matter under consideration; it would be totally unnecessary to invoke the rule of State immunity in the absence of jurisdiction. There is as such an indispensable and inseparable link between State immunity and the existence of jurisdiction of another State with regard to the matter in question.*

(2) The same initial proposition could well be formulated in reverse, taking the jurisdiction of a State as a starting-point, after having established the firm existence

of jurisdiction. Paragraph 1 stipulates an obligation to refrain from exercising such jurisdiction in so far as it involves, concerns or otherwise affects another State that is entitled to immunity and is unwilling to submit to the jurisdiction of the former. This restraint on the exercise of jurisdiction is prescribed as a proposition of international law and should be observed in accordance with detailed rules to be examined and clarified in subsequent draft articles. While this obligation to refrain from exercising jurisdiction against a foreign State may be regarded as a general rule, it is not unqualified. It should be applied in accordance with the provisions of the present articles. From the point of view of the absolute sovereignty of the State exercising its jurisdiction in accordance with its own internal law, any restraint or suspension of that exercise based on a requirement of international law could be viewed as a limitation.

(3) The first prerequisite to any question involving jurisdictional immunity is therefore the existence of a valid "jurisdiction", primarily under internal law rules of a State, and, in the ultimate analysis, the assumption and exercise of such jurisdiction not conflicting with any basic norms of public international law. It is then that the applicability of State immunity may come into play. It should, however, be emphasized that the Commission is not concerned in the consideration of this topic with the compatibility with general international law of a State's internal law on the extent of jurisdiction. Without evidence of valid jurisdiction, there is no necessity to proceed to initiate, let alone substantiate, any claim of State immunity. The authority competent to examine the existence of valid jurisdiction may vary according to internal law, although, in practice, courts are generally competent to determine the existence, extent and limits of their own jurisdiction.

(4) It is easy to overlook the question concerning jurisdiction and to proceed to decide the issue of immunity without ascertaining first the existence of jurisdiction if contested on other grounds. The court should be satisfied that it is competent before proceedings to examine the plea of jurisdictional immunity. In actual practice, there is no established order of priority for the court in its examination of jurisdictional questions raised by parties. There is often no rule requiring the court to exhaust its consideration of other pleas or objections to jurisdiction before deciding the question of jurisdictional immunity.

(5) The second part of paragraph 1 reading "and to that end shall ensure that its courts determine on their own initiative that the immunity of that other State under article 5 is respected" has been added to the text as adopted on first reading. Its purpose was to define and strengthen the obligation set forth in the first part of the provision. Respect for State immunity would be ensured all the more if the courts of the State of the forum, instead of simply acting on the basis of a declaration by the other State, took the initiative in determining whether the proceedings were really directed against that State, and whether the State was entitled to invoke immunity. Appearance before foreign courts to invoke immunity would involve significant

financial implications for the contesting State and should therefore not necessarily be made the condition on which the question of State immunity is determined. On the other hand, the present provision is not intended to discourage the court appearance of the contesting State, which would provide the best assurance for obtaining a satisfactory result. The expression "shall ensure that its courts" is used to make it quite clear that the obligation was incumbent on the forum State, which is responsible for giving effect to it in accordance with its internal procedures. The reference to article 5 indicates that the provision should not be interpreted as prejudging the question whether the State was actually entitled to benefit from immunity under the present articles.

Paragraph 2

(6) Paragraph 2 deals with the notion of proceedings before the courts of one State against another State. There are various ways in which a State can be impleaded or implicated in a litigation or a legal proceeding before the court of another State.

(7) Proceedings before the courts of one State are considered as having been instituted against another State if that other State is named as a party to the proceeding, or, in a case where that other State itself is not a party to the proceeding, if the proceeding in effect seeks to affect the property, rights, interests or activities of that other State. The wording has been modified on second reading, in order to draw a clear distinction between two cases.

Paragraph 2 (a)

(8) A State is indubitably implicated in litigation before the courts of another State if a legal proceeding is instituted against it in its own name. The question of immunity arises only when the defendant State is unwilling or does not consent to be proceeded against. It does not arise if the State agrees to become a party to the proceeding.

(9) Although, in the practice of States, jurisdictional immunity has been granted frequently in cases where a State as such has not been named as a party to the proceeding, in reality there is a surprising collection of instances of direct implication in proceedings in which States are actually named as defendants.[59]

(10) Paragraph 2, subparagraph (a), applies to all proceedings naming as a party the State itself or any of its entities or persons that are entitled to invoke jurisdictional immunity in accordance with article 2, paragraph 1, subparagraph (b).

Paragraph 2 (b)

(11) Without closing the list of beneficiaries of State immunities, it is necessary to note that actions involving seizure or attachment of public properties or properties belonging to a foreign State or in its possession or control have been considered in the

practice of States to be proceedings which in effect implicate the foreign sovereign or seek to compel the foreign State to submit to the local jurisdiction. Such proceedings include not only actions in rem or in admiralty against State-owned or State-operated vessels used for defence purposes and other peaceful uses,[60] but also measures of prejudgement attachment or seizure (saisie conservatoire) as well as execution or measures in satisfaction of judgement (saisie exécutoire). The post-judgement or execution order will not be considered in the context of the present article, since it concerns not only immunity from jurisdiction but, beyond that, also immunity from execution, a further stage in the process of jurisdictional immunities.[61]

(12) As has been seen, the law of State immunities has developed in the practice of States not so much from proceedings instituted directly against foreign States or Governments in their own name, but more indirectly through a long line of actions for the seizure or attachment of vessels for maritime liens or collision damages or salvage services.[62] State practice has been rich in instances of State immunities in respect of their men-of-war,[63] visiting forces,[64] ammunitions and weapons[65] and aircraft.[66] The criterion for the foundation of State immunity is not limited to the claim of title or ownership by the foreign Government,[67] but clearly encompasses cases of property in actual possession or control of a foreign State.[68] The Court should not so exercise its jurisdiction as to put a foreign sovereign in the position of choosing between being deprived of property or else submitting to the jurisdiction of the Court.[69]

(13) Subparagraph (b) applies to situations in which the State is not named as a party to the proceeding, but is indirectly involved, as for instance in the case of an action in rem concerning State property, such as a warship. The wording adopted on first reading has been simplified on second reading. First, the clause "so long as the proceeding in effect seeks to compel that . . . State . . . to submit to the jurisdiction of the court" was deleted as it was, in the case under consideration, meaningless. The words "to bear the consequences of a determination by the court which may affect", in the last part of the sentence was also deleted, because it appeared to create too loose a relationship between the procedure and the consequences to which it gave rise for the State in question and could thus result in unduly broad interpretations of the paragraph. To make the text more precise in that regard, those words have therefore been replaced by the words "to affect". Lastly, the Commission has deleted paragraph 3, which, given the very elaborate definition of the term "State" contained in article 2, no longer had any point.

Express consent to exercise of jurisdiction

Article 7   2.014

1. A State cannot invoke immunity from jurisdiction in a proceeding before a court of another State with regard to a matter or case if it has expressly

consented to the exercise of jurisdiction by the court with regard to the matter or case:

(a) by international agreement;

(b) in a written contract; or

(c) by a declaration before the court or by a written communication in a specific proceeding.

2. Agreement by a State for the application of the law of another State shall not be interpreted as consent to the exercise of jurisdiction by the courts of that other State.

2.015 *Commentary*

(1) In the present part of the draft articles, article 5 enunciates the rule of State immunity while article 6 sets out the modalities for giving effect to State immunity. Following these two propositions, a third logical element is the notion of "consent",[70] the various forms of which are dealt with in articles 7, 8 and 9 of this part.[71]

Paragraph 1

(a) The relevance of consent and its consequences

(2) Paragraph 1 deals exclusively with express consent by a State in the manner specified therein, namely, consent given by a State in an international agreement, in a written contract or by a declaration before the courts or by a written communication in a specific proceeding.

(i) Absence of consent as an essential element of State immunity

(3) As has been intimated in article 5 (State immunity) and more clearly indicated in article 6 (Modalities for giving effect to State immunity) with respect to the obligation to refrain from subjecting another State to its jurisdiction, the absence or lack of consent on the part of the State against which the court of another State has been asked to exercise jurisdiction is presumed. State immunity under article 5 does not apply if the State in question has consented to the exercise of jurisdiction by the court of another State. There will be no obligation under article 6 on the part of a State to refrain from exercising jurisdiction, in compliance with its rules of competence, over or against another State which has consented to such exercise. The obligation to refrain from subjecting another State to its jurisdiction is not an absolute obligation. It is distinctly conditional upon the absence or lack of consent on the part of the State against which the exercise of jurisdiction is being sought.

(4) Consent, the absence of which has thus become an essential element of State immunity, is worthy of the closest attention. The obligation to refrain from exercising jurisdiction against another State or from impleading another sovereign Government is based on the assertion or presumption that such exercise is without consent. Lack of consent appears to be presumed rather than asserted in every case.

State immunity applies on the understanding that the State against which jurisdiction is to be exercised does not consent, or is not willing to submit to the jurisdiction. This unwillingness or absence of consent is generally assumed, unless the contrary is indicated. The court exercising jurisdiction against an absent foreign State cannot and does not generally assume or presume that there is consent or willingness to submit to its jurisdiction. There must be proof or evidence of consent to satisfy the exercise of existing jurisdiction or competence against another State.

(5) Express reference to absence of consent as a condition sine qua non of the application of State immunity is borne out in the practice of States. Some of the answers to the questionnaire circulated to Member States clearly illustrate this link between the absence of consent and the permissible exercise of jurisdiction.[72] The expression "without consent" often used in connection with the obligation to decline the exercise of jurisdiction is sometimes rendered in judicial references as "against the will of the sovereign State" or "against the unwilling sovereign".[73]

(ii) Consent as an element permitting exercise of jurisdiction

(6) If the lack of consent operates as a bar to the exercise of jurisdiction, it is interesting to examine the effect of consent by the State concerned. In strict logic, it follows that the existence of consent on the part of the State against which legal proceedings are instituted should operate to remove this significant obstacle to the assumption and exercise of jurisdiction. If absence of consent is viewed as an essential element constitutive of State immunity, or conversely as entailing the disability, or lack of power, of an otherwise competent court to exercise its existing jurisdiction, the expression of consent by the State concerned eliminates this impediment to the exercise of jurisdiction. With the consent of the sovereign State, the court of another State is thus enabled or empowered to exercise its jurisdiction by virtue of its general rules of competence, as though the foreign State were an ordinary friendly alien capable of bringing an action and being proceeded against in the ordinary way, without calling into play any doctrine or rule of State or sovereign immunity.[74]

(b) The expression of consent to the exercise of jurisdiction

(7) The implication of consent, as a legal theory in partial explanation or rationalization of the doctrine of State immunity, refers more generally to the consent of the State not to exercise its normal jurisdiction against another State or to waive its otherwise valid jurisdiction over another State without the latter's consent. The notion of consent therefore comes into play in more ways than one, with particular reference in the first instance to the State consenting to waive its jurisdiction (hence another State is immune from such jurisdiction) and to the instances under consideration, in which the existence of consent to the exercise of jurisdiction by another State precludes the application of the rule of State immunity. Consent of a State to the exercise of jurisdiction by another State could be given with regard to a particular case. Furthermore, the consent of a State with regard to a matter could be

confined to a particular case only and consequently would not affect the immunity of the State with regard to a similar matter in another case. The Commission therefore slightly amended on second reading the end of the opening clause of the paragraph, to read: "with regard to the matter or case".

(8) In the circumstances under consideration, that is, in the context of the State against which legal proceedings have been brought, there appear to be several recognizable methods of expressing or signifying consent. In this particular connection, the consent should not be taken for granted, nor readily implied. Any theory of "implied consent" as a possible exception to the general principles of State immunities outlined in this part should be viewed not as an exception in itself, but rather as an added explanation or justification for an otherwise valid and generally recognized exception. There is therefore no room for implying the consent of an unwilling State which has not expressed its consent in a clear and recognizable manner, including by the means provided in article 8. It remains to be seen how consent would be given or expressed so as to remove the obligation of the court of another State to refrain from the exercise of its jurisdiction against an equally sovereign State.

(i)   Consent given in a written contract, or by a declaration or a written communication in a specific proceeding

(9) An easy and indisputable proof of consent is furnished by the State's expressing its consent in a written contract, as provided in subparagraph (b),[75] or in writing on an ad hoc basis for a specific proceeding before the authority when a dispute has already arisen, as provided in subparagraph (c). In the latter case, a State is always free to communicate the expression of its consent to the exercise of jurisdiction by the court of another State in a legal proceeding against itself or in which it has an interest, by giving evidence of such consent in the form of an oral declaration before the court properly executed by one of its authorized representatives, such as an agent or counsel, or by a written communication through diplomatic channels or any other generally accepted channels of communication. By the same method, a State could also make known its unwillingness or lack of consent, or give evidence in writing which tends to disprove any allegation or assertion of consent.[76] As originally worded, subparagraph (c) provided that the consent of the State could be expressed by a declaration before the court in a specific case. It was, however, pointed out that that wording would require a State wishing to make such a declaration to send a representative especially to appear before a national court; it should be possible to make such a declaration in a written communication to the plaintiff or to the court. The Commission therefore added on second reading the last part of subparagraph (c) to provide that the State would have the possibility of consenting to the exercise of jurisdiction by means of such a written communication. The Commission also replaced on second reading the words "in a specific case" by the words "in a specific proceeding", to ensure better coordination between sub-paragraph (c) and the introductory clause of the paragraph.

(ii) Consent given in advance by international agreement

(10) The consent of a State could be given for one or more categories or cases. Such expression of consent is binding on the part of the State giving it in accordance with the manner and circumstances in which consent is given and subject to the limitations prescribed by its expression. The nature and extent of its binding character depend on the party invoking such consent. For instance, as provided under subparagraph (a) of paragraph 1, if consent is expressed in a provision of a treaty concluded by States, it is certainly binding on the consenting State, and States parties entitled to invoke the provisions of the treaty could avail themselves of the expression of such consent.[77] The law of treaties upholds the validity of the expression of consent to jurisdiction as well as the applicability of other provisions of the treaty. Consequently, lack of privity to the treaty precludes non-parties from the benefit or advantage to be derived from the provisions thereof. If, likewise, consent is expressed in a provision of an international agreement concluded by States and international organizations, the permissive effect of such consent is available to all parties, including international organizations. On the other hand, the extent to which individuals and corporations may successfully invoke one of the provisions of the treaty or international agreement is generally dependent on the specific rules of the domestic legal order concerned on implementation of treaties.

(11) The practice of States does not go so far as to support the proposition that the court of a State is bound to exercise its existing jurisdiction over or against another sovereign State which has previously expressed its consent to such jurisdiction in the provision of a treaty or an international agreement,[78] or indeed in the express terms of a contract[79] with the individual or corporation concerned. While the State having given express consent in any of these ways may be bound by such consent under international law or internal law, the exercise of jurisdiction or the decision to exercise or not to exercise jurisdiction is exclusively within the province and function of the trial court itself. In other words, the rules regarding the expression of consent by the State involved in a litigation are not absolutely binding on the court of another State, which is free to continue to refrain from exercising jurisdiction, subject, of course, to any rules deriving from the internal law of the State concerned. The court can and must devise its own rules and satisfy its own requirements regarding the manner in which such a consent could be given with desired consequences. The court may refuse to recognize the validity of consent given in advance and not at the time of the proceeding, not before the competent authority, or not given in facie curiae.[80] The proposition formulated in draft article 7 is therefore discretionary and not mandatory as far as the court is concerned. The court may or may not exercise its jurisdiction. Customary international law or international usage recognizes the exercisability of jurisdiction by the court against another State which has expressed its consent in no uncertain terms, but actual exercise of such jurisdiction is exclusively within the discretion or the power of the court, which could require a more rigid rule for the expression of consent.

(12) Consent to the exercise of jurisdiction in a proceeding before a court of another State covers the exercise of jurisdiction by appellate courts in any subsequent stage of the proceeding up to and including the decision of the court of final instance, retrial and review, but not execution of judgement.

Paragraph 2

(13) Consent by a State to the application of the law of another State shall not be construed as its consent to the exercise of jurisdiction by a court of that other State. Questions of consent to the exercise of jurisdiction and of applicable law to the case must be treated separately. The Commission on second reading added paragraph 2 in order to provide that important clarification.

Effect of participation in a proceeding before a court

2.016 Article 8

  1. A State cannot invoke immunity from jurisdiction in a proceeding before a court of another State if it has:

    (a) itself instituted the proceeding; or

    (b) intervened in the proceeding or taken any other step relating to the merits. However, if the State satisfies the court that it could not have acquired knowledge of facts on which a claim to immunity can be based until after it took such a step, it can claim immunity based on those facts, provided it does so at the earliest possible moment.

  2. A State shall not be considered to have consented to the exercise of jurisdiction by a court of another State if it intervenes in a proceeding or takes any other step for the sole purpose of:

    (a) invoking immunity; or

    (b) asserting a right or interest in property at issue in the proceeding.

  3. The appearance of a representative of a State before a court of another State as a witness shall not be interpreted as consent by the former State to the exercise of jurisdiction by the court.

  4. Failure on the part of a State to enter an appearance in a proceeding before a court of another State shall not be interpreted as consent by the former State to the exercise of jurisdiction by the court.

2.017 *Commentary*

(1) Article 8 deals with circumstances under which participation by a State in a proceeding before the courts of another State may be regarded as evidence of consent by that participating State to the exercise of jurisdiction by the courts concerned. The expression of consent or its communication must be explicit. Consent could also be evidenced by positive conduct of the State, but it cannot be presumed to exist by

sheer implication, nor by mere silence, acquiescence or inaction on the part of that State. A clear instance of conduct or action amounting to the expression of assent, concurrence, agreement, approval or consent to the exercise of jurisdiction is illustrated by entry of appearance by or on behalf of the State contesting the case on the merits. Such conduct may be in the form of a State requesting to be joined as a party to the litigation, irrespective of the degree of its preparedness or willingness to be bound by the decision or the extent of its prior acceptance of subsequent enforcement measures or execution of judgement.[81] In point of fact, the expression of consent either in writing, which is dealt with in article 7, or by conduct, which is the subject of the present commentary, entails practically the same results. They all constitute voluntary submission by a State to the jurisdiction, indicating a willingness and readiness on the part of a sovereign State of its own free will to submit to the consequences of adjudication by the court of another State, up to but not including measures of constraint which require separate consent of that foreign State.

Paragraph 1

(2) There is unequivocal evidence of consent to the assumption and exercise of jurisdiction by the court if and when the State knowingly enters an appearance in answer to a claim of right or to contest a dispute involving the State or over a matter in which it has an interest, and when such entry of appearance is unconditional and unaccompanied by a plea of State immunity, despite the fact that other objections may have been raised against the exercise of jurisdiction in that case on grounds recognized either under general conflict rules or under the rules of competence of the trial court other than by reason of jurisdictional immunity.

(3) By choosing to become a party to a litigation before the court of another State, a State clearly consents to the exercise of such jurisdiction, regardless of whether it is a plaintiff or a defendant, or indeed is in an ex parte proceeding, or an action in rem or in a proceeding seeking to attach or seize a property which belongs to it or in which it has an interest or property which is in its possession or control.

(a) Instituting or intervening in a legal proceeding

(4) One clearly visible form of conduct amounting to the expression of consent comprises the act of bringing an action or instituting a legal proceeding before a court of another State. By becoming a plaintiff before the judicial authority of another State, the claimant State, seeking judicial relief or other remedies, manifestly submits to the jurisdiction of the forum. There can be no doubt that when a State initiates a litigation before a court of another State, it has irrevocably submitted to the jurisdiction of the other State to the extent that it can no longer be heard to complain against the exercise of the jurisdiction it has itself initially invoked.[82]

(5) The same result follows in the event that a State intervenes in a proceeding before a court of another State, unless, as stipulated in paragraph 2, the intervention is

exclusively a plea of State immunity or made purposely to object to the exercise of jurisdiction on the ground of its sovereign immunity.[83] *Similarly, a State which participates in an interpleader proceeding voluntarily submits to the jurisdiction of that court. Any positive action by way of participation in the merits of a proceeding by a State on its own initiative and not under any compulsion is inconsistent with a subsequent contention that the volunteering State is being impleaded against its will. Subparagraph (b) provides also for a possibility for a State to claim immunity in the case where a State has taken a step relating to the merits of a proceeding before it had knowledge of facts on which a claim to immunity might be based. It had been pointed out that there might be circumstances in which a State would not be famil-iar with certain facts on the basis of which it could invoke immunity. It could hap-pen that the State instituted proceedings or intervened in a case before it had acquired knowledge of such facts. In such cases, States should be able to invoke immunity on two conditions. First, the State must satisfy the court that it could only have acquired knowledge of the facts justifying a claim of immunity after it had intervened in the proceeding or had taken steps relating to the merits of the case. Secondly, the State must furnish such proof at the earliest possible moment.*[84] *The second sentence of paragraph 1 (b), which has been added on second reading, deals with that point.*

(b) Entering an appearance on a voluntary basis

(6) A State may be said to have consented to the exercise of jurisdiction by a court of another State without being itself a plaintiff or claimant, or intervening in pro-ceedings before that court. For instance, a State may volunteer its appearance or freely enter an appearance, not in answer to any claim or any writ of summons, but of its own free will to assert an independent claim in connection with proceedings before a court of another State. Unless the assertion is one concerning jurisdictional immunity in regard to the proceedings in progress, entering an appearance on a vol-untary basis before a court of another State constitutes another example of consent to the exercise of jurisdiction, after which no plea of State immunity could be successfully raised.

Paragraph 2

(7) A State does not consent to the exercise of jurisdiction of another State by enter-ing a conditional appearance or by appearing expressly to contest or challenge juris-diction on the grounds of sovereign immunity or State immunity, although such appearances accompanied by further contentions on the merits to establish its immunity could result in the actual exercise of jurisdiction by the court.[85] *Participa-tion for the limited purpose of objecting to the continuation of the proceedings will not be viewed as consent to the exercise of jurisdiction either.*[86] *Furthermore, a State may assert a right or interest in property by presenting prima facie evidence on its title at issue in a proceeding to which the State is not a party, without being*

submitted to the jurisdiction of another State, under paragraph 2 (b). But, if a State presents a claim on the property right in a proceeding, that is regarded as an intervention in the merit and accordingly the State cannot invoke immunity in that proceeding.

Paragraph 3

(8) This paragraph was introduced here on second reading to identify another type of appearance of a State, or its representatives in their official capacity, in a proceeding before a court of another State that does not constitute evidence of consent by the participating State to the exercise of jurisdiction by the court.[87] This exception to the rule of non-immunity related to a State's participation in a foreign proceeding, however, is limited to cases of appearance of the State, or its representatives as a witness, for example, to affirm that a particular person is a national of the State, and does not relate to all appearances of a State or its representatives in a foreign proceeding in the performance of the duty of affording protection to nationals of that State.[88]

Paragraph 4

(9) By way of contrast, it follows that failure on the part of a State to enter an appearance in a legal proceeding is not to be construed as passive submission to the jurisdiction. The term "failure" in the present article covers cases of non-appearance, either intentional or unintentional, in the sense of a procedural matter, and does not affect the substantive rules concerning the appearance or non-appearance of a State before foreign courts.[89] Alternatively, a claim or interest by a State in property under litigation is not inconsistent with its assertion of jurisdictional immunity.[90] A State cannot be compelled to come before a court of another State to assert an interest in a property against which an action in rem is in progress, if that State does not choose to submit to the jurisdiction of the court entertaining the proceedings.

Counter-claims

Article 9   **2.018**

1. A State instituting a proceeding before a court of another State cannot invoke immunity from the jurisdiction of the court in respect of any counter-claim arising out of the same legal relationship or facts as the principal claim.
2. A State intervening to present a claim in a proceeding before a court of another State cannot invoke immunity from the jurisdiction of the court in respect of any counter-claim arising out of the same legal relationship or facts as the claim presented by the State.
3. A State making a counter-claim in a proceeding instituted against it before a court of another State cannot invoke immunity from the jurisdiction of the court in respect of the principal claim.

2.019   *Commentary*

(1) Article 9 follows logically from articles 7 and 8. While article 7 deals with the effect of consent given expressly by one State to the exercise of jurisdiction by a court of another State, article 8 defines the extent to which consent may be inferred from a State's conduct in participating in a proceeding before a court of another State. Article 9 is designed to complete the trilogy of provisions on the scope of consent by dealing with the effect of counter-claims against a State and counter-claims by a State.

(2) A State may institute a proceeding before a court of another State under article 8, paragraph 1 (a), thereby consenting or subjecting itself to the exercise of jurisdiction by that court in respect of that proceeding, including pre-trial hearing, trial and decisions, as well as appeals. Such consent to jurisdiction is not consent to execution, which is a separate matter to be dealt with in part IV in connection with immunity of the property of States from attachment and execution. The question may arise as to the extent to which the initiative taken by a State in instituting that proceeding could entail its subjection or amenability to the jurisdiction of that court in respect of counter-claims against the plaintiff State. Conversely, a State against which a proceeding has been instituted in a court of another State may decide to make a counter-claim against the party which initiated the proceeding. In both instances, a State is to some extent amenable to the competent jurisdiction of the forum, since in either case there is clear evidence of consent by conduct or manifestation of volition to submit to the jurisdiction of that court. The consequence of the expression of consent by conduct, such as by a State instituting a proceeding, or by intervening in a proceeding to present a claim or, indeed, by making a counter-claim in a proceeding instituted against it, may indeed vary according to the effectiveness of its consent to the exercise of jurisdiction by the competent judicial authority concerned. In each of the three cases, an important question arises as to the extent and scope of the effect of consent to the exercise of jurisdiction in the event of such a counter-claim against or by a State.

(a) Counter-claims against a State

(3) The notion of "counter-claims" presupposes the prior existence or institution of a claim. A counter-claim is a claim brought by a defendant in response to an original or principal claim. For this reason, there appear to be two possible circumstances in which counter-claims could be brought against a State. The first possibility is where a State has itself instituted a proceeding before a court of another State, as in article 8, paragraph 1 (a), and in article 9, paragraph 1. The second case occurs when a State has not itself instituted a proceeding but has intervened in a proceeding to present a claim. There is an important qualification as to the purpose of the intervention. In article 8, paragraph 1 (b), a State may intervene in a proceeding or take any other step relating to the merits thereof, and by such intervention subject

itself to the jurisdiction of that court in regard to the proceeding, subject to the qualification provided in the same subparagraph. Article 9, paragraph 2, deals with cases where a State intervenes in order to present a claim; hence the possibility arises of a counter-claim being brought against the State in respect of the claim it has presented by way of intervention. There would be no such possibility of a counter-claim against an intervening State which had not also made a claim in connection with the proceeding. For instance, a State could intervene as an amicus curiae, or in the interest of justice, or to make a suggestion, or to give evidence on a point of law or of fact without itself consenting to the exercise of jurisdiction against it in respect of the entire proceeding. Such actions would not fall under paragraph 2 of article 9. Thus, as in article 8, paragraph 2 (a), a State could intervene to invoke immunity or, as in paragraph 2 (b) of that article, to assert a right or interest in property at issue in that proceeding. In the case of paragraph 2 (b) of article 8, the intervening State, in so far as it may be said to have presented a claim connected with the proceeding, could also be considered to have consented to a counter-claim brought against it in respect of the claim it has presented, quite apart from, and in addition to, its amenability to the requirement to answer a judicial inquiry or to give prima facie evidence in support of its title or claim to rights or interests in property as contemplated in article 8, paragraph 2 (b). Even to invoke immunity as envisaged in article 8, paragraph 2 (a), a State may also be required to furnish proof or [sic] the legal basis of its claim to immunity. But once the claim to immunity is sustained under article 8, paragraph 2(a), or the claim or right or title is established under paragraph 2 (b), consent to the exercise of jurisdiction ceases. The court should, therefore, in such a case, refrain from further exercise of jurisdiction in respect of the State that is held to be immune or the property in which the State is found to have an interest, for the reason that the State and the property respectively would, in ordinary circumstances, be exempt from the jurisdiction of the court. Nevertheless, the court could continue to exercise jurisdiction if the proceeding fell within one of the exceptions provided in part III or the State had otherwise consented to the exercise of jurisdiction or waived its immunity.

Paragraph 1

(4) As has been seen in article 8, paragraph 1 (a), a State which has itself instituted a proceeding is deemed to have consented to the jurisdiction of the court for all stages of the proceeding, including trial and judgement at first instance, appellate and final adjudications and the award of costs where such lies within the discretion of the deciding authority, but excluding execution of the judgement. Article 9, paragraph 1, addresses the question of the extent to which a State which has instituted a proceeding before a court of another State may be said to have consented to the jurisdiction of the court in respect of counter-claims against it. Clearly, the mere fact that a State has instituted a proceeding does not imply its consent to all other civil

actions against the State which happen to be justiciable or subject to the jurisdiction of the same court or another court of the State of the forum. The extent of consent in such an event is not unlimited, and the purpose of article 9, paragraph 1, is to ensure a more precise and better balanced limit of the extent of permissible counter-claims against a plaintiff State. A State instituting a proceeding before a court of another State is not open to all kinds of cross-actions before that court nor to cross-claims by parties other than the defendants. A plaintiff State has not thereby consented to separate and independent counter-claims. There is no general submission to all other proceedings or all actions against the State, nor for all times. The State instituting a proceeding is amenable to the court's jurisdiction in respect of counter-claims arising out of the same legal relationship or facts as the principal claim,[91] or the same transaction or occurrence that is the subject-matter of the principal claim.[92] In some jurisdictions, the effect of a counter-claim against a plaintiff State is also limited in amount, which cannot exceed that of the principal claim; or if it does exceed the principal claim, the counter-claims against the State can only operate as a set-off.[93] This is expressed in American legal terminology as "recoupment against the sovereign claimant", which normally cannot go beyond "the point where affirmative relief is sought".[94] Only defensive counter-claims against foreign States appear to have been permitted in common-law jurisdictions.[95] On the other hand, in some civil-law jurisdictions, independent counter-claims have been allowed to operate as offensive remedies, and, in some cases, affirmative relief is known to have been granted.[96]

(5) Where the rules of the State of the forum so permit, article 9, paragraph 1, also applies in the case where a counter-claim is made against a State, and that State could not, in accordance with the provisions of the present articles, notably in part III, invoke immunity from jurisdiction in respect of that counter-claim, had separate proceedings been brought against the State in those courts.[97] Thus independent counter-claims, arising out of different transactions or occurrences not forming part of the subject-matter of the claim or arising out of a distinct legal relationship or separate facts from those of the principal claim, may not be maintained against the plaintiff State, unless they fall within the scope of one of the admissible exceptions under part III. In other words, independent counter-claims or cross-actions may be brought against a plaintiff State only when separate proceedings are available against that State under other parts of the present articles, whether or not the State has instituted a proceeding as in paragraph 1 or has intervened to present a claim as in paragraph 2 of article 9.

Paragraph 2

(6) Paragraph 2 of article 9 deals with cases where a State intervenes in a proceeding before a court of another State not as an amicus curiae, but as an interested party, to present a claim. It is only in this sense that it is possible to conceive of a

counter-claim being brought against a State which has intervened as a claimant, and not as a mere witness or merely to make a declaration, as in article 8, paragraph 1 (b), without presenting a claim. Once a State has intervened in a proceeding to make or present a claim, it is amenable to any counter-claim against it which arises out of the same legal relationship or facts as the claim presented by the State. Other parts of the commentary applicable to paragraph 1 concerning the limits of permissible counter-claims against a plaintiff State apply equally to counter-claims against an intervening claimant State, as envisaged in paragraph 2. They apply in particular to the identity of the legal relationship and facts as between the claim presented by the intervening State and the counter-claim, and possibly also to the quantum of the counter-claim and the extent or absence of allowable affirmative relief, if any, or of a remedy different in kind from, or beyond the limits of, the claim presented by the intervening State.

(b) Counter-claims by a State

Paragraph 3

(7) Where a State itself makes a counter-claim in a proceeding instituted against it before a court of another State, it is taking a step relating to the merits of the proceeding within the meaning of article 8, paragraph 1. In such a case, the State is deemed to have consented to the exercise of jurisdiction by that court with respect not only to the counter-claim brought by the State itself, but also to the principal claim against it.

(8) By itself bringing a counter-claim before a judicial authority of another State, a State consents by conduct to the exercise of jurisdiction by that forum. However, the effect, extent and scope of counter-claims by a State under article 9, paragraph 3, could be wider than those of counter-claims against the plaintiff State under paragraph 1, or against the intervening claimant State under paragraph 2 of article 9. For one thing, counter-claims by a defendant foreign State, although usually limited by local law to matters arising out of the same legal relationship or facts as the principal claim, are not limited in respect of the extent or scope of the relief sought, nor in respect of the nature of the remedy requested. Indeed, if they arise out of a different legal relationship or a different set of facts from those of the principal claim or if they are truly new and separate or independent counter-claims, they are still permissible as independent claims or, indeed, as separate proceedings altogether unconnected with the principal or original claim against the State. It is clear that the defendant State has the choice of bringing a counter-claim against the plaintiff or instituting a fresh and separate proceeding. Whatever the alternative chosen, the State making the counter-claim under article 9, paragraph 3, or instituting a separate proceeding under article 8, paragraph 1, is deemed to have consented to the exercise of jurisdiction by that court. Under article 8, as has been seen, the plaintiff State has consented to all stages of the proceeding before all the courts up to judgement,

but not including its execution. Likewise, under article 9, paragraph 3, a State is deemed to have consented to the exercise of jurisdiction with regard to its counterclaims and to the principal claim instituted against it.[98]

PART III

Proceedings in which State Immunity cannot be Invoked

2.020 *Commentary*

(1) The title of part III, as adopted provisionally on first reading, contained two alternative titles in square brackets reading "[Limitations on] [Exceptions to] State immunity" which reflected, on the one hand, the position of those States which had favoured the term "limitations" subscribing to the notion that present international law did not recognize the jurisdictional immunity of States in the areas dealt with in part III and, on the other hand, the position of those which had favoured the term "exceptions" holding the view that the term correctly described the notion that State jurisdictional immunity was the rule of international law, and exceptions to that rule were made subject to the express consent of the State. The Commission adopted the present formulation on second reading to reconcile these two positions.

(2) It is to be kept in mind that the application of the rule of State immunity is a two-way street. Each State is a potential recipient or beneficiary of State immunity as well as having the duty to fulfil the obligation to give effect to jurisdictional immunity enjoyed by another State.

(3) In the attempt to specify areas of activity to which State immunity does not apply, several distinctions have been made between acts or activities to which State immunity is applicable and those not covered by State immunity. The distinctions, which have been discussed in greater detail in a document submitted to the Commission,[99] *have been drawn up on the basis of consideration of the following factors: dual personality of the State,*[100] *dual capacity of the State,*[101] *acta jure imperii and acta jure gestionis,*[102] *which also relate to the public and private nature of State acts,*[103] *and commercial and non-commercial activities.*[104] *The Commission, however, decided to operate on a pragmatic basis, taking into account the situations involved and the practice of States.*

Commercial transactions

2.021 Article 10

1. If a State engages in a commercial transaction with a foreign natural or juridical person and, by virtue of the applicable rules of private international law, differences relating to the commercial transaction fall within the jurisdiction of a court of another State, the State cannot invoke immunity from that jurisdiction in a proceeding arising out of that commercial transaction.

2. Paragraph 1 does not apply:

    (a) in the case of a commercial transaction between States; or

    (b) if the parties to the commercial transaction have expressly agreed otherwise.

3. The immunity from jurisdiction enjoyed by a State shall not be affected with regard to a proceeding which relates to a commercial transaction engaged in by a State enterprise or other entity established by the State which has an independent legal personality and is capable of:

    (a) suing or being sued; and

    (b) acquiring, owning or possessing and disposing of property, including property which the State has authorized it to operate or manage.

Commentary   2.022

(a) General observations on the draft article

(1) Article 10 as adopted by the Commission on second reading is now entitled "Commercial transactions", replacing the words "commercial contracts" originally adopted on first reading, consistent with the change made in article 2 (Use of terms), paragraph 1 (c). It constitutes the first substantive article of part III, dealing with proceedings in which State immunity cannot be invoked.

Paragraph 1

(2) Paragraph 1 represents a compromise formulation. It is the result of continuing efforts to accommodate the differing viewpoints of those who are prepared to admit an exception to the general rule of State immunity in the field of trading or commercial activities, based upon the theory of implied consent, or on other grounds, and those who take the position that a plea of State immunity cannot be invoked to set aside the jurisdiction of the local courts where a foreign State engages in trading or commercial activities. For reasons of consistency and clarity, the phrase "the State is considered to have consented to the exercise of" which appeared in the original text of paragraph 1 provisionally adopted on first reading has been amended to read "the State cannot invoke immunity", as a result of the Commission's second reading of the draft article. This change, which is also made in articles 11 to 14, does not, however, suggest any theoretical departure from various viewpoints as described above. The Commission held an extensive debate on this specified area of State activities[105] and adopted a formula in an attempt to take into account the interests and views of all countries with different systems and practices.

(3) The application of jurisdictional immunities of States presupposes the existence of jurisdiction or the competence of a court in accordance with the relevant internal law of the State of the forum. The relevant internal law of the forum may be the laws, rules or regulations governing the organization of the courts or the limits of judicial jurisdiction of the courts and may also include the applicable rules of private international law.

(4) It is common ground among the various approaches to the study of State immunities that there must be a pre-existing jurisdiction in the courts of the foreign State before the possibility of its exercise arises and that such jurisdiction can only exist and its exercise only be authorized in conformity with the internal law of the State of the forum, including the applicable rules of jurisdiction, particularly where there is a foreign element involved in a dispute or differences that require settlement or adjudication. The expression "applicable rules of private international law" is a neutral one, selected to refer the settlement of jurisdictional issues to the applicable rules of conflict of laws or private international law, whether or not uniform rules of jurisdiction are capable of being applied. Each State is eminently sovereign in matters of jurisdiction, including the organization and determination of the scope of the competence of its courts of law or other tribunals.

(5) The rule stated in paragraph 1 of article 10 concerns commercial transactions between a State and a foreign natural or juridical person when a court of another State is available and in a position to exercise its jurisdiction by virtue of its own applicable rules of private international law. The State engaging in a commercial transaction with a person, natural or juridical, other than its own national cannot invoke immunity from the exercise of jurisdiction by the judicial authority of another State where that judicial authority is competent to exercise its jurisdiction by virtue of its applicable rules of private international law. Jurisdiction may be exercised by a court of another State on various grounds, such as the place of conclusion of the contract, the place where the obligations under the contract are to be performed, or the nationality or place of business of one or more of the contracting parties. A significant territorial connection generally affords a firm ground for the exercise of jurisdiction, but there may be other valid grounds for the assumption and exercise of jurisdiction by virtue of the applicable rules of private international law.

Paragraph 2

(6) While the wording of paragraph 1, which refers to a commercial transaction between a State and a foreign natural or juridical person, implies that the State-to-State transactions are outside the scope of the present article, this understanding is clarified in paragraph 2, particularly because "foreign natural or juridical persons" could be interpreted broadly to include both private and public persons.[106]

(7) Subparagraphs (a) and (b) of paragraph 2 are designed to provide precisely the necessary safeguards and protection of the interests of all States. It is a well-known fact that developing countries often conclude trading contracts with other States, while socialist States also engage in direct State-trading not only among themselves, but also with other States, both in the developing world and with the highly industrialized countries. Such State contracts, concluded between States, are excluded by subparagraph (a) of paragraph 2 from the operation of the rule stated in paragraph 1. Thus State immunity continues to be the applicable rule in such cases. This type

of contract also includes various tripartite transactions for the better and more efficient administration of food aid programmes. Where food supplies are destined to relieve famine or revitalize a suffering village or a vulnerable area, their acquisition could be financed by another State or a group of States, either directly or through an international organization or a specialized agency of the United Nations, by way of purchase from a developing food-exporting country on a State-to-State basis as a consequence of tripartite or multilateral negotiations. Transactions of this kind not only help the needy population, but may also promote developing countries' exports instead of encouraging dumping or unfair competition in international trade. It should be understood that "a commercial transaction between States" means a transaction which involves all agencies and instrumentalities of the State, including various organs of government, as defined in article 2, paragraph (1) (b).

(8) Subparagraph (b) leaves a State party to a commercial transaction complete freedom to provide for a different solution or method of settlement of differences relating to the transaction. A State may expressly agree in the commercial transaction itself, or through subsequent negotiations, to arbitration or other methods of amicable settlement such as conciliation, good offices or mediation. Any such express agreement would normally be in writing.

Paragraph 3

(9) Paragraph 3 sets out a legal distinction between a State and certain of its entities in the matter of State immunity from foreign jurisdiction. In the economic system of some States, commercial transactions as defined in article 2, paragraph 1 (c), are normally conducted by State enterprises, or other entities established by a State, which have independent legal personality. The manner under which State enterprises or other entities are established by a State may differ according to the legal system of the State. Under some legal systems, they are established by a law or decree of the Government. Under some other systems, they may be regarded as having been established when the parent State has acquired majority shares or other ownership interests. As a rule, they engage in commercial transactions on their own behalf as separate entities from the parent State, and not on behalf of that State. Thus, in the event of a difference arising from a commercial transaction engaged in by a State entity, it may be sued before the court of another State and may be held liable for any consequences of the claim by the other party. In such a case, the immunity of the parent State itself is not affected, since it is not a party to the transaction.

(10) The application of the provision of paragraph 3 is subject to certain conditions. First, a proceeding must be concerned with a commercial transaction engaged in by a State enterprise or other entity. Secondly, a State enterprise or entity must have an independent legal personality. Such an independent legal personality must include the capacity to: (a) sue or be sued; and (b) acquire, own, possess and dispose of property, including property which the State has authorized the enterprise or entity to

operate or manage. In some socialist States, the State property which the State empowers its enterprises or other entities to operate or manage is called "segregated State property". This terminology is not used in paragraph 3, since it is not universally applicable in other States. The requirements of subparagraphs (a) and (b) are cumulative: in addition to the capacity of such State enterprises and other entities to sue or be sued, they must also satisfy certain financial requirements as stipulated in subparagraph (b). Namely, they must be capable of acquiring, owning or possessing and of disposing of property—property that the State has authorized them to operate or manage as well as property they gain themselves as a result of their activities. The term "disposing" in paragraph (b) is particularly important, because that makes the property of such entities, including the property which the State authorized them to operate or manage, potentially subject to measures of constraint, such as attachment, arrest and execution, to the satisfaction of the claimant.

(11) The text of paragraph 3 is the result of lengthy discussion in the Commission. The original proposal (former article 11 bis), which was submitted by the Special Rapporteur in response to the suggestion of some members and Governments, was an independent article relating specifically to State enterprises with segregated property. During the Commission's deliberation of the proposal, however, it was the view of some members that the provision was of limited application as the concept of segregated property was a specific feature of socialist States and should not be included in the present draft articles. However, the view of some other members was that the question of State enterprises performing commercial transactions as separate and legally distinct entities from the State had a much wider application as it was also highly relevant to developing countries and even to many developed countries. They further maintained that a distinction between such enterprises and the parent State should be clarified in the present draft articles in order to avoid abuse of judicial process against the State. The Commission, taking into account these views, adopted the present formulation which includes not only the State enterprise with segregated property but also any other enterprise or entity established by the State engaged in commercial transactions on its own behalf, having independent legal personality and satisfying certain requirements as specified in subparagraphs (a) and (b). The Commission further agreed to the inclusion of the provision as part of article 10 rather than as an independent article, since article 10 itself deals with "commercial transactions". One member, however, had serious reservations about the substance of paragraph 3 which, in his view, had been introduced to meet the concern of a limited number of States and was likely to thwart the whole object of the draft articles, which was to ensure the enforcement of commercial transactions and the performance of contractual obligations. Other members emphasized that the provisions of subparagraphs (a) and (b) did not add anything to the notion of "independent legal personality" and were therefore superfluous.

(12) Although not specifically dealt with in the draft articles, note should be taken of the question of fiscal matters particularly in relation to the provisions of article 10. It is recalled that former article 16 as provisionally adopted on first reading dealt with that particular question.[107] One member expressed strong reservations with regard to the article, since it violated the principle of the sovereign equality of States by allowing a State to institute proceedings against another State before the courts of the former State. In this connection, a proposal was made to delete the article. The reason for the proposal was that the article concerned only the relations between two States, the forum State and the foreign State; it essentially dealt with a bilateral international problem governed by existing rules of international law. In contrast, the present draft articles dealt with relations between a State and foreign natural or juridical persons, the purpose being to protect the State against certain actions brought against it by such persons or to enable those persons to protect themselves against the State. Hence, the article which dealt with inter-State relations alone was not considered to have its proper place in the draft articles. There were members, however, who opposed the deletion of the article as it was based on extensive legislative practice and had been adopted on first reading. After some discussion, it was finally decided to delete former article 16 on the understanding that the commentary to article 10 would clarify that its deletion is without prejudice to the law with respect to fiscal matters.

(b) "Commercial transactions" in the context of State immunity

(13) In order to appreciate the magnitude and complexity of the problem involved in the consideration and determination of the precise limits of jurisdictional immunities in this specified area of "commercial transactions",[108] it is useful to provide here, in a condensed form, a chronological survey of State practice relating to this question.

(i) A survey of judicial practice: international and national

(14) This brief survey, of which a more detailed version has been submitted to the Commission,[109] begins by mentioning one of the earliest cases, The "Charkieh" (1873), in which the exception of trading activities (for the purpose of the article, "commercial transactions") was recognized and applied in State practice. In this case, the court observed:

> *No principle of international law, and no decided case, and no dictum of jurists of which I am aware, has gone so far as to authorize a sovereign prince to assume the character of a trader, when it is for his benefit; and when he incurs an obligation to a private subject to throw off, if I may so speak, his disguise, and appear as a sovereign, claiming for his own benefit, and to the injury of a private person, for the first time, all the attributes of his character.[110]*

(15) The uncertainty in the scope of application of the rule of State immunity in State practice is, in some measure, accountable for the relative silence of judicial

pronouncement on an international level. Nevertheless, by not pursuing the matter on the international level, a State affected by an adverse judicial decision of a foreign court may remain silent at the risk of acquiescing in the judgement or the treatment given, though, as will be seen in part IV of the present draft articles, States are not automatically exposed to a measure of seizure, attachment and execution in respect of their property once a judgement which may adversely affect them has been rendered or obtained.

(16) The practice of States such as Italy,[111] Belgium[112] and Egypt[113] which could be said to have led the field of "restrictive" immunity, denying immunity in regard to trading activities, may now have been overtaken by the recent practice of States which traditionally favoured a more unqualified doctrine of State immunity, such as Germany,[114] the United States of America[115] and the United Kingdom.[116]

(17) In Europe, the "restrictive" view of State immunity pronounced by the Italian and Belgian courts, as already noted, was soon followed also by the French,[117] Netherlands[118] and Austrian[119] courts.

(18) The judicial practice of a certain number of developing countries can also be said to have adopted restrictive immunity. Egypt, as already noted,[120] was the pioneer in this field. In recent years, the judicial practice of Pakistan[121] and Argentina[122] has provided examples of acceptance of restrictive immunity, while in the case of the Philippines,[123] there have been some relevant cases, but no decisions on the question of the exception of commercial transactions from State immunity.

(ii) A survey of national legislation

(19) A number of Governments have recently enacted legislation dealing comprehensively with the question of jurisdictional immunities of States and their property. While these laws share a common theme, namely the trend towards "restrictive" immunity, some of them differ in certain matters of important detail which must be watched. Without going into such details here, it is significant to compare the relevant texts relating to the "commercial contracts" exception as contained in the Foreign Sovereign Immunities Act of 1976[124] of the United States of America and in the State Immunity Act of 1978[125] of the United Kingdom. The latter Act has, on this point, been followed closely by Pakistan,[126] Singapore[127] and South Africa[128] and partly by Australia[129] and Canada.[130]

(iii) A survey of treaty practice

(20) The attitude or views of a Government can be gathered from its established treaty practice. Bilateral treaties may contain provisions whereby parties agree in advance to submit to the jurisdiction of the local courts in respect of certain specified areas of activities, such as trading or investment. Thus the treaty practice of the Soviet Union amply demonstrates its willingness to have commercial relations carried on by State enterprises or trading organizations with independent legal personality

regulated by competent territorial authorities. While the fact that a State is consistent in its practice in this particular regard may be considered as proof of the absence of rules of international law on the subject, or of the permissibility of deviation or derogation from such rules through bilateral agreements, an accumulation of such bilateral treaty practices could combine to corroborate the evidence of the existence of a general practice of States in support of the limitations agreed upon, which could ripen into accepted exceptions in international practice.[131] However, at the time of first reading a member of the Commission maintained that the repeated inclusion of such an exception in specific agreements was based on consent and must not be taken to imply general acceptance of such an exception.

(21) The 1951 agreement between the Soviet Union and France,[132] typical of treaties concluded between the Soviet Union and developed countries, and paragraph 3 of the exchange of letters of 1953 between the Soviet Union and India,[133] which is an example of such agreements between the Soviet Union and developing countries, provide further illustrations of treaty practice relating to this exception.

(iv) A survey of international conventions and efforts towards codification by intergovernmental bodies

(22) One regional convention, the 1972 European Convention on State Immunity, and one global convention, the 1926 Brussels Convention, addressed the question of commercial activities as an exception to State immunity. While article 7 of the European Convention is self-evident in addressing the issue,[134] it needs to be observed that the main object of article 1 of the Brussels Convention[135] was clearly to assimilate the position of State-operated merchant ships to that of private vessels of commerce in regard to the question of immunity.

(23) While the efforts of the Council of Europe culminated in the entry into force of the 1972 European Convention on State Immunity, similar efforts have been or are being pursued also in other regions. The Central American States, the Inter-American Council and the Caribbean States have been considering similar projects.[136] Another important development concerns the work of OAS on the Inter-American Draft Convention on Jurisdictional Immunity of States. In the early 1980s, the OAS General Assembly requested the Permanent Council, a political body, to study the Inter-American Draft Convention on Jurisdictional Immunity of States approved by the Inter-American Juridical Committee in 1983,[137] which contains a provision limiting immunity in regard to "claims relative to trade or commercial activities undertaken in the State of the forum".[138] The draft has been considered by a working group, established by the Permanent Council, which prepared a revised text as well as a comparative analysis of the two OAS drafts and the ILC draft on jurisdictional immunities. The revised OAS draft has been referred to Governments for their consideration.

(24) It may be said from the foregoing survey that while the precise limits of jurisdictional immunities in the area of "commercial transactions" may not be

easily determined on the basis of existing State practice, the concept of non-immunity of States in respect of commercial activities as provided in the rule formulated in paragraph 1 of the present article finds precedent in the sources reviewed above.[139]

(25) The distinction made between a State and certain of its entities performing commercial transactions in the matter of State immunity from foreign jurisdiction appears to be generally supported by the recent treaties[140] and national legislation[141] as well as by the judicial practice of States,[142] although specific approaches or requirements may vary among them.[143]

Contracts of employment

2.023 **Article 11**

1. Unless otherwise agreed between the States concerned, a State cannot invoke immunity from jurisdiction before a court of another State which is otherwise competent in a proceeding which relates to a contract of employment between the State and an individual for work performed or to be performed, in whole or in part, in the territory of that other State.

2. Paragraph 1 does not apply if:
    (a) the employee has been recruited to perform functions closely related to the exercise of governmental authority;
    (b) the subject of the proceeding is the recruitment, renewal of employment or reinstatement of an individual;
    (c) the employee was neither a national nor a habitual resident of the State of the forum at the time when the contract of employment was concluded;
    (d) the employee is a national of the employer State at the time when the proceeding is instituted; or
    (e) the employer State and the employee have otherwise agreed in writing, subject to any considerations of public policy conferring on the courts of the State of the forum exclusive jurisdiction by reason of the subject-matter of the proceeding.

2.024 *Commentary*

(a) Nature and scope of the exception of "contracts of employment"

(1) Draft article 11 adopted by the Commission covers an area commonly designated as "contracts of employment", which has recently emerged as an exception to State immunity. "Contracts of employment" have been excluded from the expression "commercial transaction" as defined in article 2, paragraph 1 (c), of the present draft articles. They are thus different in nature from commercial transactions.

(2) Without technically defining a contract of employment, it is useful to note some of the essential elements of such a contract for the purposes of article 11. The area of exception under this article concerns a contract of employment or service between a State and a natural person or individual for work performed or to be performed in whole or in part in the territory of another State. Two sovereign States are involved, namely the employer State and the State of the forum. An individual or natural person is also an important element as a party to the contract of employment, being recruited for work to be performed in the State of the forum. The exception to State immunity applies to matters arising out of the terms and conditions contained in the contract of employment.

(3) With the involvement of two sovereign States, two legal systems compete for application of their respective laws. The employer State has an interest in the application of its law in regard to the selection, recruitment and appointment of an employee by the State or one of its organs, agencies or instrumentalities acting in the exercise of governmental authority. It would also seem justifiable that for the exercise of disciplinary supervision over its own staff or government employees, the employer State has an overriding interest in ensuring compliance with its internal regulations and the prerogative of appointment or dismissal which results from unilateral decisions taken by the State.

(4) On the other hand, the State of the forum appears to retain exclusive jurisdiction if not, indeed, an overriding interest in matters of domestic public policy regarding the protection to be afforded to its local labour force. Questions relating to medical insurance, insurance against certain risks, minimum wages, entitlement to rest and recreation, vacation with pay, compensation to be paid on termination of the contract of employment, and so forth, are of primary concern to the State of the forum, especially if the employees were recruited for work to be performed in that State, or at the time of recruitment were its nationals or habitual or permanent residents there. Beyond that, the State of the forum may have less reason to claim an overriding or preponderant interest in exercising jurisdiction. The basis for jurisdiction is distinctly and unmistakably the closeness of territorial connection between the contracts of employment and the State of the forum, namely performance of work in the territory of the State of the forum, as well as the nationality or habitual residence of the employees. Indeed, local staff working, for example, in a foreign embassy would have no realistic way to present a claim other than in a court of the State of the forum.[144] Article 11, in this respect, provides an important guarantee to protect their legal rights. The employees covered under the present article include both regular employees and short-term independent contractors.

(b) The rule of non-immunity

(5) Article 11 therefore endeavours to maintain a delicate balance between the competing interests of the employer State with regard to the application of its law

and the overriding interests of the State of the forum for the application of its labour law and, in certain exceptional cases, also in retaining exclusive jurisdiction over the subject-matter of a proceeding.

(6) Paragraph 1 thus represents an effort to state the rule of non-immunity. In its formulation, the basis for the exercise of jurisdiction by the competent court of the State of the forum is apparent from the place of performance of work under the contract of employment in the territory of the State of the forum. Reference to the coverage of its social security provisions incorporated in the original text adopted on first reading has been deleted on second reading, since not all States have social security systems in the strict sense of the term and some foreign States may prefer that their employees not be covered by the social security system of the State of the forum. Furthermore, there were social security systems whose benefits did not cover persons employed for very short periods. If the reference to social security provisions was retained in article 11, such persons would be deprived of the protection of the courts of the forum State. However, it was precisely those persons who were in the most vulnerable position and who most needed effective judicial remedies. The reference to recruitment in the State of the forum which appeared in the original text adopted on first reading has also been deleted.

(7) Paragraph 1 is formulated as a residual rule, since States can always agree otherwise, thereby adopting a different solution by waiving local labour jurisdiction in favour of immunity. Respect for treaty regimes and for the consent of the States concerned is of paramount importance, since they are decisive in solving the question of waiver or of exercise of jurisdiction by the State of the forum or of the maintenance of jurisdictional immunity of the employer State. Without opposing the adoption of paragraph 1, some members felt that paragraph 1 should provide for the immunity of the State as a rule and that paragraph 2 should contain the exceptions to that rule.

(c) Circumstances justifying maintenance of the rule of State immunity

(8) Paragraph 2 strives to establish and maintain an appropriate balance by introducing important limitations on the application of the rule of non-immunity, by enumerating circumstances where the rule of immunity still prevails.

(9) Paragraph 2 (a) enunciates the rule of immunity for the engagement of government employees of rank whose functions are closely related to the exercise of governmental authority. Examples of such employees are private secretaries, code clerks, interpreters, translators and other persons entrusted with functions related to State security or basic interests of the State.[145] Officials of established accreditation are, of course, covered by this subparagraph. Proceedings relating to their contracts of employment will not be allowed to be instituted or entertained before the courts of the State of the forum. The Commission on second reading considered that the

expression "services associated with the exercise of governmental authority" which had appeared in the text adopted on first reading might lend itself to unduly extensive interpretation, since a contract of employment concluded by a State stood a good chance of being "associated with the exercise of governmental authority", even very indirectly. It was suggested that the exception provided for in subparagraph (a) was justified only if there was a close link between the work to be performed and the exercise of governmental authority. The word "associated" has therefore been amended to read "closely related". In order to avoid any confusion with contracts for the performance of services which were dealt with in the definition of a "commercial transaction" and were therefore covered by article 11, the word "services" was replaced by the word "functions" on second reading.

(10) Paragraph 2 (b) is designed to confirm the existing practice of States[146] in support of the rule of immunity in the exercise of the discretionary power of appointment or non-appointment by the State of an individual to any official post or employment position. This includes actual appointment which under the law of the employer State is considered to be a unilateral act of governmental authority. So also are the acts of "dismissal" or "removal" of a government employee by the State, which normally take place after the conclusion of an inquiry or investigation as part of supervisory or disciplinary jurisdiction exercised by the employer State. This subparagraph also covers cases where the employee seeks the renewal of his employment or reinstatement after untimely termination of his engagement. The rule of immunity applies to proceedings for recruitment, renewal of employment and reinstatement of an individual only. It is without prejudice to the possible recourse which may still be available in the State of the forum for compensation or damages for "wrongful dismissal" or for breaches of obligation to recruit or to renew employment. In other words, this subparagraph does not prevent an employee from bringing action against the employer State in the State of the forum to seek redress for damage arising from recruitment, renewal of employment or reinstatement of an individual. The Commission on second reading replaced the words "the proceeding relates to" adopted on first reading by the words "the subject of the proceeding is" to clarify this particular point. The new wording is intended to make it clear that the scope of the exception is restricted to the specific acts which are referred to in the subparagraph and which are legitimately within the discretionary power of the employer State.

(11) Paragraph 2 (c) also favours the application of State immunity where the employee was neither a national nor a habitual resident of the State of the forum, the material time for either of these requirements being set at the conclusion of the contract of employment. If a different time were to be adopted, for instance the time when the proceeding is initiated, further complications would arise as there could be incentives to change nationality or to establish habitual or permanent residence

in the State of the forum, thereby unjustly limiting the immunity of the employer State. The protection of the State of the forum is confined essentially to the local labour force, comprising nationals of the State of the forum and non-nationals who habitually reside in that State. Without the link of nationality or habitual residence, the State of the forum lacks the essential ground for claiming priority for the exercise of its applicable labour law and jurisdiction in the face of a foreign employer State, in spite of the territorial connection in respect of place of recruitment of the employee and place of performance of services under the contract.

(12) Another important safeguard to protect the interest of the employer State is provided in paragraph 2 (d). The fact that the employee has the nationality of the employer State at the time of the initiation of the proceeding is conclusive and determinative of the rule of immunity from the jurisdiction of the courts of the State of the forum. As between the State and its own nationals, no other State should claim priority of jurisdiction on matters arising out of contracts of employment. Remedies and access to courts exist in the employer State. Whether the law to be applied is the administrative law or the labour law of the employer State, or of any other State, would appear to be immaterial at this point.

(13) Finally, paragraph 2 (e) provides for the freedom of contract, including the choice of law and the possibility of a chosen forum or forum prorogatum. This freedom is not unlimited. It is subject to considerations of public policy or ordre public or, in some systems, "good moral and popular conscience", whereby exclusive jurisdiction is reserved for the courts of the State of the forum by reason of the subject-matter of the proceeding.

(14) The rules formulated in article 11 appear to be consistent with the emerging trend in the recent legislative and treaty practice of a growing number of States.[147]

(15) It was observed in the Commission that the provision of paragraph 2 (c) might deprive persons who were neither nationals nor habitual residents of the State of the forum at the relevant time of every legal protection.

Personal injuries and damage to property

2.025 **Article 12**

Unless otherwise agreed between the States concerned, a State cannot invoke immunity from jurisdiction before a court of another State which is otherwise competent in a proceeding which relates to pecuniary compensation for death or injury to the person, or damage to or loss of tangible property, caused by an act or omission which is alleged to be attributable to the State, if the act or omission occurred in whole or in part in the territory of that other State and if the author of the act or omission was present in that territory at the time of the act or omission.

Commentary **2.026**

(1) This article covers an exception to the general rule of State immunity in the field of tort or civil liability resulting from an act or omission which has caused personal injury to a natural person or damage to or loss of tangible property.[148]

(2) This exception to the rule of immunity is applicable only to cases or circumstances in which the State concerned would have been liable under the lex loci delicti commissi. Although the State is as a rule immune from the jurisdiction of the courts of another State, for this exceptional provision immunity is withheld.

(3) The exception contained in this article is therefore designed to provide relief or possibility of recourse to justice for individuals who suffer personal injury, death or physical damage to or loss of property caused by an act or omission which might be intentional, accidental or caused by negligence attributable to a foreign State. Since the damaging act or omission has occurred in the territory of the State of the forum, the applicable law is clearly the lex loci delicti commissi and the most convenient court is that of the State where the delict was committed. A court foreign to the scene of the delict might be considered as a forum non conveniens. The injured individual would have been without recourse to justice had the State been entitled to invoke its jurisdictional immunity.

(4) Furthermore, the physical injury to the person or the damage to tangible property, resulting in death or total loss or other lesser injury, appears to be confined principally to insurable risks. The areas of damage envisaged in article 12 are mainly concerned with accidental death or physical injuries to persons or damage to tangible property involved in traffic accidents, such as moving vehicles, motor cycles, locomotives or speedboats. In other words, the article covers most areas of accidents involved in the transport of goods and passengers by rail, road, air or waterways. Essentially, the rule of non-immunity will preclude the possibility of the insurance company hiding behind the cloak of State immunity and evading its liability to the injured individuals. In addition, the scope of article 12 is wide enough to cover also intentional physical harm such as assault and battery, malicious damage to property, arson or even homicide, including political assassination.[149]

(5) Article 12 does not cover cases where there is no physical damage. Damage to reputation or defamation is not personal injury in the physical sense, nor is interference with contract rights or any rights, including economic or social rights, damage to tangible property.

(6) The existence of two cumulative conditions is needed for the application of this exception. The act or omission causing the death, injury or damage must occur in whole or in part in the territory of the State of the forum so as to locate the locus delicti commissi within the territory of the State of the forum. In addition, the author of such act or omission must also be present in that State at the time of the

act or omission so as to render even closer the territorial connection between the State of the forum and the author or individual whose act or omission was the cause of the damage in the State of the forum.

(7) The second condition, namely the presence of the author of the act or omission causing the injury or damage within the territory of the State of the forum at the time of the act or omission, has been inserted to ensure the exclusion from the application of this article of cases of trans-boundary injuries or trans-frontier torts or damage, such as export of explosives, fireworks or dangerous substances which could explode or cause damage through negligence, inadvertence or accident. It is also clear that cases of shooting or firing across a boundary or of spill-over across the border of shelling as a result of an armed conflict are excluded from the areas covered by article 12. The article is primarily concerned with accidents occurring routinely within the territory of the State of the forum, which in many countries may still require specific waiver of State immunity to allow suits for recovering damages to proceed, even though compensation is sought from, and would ultimately be paid by, an insurance company.[150]

(8) The basis for the assumption and exercise of jurisdiction in cases covered by this exception is territoriality. The locus delicti commissi offers a substantial territorial connection regardless of the motivation of the act or omission, whether intentional or even malicious, or whether accidental, negligent, inadvertent, reckless or careless, and indeed irrespective of the nature of the activities involved, whether jure imperii or jure gestionis. This distinction has been maintained in the case law of some States[151] involving motor accidents in the course of official or military duties. While immunity has been maintained for acts jure imperii, it has been rejected for acts jure gestionis. The exception proposed in article 12 makes no such distinction, subject to a qualification in the opening paragraph indicating the reservation which in fact allows different rules to apply to questions specifically regulated by treaties, bilateral agreements or regional arrangements specifying or limiting the extent of liabilities or compensation, or providing for a different procedure for settlement of disputes.[152]

(9) In short, article 12 is designed to allow normal proceedings to stand and to provide relief for the individual who has suffered an otherwise actionable physical damage to his own person or his deceased ancestor, or to his property. The cause of action relates to the occurrence or infliction of physical damage occurring in the State of the forum, with the author of the damaging act or omission physically present therein at the time, and for which a State is answerable under the law of the State of the forum, which is also the lex loci delicti commissi.

(10) The Commission has added on second reading the word "pecuniary" before "compensation" to clarify that the word "compensation" did not include any non-pecuniary forms of compensation. The words "author of the act" should be understood

to refer to agents or officials of a State exercising their official functions and not neces-sarily the State itself as a legal person. The expression "attributable to the State" is also intended to establish a distinction between acts by such persons which are not attrib-utable to the State and those which are attributable to the State. The reference to act or omission attributable to the State, however, does not affect the rules of State responsi-bility. It should be emphasized that the present article does not address itself to the ques-tion of State responsibility but strictly to non-immunity of a State from jurisdiction before a court of another State in respect of damage caused by an act or omission of the State's agents or employees which is "alleged" to be attributable to that State; the deter-mination of attribution or responsibility of the State concerned is clearly outside the scope of the present article. Neither does it affect the question of diplomatic immuni-ties, as provided in article 3, nor does it apply to situations involving armed conflicts.

(11) Some members expressed reservations about the very broad scope of the article and on the consequences that might have for State responsibility. In their view, the protection of individual victims would effectively be secured by negotiations through diplomatic channels or by insurance.

Ownership, possession and use of property

Article 13   2.027

Unless otherwise agreed between the States concerned, a State cannot invoke immunity from jurisdiction before a court of another State which is otherwise competent in a proceeding which relates to the determination of:

(a) any right or interest of the State in, or its possession or use of, or any oblig-ation of the State arising out of its interest in, or its possession or use of, immovable property situated in the State of the forum;

(b) any right or interest of the State in movable or immovable property arising by way of succession, gift or bona vacantia; or

(c) any right or interest of the State in the administration of property, such as trust property, the estate of a bankrupt or the property of a company in the event of its winding-up.

Commentary   2.028

(1) Article 13 deals with an important exception to the rule of State immunity from the jurisdiction of a court of another State quite apart from State immunity in respect of its property from attachment and execution. It is to be recalled that, under article 6, paragraph 2 (b),[153] State immunity may be invoked even though the pro-ceeding is not brought directly against a foreign State but is merely aimed at depriv-ing that State of its property or of the use of property in its possession or control. Article 13 is therefore designed to set out an exception to the rule of State immunity.

The provision of article 13 is, however, without prejudice to the privileges and immunities enjoyed by a State under international law in relation to property of diplomatic missions and other representative offices of a government, as provided under article 3.

(2) This exception, which has not encountered any serious opposition in the judicial and governmental practice of States,[154] is formulated in language which has to satisfy the differing views of Governments and differing theories regarding the basis for the exercise of jurisdiction by the courts of another State in which, in most cases, the property—especially immovable property—is situated. According to most authorities, article 13 is a clear and well-established exception, while others may still hold that it is not a true exception since a State has a choice to participate in the proceeding to assert its right or interest in the property which is the subject of adjudication or litigation.

(3) Article 13 lists the various types of proceedings relating to or involving the determination of any right or interest of a State in, or its possession or use of, movable or immovable property, or any obligation arising out of its interest in, or its possession or use of, immovable property. It is not intended to confer jurisdiction on any court where none exists. Hence the expression "which is otherwise competent" is used to specify the existence of competence of a court of another State in regard to the proceeding. The word "otherwise" merely suggests the existence of jurisdiction in normal circumstances had there been no question of State immunity to be determined. It is understood that the court is competent for this purpose by virtue of the applicable rules of private international law.

(4) Subparagraph (a) deals with immovable property and is qualified by the phrase "situated in the State of the forum". This subparagraph as a whole does not give rise to any controversy owing to the generally accepted predominance of the applicability of the lex situs and the exclusive competence of the forum rei sitae. However, the expression "right or interest" in this paragraph gives rise to some semantic difficulties. The law of property, especially real property or immovable property, contains many peculiarities. What constitutes a right in property in one system may be regarded as an interest in another system. Thus the combination of "right or interest" is used as a term to indicate the totality of whatever right or interest a State may have under any legal system. The French text of the 1972 European Convention on State Immunity used in article 9 the term droit in its widest sense, without the addition of intérêt. In this connection, it should also be noted that "possession" is not always considered a "right" unless it is adverse possession or possessio longi temporis, nec vi nec clam nec precario, which could create a "right" or "interest", depending on the legal terminology used in a particular legal system. The Spanish equivalent expression, as adopted, is derecho o interés.

(5) Subparagraph (b) concerns any right or interest of the State in movable or immovable property arising by way of succession, gift or bona vacantia. It is clearly

understood that, if the proceeding involves not only movable but also immovable property situated within the territorial jurisdiction of the State of the forum, then a separate proceeding may also have to be initiated in order to determine such rights or interests before the court of the State where the immovable property is situated, that is to say, the forum rei sitae.

(6) Subparagraph (c) need not concern or relate to the determination of a right or interest of the State in property, but is included to cover the situation in many countries, especially in the common-law systems, where the court exercises some supervisory jurisdiction or other functions with regard to the administration of trust property or property otherwise held on a fiduciary basis; of the estate of a deceased person, a person of unsound mind or a bankrupt; or of a company in the event of its winding-up. The exercise of such supervisory jurisdiction is purely incidental, as the proceeding may in part involve the determination or ascertainment of rights or interests of all the interested parties, including, if any, those of a foreign State. Taking into account the comments and observations of Governments as well as those of members of the Commission, the present subparagraph (c) combines original paragraph 1, subparagraphs (c), (d) and (e), as adopted on first reading, in a single paragraph.

(7) Former paragraph 2,[155] which was included in the text of the article adopted provisionally on first reading notwithstanding the contention of some members, has been deleted in view of the fact that the definition of the term "State" having been elaborated in article 2, paragraph 1 (b), the possibility of a proceeding being instituted in which the property, rights, interests or activities of a State are affected, although the State is not named as a party, has been much reduced. Even if such a case arose, that State could avoid its property, rights, interests or activities from being affected by providing prima facie evidence of its title or proof that the possession was obtained in conformity with the local law.

Intellectual and industrial property

Article 14   2.029

Unless otherwise agreed between the States concerned, a State cannot invoke immunity from jurisdiction before a court of another State which is otherwise competent in a proceeding which relates to:

(a) the determination of any right of the State in a patent, industrial design, trade name or business name, trade mark, copyright or any other form of intellectual or industrial property, which enjoys a measure of legal protection, even if provisional, in the State of the forum; or

(b) an alleged infringement by the State, in the territory of the State of the forum, of a right of the nature mentioned in subparagraph (a) which belongs to a third person and is protected in the State of the forum.

2.030 *Commentary*

(1) Article 14 deals with an exception to the rule of State immunity which is of growing practical importance. The article is concerned with a specialized branch of internal law in the field of intellectual or industrial property. It covers wide areas of interest from the point of view of the State of the forum in which such rights to industrial or intellectual property are protected. In certain specified areas of industrial or intellectual property, measures of protection under the internal law of the State of the forum are further strengthened and reinforced by international obligations contracted by States in the form of international conventions.[156]

(2) The exception provided in article 14 appears to fall somewhere between the exception of "commercial transactions" provided in article 10 and that of "ownership, possession and use of property" in article 13. The protection afforded by the internal system of registration in force in various States is designed to promote inventiveness and creativity and, at the same time, to regulate and secure fair competition in international trade. An infringement of a patent of invention or industrial design or of any copyright of literary or artistic work may not always have been motivated by commercial or financial gain, but invariably impairs or entails adverse effects on the commercial interests of the manufacturers or producers who are otherwise protected for the production and distribution of the goods involved. "Intellectual and industrial property" in their collective nomenclature constitute a highly specialized form of property rights which are intangible or incorporeal, but which are capable of ownership, possession or use as recognized under various legal systems.

(3) The terms used in the title of article 14 are broad and generic expressions intended to cover existing and future forms, types, classes or categories of intellectual or industrial property. In the main, the three principal types of property that are envisaged in this article include: patents and industrial designs which belong to the category of industrial property; trade marks and trade names which pertain more to the business world or to international trade and questions relating to restrictive trade practices and unfair trade competition (concurrence déloyale); and copyrights or any other form of intellectual property. The generic terms employed in this article are therefore intended to include the whole range of forms of intellectual or industrial property which may be identified under the groups of intellectual or industrial property rights, including, for example, a plant breeder's right and a right in computer-generated works. Some rights are still in the process of evolution, such as in the field of computer science or other forms of modern technology and electronics which are legally protected. Such rights are not readily identifiable as industrial or intellectual. For instance, hardware in a computer system is perhaps industrial, whereas software is more clearly intellectual, and firmware may be in between. Literary and culinary arts, which are also protected under the name of copyright, could have a separate grouping as well. Copyrights in relation to music,

*songs and the performing arts, as well as other forms of entertainment, are also pro-
tected under this heading.*

*(4) The rights in industrial or intellectual property under the present draft article
are protected by States, nationally and also internationally. The protection provided by States within their territorial jurisdiction varies according to the type of
industrial or intellectual property in question and the special regime or organized
system for the application, registration or utilization of such rights for which protection is guaranteed by domestic law.*

*(5) The voluntary entrance by a State into the legal system of the State of the forum,
for example by submitting an application for registration of, or registering
a copyright, as well as the legal protection offered by the State of the forum, provide
a strong legal basis for the assumption and exercise of jurisdiction. Protection is generally consequential upon registration, or even sometimes upon the deposit or filing
of an application for registration. In some States, prior to actual acceptance of an
application for registration, some measure of protection is conceivable. Protection
therefore depends on the existence and scope of the national legislation, as well as on
a system of registration. Thus, in addition to the existence of appropriate domestic
legislation, there should also be an effective system of registration in force to afford a
legal basis for jurisdiction. The practice of States appears to warrant the inclusion
of this article.*[157]

*(6) Subparagraph (a) of article 14 deals specifically with the determination of any
rights of the State in a legally protected intellectual or industrial property. The
expression "determination" is here used to refer not only to the ascertainment or verification of the existence of the rights protected, but also to the evaluation or assessment of the substance, including content, scope and extent of such rights.*

*(7) Furthermore, the proceeding contemplated in article 14 is not confined to an
action instituted against the State or in connection with any right owned by the
State, but may also concern the rights of a third person, and only in that connection
would the question of the rights of the State in a similar intellectual or industrial
property arise. The determination of the rights belonging to the State may be incidental to, if not inevitable for, the establishment of the rights of a third person,
which is the primary object of the proceeding.*

*(8) Subparagraph (b) of article 14 deals with an alleged infringement by a State in
the territory of the State of the forum of any such right as mentioned above which
belongs to a third person and is protected in the State of the forum. The infringement under this article does not necessarily have to result from commercial activities conducted by a State as stipulated under article 10 of the present draft articles;
it could also take the form of activities for non-commercial purposes. The existence
of two conditions is essential for the application of this paragraph. First, the alleged
infringement by a State of a copyright must take place in the territory of the State of*

the forum. Secondly, such a copyright of a third person must be legally protected in the State of the forum. Hence there is a limit to the scope of the application of the article. Infringement of a copyright by a State in its own territory, and not in the State of the forum, does not establish a sufficient basis for jurisdiction in the State of the forum under this article.

(9) Article 14 expresses a residual rule and is without prejudice to the rights of States to formulate their own domestic laws and policies regarding the protection of any intellectual or industrial property in accordance with relevant international conventions to which they are parties and to apply them domestically according to their national interests. It is also without prejudice to the extraterritorial effect of nationalization by a State of intellectual or industrial property within its territory. The question of the precise extent of the extraterritorial effects of compulsory acquisition, expropriation or other measures of nationalization brought about by the State in regard to such rights within its own territory in accordance with its internal laws is not affected by the provision of the present articles.

(10) It should be observed that the application of the exception to State immunity in subparagraph (b) of this article is confined to infringements occurring in the State of the forum. Every State is free to pursue its own policy within its own territory. Infringement of such rights in the territory of another State, for instance the unauthorized reproduction or distribution of copyrighted publications, cannot escape the exercise of jurisdiction by the competent courts of that State in which measures of protection have been adopted. The State of the forum is also equally free to tolerate or permit such infringements or to deny remedies thereof in the absence of an internationally organized system of protection for the rights violated or breached in its own territory.

Participation in companies or other collective bodies

2.031 **Article 15**

1. A State cannot invoke immunity from jurisdiction before a court of another State which is otherwise competent in a proceeding which relates to its participation in a company or other collective body, whether incorporated or unincorporated, being a proceeding concerning the relationship between the State and the body or the other participants therein, provided that the body:

   (a) has participants other than States or international organizations; and
   (b) is incorporated or constituted under the law of the State of the forum or has its seat or principal place of business in that State.

2. A State can, however, invoke immunity from jurisdiction in such a proceeding if the States concerned have so agreed or if the parties to the dispute have so provided by an agreement in writing or if the instrument establishing or regulating the body in question contains provisions to that effect.

Commentary

(1) Article 15 contains an exception to the rule of jurisdictional immunity of a State in a proceeding before the courts of another State relating to the participation by the State in a company or other collective body which has been established or has its seat or principal place of business in the State of the forum. Such a body in which the State participates may be incorporated, that is to say, with a legal personality, or unincorporated with limited legal capacity.

(2) The expression "company or other collective body, whether incorporated or unincorporated", used in article 15, has been deliberately selected to cover a wide variety of legal entities as well as other bodies without legal personality. The formulation is designed to include different types or categories of bodies, collectivities and groupings known under different nomenclatures, such as corporations, associations, partnerships and other similar forms of collective bodies which may exist under various legal systems with varying degrees of legal capacity and status.

(3) The collective body in which the State may thus participate with private partners or members from the private sector may be motivated by profit-making, such as a trading company, business enterprise or any other similar commercial entity or corporate body. On the other hand, the State may participate in a collective body which is inspired by a non-profit-making objective, such as a learned society, a temple, a religious congregation, a charity or charitable foundation, or any other similar philanthropic organization.

(4) Article 15 is thus concerned with the legal relationship within the collective body or the corporate relations—more aptly described in French as rapports sociétaires—or legal relationship covering the rights and obligations of the State as participant in the collective body in relation to that body, on the one hand, and in relation to other participants in that body on the other.

Paragraph 1

(5) The rule of non-immunity as enunciated in paragraph 1 depends in its application upon the concurrence or coexistence of two important conditions. First, the body must have participants other than States or international organizations; in other words, it must be a body with participation from the private sector. Thus international organizations and other forms of collectivity which are composed exclusively of States and/or international organizations without participation from the private sector are excluded from the scope of article 15.

(6) Secondly, the body in question must be incorporated or constituted under the law of the State of the forum, or have its seat or principal place of business in that State. The seat is normally the place from which the entity is directed; and the principal place of business means the place where the major part of its business is conducted. The reference to the place of control which appeared in the English text of paragraph 1 (b) provisionally adopted on first reading[158] has been deleted, as it was

felt that the issue of determination of how a State is in control of a corporate entity was a very controversial one. The reference is replaced by another more easily identifiable criterion, namely the "seat" of the corporate entity, which is also used in article 6 of the European Convention on State Immunity.

(7) When a State participates in a collective body, such as by acquiring or holding shares in a company or becoming a member of a body corporate which is organized and operated in another State, it voluntarily enters into the legal system of that other State and into a relationship recognized as binding under that legal system. Consequently, the State is of its own accord bound and obliged to abide by the applicable rules and internal law of the State of incorporation, of registration or of the principal place of business. The State also has rights and obligations under the relevant provisions of the charter of incorporation, articles of association or other similar instruments establishing limited or registered partnerships. The relationship between shareholders inter se or between shareholders and the company or the body of any form in matters relating to the formation, management, direction, operation, dissolution or distribution of assets of the entity in question is governed by the law of the State of incorporation, of registration or of the seat or principal place of business. The courts of such States are best qualified to apply this specialized branch of their own law.

(8) It has become increasingly clear from the practice of States[159] that matters arising out of the relationship between the State as participant in a collective body and that body or other participants therein fall within the areas covered by this exception to the rule of State immunity. To sustain the rule of State immunity in matters of such a relationship would inevitably result in a jurisdictional vacuum. One of the three links based on substantial territorial connection with the State of the forum must be established to warrant the assumption and exercise of jurisdiction by its courts. These links are: the place of incorporation indicating the system of incorporation, charter or other type of constitution or the seat or the principal place of business (siège social ou statutaire).

Paragraph 2

(9) The exception regarding the State's participation in companies or other collective bodies as provided in paragraph 1 is subject to a different or contrary agreement between the States concerned, namely the State of the forum, which in this case is also the State of incorporation or of the seat or principal place of business, on the one hand, and the State against which a proceeding is instituted on the other. This particular reservation had originally been placed in paragraph 1, but was moved to paragraph 2 on second reading, with a view to setting out clearly the general rule of non-immunity in paragraph 1 and consolidating all the reservation clauses in paragraph 2. Paragraph 2 also recognizes the freedom of the parties to the dispute to agree contrary to the rule of non-immunity as enunciated in paragraph 1. Furthermore,

parties to the corporate relationship (rapports sociétaires) may themselves agree that the State as a member or participant continues to enjoy immunity or that they may choose or designate any competent courts or procedures to resolve the differences that may arise between them or with the body itself. In particular, the instrument establishing or regulating that body itself may contain provisions contrary to the rule of non-immunity for the State, in its capacity as a member, shareholder or participant, from the jurisdiction of the courts so chosen or designated. Subscription by the State to the provisions of the instrument constitutes an expression of consent to abide by the rules contained in such provisions, including the choice of law or jurisdiction. The phrase "the instrument establishing or regulating the body in question" should be understood as intending to apply only to the two fundamental instruments of a corporate body and not to any other type of regulation.

Ships owned or operated by a State

Article 16   2.033

1. Unless otherwise agreed between the States concerned, a State which owns or operates a ship cannot invoke immunity from jurisdiction before a court of another State which is otherwise competent in a proceeding which relates to the operation of that ship if, at the time the cause of action arose, the ship was used for other than government non-commercial purposes.

2. Paragraph 1 does not apply to warships and naval auxiliaries nor does it apply to other ships owned or operated by a State and used exclusively on government non-commercial service.

3. For the purposes of this article, "proceeding which relates to the operation of that ship" means, inter alia, any proceeding involving the determination of a claim in respect of:
   (a) collision or other accidents of navigation;
   (b) assistance, salvage and general average;
   (c) repairs, supplies or other contracts relating to the ship;
   (d) consequences of pollution of the marine environment.

4. Unless otherwise agreed between the States concerned, a State cannot invoke immunity from jurisdiction before a court of another State which is otherwise competent in a proceeding which relates to the carriage of cargo on board a ship owned or operated by that State if, at the time the cause of action arose, the ship was used for other than government non-commercial purposes.

5. Paragraph 4 does not apply to any cargo carried on board the ships referred to in paragraph 2 nor does it apply to any cargo owned by a State and used or intended for use exclusively for government non-commercial purposes.

6. States may plead all measures of defence, prescription and limitation of liability which are available to private ships and cargoes and their owners.

7. If in a proceeding there arises a question relating to the government and non-commercial character of a ship owned or operated by a State or cargo owned by a State, a certificate signed by a diplomatic representative or other competent authority of that State and communicated to the court shall serve as evidence of the character of that ship or cargo.

2.034 *Commentary*

(1) Draft article 16 is concerned with a very important area of maritime law as it relates to the conduct of external trade. It is entitled "Ships owned or operated by a State". The expression "ship" in this context should be interpreted as covering all types of seagoing vessels, whatever their nomenclature and even if they are engaged only partially in seagoing traffic. It is formulated as a residual rule, since States can always conclude agreements or arrangements[160] allowing, on a reciprocal basis or otherwise, for the application of jurisdictional immunities in respect of ships in commercial service owned or operated by States or their agencies.

(2) Paragraphs 1 and 3 are mainly concerned with ships engaged in commercial service, paragraph 2 mainly with warships and naval auxiliaries and paragraphs 4 and 5 with the status of cargo. Paragraph 4 enunciates the rule of non-immunity in proceedings relating to the carriage of cargo on board a ship owned or operated by a State and used for other than government non-commercial service. Paragraph 5 maintains State immunity in respect of any cargo carried on board the ships referred to in paragraph 2 as well as of any cargo belonging to a State and used or intended for use exclusively for government non-commercial purposes.

(3) The difficulties inherent in the formulation of rules for the exception provided for under article 16 are manifold. They are more than linguistic. The English language presupposes the employment of terms that may be in current usage in the terminology of common law but are unknown to and have no equivalents in other legal systems. Thus the expressions "suits in admiralty", "libel in rem", "maritime lien" and "proceedings in rem against the ship", may have little or no meaning in the context of civil law or other non-common-law systems. The terms used in article 16 are intended for a more general application.

(4) There are also conceptual difficulties surrounding the possibilities of proceedings in rem against ships, for example by service of writs on the main mast of the ship, or by arresting the ship in port, or attaching it and releasing it on bond. In addition, there is a special process of arrest ad fundandam jurisdictionem. In some countries, it is possible to proceed against another merchant ship in the same ownership as the ship in respect of which the claim arises, on the basis of what is known as sister-ship jurisdiction, for which provision is made in the International Convention relating

to the Arrest of Seagoing Ships (Brussels, 1952). The present article should not be interpreted as recognizing such systems as arrest ad fundandam jurisdictionem or sister-ship jurisdiction as a generally applicable rule. It follows that where a claim is brought against a merchant ship owned or operated by a State, another merchant ship owned or operated by the same State could not be subject to a proceeding in rem against it.

(5) *The problem of government-owned or State-operated vessels employed in ordinary commercial activities is not new. This is apparent from the vivid account given by one author[161] and confirmed by the fact that some maritime Powers felt it necessary to convene a conference to adopt the International Convention for the Unification of Certain Rules relating to the Immunity of State-owned Vessels (Brussels, 1926) and its Additional Protocol (1934) on the subject. The main purpose of the 1926 Brussels Convention was to reclassify seagoing vessels not according to ownership but according to the nature of their operation (exploitation) or their use, whether in "governmental and non-commercial" or in "commercial" service.*

(6) *The text of article 16 as provisionally adopted on first reading[162] maintained the dichotomy of service of vessels, classified according to a dual criterion of "commercial and non-governmental" or "governmental and non-commercial" use. The term "governmental and non-commercial" is used in the 1926 Brussels Convention, and the term "government non-commercial" in conventions of a universal character such as the Convention on the High Seas (Geneva, 1958) and the 1982 United Nations Convention on the Law of the Sea, in which ships are classified according to their use, that is to say, government and non-commercial service as opposed to commercial service.*

(7) *Some members of the Commission at the time of adopting the article on first reading expressed misgivings concerning that dual criterion, as it might suggest the possibility of a very different combination of the two adjectives, such as "governmental commercial" service or "commercial and governmental" service. Other members, on the other hand, denied the likelihood of that interpretation, and considered that "commercial" and "non-governmental" could be taken cumulatively. Others again added that States, particularly developing countries, and other public entities could engage in activities of a commercial and governmental nature without submitting to the jurisdiction of national courts. Furthermore, the purchase of armaments was often concluded on a government-to-government basis, including the transport of such armaments by any type of carrier, which would not normally be subject to the exercise of jurisdiction by any national court. The diversity of views led the Commission to maintain square brackets round the phrase "non governmental" in paragraphs 1 and 4 of the draft article on first reading.*

(8) *The Commission, after further discussion, adopted on second reading the present formulation "other than government non-commercial purposes" in paragraphs 1 and 4, thereby eliminating the problem of dual criterion.*

(9) The words "operate" (exploiter) and "operation" (exploitation) in paragraph 1 must be understood against the background of the 1926 Brussels Convention and existing State practice. Both terms refer to the exploitation or operation of ships in the transport of goods and passengers by sea. The carriage of goods by sea constitutes an important subject in international trade law. A study has been undertaken by UNCITRAL, and a standard convention or legislation on maritime law or the law of carriage of goods by sea[163] has been proposed to serve as a model for developing countries which are contemplating national legislation on the subject. The subject covers a wide field of maritime activities, from organization of the merchant marine, construction and building of a merchant fleet, training of master and crew, establishment of forwarding and handling agents, and taking of marine insurance. More generally known are questions relating to the liabilities of carriers for the carriage of dangerous goods or of animals, the discharge of oil offshore away from the port, collision at sea, salvage and repair, general average, seamen's wages, maritime liens and mortgages. The concept of the operation of merchant ships or ships engaged in commerce is given some clarification by way of illustration in paragraph 3. The expression "a State which operates a ship" covers also the "possession", "control", "management" and "charter" of ships by a State, whether the charter is for a time or voyage, bare-boat or otherwise.

(10) A State owning a ship, but allowing a separate entity to operate it, could still be proceeded against owing to the special nature of proceedings in rem or in admiralty or maritime lien which might be provided for in some common-law countries, and which were directed to all persons having an interest in the ship or cargo. In practice, a State owning a ship but not operating it should not otherwise be held liable for its operation at all, as the corporation or operating entity exists to answer for all liabilities arising out of the operation of that ship. The provision of paragraph 1 should be interpreted that in a case where a ship is owned by a State but operated by a State enterprise which has independent legal personality, it is the ship-operating State enterprise and not the State owning the ship that would become subject to jurisdiction before the court of the forum State. It may be also said that it should be possible to allow actions to proceed relating to the operation of the ship without involving the State or its claim for jurisdictional immunity. There seemed to be no need in such a case to institute a proceeding in personam against the State owning the ship as such, particularly if the cause of action related to its operation, such as collision at sea, general average, or carriage of goods by sea. But if the proceeding related to repairs or salvage services rendered to the ship, it might be difficult in some legal systems to imagine that the owner did not benefit from the repairs or services rendered and that the operator alone was liable. If such an eventuality occurred, a State owning but not operating the vessel could allow the operator, which is in many cases a State enterprise, to appear in its place to answer the complaint or claim made. The practice is slowly evolving in this direction through bilateral arrangements.

(11) Paragraph 2 enunciates the rule of State immunity in favour of warships and naval auxiliaries, even though such vessels may be employed occasionally for the carriage of cargoes for such purposes as to cope with an emergency or other natural calamities. Immunity is also maintained for other government ships such as police patrol boats, customs inspection boats, hospital ships, oceanographic survey ships, training vessels and dredgers, owned or operated by a State and used or intended for use in government non-commercial service. A similar provision is found in article 3 of the 1926 International Convention for the Unification of Certain Rules relating to the Immunity of State-owned Vessels. The word "exclusively" was introduced on second reading in line with article 96 of the 1982 United Nations Convention on the Law of the Sea. Some members, however, expressed reservations about the retention of the second half of the text beginning with the words "nor does it apply" on the ground that the reference to "other ships owned or operated by a State and used exclusively on government non-commercial service" was unnecessary and illogical in light of the provision of paragraph 1. One member also expressed reservations about the use of the word "service" in paragraph 2, stating that it should be replaced by the word "purposes" as in paragraph 1; since paragraph 2 forms a consequential provision of paragraph 1, it would be confusing to use different terms for those corresponding provisions.

(12) It is important to note that paragraphs 1, 2 and 4 apply to "use" of the ship. The application of the criterion of use of the ship, which is actual and current, is thus clarified. The criterion of intended use, which was included in the text adopted provisionally on first reading, has been eliminated, for paragraph 1 presupposes the existence of a cause of action relating to the operation of the ship and such a cause of action is not likely to arise if the ship is not actually in use. The Commission therefore retained on second reading only the criterion of actual use, all the more because the criterion of intended use was considered very vague and likely to give rise to difficulties in practice. For the same reason, the criterion of intended use has been eliminated also from paragraphs 2 and 4. Some members, however, expressed reservations about the deletion of that criterion. One member pointed out that State A could order from a shipbuilding yard in a State B a ship intended for commercial use. After its construction, the ship would sail from a port in State B to a port in State A, during which the ship, though intended for commercial purposes, would not be actually used for carriage of cargo. In his view, deletion of "intended for use" therefore created a lacuna in that respect.

(13) The expression "before a court of another State which is otherwise competent in any proceeding" is designed to refer back (renvoyer) to the existing jurisdiction of the courts competent under the internal law, including the maritime law, of the forum State, which may recognize a wide variety of causes of action and may allow a possible choice of proceedings, such as in personam against the owner and

*operator or in rem against the ship itself, or suits in admiralty or actions to enforce
a maritime lien or to foreclose a mortgage. A court may be competent on a variety of
grounds, including the presence of the ship at a port of the forum State, and it need
not be the same ship as the one that caused damage at sea or had other liabilities but
a similar merchant ship belonging to the same owner. Courts in common-law systems
generally recognize the possibility of arrest or seizure of a sister ship ad fundandam
jurisdictionem, but once bond is posted the ship would be released and the proceedings allowed to continue. As stated earlier, however, the present article should not be
interpreted to recognize this common law practice as a universally applicable practice. Thus the expression "any proceeding" refers to "any type of proceeding", regardless of its nature, whether in rem, in personam, in admiralty or otherwise. The rules
enunciated in paragraphs 1 and 2 are supported by State practice, both judicial,
legislative and governmental, as well as by multilateral and bilateral treaties.[164]*

*(14) Paragraph 3 sets out some examples of the proceedings which relate to the oper-
ation of ships "used for other than government non-commercial purposes" under
paragraph 1. Paragraph 3 (d) has been introduced on second reading in response to
a suggestion put forward by a Government in the Sixth Committee at the forty-fifth
session of the General Assembly. Although the provisions of paragraph 3 are merely
illustrative, the Commission deemed it appropriate to include this additional
example in view of the importance attached by the international community to
environmental questions and of the problem of ship-based marine pollution. In
consideration of the fact that this subparagraph was not contained in the text of former article 18 adopted on first reading, both the Commission and the Drafting
Committee discussed the question in some detail. Since subparagraph (d), like sub-
paragraphs (a) to (c), serves merely as an example of the claims to which the provisions of paragraph 1 would apply, it does not affect the substance or scope of the
exception to State immunity under paragraph 1. Nor does the subparagraph establish substantive law concerning the legitimacy or receivability of a claim. Whether
or not a claim is to be deemed actionable is a matter to be decided by the competent
court. The words "consequences of" are intended to convey the concern of some
members that unqualified reference to pollution of the marine environment from
ships might encourage frivolous claims or claims without tangible loss or damage to
the claimant. One member, indeed, considered that a more qualified wording such
as "injurious consequences" would have been necessary and he therefore reserved his
position on the subparagraph. Some other members, on the other hand, felt that this
concern was unjustified since no frivolous or vexatious claims would be entertained
by a court and that furthermore it was not the function of rules of State immunity
to prevent claims on the basis of their merits.*

*(15) Paragraph 4 provides for the rule of non-immunity applicable to a cargo
belonging to a State and used or intended for use for commercial non-governmental*

purposes. Paragraph 5 is designed to maintain immunity for any cargo, commercial or non-commercial, carried on board the ships referred to in paragraph 2, as well as for any cargo belonging to a State and used, or intended for use, in government non-commercial service. This provision maintains immunity for, inter alia, cargo involved in emergency operations such as food relief or transport of medical supplies. It should be noted that, in paragraph 5, unlike in paragraphs 1, 2 and 4, the words "intended for use" have been retained because the cargo is not normally used while it is on board the ship and it is therefore its planned use which will determine whether the State concerned is or is not entitled to invoke immunity.

(16) Paragraphs 6 and 7 apply to both ships and cargoes and are designed to strike an appropriate balance between the State's non-immunity under paragraphs 1 and 4 and a certain protection to be afforded the State. Paragraph 6 reiterates that States owning or operating ships engaged in commercial service may invoke all measures of defence, prescription and limitation of liability that are available to private ships and cargoes and their owners. The rule enunciated in paragraph 6 is not limited in its application to proceedings relating to ships and cargoes. States may plead all available means of defence in any proceedings in which State property is involved. Paragraph 7 indicates a practical method for proving the government and non-commercial character of the ship or cargo, as the case may be, by a certificate signed in normal circumstances by the accredited diplomatic representative of the State to which the ship or cargo belongs. In the absence of an accredited diplomatic representative, a certificate signed by another competent authority, such as the Minister of Transport or the consular officer concerned, shall serve as evidence before the court. The communication of the certificate to the court will of course be governed by the applicable rules of procedure of the forum State. The words "shall serve as evidence" do not, however, refer to irrebuttable evidence.

(17) Article 16 does not deal with the issue of immunity of States in relation to aircraft or space objects. Hence it cannot be applied to aircraft or space objects.[165]

Effect of an arbitration agreement

Article 17   2.035

If a State enters into an agreement in writing with a foreign natural or juridical person to submit to arbitration differences relating to a commercial transaction, that State cannot invoke immunity from jurisdiction before a court of another State which is otherwise competent in a proceeding which relates to:

(a) the validity or interpretation of the arbitration agreement;
(b) the arbitration procedure; or
(c) the setting aside of the award;

unless the arbitration agreement otherwise provides.

2.036 *Commentary*

(1) Draft article 17 deals with the rule of non-immunity relating to the supervisory jurisdiction of a court of another State which is otherwise competent to determine questions connected with the arbitration agreement, such as the validity of the obligation to arbitrate or to go to arbitration or to compel the settlement of a difference by arbitration, the interpretation and validity of the arbitration clause or agreement, the arbitration procedure and the setting aside of arbitral awards.[166]

(2) The draft article as provisionally adopted on first reading included two expressions "commercial contract" and "civil or commercial matter" in square brackets as alternative confines of the exception relating to an arbitration agreement. Those expressions have now been replaced by the term "commercial transaction" in line with the provision of article 2, paragraph 1 (c).

(3) The expression "the court which is otherwise competent" in this context refers to the competence of a court, if any, to exercise supervisory jurisdiction under the internal law of the State of the forum, including in particular its rules of private international law, in a proceeding relating to the arbitration agreement. A court may be competent to exercise such supervisory jurisdiction in regard to a commercial arbitration for one or more reasons. It may be competent in normal circumstances because the seat of the arbitration is located in the territory of the State of the forum, or because the parties to the arbitration agreement have chosen the internal law of the forum as the applicable law of the arbitration. It may also be competent because the property seized or attached is situated in the territory of the forum.

(4) It should be pointed out in this connection that it is the growing practice of States to create conditions more attractive and favourable for parties to choose to have their differences arbitrated in their territory. One of the attractions is an endeavour to simplify the procedures of judicial control. Thus the United Kingdom and Malaysia have amended their legislation regarding supervisory jurisdiction applicable to arbitration in general. The fact remains that, in spite of this trend, many countries, such as Thailand and Australia, continue to maintain more or less strict judicial control or supervision of arbitration in civil, commercial and other matters taking place within the territory of the forum State. Thus it is possible, in a given instance, either that the court which is otherwise competent may decline to exercise supervisory jurisdiction, or that it may have its jurisdiction restricted as a result of new legislation. Furthermore, the exercise of supervisory jurisdiction may have been excluded, at least in some jurisdictions, by the option of the parties to adopt an autonomous type of arbitration, such as the arbitration of ICSID or to regard arbitral awards as final, thereby precluding judicial intervention at any stage. The proviso "unless the arbitration agreement otherwise provides" is designed to cover the option freely expressed by the parties concerned which may serve to take the arbitration procedure out of domestic judicial control. Some courts may still

insist on the possibility of supervision or control over arbitration despite the expression of unwillingness on the part of the parties. In any event, agreements to arbitrate are binding on the parties thereto, although their enforcement may have to depend, at some point, on judicial participation.

(5) For the reasons indicated, submission to commercial arbitration under this article constitutes an expression of consent to all the consequences of acceptance of the obligation to settle differences by the type of arbitration clearly specified in the arbitration agreement. Normally, the relevant procedural matters—for example the venue and the applicable law—are laid down in the arbitration agreement. Thus, the court which was appointed pursuant to such an agreement would deal with the question of immunity rather than the court of any other State, and the arbitration procedure prescribed in the arbitration agreement would govern such matters as referred to in subparagraphs (a)–(c). It is merely incidental to the obligation to arbitrate undertaken by a State that a court of another State, which is otherwise competent, may be prepared to exercise its existing supervisory jurisdiction in connection with the arbitration agreement, including the arbitration procedure and other matters arising out of the arbitration agreement or arbitration clause.

(6) Consent to arbitration is as such no waiver of immunity from the jurisdiction of a court which would otherwise be competent to decide the dispute or difference on the merits. However, consenting to a commercial arbitration necessarily implies consent to all the natural and logical consequences of the commercial arbitration contemplated. In this limited area only, it may therefore be said that consent to arbitration by a State entails consent to the exercise of supervisory jurisdiction by a court of another State, competent to supervise the implementation of the arbitration agreement.

(7) It is important to note that the draft article refers to "arbitration agreement" between a State and a foreign natural or juridical person, and not between States themselves or between States and international organizations. Also excluded from this article are the types of arbitration provided by treaties between States[167] or those that bind States to settle differences between themselves and nationals of other States, such as the Convention on the Settlement of Investment Disputes between States and Nationals of Other States (Washington, 1965), which is self-contained and autonomous, and contains provisions for execution of the awards. This does not prevent States and international organizations from concluding arbitration agreements that may entail consequences of submission to the supervisory jurisdiction of the forum State.

(8) It should also be added that, of the several types of arbitration available to States as peaceful means of settling various categories of disputes, only the type between States and foreign natural and juridical persons is contemplated in this article. Arbitration of this type may take any form, such as arbitration under the rules of the

International Chamber of Commerce or UNCITRAL, or other institutionalized or ad hoc commercial arbitration. Submission of an investment dispute to ICSID arbitration, for instance, is not submission to the kind of commercial arbitration envisaged in this draft article and can in no circumstances be interpreted as a waiver of immunity from the jurisdiction of a court which is otherwise competent to exercise supervisory jurisdiction in connection with a commercial arbitration, such as an International Chamber of Commerce arbitration or an arbitration under the aegis of the American Arbitration Association.[168]

(9) The article in no way seeks to add to or detract from the existing jurisdiction of the courts of any State, nor to interfere with the role of the judiciary in any given legal system in the judicial control and supervision which it may be expected or disposed to exercise to ensure the morality and public order in the administration of justice needed to implement the arbitral settlement of differences. Only in this narrow sense is it correct to state that submission to commercial arbitration by a State entails an implied acceptance of the supervisory jurisdiction of a court of another State otherwise competent in matters relating to the arbitration agreement.

PART IV

State Immunity from Measures of Constraint in Connection
With Proceedings Before a Court

2.037 *Commentary*

(1) The first three parts—"Introduction", "General principles" and "Proceedings in which State immunity cannot be invoked"—having been completed, the draft should also contain a fourth part concerning State immunity from measures of constraint in connection with proceedings. Immunity in respect of property owned, possessed, or used by States in this context is all the more meaningful for States in view of the recent growing practice for private litigants, including multinational corporations, to seek relief through attachment of property owned, possessed or used by developing countries, such as embassy bank accounts or funds of the central bank or other monetary authority, in proceedings before the courts of industrially advanced countries.

(2) Part IV of the draft is concerned with State immunity from measures of constraint upon the use of property, such as attachment, arrest and execution, in connection with a proceeding before a court of another State. The expression "measures of constraint" has been chosen as a generic term, not a technical one in use in any particular internal law. Since measures of constraint vary considerably in the practice of States, it would be difficult, if not impossible, to find a term which covers each and every possible method or measure of constraint in all legal systems. Suffice it, therefore, to mention by way of example the more notable and readily understood

measures, such as attachment, arrest and execution. The problem of finding readily translatable terms in the official languages is indubitably multiplied by the diversity of State practice in the realm of procedures and measures of constraint.

(3) Part IV is of special significance in that it relates to a second phase of the proceedings in cases of measures of execution, as well as covering interlocutory measures or pre-trial or prejudgement measures of attachment, or seizure of property ad fundandam jurisdictionem. Part IV provides in general, but subject to certain limitations, for the immunity of a State from all such measures of constraint in respect of the use of its property in connection with proceedings before a court of another State.

State immunity from measures of constraint

Article 18   2.038

1. No measures of constraint, such as attachment, arrest and execution, against property of a State may be taken in connection with a proceeding before a court of another State unless and except to the extent that:

    (a) the State has expressly consented to the taking of such measures as indicated:
       (i) by international agreement;
      (ii) by an arbitration agreement or in a written contract; or
     (iii) by a declaration before the court or by a written communication after a dispute between the parties has arisen;
    (b) the State has allocated or earmarked property for the satisfaction of the claim which is the object of that proceeding; or
    (c) the property is specifically in use or intended for use by the State for other than government non-commercial purposes and is in the territory of the State of the forum and has a connection with the claim which is the object of the proceeding or with the agency or instrumentality against which the proceeding was directed.

2. Consent to the exercise of jurisdiction under article 7 shall not imply consent to the taking of measures of constraint under paragraph 1, for which separate consent shall be necessary.

Commentary   2.039

(1) Article 18 concerns immunity from measures of constraint only to the extent that they are linked to a judicial proceeding. Theoretically, immunity from measures of constraint is separate from jurisdictional immunity of the State in the sense that the latter refers exclusively to immunity from the adjudication of litigation. Article 18 clearly defines the rule of State immunity in its second phase, concerning property, particularly measures of execution as a separate procedure from the original proceeding.

(2) The practice of States has evidenced several theories in support of immunity from execution as separate from and not interconnected with immunity from jurisdiction.[169] Whatever the theories, for the purposes of this article, the question of immunity from execution does not arise until after the question of jurisdictional immunity has been decided in the negative and until there is a judgement in favour of the plaintiff. Immunity from execution may be viewed, therefore, as the last bastion of State immunity. If it is admitted that no sovereign State can exercise its sovereign power over another equally sovereign State (par in parem imperium non habet), it follows a fortiori that no measures of constraint by way of execution or coercion can be exercised by the authorities of one State against another State and its property. Such a possibility does not exist even in international litigation, whether by judicial settlement or arbitration.[170]

(3) Article 18 is a merger and a reformulation of former articles 21 and 22 as provisionally adopted on first reading. Former article 21 dealt with State immunity from measures of constraint and former article 22 with consent to such measures. Since the ideas expressed in those two articles were closely related, the Commission agreed to the proposal of the Special Rapporteur for the merger, which was supported by many members as well as Governments. In this manner, the principle of non-execution against the property of a State at any stage or phase of proceedings is clearly set out, followed by the exceptions to that principle.

Paragraph 1

(4) The measures of constraint mentioned in this article are not confined to execution but cover also attachment and arrest, as well as other forms of saisie, saisie-arrêt and saisie-exécution, including enforcement of arbitral award, sequestration and interim, interlocutory and all other prejudgement conservatory measures, intended sometimes merely to freeze assets in the hands of the defendant. The measures of constraint indicated in paragraph 1 are illustrative and non-exhaustive.

(5) The property protected by immunity under this article is State property, including, in particular, property defined in article 19. The original text of the chapeau of former article 21 and of paragraph 1 of former article 22 as provisionally adopted on first reading contained the phrase, [or property in which it has a legally protected interest,], over which there were differences of view among members of the Commission. In their written submissions, a number of Governments criticized the phrase as being vague and permitting a broadening of the scope of immunity from execution. The bracketed phrase was therefore deleted and replaced by the words "property of a State".

(6) The word "State" in the expression "proceeding before a court of another State" refers to the State where the property is located, regardless of where the substantive proceeding takes place. Thus, before any measures of constraint are implemented, a proceeding to that effect should be instituted before a court of the State where the

property is located. Of course, in some special circumstances, such as under a treaty obligation, no further court proceeding may be required for execution once there is a final judgement by a court of another State party to the treaty.

(7) The principle of immunity here is subject to three conditions, the satisfaction of any of which would result in non-immunity: (a) if consent to the taking of measures of constraint is given by international agreement, in an arbitration agreement or in a written contract, or by a declaration before the court or by a written communication after a dispute between the parties has arisen; or (b) if the property has been allocated or earmarked by the State for the satisfaction of the claim; or (c) if the property, is specifically in use or intended for use by the State for other than government non-commercial purposes.[171] Subparagraph (c) further provides that, for there to be no immunity, the property must have a connection with the object of the claim, or with the agency or instrumentality against which the proceeding was directed.

(8) The phrase "the taking of such measures, as indicated:" in paragraph 1 (a) refers to both the measures of constraint and the property. Thus express consent can be given generally with regard to measures of constraint or property, or be given for particular measures or particular property, or, indeed, be given for both measures and property.

(9) Once consent has been given under paragraph 1 (a), any withdrawal of that consent may only be made under the terms of the international agreement (subparagraph (i)) or of the arbitration agreement or the contract (subparagraph (ii)). However, once a declaration of consent or a written communication to that effect (subparagraph (iii)) has been made before a court, it cannot be withdrawn. In general, once a proceeding before a court has begun, consent cannot be withdrawn.

(10) Under paragraph 1 (b), the property can be subject to measures of constraint if it has been allocated or earmarked for the satisfaction of the claim or debt which is the object of the proceeding. This should have the effect of preventing extraneous or unprotected claimants from frustrating the intention of the State to satisfy specific claims or to make payment for an admitted liability. Understandably, the question whether particular property has or has not been allocated for the satisfaction of a claim may in some situations be ambiguous and should be resolved by the court.

(11) The use of the word "is" in paragraph 1 (c) indicates that the property should be specifically in use or intended for use by the State for other than government non-commercial purposes at the time the proceeding for attachment or execution is instituted. To specify an earlier time would unduly fetter States' freedom to dispose of their property. It is the Commission's understanding that States would not encourage and permit abuses of this provision, for example by changing the status of their property in order to avoid attachment or execution. The words "for commercial [non-governmental] purposes" included in the text adopted on first reading have been

replaced by the phrase "for other than government non-commercial purposes" in line with the usage of that phrase in article 16.

Paragraph 2

(12) Paragraph 2 makes more explicit the requirement of separate consent for the taking of measures of constraint under part IV. Consent under article 7 of part II does not cover any measures of constraint but is confined exclusively to immunity from the jurisdiction of a court of a State in a proceeding against another State.[172]

Specific categories of property

2.040   **Article 19**

1. The following categories, in particular, of property of a State shall not be considered as property specifically in use or intended for use by the State for other than government non-commercial purposes under paragraph 1 (c) of article 18:

   (a) property, including any bank account, which is used or intended for use for the purposes of the diplomatic mission of the State or its consular posts, special missions, missions to international organizations, or delegations to organs of international organizations or to international conferences;

   (b) property of a military character or used or intended for use for military purposes;

   (c) property of the central bank or other monetary authority of the State;

   (d) property forming part of the cultural heritage of the State or part of its archives and not placed or intended to be placed on sale;

   (e) property forming part of an exhibition of objects of scientific, cultural or historical interest and not placed or intended to be placed on sale.

2. Paragraph 1 is without prejudice to paragraph 1 (a) and (b) of article 18.

2.041   *Commentary*

Paragraph 1

(1) Article 19 is designed to provide some protection for certain specific categories of property by excluding them from any presumption or implication of consent to measures of constraint. Paragraph 1 seeks to prevent any interpretation to the effect that property classified as belonging to any one of the categories specified is in fact property specifically in use or intended for use by the State for other than government non-commercial purposes under paragraph 1 (c) of article 18. The words "in particular" suggest that the enumeration in subparagraphs (a) to (e) is merely illustrative.

(2) This protection is deemed necessary and timely in view of the trend in certain jurisdictions to attach or freeze assets of foreign States, especially bank accounts,[173]

assets of the central bank[174] or other *instrumenta legati*[175] and specific categories of property which equally deserve protection. Each of these specific categories of property, by its very nature, must be taken to be in use or intended for use for governmental purposes removed from any commercial considerations.

(3) Property listed in paragraph 1 (a) is intended to be limited to that which is in use or intended for use for the "purposes" of the State's diplomatic functions.[176] This obviously excludes property, for example, bank accounts maintained by embassies for commercial purposes.[177] Difficulties sometimes arise concerning a "mixed account" which is maintained in the name of a diplomatic mission, but occasionally used for payment, for instance, of supply of goods or services to defray the running costs of the mission. The recent case law seems to suggest the trend that the balance of such a bank account to the credit of the foreign State should not be subject to an attachment order issued by the court of the forum State because of the noncommercial character of the account in general.[178] Property listed in paragraph 1 (a) also excludes property which may have been, but is no longer, in use or intended for use for diplomatic or cognate purposes. The expressions "missions" and "delegations" also include permanent observer missions and observer delegations within the meaning of the 1975 Vienna Convention on the Representation of States in their Relations with International Organizations of a Universal Character.

(4) The word "military", in the context of paragraph 1 (b), includes the navy, air force and army.[179]

(5) With regard to paragraph 1 (c), the Special Rapporteur suggested the addition of the words "and used for monetary purpose" at the end of the paragraph,[180] but they were not included for lack of general support.[181]

(6) The purpose of paragraph 1 (d) is to protect only property characterized as forming part of the cultural heritage or archives of the State which is owned by the State.[182] Such property benefits from protection under the present articles when it is not placed or intended to be placed on sale.

(7) Paragraph 1 (e) extends such protection to property forming part of an exhibition of objects of cultural or scientific or historical interest belonging to the State.[183] State-owned exhibits for industrial or commercial purposes are not covered by this subparagraph.

Paragraph 2

(8) Notwithstanding the provision of paragraph 1, the State may waive immunity in respect of any property belonging to one of the specific categories listed, or any part of such a category, by either allocating or earmarking the property within the meaning of article 18 (b), paragraph 1, or by specifically consenting to the taking of measures of constraint in respect of that category of its property, or that part thereof, under article 18 (a), paragraph 1. A general waiver or a waiver in respect of all

property in the territory of the State of the forum, without mention of any of the specific categories, would not be sufficient to allow measures of constraint against property in the categories listed in paragraph 1.

PART V

Miscellaneous Provisions

Service of process

2.042 **Article 20**

1. Service of process by writ or other document instituting a proceeding against a State shall be effected:

   (a) in accordance with any applicable international convention binding on the State of the forum and the State concerned; or

   (b) in the absence of such a convention:

   (i) by transmission through diplomatic channels to the Ministry of Foreign Affairs of the State concerned; or

   (ii) by any other means accepted by the State concerned, if not precluded by the law of the State of the forum.

2. Service of process referred to in paragraph 1 (b) (i) is deemed to have been effected by receipt of the documents by the Ministry of Foreign Affairs.

3. These documents shall be accompanied, if necessary, by a translation into the official language, or one of the official languages, of the State concerned.

4. Any State that enters an appearance on the merits in a proceeding instituted against it may not thereafter assert that service of process did not comply with the provisions of paragraphs 1 and 3.

2.043 *Commentary*

(1) Article 20 relates to a large extent to the domestic rules of civil procedure of States. It takes into account the difficulties involved if States are called upon to modify their domestic rules of civil procedure. At the same time, it does not provide too liberal or generous a regime of service of process, which could result in an excessive number of judgements in default of appearance by the defendant State. The article therefore proposes a middle ground so as to protect the interests of the defendant State and those of the individual plaintiff.

Paragraph 1

(2) Paragraph 1 is designed to indicate the normal ways in which service of process can be effected when a proceeding is instituted against a State. Three categories of means by which service of process is effected are provided: first, if an applicable

international convention binding upon the State of the forum and the State concerned exists, service of process shall be effected in accordance with the procedures provided for in the convention. Then, in the absence of such a convention, service of process shall be effected either (a) by transmission through diplomatic channels or (b) by any other means accepted by the State concerned. Thus, among the three categories of the means of service of process provided under paragraph 1, an international convention binding both States is given priority over the other two categories. The variety of means available ensures the widest possible flexibility, while protecting the interests of the parties concerned.[184]

Paragraphs 2 and 3

(3) Since the time of service of process is decisive for practical purposes, it is further provided in paragraph 2 that, in the case of transmission through diplomatic channels or by registered mail, service of process is deemed to have been effected on the day of receipt of the documents by the Ministry of Foreign Affairs. Paragraph 3 further requires that the documents be accompanied, if necessary, by a translation into the official language, or one of the official languages, of the State concerned. The Special Rapporteur made a proposal in this connection to add at the end of paragraph 3 the phrase "or at least by a translation into one of the official languages of the United Nations" so that when translation into a language not widely used gave rise to difficulties on the part of the authority serving the process, translation into one of the official languages of the United Nations might be acceptable. The proposal was, however, not adopted.

Paragraph 4

(4) Paragraph 4 provides that a State which has entered an appearance on the merits, that is to say without contesting any question of jurisdiction or procedure, cannot subsequently be heard to raise any objection based on non-compliance with the service of process provisions of paragraphs 1 and 3. The reason for the rule is self-evident. By entering an appearance on the merits, the defendant State effectively concedes that it has had timely notice of the proceeding instituted against it. The defendant State is, of course, entitled at the outset to enter a conditional appearance or to raise a plea as to jurisdiction.

Default judgment

Article 21   2.044

1. A default judgement shall not be rendered against a State unless the court has found that:
   (a) the requirements laid down in paragraphs 1 and 3 of article 20 have been complied with;
   (b) a period of not less than four months has expired from the date on which the service of the writ or other document instituting a proceeding has

been effected or deemed to have been effected in accordance with paragraphs 1 and 2 of article 20; and

(c) the present articles do not preclude it from exercising jurisdiction.

2. A copy of any default judgement rendered against a State, accompanied if necessary by a translation into the official language or one of the official languages of the State concerned, shall be transmitted to it through one of the means specified in paragraph 1 of article 20 and in accordance with the provisions of that paragraph.

3. The time-limit for applying to have a default judgement set aside shall not be less than four months and shall begin to run from the date on which the copy of the judgement is received or is deemed to have been received by the State concerned.

2.045 *Commentary*

(1) There appears to be an established practice requiring proof of compliance with the procedure for service of process and of the expiry of the time-limit before any judgement may be rendered against a foreign State in default of appearance. There is also a further requirement that such a judgement, when rendered in default of appearance, should be communicated to the State concerned through the same procedure or channel as the service of process.[185]

Paragraph 1

(2) Default judgement cannot be entered by the mere absence of a State before a court of another State. The court must establish that certain conditions have been met before rendering its judgement. These conditions are set out in paragraph 1. A proper service of process is a precondition for making application for a default judgement to be given against a State. Under paragraph 1 (a), even if the defendant State does not appear before a court, the judge still has to be satisfied that the service of process was properly effected in accordance with paragraphs 1 and 3 of article 20. Paragraph 1 (b) gives added protection to States by requiring the expiry of not less than four months from the date of service of process. The expiry period which was three months in the text adopted on first reading has been changed to four months on second reading. The judge, of course, always has the discretion to extend the minimum period of four months if the domestic law so permits. Paragraph 1 (c) further requires a court to determine on its own initiative that the State concerned was not immune from the jurisdiction of the court. This provision, which has been introduced on second reading in response to a suggestion made in the Sixth Committee and supported by several delegations, provides an important safeguard in line with the provision of paragraph 1 of article 6. The new paragraph 1 (c), however, has no bearing on the question of the competence of the court, which is a matter for each legal system to determine.

Paragraph 2

(3) Paragraph 2 is designed to ensure that a copy of any default judgement is transmitted to a State in conformity with the procedure and means established under paragraph 1 of article 20.

Paragraph 3

(4) Paragraph 3 is designed to ensure effective communication with the State concerned and to allow adequate opportunities to the defendant State to apply to have a default judgement set aside, whether by way of appeal or otherwise. If any time-limit is to be set for applying to have a default judgement set aside, another period of not less than four months must have elapsed before any measure can be taken in pursuance of the judgement. The period was three months in the text adopted on first reading but has been changed to four months on second reading.

Privileges and immunities during court proceedings

Article 22 2.046a

1. Any failure or refusal by a State to comply with an order of a court of another State enjoining it to perform or refrain from performing a specific act or to produce any document or disclose any other information for the purposes of a proceeding shall entail no consequences other than those which may result from such conduct in relation to the merits of the case. In particular, no fine or penalty shall be imposed on the State by reason of such failure or refusal.

2. A State shall not be required to provide any security, bond or deposit, however described, to guarantee the payment of judicial costs or expenses in any proceeding to which it is a party before a court of another State.

Commentary 2.046b

Paragraph 1

(1) Article 22, which is a merger of former articles 26 and 27 provisionally adopted on first reading, provides for immunity of a State from measures of coercion and procedural immunities in a court of another State.

(2) States, for reasons of security or their own domestic law, may sometimes be prevented from submitting certain documents or disclosing certain information to a court of another State. States should therefore not be subject to penalties for protecting their national security or for complying with their domestic law. At the same time, the legitimate interests of the private litigant should not be overlooked.[186]

(3) Paragraph 1 speaks of "no consequences" being entailed by the conduct in question, although it specifies that the consequences which might ordinarily result from such conduct in relation to the merits of the case would still obtain. This

reserves the applicability of any relevant rules of the internal law of the State of the forum, without requiring another State to give evidence or produce a document.

(4) Courts are bound by their own domestic rules of procedure. In the domestic rules of procedure of many States, the refusal, for any reason, by a litigant to submit evidence would allow or even require the judge to draw certain inferences which might affect the merits of the case. Such inferences by a judge under the domestic rules of procedure of the State of the forum, when permitted, are not considered a penalty. The final sentence specifies that no fine or pecuniary penalty shall be imposed.

Paragraph 2

(5) The procedural immunities provided for in paragraph 2 apply to both plaintiff States and defendant States. Some reservations were made regarding the application of those procedural immunities in the event of the State being plaintiff in a proceeding before a court of another State since, in some systems, security for costs is required only of plaintiffs and not defendants.

2.047   *[NOTE: These notes retain the numbering used in the ILC Yearbook. Notes 1–23, not here reproduced, relate to other matters.]*

   [24]   *The practice of some States appears to support the view that semi-sovereign States and even colonial dependencies are treated, although they may fall within the same constitutional grouping as the State itself, as foreign sovereign States. British courts, for instance, consistently declined jurisdiction in actions against States members of the British Commonwealth and semi-sovereign States dependent on the United Kingdom. Thus, the Maharajah of Baroda was regarded as "a sovereign prince over whom British courts have no jurisdiction": Gaekwar of Baroda State Railways v. Hafiz Habid-ul-Haq (1938) (Annual Digest . . ., 1938–1940 (London), vol. 9 (1942), case No. 78, p. 233). United States courts have adopted the same view with regard to their own dependencies: Kawananakoa v. Polybank (1907) (United States Reports, vol. 205 (1921), pp. 349 and 353), wherein the territory of Hawaii was granted sovereign immunity; and also, by virtue of the federal Constitution, with respect to member States of the Union: Principality of Monaco v. Mississippi (1934) (Annual Digest . . ., 1933–1934 (London), vol. 7 (1940), case No. 61, p. 166; cf. G. H. Hackworth, Digest of International Law (Washington, D.C., United States Government Printing Office, 1941), vol. II, p. 402). More recently, in Morgan Guaranty Trust Co. v. Republic of Palau (639 F. Supp. 706, United States District Court for the Southern District of New York, 10 July 1986, AJIL (Washington, D.C.), vol. 81 (1987), p. 220) the court held that Palau was a "foreign State" for purposes of the United States Foreign Sovereign Immunities Act (see footnote 40 below) based on the de facto degree of sovereignty exercised by Palau, even though the Compact of Free Association had not been ratified and the termination of the United Nations Trusteeship Agreement designating Palau as a "strategic trust" had not been approved by the Security Council. French courts have similarly upheld immunity in cases concerning semi-sovereign States and member States within the French Union: Bey of Tunis et consorts v. Ahmed-ben-Aïad (1893) (Recueil périodique et critique de jurisprudence, 1894 (Dalloz) (Paris), part 2, p. 421); see also cases concerning the Gouvernement chérifien, for instance, Laurans v. Gouvernement impérial chérifien et Société marseillaise de crédit (1934) (Revue critique de droit international (Darras) (Paris), vol. XXX, No. 4 (October–December 1935), p. 795, and a note by S. Basdevant-Bastid, pp. 796 et seq.). See also Duff Development Company Ltd. v. Government of Kelantan and another (1924) (United Kingdom, The Law Reports, House of Lords, Judicial Committee of the Privy Council, 1924, p. 797). See, however, Marine Steel Ltd. v. Government of the Marshall Islands (1981) 2 NZLR, High Court of New Zealand, 29 July 1981, AJIL (Washington, D.C.), vol. 77 (1983), p. 158), where the High Court of New Zealand held that United Nations Trust Territories, such as the Marshall Islands, have not yet achieved the status of a sovereign State and, therefore, are not entitled to sovereign immunity.*

   [25]   *See, for instance, Dralle v. Republic of Czechoslovakia (1950) (ILR, 1950 (London), vol. 17 (1956), case No. 41, p. 155); Etat espagnol v. Canal (1951) (Journal du droit international (Clunet) (Paris),*

vol 79, No. 1 (January–March 1952), p. 220); Patterson-MacDonald Shipbuilding Co., McLean v. Commonwealth of Australia (1923) (United States of America, The Federal Reporter, vol. 293 (1924), p. 192); De Froe v. The Russian State, now styled "The Union of Soviet Socialist Republics" (1932) (Annual Digest . . ., 1931–1932 (London), vol. 6 (1938), case No. 87, p. 170); Irish Free State v. Guaranty Safe Deposit Company (1927) (Annual Digest . . ., 1925–1926 (London), vol. 3 (1929), case No. 77, p. 100); Kingdom of Norway v. Federal Sugar Refining Co. (1923) (United States of America, The Federal Reporter, vol. 286 (1923), p. 188); Ipitrade International S.A. v. Federal Republic of Nigeria (1978) (United States of America, Federal Supplement, vol. 465 (1979), p. 824); 40 D 6262 Realty Corporation and 40 E 6262 Realty Corporation v. United Arab Emirates Government (1978) (ibid., vol. 447 (1978), p. 710); Kahan v. Pakistan Federation (1951) (United Kingdom, The Law Reports, King's Bench Division, 1951, vol. II, p. 1003); Venne v. Democratic Republic of the Congo (1968) (Canada, The Dominion Law Reports, Third series, vol. 5, p. 128).

[26] See, for example, Lakhowsky v. Swiss Federal Government and Colonel de Reynier (1921) (Annual Digest . . ., 1919–1922 (London), vol. 1, case No. 83, p. 122); U Kyaw Din v. His Britannic Majesty's Government of the United Kingdom and the Union of Burma (1948) (Annual Digest . . ., 1948 (London), vol. 15 (1953), case No. 42, p. 137); Etienne v. Government of the Netherlands (1947) (Annual Digest . . ., 1947 (London), vol. 14, case No. 30, p. 83).

[27] Sovereign immunity has sometimes been accorded to colonial dependencies of foreign States on the ground that the actions in effect impleaded the foreign Governments, States being identifiable with their Governments. See, for instance, The "Martin Behrman", Isbrandtsen Co. v. Netherlands East Indies Government (1947) Annual Digest . . ., 1947 (London), vol. 14 (1951), case No. 26, p. 75); Van Heyningen v. Netherlands Indies Government (1948) (Annual Digest . . ., 1948 (London), vol. 15 (1953), case No. 43, p. 138.

See, for instance, Bainbridge v. The Postmaster General (1905) (United Kingdom, The Law Reports, King's Bench Division, 1906, vol. I, p. 178); Henon v. Egyptian Government and British Admiralty (1947) (Annual Digest . . ., 1947 (London), vol. 14 (1951), case No. 28, p. 78); Triandafilou v. Ministère public (1942) (AJIL (Washington, D.C.), vol. 39, No. 2 (April 1945), p. 345); Piascik v. British Ministry of War Transport (1943) (Annual Digest . . ., 1943–1945 (London), vol. 12 (1949), case No. 22, p. 87); and Turkish Purchases Commission case (1920) (Annual Digest . . ., 1919–1922 (London), vol. 1 (1932), case No. 77, p. 114)

[29] See, for example, the opinion of Chief Justice Marshall in The Schooner "Exchange" v. McFaddon and others (1812) (W. Cranch, Reports of Cases . . ., (New York, 1911), vol. VII, 3rd ed., pp. 135–137). See also various status of forces agreements and foreign visiting forces acts.

[30] Embassies are subsidiary organs of the State, being part of the Ministry of Foreign Affairs or the Foreign Office of the sending State. Their status is governed by the Vienna Convention on Diplomatic Relations.

[31] Special missions are also covered by State immunity as contained in the Convention on Special Missions. See also the Vienna Convention on the Representation of States in their Relations with International Organizations of a Universal Character.

[32] See the Vienna Convention on Consular Relations.

[33] See, for example, Mackenzie-Kennedy v. Air Council (1927) (United Kingdom, The Law Reports, King's Bench Division, 1927, vol. II, p. 517); Graham and others v. His Majesty's Commissioners of Public Works and Buildings (1901) (United Kingdom, The Law Reports, King's Bench Division, 1901, vol. II, p. 781); Société Viajes v. Office national du tourisme espagnol (1936) (Annual Digest . . ., 1935–1937 (London), vol. 8 (1941), case No. 87, p. 227); Telkes v. Hungarian National Museum (1942) (Annual Digest . . ., 1941–1942 (London), vol. 10 (1945), case No. 169, p. 576).

[34] See, for example, Sullivan v. State of Sao Paulo (1941) (Annual Digest . . ., 1941–1942 (London), vol. 10 (1945), case No. 50, p. 178), where the United States State Department had recognized the claim of immunity. In that case, Judge Clark suggested that immunity could be grounded on the analogy with member States within the United States; Judge Hand expressed his doubts whether every political subdivision of a foreign State was immune which exercised substantial governmental power. See also Yale Law Journal (New Haven, Conn.), vol. 50, No. 6 (April 1941), pp. 1088 et seq.; Cornell Law Quarterly Review (Ithaca, N.Y.), vol. 26 (1940–1941), pp. 720 et seq.; Harvard Law Review (Cambridge, Mass.), vol. LV, No. 1 (November 1941), p. 149; Michigan Law Review (Ann Arbor, Mich.), vol. 40, No. 6 (April 1942), pp. 911 et seq.; Southern California Law Review (Los Angeles, Calif.), vol. 15 (1941–1942), p. 258. This was the most commented case of that time. See also Hans v. Louisiana (1890) (United States Reports, vol. 134 (1910), p. 1); South Dakota v. North Carolina (1904) (ibid., vol. 192 (1911), p. 286); United States v. North Carolina (1890) (ibid., vol. 136 (1910), p. 211); Rhode Island v. Massachusetts (1846)

(B. C. Howard, Reports of Cases . . . (New York, 1909), vol. IV, 2nd ed., p. 591); and cases cited above in footnotes 24 and 26.

See, however, the practice of France, for example, in Etat de Ceará v. Dorr et autres (1932) (Dalloz, Recueil périodique et critique de jurisprudence, 1933 (Paris), part 1, p. 196 et seq.). The Court said:

> *"Whereas this rule [of incompetence] is to be applied only when invoked by an entity which shows itself to have a personality of its own in its relations with other countries, considered from the point of view of public international law; whereas such is not the case of the State of Ceará, which, according to the provisions of the Brazilian Constitution legitimately relied upon by the lower courts, and whatever its internal status in the sovereign confederation of the United States of Brazil of which it is a part, being deprived of diplomatic representation abroad, does not enjoy from the point of view of inter-national political relations a personality of its own . . . ".*

See also Dumont v. State of Amazonas (1948) (Annual Digest . . ., 1948 (London), vol. 15, case No. 44, p. 140). For Italy, see Somigli v. Etat de Sao Paulo du Brésil (1910) (Revue de droit international privé et de droit pénal inter-national (Darras) (Paris), vol. VI (1910), p. 527), where Sao Paulo was held amenable to Italian jurisdiction in respect of a contract to promote immigration to Brazil. For Belgium, see Feldman v. Etat de Bahia (1907) (Pasicrisie belge, 1908 (Brussels), vol. II, p. 55 or Supplement to AJIL (Washington, D.C.), vol. 26, No. 3 (July 1932), p. 484), where Bahia was denied immunity although under the Brazilian Constitution it was regarded as a sovereign State. See also the case, in the United States, Molina v. Comisión Reguladora del Mercado de Henequén (1918) (Hackworth, op. cit., vol. II, pp. 402–403), where Yucatán, a member State of the United States of Mexico, was held amenable to the jurisdiction of the United States courts; and in Australia, Commonwealth of Australia v. New South Wales (1923) (Annual Digest . . ., 1923–1924 (London), vol. 2 (1933), case No. 67, p. 161). The Court said:

> *"The appellation 'sovereign State' as applied to the construction of the Commonwealth Constitution is entirely out of place, and worse than unmeaning."*

[35] *The Convention came into force on 11 June 1976 between Austria, Belgium and Cyprus and has since been ratified by the United Kingdom of Great Britain and Northern Ireland, Switzerland, the Netherlands, Luxembourg and Germany. Article 28, paragraph 1, confirms non-enjoyment of immunity by the constituent states of a federal State, but paragraph 2 permits the federal State to make a declaration that its constituent states may invoke the provisions of the Convention. The Protocol came into effect on 22 May 1985 between Austria, Belgium, Cyprus, the Netherlands and Switzerland, and has since been ratified by Luxembourg. The European Tribunal in matters of State immunity was established on 28 May 1985 pursuant to the Protocol.*

[36] *The view was expressed by some members that the expression prérogatives de la puissance publique de l'Etat in the French text, and the expression "sovereign authority of the State" in the English text, were not equivalent in meaning and could lead to different interpretations. The French expression appears to be intended to refer to public institutions and to distinguish them from private institutions. Thus not all types of prérogatives de la puissance publique are related to the sovereignty of a State, and the view of those members was that the expression "sovereign authority of the State" in the English text was too restrictive. In this connection, it was noted that the term "government" or "government authority" was used in part 1 of the draft articles on State responsibility on which the Commission had taken the view that the term was the correct translation of prérogative de la puissance publique in the French text of the draft articles. It was suggested, therefore, that the term should be interpreted as "government authority", or "State authority", which is the term in fact used in the Russian text of the present draft article.*

[37] *This possibility was pointed out by Pillet, commenting on a French case denying immunity. Ville de Genève v. Consorts de Civry (1894) (Sirey, Recueil général des lois et des arrêts, 1896 (Paris), part 1, pp. 225 et seq.). See also Rousse et Maber v. Banque d'Espagne et autres (1937) (Sirey, Recueil général des lois et des arrêts, 1938 (Paris), part 2, pp. 17 et seq.), where the Court of Appeal of Poitiers envisaged the same possibility; Rousseau, in his note, thought that provincial autonomies such as the Basque Government might at the same time be "an executive organ of a decentralized administrative unit". Compare the English Court of Appeal in Kahan v. Pakistan Federation (1951) (see footnote 25 above). See also Huttinger v. Upper Congo-Great African Lakes Railways Co. et al. (1934) (Annual Digest . . ., 1933–1934 (London), vol. 7 (1940), case No. 65, pp. 172–173), and the cases cited in footnote 27 above.*

[38] *In Van Heyningen v. Netherlands Indies Government (1948) (Annual Digest . . ., 1948 (London), vol. 15 (1953), case No. 43, pp. 138 et seq.), the Supreme Court of Queensland (Australia) granted immunity to the Netherlands Indies Government. Judge Philip said:*

"*In my view, an action cannot be brought in our courts against a part of a foreign sovereign State. Where a foreign sovereign State sets up as an organ of its Government a governmental control of part of its territory which it creates into a legal entity, it seems to me that that legal entity cannot be sued here, because that would mean that the authority and territory of a foreign sovereign would be subjected in the ultimate result to the jurisdiction and execution of this court.*"

[39] *See also footnote 35 above.*

[40] *See, for example, the United States of America Foreign Sovereign Immunities Act of 1976 (United States Code, 1982 Edition, vol. 12, title 28, chap. 97 (text reproduced in United Nations, Materials on Jurisdictional Immunities . . . , pp. 55 et seq.)), which, in sect. 1603 (b), defines "agency or instrumentality of a foreign State" as an entity "(1) which is a separate legal person, (2) which is an organ of a foreign State or political division thereof, or a majority of whose shares or other ownership interest is owned by a foreign State or political subdivision thereof, and (3) which is neither a citizen or a State of the United States as defined in section 1332 (c) and (d) of this title nor created under the laws of any third country."*

[41] *See, for example, Krajina v. The Tass Agency and another (1949) (Annual Digest . . . , 1949 (London), vol. 16 (1955), case No. 37, p. 129); compare Compaña Mercantil Argentina v. United States Shipping Board (1924) (Annual Digest . . ., 1923–1924 (London), vol. 2 (1933), case No. 73, p. 138), and Baccus S.R.L. v. Servicio Nacional del Trigo (1956) (United Kingdom, The Law Reports, Queen's Bench Division, 1957, vol. 1, p. 438 et seq.), in which Lord Justice Jenkins observed:*

"*Whether a particular ministry or department or instrument, call it what you will, is to be a corporate body or an unincorporated body seems to me to be purely a matter of governmental machinery.*"

[42] *For a different view, see the opinions of Lord Justices Cohen and Tucker in Krajina v. The Tass Agency and another (1949) (see footnote 41 above), and in Baccus S.R.L. v. Servicio Nacional del Trigo (1956) (ibid.), where Lord Justice Parker said:*

"*I see no ground for thinking that the mere constitution of a body as a legal personality with the right to make contracts and to sue and be sued is wholly inconsistent with it remaining and being a department of State.*"

See also Emergency Fleet Corporation, United States Shipping Board v. Western Union Telegraph Company (1928) (United States Reports, vol. 275 (1928), p. 415 et seq.):

"*instrumentalities like the national banks or the federal reserve banks, in which there are private interests, are not departments of the Government. They are private corporations in which the Government has an interest.*"

See, however, the certificate of the United States Ambassador regarding the status of the United States Shipping Board in the case brought by Compaña Mercantil Argentina (see footnote 41 above).

[43] *See Dollfus Mieg et Cie S.A. v. Bank of England (1950) and United States of America and Republic of France v. Dollfus Mieg et Cie S.A. and Bank of England—"Gold bars" case (1952) (Annual Digest . . ., 1949 (London), vol. 16 (1955), case No. 36, p. 103); and Monopole des tabacs de Turquie et al. v. Régie co-intéressée des tabacs de Turquie (1930) (Annual Digest . . ., 1929–1930 (London), vol. 5 (1935), case No. 79, p. 123).*

[44] *The fact that the immunities enjoyed by representatives of government, whatever their specialized qualifications, diplomatic or consular or otherwise, are in the ultimate analysis State immunities has never been doubted. Rather, it has been unduly overlooked. Recently, however, evidence of their connection is reflected in some of the replies and information furnished by Governments. The Jamaican legislation and the Moroccan decision on diplomatic immunities and Mauritian law on consular immunities are outstanding reminders of the closeness of identities between State immunities and other types of immunities traceable to the State.*

[45] *See, for example, Thai-Europe Tapioca Service v. Government of Pakistan, Ministry of Food and Agriculture, Directorate of Agricultural Supplies (1975) (The All England Law Reports, 1975 (London), vol. 3, pp. 961 et seq.).*

[46] *Immunities ratione materiae may outlive the tenure of office of the representatives of a foreign State. They are nevertheless subject to the qualifications and exceptions to which State immunities are ordinarily*

subject in the practice of States. See, for instance, Nobili v. Charles I of Austria (1921) (Annual Digest . . . , 1919–1922 (London), vol. 1 (1932), case No. 90, p. 136) and La Mercantile v. Regno de Grecia (1955) (ILR, 1955 (London), vol. 22 (1958), p. 240), where the contract concluded by the Greek Ambassador for the delivery of raw materials was imputable to the State, and subject to the local jurisdiction.

[47] *Historically speaking, immunities of sovereigns and ambassadors developed even prior to State immunities. They are in State practice regulated by different sets of principles of international law. The view has been expressed that, in strict theory, all jurisdictional immunities are traceable to the basic norm of State sovereignty. See S. Sucharitkul, State Immunities and Trading Activities in International Law (London, Stevens, 1959), chaps. 1 and 2; E. Suy, "Les bénéficiaires de l'immunité de l'Etat", L'immunité de juridiction et d'exécution des Etats, Actes du colloque conjoint des 30 et 31 janvier 1969 des Centres de droit international (Brussels, Editions de l'Institut de sociologie, 1971), pp. 257 et seq.*

[48] *Thus in The Empire v. Chang and Others (1921) (Annual Digest . . . , 1919–1922 (London), vol. 1 (1932), case No. 205, p. 288), the Supreme Court of Japan confirmed the conviction of former employees of the Chinese legation in respect of offences committed during their employment as attendants there, but unconnected with their official duties. See also Léon v. Diaz (1892) (Journal du droit international privé et de la jurisprudence comparée (Clunet) (Paris), vol. 19 (1892), p. 1137), concerning a former Minister of Uruguay in France, and Laperdrix et Penquer v. Kouzouboff et Belin (1926) (Journal du droit international (Clunet) (Paris), vol. 53 (January–February 1926), pp. 64–65), where an ex-secretary of the United States Embassy was ordered to pay an indemnity for injury in a car accident.*

[49] *See, for example, the judgement of the Court of Geneva in the case V. . . . et Dicker v. D. . . . (1927) (ibid., vol. 54 (January–February 1927, p. 1179 et seq.), where an action by a mother and newly born child was allowed to proceed against an ex-diplomat. Commenting on the decision, Nöel-Henry said:*

> ". . . the real basis of immunity is the necessity of the function. Consequently, the principle is that the diplomat is covered by immunity only when he is fulfilling his functions . . . When he has relinquished his post, he can be sued, except in connection with acts performed by him in the fulfilment of his functions; moreover, it is not so much the immunity of the diplomat that is involved as the immunity of the Government which he represents."

See also M. Brandon, "Report on diplomatic immunity by an Interdepartmental Committee on State immunities", International and Comparative Law Quarterly (London), vol. 1 (July 1952), p. 358; P. Fiore, Trattato di diritto internazionale pubblico, 3rd ed. rev. (Turin, Unione tipografico-editrice, 1887–1891), p. 331, para. 491.

[50] *See, for instance, Dessus v. Ricoy (1907) (Journal du droit international privé et de la jurisprudence comparée (Clunet) (Paris), vol. 34 (1907), p. 1086), where the Court said:*

> ". . . since the immunity of diplomatic agents is not personal to them, but is an attribute and a guarantee of the State they represent . . . the agent cannot waive his immunity, especially when he cannot produce in support of a waiver of immunity any permission to do so issued by his Government."

See also Reichenbach et Cie v. Mme Ricoy (1906) (ibid., p. 111); Cottenet et Cie v. Dame Raffalowich (1908) (ibid., vol. 36 (1909), p. 150); the Grey case (1953) (Journal du droit international, vol. 80 (April–June 1953), p. 886); and The Attorney General to the Court of Cassation v. H.E. Doctor Franco-Franco (January–March 1954) (ibid., vol. 81, No. 1 (1954), p. 787). See also the provisions of the Vienna Convention on Diplomatic Relations.

[51] *The term "commercial transaction" is in fact used in several national legislations. See, for example, the United Kingdom State Immunity Act of 1978 (sect. 3 (3)) (The Public General Acts, 1978 (H.M. Stationery Office), part 1, chap. 33, p. 715; reproduced in United Nations, Materials on Jurisdictional Immunities . . ., pp. 41 et seq.); the Singapore State Immunity Act of 1979 (sect. 5 (3)) (1979 Supplement to the Statutes of the Republic of Singapore; reproduced in United Nations, Materials on Jurisdictional Immunities . . ., pp. 28 et seq.); the Pakistan State Immunity Ordinance of 1981 (sect. 5 (3)) (The Gazette of Pakistan (Islamabad), 11 March 1981; reproduced in United Nations, Materials on Jurisdictional Immunities . . ., pp. 20 et seq.; the South Africa Foreign States Immunities Act of 1981 (sect. 4 (3)) (Government Gazette (Cape Town), vol. 196, No. 7849, 28 October 1981; reproduced in United Nations, Materials on Jurisdictional Immunities . . ., pp. 34 et seq.); the Australia Foreign States Immunities Act No. 196 of 1985 (sect. 11 (3)) (Acts of Parliament of the Commonwealth of Australia passed during the year 1985 (Canberra, 1986), vol. 2, p. 2696; reproduced in ILM (Washington, D.C.), vol. 25 (1986), p. 715).*

[52] *See the commentary to article 10 below, paras. (13)–(18). In a recent decision, a United States court held that the commercial or non-commercial character of a contract must be determined on the basis of the*

essential character of the agreement and not on the basis of auxiliary terms that are designed to facilitate the performance of the contract. See Practical Concepts, Inc. v. Republic of Bolivia (1987) (811 F.2d, p. 1543, United States Court of Appeals, D.C. Cir., 17 February 1987, AJIL (Washington, D.C.), vol. 81 (1987), p. 952).

⁵³ *For example, in the "Parlement belge" case (1879) (United Kingdom, The Law Reports, Probate Division, 1879, vol. IV, p. 129), Sir Robert Phillimore, after reviewing English and American cases, considered the Parlement belge itself as being neither a ship of war nor a vessel of pleasure and thus not entitled to immunity. This decision was reversed by the Court of Appeal (1880) (ibid., 1880, vol. V, p. 197; see Lord Justice Brett (ibid., p. 203). See also Gouvernement espagnol v. Casaux (1849) (Dalloz, Recueil périodique et critique de jurisprudence, 1849 (Paris), part 1, p. 9), concerning the purchase of boots by the Spanish Government for the Spanish army. Cf. Hanukiew v. Ministère de l'Afghanistan (1933) (Annual Digest . . ., 1933–1934 (London), vol. 7 (1940), case No. 66, pp. 174–175), concerning a contract for the purchase of arms; and various loan cases, such as the Moroccan Loan, Laurans v. Gouvernement impérial chérifien et la Société marseillaise de crédit (1934) (see footnote 24 above). See also Vavasseur v. Krupp (1878) (United Kingdom, The Law Reports, Chancery Division, 1878, vol. IX, p. 351); Trendtex Trading Corporation Ltd. v. The Central Bank of Nigeria (1977) (The All England Law Reports, 1977 (London), vol. I, p. 881), concerning an order for cement for the construction of barracks in Nigeria. Cf. Gugenheim v. State of Viet Nam (1961) (Revue générale de droit international public (Paris), vol. 66 (1962), p. 654; reproduced in United Nations, Materials on Jurisdictional Immunities . . ., p. 257), a case concerning a contract for the purchase of cigarettes for the Vietnamese national army. Other cases relevant in the present context include: Egyptian Delta Rice Mills Co. v. Comisaría General de Abastecimientos y Transportes de Madrid (1943) (Annual Digest . . ., 1943–1945 (London), vol. 12 (1949), case No. 27, pp. 103–104), cited by S. Sucharitkul in "Immunities of foreign States before national authorities", Collected Courses . . ., 1976–I (Leiden, Sijthoff, 1977), vol. 149, pp. 140–141; Khan v. Fredson Travel Inc. (1982) (133 D.L.R. (3d), p. 632, Ontario High Court, Canadian Yearbook of International Law, vol. XXI, p. 376 (1983)); X v. Empire of . . . (1963) (Entscheidungen des Bundesverfassungsgericht) (Tubingen), vol. 16 (1964), p. 27; United Nations, Materials on Jurisdictional Immunities . . ., pp. 282 et seq.).*

⁵⁴ *This is of crucial significance in view of the emerging trend in the judicial practice and legislation of some States. See the commentary to article 10 below, paras. (13)–(17).*

⁵⁵ *See, for example, the Convention on the Privileges and Immunities of the United Nations and the Convention on the Privileges and Immunities of the Specialized Agencies, as well as regional conventions.*

⁵⁶ *For the case law in this connection, see Yearbook . . . 1985, vol. II (Part One), document A/CN.4/388, paras. 119–125.*

⁵⁷ *See Yearbook . . . 1980, vol. II (Part Two), pp. 142–157. Several other States have recently adopted legislation dealing directly with the subject of State immunity, namely: the Singapore State Immunity Act of 1979; the Pakistan State Immunity Ordinance of 1981; the South Africa Foreign States Immunities Act of 1981, as amended in 1985 [and 1988 (South Africa Foreign States Immunities Amendment Act, No. 5, 3 March 1988; Not in force as of April 1991)]; and the Australia Foreign States Immunities Act of 1985 (see footnote 51 above); as well as the Canada Act to Provide for State Immunity in Canadian Courts of 1982 (The Canada Gazette, Part III (Ottawa), vol. 6, No. 15, 22 June 1982 and Revised Statutes of Canada, 1985, vol. VIII, chap. S-18. See also for the recent development of the general practice of State immunity, the second report of the Special Rapporteur (footnote 17 above) [Not here reproduced].*

⁵⁸ *Specific provisions to this effect are not uncommon in national legislation. See, for example, the United Kingdom State Immunity Act of 1978 (sect. 1 (2)); the Singapore State Immunity Act of 1979 (sect. 3 (2)); the Pakistan State Immunity Ordinance of 1981 (sect. 3 (2)); the South Africa Foreign State Immunities Act of 1981 (sect. 2 (2)) (footnote 51 above); the Canada Act to Provide for State Immunity in Canadian Courts of 1982 (sect. 3 (2)) (footnote 57 above). See also the European Convention on State Immunity, art. 15.*

⁵⁹ *See, for example, F. Advokaat v. I. Schuddinck #38; den Belgischen Staat (1923) (Annual Digest . . ., 1923–1924 (London), vol. 2 (1933), case No. 69, p. 133); United States of America v. Republic of China (1950) (ILR, 1950 (London), vol. 17 (1956), case No. 43, p. 168); The "Hai Hsuan"—United States of America v. Yong Soon Fe and another (1950) (ibid., case No. 44, p. 170); Stato de Grecia v. Di Capone (1926) (Rivista . . . (Rome), series III, vol. VI (1927), p. 102); Pauer v. Hungarian People's Republic (1956) (ILR, 1957 (London), vol. 24 (1961), p. 211); Alfred Dunhill of London, Inc. v. Republic of Cuba (1976) (ILM (Washington. D.C.), vol. 15, No. 4 (July 1976), p. 735).*

⁶⁰ *See in this connection the International Convention for the Unification of Certain Rules relating to the Immunity of State-owned Vessels; the Convention on the Territorial Sea and the Contiguous Zone, the Convention on the High Seas and the United Nations Convention on the Law of the Sea.*

[61] See draft arts. 18–19 below.

[62] See, for example, The Schooner "Exchange" v. McFaddon and others (1812) (see footnote 29 above); The "Prins Frederik" (1820) (J. Dodson, Reports of Cases Argued and Determined in the High Court of Admiralty (1815–1822) (London), vol. II (1828), p. 451); The "Charkieh" (1873) (United Kingdom, The Law Reports, High Court of Admiralty and Ecclesiastical Courts, 1875, vol. IV, p. 97).

[63] See, for example, The "Constitution" (1879) (United Kingdom, The Law Reports, Probate Division, 1879, vol. IV, p. 39); The "Ville de Victoria" and The "Sultan" (1887) (see G. Gidel, Le droit international public de la mer (Paris, Sirey, 1932), vol. II, p. 303); "El Presidente Pino" (1891) and "Assari Tewfik" (1901) (see C. Baldoni, "Les navires de guerre dans les eaux territoriales étrange res", Recueil des cours . . . 1938—III (Paris, Sirey, 1938), vol. 65, pp. 247 et seq.).

[64] See, for example, The Schooner "Exchange" case (1812) and the status of forces agreements (footnote 29 above).

[65] See, for example, Vavasseur v. Krupp (1878) (footnote 53 above).

[66] See, for example, Hong Kong Aircraft-Civil Air Transport Inc. v. Central Air Transport Corp. (1953) (United Kingdom, The Law Reports, House of Lords, Judicial Committee of the Privy Council, 1953, p. 70).

[67] See, for example, Juan Ysmael & Co. v. Government of the Republic of Indonesia (1954) (ILR, 1954 (London), vol. 21 (1957), p. 95), and also cases involving bank accounts of a foreign Government, such as Trendtex Trading Corporation Ltd. v. The Central Bank of Nigeria (1977) (footnote 53 above).

[68] See, for example, the "Philippine Admiral" (1975) (ILM (Washington, D.C.), vol. 15, No. 1 (January 1976), p. 133).

[69] Dollfus Mieg et Cie S.A. v. Bank of England (1950) (see footnote 43 above).

[70] The notion of "consent" is also relevant to the theory of State immunity in another connection. The territorial or receiving State is sometimes said to have consented to the presence of friendly foreign forces passing through its territory and to have waived its normal jurisdiction over such forces. See, for example, Chief Justice Marshall in The Schooner "Exchange" v. McFaddon and others (1812) (footnote 29 above).

[71] For the legislative practice of States, see, for example, the United States Foreign Sovereign Immunities Act of 1976 (sect. 1605 (a) (1)) (footnote 40 above); the United Kingdom State Immunity Act of 1978 (sect. 2); the Singapore State Immunity Act of 1979 (sect. 4); the Pakistan State Immunity Ordinance of 1981 (sect. 4); the South Africa Foreign States Immunities Act of 1981 (sect. 3); the Australia Foreign States Immunities Act of 1985 (sect. 10) (footnote 51 above); Canada Act to Provide for State Immunity in Canadian Courts of 1982 (sect. 4) (footnote 57 above).

[72] See, for example, the reply of Trinidad and Tobago (June 1980) to question 1 of the questionnaire addressed to Governments:

"The common law of the Republic of Trinidad and Tobago provides specifically for jurisdictional immunities for foreign States and their property and generally for non-exercise of jurisdiction over foreign States and their property without their consent*. A court seized of any action attempting to implead a foreign sovereign or State would apply the rules of customary international law dealing with the subject." (United Nations, Materials on Jurisdictional Immunities . . ., p. 610.)

[73] See, for example, Lord Atkin in The "Cristina" (1938) (Annual Digest . . . 1938–40) (London), vol. 9 (1942), case No. 36, pp. 250–252):

"The foundation for the application to set aside the writ and arrest of the ship is to be found in two propositions of international law engrafted into our domestic law, which seem to me to be well established and to be beyond dispute. The first is that the courts of a country will not implead a foreign sovereign, that is, they will not by their process make him against his will a party to legal proceedings* whether the proceedings involve process against this person or seek to recover from him specific damages."

[74] Thus, the Fundamentals of Civil Procedure of the USSR and the Union Republics, Approved in the Law of the Union of Soviet Socialist Republics dated 8 December 1961, provides in article 61:

"The filing of a suit against a foreign State, the collection of a claim against it and the attachment of the property located in the USSR may be permitted only* with the consent* of the competent organs of the State concerned." (United Nations, Materials on Jurisdictional Immunities . . ., p. 40.)

[75] See, for example, Bayerischer Rundfunk v. Schiavetti Magnani (Corte di Cassazione, 12 January 1987) (Rivista di diritto internazionale privato e processuale, vol. XXIV (1988), p. 512) concerning the employment in Italy of an Italian journalist by a German public broadcasting enterprise. The court found that the parties

having agreed in the employment contract to confer exclusive jurisdiction on the courts of Italy, Bayerischer Rundfunk could not invoke immunity from jurisdiction and should be treated as a private enterprise.

[76] *See, for example, statements submitted in writing to the Court by accredited diplomats, in Krajina v. The Tass Agency and another (1949) (footnote 41 above) and in First Fidelity Bank v. The Government of Antigua and Barbuda (1989) (877 F.2d, p. 189, United States Court of Appeals, 2nd Cir., 7 June 1989); cf. Compaña Mercantil Argentina v. United States Shipping Board (1924) and Baccus S.R.L. v. Servicio Nacional del Trigo (1956) (footnote 41 above).*

[77] *In a recent case, Frolova v. Union of Soviet Socialist Republics (761 F.2d, p. 370, United States Court of Appeals, 7th Cir., 1 May 1985, AJIL (Washington, D.C.), vol. 79 (1985), p. 1057), the United States Court of Appeals held that the Soviet Union had not implicitly waived its immunity for purposes of the Foreign Sovereign Immunities Act by signing the Charter of the United Nations and the Helsinki accords. The court noted that the Congressional committee reports on the Act refer to waiver by treaty in the context of explicit waivers, but do not include waiver by treaty in the list of examples of implicit waivers.*

[78] *There are certain multilateral treaties in point such as the European Convention on State Immunity and the 1926 Brussels Convention, and those listed in United Nations, Materials on Jurisdictional Immunities . . ., part III, sect. B, pp. 150 et seq. There are also a number of relevant bilateral trade agreements between non-socialist countries, between socialist countries and developed countries and between socialist countries and developing countries (ibid., part III, sect. A.3 and A.4, pp. 140 et seq.).*

[79] *See, for example, an agreement between the Banque Francaise du Commerce Extérieur and the Kingdom of Thailand signed on 23 March 1978 in Paris by the authorized representative of the Minister of Finance of Thailand. Art. III, para. 3.04, provides:*

"For the purpose of jurisdiction and of execution or enforcement of any judgement or award, the Guarantor certifies that he waives and renounces hereby any right to assert before an arbitration tribunal or court of law or any other authority any defence or exception based on his sovereign immunity." (Malaya Law Review (Singapore), vol. 22, No. 1 (July 1980), p. 192, note 22.)

[80] *See, for example, Duff Development Co. Ltd. v. Government of Kelantan and another (1924) (footnote 24 above), where by assenting to the arbitration clause in a deed, or by applying to the courts to set aside the award of the arbitrator, the Government of Kelantan did not submit to the jurisdiction of the High Court in respect of a later proceeding by the company to enforce the award. See also Kahan v. Pakistan Federation (1951) (footnote 25 above) and Baccus S.R.L. v. Servicio Nacional del Trigo (1956) (footnote 41 above).*

[81] *Although, for practical purposes, F. Laurent in his Le droit civil international (Brussels, Bruylant-Christophe, 1881), vol. III, pp. 80–81, made no distinction between "power to decide" (jurisdiction) and "power to execute" (execution), consent by a State to the exercise of the power to decide by the court of another State cannot be presumed to extend to the exercise of the power to execute or enforce judgement against the State having consented to the exercise of jurisdiction by appearing before the court without raising a plea of jurisdictional immunity.*

[82] *For example, the European Convention on State Immunity, which provides, in article 1, para. 1, that:*

"A Contracting State which institutes or intervenes in proceedings before a court of another Contracting State submits, for the purpose of those proceedings, to the jurisdiction of the courts of that State."

[83] *Thus, according to art. 1, para. 3, of the European Convention on State Immunity:*

"A Contracting State which makes a counter-claim in proceedings before a court of another Contracting State submits to the jurisdiction of the courts of that State with respect not only to the counter-claim but also to the principal claim."

See also The Republic of Portugal v. Algemene Olienhandel International (AOI), District Court of Rotterdam, 2 April 1982, NJ (1983), No. 722, Netherlands Yearbook of International Law, vol. XVI (1985), p. 522, in which Portugal's plea of immunity from jurisdiction must fail since it voluntarily submitted to the jurisdiction of a Dutch court when it objected to a default judgement of the Rotterdam District Court ordering Portugal to pay a sum of money to AOI.

[84] *See, for example, subsects. 4 (a) and 4 (b) of sect. 2 of the United Kingdom State Immunity Act of 1978 (footnote 51 above). Subsect. 5 does not regard as voluntary submission any step taken by a State on proceedings before a court of another State:*

". . . in ignorance of facts entitling it to immunity if those facts could not reasonably have been ascertained and immunity is claimed as soon as reasonably practicable."

Delay in raising a plea or defence of jurisdictional immunity may create an impression in favour of submission.

  [85] *There could be no real consent without full knowledge of the right to raise an objection on the ground of State immunity (Baccus S.R.L. v. Servicio Nacional del Trigo (1956) (see footnote 41 above), but see also Earl Jowitt, in Juan Ysmael & Co. v. Government of the Republic of Indonesia (1954) (footnote 67 above), where he said obiter that a claimant Government:*

> ". . . must produce evidence to satisfy the court that its claim is not merely illusory, nor founded on a title manifestly defective. The court must be satisfied that conflicting rights have to be decided in relation to the foreign government's claim."

  Cf. the Hong Kong Aircraft case (see footnote 66 above), in which Sir Leslie Gibson of the Supreme Court of Hong Kong did not consider mere claim of ownership to be sufficient (ILR, 1950 (London), vol. 17 (1956), case No. 45, p. 173). Contrast Justice Scrutton in The "Jupiter" No. 1 (1924) (United Kingdom, The Law Reports, Probate Division, 1924, p. 236), and Lord Radcliffe in the "Gold bars" case (1952) (see footnote 43 above), pp. 176–177.

  [86] *See, for example, art. 13 of the European Convention on State Immunity:*

> "Paragraph 1 of Article 1 shall not apply where a Contracting State asserts, in proceedings pending before a court of another Contracting State to which it is not a party, that it has a right or interest in property which is the subject-matter of the proceedings, and the circumstances are such that it would have been entitled to immunity if the proceedings had been brought against it."

See also Dollfus Mieg et Cie. S.A. v. Bank of England (1950) (see footnote 43 above).

  [87] *See footnote 84 above.*

  [88] *This provision, however, does not affect the privileges and immunities of members of a diplomatic mission or consular post of a State in respect of appearance before judicial or administrative proceedings of another State accorded under international law. See the Vienna Convention on Diplomatic Relations (art. 31, para. 2) and the Vienna Convention on Consular Relations (art. 44, para. 1).*

  [89] *Thus, in Dame Lizarda dos Santos v. Republic of Iraq (Supreme Court, undated) (extraits in French in Journal du droit international (Clunet) (Paris), vol. 115 (1988), p. 472), the appeal of a Brazilian national employed as a cook at the Embassy of Iraq against a court decision to refrain from exercising immunity, on its own initiative, on the ground that Iraq had implicitly renounced its immunity, was rejected by the Court which stated that it could not recognize an implied waiver based solely on the State's refusal to respond to the complaint.*

  [90] *For example, in The "Jupiter" No. 1 (1924) (see footnote 85 above), Justice Hill held that a writ in rem against a vessel in the possession of the Soviet Government must be set aside inasmuch as the process against the ship compelled all persons claiming interests therein to assert their claims before the court, and inasmuch as the USSR claimed ownership in her and did not submit to the jurisdiction.* Contrast The "Jupiter" No. 2 (1925), where the same ship was then in the hands of an Italian company and the Soviet Government did not claim an interest in her (United Kingdom, The Law Reports, Probate Division, 1925, p. 69).*

  [91] *For example, the United Kingdom State Immunity Act of 1978 (see footnote 51 above) provides in sect. 2, subsect. (6), that:*

> "A submission in respect of any proceedings extends to any appeal but not to any counter-claim unless it arises out of the same legal relationship or facts as the claim."

See also Strousberg v. Republic of Costa Rica (1881), Law Times Reports (London), vol. 44, p. 199, where the defendant was allowed to assert any claim he had by way of cross-action or counter-claim to the original action in order that justice might be done. But such counter-claims and cross-suits can only be brought in respect of the same transactions and only operate as set-offs.

  [92] *For example, the United States Foreign Sovereign Immunities Act of 1976 (see footnote 40 above) provides in sect. 1607 (Counter-claims), subsect. (b), that immunity shall not be accorded with respect to any counter-claim "arising out of the transaction or an occurrence that is the subject-matter of the claim of the foreign State". Thus, in Kunstsammlungen Zu Weimar and Grand Duchess of Saxony-Weimar v. Federal Republic of Germany and Elicofon (United States Court of Appeals, 2nd Cir., 5 May 1982, ILM (Washington, D.C.), vol. 21 (1982), p. 773) where the court was asked to determine the ownership of two priceless Albrecht Dürer portraits based on the competing claims of the German Democratic Republic, the Federal Republic of Germany, the Grand Duchess of Saxony-Weimar, and a United States citizen who had purchased the drawings in good faith without knowledge that they were Dürers, it held that the Grand*

Duchess' cross-claim for annuities under a 1921 agreement did not come under the immunity exception for counter-claims arising out of the same transaction or occurrence as the claim of the foreign State.

[93] *Sect. 1607, subsect. (c), of the United States Foreign Sovereign Immunities Act of 1976 states: "to the extent that the counter-claim does not seek relief exceeding in amount or differing in kind from that sought by the foreign State" (see footnote 40 above). See also Strousberg v. Republic of Costa Rica (1881) (footnote 91 above) and Union of Soviet Socialist Republics v. Belaiew (1925) (The All England Law Reports, 1925 (London) (reprint), p. 369).*

[94] *See, for example, South African Republic v. La Compagnie franco-belge du chemin de fer du Nord (1897) (United Kingdom, The Law Reports, Chancery Division, 1898, p. 190) and the cases cited in footnotes 91 and 93 above.*

[95] *For an indication of possible means of affirmative relief in justifiable circumstances, see Republic of Haiti v. Plesch et al. (1947) (New York Supplement, 2nd Series, vol. 73 (1947), p. 645); United States of Mexico v. Rask (1931) (Pacific Reporter, 2nd Series, vol. 4 (1931), p. 981); see also The International and Comparative Law Quarterly (London), vol. 2 (1953), p. 480; The Law Quarterly Review (London), vol. 71, No. 283 (July 1955), p. 305; The Modern Law Review (London), vol. 18 (1955), p. 417; and Minnesota Law Review (Minneapolis, Minn.), vol. 40 (1956), p. 124. See, however, Alberti v. Empresa Nicaragüense de la Carne (705 F.2d, p. 250, United States Court of Appeals, 7th Cir., 18 April 1983).*

[96] *See, for example, Etat du Pérou v. Kreglinger (1857) (Pasicrisie belge, 1857 (Brussels), part 2, p. 348); Letort v. Gouvernement ottoman (1914) (Revue juridique internationale de la locomotion aérienne (Paris), vol. V (1914), p. 142).*

[97] *See, for example, the United States Foreign Sovereign Immunities Act of 1976 (footnote 40 above), sect. 1607, subsect. (a), concerning counter-claims "for which a foreign State would not be entitled to immunity under sect. 1605 of this chapter had such claim been brought in a separate action against the foreign State". Cf. art. 1, para. 2, of the European Convention on State Immunity and Additional Protocol.*

[98] *See, for example, art. 1, para. 3, of the European Convention on State Immunity.*

[99] *See Yearbook . . . 1982, vol. II (Part One), p. 199, document A/CN.4/357, paras. 35–45.*

[100] *Ibid., para. 36.*

[101] *Ibid., para. 37.*

[102] *Ibid., paras. 38–39.*

[103] *Ibid., paras. 40–42.*

[104] *Ibid., paras. 43–45.*

[105] *See Yearbook . . . 1982, vol. I, pp. 183–199, 1728th meeting, paras. 7–45, and 1729th to 1730th meetings; the discussion is summarized in Yearbook . . . 1982, vol. II (Part Two), pp. 98–99, paras. 194–197. See also, comments and observations of Governments reproduced in Yearbook . . . 1988, vol. II (Part One), pp. 51 et seq., document A/CN.4/410 and Add. 1–5, and the Commission's discussion at its forty-first session, which is summarized in Yearbook . . . 1989, vol. II (Part Two), pp. 107–108, paras. 489–498.*

[106] *See, for example, Republic of Syria v. Arab Republic of Egypt (Supreme Court, undated) (extracts in French in Journal du droit international (Clunet) (Paris), vol. 115 (1988), p. 472) concerning the dispute of the ownership of a building purchased by Syria in Brazil, subsequently used by Egypt and retained by Egypt after the break-up of the union between the two States. By a one-vote majority, immunity from jurisdiction prevailed in the Court's split decision.*

The Government Procurator held the view that a discussion of the substantive issues could be relevant only if the Arab Republic of Egypt accepted Brazilian jurisdiction. He said that its right to refuse was clear, and would have been even according to the doctrine of restrictive immunity, still confused and hardly convincing, which made a distinction between acts jure imperii and jure gestionis. This was because the case at hand had nothing to do with any private business whatsoever, but concerned diplomatic premises within the context of State succession, which was exclusively and primarily within the domain of public international law.

[107] *See Yearbook . . . 1986, vol. II (Part Two), p. 11.*

[108] *Art. 10 has to be read in conjunction with art. 2, para. 1 (c), on the definition of "commercial transaction", and art. 2, para. 2, on the interpretation of that definition. The commentaries to those provisions should also be taken into consideration.*

[109] *See the fourth report of the former Special Rapporteur (footnote 13 above), paras. 49–92; and the second report of the Special Rapporteur (footnote 17 above), paras. 2–19.*

[110] *This was the first case in which the commercial nature of the service or employment of a public ship was held to disentitle her from State immunity.*

[111] *The courts of Italy were the first, in 1882, to limit the application of State immunity to cases where the foreign State had acted as an ente politico as opposed to a corpo morale (see Morellet ed altri v. Governo Danese*

(1882) (Giurisprudenza Italiana (Turin), vol. XXXV, part 1 (1883), p. 125)), or in the capacity of a sovereign authority or political power (potere politico) as distinguished from a persona civile (see Guttieres v. Elmilik (1886) (Il Foro Italiano (Rome), vol. XI, part 1 (1886), pp. 920–922)). See also Hamspohn v. Bey di Tunisi ed Erlanger (1887) (ibid., vol. XII, part 1 (1887), pp. 485–486).

In Italian jurisdiction, State immunity was allowed only in respect of atti d'impero and not atti di gestione. The public nature of the State act was the criterion by which it was determined whether or not immunity should be accorded. Immunity was not recognized for private acts or acts of a private-law nature. See Department of the Army of the United States of America v. Gori Savellini (Rivista . . . (Milan), vol. XXXIX (1956), pp. 91–92, and ILR, 1956 (London), vol. 23 (1960), p. 201). Cf. La Mercantile v. Regno di Grecia (1955) (see footnote 46 above). More recently, in Banco de la Nación v. Credito Varesino (Corte di Cassazione, 19 October 1984) (Rivista di diritto internazionale privato e processuale, vol. XXI (1985), p. 635) concerning the debts arising from money transfers made by an Italian bank in favour of a Peruvian bank, the court held that even assuming that the bank is a public entity, immunity from the jurisdiction of Italian courts could not be invoked with respect to a dispute arising not from the exercise of sovereign powers but from activities of a private nature.

[112] Belgian case law was settled as early as 1857 in a trilogy of cases involving the guano monopoly of Peru. These cases are: (a) Etat du Pérou v. Kreglinger (1857) (see footnote 96 above); cf. E. W. Allen, The Position of Foreign States before Belgian Courts (New York, Macmillan, 1929), p. 8; (b) the "Peruvian loans" case (1877) (Pasicrisie belge, 1877 (Brussels), part 2, p. 307); this case was brought not against Peru, but against the Dreyfus Brothers company; (c) Peruvian Guano Company v. Dreyfus et consorts et le Gouvernement du Pérou (1880) (ibid., 1881 (Brussels), part 2, p. 313). In these three cases, a distinction was drawn between the public activities of the State of Peru and its private activities with respect to which the Court of Appeals of Brussels denied immunity. Thus, like Italian courts, Belgian courts have, since 1888, also adopted the distinction between acts of the State in its sovereign (public) and civil (private) capacities: in Société pour la fabrication de cartouches v. Colonel Mutkuroff, Ministre de la guerre de la principauté de Bulgarie (1888) (ibid., 1889 (Brussels), part 3, p. 62), the Tribunal civil of Brussels held that, in concluding a contract for the purchase of bullets, Bulgaria had acted as a private person and subjected itself to all the consequences of the contract. Similarly, in Société anonyme des chemins de fer liégeois-luxembourgeois v. Etat néerlandais (Ministère du Waterstaat) (1903) (ibid., 1903 (Brussels), part I, p. 294), a contract to enlarge a railway station in Holland was made subject to Belgian jurisdiction. The distinction between acta jure imperii and acta jure gestionis has been applied by Belgian courts consistently since 1907; see Feldman v. Etat de Bahia (1907) (footnote 34 above).

[113] The current case law of post-war Egypt has confirmed the jurisprudence of the country's mixed courts, which have been consistent in their adherence to the Italo-Belgian practice of limited immunity. In Egypt, jurisdictional immunities of foreign States constitute a question of ordre public; see Decision 1173 of 1963 of the Cairo Court of First Instance (cited in United Nations, Materials on Jurisdictional Immunities . . ., p. 569). Immunity is allowed only in respect of acts of sovereign authority and does not extend to "ordinary acts" (ibid.).

[114] The practice of German courts began as early as 1885 with restrictive immunity based on the distinction between public and private activities, holding State immunity to "suffer at least certain exceptions"; see Heizer v. Kaiser Franz-Joseph-Bahn A.G. (1885) (Gesetz und Verordnungsblatt für das Königreich Bayern (Munich), vol. I (1885), pp. 15–16; cited in Harvard Law School, Research in International Law, part III, "Competence of Courts in regard to Foreign States" (Cambridge, Mass., 1932), published as Supplement to AJIL (Washington, D.C.), vol. 26 (1932), pp. 533–534). In the Republic of Latvia case (1953) (Rechtsprechung zum Wiedergutmachungsrecht (Munich), vol. 4 (1953), p. 368; ILR, 1953 (London), vol. 20 (1957), pp. 180–181), the Restitution Chamber of the Kammergericht of West Berlin denied immunity on the grounds that "this rule does not apply where the foreign State enters into commercial relations . . . viz., where it does not act in its sovereign capacity but exclusively in the field of private law*, by engaging in purely private business, and more especially in commercial intercourse". This restrictive trend has been followed by the Federal Constitutional Court in later cases; see, for example, X v. Empire of . . . (1963) (footnote 53 above), in which a contract for repair of the heating system of the Iranian Embassy was held to be "non-sovereign" and thus not entitled to immunity. In 1990, Germany ratified the European Convention on State Immunity.

[115] It has sometimes been said that the practice of the courts of the United States of America started with an unqualified principle of State immunity. The truth might appear to be the opposite upon closer examination of the dictum of Chief Justice Marshall in The Schooner "Exchange" v. McFaddon and others (1812) (see footnote 29 above). In Bank of the United States v. Planters' Bank of Georgia (1824) (H. Wheaton, Reports of Cases . . . (New York, 1911), vol. IX, 4th ed., pp. 904 and 907), it was held that, "when a

Government becomes a partner in any trading company, it divests itself, so far as concerns the transactions of that company, of its sovereign character, and takes that of a private citizen".

The first clear pronouncement of restrictive immunity by a United States court, based on the distinction between *acta jure imperii* and *acta jure gestionis*, came in 1921 in The *"Pesaro" case (United States of America, The Federal Reporter, vol. 277 (1922), p. 473, at 479–480; see also AJIL (Washington, D.C.), vol. 21 (1927), p. 108)*. This distinction was supported by the Department of State, but rejected by the Supreme Court in 1926 in *Berizzi Brothers Co. v. The S.S. "Pesaro" (United States Reports, vol. 271 (1927), p. 562)*. In subsequent cases, the courts preferred to follow the suggestion of the political branch of the Government; see, for example, *Chief Justice Stone in Republic of Mexico et al. v. Hoffman (1945) (ibid., vol. 324 (1946), pp. 30–42)*. It was not until the *"Tate Letter" of 1952 (United States of America, The Department of State Bulletin (Washington, D.C.), vol. XXVI, No. 678 (23 June 1952), pp. 984–985)* that the official policy of the Department of State was restated in general and in the clearest language in favour of a restrictive theory of immunity based upon the distinction between *acta jure imperii* and *acta jure gestionis*. See, further, *Victory Transport Inc. v. Comisaria General de Abastecimientos y Transportes (United States of America, The Federal Reporter, 2nd Series, vol. 336 (1965), p. 354; see also ILR (London), vol. 35 (1967), p. 110)*.

Since the adoption of the Foreign Sovereign Immunities Act of 1976 (see footnote 40 above), United States courts have decided on the question of immunity, without any suggestion from the Department of State in the form of a "Tate Letter". It is this 1976 Act that now provides legislative guidance for the courts with regard to the exception of commercial activity. See, for example, *West v. Multibanco Comermex, S.A. (807 F.2d 820, United States Court of Appeals, 9th Cir., 6 January 1987, AJIL (Washington, D.C.), vol. 81 (1987), p. 660); Rush-Presbyterian-St. Luke's Medical Center v. The Hellenic Republic (United States Court of Appeals, 7th Cir., 14 June 1989). Cf. De Sanchez v. Banco Central de Nicaragua (720 F.2d, p. 1385, United States Court of Appeals, 5th Cir., 19 September 1985, AJIL (Washington, D.C.), vol. 80 (1986), p. 658); Gregorian v. Izvestia (871 F.2d, p. 1515, United States Court of Appeals, 9th Cir., 12 April 1989); Harris Corporation v. National Iranian Radio and Television and Bank Melli Iran (United States Court of Appeals, 11th Cir., 22 November 1982, ILR (London), vol. 72 (1987), p. 172); America West Airlines, Inc. v. GPA Group, Ltd. (877 F.2d, p. 793, United States Court of Appeals, 9th Cir., 12 June 1989); MOL Inc. v. The People's Republic of Bangladesh (United States Court of Appeals, 9th Cir., 3 July 1984, ILR (London), vol. 80 (1989), p. 583)*.

[116] In connection with the commercial activities of a foreign State, notably in the field of shipping or maritime transport, the case law of the United Kingdom fluctuated throughout the nineteenth century. The decision which went furthest in the direction of restricting immunity was that of The *"Charkieh" case (1873) (see footnote 62 above); see also the fourth report of the former Special Rapporteur (see footnote 13 above), para. 80*. The decision which went furthest in the opposite direction was that of The *"Porto Alexandre" case (1920) (United Kingdom, The Law Reports, Probate Division, 1920, p. 30)*. Thus the principle of unqualified immunity was followed in subsequent cases concerning commercial shipping, such as *Compaña Mercantil Argentina v. United States Shipping Board (1924) (see footnote 41 above)*, and other trading activities, such as the ordinary sale of a quantity of rye in *Baccus S.R.L. v. Servicio Nacional del Trigo (1956) (ibid.)*.

However, even in The *"Cristina" case (1938) (see footnote 73 above)*, considerable doubt was thrown upon the soundness of the doctrine of immunity when applied to trading vessels, and some of the judges were disposed to reconsider the unqualified immunity held in The *"Porto Alexandre" case (1920)*. Thus, in a series of cases which include *Dollfus Mieg et Cie S.A. v. Bank of England (1950)* and *United States of America and Republic of France v. Dollfus Mieg et Cie S.A. and Bank of England (1952) (see footnote 43 above), Sultan of Johore v. Abubakar, Tunku Aris Bendahara and others (1952) (The All England Law Reports, 1952 (London), vol. 1, p. 1261; see also The Law Quarterly Review (London), vol. 68 (1952), p. 293) and Rahimtoola v. Nizam of Hyderabad (1957) (United Kingdom, The Law Reports, House of Lords, 1958, p. 379)*, a trend towards a "restrictive" view of immunity was maintained. In the *Dollfus Mieg et Cie S.A. case (1950)*, the Master of the Rolls, Sir Raymond Evershed, agreed with Lord Maugham that "the extent of the rule of immunity should be jealously watched". In the *Sultan of Johore case (1952)*, Lord Simon, per curiam, denied that unqualified immunity was the rule in England in all circumstances.

A forerunner of the ultimate reversal of the unqualified immunity held in The *"Porto Alexandre" case (1920)* came in 1975 in the *"Philippine Admiral" case (see footnote 68 above)*, in which the decision in the *"Parlement belge" case (1880) (see footnote 53 above)* was distinguished and the *Sultan of Johore case (1952)* cited as establishing that the question of unqualified immunity was an open one when it came to State-owned vessels engaged in ordinary commerce.

Then, in 1977, in *Trendtex Trading Corporation Ltd. v. The Central Bank of Nigeria (ibid.)*, the Court of Appeal unanimously held that the doctrine of sovereign immunity no longer applied to ordinary trading transactions and that the restrictive doctrine of immunity should therefore apply to actions in personam as well as actions in rem. This emerging trend was reinforced by the State Immunity Act of 1978 (see footnote 51 above), which came before the House of Lords for a decision in 1981 in the "I Congreso del Partido" case (1981) (The All England Law Reports, 1981 (London), vol. 2, p. 1064). With the 1978 Act and this recent series of cases, the judicial practice of British courts must now be said to be well settled in relation to the exception of trading activities of foreign Governments. See also, *Planmount Limited v. The Republic of Zaire* (High Court, Queen's Bench Division (Commercial Court), 29 April 1980 (ILR (London), vol. 64 (1983), p. 268).

[117] A survey of the practice of French courts discloses traces of certain limitations on State immunity, based on the distinction between the State as puissance publique and as personne privée, and between acte d'autorité and acte de gestion or acte de commerce, in the judgements of lower courts as early as 1890; see *Faucon et Cie v. Gouvernement grec* (1890) (Journal du droit international privé et de la jurisprudence comparée (Clunet) (Paris), vol. 17 (1890), p. 288). It was not until 1918, however, that the restrictive theory of State immunity was formulated and adopted by the French courts. See *Société maritime auxiliaire de transports v. Capitaine du vapeur anglais "Hungerford"* (Tribunal de commerce of Nantes, 1918) (Revue de droit international privé (Darras) (Paris), vol. XV (1919), p. 510); *Capitaine Seabrook v. Société maritime auxiliaire de transports* (Court of Appeal of Rennes, 1919) (ibid., vol. XVIII (1922–1923), p. 743); *Etat roumain v. Pascalet et Cie* (Journal du droit international (Clunet) (Paris), vol. 52 (1925), p. 113).

The current jurisprudence of France may be said to be settled in its adherence to the "restrictive" view of State immunity, based on "trading activities". The more recent decisions, however, have interpreted the theory of actes de commerce with some divergent results. For example, on the one hand, the purchase of cigarettes for a foreign army and a contract for a survey of water distribution in Pakistan were both held to be actes de puissance publique for public service; see, respectively, *Gugenheim v. State of Viet Nam* (1961) (footnote 53 above) and *Société Transshipping v. Federation of Pakistan* (1966) (ILR (London), vol. 47 (1974), p. 150). On the other hand, a contract for the commercial lease of an office for the tourist organization of a foreign Government and methods of raising loans both posed difficulties for the courts in applying the standards of actes de commerce; see, respectively, *Etat espagnol v. Société anonyme de l'Hôtel George V* (1970) (ibid. (Cambridge), vol. 52 (1979), p. 317); and *Montefiore v. Congo belge* (1955) (ibid., 1955, vol. 22 (1958), p. 226). In *Banque camerounaise de développement v. Société des Etablissements Robler* (Cour de cassation 18 November 1986) (Journal du droit international (Clunet) (Paris), vol. 114 (1987), p. 632) involving the aval guaranteed by the Banque camerounaise de développement, a public bank, on bills of exchange drawn by the State of Cameroon for the financing of the construction of a public hospital in Yaoundé, the court upheld the restrictive view of State immunity based on the distinction between the State as puissance publique and as personne privée, and held that, regardless of the cause of the difference, the aval guaranteed by the bank on behalf of the State of Cameroon is a commercial transaction entered into in the normal exercise of banking activities and is not related to the exercise of puissance publique. See also, *Banque Tejarat-Iran v. S.A. Tunzini Nessi Entreprises Equipements* (Cour d'appel de Paris, 29 November 1982) (Recueil Dalloz-Sirey, 1983, Inf. rap., p. 302).

[118] A survey of the Netherlands courts indicates that, after the passage of a bill in 1917 allowing the courts to apply State immunity with reference to acta jure imperii, the question of acta jure gestionis remained open until 1923, when a distinction between the two categories of acts was made. However, the Netherlands courts remained reluctant to consider any activities performed by Governments to be other than an exercise of governmental functions. Thus a public service of tug boats, State loans raised by public subscription and the operation of a State ship were all considered to be acta jure imperii; see, respectively, *F. Advokaat v. Schuddinck & den Belgischen Staat* (1923) (footnote 59 above), *De Froe v. The Russian State, now styled "The Union of Soviet Socialist Republics"* (1932) (footnote 25 above) and *The "Garbi"* (1938) (Weekblad van het Recht en Nederlandse Jurisprudentie (Zwolle), No. 96 (1939); Annual Digest . . ., 1919–1942 (London), vol. 11 (1947), case No. 83, p. 155).

It was not until 1947 that the Netherlands courts were able to find and apply a more workable criterion for restricting State immunity, holding that "the principles of international law concerning the immunity of States from foreign jurisdiction did not apply to State-conducted undertakings in the commercial, industrial or financial fields"; see *Weber v. USSR* (1942) (Weekblad van het Recht en Nederlandse Jurisprudentie (Zwolle), No. 757 (1942); Annual Digest . . ., 1919–1942 (London), vol. 11 (1947), case No. 74, p. 140) and *The Bank of the Netherlands v. The State Trust Arktikugol (Moscow); The Trade Delegation of the USSR in Germany (Berlin); The State Bank of the USSR (Moscow)* (1943) (Weekblad van het Recht *en Nederlandse Jurisprudentie (Zwolle), No. 600 (1943); Annual Digest . . ., 1943–1945 (London), vol. 12 (1949), case No. 26, p. 101). The exception of trading activities, however, was more clearly stated in the 1973 decision of the Netherlands Supreme Court in Société européenne d'études et d'entreprises en liquidation volontaire v. Socialist Federal Republic of Yugoslavia (Netherlands Yearbook of International Law (Leiden), vol. V (1974), p. 290; reproduced in United Nations, Materials on Jurisdictional Immunities . . ., p. 355). See also L. F. and H. M. H. K. v. Federal Republic of Germany (FRG) (District Court of Haarlem, 7 May 1986, KG (1986) No. 322, NJ (1987) No. 955, Netherlands Yearbook of International Law (Leiden), vol. XX (1989), p. 285, at 287–290).*

[119]   *The practice of Austria has fluctuated, starting with unqualified immunity in the nineteenth century, changing to restrictive immunity from 1907 to 1926, and reverting to unqualified immunity until 1950. In Dralle v. Republic of Czechoslovakia, decided in 1950, the Supreme Court of Austria reviewed existing authorities on international law before reaching a decision denying immunity for what were not found to be acta jure gestionis. The Court declared:*

> *". . . This subjection of the acta gestionis to the jurisdiction of States has its basis in the development of the commercial activity of States. The classic doctrine of immunity arose at a time when all the commercial activities of States in foreign countries were connected with their political activities . . . Today the position is entirely different; States engage in commercial activities and . . . enter into competition with their own nationals and with foreigners. Accordingly, the classic doctrine of immunity has lost its meaning, and, ratione cessante, can no longer be recognized as a rule of international law." (See footnote 25 above.)*

[120]   *See footnote 113 above.*

[121]   *In its decision in 1981 in A. M. Qureshi v. Union of Soviet Socialist Republics through Trade Representative in Pakistan and another (All Pakistan Legal Decisions (Lahore), vol. XXXIII (1981), p. 377), the Supreme Court of Pakistan, after reviewing the laws and practice of other jurisdictions, as well as relevant international conventions and opinions of writers, and confirming with approval the distinction between acta jure imperii and acta jure gestionis, held that the courts of Pakistan had jurisdiction in respect of commercial acts of a foreign Government.*

[122]   *An examination of the case law of Argentina reveals that the courts have recognized and applied the principle of sovereign immunity in various cases concerning sovereign acts of a foreign Government; see, for example, BAIMA y BESSOLINO v. Gobierno del Paraguay (1916) (Argentina, Fallos de la Corte Suprema de Justicia de la Nación (Buenos Aires), decision No. 123, p. 58), United States Shipping Board v. Dodero Hermanos (1924) (ibid., decision No. 141, p. 129) and Zubiaurre v. Gobierno de Bolivia (1899) (ibid., decision No. 79, p. 124); all cases referred to in United Nations, Materials on Jurisdictional Immunities . . ., pp. 73–74. The exception of trading activities was applied in The S.S. "Aguila" case (1892) in respect of a contract of sale to be performed and complied within the jurisdictional limits of the Argentine Republic (see Ministro Plenipotenciario de Chile v. Fratelli Lavarello (ibid., decision No. 47, p. 248). The court declared itself competent and ordered the case to proceed on the grounds that "the intrinsic validity of this contract and all matters relating to it should be regulated in accordance with the general laws of the Nation and that the national courts are competent in such matters" (see extract of the decision in United Nations, Materials on Jurisdictional Immunities . . ., p. 73). See also I. Ruiz Moreno, El Derecho Internacional Publico ante la Corte Suprema (Editorial Universitaria de Buenos Aires, 1941).*

[123]   *See the fourth report of the former Special Rapporteur (footnote 13 above), para. 92. For example, in The United States of America, Capt. James E. Galloway, William I. Collins and Robert Gohier, petitioners, v. Hon. v. M. Ruiz (Presiding Judge of Branch XV, Court of First Instance of Rizal and Eligio de Guzman & Co. Inc., respondents, No. L-35645, 22 May 1985, the Supreme Court of the Philippines, en banc, Philippine Yearbook of International Law, vol. XI (1985), p. 87), the Supreme Court of the Philippines held that contracts to repair a naval base related to the defence of a nation, a governmental function, and did not fall under the State immunity exception for commercial activities. There appear to be, however, no decisions upholding the exception of commercial transactions from State immunity. A similar situation is found in Chile, See the fourth report of the former Special Rapporteur (footnote 13 above [Not here reproduced]), para. 91.*

[124]   *See sections 1604 and 1605 (footnote 40 above).*

[125]   *See section 3 under "Exceptions from immunity" (footnote 51 above).*

[126]   *The State Immunity Ordinance of 1981, section 5 (ibid.).*

[127]   *State Immunity Act of 1979, section 5 (ibid.).*

[128]   *The South Africa Foreign States Immunities Act of 1981, section 4(1) (ibid.).*

¹²⁹ *The Australia Foreign States Immunities Act of 1985, section II (1) and (2) (ibid.).*

¹³⁰ *Act to Provide for State Immunity in Canadian Courts (State Immunity Act), section 5 (see footnote 57 above).*

¹³¹ *This view was substantiated by a member of the Commission. See the statement by Mr. Tsuruoka during the thirty-third session of the Commission, in which he referred to the trade treaties concluded by Japan with the United States of America in 1953 and with the USSR in 1957 (Yearbook . . . 1981, vol. I, p. 63, 1654th meeting, para. 23).*

¹³² *United Nations, Treaty Series, vol. 221, p. 95, art. 10. See similar provisions in treaties concluded by the USSR with Denmark (1946) (ibid., vol. 8, p. 201); Finland (1947) (ibid., vol. 217, p. 3); Italy (1948) (ibid., p. 181); Austria (1955) (ibid., vol. 240, p. 289); Japan (1957) (ibid., vol. 325, p. 35); Federal Republic of Germany (1958) (ibid., vol. 346, p. 71); the Netherlands (1971) (Tractatenblad van het Koninkrijk der Nederlanden (The Hague, 1971), No. 163). The relevant provisions of these treaties are reproduced in English in United Nations, Materials on Jurisdictional Immunities . . . , pp. 140–144.*

¹³³ *United Nations, Treaty Series, vol. 240, p. 157. See also similar provisions in treaties concluded by the USSR with other developing countries, such as Egypt (1956) (ibid., vol. 687, p. 221); Iraq (1958) (ibid., vol. 328, p. 118); Togo (1961) (ibid., vol. 730, p. 187); Ghana (1961) (ibid., vol. 655, p. 171); Yemen (1963) (ibid., vol. 672, p. 315); Brazil (1963) (ibid., vol. 646, p. 277); Singapore (1966) (ibid., vol. 631, p. 125); Costa Rica (1970) (ibid., vol. 957, p. 347); Bolivia (1970) (ibid., p. 373). The relevant provisions of these treaties are reproduced in English in United Nations, Materials on Jurisdictional Immunities . . ., pp. 145–150.*

¹³⁴ *Article 7 provides:*

> *"1. A Contracting State cannot claim immunity from the jurisdiction of a court of another Contracting State if it has on the territory of the State of the forum an office, agency or other establishment through which it engages, in the same manner as a private person, in an industrial, commercial or financial activity, and the proceedings relate to that activity of the office, agency or establishment."*
> *"2. Paragraph 1 shall not apply if all the parties to the dispute are States, or if the parties have otherwise agreed in writing."*

¹³⁵ *Article 1 provides:*

> *"Seagoing vessels owned or operated by States, cargoes owned by them, and cargoes and passengers carried on government vessels and the States owning or operating such vessels, or owning such cargoes, are subject in respect of claims relating to the operation of such vessels or the carriage of such cargoes, to the same rules of liability and to the same obligations as those applicable to private vessels, cargoes and equipment."*

¹³⁶ *See, for example, the materials submitted by the Government of Barbados: "The Barbados Government is . . . at the moment in the process of considering such legislation [as the United Kingdom State Immunity Act of 1978] and in addition is spearheading efforts for a Caribbean Convention on State Immunity." (United Nations, Materials on Jurisdictional Immunities . . ., pp. 74–75.)*

¹³⁷ *Inter-American Draft Convention on Jurisdictional Immunity of States, adopted on 21 January 1983 by the Inter-American Juridical Committee (OEA/Ser.G-CP/doc. 1352/83 of 30 March 1983). See also ILM (Washington, D. C.), vol. 22 (1983), No. 2, p. 292.*

¹³⁸ *According to the second paragraph of article 5 of the draft Convention, "trade or commercial activities of a State" are construed to mean the performance of a particular transaction or commercial or trading act pursuant to its ordinary trade operations.*

¹³⁹ *See also the contributions from non-governmental bodies surveyed in the fourth report of the former Special Rapporteur (see footnote 13 above [Not here reproduced]), pp. 226–227. See further, for recent developments, Yearbook of the Institute of International Law, 1989, vol. 63, part II, session of Santiago de Compostela, 1989; and ILA, Queensland Conference (1990), International Committee on State Immunity, First Report on Developments in the field of State Immunity since 1982.*

¹⁴⁰ *See, for example, the European Convention on State Immunity, article 27 and the Union of Soviet Socialist Republics–United States Agreement on Trade Relations of 1 June 1990, article XII (1).*

Provisions similar to the USSR–United States Agreement are found also in the Czechoslovakia–United States Agreement on Trade Relations of 12 April 1990, article XIV (1) and in the Mongolia–United States Agreement on Trade Relations of 23 January 1991, article XII (1).

¹⁴¹ *See, for example, the United Kingdom State Immunity Act of 1978, section 14 (1), (2) and (3); the Singapore State Immunity Act of 1979, section 16 (1), (2) and (3); the Pakistan State Immunity Ordinance*

of 1981, section 15 (1), (2) and (3); the South Africa Foreign States Immunities Act of 1981, sections 1 (2) and 15; the Australia Foreign Immunities Act of 1985, section 3 (1) (footnote 51 above) and the Canada Act to Provide for State Immunity in Canadian Courts of 1982, sections 2, 3 (1), 11 (3) and 13 (2) (footnote 57 above). See also, the United States Foreign Sovereign Immunities Act of 1976, section 1603 (a) and (b) and section 1606 (footnote 40 above) as well as section 452 of the Third Restatement.

National legislation specially relevant in the present context has been recently enacted in several socialist States. See, for example, Law of the Union of Soviet Socialist Republics on State enterprises (associations), dated 30 June 1987 (Vedomosti Verkhovnogo soveta SSR, 1 July 1987, No. 26 (2412) (Article 385, pp. 427–463) (section 1 (1), (2) and (6)); 1987 Decree on the Procedure for the Establishment on the Territory of the USSR and the Activities of Joint Enterprises with the Participation of Soviet Organizations and Firms of Capitalist and Developing Countries (Decree of the USSR Council of Ministers, adopted on 13 January 1987, No. 49, Sobraniye postanovlenii Pravitelstva SSSR (1987), No. 9, item 40; as amended by Decrees No. 352 of 17 March 1988 and No. 385 of 6 May 1989, Svod zakonov SSSR, IX, 50–19; Sobraniye postanovlenii Pravitelstva SSSR (1989), No. 23, item 75); Law of the Union of Soviet Socialist Republics on Cooperatives in the USSR, adopted by the Supreme Soviet of the USSR on 1 June 1988 (arts. 5, 7 and 8); Law of the People's Republic of China on Industrial Enterprises owned by the Whole People, adopted on 13 August 1988 at the first session of the Seventh National People's Congress (art. 2); General Principles of the Civil Law of the People's Republic of China, adopted at the fourth session of the Sixth National People's Congress, promulgated by Order No. 37 of the President of the People's Republic of China on 12 April 1986 and effective as of 1 January 1987 (arts. 36, 37 and 41); the Enterprise with Foreign Property Participation Act of the Czechoslovak Federal Republic, the Act of 19 April 1990 amending the Enterprise with Foreign Property Participation Act No. 173 of 1988, Coll. (arts. 2 and 4).

[142] *For the judicial practice of the United States of America, see, for example, Matter of SEDCO, Inc. (543 F. Supp., p. 561, United States District Court, Southern District, Texas, 30 March 1982); O'Connell Machinery Co. v. M. V. "Americana" and Italia Di Navigazione, SpA (734, F. 2d, p. 115, United States Court of Appeals, 2d Cir., 4 May 1984, ILR (London), vol. 81 (1990), p. 539). See, however, First National City Bank v. Banco Para el Comercio Exterior de Cuba (1983) (103 S. Ct., p. 2591, 17 June 1983, AJIL (Washington, D.C.), vol. 78 (1984), p. 230). See, further, Foremost-McKesson, Inc. v. Islamic Republic of Iran (905 F. 2d, p. 438, United States Court of Appeals, D.C. Cir., 15 June 1990), and Kalamazoo Spice Extraction Company v. The Provisional Military Government of Socialist Ethiopia (ILM (Washington, D.C.), vol. 24 (1985), p. 1277). Cf. Edlow International Co. v. Nuklearna Elektrarna Krsko (441, F. Supp., p. 827 (D.D.C. 1977), ILR (London), vol. 63 (1982), p. 100).*

For the judicial practice of the United Kingdom, see, for example, Congreso del Partido (1983) (The Law Reports, 1983, vol. I, p. 244) in which the Appeals Court said:

> *"State-controlled enterprises, with legal personality, ability to trade and to enter into contracts of private law, though wholly subject to the control of their State, are a well-known feature of the modern commercial scene. The distinction between them, and their governing State, may appear artificial, but it is an accepted distinction in the law of England and other States. Quite different considerations apply to a State-controlled enterprise acting on government directions on the one hand, and a State, exercising sovereign functions, on the other." (Ibid., p. 258, citations omitted.)*

Later in his opinion, Lord Wilberforce rejected the contention that commercial transactions entered into by State-owned organizations could be attributed to the Cuban Government:

> *"The status of these organizations is familiar in our courts, and it has never been held that the relevant State is in law answerable for their actions." (Ibid., p. 271.)*

See also Trendtex Trading Corp. v. Central Bank of Nigeria 1977) (footnote 53 above) in which the Court of Appeal ruled that the Bank was not an alter ego or organ of the Nigerian Government for the purpose of determining whether it could assert sovereign immunity; and C. Czarnikow Ltd. v. Centrala Handlu Zagranicznego Rolimpex (Court of Appeal (1978) Q. B. 176, House of Lords (1979) A.C. 351, ILR (London), vol. 64 (1983), p. 195) in which the House of Lords affirmed the decision of the lower court stating that, in the absence of clear evidence and definite findings that the foreign government took the action purely in order to extricate a State enterprise from State contract liability, the enterprise cannot be regarded as an organ of the State.

For the judicial practice of Canada, see, for example, Ferranti-Packard Ltd. v. Cushman Rentals Ltd. et al. (ibid., p. 63), and Bouchard v. J. L. Le Saux Ltée (1984) (45 O.R. (2d), p. 792, Ontario Supreme Court (Master's Chambers) (Canadian Yearbook of International Law, vol. XXIII (1985), pp. 416–417).

In the former case, the Ontario High Court of Justice (Divisional Court) held that the New York State Thruway Authority was not an organ or alter ego of the State of New York but an independent body constituted so as to conduct its own commercial activities and, therefore, was not entitled to sovereign immunity. In the latter case, although the Senior Master reached the decision to set aside the service on the James Bay Energy Corporation on the ground that the corporation was entitled to sovereign immunity as an organ of the government of Quebec, he did consider the question of whether there was any evidence to show that the corporation was engaged in purely private or commercial activities.

For the judicial practice of France, see, for example, Corporación del Cobre v. Braden Copper Corporation and Société Groupement d'Importation des Métaux (ILR, vol. 65 (1984), p. 57); Société des Ets. Poclain and Compagnie d'Assurance La Concorde v. Morflot USSR and Others (ibid., p. 67). In Société Nationale des Transports Routiers v. Compagnie Algérienne de Transit et d'Affrétement Serres et Pilaire and Another (1979) (ibid., p. 83 et seq.) the Court of Cassation held as follows:

"SNTR had a legal personality distinct from that of the Algerian State, was endowed with its own assets, against which the action of the creditors was exclusively directed, and performed commercial operations by transporting goods in the same way as an ordinary commercial undertaking. Having made these findings, the Court of Appeal correctly concluded, . . . that SNTR could not claim before a French court either to exploit assets belonging to the Algerian State or, even if such had been the case, to act pursuant to an act of public power or in the interests of a public service. It therefore followed that SNTR was not entitled either to jurisdictional immunity or immunity from execution."

For the judicial practice of Germany, which may be said to have applied both the structural and the functional tests, see, for example, Non-resident Petitioner v. Central Bank of Nigeria (1975) (ibid., p. 131) relating to a contract claim, in which the District Court of Frankfurt held that "[w]e need not decide whether, based on the responsibilities assigned to it, the respondent discharges sovereign functions and whether, under Nigerian law, the respondent acts as a legal personality and carried out in whole or in part the authority of the State in fulfilment of responsibilities under public law. The petitioner correctly points out that in accordance with general case law, legal publications and writings on international law, separate legal entities of a foreign State enjoy no immunity" (ibid., p. 134). The court added cautiously that, even if the defendant were a legally dependent government department, it would still not be entitled to immunity, since immunity from jurisdiction was only available in respect of acta jure imperii and not for acta jure gestionis. Also, in the National Iranian Oil Company Pipeline Contracts case, 1980 (ibid., p. 212), the Superior Provincial Court of Frankfurt held that there was no general rule of public international law to the effect that domestic jurisdiction was excluded for actions against a foreign State in relation to its non-sovereign activity (acta jure gestionis) and further stated as follows:

"In German case law and legal doctrine, it is predominantly argued that commercial undertakings of a foreign State which have been endowed with their own independent legal personality do not enjoy immunity . . . what is decisive is that the defendant is organized under Iranian law as a public limited company—that is as a legal person in private law enjoying autonomy vis-a-vis the Iranian State."

See further, In the Matter of Constitutional Complaints of the National Iranian Oil Company against Certain Orders of the District Court and the Court of Appeals of Frankfurt in Prejudgement Attachment Proceedings against the Complainant (37 WM Zeitschrift für Wirtschafts-und Bankrecht 722 (1983) (Federal Constitutional Court, 12 April 1983, ILM (Washington, D.C.), vol. 22 (1983), p. 1279).

For the judicial practice of Switzerland, see, for example, Banque Centrale de la République de Turquie v. Weston Compagnie de Finance et d'Investissement SA (1978) (ILR (London), vol. 65 (1984), p. 417), in which the Federal Tribunal rejected the plea of immunity on the ground that the agreement for the provision of a "time deposit" between two commercial banks, to which a State was not a party and which had been concluded according to prevailing international banking practice, was to be classified according to its nature as a contract under private law (jure gestionis) over which the Swiss courts had jurisdiction. In this case, it seems that the ratione materiae approach weighed. But, also in this case, it was indicated that the State Bank was deemed to be like a private bank as far as the transaction in question was concerned. See also Banco de la Naciön Lima v. Banco Cattolica del Veneto (1984) (ILR (London), vol. 82 (1990), p. 10); Swissair v. X and Another (Federal Tribunal, 1985, ibid., p. 36) and Banque du Gothard v. Chambre des Recours en Matière Pénale du Tribunal d'Appel du Canton du Tessin and Another (Federal Tribunal, 1987, ibid., p. 50). In the latter case the bank deposits of the Vatican City Institute were dealt with in the same manner as that of a foreign State bank.

Some other cases relevant to the question of State enterprises or other entities in relation to immunity of States from the jurisdiction of foreign courts include Belgium: S.A. "Dhlellemes et Masurel" v. Banque

Centrale de la République de Turquie (Court of Appeal of Brussels, 1963, ILR (London), vol. 45 (1972), p. 85); Italy: Hungarian Papal Institute v. Hungarian Institute (Academy) in Rome (Court of Cassation, 1960 (ibid.), vol. 40 (1970), p. 59).

The judicial practice of developing countries on foreign State enterprises or entities is not readily discernible due to the lack of information. With regard to the practice of Indian courts see, for example, New Central Jute Mills Co. Ltd. v. VEB Deutfracht Seereederei Rostock (Calcutta High Court, A.I.R. 1983, cal. 225, Indian Journal of International Law, vol. 23 (1983), p. 589) in which the Court held that VEB Deutfracht Seereederei Rostock which was a company incorporated under the laws of the German Democratic Republic was not a "State" for the purpose of national legislation requiring consent of the Indian Central Government to sue a foreign State, but did not decide whether the entity should be considered as part of a State for the purposes of jurisdictional immunity under international law.

[143] *See C. Schreuer, State Immunity: Some Recent Developments (Cambridge, Grotius Publications, 1988), pp. 92–124.*

[144] *See, for example, S. v. Etat indien (Federal Tribunal, 22 May 1984) (Annuaire suisse de droit international, vol. 41 (1985), p. 172) concerning the dismissal of a locally recruited Italian national originally employed by the Embassy of India to Switzerland as a radio-telegraphist, subsequently carrying out drafting, translation and photography, finally working as an office employee. The court held that, since the employee was an Italian national, carried out activities of a subordinate nature and had been recruited outside India, he had no link with the State of India and exercise of jurisdiction on the case could not cause any prejudice to the discharge of State functions, and, therefore, that the employment contract was not in the realm of the puissance publique of India and that the Swiss courts had jurisdiction over the case.*

[145] *See, for example, the judicial practice of Italy: Console generale britannico in Napoli v. Ferraino (Corte di Cassazione (Sezioni Unite), 17 January 1986, No. 283, The Italian Yearbook of International Law, vol. VII (1986–1987), pp. 298–299); Console generale belga in Napoli v. Esposito (Corte di Cassazione (Sezioni Unite), 3 February 1986, No. 666, ibid.); Panattoni v. Repubblica federale di Germania (Corte di Cassazione, 15 July 1987) (Rivista . . ., vol. LXXI (1988), p. 902).*

For the judicial practice of some other States, see, for example, Poland: Maria B. v. Austrian Cultural Institute in Warsaw (Supreme Court, 25 March 1987, ILR (London), vol. 82 (1990), p. 1); Germany: Conrades v. United Kingdom of Great Britain and Northern Ireland (Hanover Labour Court, 4 March 1981, ibid., vol. 65 (1984), p. 205); Belgium: Portugal v. Goncalves (Civil Court of Brussels, Second Chamber, 11 March 1982, ibid., vol. 82 (1990), p. 115); Switzerland: Tsakos v. Government of the United States of America (Labour Tribunal of Geneva, 1 February 1972, ibid., vol. 75 (1987), p. 78); United Kingdom: Sengupta v. Republic of India (Employment Appeal Tribunal, 17 November 1982, ibid., vol. 64 (1983), p. 352).

[146] *See, for example, in the judicial practice of Italy, the interesting decision rendered in 1947 by the Corte di Cassazione (Sezioni Unite) in Tani v. Rappresentanza commerciale in Italia dell'U.R.S.S. (Il Foro Italiano (Rome), vol. LXXI (1948), p. 855; Annual Digest . . ., 1948 (London), vol. 15 (1953), case No. 45, p. 141), in which the Soviet Trade Delegation was held to be exempt from jurisdiction in matters of employment of an Italian citizen, being acta jure imperii, notwithstanding the fact that the appointing authority was a separate legal entity, or for that matter a foreign corporation established by a State. Also in this case, no distinction was made between diplomatic and commercial activities of the trade agency. Similarly, in 1955, in Department of the Army of the United States of America v. Gori Savellini (see footnote 111 above), the Corte di Cassazione declined jurisdiction in an action brought by an Italian citizen in respect of his employment by a United States military base established in Italy in accordance with the North Atlantic Treaty, this being an attività publicistica connected with the funzioni pubbliche o politiche of the United States Government. The act of appointment was performed in the exercise of governmental authority, and as such considered to be an atto di sovranità.*

In Rappresentanza commerciale dell' U.R.S.S. v. Kazmann (1933), Rivista . . . (Rome), vol. XXV (1933), p. 240; Annual Digest . . ., 1933–1934 (London), vol. 7 (1940), case No. 69, p. 178, concerning an action for wrongful dismissal brought by an ex-employee of the Milan branch of the Soviet Trade Delegation, the Italian Supreme Court upheld the principle of immunity. This decision became a leading authority followed by other Italian courts in other cases, such as Little v. Riccio e Fischer (Court of Appeal of Naples, 1933) (Rivista . . ., vol. XXVI (1934), p. 110) (Court of Cassation, 1934) (Annual Digest . . ., 1933–1934, case No. 68, p. 177); the Court of Appeal of Naples and the Court of Cassation disclaimed jurisdiction in this action for wrongful dismissal by Riccio, an employee in a cemetery the property of the British Crown and "maintained by Great Britain jure imperii for the benefit of her nationals as such, and not for them as individuals". Furthermore, in another case, Luna v. Repubblica socialista di Romania

(1974) (Rivista . . . (Milan), vol. LVIII (1975), p. 597), concerning an employment contract concluded by an economic agency forming part of the Romanian Embassy, the Supreme Court dismissed Luna's claim for 7,799,212 lire as compensation for remuneration based on the employment contract. The court regarded such labour relations as being outside Italian jurisdiction.

See the practice of Dutch courts, for example, in M.K. v. Republic of Turkey (The Hague Sub-District Court, 1 August 1985, Institute's Collection No. R 2569; Netherlands Yearbook of International Law, vol. XIX (1988), p. 435) concerning the application for a declaration of nullity in respect of the dismissal of a Dutch secretary employed at the Turkish Embassy in The Hague. The court held that the conclusion of a contract of employment with a Dutch clerical worker who had no diplomatic or civil service status was an act which the defendant performed on the same footing as a natural or legal person under private law and that there was no question whatsoever there of a purely governmental act; the defendant, who was represented by his ambassador, entered into a legal transaction on the same footing as a natural or legal person under private law. The court accordingly decided that the defendant's plea of immunity must therefore be rejected and further that since the defendant gave notice of dismissal without the consent of the Director of the Regional Employment Office [Gewestelijk Arbeidsbureau], without K's consent and without any urgent reason existing or even having been alleged, the dismissal was void.

See also the practice of Spanish courts, for example, in E.B.M. v. Guinea Ecuatorial (Tribunal Supremo, 10 February 1986, abstract in Revista Española de Derecho Internacional, vol. 40, II (1988), p. 10) concerning the application of a Spanish national for reinstatement as a receptionist at the Embassy of Equatorial Guinea. The court said that granting Equatorial Guinea immunity from jurisdiction would imply an extension by analogy of the rules on diplomatic immunity and the recognition of absolute immunity of States from jurisdiction as a basic principle or customary rule of international law, while this principle was presently being questioned by the doctrine, and national courts were exercising their jurisdiction over sovereign States in matters in the sphere of acta jure gestionis; and in D. A. v. Sudáfrica (Tribunal Supremo, 1 December 1986, ibid., p. 11) in which the court upheld the application of a non-Spanish national for reinstatement as a secretary in the Embassy of South Africa, stating that acta jure gestionis were an exception to the general rules on jurisdictional immunity of States.

With regard to the practice of Belgian courts see, for example, Castanheira v. Office commercial du Portugal (1980) (Tribunal du travail de Bruxelles, abstract in Revue belge de droit international, vol. 19 (1986), p. 368) which related to an employment contract between a Portuguese national and the Portuguese public entity Fundo de Fomenteo de Exportacao. The Tribunal held that while, as an emanation of the State, the entity could in principle enjoy immunity from jurisdiction, the employment contract had the characteristics of an acte de gestion privée.* Immunity was therefore denied.

[147] *With regard to the provision of paragraph 2 (c) of article 11, see, for example, the United Kingdom State Immunity Act of 1978 which provides in subsection (2) (b) of section 4 that the non-immunity provided for in subsection (1) of that section does not apply if:*

"(b) at the time when the contract was made the individual was neither a national of the United Kingdom nor habitually resident there; . . ."

Subsection (2) (b) of section 6 of the Pakistan State Immunity Ordinance of 1981, subsection (2) (b) of section 6 of the Singapore State Immunity Act of 1979, subsection (1) (b) of section 5 of the South Africa Foreign States Immunities Act of 1981 (ibid.), section 12 (3) of the Australia Foreign States Immunities Act of 1985 (see footnote 51 above), and paragraph 2 (b) of article 5 of the European Convention on State Immunity are worded in similar terms.

The United Kingdom State Immunity Act of 1978 (sect. 4, subsect. (2) (a)), the Pakistan State Immunity Ordinance of 1981 (sect. 6, subsect. (2) (a)), the Singapore State Immunity Act of 1979 (sect. 6, subsect. 2 (a)), the South Africa Foreign States Immunities Act of 1981 (sect. 5, subsect. (1) (c)) and the European Convention (art. 5, para. 2 (a)) grant immunity to the employer State if the employee is a national of that State at the time when the proceeding is instituted.

[148] *See the State practice cited in the fifth report of the former Special Rapporteur (footnote 13 above), paras. 76–99. See also Australia Foreign States Immunities Act of 1985, section 13 (footnote 51 above).*

[149] *See, for example, the possibilities unfolded in Letelier v. Republic of Chile (1980) (United States of America, Federal Supplement, vol. 488 (1980), p. 665); see also H. D. Collums, "The Letelier case: Foreign sovereign liability for acts of political assassination", Virginia Journal of International Law (Charlottesville, Va.), vol. 21 (1981), p. 251. Chile-United States Agreement to Settle Dispute Concerning Compensation for the Deaths of Letelier and Moffit. Done at Santiago, 11 June 1990, ILM (Washington, D.C.), vol. 30 (1991), p. 421.*

See also Olsen v. Mexico (729 F.2d, p. 641, United States Court of Appeals, 9th Cir., 30 March 1984, as amended 16 July 1984); Frolova v. Union of Soviet Socialist Republics (1985) (see footnote 77 above); Gerritsen v. De La Madrid (819 F.2d, p. 1511, United States Court of Appeals, 9th Cir., 18 June 1987); Helen Liu v. The Republic of China (Court of Appeals, 9th Cir., 29 December 1989, ILM (Washington, D.C.), vol. 29 (1990), p. 192). However, acts committed outside the territory of the State of the forum are excluded from the application of this article. See, for example, United States: McKeel v. Islamic Republic of Iran (United States Court of Appeals, 9th Cir., 30 December 1983, ILR (London), vol. 81 (1990), p. 543); Perez et al v. The Bahamas, Court of Appeals, District of Columbia Circuit, 28 April 1981, ibid., vol. 63 (1982), p. 601; Berkovitz v. Islamic Republic of Iran and Others, United States Court of Appeals, 9th Cir., 1 May 1984, ibid., vol. 81 (1990), p. 552; Argentine Republic v. Amerada Hess Shipping Corp. (488 US428, United States Supreme Court, 23 January 1989, AJIL (Washington, D.C.), vol. 83 (1989), p. 565).

[150] *In some countries, where proceedings cannot be instituted directly against the insurance company, this exception is all the more necessary. In other countries, there are legislative enactments making insurance compulsory for representatives of foreign States, such as the United States Foreign Missions Amendments Act of 1983 (Public Law 98–164 of 22 November 1983, title VI, sect. 603 (United States Statutes at Large, 1983, vol. 97, p. 1042)), amending the United States Code, title 22, section 204.*

[151] *See, for example, the judgements delivered in Belgium, in S.A. "Eau, gaz, électricité et applications" v. Office d'aide mutuelle (1956) (Pasicrisie belge (Brussels), vol. 144 (1957), part 2, p. 88; ILR, 1956 (London), vol. 23 (1960), p. 205); in the Federal Republic of Germany, in Immunity of United Kingdom from Jurisdiction (Germany) (1957) (ibid., 1957, vol. 24 (1961), p. 207); in Egypt, in Dame Safia Guebali v. Colonel Mei (1943) (Bulletin de législation et de jurisprudence égyptiennes (Alexandria), vol. 55 (1942–1943), p. 120; Annual Digest . . ., 1943–1945 (London), vol. 12 (1949), case No. 44, p. 164); in Austria, in Holubek v. Government of the United States (1961) (Juristische Biätter (Vienna), vol. 84 (1962), p. 43; ILR (London), vol. 40 (1970), p. 73); in Canada, in Carrato v. United States of America (1982) (141 D.L.R. (3d), p. 456, Ontario High Court; Canadian Yearbook of International Law, vol. XXII (1984), p. 403); and in the United States, in Tel-Oren v. Libyan Arab Republic, United States Brief Submitted to Supreme Court in Response to Court's Invitation in Reviewing Petition for a Writ of Certiorari (ILM (Washington, D.C.), vol. 24 (1985), p. 427).*

[152] *Examples include the various status of forces agreements and international conventions on civil aviation or on the carriage of goods by sea.*

[153] *See article 6 and the commentary thereto.*

[154] *See the fifth report of the former Special Rapporteur (footnote 13 above), where he discusses the decision and dictum of a Tokyo court in Limbin Hteik Tin Lat v. Union of Burma (1954) (ibid., para. 117) as well as the dictum of Lord Denning, Master of the Rolls, in Thai-Europe Tapioca Service Ltd v. Government of Pakistan, Ministry of Food and Agriculture, Directorate of Agricultural Supplies (1975) (ibid., para 118; see also footnote 45 above). For the English doctrine of trust, see the cases cited in paras. 120–121 of the fifth report. The case law of other countries has also recognized this exception, especially Italian case law (ibid., para. 122). See, however, the decision of a Brazilian court in Republic of Syria v. Arab Republic of Egypt (footnote 106 above).*

[155] *See footnote 14 above [Not here reproduced].*

[156] *See, for example, the Universal Copyright Convention. There is also a United Nations specialized agency, WIPO, involved in this field.*

For relevant legislative provisions, reference may be made to section 56 of Hungary's Law Decree No. 13 of 1979, to article 29 of Madagascar's Ordinance No. 62–041 of 19 September 1962 and to the information given in other replies to the secretariat's questionnaire (paras. 125–129 of the fifth report), as well as to section 14 of the Australia Foreign States Immunities Act of 1985 (see footnote 51 above). For discussion of other legislative provisions, international conventions and international opinions, see fifth report, paras. 130–139. See, further, comments and observations of Governments analysed in the present Special Rapporteur's preliminary report (see footnote 16 above [Not here reproduced]), paras. 1, 2 and 7–9).

[157] *Domestic legislation adopted since 1970 supports this view, see section 7 of the United Kingdom State Immunity Act of 1978; section 9 of the Singapore State Immunity Act of 1979; section 8 of the Pakistan State Immunity Ordinance of 1981; section 8 of the South Africa Foreign States Immunities Act of 1981; section 15 of the Australia Foreign States Immunities Act of 1985 (see footnote 51 above). The United States Foreign Sovereign Immunities Act of 1976 (see footnote 40 above) contains no direct provision on this. Section 1605 (a) (2) of the Act may in fact be said to have overshadowed, if not substantially overlapped, the use of copyrights and other similar rights. The European Convention on State Immunity, in*

its article 8, supports the above view. A leading case in support of this view is the decision of the Austrian Supreme Court in Dralle v. Republic of Czechoslovakia (1950) (see footnote 25 above).

[158] *See footnote 14 above [Not here reproduced].*

[159] *Recent national legislation on jurisdictional immunities of States may be cited in support of this exception. See, for example, section 8 of the United Kingdom State Immunity Act of 1978; section 10 of the Singapore State Immunity Act of 1979; section 9 of the Pakistan State Immunity Ordinance of 1981; section 9 of the South Africa Foreign States Immunities Act of 1981; and section 16 of the Australia Foreign States Immunities Act of 1985 (see footnote 51 above).*

This exception appears to have been included in the broader exception of trade or commercial activities conducted or undertaken in the State of the forum provided in the United States of America Foreign Sovereign Immunities Act of 1976, section 1605 (a) (2) (see footnote 40 above), in the European Convention, and in the Inter-American Draft Convention on Jurisdictional Immunity of States (see footnote 137 above).

[160] *See, for example, the Protocol of 1 March 1974 to the Treaty of Merchant Navigation of 3 April 1968 between the United Kingdom and the Soviet Union (United Kingdom, Treaty Series No. 104 (1977)). See also the treaties on maritime navigation concluded between the Soviet Union and the following States: France, Maritime Agreement of 20 April 1967 (art. 14) (United Nations, Treaty Series, vol. 1007, p. 183); Netherlands, Agreement of 28 May 1969 concerning shipping (art. 16) (ibid., vol. 815, p. 159); Bulgaria, Czechoslovakia, German Democratic Republic, Hungary, Poland, Romania, Agreement of 3 December 1971 on cooperation with regard to maritime merchant shipping (art. 13) (ibid., vol. 936, p. 19); Algeria, Agreement of 18 April 1973 concerning maritime navigation (art. 16) (ibid., vol. 990, p. 211); Iraq, Agreement of 25 April 1974 on maritime merchant shipping (art. 15); Portugal, Agreement of 20 December 1974 on maritime navigation (art. 15). Cf. M.M. Boguslavsky, "Foreign State immunity: Soviet doctrine and practice", Netherlands Yearbook of International Law (Alphen aan den Rijn), vol. X (1979), pp. 173–174.*

[161] *See G. van Slooten, "La Convention de Bruxelles sur le statut juridique des navires d'État", Revue de droit international et de législation comparée (Brussels), 3rd series, vol. VII (1926), p. 453, in particular p. 457.*

[162] *See footnote 14 above [Not here reproduced].*

[163] *See the United Nations Convention on the Carriage of Goods by Sea.*

[164] *See the sixth report of the former Special Rapporteur (footnote 13 above), paras. 136–230.*

See also for recent legislative practice, the South Africa Foreign States Immunities Act of 1981 (section 11) (footnote 51 above); the United States Act to amend the Foreign Sovereign Immunities Act with respect to admiralty jurisdiction of 1988, Public Law 100–640, 102 stat. 3333 (section 1605 (b), as amended, and section 1610 as amended).

For the recent judicial practice, see, for example, Canada: Lorac Transport Ltd. v. The Ship "Atra" (1984) (9 D.L.R. (4th) 129, Federal Court, Trial Division, Canadian Yearbook of International Law, vol. XXIII (1985), pp. 417–418; The Netherlands: USSR v. I.C.C. Handel-Maatschappij; the United States of America: Trans-american Steamship Corp. v. Somali Democratic Republic (767 F.2d, p. 998, United States Court of Appeals, D.C. Cir., 12 July 1985, AJIL (Washington, D.C.), vol. 80 (1986), p. 357); China National Chemical Import and Export Corporation and Another v. M/V Lago Hualaihue and Another (District Court, Maryland, 6 January 1981, ILR (London), vol. 63 (1982), p. 528).

[165] *This issue was discussed in the Drafting Committee and referred to in the Commission (see Yearbook . . . 1991, vol. I, 2221st meeting, paras. 82–84).*

Treaties relating to international civil aviation law include the following:

    (a) Convention on International Civil Aviation, Chicago, 1944 (see, in particular, chapters I and II);

    (b) Convention for the Unification of Certain Rules Relating to International Carriage by Air, War-saw, 1929 (see arts. 1, 2 and the Additional Protocol);

    (c) Protocol to Amend the Convention for the Unification of Certain Rules Relating to International Carriage by Air Signed at Warsaw on 12 October 1929, The Hague, 1955 (see art. XXVI);

    (d) Convention supplementary to the Warsaw Convention for the Unification of Certain Rules Relating to International Carriage by Air Performed by a Person Other than the Contracting Carrier, Guadalajara, 1961;

    (e) Convention on the International Recognition of Rights in Aircraft, Geneva, 1948 (see arts. XI, XII and XIII);

    (f) Convention on Damage Caused by Foreign Aircraft to Third Parties on the Surface, Rome, 1952 (see arts. 1, 2, 20, 23 and 26);

    (g) Convention on Offences and Certain Other Acts Committed on Board Aircraft, Tokyo, 1963 (see art. 1);

(h) Convention for the Suppression of Unlawful Seizure of Aircraft, The Hague, 1970 (see art. 3);

(i) Convention for the Suppression of Unlawful Acts against the Safety of Civil Aviation, Montreal, 1971 (see art. 4).

Treaties relevant to space activities and space objects include the following:

(a) Treaty on Principles Governing the Activities of States in the Exploration and Use of Outer Space, including the Moon and Other Celestial Bodies (Outer Space Treaty) 1967;

(b) Agreement on the Rescue of Astronauts, the Return of Astronauts and the Return of Objects Launched into Outer Space 1968 (General Assembly resolution 2345 (XXII));

(c) Convention on International Liability for Damage Caused by Space Objects (Liability Convention) 1972;

(d) Convention on Registration of Objects Launched into Outer Space 1975;

(e) Agreement Governing the Activities of States on the Moon and Other Celestial Bodies (General Assembly resolution 34/68).

[166] See the sixth report of the former Special Rapporteur (footnote 13 above [Not here reproduced]), paras. 247–253. See, for example, France: Court of Cassation decision in Southern Pacific Properties Ltd. et al. v. Arab Republic of Egypt (6 January 1987, ILM (Washington, D.C.), vol. 26 (1987), p. 1004); Société Européenne d'Etudes et d'Entreprises v. Yougoslavie et al. (Court of Cassation, 18 November 1986, ILM (Washington, D.C.), vol. 26 (1986), p. 377). See also Switzerland: Decisions of the Court of Justice of Geneva and the Federal Tribunal (Excerpts) Concerning Award in Westland Helicopters Arbitration (19 July 1988, ibid., vol. 28 (1989), p. 687).

See further the United States Foreign Sovereign Immunities Act of 1976 (footnote 40 above); the United States has since adopted an Act to Implement the Inter-American Convention on International Commercial Arbitration of 1988, Public Law 100–669, 102 stat. 3969, amending sections 1605 (a) and 1610 (a) of the United States Foreign Sovereign Immunities Act of 1976.

[167] See, for example, the Agreement between Japan and the People's Republic of China concerning the Encouragement and Reciprocal Protection of Investment, article 11.

[168] See, for example, Maritime International Nominees Establishment v. Republic of Guinea (United States of America, intervenor) (1982) (The Federal Reporter, 2nd Series, vol. 693 (1983), p. 1094); Guinea v. Maritime International Nominees Establishment (Belgium, Court of First Instance of Antwerp, 27 September 1985, ILM (Washington, D.C.), vol. 24 (1985), p. 1639); Senegal v. Seutin as Liquidator of the West African Industrial Concrete Co. (SOABI) (France, Court of Appeal of Paris, 5 December 1989, ILM (Washington, D.C.), vol. 29 (1990), p. 1341); Socialist Libyan Arab Popular Jamahiriya v. Libyan American Oil Company (LIAMCO) (Switzerland, Federal Supreme Court, First Public Law Department, 19 June 1980, ILR (London), vol. 62 (1982), p. 228); Tekno-Pharma AB v. State of Iran (Sweden, Svea Court of Appeal, 24 May 1972, ibid., vol. 65 (1984), p. 383); Libyan American Oil Company v. Socialist People's Arab Republic of Libya (Sweden, Svea Court of Appeal, 18 June 1980, ibid., vol. 62 (1982), p. 225); Libyan American Oil Company v. Socialist People's Libyan Arab Jamahiriya, formerly Libyan Arab Republic (United States District Court, District of Columbia, 18 January 1980, ibid., p. 220). See, however, Atlantic Triton Company v. Popular Revolutionary Republic of Guinea and Société guinéenne de pêche (Soguipêche) (France, Court of Cassation, First Civil Chamber, 18 November 1986, ibid., vol. 82 (1990), p. 83), in which the court took the position that the exclusive character of ICSID arbitration set forth in article 26 of the ICSID Convention did not prevent a party to an ICSID proceeding from seeking in the French courts provisional measures in the form of attachment.

[169] See the jurisprudence cited in the former Special Rapporteur's seventh report (footnote 13 above [Not here reproduced]), paragraphs 73–77. See also the second report of the present Special Rapporteur (footnote 17 above [Not here reproduced]), paragraphs 42–44. Citing Schreuer (State Immunity: Some Recent Developments, p. 125) (see footnote 143 above), the Special Rapporteur observed that there were some writers who argued that allowing plaintiffs to proceed against foreign States and then to withhold from them the fruits of successful litigation through immunity from execution might put them into the doubly frustrating position of being left with an unenforceable judgement with expensive legal costs, although the majority views of Governments as well as writers were that immunity from measures of constraint was separate from the jurisdictional immunity of a State.

[170] See, for example, in the Société Commerciale de Belgique case, the judgement of PCIJ of 15 June 1939 concerning the arbitral awards of 3 January and 25 July 1936 (P.C.I.J. Series A/B, No. 78, p. 160) and the decision of 30 April 1951 of the Tribunal civil of Brussels (Journal de droit international (Clunet) (Paris), vol. 79 (1952), p. 244).

[171] *For the case law, international opinion, treaties and national legislation dealing with immunity from measures of constraint, see the seventh report of the former Special Rapporteur (footnote 13 above [Not here reproduced]), paragraphs 33–82, and the second report of the Special Rapporteur (footnote 17 above [Not here reproduced]), paras. 42–44.*

For recent legislation, see further the Australia Foreign States Immunities Act of 1985 (sections 30–35); the South Africa Foreign States Immunities Amendment Act of 1988 (section 14 (b)) (footnote 51 above); the United States Act to Implement the Inter-American Convention on International Commercial Arbitration (footnote 166 above).

For recent cases concerning the provision of paragraph 1 (a), see, for example, with respect to the require-ment of express consent by international agreement under subparagraph (i), O'Connell Machinery Co. v. MV Americana and Italia Di Navigazione, SpA (footnote 142 above), in which, despite an express waiver of immunity in article XXIV (6) of the Italy–United States Treaty of Friendship, Commerce and Naviga-tion, 1965, the Court did not interpret the treaty as providing for waiver of prejudgement attachment. See also, New England Merchants National Bank v. Iran Power Generation and Transmission Co., et al. (502 F. Supp 120, United States District Court for the Southern District of New York, 26 September 1980, AJIL (Washington, D.C.), vol. 75 (1981), p. 375); E-Systems Inc. v. Islamic Republic of Iran and Bank Melli Iran (United States District Court, Northern District, Texas, 19 June 1980, ILR (London), vol. 63 (1982), p. 424).

With regard to the requirement of express consent in a written contract under subparagraph (ii), see, for example, Libra Bank Limited v. Banco Nacional de Costa Rica (1982) (676 F.2d, p. 47, United States Court of Appeals, 2nd Cir., 12 April 1982, ILM (Washington, D.C.), vol. 21 (1982), p. 618), in which the court held that a written waiver by a foreign State of any right of immunity from suit with respect to a loan agreement constitutes an explicit waiver of immunity for prejudgement attachment for purposes of the Foreign Sovereign Immunities Act, section 1610 (d) (1). See, however, on the requirement of express consent by an arbitration agreement under subparagraph (ii), Birch Shipping Corp. v. Embassy of Tanzania (1980) (Misc. No. 80–247, United States District Court, District of Columbia, 18 November 1980, AJIL (Washington, D.C.), vol. 75 (1981), p. 373) in which the court found that the defendant in its submission to arbitration had implicitly agreed to waive immunity, including entry of judgement on any resulting award.

Cf. cases concerning measures of constraint in connection with ICSID proceedings: Popular Revolution-ary Republic of Guinea and Société guinéenne de pêche (Soguipêche) v. Atlantic Triton Company (France, Court of Appeal of Rennes, Second Chamber, 26 October 1984, ILR (London), vol. 82 (1990), p. 76); Atlantic Triton Company v. Popular Revolutionary Republic of Guinea and Société guinéenne de pêche (Soguipêche) (see footnote 168 above); Senegal v. Seutin as Liquidator of the West African Industrial Con-crete Co. (SOABI) (ibid.); Benvenuti et Bonfant SARL v. Government of the People's Republic of the Congo (France, Court of Appeal of Paris, 26 June 1981, ILR (London), vol. 65 (1984), p. 88); Société Benvenuti et Bonfant v. Banque commerciale congolaise (France, Cour de Cassation, 21 July 1987, Journal du droit international (Clunet) (Paris), vol. 115 (1988), p. 108); Guinea v. Maritime International Nominees Establishment (see footnote 168 above); Liberian Eastern Timber Corporation (LETCO) v. The Govern-ment of the Republic of Liberia (United States District Court for the Southern District of New York, 12 December 1986, ILM (Washington, D.C.), vol. 26 (1987), p. 695).

For recent cases concerning the provision of paragraph 1 (c), see, for example, Islamic Republic of Iran and Others v. Société Eurodif and Others (France, Court of Cassation, First Civil Chamber, 14 March 1984, ILR (London), vol. 77 (1988), p. 513) in which the court stated that notwithstanding the fact that foreign States enjoyed immunity from execution as a matter of principle, the immunity could be set aside where the assets attached had been allocated for a commercial activity of a private law nature upon which the claim was based. See also, General National Maritime Transport Company v. Société Marseille Fret (France, Court of Cassation, First Civil Chamber, 4 February 1986, ibid., p. 530); Re Royal Bank of Canada and Corriveau et al. (Canada, Ontario High Court, 22 October 1980, ibid., vol. 64 (1983), p. 69); Banque du Gothard v. Chambre des Recours en Matière Pénale du Tribunal d'Appel du Canton du Tessin and Another (footnote 142 above); Giamahiria araba libica popolare socialista v. Rossbeton Officine Meccaniche s.r.l. e Libyan Arab Airlines, Ministero degli affari esteri e Ministero di grazia e giustizia (Italy, Corte di Cassazione, 25 May 1989, Rivista di diritto inter-nazionale privato e processuale (Padua), vol. XXVI (1990), p. 663); cf. International Consolidated Companies Inc. v. Nigerian National Petroleum Corporation (Italy, Tribunale di Taranto, 18 December 1987, order, Rivista . . . (Milan), vol. LXXII (1989), p. 110).

On the question of the measures of constraint involving the property of State enterprises, see, for example, In the Matter of Constitutional Complaints of the National Iranian Oil Company Against Certain Orders of the District Court and the Court of Appeals of Frankfurt in Prejudgement Attachment Proceedings against the Complainant (footnote 142 above), in which the court found that there exists no general rule of international law mandating that accounts maintained in domestic banks and designated as accounts of a foreign government agency with separate legal personality be treated as property of the foreign State. The court indicated additionally that general international law does not require absolute immunity from execution of accounts standing in the name of the foreign State itself, but that immunity of accounts of a foreign Government held in banks located in the forum is to be accorded only if the account itself at the time of the levy is designed to be used for internationally protected governmental purposes. In Société Nationale Algérienne de Transport et de Commercialisation des Hydrocarbures (Sonatrach) v. Migeon (France, Court of Cassation, First Civil Chamber, 1 October 1985, ILM (Washington, D.C.), vol. 26 (1987), p. 998); ILR (London), vol. 77 (1988), p. 525), the court stated that, while the assets of a foreign State were not subject to attachment unless they had been allocated for a commercial activity under private law upon which the claim was based, the assets of a State-owned entity which was legally distinct from the foreign State concerned could be subjected to attachment by all debtors of that entity, of whatever type, provided that the assets formed part of a body of funds allocated for a principal activity governed by private law. See also, Société Air Zaire v. Gauthier and van Impe (France, Court of Appeal of Paris, First Chamber, 31 January 1984, ibid., p. 510).

In some legal systems, a sufficient legal relationship between the subject-matter and the State of the forum is also required for its courts to consider any order of attachment against property of a foreign State which is located in the territory of the State of the forum. See, for example, Socialist Libyan Arab Popular Jamahiriya v. Libyan American Oil Company (LIAMCO) (see footnote 168 above).

[172]   *For a more detailed account of the judicial and treaty practice of States and government contracts, see the former Special Rapporteur's seventh report (footnote 13 above [Not here reproduced]), paras. 85–102. In some jurisdictions, for example in Switzerland, execution is based on the existence of a sufficient connection with Swiss territory (Binnenbeziehung). See, for example, Greek Republic v. Walder and others (1930) (Recueil officiel des arrêts du Tribunal fédéral suisse, 1930, vol. 56, p. 237; Annual Digest . . ., 1929–1930 (London), vol. 5 (1935), case No. 78, p. 121); J.-F. Lalive, "Swiss law and practice in relation to measures of execution against the property of a foreign State", Netherlands Yearbook of International Law (Alphen aan den Rijn), vol. X (1979), p. 160; and I. Sinclair, "The law of sovereign immunity: Recent developments", Collected Courses . . ., 1980-II (Alphen aan den Rijn, Sijthoff and Noordhoff, 1981), vol. 167, p. 236. See also Lord Denning's observations in Thai-Europe Tapioca Service Ltd. v. Government of Pakistan, Ministry of Food and Agriculture, Directorate of Agricultural Supplies (1975) (footnote 45 above). On the requirement of a separate or second consent to execution, see the judgement of the Court of Appeal of Aix-en-Provence in Banque d'Etat tchécoslovaque v. Englander (1966) (Annuaire français de droit international, 1967 (Paris), vol. 13, p. 825; ILR (London), vol. 47 (1974), p. 157)—however, this judgement was set aside by the Court of Cassation (1969) (Journal du droit international (Clunet) (Paris), vol. 96 (1969), p. 923; ILR (Cambridge), vol. 52 (1979), p. 335); and Clerget v. Représentation commerciale de la République démocratique du Viet Nam (1969) (Annuaire français de droit international, 1970 (Paris), vol. 16, p. 931).*

[173]   *See, for example, Birch Shipping Corp. v. Embassy of Tanzania (1980) (footnote 171 above); the decision of 13 December 1977 of the Federal Constitutional Court of the Federal Republic of Germany in X v. Republic of the Philippines (United Nations, Materials on Jurisdictional Immunities . . ., p. 297); and Alcom Ltd. v. Republic of Colombia (1984) (The All England Law Reports, 1984, vol. 2, p. 6). See, also, Banco de la Nación Lima v. Banco Cattolica del Veneto (footnote 142 above).*

[174]   *See, for example, Hispano Americana Mercantil S.A. v. Central Bank of Nigeria (1979) (Lloyd's Law Reports, 1979, vol. 2, p. 277; reproduced in United Nations, Materials on Jurisdictional Immunities . . ., p. 449); Re Royal Bank of Canada and Corriveau et al. (1980) (footnote 171 above); Libra Bank Ltd. v. Banco Nacional de Costa Rica (1982) (ibid.); and Trendtex Trading Corporation Ltd. v. Central Bank of Nigeria (1977) (footnote 53 above). See also, Libyan Arab Socialist People's Jamahiriya v. Actimon SA (Switzerland, Federal Tribunal, 24 April 1985, ILR (London), vol. 82 (1990), p. 30). Cf. Banque Compafina v. Banco de Guatemala et al. (United States District Court for the Southern District of New York, 23 March 1984, ILM (Washington, D.C.), vol. 23 (1984), p. 782).*

[175]   *See, for example, the Romanian legation case (1949) (Revue hellénique de droit international (Athens), vol. 3 (1950), p. 331); and, in a case concerning a contract of employment at the Indian Embassy in Berne, J. Monnier, "Note à l'arrêt de la première Cour civile du Tribunal fédéral du 22 mai 1984 dans l'affaire S. contre Etat indien", Annuaire suisse de droit international (Zurich), vol. 41 (1985), p. 235.*

[176]   *See, for example, Alcom Ltd. v. Republic of Colombia (1984) (footnote 173 above). See also, Republic of "A" Embassy Bank Account Case (Austria, Supreme Court, 3 April 1986, ILR (London), vol. 77*

(1988), p. 489); M.K. v. State Secretary for Justice, Council of State, President of the Judicial Division (Netherlands, 24 November 1986, KG (1987) No. 38, AROB tB/S (1986) No. 189). Cf. Benamar v. Embassy of the Democratic and Popular Republic of Algeria (Italy, Corte di Cassazione, plenary session, 4 May 1989, AJIL (Washington, D.C.), vol. 84 (1990), p. 573).

[177] *See, for example, Griessen (Switzerland, Federal Tribunal, 23 December 1982, ILR (London), vol. 82 (1990), p. 5).*

[178] *See, for example, Benamar v. Embassy of the Democratic and Popular Republic of Algeria (footnote 176 above); Birch Shipping Corporation v. Embassy of Tanzania (footnote 171 above). See, however, Republic of "A" Embassy Bank Account Case (footnote 176 above).*

[179] *See, for example, Wijsmuller Salvage BV v. ADM Naval Services (Netherlands, District Court of Amsterdam, 19 November 1987, KG (1987), No. 527, S&S (1988), No. 69).*

[180] *Yearbook . . . 1990, vol. II (Part Two), para. 219.*

[181] *Ibid., p. 42, para. 227.*

[182] *See, for example, Italian State v. X and Court of Appeal of the Canton of the City of Basel (Switzerland, Federal Tribunal, 6 February 1985, ILR (London), vol. 82 (1990), p. 30).*

[183] *See, for example, the note dated 26 October 1984 of the Département fédéral des affaires étrangères, Direction du droit international public, of Switzerland (Annuaire suisse du droit international, vol. 41 (1985), p. 178).*

[184] *Cf. European Convention on State Immunity, article 16, paras. 1–3.*

For the relevant provisions in national legislation, see, for example, the United States Foreign Sovereign Immunities Act of 1976 (section 1608 (a)-(d)) (footnote 40 above); the United Kingdom State Immunity Act of 1978 (section 12 (1), (2), (3), (6) and (7)); the Singapore State Immunity Act of 1979 (section 14 (1), (2), (3), (6) and (7)); the Pakistan State Immunity Ordinance of 1981 (section 13 (1), (2), (3) and (6)); the South Africa Foreign States Immunities Act of 1981 (section 13 (1), (2), (3), (6) and (7)); the Australia Foreign States Immunities Act of 1985 (sections 23 to 26) (footnote 52 above) (ibid.); the Canada Act to Provide for State Immunity in Canadian Courts of 1982 (section 9) (footnote 57 above).

With regard to recent judicial practice, see, for example, Garden Contamination Case (1) (Federal Republic of Germany, Provincial Court (Landgericht) of Bonn, 11 February 1987, ILR (London), vol. 80 (1989), p. 367); New England Merchants National Bank and Others v. Iran Power Generation and Transmission Company and Others (see footnote 171 above); International Schools Service v. Government of Iran (United States District Court, New Jersey, 19 January 1981, ILR (London), vol. 63 (1982), p. 550); Velidor v. L.P.G. Benghazi (653 F.2d, p. 812, United States Court of Appeals, Third Circuit, 30 June 1981, ILM (Washington, D.C.), vol. 21 (1982), p. 621).

[185] *Cf. European Convention on State Immunity, article 16, para. 7.*

Comparable provisions are found, for example, in: the United States Foreign Sovereign Immunities Act of 1976 (section 1608 (e)) (see footnote 40 above); the United Kingdom State Immunity Act of 1978 (section 12 (4) and (5)); the Singapore State Immunity Act of 1979 (section 14 (4) and (5)); the Pakistan State Immunity Ordinance of 1981 (section 13 (4) and (5)); the South Africa Foreign States Immunities Act of 1981 (section 13 (4) and (5)); the Australia Foreign States Immunities Act of 1985 (sections 27 and 28) (see footnote 51 above); South Africa Foreign States Immunities Amendment Act of 1988 (section 13 (5)); the Canada Act to Provide for State Immunity in Canadian Courts of 1982 (section 10) (see footnote 57 above).

For the recent judicial practice, see, for example, Azeta BV v. Republic of Chile (Netherlands, District Court of Rotterdam, 5 December 1984, Institute's Collection No. 2334); Murphy v. Republic of Panama d.b.a Air Panama International (751 F. Suppl., p. 1540, United States District Court, Southern District, Florida, 12 December 1990).

[186] *Cf. European Convention on State Immunity, articles 17 and 18.*

For the relevant provisions in national legislation, see, for example: The Australia Foreign States Immunities Act of 1985 (section 29); the Pakistan State Immunity Ordinance of 1981 (section 14, 14 (2) (a), (3) and (4)); the Singapore State Immunity Act of 1979 (section 15 (1), (2), (3) and (5)); the South Africa Foreign States Immunities Act of 1981 (section 14 (1) (a) and (2)); the United Kingdom State Immunity Act of 1978 (section 13 (1), (2a), (3) and (5)) (footnote 51 above).

**Report of the Ad Hoc Committee on Jurisdictional Immunities 2.048
of States and Their Property (24–28 February 2003)³**

[Original: English and Spanish]

[28 February 2003]

Contents

CHAPTER I

Introduction

1. The Ad Hoc Committee on Jurisdictional Immunities of States and Their Property, established by the General Assembly in its resolution 55/150 of 12 December 2000, was reconvened in accordance with paragraph 2 of General Assembly resolution 57/16 of 19 November 2002. The Ad Hoc Committee met at Headquarters from 24 to 28 February 2003.
2. In accordance with paragraph 3 of General Assembly resolution 55/150, the Ad Hoc Committee was open to all States Members of the United Nations and to States members of the specialized agencies.
3. The Chairman of the Ad Hoc Committee, Gerhard Hafner (Austria), opened the session.
4. At its 5th plenary meeting, on 24 February, the Ad Hoc Committee elected Manimuthu Gandhi (India) to replace Narinder Singh (India) and Ana Carlina Plazas (Colombia) to replace Guillermo Reyes (Colombia) on the Bureau. Thus, the Bureau was constituted as follows:

Chairman:

Gerhard Hafner (Austria)

---

³ General Assembly Official Records Fifty-eighth Session Supplement No 22 (A/58/22). Source: http://www.un.org/law/jurisdictionalimmunities/. Endnotes 1 to 5 in bold from original text.

Vice-Chairpersons:

Karim Medrek (Morocco)
Piotr Ogonowski (Poland)
Manimuthu Gandhi (India)

Rapporteur:

Ana Carlina Plazas (Colombia)

5. The Director of the Codification Division of the Office of Legal Affairs, Václav Mikulka, acted as Secretary of the Ad Hoc Committee. The Deputy Director of the Division, Mahnoush H. Arsanjani, acted as Deputy Secretary of the Ad Hoc Committee and Secretary to the Working Group of the Whole. The Codification Division provided the substantive services for the Ad Hoc Committee and the Working Group of the Whole and its working groups.

6. Also at its 5th plenary meeting, the Ad Hoc Committee adopted the following agenda (A/AC.262/L.3):

1. Opening of the session.
2. Election of officers.
3. Adoption of the agenda.
4. Organization of work.
5. Making a final attempt at consolidating areas of agreement and resolving outstanding issues, with a view to elaborating a generally acceptable instrument based on the draft articles on jurisdictional immunities of States and their property adopted by the International Law Commission at its forty-third session, and also on the discussions of the open-ended working group of the Sixth Committee and the Ad Hoc Committee and their results, as well as to recommending a form for the instrument.
6. Adoption of the report.

7. The Ad Hoc Committee had before it its report on the 2002 session[1] and, for reference purposes, comments submitted by States in accordance with General Assembly resolution 49/61 of 9 December 1994 and on the reports of the open ended working group of the Sixth Committee established under Assembly resolutions 53/98 of 8 December 1998 and 54/101 of 9 December 1999, as contained in the reports of the Secretary-General.[2] The Committee also had, for reference purposes, the 1999 and 2000 reports of the Chairman of the working group of the Sixth Committee;[3] the draft articles on jurisdictional immunities of States and their property adopted by the International Law Commission at its forty-third session in 1991;[4] and the comments and suggestions made by the Commission at its fifty-fourth session in 1999,[5] in accordance with Assembly resolution 53/98.

CHAPTER II

Proceedings

8. At its 5th plenary meeting, the Ad Hoc Committee adopted its organization of work and decided to proceed with its work in a Working Group of the Whole.

9. The Working Group proceeded with the substantive discussion of the outstanding issues and established two informal consultative groups. The first group, coordinated by Chusei Yamada (Japan), dealt with the criteria for determining the commercial character of a contract or transaction under paragraph 2 of article 2. The second group, coordinated by Michael Bliss (Australia), considered outstanding issues relating to the concept of a State enterprise or other entity in relation to commercial transactions under paragraph 3 of article 10, contracts of employment under paragraph 2 of article 11, the question of non-applicability of the draft articles to criminal proceedings, and their relationship with other agreements. Pending issues concerning articles 13, 14, 17, 18 and the form of the future instrument were considered by the Working Group of the Whole.

10. The Working Group of the Whole discussed and resolved all the outstanding issues.

11. At its 6th plenary meeting, on 28 February 2003, the Ad Hoc Committee adopted its report containing the text of the draft articles on jurisdictional immunities of States and their property (see annex I), together with understandings with regard to some of the provisions of the draft articles (see annex II).

12. At the same meeting, the Ad Hoc Committee decided to recommend that the General Assembly take a decision on the form of the draft articles. If and when the General Assembly decided to adopt the draft articles as a convention, the draft articles would need a preamble and final clauses, including a general saving provision concerning the relationship between the articles and other international agreements relating to the same subject.

Notes   2.051

1. *Official Records of the General Assembly, Fifty-seventh Session, Supplement No. 22* (A/57/22).
2. A/52/294, A/53/274 and Add.1, A/54/266, A/55/298 and A/56/292 and Add.1 and 2.
3. A/C.6/54/L.12 and A/C.6/55/L.12.
4. *Yearbook of the International Law Commission, 1991*, vol. II (Part Two) (United Nations publication, Sales No. E.93.V.9 (Part 2)), document A/46/10, chap. II, para. 28.
5. *Official Records of the General Assembly, Fifty-fourth Session, Supplement No. 10* and corrigenda (A/54/10 and Corr.1 and 2), annex.

Annex I   2.052

Draft articles on jurisdictional immunities of States and their property

PART I

Introduction

2.053 **Article 1**

Scope of the present articles

The present articles apply to the immunity of a State and its property from the jurisdiction of the courts of another State.

2.054 **Article 2**

Use of terms

1. For the purpose of the present articles:
    (a) "court" means any organ of a State, however named, entitled to exercise judicial functions;
    (b) "State" means:
        (i)   The State and its various organs of government;
        (ii) Constituent units of a federal State or political subdivisions of the State, which are entitled to perform acts in the exercise of the sovereign authority, and are acting in that capacity;
        (iii) Agencies or instrumentalities of the State or other entities, to the extent that they are entitled to perform and are actually performing acts in the exercise of sovereign authority of the State;
        (iv) Representatives of the State acting in that capacity;
    (c) "commercial transaction" means:
        (i)   Any commercial contract or transaction for the sale of goods or supply of services;
        (ii) Any contract for a loan or other transaction of a financial nature, including any obligation of guarantee or of indemnity in respect of any such loan or transaction;
        (iii) Any other contract or transaction of a commercial, industrial, trading or professional nature, but not including a contract of employment of persons.
2. In determining whether a contract or transaction is a "commercial transaction" under paragraph 1 (c), reference should be made primarily to the nature of the contract or transaction, but its purpose should also be taken into account if the parties to the contract or transaction have so agreed, or if, in the practice of the State of the forum, that purpose is relevant to determining the non-commercial character of the contract or transaction.

3. The provisions of paragraphs 1 and 2 regarding the use of terms in the present articles are without prejudice to the use of those terms or to the meanings which may be given to them in other international instruments or in the internal law of any State.

Article 3   2.055

Privileges and immunities not affected by the present articles

1. The present articles are without prejudice to the privileges and immunities enjoyed by a State under international law in relation to the exercise of the functions of:

    (a) Its diplomatic missions, consular posts, special missions, missions to international organizations or delegations to organs of international organizations or to international conferences; and

    (b) Persons connected with them.

2. The present articles are without prejudice to privileges and immunities accorded under international law to heads of State *ratione personae*.

3. The present articles are without prejudice to the immunities enjoyed by a State under international law with respect to aircraft or space objects owned or operated by a State.

Article 4   2.056

Non-retroactivity of the present articles

Without prejudice to the application of any rules set forth in the present articles to which jurisdictional immunities of States and their property are subject under international law independently of the present articles, the articles shall not apply to any question of jurisdictional immunities of States or their property arising in a proceeding instituted against a State before a court of another State prior to the entry into force of the present articles for the States concerned.

PART II

General principles

Article 5   2.057

State immunity

A State enjoys immunity, in respect of itself and its property, from the jurisdiction of the courts of another State subject to the provisions of the present articles.

2.058 Article 6

Modalities for giving effect to State immunity

1. A State shall give effect to State immunity under article 5 by refraining from exercising jurisdiction in a proceeding before its courts against another State and to that end shall ensure that its courts determine on their own initiative that the immunity of that other State under article 5 is respected.

2. A proceeding before a court of a State shall be considered to have been instituted against another State if that other State:

   (a) Is named as a party to that proceeding; or
   (b) Is not named as a party to the proceeding but the proceeding in effect seeks to affect the property, rights, interests or activities of that other State.

2.059 Article 7

Express consent to exercise of jurisdiction

1. A State cannot invoke immunity from jurisdiction in a proceeding before a court of another State with regard to a matter or case if it has expressly consented to the exercise of jurisdiction by the court with regard to the matter or case:

   (a) By international agreement;
   (b) In a written contract; or
   (c) By a declaration before the court or by a written communication in a specific proceeding.

2. Agreement by a State for the application of the law of another State shall not be interpreted as consent to the exercise of jurisdiction by the courts of that other State.

2.060 Article 8

Effect of participation in a proceeding before a court

1. A State cannot invoke immunity from jurisdiction in a proceeding before a court of another State if it has:

   (a) Itself instituted the proceeding; or
   (b) Intervened in the proceeding or taken any other step relating to the merits. However, if the State satisfies the court that it could not have acquired knowledge of facts on which a claim to immunity can be based until after it took such a step, it can claim immunity based on those facts, provided it does so at the earliest possible moment.

2. A State shall not be considered to have consented to the exercise of jurisdiction by a court of another State if it intervenes in a proceeding or takes any other step for the sole purpose of:

   (a) Invoking immunity; or
   (b) Asserting a right or interest in property at issue in the proceeding.

3. The appearance of a representative of a State before a court of another State as a witness shall not be interpreted as consent by the former State to the exercise of jurisdiction by the court.

4. Failure on the part of a State to enter an appearance in a proceeding before a court of another State shall not be interpreted as consent by the former State to the exercise of jurisdiction by the court.

Article 9 2.061

Counter-claims

1. A State instituting a proceeding before a court of another State cannot invoke immunity from the jurisdiction of the court in respect of any counter-claim arising out of the same legal relationship or facts as the principal claim.

2. A State intervening to present a claim in a proceeding before a court of another State cannot invoke immunity from the jurisdiction of the court in respect of any counter-claim arising out of the same legal relationship or facts as the claim presented by the State.

3. A State making a counter-claim in a proceeding instituted against it before a court of another State cannot invoke immunity from the jurisdiction of the court in respect of the principal claim.

PART III

Proceedings in which State immunity cannot be invoked

Article 10 2.062

Commercial transactions

1. If a State engages in a commercial transaction with a foreign natural or juridical person and, by virtue of the applicable rules of private international law, differences relating to the commercial transaction fall within the jurisdiction of a court of another State, the State cannot invoke immunity from that jurisdiction in a proceeding arising out of that commercial transaction.

2. Paragraph 1 does not apply:

   (a) In the case of a commercial transaction between States; or
   (b) If the parties to the commercial transaction have expressly agreed otherwise.

3. Where a State enterprise or other entity established by a State which has an independent legal personality and is capable of:

(a) Suing or being sued; and

(b) Acquiring, owning or possessing and disposing of property, including property which that State has authorized it to operate or manage, is involved in a proceeding which relates to a commercial transaction in which that entity is engaged, the immunity from jurisdiction enjoyed by that State shall not be affected.

2.063 **Article 11**

Contracts of employment

1. Unless otherwise agreed between the States concerned, a State cannot invoke immunity from jurisdiction before a court of another State which is otherwise competent in a proceeding which relates to a contract of employment between the State and an individual for work performed or to be performed, in whole or in part, in the territory of that other State.

2. Paragraph 1 does not apply if:

(a) The employee has been recruited to perform particular functions in the exercise of governmental authority;

(b) The employee is:

(i) A diplomatic agent, as defined in the Vienna Convention on Diplomatic Relations of 1961;

(ii) A consular officer, as defined by the Vienna Convention on Consular Relations of 1963;

(iii) A member of diplomatic staff of permanent missions to international organizations, of special missions, or is recruited to represent a State at international conferences; or

(iv) Any other person enjoying diplomatic immunity;

(c) The subject of the proceeding is the recruitment, renewal of employment or reinstatement of an individual;

(d) The subject of the proceeding is the dismissal or termination of employment of an individual and, as determined by the head of State, the head of Government or the Minister for Foreign Affairs of the employer State, such a proceeding would interfere with the security interests of that State;

(e) The employee is a national of the employer State at the time when the proceeding is instituted, unless this person has the permanent residence in the State of the forum; or

(f) The employer State and the employee have otherwise agreed in writing, subject to any considerations of public policy conferring on the courts of the State of the forum exclusive jurisdiction by reason of the subject matter of the proceeding.

Article 12   2.064
Personal injuries and damage to property

Unless otherwise agreed between the States concerned, a State cannot invoke immunity from jurisdiction before a court of another State which is otherwise competent in a proceeding which relates to pecuniary compensation for death or injury to the person, or damage to or loss of tangible property, caused by an act or omission which is alleged to be attributable to the State, if the act or omission occurred in whole or in part in the territory of that other State and if the author of the act or omission was present in that territory at the time of the act or omission.

Article 13   2.065
Ownership, possession and use of property

Unless otherwise agreed between the States concerned, a State cannot invoke immunity from jurisdiction before a court of another State which is otherwise competent in a proceeding which relates to the determination of:

(a) Any right or interest of the State in, or its possession or use of, or any obligation of the State arising out of its interest in, or its possession or use of, immovable property situated in the State of the forum;

(b) Any right or interest of the State in movable or immovable property arising by way of succession, gift or *bona vacantia*; or

(c) Any right or interest of the State in the administration of property, such as trust property, the estate of a bankrupt or the property of a company in the event of its winding up.

Article 14   2.066
Intellectual and industrial property

Unless otherwise agreed between the States concerned, a State cannot invoke immunity from jurisdiction before a court of another State which is otherwise competent in a proceeding which relates to:

(a) The determination of any right of the State in a patent, industrial design, trade name or business name, trademark, copyright or any other form of intellectual or industrial property which enjoys a measure of legal protection, even if provisional, in the State of the forum; or

(b) An alleged infringement by the State, in the territory of the State of the forum, of a right of the nature mentioned in subparagraph (a) which belongs to a third person and is protected in the State of the forum.

2.067 Article 15

Participation in companies or other collective bodies

1. A State cannot invoke immunity from jurisdiction before a court of another State which is otherwise competent in a proceeding which relates to its participation in a company or other collective body, whether incorporated or unincorporated, being a proceeding concerning the relationship between the State and the body or the other participants therein, provided that the body:

   (a) Has participants other than States or international organizations; and
   (b) Is incorporated or constituted under the law of the State of the forum or has its seat or principal place of business in that State.

2. A State can, however, invoke immunity from jurisdiction in such a proceeding if the States concerned have so agreed or if the parties to the dispute have so provided by an agreement in writing or if the instrument establishing or regulating the body in question contains provisions to that effect.

2.068 Article 16

Ships owned or operated by a State

1. Unless otherwise agreed between the States concerned, a State which owns or operates a ship cannot invoke immunity from jurisdiction before a court of another State which is otherwise competent in a proceeding which relates to the operation of that ship if, at the time the cause of action arose, the ship was used for other than government non-commercial purposes.

2. Paragraph 1 does not apply to warships, or naval auxiliaries, nor does it apply to other vessels owned or operated by a State and used, for the time being, only on government non-commercial service.

3. Unless otherwise agreed between the States concerned, a State cannot invoke immunity from jurisdiction before a court of another State which is otherwise competent in a proceeding which relates to the carriage of cargo on board a ship owned or operated by that State if, at the time the cause of action arose, the ship was used for other than government non-commercial purposes.

4. Paragraph 3 does not apply to any cargo carried on board the ships referred to in paragraph 2, nor does it apply to any cargo owned by a State and used or intended for use exclusively for government non-commercial purposes.

5. States may plead all measures of defence, prescription and limitation of liability which are available to private ships and cargoes and their owners.

6. If in a proceeding there arises a question relating to the government and non-commercial character of a ship owned or operated by a State or cargo owned by a State, a certificate signed by a diplomatic representative or other

competent authority of that State and communicated to the court shall serve as evidence of the character of that ship or cargo.

Article 17 2.069

Effect of an arbitration agreement

If a State enters into an agreement in writing with a foreign natural or juridical person to submit to arbitration differences relating to a commercial transaction, that State cannot invoke immunity from jurisdiction before a court of another State which is otherwise competent in a proceeding which relates to:

(a) The validity, interpretation or application of the arbitration agreement;

(b) The arbitration procedure; or

(c) The confirmation or the setting aside of the award, unless the arbitration agreement otherwise provides.

PART IV

State immunity from measures of constraint in connection with proceedings before a court

Article 18 2.070

State immunity from pre-judgement measures of constraint

No pre-judgement measures of constraint, such as attachment or arrest, against property of a State may be taken in connection with a proceeding before a court of another State unless and except to the extent that:

(a) The State has expressly consented to the taking of such measures as indicated:

    (i) By international agreement;

    (ii) By an arbitration agreement or in a written contract; or

    (iii) By a declaration before the court or by a written communication after a dispute between the parties has arisen; or

(b) The State has allocated or earmarked property for the satisfaction of the claim which is the object of that proceeding.

Article 19 2.071

State immunity from post-judgement measures of constraint

No post-judgement measures of constraint, such as attachment, arrest or execution, against property of a State may be taken in connection with a proceeding before a court of another State unless and except to the extent that:

(a) The State has expressly consented to the taking of such measures as indicated:

    (i) By international agreement;

    (ii) By an arbitration agreement or in a written contract; or

(iii) By a declaration before the court or by a written communication after a dispute between the parties has arisen; or

(b) The State has allocated or earmarked property for the satisfaction of the claim which is the object of that proceeding; or

(c) It has been established that the property is specifically in use or intended for use by the State for other than government non-commercial purposes and is in the territory of the State of the forum, provided that post-judgement measures of constraint may only be taken against property that has a connection with the entity against which the proceeding was directed.

2.072 **Article 20**

Effect of consent to jurisdiction to measures of constraint

Where consent to the measures of constraint is required under articles 18 and 19, consent to the exercise of jurisdiction under article 7 shall not imply consent to the taking of measures of constraint.

2.073 **Article 21**

Specific categories of property

1. The following categories, in particular, of property of a State shall not be considered as property specifically in use or intended for use by the State for other than government non-commercial purposes under article 19, paragraph (c):

   (a) Property, including any bank account, which is used or intended for use in the performance of the functions of the diplomatic mission of the State or its consular posts, special missions, missions to international organizations, or delegations to organs of international organizations or to international conferences;

   (b) Property of a military character or used or intended for use in the performance of military functions;

   (c) Property of the central bank or other monetary authority of the State;

   (d) Property forming part of the cultural heritage of the State or part of its archives and not placed or intended to be placed on sale;

   (e) Property forming part of an exhibition of objects of scientific, cultural or historical interest and not placed or intended to be placed on sale.

2. Paragraph 1 is without prejudice to article 18 and article 19, subparagraphs (a) and (b).

PART V

Miscellaneous provisions

Article 22

2.074

Service of process

1. Service of process by writ or other document instituting a proceeding against a State shall be effected:

    (a) In accordance with any applicable international convention binding on the State of the forum and the State concerned; or

    (b) In accordance with any special arrangement for service between the claimant and the State concerned, if not precluded by the law of the State of the forum; or

    (c) In the absence of such a convention or special arrangement:

        (i) By transmission through diplomatic channels to the Ministry of Foreign Affairs of the State concerned; or

        (ii) By any other means accepted by the State concerned, if not precluded by the law of the State of the forum.

2. Service of process referred to in paragraph 1 (c) (i) is deemed to have been effected by receipt of the documents by the Ministry of Foreign Affairs.

3. These documents shall be accompanied, if necessary, by a translation into the official language, or one of the official languages, of the State concerned.

4. Any State that enters an appearance on the merits in a proceeding instituted against it may not thereafter assert that service of process did not comply with the provisions of paragraphs 1 and 3.

Article 23

2.075

Default judgement

1. A default judgement shall not be rendered against a State unless the court has found that:

    (a) The requirements laid down in article 22, paragraphs 1 and 3, have been complied with;

    (b) A period of not less than four months has expired from the date on which the service of the writ or other documents instituting a proceeding has been effected or deemed to have been effected in accordance with article 22, paragraphs 1 and 2;

    and

    (c) The present articles do not preclude it from exercising jurisdiction.

2. A copy of any default judgement rendered against a State, accompanied if necessary by a translation into the official language or one of the official languages of the State concerned, shall be transmitted to it through one of the means specified in article 22, paragraph 1, and in accordance with the provisions of that paragraph.

3. The time limit for applying to have a default judgement set aside shall not be less than four months and shall begin to run from the date on which the copy of the judgement is received or is deemed to have been received by the State concerned.

2.076 Article 24

Privileges and immunities during court proceedings

1. Any failure or refusal by a State to comply with an order of a court of another State enjoining it to perform or refrain from performing a specific act or to produce any document or disclose any other information for the purposes of a proceeding shall entail no consequences other than those which may result from such conduct in relation to the merits of the case. In particular, no fine or penalty shall be imposed on the State by reason of such failure or refusal.

2. A State shall not be required to provide any security, bond or deposit, however described, to guarantee the payment of judicial costs or expenses in any proceeding to which it is a respondent party before a court of another State.

2.077 Annex II

Understandings with respect to certain provisions of the draft articles

With respect to article 10

The term "immunity" in article 10 is to be understood in the context of the draft articles as a whole.

Article 10, paragraph 3, does not pre-judge the question of "piercing the corporate veil", questions relating to a situation where a State entity has deliberately misrepresented its financial position or subsequently reduced its assets to avoid satisfying a claim, or other related issues.

With respect to article 11

The reference in article 11, paragraph 2 (d), to the "security interests" of the employer State was intended primarily to address matters of national security and the security of diplomatic missions and consular posts.

Under article 41 of the 1961 Vienna Convention on Diplomatic Relations and article 55 of the 1963 Vienna Convention on Consular Relations, all persons referred to in those articles have the duty to respect the laws and regulations, including the respect of labour laws, of the host country. At the same time, under article 38 of the 1961 Vienna Convention on Diplomatic Relations and article 71 of the 1963 Vienna Convention on Consular Relations, the receiving State has a duty to exercise its jurisdiction in such a manner as not to interfere unduly with the performance of the functions of the mission or the consular post.

With respect to articles 13 and 14

The expression "determination" is used to refer not only to the ascertainment or verification of the existence of the rights protected, but also to the evaluation or assessment of the substance, including content, scope and extent, of such rights.

With respect to article 17

The expression "commercial transaction" includes investment matters.

With respect to article 19

The expression "entity" in subparagraph (c) means the State as an independent legal personality, a constituent unit of a federal State, a subdivision of a State, agency or instrumentality of a State or other entity, which enjoys independent legal personality.

The words "property that has a connection with the entity" in subparagraph (c) are to be understood as broader than ownership or possession.

Article 19 does not pre-judge the question of "piercing the corporate veil", questions relating to a situation where a State entity has deliberately misrepresented its financial position or subsequently reduced its assets to avoid satisfying a claim, or other related issues.

With respect to criminal proceedings

There was the general understanding that the draft articles do not cover criminal proceedings.

2.078

**International Law Association Revised
Draft Articles for a Convention on State Immunity
(Buenos Aires, 14–20 August 1994)**[4]

The States Party to this Convention,
DESIRING to achieve a further harmonization of the law of State Immunity,
AGREE upon the following Articles:

2.079 Article I

Definitions

A. Tribunal

The term "tribunal" includes any court and any administrative body acting in an adjudicative capacity.

B. Foreign State

The term "foreign State" includes:

1. The government of the State;
2. Any other State organs;
3. Agencies and instrumentalities of the State not possessing legal personality distinct from the State.

An agency or instrumentality of a foreign State which possesses legal personality distinct from the State shall be treated as a foreign State only for acts or omissions performed in the exercise of sovereign authority, i.e. *jure imperii*.

C. Commercial Activity

The term "commercial activity" refers either to a regular course of commercial conduct or a particular commercial transaction or act. It shall include any activity or transaction into which a foreign State enters or in which it engages otherwise than in the exercise of sovereign authority and in particular:

1. Any arrangement for the supply of goods or services;
2. Any financial transaction involving lending or borrowing or guaranteeing financial obligations.

In applying this definition, the commercial character of a particular act shall be determined by reference to the nature of the act, rather than by reference to its purpose.

---

[4] Revising the Draft Convention approved at Montreal (4 September 1982). See Report of the Sixtieth Conference (1982), 5–10, 325–337; Report of the Sixty Fourth Conference (1990), 393–431; Report of the Sixty Fifth Conference (1992), 290–330; Report of the Sixty Sixth Conference (1994), 21–27, 452–499.

Article II 2.080

Immunity of a Foreign State from Adjudication

In principle, a foreign State shall be immune from the adjudicatory jurisdiction of a forum State for acts performed by it in the exercise of its sovereign authority, i.e. *jure imperii*. It shall not be immune in the circumstances provided in Article III.

Article III 2.081

Exceptions to Immunity from Adjudication

A Foreign State shall not be immune from the jurisdiction of the forum State to adjudicate in the following instances *inter alia*.

A. Where the foreign State has waived its immunity from the jurisdiction of the forum State either expressly or by implication, a waiver may not be withdrawn except in accordance with its terms.

   1. An express waiver may be made *inter alia*:

      (a) by unilateral declaration; or
      (b) by international agreement; or
      (c) by a provision in a contract; or
      (d) by an explicit agreement.

   2. An implied waiver may be made *inter alia*:

      (a) by participating in proceedings before a tribunal of the forum State
         (i) Subsection 2(a) above shall not apply if a foreign State intervenes or takes steps in the proceedings for the purpose of:

            (A) claiming immunity; or
            (B) asserting an interest in the proceedings in circumstances such that it would have been entitled to immunity if the proceedings had been brought against it;

         (ii) In any action in which a foreign State participates in a proceeding before a tribunal in the forum State, the foreign State shall not be immune with respect to any counterclaim or setoff (irrespective of the amount thereof):

            (A) for which a foreign State would not be entitled to immunity under other provisions of this Convention had such a claim been brought in a separate action against the foreign State; or
            (B) arising out of the transaction or occurrence that is the subject matter of the claim of the foreign State;

(iii) In any action not within the scope of subsection 2(a)(ii) above in which a foreign State participates in a proceeding before a tribunal in the forum State, the foreign State shall not be immune with respect to claims arising between the parties from unrelated transactions up to the amount of its adverse claim.

(b) by agreeing in writing to submit a dispute which has arisen, or may arise, to arbitration in the forum State or in a number of States which may include the forum State. In such an instance a foreign State shall not be immune with respect to proceedings in a tribunal of the forum State which relate to:

  (i) the constitution or appointment of the arbitral tribunal; or

  (ii) the validity or interpretation of the arbitration agreement or the award; or

  (iii) the arbitration procedure; or

  (iv) the setting aside of the award.

B. Where the cause of action arises out of:

1. A commercial activity carried on by the foreign State, or

2. An obligation of the foreign State arising out of a contract (whether or not a commercial transaction but excluding a contract of employment) unless the parties have otherwise agreed in writing.

C. Where the foreign State enters into a contract of employment in the forum State, or where work under such a contract is to be performed wholly or partly in the forum State and the proceedings relate to the contract. This provision shall not apply if:

1. The employee was appointed under the public (administrative) law of the foreign State, such as, *inter alia*, members of the mission, diplomatic, consular or military staff.

2. At the time the proceedings are brought the employee is a national of the foreign State; or

3. At the time the contract for employment was made the employee was neither a national nor a permanent resident of the forum State; or

4. The employer and employee have otherwise agreed in writing; or

D. Where the cause of action relates to:

1. The foreign State's rights or interests in, or its possession or use of, immovable property in the forum State; or

2. Obligations of the foreign State arising out of its rights or interests in, or its possession or use of, immovable property in the forum State; or

3. Rights or interests of the foreign State in movable or immovable property in the forum State arising by way of succession, gift or *bona vacantia*.

E. Where the cause of action relates to:

1. Intellectual or industrial property rights (patent, industrial design, trademark, copyright, or other similar rights) belonging to the foreign State in the forum State or for which the forum State has applied in the forum State; or
2. A claim for infringement by the foreign State of any patent, industrial design, trademark, copyright or other similar right; or
3. The right to use a trade or business name in the forum State.

F. Where the cause of action relates to:

1. Death or personal injury; or
2. Damage to or loss of property,

and the act or omission which caused the death, injury or damage either occurred wholly or partly in the forum State or if that act or omission had a direct effect in the forum State.

G. Where the cause of action relates to rights in property taken in violation of international law and that property or property exchanged for that property is:

1. In the forum State in connection with a commercial activity carried on in the forum State by the foreign State; or
2. Owned or operated by an agency or instrumentality of the foreign State and that agency or instrumentality is engaged in a commercial activity in the forum State.

Article IV   2.082

Service of Process and Other Procedural Documents

In proceedings against a foreign State under theses articles the following rule shall apply:

A. Service shall be made upon a foreign State:

1. By transmittal of a copy of the summons, notice of suit, complaint, and any resulting default judgment in accordance with any special arrangement in writing for service between the plaintiff and the foreign State; or
2. By transmittal of a copy of the summons, notice of suit, complaint, and any resulting default judgment in accordance with any international agreement on service of judicial documents; or
3. By transmittal of a copy of the summons, notice of suit, complaint, and any resulting default judgment through diplomatic channels to the ministry of foreign affairs of the foreign State; or
4. By transmittal of a copy of the summons, notice of suite, complaint, and any resulting default judgment in any other manner agreed between the foreign State and the forum State.

5. By transmittal of a copy of the summons, notice of suit, complaint, and any resulting default judgment by registered mail to the ministry of foreign affairs of the foreign State; or

6. By any other means of constructive or substitute service which satisfies the court of the forum State and the requirements of international law.

B. Service of documents shall be deemed to have been effected upon their receipt by the ministry of foreign affairs unless some other time of service has been prescribed in an applicable international convention or arrangement or agreement with the foreign State.

C. The time limit in which a State must enter an appearance or appeal against any judgment or order shall begin to run sixty days after the date on which the summons or notice of suit or complaint is deemed to have been effectively received in accordance with this article.

D. Service of other procedural documents, i.e. procedural documents which have not been mentioned in Art. IV A, may be accomplished according to the rules of the forum State.

2.083 Article V

Default Judgments

No default judgment may be entered by a tribunal in a forum State against a foreign State, unless service has been effected in accordance with Art. IV and an exception to immunity from adjudication under Art. III has been established to the satisfaction of the tribunal.

2.084 Article VI

Extent of Liability

A. As to any claim with respect to which a foreign State is not entitled to immunity under the Convention, the foreign State shall be liable as to amount to the same extent as a private individual under like circumstances; but a foreign State shall not be liable for punitive damages. If, however, in any case where the jurisdiction of the forum State can be established under Art. III F of this Convention, the applicable law provides, or has been construed to provide, for damages only punitive in nature, the foreign State shall be liable for actual or compensatory damages measured by the primary loss incurred by the persons for whose benefit the suit was brought.

B. Judgments enforcing maritime liens against a foreign State may not exceed the value of the vessel or cargo, with value assessed as of the date notice of suit was served.

Article VII
2.085

Immunity from Attachment and Execution

A foreign State's property in the forum State shall be immune from attachment, arrest and execution, except as provided in Article VIII.

Article VIII
2.086

Exceptions to Immunity from Attachment and Execution

A. A foreign State's property in the forum State, shall not be immune from any measure for the enforcement of a judgment or an arbitration award if:

1. The foreign State has waived its immunity either expressly or by implication from such measures. A waiver may not be withdrawn except in accordance with its terms; or
2. The property is in use for the purpose of commercial activity or was in use for the commercial activity upon which the claim is based; or
3. Execution is against property which has been taken in violation of international law, or which has been exchanged for property taken in violation of international law and is pursuant to a judgment or an arbitral award establishing rights in such property.

B. In case of mixed financial accounts that proportion duly identified of the account used for non-commercial activity shall be entitled to immunity.

C. Attachment or execution shall not be permitted, if:

1. The property against which execution is sought to be had is used for diplomatic or consular purposes; or
2. The property is of a military character or is used or intended for use for military purposes; or
3. The property is that of a State central bank held by it for central banking purposes; or
4. The property is that of a State monetary authority held by it for monetary purposes; unless the State has made an explicit waiver with respect to such property.

D. In exceptional circumstances, a tribunal of the forum State may order interim measures against the property of a foreign State, available under Art. VIII A to C of this convention for attachment, arrest or execution, including prejudgment attachment of assets and injunctive relief, if a party presents a *prima facie* case that such assets within the territorial limits of the forum State may be removed, dissipated or otherwise dealt with by the foreign State before the tribunal renders judgment and there is a reasonable probability that such action will frustrate execution of any such judgment.

2.087 Article IX

Miscellaneous Provisions

A. This Convention is without prejudice to:

1. Other applicable international agreements;
2. The rules of international law relating to diplomatic and consular privileges and immunities, to the immunities of foreign public ships and to the immunities of international organizations.

B. Nothing in this Convention shall be interpreted as conferring on tribunals in the foreign State any additional competence with respect to subject matter.

Organization of American States: Inter-American Draft Convention on Jurisdictional Immunity of States[5]   2.088

I JURISDICTIONAL IMMUNITY

Article 1   2.089

A State is immune from the jurisdiction of any other State.

Article 2   2.090

For purposes of this Convention, the definition of State includes:

a) the government and its departments, its decentralized agencies and self-governing or self-sustaining entities;

b) its agencies, whether or not endowed with a separate legal personality, and any other entity, of legal national interest, whatever its technical and legal form;

c) national, regional or local political or administrative institutions.

The preceding list is not all-inclusive.

Article 3   2.091

A State is granted immunity from jurisdiction for acts performed by virtue of governmental powers.

Immunity from jurisdiction applies equally to activities regarding property owned and to assets which the State uses by virtue of its governmental powers.

Article 4   2.092

Notwithstanding Article 1 provisions, a State may be brought before the adjudicatory authorities of another State under the circumstances foreseen in this Convention.

II EXCEPTIONS TO JURISDICTIONAL IMMUNITY

Article 5   2.093

States shall not invoke immunity against claims relative to trade or commercial activities undertaken in the State of the *forum*.

---

[5] The draft was approved by the Inter-American Juridical Committee on 21 January 1983. For materials relating to the Organization of American States, see http://www.oas.org.

Trade or commercial activities of a State are construed to mean the performance of a particular transaction or commercial or trading act pursuant to its ordinary trade operations.

2.094   Article 6

States shall not claim immunity from jurisdiction either:

a) in labour affairs or employment contracts between any State and one or more individuals, when the work is performed in the *forum* State;

b) in proceedings for the distribution of assets, be they of a civil, trade or commercial nature;

c) in actions involving real property located in the State of the *forum* with the exceptions contained in international treaties or in diplomatic or consular practices;

d) in tax matters regarding activities under paragraph one of Article 5, for property located in the *forum* State;

e) in proceedings for losses and damages on tort liabilities arising from the activities mentioned in Article 5, paragraph one; and

f) when the judgement includes court costs.

2.095   Article 7

Otherwise, the adjudicatory authorities of a State shall exercise jurisdiction over another State, subject to this Convention, when the latter State:

a) institutes proceedings before them;

b) defends a suit or joins in proceedings or brings legal action against the merits of the case without explicitly claiming immunity, when such immunity would be applicable;

c) counterclaims or brings a third-party claim.

A State is not deemed to have accepted the jurisdiction of the adjudicatory authorities merely by appearing before a court of another State in order to assert immunity.

III RULES OF PROCEDURE

2.096   Article 8

Notwithstanding the provisions of this Convention, a State Party to proceedings filed before an adjudicatory authority of another State shall be subject to the procedural rules of the *forum*.

2.097   Article 9

To summon or notify a foreign State of a claim, the competent adjudicatory authority of the *forum* State shall send letters rogatory to the applicable adjudicatory authority of the foreign State through the Ministry of Foreign Affairs of the *forum* State. The latter shall forward said letters rogatory to the Ministry of Foreign Affairs of the foreign State through diplomatic channels within fifteen working days. The Ministry in turn shall notify the addressee of the summons or notice, within an identical time-limit, in accordance with due legal procedure.

Article 10   2.098

The letters rogatory shall be supplemented by certified copies of the claim filed and attachments thereto, and a copy of the resolution supporting the summons or notice served the defendant.

The above documents shall be exempt from authentication but must be translated into the language of the receiving State, if required. Compliance with the letters rogatory shall not imply recognition of competence of the plaintiff adjudicatory authority.

Article 11   2.099

The foreign State shall have a time limit of forty working days from the date in which the notice mentioned at the end of Article 9 is served to come before the appropriate adjudicatory authorities to exercise its rights and, at its discretion, to claim immunity from jurisdiction.

Upon a well-founded request by the foreign State, the court should extend the above-mentioned time limit by a maximum of another forty working days.

Article 12   2.100

Should the foreign State claim immunity from jurisdiction it shall be free to appoint to the proceeding a special agent assisted by an attorney registered in the State of the *forum*.

Article 13   2.101

A foreign State claiming immunity from jurisdiction shall not be required to go into the substance of the dispute nor submit evidence at such occasion.

Nevertheless, should a challenge arise as to the qualification of an entity as per Article 2 of this Convention, the burden of proof shall fall upon the challenger.

Should immunity be disputed, the adjudicatory authority shall issue a decision on the matter without going into the merit of the claim.

Article 14   2.102

Final judgement given in accordance with this Convention shall be executed in the foreign State Party to the proceeding, subject to the provisions of treaties in effect between the States involved or, in default thereof, to its national legislation.

2.103 Article 15

The foreign State shall always be immune to foreclosure or other preventive measures, unless it formally waives immunity.

Actions on real property listed under Article 6 item d) are excepted from the provisions of the foregoing paragraph, unless granted international protection.

IV SPECIAL RULES

2.104 Article 16

No provision of this Convention shall affect privileges and immunities applicable under international treaties currently in force.

V GENERAL PROVISIONS

2.105 Article 17

This Convention applies only to proceedings initiated after it has entered into force.

For States acceding hereto after enforcement date, this Convention shall be in effect for any proceeding commenced immediately following the thirtieth day after the respective ratification document is deposited.

2.106 Article 18

Should any dispute arise between Contracting Parties regarding acceptance or rejection of immunity from jurisdiction under this Convention, the defendant State shall be entitled to appeal to the International Court of Justice without need of prior agreement, for a definitive judgement on the matter, unless said parties agree to resolve the dispute otherwise.

Enforcement of this article shall cause the immediate stay of the proceedings.

VI FINAL PROVISIONS

2.107 Article 19

This Convention shall be open to the signature of Member States of the Organization of American States.

2.108 Article 20

This Convention is subject to ratification. The instruments of ratification shall be deposited with the General Secretariat of the Organization of American States.

Article 21 **2.109**

This Convention shall remain open for accession by any other State. The instruments of accession shall be deposited with the General Secretariat of the Organization of American States.

Article 22 **2.110**

This Convention shall enter into force on the thirtieth day following the date of deposit of the second instrument of ratification.

For each State ratifying or acceding to the Convention after the deposit of the second instrument of ratification, the Convention shall enter into force on the thirtieth day after deposit by such State of its instrument of ratification or accession.

Article 23 **2.111**

One third of the Contracting Parties may request that a Conference be called to revise or amend this Convention five years after it has entered into force.

The Conference shall be called by the Secretary General of the Organization of American States within one year of the request, in accordance with this article.

Article 24 **2.112**

This Convention shall remain in force indefinitely, but any of the States Parties may denounce it. The instrument of denunciation shall be deposited with the General Secretariat of the Organization of American States. After one year from the date of deposit of the instrument of denunciation, the Convention shall no longer be in force for the denouncing State, except for proceedings under way in which such State is a party, but shall remain in force for the other States.

Article 25 **2.113**

The original instrument of this Convention, the English, French, Portuguese and Spanish texts of which are equally authentic, shall be deposited with the General Secretariat of the Organization of American States, which will forward an authenticated copy of the text to the Secretariat General of the United Nations for registration and publication in accordance with Article 102 of its Charter. The General Secretariat of the Organization of American States shall notify Member States of that Organization and the States that have acceded to the Convention of the signatures and deposits of instruments of ratification, accession and denouncement.

Rio de Janeiro, 21 January 1983

[List of signatories omitted]

2.114   Resolution of L'Institut de Droit International on
Contemporary Problems Concerning the Immunity of
States in Relation to Questions of Jurisdiction and
Enforcement (Basle, 2 September 1991)[6]

(Fourteenth Commission, Rapporteur: Mr Ian Brownlie)
The Institute of International Law,

Whereas significant trends have appeared both in the practice of States and in doctrine and jurisprudence since the Resolution on the immunities of foreign States adopted at the Aix-en-Provence Session of the Institute in 1954;

Whereas it is helpful to propose formulations pertinent to the application within the various national legal systems of the rules relating to the jurisdictional immunity of States with a view to limiting the immunity, while maintaining the protection of essential States interests;

Adopts the following Resolution:

2.115 Article 1

Scope of the Resolution

The present Resolution is concerned exclusively with the competence of the relevant organs of the State of the forum in respect of the acts or omissions of a State which is a party to proceedings in the courts of the forum State or in other organs of that State with powers of a quasi-judicial character.

2.116 Article 2

Criteria Indicating the Competence of Courts or Other Relevant
Organs of the Forum State in Relation to Jurisdictional Immunity

1. In determining the question of the competence of the relevant organs of the forum State, each case is to be separately characterised in the light of the relevant facts and the relevant criteria, both of competence and incompetence; no presumption is to be applied concerning the priority of either group of criteria.

2. In the absence of agreement to the contrary, the following criteria are indicative of the competence of the relevant organs of the forum State to

---

[6] For further information concerning the work of the Institut de Droit International, see http://www.idi-iil.org/index.html. The Resolution of the Institut de Droit International on the Immunities from Jurisdiction and Execution of Heads of State and of Government in International Law is reproduced at paras. 2.123 to 2.138 below.

determine the substance of the claim, notwithstanding a claim to jurisdictional immunity by a foreign State which is a party:

a) The organs of the forum State are competent in respect of proceedings relating to a commercial transaction to which a foreign State (or its agent) is a party.

b) The organs of the forum State are competent in respect of proceedings concerning legal disputes arising from relationships of a private law character to which a foreign State (or its agent) is a party; the class of relationships referred to includes (but is not confined to) the following legal categories: commercial contracts; contracts for the supply of services; loans and financing arrangements; guarantees or indemnities in respect of financial obligations; ownership, possession and use of property; the protection of industrial and intellectual property; the legal incidents attaching to incorporated bodies, unincorporated bodies and associations, and partnerships; actions *in rem* against ships and cargoes; and bills of exchange.

c) The organs of the forum State are competent in respect of proceedings concerning contracts of employment and contracts for professional services to which a foreign State (or its agent) is a party.

d) The organs of the forum State are competent in respect of proceedings concerning legal disputes arising from relationships which are not classified in the forum as having a "private law character" but which nevertheless are based upon elements of good faith and reliance (legal security) within the context of the local law.

e) The organs of the forum State are competent in respect of proceedings concerning the death of, or personal injury to, a person, or loss of or damage to tangible property, which are attributable to activities of a foreign State and its agents within the national jurisdiction of the forum State.

f) The organs of the forum State are competent in respect of proceedings relating to any interests of a foreign State in movable or immovable property, being a right or interest arising by way of succession, gift or *bona vacantia*; or a right or interest in the administration of property forming part of the estate of a deceased person or a person of unsound mind or a bankrupt; or a right or interest in the administration of property of a company in the event of its dissolution or winding up; or a right or interest in the administration of trust property or property otherwise held on a fiduciary basis.

g) The organs of the forum State are competent in so far as it has a supervisory jurisdiction in respect of an agreement to arbitrate between a foreign State and a natural or juridical person.

h) The organs of the forum State are competent in respect of transactions in relation to which the reasonable inference is that the parties did not intend that the settlement of disputes would be on the basis of a diplomatic claim.

i) The organs of the forum State are competent in respect of proceedings relating to fiscal liabilities, income tax, customs duties, stamp duty, registration fees, and similar impositions provided that such liabilities are the normal concomitant or commercial and other legal relationships in the context of the local legal system.

3. In the absence of agreement to the contrary, the following criteria are indicative of the incompetence of the organs of the forum State to determine the substance of the claim, in a case where the jurisdictional immunity of a foreign State party is in issue:

a) The relation between the subject-matter of the dispute and the validity of the transactions of the defendant State in terms of public international law.

b) The relation between the subject-matter of the dispute and the validity of the internal administrative and legislative acts of the defendant State in terms of public international law.

c) The organs of the forum State should not assume competence in respect of issues the Resolution of which has been allocated to another remedial context.

d) The organs of the forum State should not assume competence to inquire into the content or implementation of the foreign defence and security policies of the defendant State.

e) The organs of the forum State should not assume competence in respect of the validity, meaning and implementation of an intergovernmental agreement or decision creating agencies, institutions or funds subject to the rules of public international law.

2.117 Article 3

State Agencies and Political Subdivisions

1. The general criteria of competence and incompetence set forth above are applicable to the activities of the agencies and political subdivisions of foreign States whatever their formal designation or constitutional status in the State concerned.

2. The fact that an agency or political subdivision of a foreign State possesses a separate legal personality as a consequence of incorporation or otherwise

under the law of the foreign State does not in itself preclude immunity in respect of its activities.

3. The fact that an entity has the status of a constituent unit of a federal State, or a comparable status of special autonomy, under the law of the foreign State does not preclude immunity in respect of its activities.

Article 4   2.118

Measures of Constraint

1. The property of a foreign State is not subject to any process or order of the courts or other organs of the forum State for the satisfaction or enforcement of a judgment or order, or for the purpose of prejudgment measures in preparation for execution (hereafter referred to as measures of constraint), except as provided for by this Article and by Article 5.

2. The following categories of property of a State in particular are immune from measures of constraint:

   a) property used or set aside for use by the State's diplomatic or consular missions, its special missions or its missions to international organizations;

   b) property in use or set aside for use by the armed forces of the State for military purposes;

   c) property of the central bank or monetary authority of the State in use or set aside for use for the purposes of the central bank or monetary authority;

   d) property identified as part of the cultural heritage of the State, or of its archives, and not placed or intended to be placed on sale.

3. Subject to paragraph (2) above, the following property of a State is not immune from measures of constraint:

   a) property allocated or earmarked by the State for the satisfaction of the claim in question;

   b) where the property referred to in sub-paragraph (a) has been exhausted or is shown to be clearly inadequate to satisfy the claim, other property of the State within the territory of the forum State which is in use or intended for use for commercial purposes.

4. This Article applies to property of or in the possession of State agencies and political subdivisions of a State, whatever their formal designation or constitutional status; but this is without prejudice to the due identification of:

   a) the legal entity liable in respect of the claim, and

   b) the property which belongs to that entity and which may accordingly be liable in accordance with paragraph (3) to measures of prejudgment attachment and seizure in execution to satisfy its liabilities.

5. The courts and other organs of the forum State shall give appropriate effect to the principle of proportionality as between the remedy sought and the consequences of enforcement measures.

2.119 **Article 5**

Consent or Waiver

1. A foreign State may not invoke immunity from jurisdiction or from measures of constraint if it has expressly consented to the exercise of the relevant type of jurisdiction by the relevant court or other organs of the forum State:

   a) by international agreement;

   b) in a written contract;

   c) by a declaration relating to the specific case;

   d) by a voluntary submission to jurisdiction in the form of the institution of proceedings in the relevant organs of the forum State, or of intervention in proceedings for the purpose of pursuing issues related to the merits of those proceedings, or of a comparable step in the proceedings.

2. Consent to the exercise of jurisdiction does not imply consent to measures of constraint, for which separate and explicit consent is required.

2.120 **Article 6**

The Principle of Good Faith

The principle of good faith is to be given appropriate weight in applying the present Resolution.

2.121 **Article 7**

Saving Clauses

1. The present Resolution is not intended to indicate either directly or indirectly the validity or otherwise of doctrines affecting the competence of municipal courts which form part of one or more systems of municipal law and of which the act of State doctrine is an example.

2. The present Resolution is not intended to regulate the general question of the recognition, as a matter of private international law, of the validity of foreign governmental acts.

3. A foreign State which asserts its jurisdictional immunity in respect of a claim before a relevant organ of the forum State is not thereby precluded from arguing that the organ lacks competence to determine the subject-matter of the claim for reasons other than jurisdictional immunity.

4. The present Resolution is without prejudice to the privileges and immunities accorded to a State under international law in relation to the exercise of the functions of:

   a) its diplomatic missions, consular posts, special missions, missions to international organizations or delegations to organs of international organizations or to international conferences; and

   b) persons connected with them.

5. The present Resolution is without prejudice to the personal privileges and immunities accorded to Heads of States under international law.

*

(2 September 1991)

2.122   Resolution of L'Institut de Droit International on Immunities from Jurisdiction and Execution of Heads of State and of Government in International Law[7]

The Institute of International Law,

Recalling the draft international rules on the jurisdiction of courts in proceedings against foreign States, sovereigns and Heads of State it adopted at its 11th Session (Hamburg, 1891), as well as the Resolutions on "Immunity of Foreign States from Jurisdiction and Measure of Execution", and on the "Contemporary Problems Concerning the Immunity of States in Relation to Questions of Jurisdiction and Enforcement", adopted respectively at its 46th (Aix-en-Provence, 1954) and 65th (Basel, 1991) Sessions;

Wishing to dispel uncertainties encountered in contemporary practice pertaining to the inviolability and immunity from jurisdiction and enforcement that a Head of State or Head of Government can invoke before the authorities of another State;

Affirming that special treatment is to be given to a Head of State or a Head of Government, as a representative of that State and not in his or her personal interest, because this is necessary for the exercise of his or her functions and the fulfilment of his or her responsibilities in an independent and effective manner, in the well-conceived interest of both the State or the Government of which he or she is the Head and the international community as a whole;

Recalling that the immunities afforded to a Head of State or Head of Government in no way imply that he or she is not under an obligation to respect the law in force on the territory of the forum;

Emphasising that these immunities of Heads of State or of Heads of Government should not be understood as allowing him or her to misappropriate the assets of the State which they represent, and that all States shall render each other mutual assistance in the recovery of such funds by the State to whom they belong, in conformity with the principles stressed in the Institute's Resolution on "Public Claims Instituted by a Foreign Authority or a Foreign Public Body" adopted at the Oslo Session (1977);

Adopts the following Resolution:

---

[7] Text adopted by the Thirteenth Commission (Rapporteur: Mr Joe Verhoeven) on 26 August 2001. The English text is a translation of the authoritative French text. Source: http://www.idi-iil.org.

1st Part: Serving Heads of State

Article 1   2.123

When in the territory of a foreign State, the person of the Head of State is inviolable.

While there, he or she may not be placed under any form or arrest or detention. The Head of State shall be treated by the authorities with due respect and all reasonable steps shall be taken to prevent any infringement of his or her person, liberty, or dignity.

Article 2   2.124

In criminal matters, the Head of State shall enjoy immunity from jurisdiction before the courts of a foreign State for any crime he or she may have committed, regardless of its gravity.

Article 3   2.125

In civil and administrative matters, the Head of State does not enjoy any immunity from jurisdiction before the courts of a foreign State, unless that suit relates to acts performed in the exercise of his or her official functions. Even in such a case, the Head of State shall enjoy no immunity in respect of a counterclaim. Nonetheless, nothing shall be done by way of court proceedings with regard to the Head of State while he or she is in the territory of that State, in the exercise of official functions.

Article 4   2.126

1. Property belonging personally to a Head of State and located in the territory of a foreign State may not be subject to any measure of execution except to give effect to a final judgement, rendered against such Head of State. In any event, no measure of execution may be taken against such property when the Head of State is present in the territory of the foreign State in the exercise of official functions.

2. When serious doubt arises as to the legality of the appropriation of a fund or any other asset held by, or on behalf of, the Head of State, nothing in these provisions prevents the State authorities of the territory on which those funds or other assets are located, from taking provisional measures with respect to those funds or assets, as are necessary for the maintenance of control over them while the legality of the appropriation remains insufficiently established.

3. In conformity with their obligations of cooperation, States should take all appropriate measures to combat illegal practices, in particular to clarify the origin of deposits and dealings in assets and to supply all relevant information in this respect.

2.127 Article 5

Neither family members nor members of the suite of the Head of State benefit from immunity before the authorities of a foreign State, unless afforded as a matter of comity. This is without prejudice to any immunities they may enjoy in another capacity, in particular as a member of a special mission, while accompanying a Head of State abroad.

2.128 Article 6

The authorities of the State shall afford to a foreign Head of State, the inviolability, immunity from jurisdiction and immunity from measures of execution to which he or she is entitled, as soon as that status is known to them.

2.129 Article 7

1. The Head of State may no longer benefit from the inviolability, immunity from jurisdiction or immunity from measures of execution conferred by international law, where the benefit thereof is waived by his or her State. Such waiver may be explicit or implied, provided it is certain.

   The domestic law of the State concerned determines which organ is competent to effect such a waiver.

2. Such a waiver should be made when the Head of State is suspected of having committed crimes of a particularly serious nature, or when the exercise of his or her functions is not likely to be impeded by the measures that the authorities of the forum may be called upon to take.

2.130 Article 8

1. States may, by agreement, derogate to the extent they see fit, from the inviolability, immunity from jurisdiction and immunity from measures of execution accorded to their own Heads of State.

2. In the absence of an express derogation, there is a presumption that no derogation has been made to the inviolability and immunities referred to in the preceding paragraph; the existence and extent of such a derogation shall be unambiguously established by any legal means.

2.131 Article 9

Nothing in this Resolution prohibits a State from unilaterally granting to a foreign Head of State, in conformity with international law, larger immunities than those laid down by the present provisions.

Article 10

Nothing in this Resolution affects any right of, or obligation incumbent upon, a State to grant or refuse to the Head of a foreign State access to, or sojourn on, its territory.

Article 11

1. Nothing in this Resolution may be understood to detract from:
   a. obligations under the Charter of the United Nations;
   b. the obligations under the statutes of the international criminal tribunals as well as the obligations, for those States that have become parties thereto, under the Rome Statute for an International Criminal Court.
2. This Resolution is without prejudice to:
   a. the rules which determine the jurisdiction of a tribunal before which immunity may be raised;
   b. the rules which relate to the definition of crimes under international law;
   c. the obligations of cooperation incumbent upon States in these matters.
3. Nothing in this Resolution implies nor can be taken to mean that a Head of State enjoys an immunity before an international tribunal with universal or regional jurisdiction.

Article 12

This Resolution is without prejudice to the effect of recognition or non-recognition of a foreign State or government on the application of its provisions.

2nd Part: Former Heads of State

Article 13

1. A former Head of State enjoys no inviolability in the territory of a foreign State.
2. Nor does he or she enjoy immunity from jurisdiction, in criminal, civil or administrative proceedings, except in respect of acts which are performed in the exercise of official functions and relate to the exercise thereof. Nevertheless, he or she may be prosecuted and tried when the acts alleged constitute a crime under international law, or when they are performed exclusively to satisfy a personal interest, or when they constitute a misappropriation of the State's assets and resources.
3. Neither does he or she enjoy immunity from execution.

2.136 **Article 14**

Article 4, paragraphs 2 and 3, and Articles 5 to 12 of this Resolution apply *mutatis mutandis* to former Heads of State to the extent that they enjoy immunity under Article 13.

3rd Part: Heads of Government

2.137 **Article 15**

1. The Head of Government of a foreign State enjoys the same inviolability, and immunity from jurisdiction recognised, in this Resolution, to the Head of the State. This provision is without prejudice to any immunity from execution of a Head of Government.

2. Paragraph 1 is without prejudice to such immunities to which other members of the government may be entitled on account of their official functions.

2.138 **Article 16**

Articles 13 and 14 are applicable to former Heads of Government.

*

(26th August 2001)

PART 3
UNITED STATES OF AMERICA

The Foreign Sovereign Immunities Act 1976[1]

Introduction

President Gerald R Ford signed the FSIA into law on 21 October 1976.[2] In doing so, the United States codified the restrictive theory of sovereign immunity that had been adopted by the United States Department of State some 24 years earlier.[3] More importantly, the FSIA removed the question of sovereign immunity from the executive branch to the judicial branch of the United States government. Prior to the enactment of the FSIA the courts normally deferred to the "suggestions of immunity" of the Department of State.[4] After the enactment of the FSIA, the question of sovereign immunity was left to solely the courts.

The FSIA was intended to remove the uncertainty created by the Department of State's discretionary role in matters of sovereign immunity. President Ford himself stated, "[i]n this modern world where private citizens increasingly come

---

[1] 28 USC §§ 1330, 1391(f), 1441(d), and 1602–1611. Referred to below as the "FSIA".

[2] As enacted, the Foreign Sovereign Immunities Act of 1976 (HR 11315) is Public Law 94-583, approved 21 October 1976.

[3] See *Letter from Jack B. Tate, Acting Legal Advisor, Department of State, to Phillip B. Perlman, Acting Attorney General of the United States* (19 May 1952) (the "Tate Letter") (reprinted in 26 Dep't of State Bull. 984 (1952); also reprinted in *Alfred Dunhill of London, Inc. v Cuba*, 425 US 682, 711–715, cert. denied, 425 US 1991 (1976)). Prior to the Tate Letter, foreign sovereigns enjoyed absolute immunity from the jurisdiction of the courts of the United States. See *The Schooner Exchange v McFaddon*, 11 US (7 Cranch) 116 (1812).

[4] "The central principle of the [FSIA] is to make the question of a foreign state's entitlement to immunity an issue justiciable by the courts, without participation by the Department of State. As the situation now stands, the courts normally defer to the views of the Department of State, which puts the Department in the difficult position of effectively determining whether the plaintiff will have his day in court . . . The transfer of this function to the courts will . . . free the Department from pressures by foreign states to suggest immunity and from any adverse consequences resulting from the unwillingness of the Department to suggest immunity. The Department would be in a position to assert that the question of immunity is entirely one for the courts." (Attorney General Richard G Kleindienst and Secretary of State William Rogers, *Immunities of Foreign States*, hearing before the Sub-committee on Claims and Governmental Relations, House Judiciary Committee, 93rd Cong. (7 June 1973) at 34.) See HR Rep No 94-1487, *Jurisdiction of United States Courts in Suits Against Foreign States*, 94th Cong. (9 September 1976) 12 (reprinted in 1976 USCCAN 6604, 6610) ("[The FSIA] is also designed to bring US practice into conformity with that of most other nations by leaving sovereign immunity decisions exclusively to the courts, thereby discontinuing the practice of judicial deference to 'suggestions of immunity' from the executive branch"). See also *Ex parte Republic of Peru*, 318 US 578, 586–587 (1943) ("the judicial department . . . follows the action of the political branch, and will not embarrass the latter by assuming an antagonistic jurisdiction"); *Republic of Mexico v Hoffman*, 324 US 30 (1945).

into contact with foreign government activities, it is important to know when the courts are available to redress legal grievances".[5]

As stated in the House Report on the FSIA:

> [c]onstitutional authority for enacting such legislation derives from the constitutional power of Congress to prescribe the jurisdiction of the Federal courts (art. I, sec. 8, cl. 9; Art. III, sec. 1); to define offenses against the Law of Nations (art. I, sec. 8, cl. 10); to regulate commerce with foreign nations (art. I, sec. 8, cl. 3); and to make all Laws which shall be necessary and proper for carrying into execution all Powers vested in the Government of the United States, including the judicial power of the United States over controversies between a State, or the Citizens thereof, and foreign states (art. I, sec. 8, cl. 18; art III, sec. 2, cl. 1).[6]

The FSIA was "the product of many years of work by the Department of State and Justice in consultation with members of the bar and the academic community".[7] Study of possible legislation began in the mid-1960s. A draft of the FSIA was first introduced on the floor of the House of Representatives on 31 January 1973 and then referred to the Judiciary Committee. A sub-committee hearing on the bill was heard on 7 June 1973.[8] Further sub-committee hearings were held on June 2 and June 4, 1976.[9] The bill enacted in 1976 was "essentially the same bill as was introduced in 1973, except for . . . technical improvements".[10] The FSIA has been amended and modified on several occasions and is currently codified in Title 28 of the United States Code at ss 1330 (jurisdiction), 1391(f) (venue), 1441(d) (removal), and 1602 through 1611 (immunity).

3.002 28 U.S.C. § 1330

Actions against foreign states

(a) The district courts shall have original jurisdiction without regard to amount in controversy of any nonjury civil action against a foreign state as defined in section 1603(a) of this title as to any claim for relief *in personam* with respect to which the foreign state is not entitled to immunity either

---

[5] Statement by President Gerald Ford on signing HR 11315 into law. Foreign Sovereign Immunities Act, 12 Weekly Compilation of Presidential Documents 1556 (1976).

[6] HR Rep No 94-1487, *Jurisdiction of United States Courts in Suits Against Foreign States*, 94th Cong. (9 September 1976) at 12 (reprinted in 1976 USCCAN 6604, 6611). See *Verlinden B. V. v Central Bank of Nigeria*, 461 US 480, 485 (1983) (FSIA does not exceed bounds of Art III of the United States Constitution).

[7] HR Rep No 94-1487, *Jurisdiction of United States Courts in Suits Against Foreign States*, 94th Cong. (9 September 1976) at 9 (reprinted in 1976 USCCAN 6604, 6608).

[8] *Immunities of Foreign States*, hearings before the Sub-committee on Claims and Governmental Relations, House Judiciary Committee, 93rd Cong. (7 June 1973).

[9] *Jurisdiction of US Courts in Suits Against Foreign States*, hearings before the Sub-committee on Administrative Law and Governmental Relations, House Judiciary Committee, 94th Cong. (2, 4 June 1976).

[10] HR Rep No 94-1487, *Jurisdiction of United States Courts in Suits Against Foreign States*, 94th Cong. (9 September 1976) at 10 (reprinted in 1976 USCCAN 6604, 6608).

under sections 1605–1607 of this title or under any applicable international agreement.

(b) Personal jurisdiction over a foreign state shall exist as to every claim for relief over which the district courts have jurisdiction under subsection (a) where service has been made under section 1608 of this title.

(c) For purposes of subsection (b), an appearance by a foreign state does not confer personal jurisdiction with respect to any claim for relief not arising out of any transaction or occurrence enumerated in sections 1605–1607 of this title.

Commentary

Legislative history   3.003

Section 1330, the jurisdiction-conferring provision of the FSIA, provides the sole basis for obtaining jurisdiction over a foreign state in the courts of the United States.[11]

Congress reasoned that "[s]uch broad jurisdiction in the Federal courts should be conducive to uniformity in decision, which is desirable since a disparate treatment of cases involving foreign governments may have adverse foreign relations consequences".[12]

Until the FSIA's passage in 1976, 28 USC § 1332 provided for federal diversity jurisdiction over cases brought by a party against a foreign state.[13] However, in 1976 the provisions of former subsections 1332 (a)(2) and (3) were deleted and replaced by s 1330(a) of the FSIA.[14] The House Report on the FSIA explained that "[s]ince jurisdiction in actions against foreign states is comprehensively treated by the new section 1330, a similar jurisdictional basis under s 1332 becomes superfluous".[15] Moreover, s 1332 contained an amount in controversy requirement of $10,000 before a party could bring a claim against a foreign state in federal court. Congress purposely excluded any amount in controversy

---

[11] See *Argentine Republic v Amerada Hess Shipping Corp.*, 488 US 428, 434 (1989) ("We think that the text and structure of the FSIA demonstrate Congress' intention that the FSIA be the sole basis for obtaining jurisdiction over a foreign state in our courts"). See also *Saudi Arabia v Nelson*, 507 US 349 (1993); *Fagot Rodriguez v Republic of Costa Rica*, 297 F 3d 1, 3 (1st Cir. 2002); *In re Republic of Philippines*, 309 F 3d 1143, 1149 (9th Cir. 2002); *Virtual Countries, Inc. v Republic of South Africa*, 300 F 3d 230, 235 (2d Cir. 2002); *Transatlantic Shiffahrtskontor GmbH v Shanghai Foreign Trade Corp.*, 204 F 3d 384, 388 (2d Cir. 2000), cert. denied, 532 US 904 (2001); *Cabiri v Government of Republic of Ghana*, 165 F 3d 193, 196 (2d Cir. 1999), cert. denied, 527 US 1022; *Creighton Ltd. v Government of State of Qatar*, 181 F 3d 118, 121 (DC Cir 1999); *Universal Consolidated Companies, Inc. v Bank of China*, 35 F 3d 243, 246 (6th Cir. 1994).

[12] HR Rep No 94-148/, *Jurisdiction of United States Courts in Suits Against Foreign States*, 94th Cong. (9 September 1976) at 13 (reprinted in 1976 USCCAN 6604, 6611).

[13] See *Princz v Federal Republic of Germany*, 26 F 3d 1166, 1176 (DC Cir 1994).

[14] See *Ruggiero v Compania Peruana de Vapores "Inca Capac Yupanqui"*, 639 F 2d 872, 875 (2d Cir. 1981).

[15] HR Rep No 94-1487, *Jurisdiction of United States Courts in Suits Against Foreign States*, 94th Cong. (9 September 1976) at 14 (reprinted in 1976 USCCAN 6604, 6613).

requirement from the FSIA because it "intended to encourage the bringing of actions against foreign states in Federal courts".[16] Congress, however, did not grant the federal courts exclusive jurisdiction over cases involving foreign states and therefore plaintiffs may elect to proceed in either federal court or in a court of a state, subject to the liberal removal provisions applicable to foreign sovereigns.[17]

3.004   Application

Both subject matter jurisdiction and personal jurisdiction turn on the application of the substantive provisions of the FSIA.[18] With respect to subject matter jurisdiction, "[s]ections 1604 and 1330(a) work in tandem: section 1604 bars federal and state courts from exercising jurisdiction when a foreign state is entitled to immunity, and section 1330(a) confers jurisdiction on district courts to hear suits brought by United States citizens and aliens when a foreign state is not entitled to immunity".[19] If one of the specified exceptions to sovereign immunity applies, a federal district court may exercise subject matter jurisdiction under s 1330(a). If, however, the claim does not fall within one of the exceptions, the courts of the United States lack subject matter jurisdiction over foreign sovereign defendants.[20]

There are two requirements to establish personal jurisdiction over a foreign sovereign defendant under the FSIA: (1) subject matter jurisdiction, and (2) proper service of process.[21] Section 1608 sets forth the methods by which service may be effected on a foreign state.[22]

The law is currently unclear as to whether the Constitution of the United States affords foreign sovereigns with the jurisdictional protections of the due process clauses of the Fifth and Fourteenth Amendments.[23] The uncertainty concerns whether foreign sovereigns are "persons" as contemplated by the Constitution.[24]

---

[16] HR Rep No 94-1487, *Jurisdiction of United States Courts in Suits Against Foreign States*, 94th Cong. (9 September 1976) at 13 (reprinted in 1976 USCCAN 6604, 6612).

[17] HR Rep No 94-1487, *Jurisdiction of United States Courts in Suits Against Foreign States*, 94th Cong. (9 September 1976) at 13 (reprinted in 1976 USCCAN 6604, 6612). The removal provision applicable to foreign sovereigns can be found at 28 USC § 1441(d). See discussion at 3.009–3.011 above.

[18] See, eg, *Verlinden B. V. v Central Bank of Nigeria*, 461 US 480, 485 (1983).

[19] *Amerada Hess Shipping Corp.*, 488 US at 434.   [20] *Verlinden*, 461 US at 489.

[21] See, eg, *Texas Trading & Milling Corp. v Fed. Republic of Nigeria*, 647 F 2d 300, 308 (2d Cir. 1981), cert. denied, 454 US 1148 (1982). See HR Rep No 94-1487, *Jurisdiction of United States Courts in Suits Against Foreign States*, 94th Cong. (9 September 1976) at 13 (reprinted in 1976 USCCAN 6604, 6612).   [22] See discussion at 3.082–3.084 below.

[23] The due process clauses require that a defendant have "certain minimum contacts with the forum such that maintenance of the suit does not offend traditional notions of fair play and substantial justice". *Helicopteros Nationales de Colombia, S.A. v Hall*, 466 US 408, 413–414 (1984) (quoting *International Shoe Co. v Washington*, 326 US 310, 316 (1945)).

[24] The Supreme Court has explicitly reserved judgment on this issue. See *Republic of Argentina v Weltover, Inc.*, 504 US 607, 619 (1992) (assuming without deciding that a foreign state is a person for purposes of the due process clause). The Second Circuit has described the genesis of the uncertainty in *Hanil Bank v PT. Bank Negara Indonesia (Persero)*, 148 F 3d 127, 134 (2d Cir. 1998):

In *Texas Trading & Milling Corp. v. Federal Republic of Nigeria*, 647 F.2d 300 (2d Cir.1981), we held that the exercise of jurisdiction over foreign states sued under the FSIA was subject to the

Several courts have held that foreign sovereigns are "persons" and therefore entitled to the due process protections.[25] Recently, however, the influential Circuit Court for the District of Columbia has held to the contrary.[26]

It is noteworthy that even if a court may exercise jurisdiction over a foreign sovereign under this section, the court may decline to do so based upon principles such as *forum non conveniens* or the act of state doctrine.[27]

Finally, s 1330 is important for an additional reason. Pursuant to s 1330(a)   **3.005**
a foreign sovereign can only be tried before a judge.[28] Congress reasoned that bench trials would create more uniformity in the treatment of foreign sovereigns.[29] This provision is mandatory and cannot be waived by the foreign sovereign defendant.[30] However, "it does not necessarily follow that the plaintiff will be deprived of a jury trial with respect to non-sovereign codefendants. The court, in its discretion, may rule on all issues relating to [the sovereign defendant] while empaneling [*sic*] a jury for the other defendants."[31]

28 U.S.C. § 1391—Venue   **3.006**

(f) A civil action against a foreign state as defined in section 1603(a) of this title may be brought—

(1) in any judicial district in which a substantial part of the events or omissions giving rise to the claim occurred, or a substantial part of property that is the subject of the action is situated;

(2) in any judicial district in which the vessel or cargo of a foreign state is situated, if the claim is asserted under section 1605(b) of this title;

same constitutional constraints which "otherwise regulate every exercise of personal jurisdiction." See *id.* at 313 (holding that a foreign state is a "person" within the meaning of the Due Process Clause). However, since the Supreme Court decided *Weltover*, we are uncertain whether our holding remains good law. In *Weltover*, the Supreme Court "[a]ssum[ed], without deciding, that a foreign state is a 'person' for purposes of the Due Process Clause." See 504 US at 619. But, immediately after making that statement, the Court cited *South Carolina v Katzenbach*, 383 US 301, 323–24 (1966), in which it had held that States of the Union were not 'persons' under the Due Process Clause.

[25] See *Texas Trading & Milling Corp.*, 647 F 2d at 313; *Thos. P. Gonzalez Corp. v Consejo Nacional de Produccion de Costa Rica*, 614 F 2d 1247, 1250–1255 (9th Cir. 1980); *Purdy Co. v Argentina*, 333 F 2d 95, 98 (7th Cir. 1964), cert. denied 379 US 962 (1965).
[26] See *Price v Socialist People's Libyan Arab Jamahiriya*, 294 F 3d 82 (DC Cir 2002).
[27] See the *Verlinden* case, 461 US at 485. See also *Honduras Aircraft Registry, Ltd. v Government of Honduras*, 129 F 3d 543 (11th Cir. 1997).   [28] See the *Ruggiero* case, 639 F 2d at 875.
[29] See HR Rep No 94-1487, *Jurisdiction of United States Courts in Suits Against Foreign States*, 94th Cong. (9 September 1976) at 13 (reprinted in 1976 USCCAN 6604, 6611–6612) ("As in suits against the US Government, jury trials are excluded. See 28 USC 2402. Actions tried by a court without a jury will tend to promote a uniformity in decision where foreign governments are involved").
[30] See *Lehman Bros. Commercial Corp. v Minmetals Intern. Non-Ferrous Metals Trading Co.*, 169 F Supp 2d 186, 191 (SDNY 2001).
[31] *Mori v Port Authority of New York and New Jersey*, 100 FRD 810 (SDNY 1984) (citing *Outboard Motor v Pezetel*, 461 F Supp 384, 396 (D Del 1978)).

(3) in any judicial district in which the agency or instrumentality is licensed to do business or is doing business, if the action is brought against an agency or instrumentality of a foreign state as defined in section 1603(b) of this title; or

(4) in the United States District Court for the District of Columbia if the action is brought against a foreign state or political subdivision thereof.

Commentary

3.007   Legislative history

Under this subsection there are four express provisions for venue in civil actions brought against foreign states, political subdivisions or their agencies or instrumentalities as follows:

(1) The action may be brought in the judicial district wherein a substantial part of the events or omissions giving rise to the claim occurred. This provision is analogous to 28 U.S.C. § 1391(e), which allows an action against the United States to be brought, *inter alia*, in any judicial district in which the "cause of action arose." The test adopted, however, is the newer test recommended by the American Law Institute and incorporated into section 1876, 92d Congress, 1st session, which does not imply that there is only one such district applicable in each case. In cases under section 1605(a)(2), involving a commercial activity abroad that causes a direct effect in the United States, venue would exist wherever the direct effect generated "a substantial part of the events" giving rise to the claim. In cases where property or rights in property are involved, the action may be brought in the judicial district in which "a substantial part of the property that is the subject of the action is situated." No hardship will be caused to the foreign state if it is subject to suit where it has chosen to place property that gives rise to the dispute.

(2) If the action is a suit in admiralty to enforce a maritime lien against a vessel or cargo of a foreign state, and if the action is brought under the new section 1605(b) . . . the action may be brought in the judicial district in which the vessel or cargo is situated at the time notice is delivered pursuant to section 1605(b)(1).

(3) If the action is brought against an agency or instrumentality of a foreign state . . . it may be brought in the judicial district where the agency or instrumentality is licensed to do business. This provision is based on 28 U.S.C. § 1391(c).

(4) If the action is brought against a foreign state or a political subdivision, it may be brought in the U.S. District of Columbia. It is in the District of Columbia that foreign states have diplomatic representatives and where it may be easiest for them to defend. This subsection would, of course, not apply to entities that are owned by a foreign state and are also citizens of a state of the United States as defined in 28 U.S.C. § 1332(c)

and (d). For purposes of [the FSIA] such entities are not agencies or instrumentalities of a foreign state. (See analysis to sec. 1603(b).)[32] As with other provisions in 28 U.S.C. § 1391, venue in any court could be waived by a foreign state, such as by failing to object to improper venue in a timely manner. (See rule 12(h), F.R. Civ. P.).[33]

Application   **3.008**

Section 1391(f) only applies to actions which are originally brought in a federal court.[34] Actions removed from state court are not subject to this venue provision. Where an action is removed from state court, s 1441 governs and the proper venue is in "the judicial district embracing the place where such action is pending".[35] However, if the court decides to transfer venue pursuant to s 1404(a), the transferee court must meet the requirements of s 1391(f).[36]

Subsection 1391(f)(1) provides that venue is proper in any judicial district in which a *substantial* part of the events giving rise to the claim occurred, or a *substantial* part of the property that is the subject of the action is situated. In a provision similar to s 1391(f)(1), "substantial" has been construed as more than a tangential connection so as to preserve the element of fairness so that a defendant is not hauled into a remote district having no real relationship with the dispute.[37]

With respect to s 1391(f)(1) "property" has been construed to include intangible property such as accounts receivables.[38] One court has stated that this subsection is "applicable to suits involving property disputes or *in rem* actions, not . . . to suits alleging financial damages to a corporation".[39]

28 U.S.C. § 1441—Removal   **3.009**

(d) Any civil action brought in a State court against a foreign state as defined in section 1603(a) of this title may be removed by the foreign state to the district court of the United States for the district and division embracing the place where such action is pending. Upon removal the action shall be tried by the court without jury. Where removal is based upon this subsection, the time limitations of section 1446(b) of this chapter[40] may be enlarged at any time for cause shown.

---

[32] See § 1603(b) (3.015–3.018 below).

[33] HR Rep No 94-1487, *Jurisdiction of United States Courts in Suits Against Foreign States*, 94th Cong. (9 September 1976) at 31–32 (reprinted in 1976 USCCAN 6604, 6630–6631).

[34] See *Translinear Inc. v Republic of Haiti*, 538 F Supp 141, 144 (DDC 1982).

[35] 28 USC § 1441(d) (see 3.009–3.011 below).

[36] See *Translinear*, 538 F Supp, at 144, n. 2.

[37] See *Siegel v Homestore Inc.*, 255 F Supp 2d 451, 454 (ED Pa 2003) (citing *Cottman Transmission Systems Inc. v Martino*, 36 F 3d 291, 294 (3d Cir. 1994) (construing 28 USC § 1391(a)(2)).

[38] See *Kalamazoo Spice Extraction Company v Provisional Military Government of Socialist Ethiopia*, 616 F Supp 660, 666 (WD Mich 1985).

[39] *Falcoal Inc. v Turkiye Komur Isletmeleri Kurumu*, 660 F Supp 1536, 1542 (SD Tex 1987).

[40] 28 USC § 1446(b) states in relevant part: "The notice of removal of a civil action or proceeding shall be filed within thirty days after the receipt by the defendant, through service or otherwise, of

Commentary

3.010   Legislative history

Congress provided foreign states with an absolute right to remove cases brought in state court. Congress reasoned that:

> [i]n view of the potential sensitivity of actions against foreign states and the importance of developing a uniform body of law in this area, it is important to give foreign states clear authority to remove to a Federal forum actions brought against them in the State courts. [Section 1441(d)] permits the removal of any such action at the discretion of the foreign state, even if there are multiple defendants and some of these defendants desire not to remove the action or are citizens of the State in which the action has been brought.[41]

Upon removal, the action would be heard and tried by the appropriate district court sitting without a jury. Thus, one effect of removing an action will be to extinguish a demand for a jury trial made in the state court.[42]

3.011   Application

Where a sovereign defendant in a multi-party suit removes under s 1441(d), "the entire action against all defendants accompanies it to federal court".[43] Removal by foreign state third-party defendants has the same effect.[44] Jurisdiction over

---

a copy of the initial pleading setting forth the claim for relief upon which such action or proceeding is based, or within thirty days after the service of summons upon the defendant if such initial pleading has then been filed in court and is not required to be served on the defendant, whichever period is shorter."

[41] HR Rep No 94-1487, *Jurisdiction of United States Courts in Suits Against Foreign States*, 94th Cong. (9 September 1976) at 32 (reprinted in 1976 USCCAN 6604, 6631).

[42] HR Rep No 94-1487, *Jurisdiction of United States Courts in Suits Against Foreign States*, 94th Cong. (9 September 1976) at 33 (reprinted in 1976 USCCAN 6604, 6632).

[43]   *Chuidian v Philippine Nat. Bank*, 912 F 2d 1095 (9th Cir. 1990). Accord *In re Air Crash Disaster Near Roselawn, Ind. on Oct. 31, 1994*, 96 F 3d 932, 943 (7th Cir. 1996); *In re Surinam Airways Holding Co.*, 974 F 2d 1255, 1258–1260 (11th Cir. 1992); *Nolan v Boeing Co.*, 919 F 2d 1058, 1064–1066 (5th Cir. 1990), cert. denied, 499 US 962 (1991); *Teledyne, Inc. v Kone Corp.*, 892 F 2d 1404 (9th Cir. 1989); *Arango v Guzman Travel Advisors Corp.*, 621 F 2d 1371, 1375–1377 (5th Cir. 1980); see also *Colgan v Port Authority of New York, New Jersey*, 1991 WL 180384, *4 (14 August 1991 EDNY); *Liberty Mutual Insurance Co. v Insurance Corp. of Ireland*, 693 F Supp 340, 345 (WD Pa 1988); *Tucker v Whitaker Travel, Ltd.*, 620 F Supp 578, 581–582 (ED Pa 1985), aff'd, 800 F 2d 1140 (3d Cir.), cert. denied, 479 US 986 (1986); *Mori v Port Authority of New York and New Jersey*, 100 FRD 810, 812 (SDNY 1984); *In re Disaster at Riyadh Airport, Saudi Arabia*, 540 F Supp 1141, 1143 n. 1 (DDC 1982). But see *Admiral Insurance Co. v L'Union des Assurances de Paris*, 758 F Supp 293, 293–294 (ED Pa 1991) (non-sovereign co-defendants are not automatically removed to federal court) (citing *Finley v United States*, 490 US 545 (1989)).

[44]   See *Nolan v Boeing Co.*, 919 F 2d 1058 (5th Cir. 1990), cert. denied, 499 US 962 (1991) ("[W]e can perceive no significant distinction between the authorization for removal of an entire action by a sovereign co-defendant, and removal of an entire action by a sovereign third-party defendant. In fact, the interest of a sovereign third-party defendant in removing the entire case may be more compelling, because its liability is logically dependent on the liability of a defendant in the main action").

the non-sovereign defendants, however, does not attach until the court determines that the foreign state lacks immunity.[45]

While removal by a foreign state will extinguish a jury demand with respect to the foreign state defendants, "it does not necessarily follow that the plaintiff will be deprived of a jury trial. The court, in its discretion, may rule on all issues relating to [the sovereign defendant] while empaneling a jury for the other defendants".[46]

Several circuit courts have held that a foreign sovereign may contractually waive the right to remove an action from state court to federal court, but such waiver must be "clear and unequivocal".[47] A forum selection clause "that merely puts jurisdiction in either a federal or state court does not constitute an express or implied waiver of the sovereign's right to remove under § 1441(d)".[48]

28 U.S.C. § 1602   3.012

Findings and declaration of purpose

The Congress finds that the determination by United States courts of the claims of foreign states to immunity from the jurisdiction of such courts would serve the interests of justice and would protect the rights of both foreign states and litigants in United States courts. Under international law, states are not immune from the jurisdiction of foreign courts insofar as their commercial activities are concerned, and their commercial property may be levied upon for the satisfaction of judgments rendered against them in connection with their commercial activities. Claims of foreign states to immunity should henceforth be decided by courts of the United States and of the States in conformity with the principles set forth in this chapter.

Commentary

Legislative history   3.013

The FSIA was:

> not intended to affect the substantive law of liability. Nor [was] it intended to affect neither diplomatic or consular immunity, or the attribution of responsibility between or among entities of a foreign state; for example, whether the proper entity of a foreign state has been sued, or whether an entity sued is liable in whole or in part for the claimed wrong.[49]

[45] See *Jones v Petty-Ray Geophysical Geosource, Inc.*, 954 F 2d 1061 (5th Cir. 1992), cert. denied, 506 US 867 (1992).

[46] *Mori*, 100 FRD, 810 (citing *Outboard Motor v Pezetel*, 461 F Supp 384, 396 (D Del 1978)).

[47] *In re Delta America re Insurance Co.*, 900 F 2d 890, 893 (6th Cir.), cert. denied 498 US 890 (1990). Accord *In re Texas Eastern Transmission Corp. PCB Contamination Ins. Coverage Litigation*, 15 F 3d 1230 (3d Cir.), cert. denied 513 US 915 (1994); *Proyecfin de Venezuela, S.A. v Banco Industrial de Venezuela, S.A.*, 760 F 2d 390 (2d Cir. 1985); *Hamakua Sugar Co., Inc. v Fiji Sugar Corp., Ltd.*, 778 F Supp 503 (D. Hawaii 1991).   [48] *Proyecfin de Venezuela*, 760 F 2d at 390.

[49] HR Rep No 94-1487, *Jurisdiction of United States Courts in Suits Against Foreign States*, 94th Cong. (9 September 1976) at 11–12 (reprinted in 1976 USCCAN 6604, 6610).

The purpose of enacting the FSIA was four-fold: (1) to codify the so-called restrictive principle of sovereign immunity (2) to ensure that the restrictive principle of sovereign immunity was always applied in litigation before US courts (3) to provide a statutory procedure to effect service of process on a foreign government and (4) to provide some means for plaintiffs to execute judgments obtained against foreign governments.[50]

Section 1602 of the FSIA, the findings and declaration of purpose section, introduces the important distinction between the "governmental" acts (*acta jure imperii*) and the "private" or "commercial" acts (*acta jure gestionis*) of a foreign state.[51] This distinction is representative of the "restrictive view" of sovereign immunity, which succeeded the older "absolutist" view, in a process of evolution described below.[52]

The US approach to questions of foreign sovereign immunity has evolved over the past two centuries. From about 1812 to 1952, the US granted foreign sovereigns almost absolute immunity from suit in US courts.[53] During this early period of US sovereign immunity law, courts generally deferred to the Executive Branch on whether or not to exercise jurisdiction over foreign sovereigns, and the State Department "ordinarily requested immunity in all actions against friendly foreign sovereigns".[54]

However, in 1952, the Executive Branch formally adopted the restrictive theory of immunity in a letter written by Jack B Tate, acting legal adviser for the Secretary of State, to the Attorney General (the "Tate Letter").[55] In the Tate Letter, the State Department announced that it would no longer recommend to US courts that foreign states be granted immunity in certain types of cases, namely those involving *jure gestionis*.[56] Section 1602 of the FSIA sets forth Congress's intention to codify the restrictive theory of immunity described in the Tate Letter.[57]

---

[50] HR Rep No 94-1487, *Jurisdiction of United States Courts in Suits Against Foreign States*, 94th Cong. (9 September 1976) at 7-8 (reprinted in 1976 USCCAN 6604, 6605–6606).

[51] See HR Rep No 94-1487, *Jurisdiction of United States Courts in Suits Against Foreign States*, 94th Cong. (9 September 1976) at 14 (reprinted in 1976 USCCAN 6604, 6613). See also *Letelier v Republic of Chile*, 748 F 2d 790, 796 (2d Cir. 1984), cert. denied, 471 US 1125 (1985).

[52] "According to the classical or absolute theory of sovereign immunity, a sovereign cannot, without his consent, be made a respondent in the courts of another sovereign." See *Letter from Jack B. Tate, Acting Legal Advisor, Department of State, to Phillip B. Perlman, Acting Attorney General of the United States* (19 May 1952) (reprinted in 26 Dep't of State Bull. 984 (1952)). See also discussion at 3.001 above.

[53] See *Verlinden B.V. v Central Bank of Nigeria*, 461 US 480, 486 (1983) (citing *The Schooner Exchange v M'Fadden*, 11 US (7 Cranch) 116, 136–137 (1812)).   [54] *Verlinden*, 461 US at 486.

[55] See *Letter from Jack B. Tate, Acting Legal Advisor, Department of State, to Phillip B. Perlman, Acting Attorney General of the United States* (19 May 1952) (reprinted in 26 Dep't of State Bull. 984 (1952)). See also discussion at 3.001 above. See also *Letelier*, 748 F 2d at 796 (citing *National City Bank of New York v Republic of China*, 348 US 356 (1955)).

[56] See the Tate Letter. See also *Verlinden*, 461 US at 486–487.

[57] "[S]overeign immunity of foreign states should be 'restricted' to cases involving acts of a foreign state which are sovereign or governmental in nature, as opposed to acts which are either commercial in nature or those which private persons normally perform." See HR Rep No 94-1487, *Jurisdiction of United States Courts in Suits Against Foreign States*, 94th Cong. (9 September 1976), 14 (reprinted in 1976 USCCAN 6604, 6613). See also *Verlinden*, 461 US, 488; *Princz v Federal Republic of Germany*,

Application **3.014**

Section 1602 is not a heavily litigated section of the FSIA. The primary issue that has arisen with respect to this section is the correct interpretation of "henceforth," and whether to apply the FSIA retroactively.[58] Traditionally, absent clear legislative intent to the contrary, courts have refused to apply non-remedial statutes with retrospective effect.[59] The courts have adopted this doctrine because "[e]lementary considerations of fairness dictate that individuals should have an opportunity to know what the law is and to conform their conduct accordingly; settled expectations should not be lightly disrupted".[60]

Accordingly, in *Carl Marks & Co., Inc. v Union of Soviet Socialist Republics*,[61] the court refused to apply the FSIA in actions to recover on debt instruments issued by the Imperial Russian Government in 1916.[62] The Second Circuit affirmed the court's judgment stating: "[w]e believe, as did the district court, that only after 1952 was it reasonable for a foreign sovereign to anticipate being sued in the United States courts on commercial transactions".[63] The court reasoned that "[s]uch a retroactive application of the FSIA would affect adversely the USSR's settled expectation, rising to the level of an antecedent right, of immunity from suit in American courts".[64] The Second Circuit explicitly reserved judgment on whether the FSIA would apply to such contracts if they arose after the issuance of the Tate Letter.[65]

Subsequently, in a non-FSIA case, the Supreme Court clarified the rule against the retroactive application of a statute. In *Landgraf v USI Film Products*,[66] the

---

26 F 3d 1166, 1169 (DC Cir 1994), cert. denied, 513 US 1121 (1995); *Carl Marks & Co., Inc. v Union of Soviet Socialist Republics*, 665 F Supp 323, 336 (SDNY 1987), aff'd, 841 F 2d 26 (2d Cir.), cert. denied, 487 US 1219 (1988) ("Congress enacted the FSIA in 1976, at the urging of the Department of State, because some thought the policy embodied in the Tate Letter had proved awkward to implement and required codification").

[58] See, eg, *Carl Marks & Co. v Union of Soviet Socialist Republics*, 441 F 2d 26 (2d Cir. 1988).

[59] "To say that a statute is remedial is simply to say that it does not prejudice antecedent rights" (*Carl Marks*, 665 F Supp at 337). [60] *Landgraf v USI Film Products*, 511 US 244, 265 (1994).

[61] 665 F Supp at 323.

[62] *Carl Marks*, 665 F Supp at 323. The district court refused to read the FSIA's plain language, and its legislative history, as giving it retrospective effect. Indeed, the court looked at the provision of a 90-day grace period between the passage of the FSIA and its effective date, "to put foreign sovereigns on notice of the codification of United States policy [as evidence] of the legislature's desire that it be given prospective application only". 665 F Supp at 336 (quoting *Buccino v Continental Assurance Co.*, 578 F Supp 1518, 1527 (SDNY 1983)).

[63] *Carl Marks*, 841 F 2d at 26. The Second Circuit limited its decision to the applicability of the FSIA to actions which arose prior to the Tate Letter. 841 F 2d, at 26.

[64] *Carl Marks*, 841 F 2d at 27 (citing *Jackson v People's Republic of China*, 794 F 2d 1490, 1497–1498 (11th Cir. 1986)); *Slade v United States of Mexico*, 617 F Supp 351, 358 (DDC 1985), aff'd, 790 F 2d 163 (DC Cir. 1986), cert. denied, 479 US 1032 (1987), *Schmidt v Polish People's Republic*, 742 F 2d 67, 71 (2d Cir. 1984). Accord *Corporacion Venezolana de Fomento v Vintero Sales Corp.*, 629 F 2d 786, 791 (2d Cir. 1980), cert. denied, 449 US 1080 (1981).

[65] 841 F 2d at 27 ("we need not decide the effect of the FSIA on causes of action arising between 1952 and the enactment of the Act"). Accord *Slade*, 617 F Supp at 351; *Jackson*, 596 F Supp 386 (ND Ala 1984). [66] 511 US at 244.

Supreme Court held that a "statute does not operate 'retrospectively' merely because it is applied in a case arising from conduct antedating the statute's enactment".[67] In the *Landgraf* case, the Supreme Court established a two-step approach to determine whether a statute applies to events predating its enactment. First, a court must ask whether Congress has expressly prescribed the statute's proper reach. If Congress has done so, the inquiry ends. If not, the court must determine whether applying the statute to pre-enactment events would have retroactive effect, ie, whether it would impair rights a party possessed when he acted, increase a party's liability for past conduct, or impose new duties with respect to transactions already completed.[68]

Several courts have held that the Supreme Court's decision in the *Landgraf* case "establishes the full retroactivity of the FSIA and thus effectively overrules the Second Circuit's decision in *Carl Marks*".[69] Other courts have disagreed with this interpretation of the *Landgraf* case as applied to the FSIA. In *Garb v Republic of Poland*, the court wrote:

> [n]othing in the Court's decision in *Landgraf* overruled the Second Circuit's ruling in *Carl Marks* that a foreign state's settled expectation of immunity from the jurisdiction of the United States courts rises to the level of an antecedent right. Indeed . . . the Court simply reaffirmed in *Landgraf* the principles of retroactivity that it had been applying since at least as early as its decision in *Hallowell v. Commons*, 239 U.S. 506 (1916).[70]

Recently, the Second Circuit in *Abrams v Société Nationale des Chemins de Fer Français*[71] did not rely on the *Carl Marks* case in addressing the retroactive application of the FSIA. Instead, the court engaged in a detailed analysis of the FSIA in light of the test set forth in the *Landgraf* case. The court expressly rejected the dicta of the DC Circuit in *Princz v Federal Republic of Germany* and held that "the FSIA's application to the present litigation would be retroactive in the *Landgraf* sense if . . . it fully barred claims that previously could have been

---

[67] *Landgraf*, 511 US at 269.
[68] See *Abrams*, 332 F 3d 173, 180–181 (2d Cir. 2003) (citations and quotation marks omitted). After *Landgraf* the court decided *Lindh v Murphy*, 521 US 320 (1997), which held that normal rules of statutory construction also apply in deciding whether Congress intended a statute to apply prospectively.
[69] *Garb v Republic of Poland*, 207 F Supp 2d 16, 27–28 (EDNY 2002) (citing *Haven v Rzeczpospolita Polska (Republic of Poland)*, 68 F Supp 2d 943, 946 (ND Ill 1999) (FSIA applicable to claims brought on behalf of Polish Jews against Polish government agency seeking compensation for post-World War II expropriation of property); *Altmann v Republic of Austria*, 142 F Supp 2d 1187, 1201 (CD Cal 2001) (FSIA applicable to claim for taking of artwork by Nazis in 1938), aff'd 317 F 3d 954 (9th Cir. 2002), cert. granted, —S Ct— , 2003 WL 21692136 (30 September 2003)). See also *Creighton Limited v Government of the State of Qatar*, 181 F 3d 118 (DC Cir 1999) (the arbitration exception to sovereign immunity held to apply where the arbitration agreement and the actual commencement of arbitration antedated the 1988 enactment of the exception); *Princz*, 26 F 3d at 1170 (suggesting, but not deciding, that "all questions of foreign sovereign immunity, including those that involve an act of a foreign government taken before 1976, are to be decided under the FSIA").
[70] *Garb*, 207 F Supp 2d at 27–28 (internal citations and quotation marks omitted). See *Hwang Geum Joo v Japan*, 332 F 3d 679, 683–684 (DC Cir 2003).   [71] 332 F 3d 173 (2d Cir. 2003).

adjudicated in the United States".[72] The court then asked "whether plaintiffs could have legitimately expected to have their claims adjudicated in the United States prior to the FSIA's enactment".[73] Citing a lack of evidence in the record, the court remanded the case for further proceedings to establish the State Department's policies with respect to plaintiffs' claims at the time they accrued.[74] This reasoning suggests that the Second Circuit would apply the FSIA only to actions which accrued after the issuance of the Tate Letter.

Most recently, the Supreme Court certified *Altmann v Republic of Austria*[75] for review. In that case the Ninth Circuit held that the expropriation exception of s 1605(a)(3) could be applied retroactively to activities of the German and Austrian governments in the 1930s and 1940s. The split of authority occasioned by the *Landgraf* case, therefore, should be resolved shortly by the Supreme Court.

28 U.S.C § 1603   3.015

Definitions

For purposes of this chapter—

(a) A "foreign state", except as used in section 1608 of this title, includes a political subdivision of a foreign state or an agency or instrumentality of a foreign state as defined in subsection (b).

(b) An "agency or instrumentality of a foreign state" means any entity—

    (1) which is a separate legal person, corporate or otherwise, and

    (2) which is an organ of a foreign state or political subdivision thereof, or a majority of whose shares or other ownership interest is owned by a foreign state or political subdivision thereof, and

    (3) which is neither a citizen of a State of the United States as defined in section 1332(c) and (d) of this title, nor created under the laws of any third country.

(c) The "United States" includes all territory and waters, continental or insular, subject to the jurisdiction of the United States.

(d) A "commercial activity" means either a regular course of commercial conduct or a particular commercial transaction or act. The commercial character of an activity shall be determined by reference to the nature of the course

---

[72] 332 F 3d 173 at 186. The reasoning of *Abrams* suggests that the opposite would be true as well; if states could be subjected to claims that previously had been barred the FSIA has a retroactive effect. See *Garb v Republic of Poland*, 2003 WL 21890843 (2d Cir 6 August 2003) (unpublished).

[73] 332 F 3d 173 at 186.

[74] 332 F 3d 173 at 187–188 (citing by way of example a 1949 State Department press release which "announced the Department's policy to 'relieve American courts from any restraint upon the exercise of their jurisdiction' with respect to claims for restitution of identifiable property wrongfully taken as a result of the Nazi persecution in Germany").

[75] 317 F 3d 954 (9th Cir. 2002), cert. granted —S Ct—, 2003 WL 21692136 (30 September 2003).

of conduct or particular transaction or act, rather than by reference to its purpose.

(e) A "commercial activity carried on in the United States by a foreign state" means commercial activity carried on by such state and having substantial contact with the United States.

Commentary

3.016 Legislative history

Section 1603 defines five terms that are used in the FSIA.[76]

3.017 Application

(1) *Foreign state*

Only a foreign state is entitled to the immunity from jurisdiction granted by the FSIA. As defined by s 1603, a foreign state includes political subdivisions, agencies and instrumentalities of a foreign state.

A court may take judicial notice of the existence of a foreign state.[77] When the existence of a foreign state is controverted, the party claiming immunity must present *prima facie* evidence that establishes that it is a foreign state.[78] This evidence typically takes the form of a letter from the ambassador of the foreign state.[79] Once the *prima facie* evidence is presented, the burden shifts to the opposing party to demonstrate an exception to the state's presumptive immunity.[80]

There is usually no dispute that an established nation is a foreign state for purposes of the FSIA.[81] A foreign state is an entity that has a defined territory and a permanent population that is under the control of their own government, and that engages in or has the capacity to engage in formal relations with other

[76] HR Rep No 94-1487, *Jurisdiction of United States Courts in Suits Against Foreign States*, 94th Cong. (9 September 1976) at 15–17 (reprinted in 1976 USCCAN 6604, 6613–6616).

[77] See *Jet Line Services Inc. v M/V Marsa El Hariga*, 462 F Supp 1165, 1171 (D Md 1978). See also *Adler v Federal Republic of Nigeria*, 107 F 3d 720, 723 (9th Cir. 1997) (acknowledging that the Republic of Nigeria was a foreign state).

[78] See *Outbound Maritime Co. P.T. Indonesian Consortium of Constr. Indus.*, 575 F Supp 1222, 1224 (SDNY 1983) (company attempted to claim sovereign immunity, stating that it had recently been nationalized by the Indonesian government) (citing *Victory Transport Inc. v Comisaria General de Abastecimientos y Transportes*, 336 F 2d 354, 359–358, n 7 (2d Cir. 1964), cert. denied, 381 US 934 (1965) (affidavit of Spanish consul in New York not sufficient to raise defense of sovereign immunity)).

[79] See *Garb v Republic of Poland*, 207 F Supp 2d 16, 35 (EDNY 2002); *Harris v VAO Intourist, Moscow*, 481 F Supp 1056, 1058 (EDNY 1979) (citing *Yessenin-Volpin v Novosti Press Agency, Tass*, 443 F Supp 849, 854 (SDNY 1978). See *Outbound Maritime*, 575 F Supp 1222, at 1224; *Jet Line Services*, 462 F Supp at 1165.

[80] *Outbound Maritime*, 575 F Supp at 1224. *Alberti v Empresa Nicaraguense De La Carne*, 705 F 2d 250, 255 (7th Cir. 1983); *Jet Line Services*, 462 F Supp at 1171. For a discussion of burden shifting under the FSIA see 3.027 below.

[81] See, eg, *Adler v Federal Republic of Nigeria*, 107 F 3d 720, 723 (9th Cir. 1997) (acknowledging that the Republic of Nigeria was a foreign state) citing *Joseph v Office of Consulate General of Nigeria*, 830 F 2d 1018, 1021 (9th Cir. 1987), cert. denied, 485 US 905 (1988).

entities.[82] Instances do arise, however, where the existence of a nation is litigated. In *Klinghoffer v S.N.C. Achille Lauro*, the court held that the Palestinian Liberation Organization was not a foreign state, despite the fact that some countries had "recognized" it as such.[83]

When "foreign state" is used in s 1608,[84] the scope of the definition excludes a foreign state's agencies and instrumentalities.[85] Thus, when applied to s 1608, a distinction must be made between the state and its agencies.[86] Two tests have emerged from the courts to determine whether an entity is a foreign state or political subdivision, or an agency or instrumentality thereof.[87] The "core function" test looks at the entity's main purpose and activities and, if its core function is governmental in nature, the entity is a foreign state and not an agency of that state.[88] Other courts have applied the more bright line "legal characteristics" test.[89] Under this test an entity would be considered an agency or instrumentality if it would be a separate entity under the foreign state's own domestic law.[90] This would be demonstrated by showing that the entity was able to "sue and be sued in its own name, contract in its own name, or hold property in its own name".[91]

---

[82] *Klinghoffer v S.N.C. Achille Lauro*, 937 F 2d 44, 47 (2d. Cir. 1991) (citing *National Petrochemical Co. v M/T Stolt Shef*, 860 F 2d 551, 553 (2d Cir. 1988) (quoting *Restatement (Third) of the Foreign Relations Law of The United States* § 201 (1987)). See *Doe v Unocal*, 963 F Supp 880 (CD Cal 1997) (recognizing Myanmar as foreign state) (citing *National Coalition Government of the Union of Burma v Unocal, Inc.*, 176 FRD 329 (CD Cal 1997)).

[83] See *Klinghoffer*, 937 F 2d at 47–48 ("contemplation" of territories such as the Gaza Strip, West Bank and east Jerusalem is insufficient for there to be a finding of a sovereign state).

[84] See 3.082–3.084 below.

[85] 28 USC § 1603(a) reads that a foreign state, "*except as used in section 1608 of this title*, includes a political subdivision of a foreign state or an agency or instrumentality of a foreign state as defined in section (b)." See also HR Rep No 94-1487, *Jurisdiction of United States Courts in Suits Against Foreign States*, 94th Cong. (9 September 1976) at 15 (reprinted in 1976 USCCAN 6604, 6613).

[86] See *Magness v Russian Fed'n*, 247 F 3d 609, 613 n 7 (5th Cir. 2001), cert. denied, 534 US 892 (2001) (characterizing Russian Ministry of Culture as political subdivision of Russia for purposes of service of process); *Filus v LOT Polish Airlines*, 819 F Supp 232, 236–237 (EDNY 1993) (characterizing Ministry of Civil Aviation of USSR alternately as foreign state itself and as political subdivision thereof for purposes of service of process).

[87] *Hyatt Corp. v Stanton*, 945 F Supp 675 (SDNY 1996).

[88] See *Transaero, Inc. v La Fuerrza Aerea Boliviana*, 30 F 3d 148, 151–153 (DC Cir 1994), cert. denied, 513 US 1150 (1995) (finding that Bolvian Air Force was part of a "foreign state" for purposes of the FSIA). See also *Gerritsen v de la Madrid Hurtado*, 819 F 2d 1511, 1517 (9th Cir. 1987) (Mexican consulate is an "organ or political subdivision" of the Mexican state), *Garb v Republic of Poland*, 207 F Supp 2d 16, 37 (EDNY 2002) (denying plaintiff's argument that the Polish Department of Treasury was an agency under s 1605(a)(3) exemption to immunity, merely because it had some characteristics of legal separateness such as the ability to own property), citing *Banco Nacional de Cuba v First Nat'l City Bank of New York*, 478 F 2d 191, 194 (2d Cir. 1973) (facts of case showed that National Bank of Cuba's function in expropriation of property made it "a mere arm or division of the Cuban government"), *Segni v Commercial Office of Spain*, 650 F Supp 1040, 1041 (ND Ill. 1986) (finding that the Commercial Office of Spain was a political subdivision of the government of Spain).

[89] See *Hyatt*, 945 F Supp at 681.

[90] See *Hyatt*, 945 F Supp at 681; *Bowers v Transportes Navieros Ecuadoriano (Transnave)*, 719 F Supp 166, 170 (SDNY 1989); *Unidyne Corp. v Aerolineas Argentinas*, 590 F Supp 398, 400 (ED Va 1984).

[91] *Hyatt*, 945 F Supp at 681, citing *Bowers*, 719 F Supp at 170.

3.018   (2) *Agency or instrumentality*

Under s 1603(a) political subdivisions,[92] instrumentalities and agencies of foreign states are included within the meaning of "foreign state". Section 1603(b) defines "agency or instrumentality" as (1) a separate legal person, corporate or otherwise; which is (2) an organ of a foreign state or political subdivision thereof, or a majority of whose shares or other ownership interests are owned by a foreign state or political subdivision thereof; and is (3) neither a citizen of a state of the US as defined in s 1332(c) and (d) of this title, nor created under the laws of any third country.[93]

The first criterion, that the entity be a separate legal person, is intended to include a corporation, association, foundation, or any other entity which under the laws of the foreign state where it was created can sue or be sued in its own name, contract in its own name or hold property in its own name.[94] "[A] state trading corporation, a mining enterprise, a transport organization such as a shipping line or airline, a steel company, a central bank, an export association, a governmental procurement agency" have all been held to constitute a separate legal entity under the FSIA.[95]

The second criterion prescribes two types of entities that can be agents or instrumentalities. Section 1603(b)(2) states that the entity may be either an "organ of a foreign state" or an entity in which the foreign state has a majority ownership interest.

Organs of the state would be any organizational unit of the state such as an administrative arm of a governmental body.[96] An entity is an organ of a foreign state if it, "engages in a public activity on behalf of the foreign government".[97]

---

[92] HR Rep No 94-1487, *Jurisdiction of United States Courts in Suits Against Foreign States*, 94th Cong. (9 September 1976) at 15 (reprinted in 1976 USCCAN 6604, 6613) (political subdivisions "includes all governmental units beneath the central government, including local governments"). See *Marlowe v Argentine Naval Com'n*, 604 F Supp 703 (DDC 1985).

[93] See *Finanz Ag Zurich v Banco Economico, S.A.*, 192 F 3d 240, 245, aff'd, 192 F 3d 240 (2d Cir. 1999) (finding that a liquidator appointed by the Central Bank of Brazil is an agency and instrumentality of a foreign state); *Gerritsen*, 819 F 2d at 1517 (Mexican Consulate is a foreign state, as it is agency and instrumentality of the Mexican government).

[94] HR Rep No 94-1487, *Jurisdiction of United States Courts in Suits Against Foreign States*, 94th Cong. (9 September 1976) at 15 (reprinted in 1976 USCCAN 6604, 6614).

[95] *Chuidian v Philippine Nat'l Bank*, 912 F 2d 1095, 1101–1103 (9th Cir. 1990) citing HR Rep No 94-1487 *Jurisdiction of United States Courts in Suits Against Foreign States*, 94th Cong. (9 September 1976) at 15 (reprinted in 1976 USCCAN 6604, 6614); see also *Gerritsen v Consulado General de Mexico*, 989 F 2d 340, 345 (9th Cir.), cert. denied, 510 US 828 (1993) (finding that the Mexican Consulate was a separate legal person); *Atwood Turnkey Drilling, Inc. v Petroleo Brasileiro, S.A.*, 875 F 2d 1174, 1176 (5th Cir. 1989), cert. denied, 493 US 1075 (1990) (finding Brazilian company to be a separate legal person as the laws creating it provided that it was), *Nazarian v Compagnie Nationale Air France*, 989 F Supp 504, 507 (SDNY 1998). "The Republic of France owns the majority of the shares of Air France, making Air France an instrumentality of a foreign state under 28 USC § 1603(b)(2)."

[96] See *Rios v Marshall*, 530 F Supp 351, 371 (SDNY 1981). See also *S & S Mach. Co. v Masinexportimport*, 706 F 2d 411, 414 (2d Cir.), cert. denied, 464 US 850 (1983) (finding that Romanian Bank was an agent and instrumentality as it was both owned by the state *and* was an organ of the state due to its mission to further the foreign trade goals of the state).

[97] *Patrickson v Dole Food Co.*, 251 F 3d 795, 807–808 (9th Cir. 2001); *Mendenhall v Saudi Aramco*, 991 F Supp 856 (SD Tex 1998).

Factors that a court should use in determining whether an entity is an organ of the state include, "the circumstances surrounding the entity's creation, the purpose of its activities, its independence from the government, the level of government financial support, its employment policies, and its obligations and privileges under state law."[98] If an entity is not directly an organ of a foreign state, it could still be considered an agent if the foreign state has ownership and control of the entity.[99]

It is generally recognized that employees of foreign sovereigns are organs entitled to immunity for actions taken within the official capacity of their positions. In *Chuidian v Philippine Nat'l Bank* the Ninth Circuit reasoned that a "separate legal person" includes individuals acting for a foreign state.[100] Natural individuals will not be entitled to immunity, however, if they act beyond the scope of their governmental authority.[101] Courts have distinguished the *Chuidian* rule as it applies to foreign heads of state.[102] These courts have held that the FSIA does not supersede the common law rule of head of state immunity.[103]

An entity is also an agent or instrumentality of a state if a majority share or other ownership interest in the entity is owned by a foreign state or political subdivision thereof:[104]

[98] *Patrickson*, 251 F 3d, 807.

[99] See *Karaho Bodas Co. LLC v Perusahaan Pertambangan Min Yak Dan Gas Bumi Negara*, 313 F 3d 70, 75–76 (2d Cir. 2002), cert. denied, 123 S Ct 2256 (2003) (where state owned all equity in company and controlled a supervisory board that oversaw management).

[100] See *Chuidian*, 912 F 2d, 1101–1103 (citing HR Rep No 94-1487, *Jurisdiction of United States Courts in Suits Against Foreign States*, 94th Cong. (9 September 1976) at 15 (reprinted in 1976 USCCAN 6604, 6614)); See also *Jungquist v Sheikh Sultan Bin Khalifa Al Nahyan*, 115 F 3d 1020, 1027 (CADC 1997) (finding that individuals are covered by the FSIA and adopting the official capacity test into the District Court Circuit); *El-Fadl v Central Bank of Jordan*, 75 F 3d 668, 671 (DC Cir 1996). Other courts have assumed that a person could be sued under the FSIA when working for a foreign state: *Kline v Kaneko*, 685 F Supp 386 (SDNY 1988) (holding Mexican Secretary of Government can be sued in his official capacity and is entitled to FSIA protection). See also *In re Estate of Ferdinand E. Marcos Human Rights Litigation*, 978 F 2d 493 (9th Cir. 1992), cert. denied, 508 US 972 (1993);. *Leutwyler v Office of Her Majesty Queen Rania Al-Abdullah*, 184 F Supp 2d 277, 286–287 (SDNY 2001) ("Although § 1605(b) does not specifically refer to natural persons, it has been generally recognized that individuals employed by a foreign state's agencies or instrumentalities are deemed 'foreign states' when they are sued for actions undertaken within the scope of their official capacities") (citing *Bryks v Canadian Broadcasting Corp.*, 906 F Supp 204, 210 (SDNY 1995)), *Doe v Bolkiah*, 74 F Supp 2d 969 (D Hawaii 1998).

[101] See *Byrd v Corporacion Forestal y Industrial de Olancho S.A.*, 182 F 3d 380, 389 (5th Cir. 1999) (two individual officers of a state corporation qualified as state entities and that the FSIA accorded immunity for their official acts); *Jungquist*, 115 F 3d at 1028 (DC Cir 1997) (the son of a Crown Prince not entitled to FSIA immunity in connection with allegedly fraudulent agreement in furtherance of personal and private interests); *El-Fadl*, 75 F 3d at 671 (finding no evidence that actions by the Deputy Governor of the foreign state's central bank were private or personal, but were taken only in his official capacity on behalf of the bank).

[102] See *Tachiona v Mugabe*, 169 F Supp 2d 259, 290–293 (SDNY 2001) (the president of Zimbabwe and his minister where not subject to the FSIA); *Lafontant v Aristide*, 844 F Supp 128 (EDNY 1994).

[103] See *Tachiona v Mugabe*, 169 F Supp 2d 259, 290–293 (SDNY 2001). See also *Leutwyler*, 184 F Supp 2d at 289–290.

[104] See *Carey v National Oil Corp.*, 592 F 2d 673, n 1 676 (2d Cir. 1979) (finding that the National Oil Company was an agency and instrumentality of the Libyan government which holds a majority

If [an entity] is entirely owned by a foreign state, they would of course be included within the definition. Where ownership is divided between a foreign state and private interests, the entity will be deemed an agency or instrumentality of a foreign state only if a majority of the ownership interests (shares of stock or otherwise) is owned by a foreign state or by a foreign state's political subdivision.[105]

The foreign state must hold the ownership interests of the entity directly. Tiered subsidiaries of an agency or instrumentality are not considered an agency or instrumentality of the state.[106]

The third criterion for determining whether an entity is an agency or instrumentality of a foreign state "excludes entities which are citizens of a State of the United States . . . for example a corporation organized and incorporated under the laws of New York but owned by a foreign state. Also excluded are entities which are created under the laws of third countries".[107] Citizenship of an entity under s 1603(b) is defined by 28 USC 1332(c) which states that "a corporation shall be deemed a citizen of any State by which it has been incorporated and of the State where it has its principal place of business . . .".[108] Entities incorporated in third party countries are excluded as agents because, "if a foreign state acquires or establishes a company or other legal entity in a foreign country, such an entity is presumptively engaging in activities that are either commercial or private in nature".[109]

Finally, the time of inquiry with respect to whether an entity is a foreign state is limited to the time of the suit rather than the time at which the alleged action or injury occurred.[110]

---

ownership interest in the company); see *Transport v Navimpex*, 989 F 2d 572, 576 (2d Cir. 1993) (finding that a wholly owned company organized under the foreign state's law was an agency and instrumentality of that state).

[105] HR Rep No 94-1487, *Jurisdiction of United States Courts in Suits Against Foreign States*, 94th Cong. (9 September 1976) at 15 (reprinted in 1976 USCCAN 6604, 6614). See *Mangattu v M/V Ibn Hayyan*, 35 F 3d 205 (5th Cir. 1994) (Shipping company, which was entirely owned by six nations, was not "created under the laws of a third country" within meaning of the FSIA, even though it was incorporated under laws of one member nation, which owned less than 20% of company). See also *In re Tamimi*, 176 F 3d 274, 278 (4th Cir. 1999) (finding that Saudi Arabian Airlines, wholly owned by Saudi Arabia, was an agent and instrumentality).

[106] See *Dole Food Company v Patrickson*, 123 S Ct 1655 (22 April 2003).

[107] HR Rep No 94-1487, *Jurisdiction of United States Courts in Suits Against Foreign States*, 94th Cong. (9 September 1976) at 15 (reprinted in 1976 USCCAN 6604, 6614).

[108] This includes, *per* 28 USC 1332(d), United States territories, the District of Columbia, and the Commonwealth of Puerto Rico. The principal place of business is usually determined by factors such as where the corporate decision-making authority and overall control is located or where the company's production and service activities occur. See *Gafford v General Elec. Co.*, 997 F 2d 150, 162 (6th Cir. 1993); *Bailey v Grand Trunk Lines New England*, 805 F 2d 1097, 1100 (2d Cir. 1986), cert. denied, 484 US 826 (1987).

[109] HR Rep No 94-1487, *Jurisdiction of United States Courts in Suits Against Foreign States*, 94th Cong. (9 September 1976) at 15 (reprinted in 1976 USCCAN 6604, 6614).

[110] See *Dole Food Company*, 123 S Ct at 1655.

(3) *United States*   **3.019**

A number of sections in the FSIA refer to the "United States" within their sections. For instance, s 1603(b)(3) requires that an entity not be a citizen of the United States, and in s 1603(a) commercial activity must be carried on in the United States. Section 1603(c) defines the United States as "all territory and waters, continental or insular, subject to the jurisdiction of the United States." While the statute uses the broad language of "subject to jurisdiction", this language has been limited to the "territorial jurisdiction" of the United States.[111] Although, the United States has jurisdiction over limited activities and events occurring in its embassies, it does not have territorial based jurisdiction.[112] Thus, under this section the area claimed to be the "United States" must be subject to the more pervasive territorial jurisdiction of the Untied States government. For instance, the Trust Territories of the Pacific are within the United States for the purposes of the FSIA as they are protected and subject to significant control of the United States through its trusteeship.[113] Yet, territory within a Congressionally created conservation zone would probably not be considered the United States for purposes of the Act.[114]

(4) *Commercial activity*   **3.020**

Commercial activity as used in the FSIA is "regular commercial conduct or a particular commercial transaction or act. The commercial character of the activity shall be determined by reference to the nature of the course of conduct or particular transaction or act, rather than by reference to its purpose".[115] Therefore, courts look to the nature of the conduct and if it is private in nature, or is an activity that a private party could do, then it is a commercial act.[116]

---

[111] *McKeel v Islamic Republic of Iran*, 722 F 2d 582, 589 (9th Cir. 1983), cert. denied, 469 US 880 (1984) (where plaintiff attempted to define s 1603(c) to include embassies so as to get the territorial tort exception to immunity under the FSIA for the Iranian embassy hostage crisis); see also *Amerada Hess*, 408 US at 441 (high seas not included); *Smith v Socialist People's Libyan Arab Jamahiriya*, 101 F 3d 239, 246 (2nd Cir. 1996), cert. denied, 520 US 1204 (1997) (US airplanes flying over foreign land not included); *Persinger v Iran*, 729 F 2d 835, 839 (DC Cir), cert. denied, 469 US 881 (1984) (US embassies overseas not included); *McKeel*, 722 F 2d at 588–589 (same); *Perez v Bahamas*, 652 F 2d 186, 189 n 1 (DC Cir), cert. denied, 454 US 865 (1981).   [112] See *McKeel*, 722 F 2d at 589.
[113] See *Sablan Const. Co. v Government of Trust Territory of Pac. Islands*, 526 F Supp 135, 137–138 (DN Mariana Islands 1981).   [114] See *Perez*, 652 F 2d at 189 fn 1.
[115] 28 USC § 1603(d).
[116] See *Republic of Argentina v Weltover*, 504 US 607, 614 (1992); see also *Holden v Canadian Consulate*, 92 F 3d 918 (9th Cir. 1996), cert. denied, 519 US 1091 (1997) (an employee of the consulate who had no ministerial duties, but rather promoted business engaged in commercial activity); *Rush-Presbyterian-St. Luke's Medical Center v Hellenic Republic*, 877 F 2d 574 (7th Cir.), cert. denied, 493 US 937 (1989); *Letelier v Republic of Chile*, 748 F 2d 790 (2d Cir 1984), cert. denied, 471 US 1125 (1985); *Texas Trading & Miller Corp. v Federal Republic of Nigeria*, 647 F 2d 300 (2d Cir. 1981), cert. denied, 454 US 1148 (1982) (purchasing of cement contracts and related letters of credit was commercial activity even if purchased for purposes of developing country's infrastructure); *LeDonne v Gulf Air, Inc.*, 700 F Supp 1400 (ED Va 1988); *International Ass'n of Machinists and Aerospace Workers (IAM) v Organization of Petroleum Exporting Countries (OPEC)*, 477 F Supp 553 (CD Cal 1979), aff'd, 649 F 2d 1354 (9th Cir. 1987), cert. denied, 454 US 1163 (1982).

[T]he question is not whether the foreign government is acting with a profit motive or instead with the aim of fulfilling uniquely sovereign objectives . . . the issue is whether the particular actions that the foreign state performs (whatever the motive behind them) are the *type* of actions by which a private party engages in trade and traffic or commerce.[117]

Thus, a contract by a foreign government to buy provisions or equipment for its armed forces or to construct a government building constitutes a commercial activity.[118] Similarly, the extension of time for payment of bonds by the Republic of Argentina to stabilize its economy is a commercial activity.[119] As the Second Circuit has noted:

[f]oreign sovereigns constantly implement broad programs intended to stimulate their economy or to avoid economic catastrophe. Each of these programs, however, is implemented through numerous individual transactions. To imbue each transaction with a sovereign character simply because it is part of a broader governmental scheme would run afoul of the FSIA's restrictive theory of foreign sovereign immunity.[120]

The mere connection to a commercial activity, alone, does not necessarily make an action commercial.[121] In *Saudi Arabia v Nelson*, the court ruled that the operation of a state-owned hospital could be considered a commercial activity, but the alleged arrest, detention and torture of a hospital employee for reporting safety violations at the hospital could not.[122] As the Supreme Court noted, "however monstrous such abuse undoubtedly may be, a foreign state's exercise of the power of its police has long been understood for purposes of the restrictive theory as peculiarly sovereign in nature".[123]

The licensing and regulating of natural resources is a sovereign act and not commercial, although the state may have entered into a contract for the license and sale of that resource.[124] However, assigning a contract regarding the computerization of oil fields is commercial activity, although it does touch on natural resources.[125]

---

[117] *Saudi Arabia v Nelson*, 507 US 349, 360–361 (1993).

[118] HR Rep No 94-1487, *Jurisdiction of United States Courts in Suits Against Foreign States*, 94th Cong. (9 September 1976) at 16 (reprinted in 1976 USCCAN 6604, 6615). See *McDonnell Douglas Corp. v Islamic Republic of Iran*, 758 F 2d 341, 349 (8th Cir. 1985); accord *Walter Fuller Aircraft Sales, Inc. v Republic of the Philippines*, 965 F 2d 1375, 1384–1385 (5th Cir. 1992).

[119] See *Weltover, Inc. v Republic of Argentina*, 941 F 2d 145, 150 (2d. Cir. 1991), cert. granted, 502 US 1024, aff'd, 504 US 607 (1992).　　　　[120] *Weltover*, 504 US at 614–615.

[121] See *Nelson*, 507 US at 361–362. See also *Alberti v Empresa Nicaraguense De La Carne*, 705 F 2d 250, 254 (7th Cir. 1983) (noting that nationalization of a private company is "a quintessential Government Act".)　　　　[122] See *Nelson*, 507 US at 361–362.

[123] *Nelson*, 507 US at 361.

[124] See *MOL, Inc. v People's Republic of Bangladesh*, 736 F 2d 1326, 1327 (9th Cir.), cert. denied, 469 US 1037 (1984) (holding that the licensing for the sale of rhesus monkeys was the exploiting of a natural resource and a sovereign act); *Jones v Petty Ray Geophysical Geosource, Inc*, 722 F Supp 343 (SD Tex 1989); *International Ass'n of Machinists and Aerospace Workers (IAM)*, 477 F Supp at 553.

[125] See *Adler v Federal Republic of Nigeria*, 107 F 3d 720, 724–725 (9th Cir. 1997); *Connecticut Bank of Commerce v Republic of Congo*, 309 F 3d 240, 263–264 (5th Cir. 2002).

(5) *Commercial activity carried on in the United States by a foreign state* **3.021**

A commercial activity is "carried on in the United States" if it has "substantial contact with the United States".[126] Thus, a foreign state's commercial activity may be "carried on" in several jurisdictions simultaneously if that activity has a substantial contact with each.[127]

The DC Circuit has suggested that proof of substantial contact requires more than the minimum contacts sufficient to satisfy due process in establishing personal jurisdiction.[128] Courts have been reluctant to declare single visits to the United States by representatives of foreign sovereigns to constitute substantial contact.[129]

Substantial contact with the United States includes:

commercial transactions performed in whole or in part in the United States, import-export transactions involving sales to, or purchases from, concerns in the United States, and an indebtedness incurred by a foreign state which negotiates or executes a loan agreement in the United States, or which receives financing from a private or public lending institution located in the United States.[130]

In the *Weltover* case, the Supreme Court held that Argentina's issuance of negotiable debt instruments denominated in United States dollars and payable in New York and its appointment of a financial agent in New York arose to the level of substantial contacts with the United States for purposes of s 1603.[131] Receiving financing from a United States lending institution, whether private or public, also arises to the level of "substantial contact" with the United States.[132] But the recruitment of an engineer from the United States did not arise to the level of substantial contact with the United States when the work and all other connections to the activity occurred on foreign soil.[133] However, actually entering into a contract within the United States does arise to the level of substantial contact.[134]

---

[126] 28 USC § 1603(e).   [127] See *Texas Trading & Milling*, 647 F 2d, 311 n 30.

[128] See *Maritime Int'l Nominees Establishment v Republic of Guinea*, 693 F 2d 1094, 1109 n 23 (DC Cir), cert. denied, 464 US 815 (1983).

[129] See *BP Chemicals Ltd. v Jiangsu Sopo Corp.*, 285 F 3d 677, 686–687 (8th Cir.), cert. denied, 537 US 942 (2002); *Soudavar v Islamic Republic of Iran*, 186 F 3d 671, 674 (5th Cir. 1999), cert. denied, 528 US 1157 (2000).

[130] HR Rep No 94-1487, *Jurisdiction of United States Courts in Suits Against Foreign States*, 94th Cong. (9 September 1976) at 17 (reprinted in 1976 USCCAN 6604, 6617).

[131] See 504 US at 614; see also *Zedan v Kingdom of Saudi Arabia*, 849 F 2d 1511, 1513 (DC Cir 1988) (citing *Maritime Int'l Nominees Establishment v Guinea*, 693 F 2d 1094, 1109 (DC Cir 1982)); *Gemini Shipping v Foreign Trade Organization for Chemicals and Foodstuffs*, 647 F 2d 317, 319 (2d Cir. 1981) ("Defendants' conduct certainly satisfies that standard, for Syria solicited bids in the United States, and paid under the contract through a letter of credit confirmed by a New York bank").

[132] See *Gemini Shipping*, 647 F 2d at 319.   [133] See *Zedan*, 849 F 2d, 1512–1514.

[134] See *Gibbons v Údaras na Gaeltachta*, 549 F Supp 1094, 1112–1113 (SDNY 1982).

3.022   28 U.S.C. § 1604

Immunity of a foreign state from jurisdiction

Subject to existing international agreements to which the United States is a party at the time of enactment of this Act a foreign state shall be immune from the jurisdiction of the courts of the United States and of the States except as provided in sections 1605 to 1607 of this chapter.

3.023   Commentary

Legislative history

As discussed above,[135] Congress intended the FSIA to codify "when and how parties can maintain a lawsuit against a foreign state . . . in the Courts of the United States and to provide when a foreign state is entitled to sovereign immunity".[136] Section 1604 serves this purpose, providing that a foreign state is generally immune from the jurisdiction of federal and state courts unless an international agreement or one of the exceptions set forth in ss 1605–1607 apply.[137]

Congress added the qualification "subject to existing international agreements" to s 1604 to accommodate the possibility that foreign sovereign immunity might be addressed in international conventions, in which case the international agreement would supercede the statute insofar as it conflicted with the provisions of the FSIA.[138] "To the extent such international agreements are silent on a question of immunity, the [FSIA] would control; the international agreement would control only where a conflict was manifest".[139]

"The immunity from jurisdiction provided by section 1604 applies to proceedings in both Federal and State courts. Section 1604 [is] the only basis under which a foreign state [can] claim immunity from the jurisdiction of any Federal or State court in the United States".[140]

---

[135] See 3.002 to 3.005.

[136] HR Rep No 94-1487, *Jurisdiction of United States Courts in Suits Against Foreign States*, 94th Cong. (9 September 1976) at 6 (reprinted in 1976 USCCAN 6604, 6604).

[137] See HR Rep No 94-1487, *Jurisdiction of United States Courts in Suits Against Foreign States*, 94th Cong. (9 September 1976) at 17 (reprinted in 1976 USCCAN 6604, 6616) ("[The Act] starts from a premise of immunity and then creates exceptions to the general principle. This chapter is thus cast in a manner consistent with the way in which the law of sovereign immunity has developed").

[138] HR Rep No 94-1487, *Jurisdiction of United States Courts in Suits Against Foreign States*, 94th Cong. (9 September 1976) at 10, 17 (reprinted in 1976 USCCAN 6604, 6616) ("Thus the bill would not alter the rights or duties of the United States under the NATO Status of Forces Agreement or similar agreements . . . to which the United States is a party, calling for exclusive non-judicial remedies through arbitration or other procedures for the settlement of disputes").

[139] HR Rep No 94-1487, *Jurisdiction of United States Courts in Suits Against Foreign States*, 94th Cong. (9 September 1976) at 18 (reprinted in 1976 USCCAN 6604, 6616).

[140] HR Rep No 94-1487, *Jurisdiction of United States Courts in Suits Against Foreign States*, 94th Cong. (9 September 1976) at 17 (reprinted in 1976 USCCAN 6604, 6616).

[141] See 3.002–3.004.

[142] Throughout this chapter "jurisdiction" will be used to refer to the subject matter jurisdiction of the courts. Under § 1330(b) of the FSIA, the district court will have statutory personal jurisdiction

Application **3.024**

As discussed above,[141] the FSIA is the sole basis for obtaining jurisdiction[142] over foreign states or their agencies or instrumentalities in the federal district courts.[143] Under s 1604, a foreign state is generally and presumptively immune from the exercise of jurisdiction by federal and state courts.[144] In keeping with the restrictive principle of sovereign immunity, a foreign sovereign will be immune under s 1604 unless the exceptions set forth in ss 1605–1607 apply.[145] In other words, subject matter jurisdiction is predicated upon the existence of an exception to foreign sovereign immunity.[146]

It is important to distinguish between the jurisdictional requirements presented by the FSIA and a defense on the merits. Under the FSIA, a foreign sovereign has "an immunity from trial and the attendant burdens of litigation, and not just a defense to liability on the merits".[147]

when subject matter jurisdiction exists under s 1330(a) and service of process had been made under § 1608 of the Act. See 3.002–3.004 above.

[143] 28 USC § 1330. See also *Argentine Republic v Amerada Hess Shipping Co.*, 488 US 428 (1989) (noting that subject matter jurisdiction in an action against a foreign sovereign cannot be based on diversity of citizenship); *Saudi Arabia v Nelson*, 507 US 349 (1993); *Fagot Rodriguez v Republic of Costa Rica*, 297 F 3d 1, 3 (1st Cir. 2002); *In re Republic of Philippines*, 309 F 3d 1143, 1149 (9th Cir. 2002); *Virtual Countries, Inc. v Republic of South Africa*, 300 F 3d 230, 235 (2d Cir. 2002). As the Supreme Court explained in *Amerada Hess* at 434: "Sections 1604 and 1330(a) work in tandem: § 1604 bars federal and state courts from exercising jurisdiction when a foreign state *is* entitled to immunity, and § 1330(a) confers jurisdiction on district courts to hear suits brought by United States citizens and by aliens when a foreign state is *not* entitled to immunity" (emphasis in original). See also *Bryks v Canadian Broad. Corp.*, 906 F Supp 204, 206 (SDNY 1995) (finding that subject matter jurisdiction in action against foreign sovereign cannot be based on diversity of citizenship).

[144] See, eg, *Nelson*, 507 US at 355; *Price v Socialist Peoples Libyan Arab Jamahiriya*, 294 F 3d 82, 87 (DC Cir 2002); *Sampson v Fed. Republic of Germany*, 250 F 3d 1145, 1149 (7th Cir. 2001); *Adler v Fed. Republic of Nigeria*, 219 F 3d 869, 874 (9th Cir. 2000); *Transatlantic Shiffahrtskontor GMBH v Shanghai Foreign Trade Corp.*, 204 F 3d 384, 388 (2d Cir. 2000), cert. denied, 532 US 904 (2001).

[145] See, eg, *Phoenix Consulting, Inc. v Republic of Angola*, 216 F 3d 36 (DC Cir 2000); *Siderman de Blake v The Republic of Argentina*, 965 F 2d 699 (9th Cir. 1992), cert. denied, 507 US 1017 (1993); *Forsythe v Saudi Arabian Airlines Corp.*, 885 F 2d 285 (5th Cir. 1989).

[146] See *Jones v Petty-Ray Geophysical, Geosource, Inc.*, 954 F 2d 1061 (5th Cir. 1992), cert. denied, 506 US 867 (1992); *Brewer v The Socialist People's Republic of Iraq*, 890 F 2d 97, 100 (8th Cir. 1989) ("The district court has jurisdiction only if defendants are without immunity"); *Security Pacific Nat'l Bank v Derderian*, 872 F 2d 281, 283 (9th Cir. 1989); *Frolova v Union of Soviet Socialist Republics*, 761 F 2d 370, 372–373 (7th Cir. 1985).

[147] *Foremost-McKesson, Inc. v The Islamic Republic of Iran*, 905 F 2d 438, 443 (DC Cir 1990) (quoting *Rush-Presbyterian-St. Luke's Medical Center v Hellenic Republic*, 877 F 2d 574, 576 n 2 (7th Cir. 1989)). Accord *Kelly v Syria Shell Petroleum Dev B.V.*, 213 F 3d 841, 847 (5th Cir.), cert. denied, 531 US 979 (2000); *Phoenix Consulting*, 216 F 3d at 39; *Rein v Socialist People's Libyan Arab Jamahiriya*, 162 F 3d 748, 756 (2d Cir. 1998), cert. denied, 527 US 1003 (1999); *Fed. Ins. Co. v Richard I. Rubin & Co., Inc.*, 12 F 3d 1270, 1281 (3d Cir. 1993), cert. denied, 511 US 1107 (1994). Cf. *Southway v Central Bank of Nigeria*, 198 F 3d 1210, 1215 (10th Cir. 1999) ("Congress viewed sovereign immunity under the FSIA as an affirmative defense to be specially pleaded or waived, rather than a jurisdictional bar to suit"). Courts have also taken issue with the characterization of sovereign immunity as an "affirmative defense" rather than as a jurisdictional prerequisite to suit. See, eg, *Frolova*, 761 F 2d at 373.

It should be noted that the jurisdictional immunity conferred by the FSIA does not supercede and is distinct from the act of state doctrine.[148] Whereas the FSIA provides a jurisdictional grant of immunity, the act of state doctrine allows a court to dismiss a claim for failure to state a claim on which relief can be granted based on prudential grounds when a sovereign act within the sovereign's own territory is called into question.[149] This prudential doctrine embodies a concern that decisions by the judiciary may interfere with United States foreign policy.[150] As discussed in the following section, because immunity under the FSIA is jurisdictional, courts must reach a decision as to immunity before considering an "act of state" defense.[151]

3.025   *Time and manner to raise immunity defense*

In order to avoid improperly exercising jurisdiction and subjecting the foreign sovereign to the burdens of litigation, a party's claim of immunity "must be decided before the suit can proceed".[152] As such, the district court must make an immunity determination prior to considering merits-based defenses.[153] Thus, immunity is typically claimed in the responsive pleading and any pre-pleading motion, such as a motion to dismiss. Further, the district court cannot postpone

---

[148] See, eg, *Int'l Ass'n of Machinists and Aerospace Workers (IAM) v Org. of Petroleum Exporting Countries (OPEC)*, 649 F 2d 1354 (9th Cir. 1981), cert. denied, 454 US 1163 (1982).

[149] See, eg, *Siderman de Blake*, 965 F 2d at 707.   [150] See *Siderman de Blake*, 965 F 2d at 707.

[151] See *Siderman de Blake*, 965 F 2d at 707.

[152] *Phaneuf v Republic of Indonesia*, 106 F 3d 302, 305 (9th Cir. 1997) (stating that "[t]he district court improvidently postponed its final determination of subject matter jurisdiction under the FSIA"). Accord *Robinson v Gov't of Malaysia*, 269 F 3d 133, 141 (2d Cir. 2001) ("The district court's review of the evidence before it on a motion to dismiss based on an assertion of sovereign immunity has particular significance because of the necessity of resolving that issue early on if possible. Sovereign immunity under the FSIA is immunity from suit, not just from liability. Such immunity is effectively lost if a case is permitted to go to trial") (internal citations omitted); *Phoenix Consulting*, 216 F 3d at 39 (DC Cir 2000) ("In order to preserve the full scope of . . . immunity, the district court must make the critical preliminary determination of its own jurisdiction as early in the litigation as possible; to defer the question is to frustrate the significance and benefit of entitlement to immunity from suit") (internal quotations omitted) (citing *Foremost-McKesson*, 905 F 2d at 449).

[153] See *In re Republic of Philippines*, 309 F 3d 1143, 1149 (9th Cir. 2002). In this interpleader action, the court held that the district court erred when it decided creditors' motion to dismiss the Republic of Philippines (the "Republic") and an instrumentality of it on the grounds that they were not real parties in interest, without first deciding Republic's motion to dismiss on immunity ground under the FSIA. "The effect" of doing so "was to adjudicate the merits of the Republic's claim to the assets and thus effectively deny its claim to sovereign immunity." It should be noted that the Republic's ultimate aim was not only to be dismissed from the suit, but to have the interpleader action itself dismissed. Under the Federal Rules of Civil Procedure r 19(b), an interpleader action can only proceed—subject to certain equitable exceptions—if all indispensable parties are present. 309 F 3d at 1143, 1152–1153. Here, the Circuit Court found that the Republic and the instrumentality were immune from jurisdiction, and also opined that they were indispensable parties (309 F 3d, 1153) The court, however, weighing its equitable options, chose not to dismiss the action but to stay the preceding, a result that the Republic agreed to as an alternative to dismissal. See also *Siderman de Blake*, 965 F 2d, 699 (finding that the court must decide a sovereign immunity claim before an Act of State claim); *Whiteman v Federal Republic of Austria*, No. 00 Civ 8006, 2002 WL 31368236 at *1–2 (SDNY 21 October 2002).

determination of sovereign immunity until after discovery on issues that go to the merits of the case.[154]

If a foreign sovereign appears in an action and fails to raise foreign sovereign immunity as a defense, however, the sovereign may be deemed to have waived its immunity under section 1605(a)(1)[155] of the FSIA.[156] As explained in the *Phoenix Consulting* case:

> As a threshold matter, if the sovereign makes a conscious decision to take part in the litigation, then it must assert its immunity under the FSIA either before or in its responsive pleading. This requirement holds even though FSIA immunity is jurisdictional because failure to assert the immunity after consciously deciding to participate in the litigation may constitute an implied waiver of immunity, 28 U.S.C. § 1605(a)(1), which invests the court with subject matter jurisdiction under 28 U.S.C. § 1330(a).[157]

When a party appears but does not raise its jurisdictional defense, and jurisdiction depends on application of the FSIA, the district court may raise the issue of its own motion.[158] Similarly, the Court of Appeals for the Ninth Circuit raised the jurisdictional issue of its own motion in a case where the issue was not raised by either party on appeal.[159]

If a party fails to enter an appearance at all, the putative sovereign is not deemed to have waived its sovereign immunity defense, but, rather, the court must determine whether immunity is available to the absent party.[160]

---

[154] See *Phaneuf*, 106 F 3d at 302. As discussed above, however, the district court may allow or require discovery on the issue of immunity.

[155] 28 USC § 1605(a)(1) provides that a foreign state shall be immune from jurisdiction in any case "(1) in which the foreign state has waived its immunity either explicitly or by implication, notwithstanding any withdrawal of the waiver which the foreign state may purport to effect except in accordance with the terms of the waiver". The waiver exception is discussed at 3.033 below.

[156] See, eg, *Phoenix Consulting*, 216 F 3d at 39; *Aquamar S.A. v Del Monte Fresh Produce N.A., Inc.*, 179 F 3d 1279, 1290 (11th Cir. 1999); *Foremost-McKesson*, 905 F 2d at 443 ("Foremost is correct in asserting that, in most instances, a state's failure to assert sovereign immunity in a responsive pleading will constitute a waiver of the defense. But the situation here is different . . . Iran did not respond substantively to any of the averments of the complaint or pose any defenses to the claims; instead, Iran . . . argued that the action should proceed in a another forum and it then did . . . [this action] did not constitute an implied waiver").

[157] *Phoenix Consulting*, 216 F 3d at 39 (internal citations and quotations omitted) (citing *Foremost-McKesson*, 905 F 2d, 443–445).

[158] See *Aquamar*, 179 F 3d at 1290 ("When the court's jurisdiction rests on the presence of the foreign sovereign, however, the court may address the issue independently") (citing *Verlinden B.V. v Central Bank of Nigeria*, 461 US 480, 493 n 20 (1983)).

[159] See *Randolph v Budget Rent-A-Car*, 97 F 3d 319, 323 (9th Cir. 1996) ("Although neither party challenged the district court's jurisdiction on appeal, we are obliged to raise *sua sponte* issues concerning district court's subject matter jurisdiction. This examination is particularly important in appeals examining the liability of foreign governments and their instrumentalities") (internal citations omitted).

[160] See, eg, *Brewer*, 890 F 2d at 101 (8th Cir. 1989) (upholding entry of default judgment where district court entered into jurisdictional analysis prior to award of judgment); *Frolova*, 761 F 2d at 373 (rejecting claim that failure to appear waives sovereign immunity defense); *Kao Hwa Shipping Co., S.A. v China Steel Corp.*, 816 F Supp 910, 917 (SDNY 1993). See also *Verlinden B.V. v Central Bank of Nigeria*, 461 US 480, 493 n 20 (1983) ("Under the Act . . . subject matter jurisdiction turns on the

3.026   *Who may raise sovereign immunity under the FSIA*

Ordinarily a party other than a putative foreign sovereign does not have standing to raise the jurisdictional defense of immunity.[161] In the *Wilmington Trust* case, for example, the Ninth Circuit held that a party did not have standing to invoke the sovereign immunity of a nonparty sovereign that had not sought to intervene in the action.[162]

As discussed in the preceding section, however, the court may raise the issue of sovereign immunity of its own motion when a foreign sovereign appears in an action and does not assert the defense.[163] The court in the *Aquamar* case held that in such a case the court was not precluded from adjudicating a foreign sovereign immunity claim even though it was the plaintiff and not the sovereign defendant that raised the issue.[164] As also discussed in the preceding section, the court must address the issue of sovereign immunity if a putative sovereign does not make an appearance.[165]

It should also be noted that the FSIA does not address the issue of head of state immunity and the courts that have considered the issue have found that the FSIA does not impact upon the head of state doctrine.[166]

existence of an exception to foreign sovereign immunity, 28 USC § 1330(a). Accordingly, even if the foreign state does not enter an appearance to assert an immunity defense, a District Court still must determine that immunity is unavailable under the Act").

[161] See *Aquamar*, 179 F 3d at 1290 (citing *Wilmington Trust v United States Dist. Court*, 934 F 2d 1026, 1033 (9th Cir. 1991) ("Congress intended requests for protection under the FSIA to originate from the foreign state party"); *Republic of Philippines v Marcos*, 806 F 2d 344 (2d Cir. 1986), *cert. dismissed*, 480 US 942 (1987). See also *The Presbyterian Church of Sudan v Talisman Energy Inc.*, 244 F Supp 2d 289, n 42 (SDNY 2003) ("Certainly, as a sovereign country, Sudan is potentially entitled to immunity under [the FSIA] . . . However, Talisman [a non-sovereign] lacks standing to raise an FSIA defense on Sudan's behalf").

[162] See *Wilmington Trust*, 934 F 2d 1026 at 1032–1033. In *Wilmington Trust*, the petitioners (the "Union"), requested that the court issue a writ of mandamus directing the district court to hear its claims before a jury. The respondent ("Connecticut Bank") had brought the underlying *in rem* action against a vessel (and a related *in personam* action against the owner of the vessel), as indenture trustee for a Finnish Corporation ("Wartsila"). Although not named as a defendant, the Union answered the complaint and brought counterclaims against Wartsila. The district court (at 1028) ordered the interlocutory sale of the vessel and Connecticut Bank purchased the ship on behalf of Wartsila. Wartsila alleged (at 1028) that it was involved in bankruptcy proceedings in Finland, "and the Finish Guaranty Board ('FGB'), a 'foreign state' within the [FSIA] . . . extended a letter of credit to Connecticut Bank on behalf of Wartsila enabling the bank to purchase the vessel at the interlocutory sale". The Union made a request for a jury trial on its claims, which the district court denied on two bases, one of which was that Wartsila had a right to a non-jury trial pursuant to the FSIA. In making its case that the FSIA applied to the Union's claims, Wartsila did not argue that it was entitled to sovereign immunity, but instead argued that the Union's claims were against a foreign state at least with respect to the letter of credit posted by the FGB. Reversing the district court's ruling, the circuit court found (at 1033) that "respondents are without standing to invoke the FSIA . . . [as n]either Finland nor FGB is a party in the action[, n]either party has sought to intervene, and neither entity has requested that the FSIA be applied[, and n]either Wartsila nor the Connecticut Bank is a foreign state and counsel for respondents have not suggested that they represent the FGB".

[163] See *Aquamar*, 179 F 3d at 1290.   [164] See *Aquamar*, 179 F 3d at 1290.

[165] See, eg, *Brewer*, 890 F 2d at 101; *Frolova*, 761 F 2d at 373.

[166] See *United States v Noriega*, 117 F 3d 1206, 1212 (11th Cir. 1997) (stating that the FSIA does not address head of state immunity); *Tachiona v Mugabe*, 169 F Supp 2d 259, 290–291 (SDNY 2001); *First American Corp. v Al-Nahyan*, 948 F Supp 1107, 1119 (DDC 1996) ("[T]he enactment

Presumptions and burden shifting under the FSIA   **3.027**

The party claiming immunity bears the initial burden of proof to make a *prima facie* showing that it is either a foreign state or agency or instrumentality of a foreign state as defined in section 1603 of the FSIA.[167] Once the party claiming immunity makes this showing, the burden shifts to the opposing party to raise the exceptions it believes applies and prove that they apply.[168] If the opposing party makes such a showing, the burden then shifts back to the party claiming immunity to show that the exception does not apply.[169] Courts have generally required a defendant to show that an exception to immunity does not apply by a preponderance of evidence.[170] Throughout this process, the party claiming immunity retains the ultimate burden of persuasion.[171]

Two Ninth Circuit decisions (*Siderman* and *Meadows*), however, suggest that the initial burden on the party claiming immunity is to show not only that it is a foreign sovereign but to make a *prima facie* case that plaintiff's claim arose from a public act.[172] Circuit courts that have considered this suggestion—or the suggestion that defendant has the initial burden of showing that an exception to

of the FSIA was not intended to affect the power of the State Department, on behalf of the President as Chief Executive, to assert immunity for heads of state or for diplomatic and consular personnel"); *Lafontant v Aristide*, 844 F Supp 128 (EDNY 1994).

[167] See, eg, *International Insurance Company v Caja Nacional de Ahorro y Seguro*, 293 F 3d 392, 397 (7th Cir. 2002); *Keller v Central Bank of Nigeria*, 277 F 3d 811, 815 (6th Cir. 2002); *Kelly*, 213 F 3d at 847; *Cargill Int'l SA v M/T Pavel Dybenko*, 991 F 2d 1012, 1016 (2d Cir. 1993).

[168] See, eg, *International Insurance*, 293 F 3d at 397; *Byrd v Corporacion Forestal y Industrial de Olancho S.A.*, 182 F 3d 380, 388 (5th Cir. 1999); *Cabari v Gov't of Republic of Ghana*, 165 F 3d 193, 196 (2d Cir. 1999); *Dalibert v Republic of Iraq*, 97 F Supp2d 38, 42 (DDC 2000).

[169] See, eg, *Aquamar*, 179 F 3d at 1290 ("Where a party . . . has asserted facts suggesting that an exception to foreign sovereign immunity exists, the party arguing for immunity . . . bears the burden of proving by a preponderance of evidence that the exception does not apply"); *Siderman de Blake*, 965 F 2d, 699. See also *Dalibert*, 97 F Supp 2d at 43.

[170] See, eg, *A & Davis Int'l, Inc. v The Republic of Yemen*, 218 F 3d 1292, 1300 (11th Cir. 2000) (citing *Aquamar*, 179 F 3d at 1290); *Joseph v Office of Consulate General of Nigeria*, 830 F 2d 1018, 1021 (9th Cir. 1987), cert. denied, 485 US 905 (1988); *Albert v Empresa Nicaraguense De La Carne*, 705 F 2d 250, 255–256 (7th Cir. 1983); *Kao Hwa Shipping*, 816 F Supp at 915.

[171] See *Keller v Central Bank of Nigeria*, 277 F 3d 811, 815 (6th Cir. 2002); *Cabari v Gov't of Republic of Ghana*, 165 F 3d 193, 196 (2d Cir. 1999) ("Once the defendant presents a *prima facie* case that it is a foreign sovereign, the plaintiff has the burden of going forward with evidence showing that, under exceptions to the FSIA, immunity should not be granted although the ultimate burden of persuasion remains with the alleged sovereign") (citing *Cargill Int'l S.A. v M/T Pavel Dybenko*, 991 F 2d 1012, 1016 (2d Cir. 1993)); *Voest-Alpine Trading USA Corp. v Bank of China*, 142 F 3d 887, 896 (5th Cir. 1998) (affirming the district court's denial of motion to dismiss for lack of jurisdiction citing Bank of China's failure to produce sufficient evidence that the commercial activity exception did not apply: "[a]lthough Voest–Alpine bore the initial burden of alleging facts which demonstrated that the commercial activity exception applied (*ie*, it bore a burden of production), the Bank of China bore the ultimate burden of persuasion on the question of immunity"); *Dalibert*, 97 F Supp 2d at 42 ("[I]f any of the exceptions appears in the pleadings or is not refuted by the foreign state asserting the defense, the motion to dismiss the complaint must be denied") (quoting *Baglab Ltd. v Johnson Matthey Bankers Ltd.*, 665 F Supp 289, 294 (SDNY 1987)).

[172] See *Siderman de Blake*, 965 F 2d 699, 708 n 9; *Meadows v Dominican Republic*, 817 F 2d 517 (9th Cir. 1987) (denying claim of immunity where defendant failed to make a *prima facie* showing that the commercial activity exception did not apply).

immunity does not exist—have rejected this approach.[173] Indeed, in the *Phaneuf* case the Ninth Circuit explicitly rejected the approach taken in the cases of *Siderman* and *Meadows*.[174] As the court in the *Phaneuf* case explained, the *Meadows* public act requirement was in part based on the following passage in the House Report:

> [T]he burden will remain on the foreign state to produce evidence in support of its claim of immunity. Thus, evidence must be produced to establish that a foreign state or one of its subdivisions, agencies or instrumentalities is the defendant in the suit and that the plaintiff's claim relates to a public act of the foreign state—that is, an act not within the exceptions in sections 1605–1607.[175]

As further explained in the *Phaneuf* case, however, "[t]his legislative history . . . clarifies only that the defendant bears the burden of establishing its immunity, including the burden of proof that no exception applies. It does not necessitate a *prima facie* showing of a public act."[176]

Thus, while the party asserting immunity is not required to make an initial showing that an exception to immunity does not apply, if the party opposing the motion to dismiss produces evidence of an exception to immunity, the party asserting immunity must show by a preponderance of the evidence that the exception does not apply or the motion will be denied.[177]

3.028   *Evidence considered*

If only the legal sufficiency of plaintiff's jurisdictional allegations are challenged, the "district court should take the plaintiff's factual allegations as true and determine whether they bring the case within any of the exceptions to immunity invoked by the plaintiff."[178]

If, however, the defendant challenges the plaintiff's factual allegations regarding jurisdiction, the district court must go beyond the pleadings to resolve the dispute.[179] The district court has discretion to devise the scope and procedure

---

[173] See, eg, *Phaneuf*, 106 F 3d at 305–306; *Gerding v Republic of France*, 943 F 2d 521, 526 (4th Cir. 1991), cert. denied, 507 US 1017 (1993) (rejecting outright the contention that the party asserting immunity must establish that the exceptions do not apply in making its *prima facie* case: "the party seeking immunity has no obligation to affirmatively eliminate all possible exceptions to sovereign immunity. Once a party demonstrates to the district court that it is a 'foreign state' . . . the burden shifts to the opposing party to raise the exceptions to . . . immunity and assert at least some facts that would establish the exceptions") (quoting *Stena Rederi AB v Comision de Contratos del Comite*, 923 F 2d 380, 390 n 14 (5th Cir. 1991)). See also *Byrd v Corporacion Forestal y Industrial de Olancho S.A.*, 182 F 3d 380, 388 (5th Cir. 1999) ("The threshold issue is whether the party claiming FSIA immunity is a "foreign state" within the meaning of the statute").

[174] See *Phaneuf*, 106 F 3d at 305–306.   [175] *Phaneuf*, 106 F 3d at 306.

[176] *Phaneuf*, 106 F 3d at 306.

[177] See, eg, *Voest-Alpine Trading USA*, 142 F 3d at 896 (5th Cir. 1998); *Dalibert*, 97 F Supp 2d 38, 42 (DDC 2000).   [178] See, eg, *Phoenix Consulting*, 216 F 3d at 40 (DC Cir 2000).

[179] See, eg, *Phoenix Consulting*, 216 F 3d at 40 (DC Cir 2000) (finding that the district court erred by assuming the truth of a contested fact); *Moran v Kingdom of Saudi Arabia*, 27 F 3d 169 at 172 (5th Cir. 1994).

for obtaining evidence to make an immunity determination.[180] This procedure "may include considering affidavits, allowing . . . discovery, hearing oral testimony, [and] conducting an evidentiary hearing".[181] While the party opposing immunity must have ample opportunity to secure and present evidence relevant to the existence of jurisdiction, "[i]n order to avoid burdening a sovereign that proves to be immune from suit . . . jurisdictional discovery should be carefully controlled and limited."[182] As explained by the court in the *Rafidain Bank* case, "the comity concerns implicated by allowing jurisdictional discovery from a foreign sovereign . . . require a delicate balancing between permitting discovery to substantiate exceptions to . . . immunity and protecting a sovereign's . . . legitimate claim to immunity from discovery".[183] Courts will, however, generally allow limited discovery in factual disputes regarding jurisdiction under the FSIA.[184]

Appeal   3.029

Denial of a motion to dismiss for lack of subject matter jurisdiction under the FSIA is immediately appealable under the collateral order doctrine[185] as a final decision.[186] The rationale for interlocutory appeal is clear, as "denial of a motion to dismiss on grounds of foreign sovereign immunity may result in the parties having to litigate claims over which the court lacks jurisdiction".[187]

A district court's conclusions of law are reviewed *de novo* by the Court of Appeals.[188] A district court's findings of fact relevant to its determination of subject matter jurisdiction will be set aside only if they are clearly erroneous.[189]

---

[180] See, eg, *Phoenix Consulting*, 216 F 3d at 40 (DC Cir 2000); *Moran*, 27 F 3d at 172.

[181] *Moran*, 27 F 3d at 172.

[182] *Phoenix Consulting*, 216 F 3d at 40 (citing *Foremost-McKesson*, 905 F 2d at 449). See also *First City, Texas-Houston, N.A. v Rafidain Bank*, 150 F 3d 172, 176–177 (2d Cir. 1998); *Gould, Inc. v Pechiney Ugine Kuhlmann*, 853 F 2d 445, 451 (6th Cir. 1988).

[183] *Rafidain Bank*, 150 F 3d at 176 (internal quotation omitted). Accord *Arriba Ltd. v Petroleos Mexicanos*, 962 F 2d 528, 534 (5th Cir.), cert. denied, 506 US 956 (1992) ("[D]iscovery should be ordered circumspectly and only to verify allegations of specific facts crucial to an immunity determination").

[184] See, eg, *Filus v Lot Polish Airlines*, 907 F 2d 1328, 1332 (2d Cir. 1990) ("[G]enerally a plaintiff may be allowed limited discovery with respect to the jurisdictional issue; but until she has shown a reasonable basis for assuming jurisdiction, she is not entitled to any other discovery").

[185] See *Aquamar*, 179 F 3d at 1287 (explaining the collateral order doctrine: "Under the collateral order doctrine . . . we may review a decision that (1) conclusively determines a disputed question that is (2) important and completely separate from the merits of the action and is (3) effectively unreviewable on appeal from final judgment") (internal citation omitted). For a general discussion of the collateral order doctrine see *Cohen v Beneficial Indus. Loan Corp.*, 337 US 541, 546 (1949) and *Mitchell v Forsyth*, 472 US 511, 524–527 (1985).

[186] See, eg, *Keller*, 277 F 3d 811, 815 (6th Cir. 2002); *Jungquist v Al Nahyan*, 115 F 3d 1020 (DC Cir 1997); *Phaneuf*, 106 F 3d 302; *Transaero, Inc. v La Fuerza Aerea Boliviana*, 99 F 3d 538 (2d Cir. 1996), cert. denied, 520 US 1240.

[187] *In re Republic of Philippines*, 309 F 3d 1143, 1148 (9th Cir. 2002).

[188] See, eg, *Cabiri*, 165 F 3d at 196; *Pere v Nuovo Pignone, Inc.*, 150 F 3d 477, 480 (5th Cir. 1998); *Adler*, 107 F 3d at 720; *Jungquist*, 115 F 3d, 1020.

[189] See, eg, *Aquamar*, 179 F 3d at 1290; *Adler*, 107 F 3d at 723 ("A district court's factual findings on jurisdictional issues are reviewed for clear error"); *Moran*, 27 F 3d at 172.

If the district court has not made findings of fact, the Court of Appeals will "accept the facts alleged in the complaint as true".[190]

3.030   **28 U.S.C. § 1605**

(a) A foreign state shall not be immune from the jurisdiction of courts of the United States or of the States in any case—

  (1) in which the foreign state has waived its immunity either explicitly or by implication, notwithstanding any withdrawal of the waiver which the foreign state may purport to effect except in accordance with the terms of the waiver;

. . .

Commentary

3.031   Legislative history

Section 1605(a)(1) treats explicit and implied waivers by foreign states of sovereign immunity. With respect to explicit waivers, a foreign state may renounce its immunity by treaty, as has been done by the United States with respect to commercial and other activities in a series of treaties of friendship, commerce, and navigation, or a foreign state may waive its immunity in a contract with a private party. Since the sovereign immunity of a political subdivision, agency or instrumentality of a foreign state derives from the foreign state itself, the foreign state may waive the immunity of its political subdivisions, agencies or instrumentalities.

> With respect to implicit waivers, the courts have found such waivers in cases where a foreign state has agreed to arbitration in another country or where a foreign state has agreed that the law of a particular country should govern a contract. An implicit waiver would also include a situation where a foreign state has filed a responsive pleading in an action without raising the defense of sovereign immunity.
>
> The language, "notwithstanding any withdrawal of the waiver which the foreign state may purport to effect except in accordance with the terms of the waiver," is designed to exclude a withdrawal of the waiver both after and before a dispute arises except in accordance with the terms of the original waiver. In other words, if the foreign state agrees to a waiver of sovereign immunity in a contract, that waiver may subsequently be withdrawn only in a manner consistent with the expression of the waiver in the contract. Some court decisions have allowed subsequent and unilateral rescissions of waivers by foreign states. But the better view, and the one followed in this section, is that a foreign state which has induced a private person into a contract by promising not to invoke its immunity cannot, when

---

[190] *The Export Group v Reef Industries, Inc.*, 54 F 3d at 1468 (citing *Siderman de Blake*, 965 F 2d at 706).

a dispute arises, go back on its promise and seek to revoke the waiver unilaterally.[191]

Application **3.032**

Waiver of sovereign immunity may be either express or implied.

(1) *Express waiver*

To establish express waiver, there must be a "clear, complete, unambiguous and unmistakable" manifestation of a sovereign's intent to waive its immunity.[192] In the legislative history to s 1605, Congress described two ways in which a foreign sovereign could expressly waive immunity under the FSIA.[193] The first is by conventions and treaties, and the second is by contract.

(i) *Conventions and treaties*

Although a foreign sovereign may waive its immunity under s 1605 by signing a treaty or convention, the treaty must contain mention of a waiver of immunity to suit in United States courts, or at least the availability of a cause of action in the United States for the waiver to be effective.[194]

(ii) *Contractual waiver*

Courts narrowly construe contractual waiver. "Explicit waiver is generally found when the contract language itself clearly and unambiguously states that the parties intended a waiver, and therefore adjudication in the United States."[195] An example of language which has been found to constitute an explicit waiver follows:

> Borrower . . . hereby waives such immunity to the full extent permitted by the laws of such jurisdiction and, in particular, to the intent [*sic*] that in any

[191] HR Rep No 94-1487, *Jurisdiction of United States Courts in Suits Against Foreign States*, 94th Cong. (9 September 1976) at 18 (reprinted in 1976 USCCAN 6604, 6617).

[192] *Aquinda v Texaco*, 175 FRD 50, 52 (SDNY 1997), vacated on other grounds *sub. nom Jota v Texaco, Inc.*, 157 F 3d 153 (2d Cir. 1998); *Libra Bank Ltd. v Banco Nacional De Costa Rica, S.A.*, 676 F 2d 47, 49 (2d Cir. 1982) ("The word 'explicit' has been defined as follows: 'Not obscure or ambiguous, having no disguised meaning or reservation. Clear in understanding.' Black's Law Dictionary 519 (5th ed. 1979)").

[193] See HR Rep No 94-1487, *Jurisdiction of United States Courts in Suits Against Foreign States*, 94th Cong. (9 September 1976) at 17(reprinted in 1976 USCCAN 6604, 6616).

[194] A foreign sovereign does not waive its sovereign immunity "by signing an international agreement that contains no mention of a waiver of immunity to suit in United States courts or even the availability of a cause of action in the United States" (*Argentine Republic v Amerada Hess Shipping Corp.*, 488 US 428, 442–443, (1989)). See *Haven v Polska*, 215 F 3d 727, 734 (7th Cir.), cert. denied, 531 US 1014 (2000); *Creighton Ltd. v Government of the State of Qatar*, 181 F 3d 118, 123 (DC Cir 1999); *Smith v Socialist People's Libyan Arab Jamahiriya*, 101 F 3d 239, 246–247 (2d Cir. 1996), cert. denied, 520 US 1204 (1997); *Frolova v Union of Soviet Socialist Republics*, 761 F 2d 370 (7th Cir. 1985).

[195] *Eaglet Corp. Ltd. v Banco Cent. De Nicaragua*, 23 F 3d 641 (2d Cir. 1994) (adopting 839 F Supp 232, 243 (SDNY 1993) (citing *Proyecfin de Venezuela, S.A. v Banco Indus. De Venezuela*, 760 F 2d 390, 393 (2d Cir. 1985)).

proceedings taken in New York the foregoing waiver of immunity shall have effect.[196]

Generally the waiver of immunity must appear in the contract which is the subject of the suit for s 1605(a)(1) to apply.[197] However, where an express waiver of immunity from one agreement is incorporated into another contemporaneous agreement, courts have construed the waiver to apply to both agreements.[198]

Express waiver of sovereign immunity in the courts of another country does not automatically confer jurisdiction over that sovereign in the United States. For example, in *Eaglet Corp. Ltd. v Banco Central De Nicaragua*, the Second Circuit held that a Nicaraguan state entity's submission to the non-exclusive jurisdiction of the United Kingdom for disputes arising out of a debt restructuring agreement, was neither an express nor implied waiver of sovereign immunity in the United States.[199]

3.033   (2) *Implied waiver*

To find an implied waiver, there must be some manifestation of the state's intent to waive.[200] Courts have held that the "implied waiver" provision of s 1605(a)(1) must be narrowly construed.[201] Courts have done this by limiting its application to three instances set forth in the legislative history to the FSIA.[202]

---

[196] *Proyecfin de Venezuela*, 760 F 2d at 393. But see *Dayton v Czechoslovak Socialist Republic*, 834 F 2d 203, 205 (DC Cir 1987), cert. denied, 486 US 1054 (1988) (giving corporation the power "to sue and be sued" is not a waiver of immunity).

[197] See *World Wide Minerals, Ltd. v Republic of Kazakhstan*, 296 F 3d 1154, 1162–1163 (DC Cir 2002), cert. denied, 123 S Ct 1250 (2003). (In considering four related agreements between a Canadian corporation and Kazakhstan, the DC Circuit found express waivers of sovereign immunity in two of the contracts. However, the court did not extend the waiver to the other two contracts, which did not contain express waiver provisions).

[198] In *Proyecfin de Venezuela*, 760 F 2d at 393, a Venezuelan bank argued that a waiver provision in a loan agreement did not extend to another action for breach of a separate supervisory agreement. The Second Circuit held that the waiver provision was not limited by its terms to actions arising under the loan agreement, which did not preclude it from being incorporated into the supervisory agreement. The supervisory agreement contained a clause that provided that the loan agreement was "totally reproduced herein." The court interpreted this clause to incorporate all loan agreement provisions—including the waiver of immunity—into the supervisory agreement. The court further reasoned (at 393) that "the related agreements were nearly contemporaneous," and that the parties to both agreements were identical.   [199] See *Eaglet Corp*, 23 F 3d at 641.

[200] See *Smith*, 101 F 3d at 243 ("We have previously given some indication that the requisite intent is subjective . . . waiver would not be found absent a conscious decision to take part in the litigation"). See also *Princz v Federal Republic of Germany*, 26 F 3d 1116, 1174 (DC Cir 1994).

[201] See *Corzo v Banco Central de Reserva del Peru*, 243 F 3d 519, 524 (9th Cir. 2001); *Sampson v Federal Republic of Germany*, 250 F 3d 1145, 1150 (7th Cir. 2001); *S Davis Int'l, Inc. v The Republic of Yemen*, 218 F 3d 1292, 1301 (11th Cir. 2000); *In re Taminimi*, 176 F 3d 274, 278 (4th Cir. 1999); *Smith*, 101 F 3d 239, 242 (2d. Cir. 1997); *Rodriguez v Transnave, Inc.*, 8 F 3d 284, 289 (5th Cir. 1993); *Shapiro v Republic of Bolivia*, 930 F 2d 1013, 1017 (2d Cir. 1991); *Foremost-McKesson, Inc. v Islamic Republic of Iran*, 905 F 2d 438, 444 (DC Cir 1990); *Joseph v Office of the Consulate General of Nigeria*, 830 F 2d 1018, 1022–1023 (9th Cir. 1987), cert. denied, 485 US 905 (1988); *Frolova v Union of Soviet Socialist Republics*, 761 F 2d 370, 377 (7th Cir. 1985); *Canadian Overseas Ores Ltd. v Compania de Acero del Pacifico S.A.*, 727 F 2d 274 (2d Cir.1984).

[202] See *Aquamar, S.A. v Del Monte Fresh Produce N.A., Inc.*, 179 F 3d 1279, 1291, n 24 (11th Cir. 1999) ("The courts, loath to broaden the scope of the implied waiver provision"); *Shapiro v Republic*

The House Report on the FSIA stated that:

> With respect to implicit waivers, the courts have found such waivers in cases where a foreign state has agreed to arbitration in another country or where a foreign state has agreed that the law of a particular country should govern a contract. An implicit waiver would also include a situation where a foreign state has filed a responsive pleading in an action without raising the defense of sovereign immunity.[203]

Implied waiver, therefore, generally can only be found where there is (i) an arbitration clause, (ii) a choice of law clause, or (iii) a failure to plead. Courts have held that even the examples in the House Report must be construed narrowly.[204] Each of these instances is addressed in turn.

(i) *Arbitration*

In 1988 Congress amended the FSIA to codify "that an agreement to arbitrate constitutes a waiver of immunity in an action to enforce that agreement or the resultant award".[205] That amendment is codified at s 1605(a)(6). Nevertheless, parties continue to argue under s 1605(a)(1) that an arbitration clause constitutes an implied waiver of immunity with respect to actions both to enforce an award and to construe the underlying contract.[206]

With respect to implied waiver, the courts have generally held that an agreement to arbitrate in a country other than the United States does not reflect an intention to waive sovereign immunity to actions brought against the foreign state in the courts of the United States.[207]

---

of Bolivia, 930 F Supp 1013, 1017 (2d Cir. 1991*)* ("This approach is derived from the legislative history of the FSIA, in which Congress specified three examples of implied waiver"); accord *Frolova*, 761 F 2d at 377. See also *Commercial Corporation Sovrybflot v Corporacion de Fomento de la Produccion*, 980 F Supp 710, 711 (SDNY 1997) ("Waiver by implication exists in only three, narrowly construed situations"); *Eaglet*, 839 F Supp at 234 ("The legislative history narrows the scope of implied waiver by delineating only three examples of waiver").

[203] HR Rep No 94-1487, *Jurisdiction of United States Courts in Suits Against Foreign States*, 94th Cong. (9 September 1976) at 18 (reprinted in 1976 USCCAN 6604, 6617).

[204] See *Eaglet*, 23 F 3d 641 adopting 839 F Supp at 235 ("Moreover, courts have even construed these three examples narrowly"); *Cargill Int'l S.A. v M/T Pavel Dybenko*, 991 F 2d 1012, 1017 (2d Cir. 1993); *Frolova*, 761 F 2d 370, 377 (7th Cir. 1985); *Kao Hwa Shipping Co., v China Steel Corp.*, 816 F Supp 910, 916–917 (SDNY 1993); *L'Europeenne de Banque v La Republica de Venezuela*, 700 F Supp 114, 123 (SDNY 1988).

[205] 131 Cong.Rec. S5369 (daily ed. May 3, 1985) (Statement of Sen. Mathias) cited in *Cargill Int'l*, 991 F 2d at 1017.

[206] See *Cargill Int'l*, 991 F 2d at 1017; *S & Davis Int'l*, 218 F 3d at 1292; *Creighton Ltd.*, 181 F 3d 118 (DC Cir 1999).

[207] See *Cargill Int'l*, 991 F 2d at 1017 (finding that an agreement to arbitrate in a foreign country ought not to operate as a waiver of sovereign immunity in United States courts); *Frolova*, 761 F 2d at 377 ("most courts have refused to find an implicit waiver of immunity to suit in American courts from a contract clause providing for arbitration in a country other than the United States"). See also *Zernicek v Petroleos Mexicanos*, 614 F Supp 407, 411 (SD Tex 1985), aff'd, 826 F 2d 415 (5th Cir.1987), cert. denied, 484 US 1043 (1988); *Ohntrup v Firearms Center Inc.*, 516 F Supp 1281, 1285 (ED Pa 1981) ("a waiver of immunity by a state as to one jurisdiction cannot be interpreted to be a waiver as to all jurisdictions"); *Texas Trading & Milling Corp. v Federal Republic of Nigeria*, 500 F Supp 320, 323

Courts have found an implicit waiver of immunity when a cause of action arises which is closely related to the enforcement of an arbitral award and the sovereign party is a signatory to the Convention on the Recognition and Enforcement of Arbitral Awards.[208]

(ii) *Choice of law provisions*

In passing the FSIA, Congress stated that a foreign sovereign will be deemed to have implicitly waived its immunity "where [it] has agreed that the law of a particular country should govern a contract". The courts have narrowly construed this legislative intent. In *Maritime Ventures Int'l v Caribbean Trading & Fidelity*,[209] the Southern District of New York stated:

> A literal interpretation of the House Report would subject a foreign government to jurisdiction in the United States whenever it agreed to be governed by the laws or arbitrate in the forum of any country other than its own, even when the contract makes no mention of the United States. This would result in a vast increase in the jurisdiction of the federal courts over matters involving sensitive foreign relations.[210]

Courts, therefore, despite the congressional language, have refused to find an implicit waiver where a foreign state enters into an agreement to be bound by the laws of another nation.[211] However, where a foreign government expressly agrees to contractual interpretation under state law in the United States, courts have found an implicit waiver of sovereign immunity.[212] However, at least one circuit court has held that by itself, the contractual choice of US law does not amount to a waiver of immunity.[213]

(SDNY 1980) ("An agreement that the contract will be . . . submitted to arbitration in another country does not reflect intention to waive governmental immunity to actions brought against the foreign state in the courts of the United States").

[208] See *Seetransport Wiking Trader Schiffahrtgesellschaft MBH & Co, Kommanditgesellschaft v Navimpex Centrala Navala*, 989 F 2d 572, 578–579 (2d Cir. 1993).

[209] *Maritime Ventures Int'l v Caribbean Trading & Fidelity*, 689 F Supp 1340 (SDNY 1988).

[210] *Maritime Ventures Int'l*, 689 F Supp at 1351.

[211] See *Marra v Papandreou*, 216 F 3d 1119, 1122–1123 (DC Cir 2000); *Eaglet*, 839 F Supp at 235 (holding that a bank's agreement to submit to the laws and jurisdiction of England for a dispute arising out of a debt restructuring agreement did not constitute an implied waiver of the bank's sovereign immunity for purposes of an enforcement action in the United States); *Joseph*, 830 F 2d at 1018; *Zernicek v Brown & Root, Inc.*, 826 F 2d 415 (5th Cir. 1987); *Kao Hwa Shipping Co., S.A. v China Steel Corporation*, 816 F Supp at 916–917 (holding that defendant did not waive immunity to United States courts by virtue of a contract provision that expressly stated that the contract would be governed by Japanese law); *Verlinden B.V. v Central Bank of Nigeria*, 488 F Supp 1284, 1302 (SDNY 1980), aff'd, 647 F 2d 320 (2d Cir. 1981), rev'd on other grounds, 461 US 480 (1983). See also *Transatlantic Shiffahrtskontor v Shanghai Foreign Trade Corp.*, 204 F 3d 384, 391 (2d Cir. 2000) (cert. denied, 532 US 904 (2001) (refusing to find implied waiver to enforce Hong Kong indemnification award); *Seetransport Wiking Trader Schiffarhtsgesellschaft MBH & Co., Kommanditgesellschaft*, 989 F 2d, 577, *as amended, on remand* 837 F Supp 79 (1993).

[212] See *Eckert Int'l, Inc. v Gov't of Sovereign Democratic Republic of Fiji*, 32 F 3d 77, 80 (4th Cir. 1994) (contract stating it was to be "interpreted" in accordance with the laws of Virginia had the same effect for FSIA waiver purposes as if it had stated that Virginia law "controlled").

[213] *Pere v Nuovo Pignone, Inc.*, 150 F 3d 477, 482 (5th Cir. 1998), cert. denied, 525 US 1141 (1999).

(iii) *Failure to raise the defense of sovereign immunity in a responsive pleading*

If a foreign state appears to defend a suit, the failure to raise the defense of sovereign immunity in a responsive pleading is sufficient to imply waiver.[214] However, courts are loathe to find implicit waiver and therefore will often allow a foreign sovereign to amend their responsive pleading to assert immunity.[215] For example, in a case involving "unusual circumstances", Iran argued sovereign immunity in a motion to dismiss but failed to raise the defense in its answer. The court held that Iran's failure to raise sovereign immunity in its responsive pleading did not constitute an implied waiver.[216]

Unlike with responsive pleadings, a court may not find an implied waiver from a failure to raise a sovereign immunity defense in pre-pleading motions or letters.[217]

Jus cogens—The violation of *jus cogens* norms does not, by itself, rise to the level of an implied waiver of sovereign immunity under the FSIA.[218]

Effect of appearance in US court—The filing of an appearance does not constitute an implied waiver of sovereign immunity.[219] The filing of an *amicus curiae* brief does not constitute an implied waiver of sovereign immunity.[220] Similarly the removal of an action to federal court is not sufficient to find an implied waiver.[221] The mere failure to enter an appearance also is insufficient to imply a waiver of sovereign immunity.[222] However, at least one court has held that, by affirmatively enlisting the aid of US courts, a foreign state waives its immunity under the FSIA with respect to actions brought in connection with the assistance sought.[223]

28 U.S.C. § 1605   3.034

(a) A foreign state shall not be immune from the jurisdiction of courts of the United States or of the States in any case—

. . .

[214] See *Barragan v Banco BCH*, 188 Cal. App. 3d 283, 294 (1986); *Foremost-McKesson*, 905 F 2d at 438 ("In most instances, a state's failure to assert sovereign immunity in a responsive pleading will constitute a waiver of the defense"); *US v Crawford Enterprises, Inc.*, 643 F Supp 370 (SD Tex 1986) (finding immunity implicitly waived by failure to assert immunity in response to order to show cause); *Aboujdid v Singapore Airlines, Ltd.*, 108 A.D.2d 330 (1st Dept. 1985), aff'd, 67 NY 2d 450 (1986).
[215] See *Drexel Burnham Lambert Group Inc. v Committee of Receivers for Galadari*, 12 F 3d 317, 326 (2d Cir. 1993), cert. denied, 511 US 1069 (1994); *Foremost-McKesson*, 905 F 2d at 441; *Alpha Therapeutic Corp. v Nippon Hoso Kyoka*, 1999 F 3d 1078 (9th Cir. 1999) (withdrawn by 237 F 3d 1007 (9th Cir. 2001)).   [216] See *Foremost-McKesson*, 905 F 2d, 445.
[217] See *Haven*, 215 F 3d at 731–732; *Smith*, 101 F 3d, 245–246; *Canadian Overseas Ores Ltd.*, 727 F 2d at 277–278; *Hirsh v State of Israel*, 962 F Supp 377, 380 (SDNY 1997), aff'd, 133 F 3d 907 (2d Cir. 1997), cert. denied, 523 US 1062 (1998).
[218] *Sampson v Federal Republic of Germany*, 250 F 3d 1145 (7th Cir. 2001); see also *Smith v Socialist People's Libyan Arab Jamahiriya*, 886 F Supp 306 (EDNY 1995); and see *Princz*, 26 F 3d at 1166
[219] See *Haven v Polska*, 215 F 3d 727 (7th Cir. 2000), cert. denied, 531 US 1014; *Jet Line Services, Inc. v M/V Marsa El Hariga*, 462 F Supp 1165 (DC Md 1978).
[220] *In re Estate of Ferdinand Marcos Human Rights Litig.*, 94 F 3d 539 (9th Cir. 1996).
[221] See, eg, *Rodriguez*, 8 F 3d at 287.   [222] *Frolova*, 761 F 2d at 377.
[223] See *Siderman de Blake v Republic of Argentina*, 965 F 2d 699 (9th Cir. 1992) (government applied to the district court through a letter rogatory for assistance in serving papers). But see

(2) in which the action is based upon a commercial activity carried on in the United States by the foreign state; or upon an act performed in the United States in connection with a commercial activity of the foreign state elsewhere; or upon an act outside the territory of the United States in connection with a commercial activity of the foreign state elsewhere and that act causes a direct effect in the United States;

. . .

Commentary

3.035   Legislative history

Section 1605(a)(2) treats what is probably the most important instance in which foreign states are denied immunity, that in which the foreign state engages in a commercial activity. The definition of a "commercial activity" is set forth in s 1603(d) and is discussed in the analysis to that section.[224]

Section 1605(a)(2) mentions three situations in which a foreign state would not be entitled to immunity with respect to a claim based upon a commercial activity. The first of these situations is where the "commercial activity [is] carried on in the United States by the foreign state." This phrase is defined in s 1603(e) of the bill. See the analysis to that section.[225]

The second situation, an "act performed in the United States in connection with a commercial activity of the foreign state elsewhere," looks to conduct of the foreign state in the United States which relates either to a regular course of commercial conduct elsewhere or to a particular commercial transaction concluded or carried out in part elsewhere. Examples of this type of situation might include: a representation in the United States by an agent of a foreign state that leads to an action for restitution based on unjust enrichment; an act in the United States that violates US securities laws or regulations; the wrongful discharge in the United States of an employee of the foreign state who has been employed in connection with a commercial activity carried on in some third country.

Although some or all of these acts might also be considered to be a "commercial activity carried on in the United States," as broadly defined in s 1603(e), it has seemed advisable to provide expressly for the case where a claim arises out of a specific act in the United States which is commercial or private in nature and which relates to a commercial activity abroad. It should be noted that the acts (or omissions) encompassed in this category are limited to those which in and of themselves are sufficient to form the basis of a cause of action.

Blaxland v Commonwealth Director of Public Prosecutions, 323 F 3d 1198 (9th Cir. 2003) (distinguishing communications with the executive branch); *Cabiri v Gov't of Republic of Ghana*, 165 F 3d 193, 202 (2d Cir.), cert. denied, 527 US 1022 (1999) (describing the reasoning of *Siderman* as "dubious").

[224] See 3.020 above.   [225] See 3.021 above.

The third situation—"an act outside the territory of the United States in connection with a commercial activity of the foreign state elsewhere and that act causes a direct effect in the United States"—would embrace commercial conduct abroad having direct effects within the United States which would subject such conduct to the exercise of jurisdiction by the United States consistent with principles set forth in s 18, *Restatement of the Law, Second, Foreign Relations Law of the United States* (1965).

Neither the term "direct effect" nor the concept of "substantial contacts" embodied in s 1603(e) is intended to alter the application of the Sherman Antitrust Act, 15 USC 1, et seq., to any defendant. Thus, the bill does not affect the holdings in such cases as *United States v. Pacific & A R & Nav. Co.*, 228 US 87 (1913), or *Pacific Seafarers, Inc. v. Pacific Far East Line, Inc.*, 404 F 2d 804 (DC Cir 1968), *cert. denied*, 393 US 1093 (1969).[226]

Application   **3.036**

Foreign states do not enjoy sovereign immunity in actions based upon: (1) a commercial activity carried on in the United States by the foreign state; (2) an act performed in the United States in connection with a commercial activity of the foreign state elsewhere; or (3) an act outside the territory of the United States in connection with a commercial activity of the foreign state elsewhere and that act causes a direct effect in the United Sates.

The so-called "commercial activity exception" is undoubtedly the most frequently litigated exception to sovereign immunity in the courts of the United States.[227] Courts apply a three-part test to determine whether the commercial activity exception applies. At the outset, the court must determine if the action involves a "commercial activity" as defined by the FSIA.[228] If the action involves a commercial activity the court must determine if there is a "sufficient jurisdictional connection or nexus between the commercial activity and the United States."[229] Finally, the court must determine if there is "a substantive connection or nexus between the commercial activity and the subject matter of the cause of

---

[226] HR Rep No 94-1487, *Jurisdiction of United States Courts in Suits Against Foreign States*, 94th Cong. (9 September 1976), 18–19 (reprinted in 1976 USCCAN 6604, 6617–6618).

[227] See *De Sanchez v Banco Central de Nicaragua*, 770 F 2d 1385, 1390 (5th Cir. 1985).

[228] "Commercial activity" is defined at 28 USC § 1603(d) (see 3.020 above). "The determination of whether particular behavior is 'commercial' is perhaps the most important decision a court faces in a FSIA suit . . . If the activity is not 'commercial' it satisfies none of the three clauses of § 1605(a)(2), and the foreign state is (at least under that subsection) immune from suit." *Texas Trading & Milling Corp. v Federal Republic of Nigeria*, 647 F 2d 300, 308 (2d Cir. 1981), cert. denied, 454 US 1148 (1982).

[229] *Federal Ins. Co. v Richard I. Rubin & Co.*, 12 F 3d 1270, 1286 (3d Cir. 1993), cert. denied, 511 US 1107 (1994).

action."[230] Courts have allowed plaintiffs limited discovery in certain instances to determine if the commercial activity exception applies.[231]

(1) Claims "Based Upon" Activity that has "Substantial Contact" with the United States

3.037 A foreign state is not immune from the jurisdiction of the courts of the United States for claims "based upon" a foreign state's commercial activity that has "substantial contact" with the United States.[232]

The FSIA contains no definition of "based upon." Courts have held that:

> a claim is "based upon" events in the United States if those events establish a legal element of the claim . . . An action is based upon the elements that prove the claim, no more and no less. If one of those elements consists of commercial activity within the United States or other conduct specified in the Act, this country's courts have jurisdiction.[233]

The Eighth Circuit has found that, where plaintiff has brought multiple claims, "[w]e need not consider each of these claims separately, since only one claim or element of a claim need concern commercial activity in the United States to erode [defendant's] presumptive immunity".[234]

In the *Saudi Arabia v Nelson* case, the plaintiff was recruited and trained in the United States to work at a state-owned hospital in Saudi Arabia. The plaintiff alleged that he was arrested and beaten by Saudi authorities for raising safety concerns at the hospital. The court held that the Saudi government enjoyed immunity from plaintiffs' claims.[235] The court reasoned that while the recruitment and employment of the plaintiff in the United States (undoubtedly commercial activity) led to the conduct that eventually injured the plaintiff, the commercial activity was not the basis of the suit. The court noted that Nelson's suit alleged injuries caused by torts such as intentional wrongs or negligence rather than by breach of contract. Because these torts, rather than the commercial activities

---

[230] 12 F 3d at 1286.

[231] See *Filus v Lot Polish Airlines*, 907 F 2d 1328, 1332–1333 (2d Cir. 1990) (citing *Oppenheim Fund Inc. v Danders*, 437 US 340, 351 & n 13 (1978)) (allowing plaintiff's discovery regarding defendants' United States commercial activities to proceed, conditioned on a showing that defendant is a foreign state and has been properly served).

[232] "Commercial activity carried on in the United States" is defined at 28 USC § 1603(e) (see 3.021 above). See *Saudi Arabia v Nelson*, 507 US 349, 356–357 (1993); *BP Chemicals Ltd. v Jiangsu Sopo Corp.*, 285 F 3d 677 (8th Cir.), cert. denied, 537 US 942 (2002); *Gould v Mitsui Mining & Smelting Co.*, 947 F 2d 218, 220 (6th Cir. 1991), cert. denied, 503 US 978 (1992).

[233] *Santos v Compagnie Nationale Air France*, 934 F 2d 890, 893 (7th Cir. 1991). See also *Fagot Rodriguez v the Republic of Costa Rica*, 139 F Supp 2d 173 (D. P.R. 2001), aff'd 297 F 3d 1 (2002) (finding immunity against a claim based on defendant's operation of a consulate without its landlord's permission because the claim was based on the sovereign act of establishing or operating of a consulate, rather than on the commercial activity of entering into a lease).

[234] *BP Chemicals Ltd.*, 285 F 3d at 682. "[A]n action is based on commercial activity in the United States if an element of the plaintiff's claim consists in conduct that occurred in commercial activity carried on in the United States." Accord *Sugimoto v Exportadora De Sal, S.A. De C.V.*, 19 F 3d 1309, 1311 (9th Cir.), cert. denied, 513 US 1018 (1994).   [235] See *Nelson*, 507 US at 356.

preceding those torts, "form[ed] the basis for" the suit, the Saudi government was immune from plaintiff's claims.[236]

A foreign sovereign, however, does not abrogate its sovereign immunity simply because it conducts commercial operations that have a connection with the United States. Not only must there be a jurisdictional nexus between the United States and the commercial acts of the foreign sovereign, there must be a connection between the plaintiff's cause of action and the commercial acts of the foreign sovereign.[237]

The conduct forming the basis of the action requires "something more than a mere connection with, or relation to, the commercial activity".[238] "In order to satisfy the commercial activities exception to sovereign immunity, the commercial activity that provides the jurisdictional nexus with the United States must also be the activity on which the lawsuit is based".[239] Moreover, the connection between the cause of action and the sovereign's commercial acts in the United States must be material.[240]

(2) *Activity in the United States "in connection with" a commercial activity elsewhere*

3.038

A foreign state is not immune from the jurisdiction of the courts of the United States for claims based on an act performed in the United States "in connection with" commercial activity outside the United States. Few authorities have discussed this element of s 1605(2).

---

[236] *Nelson*, 507 US at 358.

[237] *Stena Rederi AB v Comision de Contratos del Comite Ejecutivo General del Sindicato Revolucionario de Trabajadores Petroleros de la Republica Mexicana, S.C.*, 923 F 2d 380, 386–387 (5th Cir. 1991) (citing *Vencedora Oceanica Navigacion v Compagnie Nationale Algerienne de Navigation*, 730 F 2d 195, 200 (5th Cir. 1984); *Gould, Inc. v Pechiney Ugine Kuhlmann & Trefimetaux*, 853 F 2d 445, 452 (6th Cir. 1988) ("there must be a connection between that [commercial] activity and the act complained of in the lawsuit"); *Joseph v Office of the Consulate General*, 830 F 2d 1018, 1023 (9th Cir. 1987), cert. denied, 485 US 905 (1988) ("In determining whether the commercial activity exception applies, the courts focus only on those specific acts that form the basis of the suit"); *Arango v Guzman Travel Advisors Corp.*, 621 F 2d 1371, 1379 (5th Cir. 1980) (focus of the commercial activity exception is on "whether the particular conduct giving rise to the claim in question actually constitutes or is in connection with commercial activity, regardless of the defendant's generally commercial or governmental character").

[238] *Nelson*, 507 US at 356–358. See *NYSA-ILA Pension Trust Fund v Garuda Indonesia*, 7 F 3d 35 (2d Cir. 1993), cert. denied, 510 US 1116 (1994) ("In construing the commercial activity exception, courts have required that a significant nexus exist between the commercial activity in this country upon which the exception is based and a plaintiff's cause of action"); *Stena Rederi AB*, 923 F 2d, 386–387; *Barkanic v General Admin. of Civil Aviation of the People's Republic of China*, 822 F 2d 11, 13 (2d Cir. 1987), cert. denied, 484 US 964 (1987).

[239] *Stena Rederi AB*, 923 F 2d at 386–387. See *Nelson*, 507 US at 357 (citing *Callejo v Bancomer, S.A.*, 764 F 2d 1101, 1109 (5th Cir. 1985); *Santos*, 934 F 2d, 893; *Millen Industries, Inc., v Coordination Council for North American Affairs*, 855 F 2d 879, 885 (DC Cir 1988).

[240] See *Stena Rederi AB*, 923 F 2d at 387 (citing *America West Airlines, Inc. v GPA Group, Ltd*, 877 F 2d 793, 797 (9th Cir. 1989); *Compania Mexicana de Aviacion v United States District Court*, 859 F 2d 1354, 1360 (9th Cir. 1988); *Alberti v Empresa Nicaraguense de la Carne*, 705 F 2d 250, 254 (7th Cir. 1983)).

Acts are "in connection with" a commercial activity so long as there is a "substantive connection" or a "causal link" between them and the commercial activity.[241] An act need not be "substantial" to satisfy the second clause of s 1605(a)(2).[242] However, there must be an affirmative act by the foreign state in the United States. In *Filus v LOT Polish Airlines*,[243] the court held that a failure to warn did not constitute an act within the United States.[244]

The Fifth Circuit has held that this clause exclusively applies "to non-commercial acts in the United States that relate to commercial acts abroad".[245] In *Byrd v Corparacion Forestal y Industrialde Olancho S.A.*,[246] the court held that a state owned bank's demand on a bank guarantee in the United States was a commercial act and therefore not the type of act covered by the second clause of s 1605(a)(2). Recently, however, an American Bar Association Working Group argued that "[t]his interpretation is not correct. Nothing in the [FSIA], the legislative history, or the Supreme Court decision on which the remarks are based limits the act specified in the second clause to non-commercial acts".[247]

With respect to the nexus between the commercial act and the cause of action:

> [a]ny material connection between "commercial activity elsewhere" and the plaintiff's complaint . . . is irrelevant . . . Under the plain language of the FSIA, the plaintiff's action must be based upon the "act performed in the United States in connection with a commercial activity of the foreign state elsewhere." Thus, the material connection required by the commercial activities exception to sovereign immunity must exist between the plaintiff's cause of action and the act performed in the United States.[248]

3.039   (3) *Activity outside the United States which causes a "direct effect" in the United States*

Foreign states do not enjoy sovereign immunity from suits based upon an act outside the territory of the United States which is performed in connection with a commercial activity of the foreign state elsewhere and that causes a direct effect in the United States.

An effect is "direct" if it "follows as an immediate consequence of the defendant's activity".[249] To satisfy this exception, the plaintiff need not establish that

---

[241] See *Hanil Bank v PT. Bank Negara Indonesia (Persero)*, 148 F 3d 127, 131 (2d Cir. 1998) (citing *Adler v Federal Republic of Nigeria*, 107 F 3d 720, 726 (9th Cir. 1997) (quoting *Federal Ins. Co. v Richard I. Rubin & Co.*, 12 F 3d 1270, 1289–1291 (3d Cir. 1993), cert. denied, 511 US 1107 (1994)).

[242] See *Stena Rederi AB*, 923 F 2d at 389, n 11 ("FSIA does not impose a similar 'substantial contact' requirement on acts performed in the United States in connection with commercial activity elsewhere").

[243] 907 F 2d at 1328.   [244] 907 F 2d at 1333.

[245] *Voest-Alpine Trading USA Corp. v Bank of China*, 142 F 3d 887, 892, n 5 (5th Cir. 1998); see also *Byrd v Corporacion Forestal y Industrial de Olancho S.A.*, 182 F 3d 380, 390 (5th Cir. 1999).

[246] 182 F 3d at 390.

[247] American Bar Association Working Group, *Reforming the Foreign Sovereign Immunities Act*, 40 Colum J Transnat'l L 489, 554 (2002).

[248] *Stena Rederi AB*, 923 F 2d at 388 (citing *Gilson v Republic of Ireland*, 682 F 2d 1022, 1027, n 22 (DC Cir 1982)).   [249] *Stena Rederi AB*, 923 F 2d at 388.

the effect in the United States was either substantial or foreseeable.[250] However, "jurisdiction may not be predicated on purely trivial effects in the United States".[251]

In the *Weltover* case, the court held that Argentina's unilateral rescheduling of its foreign debt caused a direct effect within the United States because the United States was the place of performance.[252] Following the *Weltover* case, the Second Circuit in *Hanil Bank v PT. Bank Negara Indonesia*,[253] held that an Indonesian bank caused a direct effect in the United States when it failed to make payment on a letter of credit after a party had designated an account in New York City as the place of payment. Similarly, the Fifth Circuit held that the Bank of China's failure to remit payment to a bank in Texas caused a direct effect in the United States.[254]

There is currently a split of authority concerning the test to be applied. Some courts hold that plaintiffs must show that something legally significant has happened in the United States for this clause to apply.[255] In these circuits, financial injury to a US business or personal injury to a US person is not a sufficiently direct effect to deny a state sovereign immunity.[256] The Fifth Circuit has expressly rejected this test.[257]

---

[250] See *Republic of Argentina v Weltover*, 504 US 607, 617–619 (1992).

[251] See *Weltover*, 504 US at 618. Jurisdiction also may not be predicated on purely speculative effects. See *Croesus EMTR Master Fund L.P. v Federative Republic of Brazil*, 212 F Supp 2d 30 (DDC 2002) (finding no direct effect in the United States where plaintiffs did not attempt to designate the United States as a place of payment, but argued that defendant would be "likely" to have honored a designation of the United States as payment if plaintiffs had attempted this designation).

[252] "Money that was supposed to have been delivered to a New York bank for deposit was not forthcoming." *Weltover*, 504 US at 619.

[253] *Hanil Bank v PT. Bank Negara Indonesia (Persero)*, 148 F 3d 127 (2d Cir. 1998).

[254] *Voest-Alpine Trading USA Corp*, 142 F 3d at 895–896.

[255] See *Virtual Countries Inc. v Republic of South Africa*, 300 F 3d 230, 240–241 (2d Cir. 2002); *Princz v Federal Republic of Germany*, 26 F 3d 1166, 1173 (DC Cir 1994), cert. denied, 513 US 1121 (1995); *Adler v Federal Republic of Nigeria*, 107 F 3d 720, 727 (9th Cir. 1997) (determining that, although the Supreme Court in *Weltover* did not apply the "legally significant acts" test, the Ninth Circuit would follow the Second, Eighth, and Tenth Circuit in deciding that the *Weltover* analysis was similar and that the "legally significant acts" test still survived); *United World Trade, Inc. v Mangyshlakneft Oil Prod. Ass'n*, 33 F 3d 1232 (10th Cir. 1994); *Antares Aircraft, L.P. v Federal Republic of Nigeria*, 999 F 2d 33 (2d Cir. 1993), cert. denied, 510 US 1071 (1994); *Human Rights in China v Bank of China*, 2003 WL 22170648 (SDNY 18 September, 2003).

[256] See *Virtual Countries*, 300 F 3d at 240 ("The plaintiffs' more expansive theory, that any US corporation's financial loss constitutes a direct effect in the United States is plainly flawed"); *Dominican Energy Ltd. v Dominican Republic*, 903 F Supp 1507 (M.D. Fla. 1995) (financial loss by a person in the United States is not sufficient to constitute a direct effect); *Coleman v Alcolac, Inc.*, 888 F Supp 1388 (SD Tex 1995); *Maizus v Weldor Trust Reg.*, 820 F Supp 101 (SDNY 1993); but see *McKesson HBOC, Inc. v Islamic Republic of Iran*, 271 F 3d 1101, 1105–1106 (DC Cir 2001), cert. denied, 537 US 941 (2002) (exercising jurisdiction because expropriation of a minority equity interest in Iranian dairy stopped the flow of capital, machinery, equipment, materials, and data between the companies and stopped the payment of dividends to the US company).

[257] See *Voest-Alpine Trading USA Corp*, 142 F 3d at 894 ("In *Weltover*, the Supreme Court expressly admonished the circuit courts not to add 'any unexpressed requirement[s]' to the third clause . . . The legally significant act requirement is unexpressed in the third clause and, thus, has been renounced by *Weltover*").

3.040 **28 U.S.C. § 1605**

(a) A foreign state shall not be immune from the jurisdiction of courts of the United States or of the States in any case—

. . .

(3) in which rights in property taken in violation of international law are in issue and that property or any property exchanged for such property is present in the United States in connection with a commercial activity carried on in the United States by the foreign state; or that property or any property exchanged for such property is owned or operated by an agency or instrumentality of the foreign state and that agency or instrumentality is engaged in a commercial activity in the United States;

. . .

Commentary

3.041   Legislative history

Section 1605(3) is often referred to as the expropriation exception. This exception denies immunity to foreign states in two categories of cases where:

> rights in property taken in violation of international law are in issue. The first category involves cases where the property in question or any property exchanged for such property is present in the United States, and where such presence is in connection with a commercial activity carried on in the United States by the foreign state, or political subdivision, agency or instrumentality of the foreign state. The second category is where the property, or any property exchanged for such property, is (i) owned or operated by an agency or instrumentality of a foreign state and (ii) that agency or instrumentality is engaged in a commercial activity in the United States. Under the second category, the property need not be present in connection with a commercial activity of the agency or instrumentality.[258]

The term "taken in violation of international law" would include the nationalization or expropriation of property without payment of the prompt adequate and effective compensation required by international law. It would also include takings which are arbitrary or discriminatory in nature. Since, however, this section deals solely with issues of immunity, it in no way affects existing law on the extent to which, if at all, the act of state doctrine may be applicable.[259]

---

[258] HR Rep No 94-1487, *Jurisdiction of United States Courts in Suits Against Foreign States*, 94th Cong. (9 September 1976) at 19 (reprinted in 1976 USCCAN 6604, 6618).
[259] HR Rep No 94-1487, *Jurisdiction of United States Courts in Suits Against Foreign States*, 94th Cong. (9 September 1976) at 19–20 (reprinted in 1976 USCCAN 6604, 6618).

The expropriation exception:

> parallels the so-called "Hickenlooper Exception" to the act of state doctrine, 22 U.S.C. § 2370(e)(2) (1982),[260] under which courts may not invoke the act of state doctrine in cases where a claim to property is asserted based upon "a confiscation or other taking . . . by an act of [a foreign] state in violation of the principles of international law".[261]

Application   **3.042**

Courts have generally analyzed the expropriation exception in terms of four discrete elements.[262] To bring a claim under the expropriation exception "a plaintiff must show that: (1) rights in property are in issue, (2) that the property was 'taken', (3) that the taking was in violation of international law, and (4) that one of the two nexus requirements is satisfied".[263]

(1) *Rights in property*

There is a split at the circuit court level concerning whether the expropriation exception applies solely to tangible property.[264] The Second Circuit has held that it is so limited.[265] The Ninth Circuit, on the other hand, has adopted a broader construction of "rights in property" which includes at least certain rights in intangible personal property.[266]

---

[260] The Second Hickenlooper Amendment effectively overturns the act of state doctrine with respect to expropriation claims. It states that "[n]o court in the United States shall decline on the ground of the federal act of state doctrine to make a determination on the merits giving effect to the principles of international law in a case in which a claim of title or other rights to property is asserted by any party . . . based upon (or traced through) a confiscation or other taking . . . by an act of that state in violation of the principles of international law, including the principles of compensation . . ." 22 USC § 2370(e)(2).

[261] See *De Sanchez v Banco Central de Nicaragua*, 770 F 2d 1385, 1395 (5th Cir. 1985). Courts will rely on cases arising under the Second Hinkenlooper Amendment in construing the language of the FSIA. See 770 F 2d at 1395.

[262] See, eg, *Zappia Middle East Construction Co., Ltd. v Emirate of Abu Dhabi*, 215 F 3d 247, 251 (2d Cir. 2000).   [263] 215 F 3d at 247.

[264] See *Brewer v Socialist People's Republic of Iraq*, 890 F 2d 97, 101 (8th Cir. 1989); *De Sanchez*, 770 F 2d at 1395; *Intercontinental Dictionary Series v De Gruyter*, 822 F Supp 662, 678 (CD Cal 1993); *Friedar v Government of Israel*, 614 F Supp 395, 399 (SDNY 1985); *Canadian Overseas Ores Ltd. v Compania de Acero del Pacifico*, 528 F Supp 1337, 1346 (SDNY 1982) aff'd, 727 F 2d 274 (2d Cir. 1984).

[265] See *Menendez v Saks & Co.*, 485 F 2d 1355, 1372 (2nd Cir. 1973), rev'd in part on other grounds sub nom. *Alfred Dunhill of London, Inc. v Republic of Cuba*, 425 US 682 (1976); *Leutwyler v Office of Her Majesty Queen Rania Al-Abdullah*, 184 F Supp 2d 277, 289 n 13 (SDNY 2001) (expropriation exception not applicable to taking of usage rights to intellectual property); *Lord Day & Lord v Socialist Republic of Vietnam*, 134 F Supp 2d 549 (SDNY 2001) (noting in dicta that less than a majority stock interest does not constitute rights in property); *Braka v Bancomer, S.A.*, 589 F Supp 1465, 1472–1473 (SDNY 1984), aff'd, 762 F 2d 222 (2d Cir. 1985); *Canadian Overseas Ores Ltd*, 528 F Supp at 1346 (holding that s 1605(a)(3) is not applicable to a contractual right to be paid). See also *Sampson v Federal Republic of Germany*, 975 F Supp 1108, 1117 (ND Ill 1997), aff'd, 250 F 3d 1145 (7th Cir. 2001) (right to receive payments does not constitute property) (citing *Hirsh v State of Israel*, 962 F Supp 377, 382–383 (SDNY 1997)).

[266] See *West v Multibanco Comermex, S.A.*, 807 F 2d 820, 826, 830–831 (9th Cir. 1987) (holding that at least some intangible property rights, including contractual rights involved in certificates of

(2) *Taking*

The FSIA does not define the term "taken." However, the legislative history makes clear that the phrase "taken in violation of international law" refers to the nationalization or expropriation of property without payment of the prompt adequate and effective compensation required by international law, including takings which are arbitrary or discriminatory in nature.[267]

Courts have held that a taking requires the "acts of a sovereign, not a private enterprise".[268] The Second Circuit has held that a private enterprise, even if deemed to be a government instrumentality, cannot commit a taking unless the claimant shows that it "is so extensively controlled by the sovereign that the latter is effectively the agent of the former, or if recognizing the corporate entity as independent would work a fraud or injustice."[269]

(3) *Violation of international law*

At the jurisdictional stage, the court "need not decide whether the taking actually violated international law; as long as a claim is substantial and non-frivolous, it provides a sufficient basis for the exercise of [its] jurisdiction".[270]

Not all government takings violate international law. For example, a state's expropriation of the property of its own nationals does not violate settled principles of international law.[271] Therefore to bring an action under the expropriation exception the claimant must not have been a citizen of the defendant state at the time of the expropriation.[272]

In *West v Multibanco Comermex, S.A*, the Ninth Circuit described when a taking is "valid", or in accordance with international law. First, valid expropriations must always serve a public purpose.[273] Second, aliens must not be discriminated against or singled out for regulation by the state.[274] Finally, an otherwise valid taking is illegal without the payment of just compensation.[275] At least one

---

deposits, are rights in property for purposes of the expropriation exception). See also *Kalamazoo Spice Extraction Co. v Provisional Military Gov't of Socialist Ethiopia*, 616 F Supp 660, 663 (WD Mich 1985) (holding that a majority interest in a company's stock does constitute rights in property).

[267] *Zappia*, 215 F 3d, 251 (citing HR Rep No 94-1487, *Jurisdiction of United States Courts in Suits Against Foreign States*, 94th Cong. (9 September 1976) at 19 (reprinted in 1976 USCCAN 6604, 6618) (internal quotation marks omitted).

[268] 215 F 3d at 251. ("The term 'taken' thus clearly refers to acts of a sovereign, not a private enterprise, that deprive a plaintiff of property without adequate compensation") (citing *Alfred Dunhill of London, Inc.*, 425 US at 685).   [269] *Zappia*, 215 F 3d at 252.

[270] *Altmann v Republic of Austria*, 317 F 3d 954, 968 (9th Cir. 2002); *Siderman de Blake v Republic of Argentina*, 965 F 2d 699, 711 (9th Cir. 1992), *West*, 807 F 2d at 826.

[271] See *Restatement (Third) of the Foreign Relations Law of the United States* § 712-713.

[272] See *Altmann*, 317 F 3d at 968 (noting that expropriation of the property of a state's own nationals does not violate settled international law). See also *Siderman de Blake*, 965 F 2d, 711; *De Sanchez*, 770 F 2d at 1395; *Dreyfus v Von Finck*, 534 F 2d 24, 30–31 (2d Cir.), cert. denied, 429 US 835 (1976).

[273] See *West*, 807 F 2d at 831.   [274] See *West*, 807 F 2d at 832.

[275] See *West*, 807 F 2d. at 832. See also *Altmann*, 317 F 3d at 968. Just compensation has also been termed "prompt, adequate, and effective" compensation (*Banco National de Cuba v Chase Manhattan Bank*, 658 F 2d 875, 888 (2d Cir. 1981), modified in part, 514 F Supp 5 (SDNY 1980), affirmed in part and remanded in part, 658 F 2d 875 (2nd Cir. 1981); *Alberti v Empresa Nicaraguense de la*

court has held that a plaintiff must exhaust domestic remedies (ie, remedies within the state alleged to have expropriated the property) before a taking will be found to violate international law.[276]

(4) *Commercial nexus*

Because Congress intended this exception to provide a means to remedy a foreign government's expropriation of property in the United States, jurisdiction over a foreign state exists only where rights in property taken in violation of international law are in issue and that property or any property exchanged for such property is present in the United States in connection with a commercial activity carried on in the United States by the foreign state.[277]

First, assuming the property or any property exchanged therefor is located in the United States, a claimant must allege that it is there in connection with a commercial activity carried on by the foreign state in the US.[278]

Assuming that the property or any property exchanged therefor is not located in the United States, a claimant must show that the property is owned by an agency or instrumentality of the foreign state which is engaged in commercial activity in the United States. The Fifth Circuit has held that the property must be used for the benefit of the foreign state in order for any seizure to rise to the level of ownership or operation.[279] For purposes of the nexus requirement, the commercial activity of the foreign state cannot be imputed to the instrumentality.[280] This is because "government instrumentalities established as

---

Carne, 705 F 2d 250, 255 (7th Cir. 1983)). In *Alberti*, the court defined "prompt payment" in dicta to mean payment "made within a reasonable time *after* nationalization" (emphasis in original).

[276] Two district courts have held that a claimant must also first exhaust domestic remedies (or show them to be futile) in order to demonstrate lack of just compensation, see *Millicom International Cellular, S.A. v Republic of Costa Rica*, 995 F Supp 14, 23 (DDC 1998); *Greenpeace, Inc. (USA) v State of France*, 946 F Supp 773, 783 (CD Cal 1996) ("As a threshold matter, a claimant cannot complain that a taking or other economic injury has not been fairly compensated, and hence violates international law unless the claimant has first pursued and exhausted domestic remedies in the foreign state that is alleged to have caused the injury") (citing *Interhandel Case (Switzerland v United States)* [1959] ICJ Rep 6, 26–27 (the state where the violation has occurred should have an opportunity to redress takings by its own means, within the framework of its own domestic legal system); *Restatement (Third) of the Foreign Relations Law of the United States* § 713 cmt. f).

[277] *Hirsh v State of Israel*, 962 F Supp at 383 (citing *Canadian Overseas Ores Ltd. v Compania De Acero Del Pacifico S.A.*, 528 F Supp 1337, 1346 (SDNY 1982), aff'd, 727 F 2d 274 (2d Cir.1984).

[278] See *Dayton v Czechoslovak Socialist Republic*, 834 F 2d 203, 205–206 (DC Cir 1987), cert. denied, 486 US 1054 (1988); *Crist v Republic of Turkey*, 995 F Supp 5, 11 (DDC 1998); *Hirsh v State of Israel*, 962 F Supp at 383.

[279] See *Vencedora Oceanica Navigacion, S.A. v Compagnie Nationale Algerienne de Navigation*, 730 F 2d 195, 204 (5th Cir. 1984) (holding that "possession" or "control" of a damaged ship in order to tow it to port for safety purposes fell short of "ownership" or "operation" because it was not for the benefit of the foreign state). See also *Greenpeace, Inc. (USA)*, 946 F Supp at 784 (same).

[280] *Antares Aircraft, L.P. v Federal Republic of Nigeria*, 948 F 2d 90, 97 (2nd Cir. 1991), vacated on other grounds, 505 US 1215 (1992) (citing *First Nat'l City Bank v Banco Para El Comercio Exterior de Cuba*, 462 US 611, 626–627 (1983); *Dayton v Czechoslovak Socialist Republic*, 672 F Supp 7, 10 (DDC 1986).

juridical entities distinct and independent from their sovereign should normally be treated as such".[281]

As a final matter, courts have held that failed takings or expropriations claims cannot be recast as tortious conversion claims.[282]

3.043 28 U.S.C. § 1605

(a) A foreign state shall not be immune from the jurisdiction of courts of the United States or of the States in any case—

. . .

(4) in which rights in property in the United States acquired by succession or gift or rights in immovable property situated in the United States are at issue;

. . .

Commentary

3.044 Legislative history

Section 1605(a)(4):

> denies immunity in litigation relating to rights in real estate and inherited or gifted property located in the United States. It establishes that, as set forth in the Tate Letter of 1952, sovereign immunity should not be granted in actions with respect to real property, diplomatic and consular property excepted. It does not matter whether a particular piece of property is used for commercial or public purposes.[283]

When passing s 1605(a)(4) Congress took note that:

> the Vienna Convention on Diplomatic Relations, concluded in 1961 23 UST 3227, TIAS 7502 (1972), provides in article 22 that the premises of the mission, their furnishings and other property thereon and the means of transport of the mission shall be immune from search, requisition, attachment or execution.[284]

Congress reasoned that:

> [a]ctions short of attachment or execution seem to be permitted under the Convention, and a foreign state cannot deny to the local state the right to

---

[281] See *Antares Aircraft, L.P.*, 948 F 2d at 97. See also *Gabay v Mostazafan Foundation of Iran*, 968 F Supp 895, 898–899 (SDNY 1997), aff'd, 152 F 3d 918 (2d Cir.), cert. denied, 525 US 1040 (1998).

[282] See *Chuidian v Philippine National Bank*, 912 F 2d 1095, 1105 (9th Cir. 1990) (if an action such as a stop payment order "is properly characterized as a taking rather than a tort, it is not cognizable under section 1605(a)(5)"); *De Sanchez*, 770 F 2d at 1398–1399 ("We do not believe that Congress intended plaintiffs to be able to rephrase their takings claims in terms of conversion and thereby bring the claims even where the takings are permitted by international law").

[283] HR Rep No 94-1487, *Jurisdiction of United States Courts in Suits Against Foreign States*, 94th Cong. (9 September 1976) at 20 (reprinted in 1976 USCCAN 6604, 6619).

[284] HR Rep No 94-1487, *Jurisdiction of United States Courts in Suits Against Foreign States*, 94th Cong. (9 September 1976) at 20 (reprinted in 1976 USCCAN 6604, 6619) (internal quotation marks omitted).

adjudicate questions of ownership, rent, servitudes, and similar matters, as long as the foreign state's possession of the premises is not disturbed.[285]

With respect to inherited or gifted property, Congress noted a "general agreement that a foreign state may not claim immunity when the suit against it relates to rights in property, real or personal, obtained by gift or inherited by the foreign state and situated or administered in the country where the suit was brought".[286]

Application **3.045**

Section 1605(a)(4)[287] has to date been the subject of very little litigation.

(1) *Proceedings involving immovable property*

"Immovable property" under the FSIA, is limited to real property.[288] A "right in property" subject to this exception is limited to claims directly affecting ownership or possession of land that is located within the United States.[289] This exception does not apply to claims that merely touch upon real property. For example, the First Circuit in *Fagot Rodriguez v Republic of Costa Rica* held that s 1605(a)(4) did not apply in a dispute over unpaid rent where the foreign state had already surrendered possession of the property.[290] The court reasoned that s 1604(a)(4) did not apply because the claim for unpaid rent did not affect ownership or control of the land.[291] An action to regain possession of an apartment from a foreign state does directly affect the possession of land and therefore has been found to fall within the exception.[292]

One district court has held that the expropriation exception applies to diplomatic and consular property despite language in the House Report which indicates

---

[285] HR Rep No 94-1487, *Jurisdiction of United States Courts in Suits Against Foreign States*, 94th Cong. (9 September 1976) at 20 (reprinted in 1976 USCCAN 6604, 6619).

[286] HR Rep No 94-1487, *Jurisdiction of United States Courts in Suits Against Foreign States*, 94th Cong. (9 September 1976) at 20 (reprinted in 1976 USCCAN 6604, 6619).

[287] At least one court has referred to s 1605(a)(4) as the "successor exception." (See *In re Republic of the Philippines*, 309 F 3d 1143, 1150 (9th Cir. 2002)).

[288] See *In the Matter of Rio Grande Transport, Inc.*, 516 F Supp 1155, 1160 (SDNY 1981) ("The legislative history of s 1605(a)(4) unequivocally indicates that immovable property refers only to real estate").

[289] See *Fagot Rodriguez v Republic of Costa Rica*, 297 F 3d 1, 11 (1st Cir. 2002) ("We conclude that the immovable property exception applies only in cases in which rights of ownership, use, or possession are at issue"); *City of Englewood v Socialist People's Libyan Arab Jamahiriya*, 773 F 2d 31 (3rd Cir. 1985) (unpaid real estate taxes insufficient to sustain jurisdiction under (a)(4)); *Asociacion de Reclamantes v United Mexican States*, 735 F 2d 1517, 1523 (DC Cir 1984), 470 US 1051 (1985) (same). Compare s 6(1) of the UK State Immunity Act 1978 (see 4.054 and 4.057 below).

[290] See *Fagot Rodriguez*, 297 F 3d at 13.

[291] See 297 F 3d at 13. See also *MacArthur Area Citizens Ass'n v Republic of Peru*, 809 F 2d 918, 921 (DC Cir 1987), modified in part, 823 F 2d 606 (DC Cir 1987) (holding that alleged zoning violations claim "sounds not in the law of real property at all, but the law of nuisance," and is therefore not actionable under s 1605(a)(4)); but see *Pulaski v Republic of India*, 212 F Supp 2d 653, 655 (SD Tex 2002) (holding that trespass by encroachment "depends on title, license, or other concept of property law" and therefore involves "rights in" real property even absent a claim of ownership or possession).

[292] See *York River House v Pakistan Mission to the United Nations*, 1991 WL 206286 at *1 (SDNY 1991) (suit against holdover foreign-state tenant to regain possession falls within the immovable property exception).

that Congress intended to exempt such property from s 1605(a)(4).[293] No other court to date has addressed this issue.

(2) Proceedings involving movable property

An action concerning movable property falls within this section only if the property is located within the United States and it was "acquired by succession or gift." Courts have stated that property is acquired by succession or gift when it is acquired in the same way in which a private party could acquire property in a non-commercial transaction.[294] In *Asociacion de Reclamantes v United Mexican States*, the court stated that Congress "did not intend to open the courts to all suits involving inherited or donated property."[295] Rather s 1604(a)(4) applies when "a foreign sovereign steps into the shoes of a private litigant by obtaining rights in property through gift or inheritance."[296] One district court has indicated that with respect to movable property, "the right in property" must account to ownership or control of the property for s 1604(a)(4) to apply.[297]

3.046   28 U.S.C. § 1605

(a) A foreign state shall not be immune from the jurisdiction of courts of the United States or of the States in any case—

. . .

(5) not otherwise encompassed in paragraph (2) above, in which money damages are sought against a foreign state for personal injury or death, or damage to or loss of property, occurring in the United Sates and caused by the tortious act or omission of that foreign state or of any official or employee of that foreign state while

---

[293]   See 1991 WL 206286 at *1 ("The Pakistan Mission, relying on comments in the House Report, asserts that there is an exception to the immovable property exception to immunity in cases of diplomatic or consular property. See HR Rep No 1487, 94th Cong., 2d Sess. 6604, 6618–6619 (1976) ('It is established that . . . sovereign immunity should not be granted in actions with respect to real property, diplomatic and consular property excepted'). There is neither a clear assertion of, nor even an ambiguous reference to, such an exception in the language of the statute. Although legislative reports can be helpful in clarifying ambiguous language in a statute, when a House Report conflicts with the clear language of the statute, as in this case, the court must be governed by the statutory language").

[294]   See *767 Third Avenue Associates. v Consulate General of Socialist Federal Republic of Yugoslavia*, 218 F 3d 152, 162 n 8 (2d Cir. 2000) (noting that the property exception governs acquisition of property through bequests or gifts [as opposed to a commercial transaction]); *In re Republic of the Philippines*, 309 F 3d at 1150 ("exception applies only when the sovereign's claim is as a successor to a private party"). This excludes rights in property acquired through state succession. See *767 Third Avenue Associates*, 218 F 3d at 162.

[295]   *Asociacion de Reclamantes v United Mexican States*, 561 F Supp 1190, 1197 (DDC 1983), aff'd on other grounds, 735 F 2d 1517 (DC Cir 1984), cert. denied, 470 US 1051 (1985).

[296]   591 F Supp at 1197.

[297]   *Fickling v Commonwealth of Australia*, 775 F Supp 66, 72 (EDNY 1991) (holding that freezing of assets pending resolution of marital dispute does not amount to claim of ownership or control).

acting within the scope of his office or employment; except this paragraph shall not apply to—

(A) any claim based upon the exercise or performance or the failure to exercise or perform a discretionary function regardless of whether the discretion be abused, or

(B) any claim arising out of malicious prosecution, abuse of process, libel, slander, misrepresentation, deceit, or interference with contract rights;

. . .

Commentary

Legislative history **3.047**

This section is often referred to as the tort exception. This section:

> is directed primarily at the problem of traffic accidents but is cast in general terms as applying to all tort actions for money damages, not otherwise encompassed by section 1605(a)(2) relating to commercial activities. It denies immunity as to claims for personal injury or death, or for damage to or loss of property, caused by the tortious act or omission of a foreign state or its officials or employees, acting within the scope of their authority; the tortious act must occur within the jurisdiction of the United States, and must not come within one of the exemptions enumerated in the second paragraph of the subsection.[298]
>
> . . .
>
> [T]he phrase "tortious act or omission" is meant to include causes of action which are based on strict liability as well as on negligence.
>
> Like other provisions in the [FSIA], section 1605 is subject to existing international agreements (see section 1604), including Status of Forces Agreements; if remedy is available under a Status of Forces Agreement, the foreign state is immune from such tort claims as are encompassed in sections 1605(a)(2) and 1605(a)(5).[299]

Section 1605(a)(5) does not:

> govern suits against diplomatic or consular representatives but only suits against the foreign state . . . [N]o case relating to a traffic accident can be brought against a member of a diplomatic mission . . . The purpose of section 1605(a)(5) is to permit the victim of a traffic accident or otherwise noncommercial tort to maintain an action against the foreign state to the extent otherwise provided by law.[300]

---

[298] HR Rep No 94-1487, *Jurisdiction of United States Courts in Suits Against Foreign States*, 94th Cong. (9 September 1976) at 21 (reprinted in 1976 USCCAN 6604, 6619).

[299] HR Rep No 94-1487, *Jurisdiction of United States Courts in Suits Against Foreign States*, 94th Cong. (9 September 1976) at 21 (reprinted in 1976 USCCAN 6604, 6620).

[300] HR Rep No 94-1487, *Jurisdiction of United States Courts in Suits Against Foreign States*, 94th Cong. (9 September 1976) at 21 (reprinted in 1976 USCCAN 6604, 6620).

3.048   Application

For the tort exception to apply, both the tort and the injury must occur within the United States.[301] The applicable definition of the United States is contained in s 1603(c).[302] Courts have indicated that the commission of the tort must occur entirely within the United States to fall under the tort exception.[303] In determining if the alleged act or omission is tortious, courts have looked to the tort law of the forum.[304] If the act or omission could not render the foreign state liable under the tort law of the forum, then the tort exception does not apply.[305] Similarly, courts have applied the state law doctrine of *respondeat superior* to determine whether an official or employee has acted within the scope of their employment.[306] If the official has acted within the scope of their employment the tort exception may apply.[307] If the court determines that the act or omission occurred outside the scope of employment, the exception cannot apply.[308]

Discretionary function

A foreign state's tortious conduct that is deemed "discretionary" is excluded from the tort exception. The so-called "discretionary function" limitation set out in

---

[301] See *Argentine Republic v Amerada Hess Shipping Corp.*, 488 US 428, 441 (1989) (noting that unlike the commercial activity exception, the non-commercial torts exception makes no mention of territory outside the United States). The language in *Amerada Hess* would seem almost to foreclose the issue, but circuit courts have found the Supreme Court's language to be both *obiter dictum* and unclear. See *Cabiri v Government of Republic of Ghana*, 165 F 3d 193, 200 n 3 (2nd Cir.), cert. denied, 527 US 1022 (1999); *Wolf v Federal Republic of Germany*, 95 F 3d 536, 542 (7th Cir. 1996), cert. denied, 520 US 1106 (1997); *Cicippio v Iran*, 30 F 3d 164, 169 (DC Cir 1994), cert. denied, 513 US 880 (1995); *Jones v Petty-Ray Geophysical*, 954 F 2d 1061, 1065 (5th Cir.), cert. denied, 506 US 867 (1992); *Frolova v Union of Soviet Socialist Republics*, 761 F 2d 370, 379 (7th Cir. 1985); *Greenpeace, Inc. (USA) v State of France*, 946 F Supp 773 (CD Cal 1996).   [302] See 3.019 above.

[303] See *Coleman v Alcolac, Inc.*, 888 F Supp 1388, 1403 (SD Tex 1995); *Fickling v Commonwealth of Australia*, 775 F Supp 66, 72 (EDNY 1991) ("Although not specifically stated in the statute, section 1605(a)(5) applies only when the entire tort takes place in the United States"). See also *Von Dardel v USSR*, 736 F Supp 1 (DDC 1990); *Frolova*, 761 F 2d, 379; *Ledgerwood v State of Iran*, 617 F Supp 311 (DDC 1985); *McKeel v Islamic Republic of Iran*, 722 F 2d 582 (9th Cir. 1983), cert. denied, 469 US 880 (1984).

[304] See *Robinson v Government of Malaysia*, 269 F 3d 133, 142 (2nd Cir. 2001). For a discussion concerning the split in authority over whether the choice of law provisions of the forum or the Federal common law apply see 3.078 below.   [305] *Robinson*, 269 F 3d at 142.

[306] *Joseph v Office of Consulate General of Nigeria*, 830 F 2d 1018, 1025 (9th Cir. 1987) (citing *Skeen v Federative Republic of Brazil*, 566 F Supp 1414, 1417–1418 (DDC 1983)). See also *Guzel v State of Kuwait*, 818 F Supp 6, 10 (DDC 1993).

[307] See *Liu v China*, 892 F 2d 1419, 1425 (9th Cir. 1989), cert. denied, 497 US 1058 (1990) (murder enabled by the use of the employer's facilities and intended to benefit the employer was within the scope of employment). See also *Rendall-Speranza v Nassim*, 942 F Supp 621, 628 (D DC 1996), rev'd on other grounds, 107 F 3d 913 (DC Cir 1997) (protecting office from theft and unauthorized entry within the scope of employment); *Letelier v Chile*, 488 F Supp 665 (DDC 1980) (murder at the direction of the employer within the scope of employment).

[308] See *MCI Telecommunications Corp. v Alhadhood*, 82 F 3d 658, 664 (5th Cir. 1996) (making unauthorized long distance phone calls not within the scope of employment); *Moran v Saudi Arabia*, 27 F 3d 169, 173–174 (5th Cir. 1994) (driving to the hospital for personal reasons, even during duty hours, not within scope of employment; *Guzel*, 818 F Supp at 10–12 (sexual assault not within the scope of employment); *Skeen*, 566 F Supp at 1417 (shooting in a nightclub not within the scope of employment).

s 1605(a)(5)(A) of the FSIA is modeled on a similar exception to jurisdiction under the Federal Tort Claims Act ("FTCA"), 28 USC § 2680(a).[309] Courts have referred to decisions applying the FTCA law in construing the FSIA.[310]

The purpose of the exception is to prevent judicial second guessing of decisions grounded in social, economic and political policy through the medium of an action in tort. Thus, it protects only governmental actions and decisions based on considerations of public policy.[311]

Courts have applied a two-prong test to determine whether an action is discretionary. The test asks first whether the conduct in question "is a matter of choice for the acting employee".[312] Second, assuming the conduct does involve an element of judgment, is that judgment "of the kind that the discretionary function exception was designed to shield?"[313] Courts have applied the test to a variety of governmental conduct.[314] Even illegal acts can fall within the discretionary function exception, particularly if the violation is not found to be an act *malum in se*.[315] However, certain illegal sovereign acts have been held to be non-discretionary per se.[316]

---

[309] *Fagot Rodriguez v Republic of Costa Rica*, 297 F 3d 1, 8–9 (1st Cir. 2002) (citing House Report at 21).

[310] 297 F 3d 1 at 8.

[311] *Fagot Rodriguez*, 297 F 3d at 8. See *Berkovitz v United States*, 486 US 531 (1988) (citing *Dalehite v United States*, 346 US 15, 36 (1953) ("Where there is room for policy judgment and decision there is discretion")); *United States v S.A. Empresa de Viacao Aerea Rio Grandense (Varig Airlines)*, 467 US 797 (1984).

[312] *Berkovitz*, 486 US at 536. The court goes on to note (at 536) that if a "federal statute, regulation or policy specifically prescribes a course of action for an employee to follow," then the discretionary function exception does not apply.

[313] *Berkovitz*, 486 US at 537 (only "governmental actions and decisions based on considerations of public policy" are shielded).

[314] See *Fagot Rodriguez*, 297 F 3d at 11 (establishing and maintaining a Consulate fall within the discretionary function); *Risk v Halvorsen*, 936 F 2d 393, 396–397 (9th Cir. 1991), cert. denied, 502 US 1035 (1992) (issuing travel documents and aiding of nationals by consular official falls within discretionary function); *Travel Associates, Inc. v Kingdom of Swaziland*, 1990 WL 134512 at *3 (DDC 1990) (training and supervision of ambassador are discretionary functions); *MacArthur Area Citizens Ass'n v Republic of Peru*, 809 F 2d 918, 922 (DC Cir 1987) (same); *Joseph*, 830 F 2d at 1020 n 1, 1027 (finding that acquisition and operation of a consular residence are discretionary, but purely destructive acts, such as property damage and removal of fixtures, are not); *Panton v Jamaica*, 1993 WL 394775 at *3 (SD Fla 1993) (issuance of tax summons is a discretionary function). But see *Gerritsen v de la Madrid Hurtado*, 819 F 2d 1511, 1518 (9th Cir. 1987) (assault and kidnapping not discretionary); *Olsen by Sheldon v Mexico*, 729 F 2d 641, 647 (9th Cir. 1984) (maintaining, directing, and piloting an aircraft not discretionary); *Olson v Singapore*, 636 F Supp 885, 886 (DDC 1986) (placing tables and maintaining the condition of the floor not discretionary).

[315] See *Fagot Rodriguez*, 297 F 3d at 10 (finding that a violation of landlord–tenant law is by itself insufficient to render an action non-discretionary); *Risk*, 936 F 2d at 396–397 (finding that intentional violation of a custody order or the rights of a parent, even though a felony, does not render actions non discretionary); *MacArthur Area Citizens Ass'n*, 809 F 2d at 923 (violations of zoning ordinance do not rise to the level of actions *malum in se*).

[316] *Liu*, 892 F 2d at 1431 (an assassination in violation of the foreign state's own law is not a discretionary function); *Letelier v Republic of Chile*, 488 F Supp 665, 673 (DDC 1980) ("action that is clearly contrary to the precepts of humanity," such as assassination, is non-discretionary); *Estate of Domingo v Republic of the Philippines*, No C82-1055V, 1984 WL 3140 at *1 (WD Wash July 18, 1984)

Excluded torts

Congress excluded certain tortious conduct from the tort exception; namely: malicious prosecution, abuse of process, libel, slander, misrepresentation, deceit, and interference with contract rights.[317] In applying this subsection, courts look beyond the characterization of the claims in the complaint to the conduct on which the claim is based.[318]

It is currently unclear whether the excluded torts limitation of s 1605(a)(5)(B) also serves to limit the commercial activity exception of s 1605(a)(2). The majority of cases that have addressed this issue have held that the two sections do not affect one another.[319] Other courts have held that s 1605(a)(5)(B) limits both the commercial activity and the non-commercial tort exceptions to sovereign immunity.[320]

3.049   28 U.S.C. § 1605

(a) A foreign state shall not be immune from the jurisdiction of courts of the United States or of the States in any case—

. . .

(6) in which the action is brought, either to enforce an agreement made by the foreign state with or for the benefit of a private party to submit to arbitration all or any differences which have arisen or which may arise between the parties with respect to a defined legal relationship, whether contractual or not, concerning a subject matter capable of settlement by arbitration under the laws of the United States, or to confirm an award made pursuant to such an agreement

("clear and unquestioned illegality of [act such as assassination] makes the distinction between operation and planning inapplicable").

[317] 28 USC § 1605(a)(5)(B).

[318] See *Blaxland v Commonwealth Director of Public Prosecutions*, 323 F 3d 1198, 1202–1203 (9th Cir. 2003) (holding that emotional distress and loss of consortium claims are barred when they arise from core claims of malicious prosecution and abuse of process); *Cabiri*, 165 F 3d at 200 (barring claim of intentional infliction of emotional distress as arising out of misrepresentation claim); *Leutwyler v Office of Her Majesty Queen Rania Al-Abdullah*, 184 F Supp 2d 277, 299 (SDNY 2001) (barring claim of intentional infliction of emotional distress as arising out of defamation and abuse of process claims).

[319] See *El-Hadad v United Arab Emirates*, 216 F 3d 29, 35–36 (DC Cir 2000); *Southway v Central Bank of Nigeria*, 198 F 3d 1210, 1219 (10th Cir. 1999); *Export Group v Reef Indus., Inc.*, 54 F 3d 1466, 1477 (9th Cir. 1995); *Mukaddam v Permanent Mission of Saudi Arabia to the United Nations*, 111 F Supp 2d 457, 474 (SDNY 2000); *Yucyco, Ltd. v Republic of Slovenia*, 984 F Supp 209, 224 (SDNY 1997); *WMW Machinery, Inc., v Werkzeugmaschinenhandel GmbH IM Aufbau*, 960 F Supp 734, 742 (SDNY 1997); *Ratnaswamy v Air Afrique*, No. 95C 7670, 1996 WL 507267 at *7 (ND Ill. Sept. 4, 1996); *Foremost-McKesson Inc. v Islamic Republic of Iran*, 759 F Supp 855, 859 (DDC 1991); *LeDonne v Gulf Air, Inc.*, 700 F Supp 1400, 1411 (ED Va 1988); *Tifa Ltd. v Republic of Ghana*, 692 F Supp 393, 404 (DNJ 1988); *United Euram Corp. v Union of Soviet Socialist Republics*, 461 F Supp 609, 612 (SDNY 1978); *Yessenin-Volpin v Novosti Press Agency*, 443 F Supp 849, 855 (SDNY 1978).

[320] See *Gregorian v Izvestia*, 871 F 2d 1515, 1522 (9th Cir. 1989), overruled as dictum, *Export Group v Reef Indus., Inc.*, 54 F 3d 1466 (9th Cir. 1995); *Bryks v Canadian Broad. Corp.*, 906 F Supp 204, 210 (SDNY 1995); *Travel All Over The World v Kingdom of Saudia Arabia*, No 91-C-3306, 1994 WL 673025 at *4 (ND Ill 28 November 1994), rev'd on other grounds, 73 F 3d 1423 (7th Cir. 1996).

to arbitrate, if (A) the arbitration takes place or is intended to take place in the United States, (B) the agreement or award is or may be governed by a treaty or other international agreement in force for the United States calling for the recognition and enforcement of arbitral awards, (C) the underlying claim, save for the agreement to arbitrate, could have been brought in a United States court under this section or section 1607, or (D) paragraph (1) of this section is otherwise applicable; or

. . .

Commentary

Legislative history   **3.050**

Congress amended the FSIA by adding the arbitration exception of s 1605(a)(6) in 1988.[321] Prior to the addition of the arbitration exception, most arbitration cases under the FSIA were litigated under the waiver exception of s 1605(a)(1).[322] According to the main sponsor of the bill, the arbitration amendment was added to "say that an agreement to arbitrate constitutes a waiver of immunity in an action to enforce that agreement or the resultant award".[323]

Application   **3.051**

"Section 1605(a)(6) does not affect the contractual right of the parties to arbitration but only the tribunal that may hear a dispute concerning the enforcement of an arbitral award."[324] The arbitration exception can only be invoked to enforce an agreement to arbitrate or confirm an arbitral award, and not, for example, to vacate an award.[325] The arbitration exception applies to agreements or contracts entered into before 1988.[326]

---

[321] An Act to implement the Inter-American Convention on International Commercial Arbitration, Pub L No 100-669 § 2, 102 Stat. 3969, 3970 (16 November 1988).

[322] See 3.033 above. See also *Maritime Ventures Int'l, Inc. v Caribbean Trading & Fidelity, Ltd.*, 722 F Supp 1032 (SDNY 1989) ("sovereign immunity is impliedly waived where the foreign state has agreed to arbitration in another country or where a foreign state has agreed that the law of another country should govern a contract") (internal citations omitted); *Liberian Eastern Timber Corp. v Gov't of Republic of Liberia*, 650 F Supp 73 (SDNY 1986), aff'd, 854 F 2d 1314 (2nd Cir. 1987) (implied waiver found). But see *Maritime Int'l Nominees Establishment v Republic of Guinea*, 693 F 2d 1094 (DC Cir 1982) (no implied waiver found). S 1605(a)(6)(D) preserves the opportunity for litigants to argue arbitration cases under the waiver exception (which may offer certain procedural advantages, as mentioned in the notes and text hereinafter). See *Seetransport Wiking Trader Schifffahrtsgesellschaft MBH & Co. v Navimpex Centrala Navala*, 989 F 2d 572 (2nd Cir. 1993) (court found jurisdiction under s 1605(a)(1) after claimant pleaded both implied waiver and arbitration jurisdiction); *M.B.L. Contractors, Inc. v Trinidad and Tobago*, 725 F Supp 52, 56 (DDC 1989).

[323] *Cargil Int'l S.A. v M/T Pavel Dybenko*, 991 F 2d 1012, 1018 (2nd Cir. 1993) (citing 131 CONG. REC. S5369 (daily ed. 3 May 1985) (statement of Sen Mathias)).

[324] *S & Davis Int'l, Inc. v Yemen*, 218 F 3d 1292, 1302 (11th Cir. 2000) (citing *Creighton Ltd. v Qatar*, 181 F 3d 118, 123–124 (DC Cir 1999)).

[325] See *HSMV Corp. v ADI Ltd.*, 72 F Supp 2d 1122, 1127 n 7 (CD Cal 1999).

[326] See *Creighton Ltd. v Gov't of the State of Qatar*, 181 F 3d 118, 124 (DC Cir 1999).

Section 1605(a)(6)(A) makes clear that the designation of an arbitral site within the US suffices to confer jurisdiction, whether or not the arbitration actually takes place there.[327] Section 1605(a)(6)(B) relates to international arbitration conventions such as the New York Convention[328] and the Inter-American Convention.[329] Section 1605(a)(6)(D) makes clear that the arbitration section in no way limits the waiver exception.[330]

There is a split of authority concerning whether an arbitration agreement entered into by an agency or instrumentality may subject the foreign state itself to jurisdiction under the arbitration exception to immunity.[331]

3.052   28 U.S.C. § 1605

(a) A foreign state shall not be immune from the jurisdiction of courts of the United States or of the States in any case—

. . .

(7) not otherwise covered by paragraph (2), in which money damages are sought against a foreign state for personal injury or death that was caused by an act of torture, extrajudicial killing, aircraft sabotage, hostage taking, or the provision of material support or resources (as defined in section 2339A of title 18) for such an act if such act or provision of material support is engaged in by an official, employee, or agent of such foreign state while acting within the scope of his or her office, employment, or agency, except that the court shall decline to hear a claim under this paragraph—

(A) if the foreign state was not designated as a state sponsor of terrorism under section 6(j) of the Export Administration Act of 1979 (50 U.S.C.

---

[327] See, eg, *Int'l Ins. Co. v Caja Nacional de Ahorro y Seguro*, 293 F 3d 392, 397 (7th Cir. 2002) ("By agreeing to a contract designating Chicago, Illinois as the site of arbitration, even if it is a foreign instrumentality, Caja waived its immunity in a proceeding to confirm the arbitral award").

[328] The Convention on the Recognition and Enforcement of Foreign Arbitral Awards of June 10, 1958, 21 UST 2517 (1970), reprinted in 9 USC § 201. See *Creighton*, 181 F 3d at 123–124 (noting that "the New York Convention is exactly the sort of treaty Congress intended to include in the arbitration exception.") See also *Cargill Int'l S.A.*, 991 F 2d at 1018; *S & Davis Int'l*, 218 F 3d at 1302.

[329] Inter-American Convention on International Commercial Arbitration of 1975, 14 ILM 336 (1975), reprinted in 9 USC § 301.

[330] At least one court has distinguished the arbitration exception from the waiver exception. See *Creighton*, 181 F 3d at 126 ("[U]nlike [section] 1605(a)(1), section 1605(a)(6) deals not with waiver but with forfeiture").

[331] See *S & Davis*, 218 F 3d at 1302 ("The Ministry contends that because it was not a party to the contract, it is not subject to the arbitration agreement or award . . . given our determination that there was sufficient evidence to show the General Corporation is an agency or instrumentality under the control of the Ministry, we find that the district court has subject matter jurisdiction pursuant to the arbitration exception under § 1605(a)(6)(B)"). But see *Glencore Denrees Paris v Dep't of National Store Branch 1*, No 99 Civ 8607 (NRB), 2000 WL 913843 at *2 (SDNY 7 July 2000), vacated on other grounds, 2002 WL 24145 (2nd Cir. 2002) ("the enforcement of an award pursuant to the Convention based upon a contractual provision entered into by an instrumentality of a foreign state would only seem to create a waiver of the sovereign immunity of that instrumentality or agency and not a waiver of the sovereign immunity of the foreign state itself") (citing *Seetransport Wiking Trader v Navimplex Centrala Navales*, 989 F 2d 572, 578–579 (2d Cir. 1993)).

App. 2405(j)) or section 620A of the Foreign Assistance Act of 1961 (22 U.S.C. 2371) at the time the act occurred, unless later so designated as a result of such act or the act is related to Case Number 1:00CV03110(EGS) in the United States District Court for the District of Columbia; and

(B) even if the foreign state is or was so designated, if —

(i) the act occurred in the foreign state against which the claim has been brought and the claimant has not afforded the foreign state a reasonable opportunity to arbitrate the claim in accordance with accepted international rules of arbitration; or

(ii) neither the claimant nor the victim was a national of the United States (as that term is defined in section 101(a)(22) of the Immigration and Nationality Act) when the act upon which the claim is based occurred.

Commentary

Legislative history   **3.053**

In 1996, Congress amended the FSIA "in response to the revelation that the Libyan government assisted in blowing up Pan Am 103 over Lockerbie, Scotland".[332] Section 1605(a)(7) was added to the FSIA as part of the Anti-Terrorism and Effective Death Penalty Act 1996 ("Anti-Terrorism Act").[333] The stated purpose of the Anti-Terrorism Act is to deter terrorist acts against US nationals by foreign sovereigns or their agents and to provide for justice for victims of such terrorism.[334] Prior to the amendment, most overseas "human rights" cases under the FSIA were litigated, without success, under the implied waiver provision of s 1605(a)(1).[335]

---

[332] HR 105-48, *To Make A Technical Correction To Title 28 United States Code, Relating to Jurisdiction For Law Suits Against Terrorist States*, 2, 10 April 1997.

[333] Antiterrorism and Effective Death Penalty Act 1996, Pub L No 104-132, 110 Stat. 1214, 1241 (24 April 1996).

[334] See HR 103–702, *Foreign Sovereign Immunities Amendments*, 103d Congress at 3–4 (16 August 1995). See also *A Bill to Amend Title 28 of the United States Code to Permit a Foreign State to be Subject to the Jurisdiction of Federal or State Courts in any Case Involving an Act of International Terrorism: Hearing on H.R. 1877 Before the Senate Subcomm. On Courts and Administrative Practice of the Comm. on the Judiciary*, 103d Cong., 2–3 (21 June 1994) (statement of the Hon Romano L Mazzoli, Representative, KY). ("The Foreign Sovereign Immunities Act currently allows US citizens to sue foreign governments for commercial disputes that arise outside the United States, but it does not allow suits for physical violence, such as torture or murder or, in the case of Senator Specter's bill, terrorism which occurs abroad. If we allow a businessman or woman to bring suit under the FSIA against a foreign government which has breached a contract, it seems logical that we should allow a citizen who was tortured or otherwise physically mistreated by the very self same government to bring suit under the act").

[335] See *Smith v Socialist People's Libyan Arab Jamahiriya*, 101 F 3d 239 (2d Cir. 1996), cert. denied, 520 US 1204 (1997). The *Smith* court dismissed arguments for an implied waiver based on *jus cogens* and UN Charter violations. 101 F 3d at 244, 246. See also *Princz v Federal Republic of Germany*, 26 F 3d 1166, 1174 (DC Cir 1994), cert. denied, 513 US 1121 (1995); *Siderman de Blake v Republic of Argentina*, 965 F 2d 699, 721 (9th Cir. 1992), cert. denied, 507 US 1017 (1993). See generally *Price v Socialist People's Libyan Arab Jamahiriya*, 294 F 3d 82, 88 (DC Cir 2002) (collecting cases).

Shortly after the passage of the Anti-Terrorism Act, Congress "passed an amendment designed to enhance the penalties available in suits implicating 28 USC § 1605(a)(7)."[336] The amendment is entitled "Civil Liability for Acts of State Sponsored Terrorism" and is commonly referred to as the "Flatow Amendment."[337]

Both the Flatow Amendment and 28 USC § 1605(a)(7) address the same subject matter, and were enacted during the same session of Congress, only five months apart. Interpretation *in pari materia* is therefore the most appropriate approach to the construction of both provisions. The amendment should be considered to relate back to the enactment of 28 USC § 1605(a)(7) as if they had been enacted as one provision and the two provisions should be construed together and in reference to one another.[338]

3.054   Application

In the Anti-Terrorism Act:

Congress lifted the sovereign immunity of foreign states for acts of state sponsored terrorism. The Antiterrorism Act specifically creates an exception to the immunity of those foreign nations officially designated by the Department of State as terrorist states when that nation commits a terrorist act, or provides material support and resources to an individual or entity that commits such an act, resulting in the death or personal injury of a United States national.[339]

Section 1605(a)(6)(C) relates to counterclaims. Courts have referred to this exception as the "state-sponsored terrorism exception".[340] This exception addresses acts of torture, extrajudicial killing, aircraft sabotage, hostage taking, or the provision of material support or resources for the commission of such acts.[341]

Traditionally, it was the State Department's role to seek redress on behalf of an aggrieved citizen, however, in considering the Anti-Terrorism Act, the House of Representatives noted a potential conflict between the State Department's role in maintaining foreign relations and in espousing the grievances of the victim. See HR 103–702, *Foreign Sovereign Immunities Amendments*, 103d Congress at 3–4 (16 August 1995) (citing *Saudi Arabia v Nelson*, 507 US 349 (1993) (holding that Saudi Arabia was immune from a claim arising from the detention and torture of an American citizen in Saudi Arabia).

[336] *Elahi v Islamic Republic of Iran*, 124 F Supp 2d 97, 105–106 (DDC 2000).

[337] See Omnibus Consolidated Appropriations Act, Omnibus Consolidated Appropriations Act, 1997 Pub L No 104-208, 110 Stat. 3009, 3009-172 (30 September 1996), codified at 28 USC 1605. See *Bettis v Islamic Republic of Iran*, 315 F 3d 325, 329–330 (DC Cir 2003). See discussion at 3.055–3.057 below.

[338] *Flatow v Islamic Republic of Iran*, 999 F Supp 1, 12 (DDC 1998). See discussion at 3.055–3.057 below.

[339] *Elahi*, 124 F Supp 2d at 105–106. As amended in 1997, the Anti-Terrorism exception includes survivors of the victim who were American nationals at the time of the terrorist act. See Jurisdiction for Lawsuits Against Terrorist States: Technical Correction, Pub Law 105-111, 111 Stat. 22, 25 April 1997.   [340] *Flatow*, 999 F Supp at 12.

[341] Torture, extrajudicial killing, aircraft sabotage and hostage taking are defined at s 1605(e). See 3.068–3.070.

Congress explicitly made the Anti-Terrorism Act retroactive,[342] and although it is a relatively new provision, s 1605(a)(7) has seen frequent use since its addition to the FSIA. The bulk of the litigation arising under it has been in the district courts of the District of Columbia, though even the case law there is still unsettled.[343]

(1) Elements

The Anti-Terrorism exception to sovereign immunity comprises seven elements: (1) an injury; (2) an act perpetrated by a foreign state or agent receiving material support from the state; (3) the provision of the support was authorized by the foreign state; (4) the foreign state has been designated a sponsor of terrorism; (5) the foreign state has been afforded a reasonable opportunity to arbitrate; (6) either the victim or claimant was a United States national at the time of the incident; and (7) similar conduct by the US or its agents would be actionable.[344]

(2) Provision of material support

It is a crime under US Federal law to provide material support or resources to terrorists.[345] In adopting s 1605(a)(7), Congress incorporated, by reference, the definition of "material support or resources" from the criminal code. That definition states that:

> [t]he term "material support or resources" means currency or other financial securities, financial services, lodging, training, expert advise or assistance, safehouses, false documentation or identification, communications equipment, facilities, weapons, lethal substances, explosives, personnel, transportation, and other physical assets, except medicine or religious materials.[346]

It is unclear whether a claimant must link the alleged material support or resources directly to the terrorist act at issue in the case.[347] In the *Flatow* case, the court held that:

> a plaintiff need not establish that the material support or resources provided by a foreign state for a terrorist act contributed directly to the act

---

[342] See Antiterrorism and Effective Death Penalty Act 1996, Pub L No 104-132, § 221(c), 110 Stat. 1214, 1243 (reprinted at 28 USC § 1605 note (West Supp. 1997)). See also *Wagner v Islamic Republic of Iran*, 172 F Supp 2d 128, 134 n 7 (DDC 2001).

[343] "Most of the cases involving the provision of material support or resources to terrorists . . . have involved defaulting defendants, and appellate courts have not yet had an opportunity to review the standards being used by district judges to analyze the liability of state sponsors of terrorism . . ." *Ungar v Islamic Republic of Iran*, 211 F Supp 2d 91, 101 (DDC 2002). But see *Simpson v Socialist People's Libyan Arab Jamahiriya*, 326 F 3d 230 (DC Cir 2003).

[344] See *Wagner v Socialist People's Libyan Arab Jamahiriya*, 180 F Supp 2d 78, 82 (DDC 2001) affirmed in part, vacated in part, reversed in part by *Simpson v Socialist People's Libyan Arab Jamahiriya*, 326 F 3d 230, 356 (DC Cir 2003); *Elahi*, 124 F Supp 2d 97, 106–107 (DDC 2000); *Flatow*, 999 F Supp 1, 16 (DDC 1998). See also *Weinstein v Islamic Republic of Iran*, 184 F Supp 2d 13, 21 (DDC 2002) (similar, but neglecting the arbitration requirement).

[345] See 18 USC § 2339A (2003).   [346] 18 USC § 2339A (2003).

[347] See *Flatow*, 999 F Supp at 18.

from which his claim arises in order to satisfy 28 U.S.C. section 1605(a)(7)'s statutory requirements for subject matter jurisdiction. Sponsorship of a terrorist group which causes the personal injury or death of a United States national alone is sufficient to invoke jurisdiction.[348]

Another court in the same district has held that the court's reasoning in the *Flatow* case "sidesteps the causation question".[349] Most courts have not required claimants to allege a direct link to the terrorist act.[350]

(3) *State sponsors of terrorism*

"Not all foreign states may be sued. Instead, only a defendant that has been specifically designated by the State Department as a 'state sponsor of terrorism' is subject to the loss of its sovereign immunity [under this section]".[351] The countries in this category at the time of writing are Cuba, Iran, Iraq,[352] Libya, North Korea, Sudan and Syria. These are the same countries that are identified pursuant to the Export Administration Act, s 6(j), as amended (50 USC App. 2405(j)).[353]

This exception applies only if the foreign state was designated a state sponsor of terrorism at the time the act at issue occurred, or is later so designated as a result of such act.[354] In addition, claims can be brought against Iran for acts "related to Case Number 1:00CV03110(EGS) in the United States District Court for the District of Columbia".[355]

---

[348] 999 F Supp at 18.

[349] *Ungar*, 211 F Supp 2d at 97–98 (Anti-Terrorism exception provides "jurisdiction over suits 'for personal injury or death' that *was caused* by . . . the provision of material support or resources").

[350] See *Weinstein v Islamic Republic of Iran*, 184 F Supp 2d 13, 19–22 (DDC 2002), *Mousa v Islamic Republic of Iran*, 238 F Supp 2d 1, 11 (DDC 2001), and *Eisenfeld v Islamic Republic of Iran*, 172 F Supp 2d 1, 5–8 (DDC 2000) (all finding but-for causation where terrorist bombers were trained in the use of explosives in Iran or by Iranian officials). See also *Flatow*, 999 F Supp, 9 (showing that foreign state was sole source of funding for terrorist organization sufficient to find causation); *Cicippio v Islamic Republic of Iran*, 18 F Supp 2d 62, 68 (DDC 1998) (showing that foreign state officials had approval authority or control over terrorist group sufficient to find causation); *Sutherland v Islamic Republic of Iran*, 151 F Supp 2d 27, 46 (DDC 2001) (same).

[351] *Bettis*, 315 F 3d at 329. There is an issue as to whether the State Department designation is an unconstitutional delegation of legislative authority to the executive branch to determine the jurisdiction of the federal courts. To date the courts have avoided this issue. See *Rein v Socialist People's Libyan Arab Jamahiriya*, 162 F 3d 748 (2d Cir. 1998), cert. denied, 527 US 1003 (1999). See also *Simpson v Socialist People's Libyan Arab Jamahiriya*, 180 F Supp 2d 78, 84–85 (DDC 2001).

[352] On 7 May 2003 President George W Bush issued a determination making "inapplicable with respect to Iraq . . . any other provision of law that applies to countries that have supported terrorism." Presidential Determination No 2003–23 of 7 May 2003 (pursuant to the authority of the Emergency Wartime Supplemental Appropriations Act, § 1503, Pub L 108-111, 117 Stat. 579 (16 April 2003)). See *Smith ex rel. Estate of Smith v Federal Reserve Bank of New York*,-F 3d-, 2003 WL 22272577 (2d Cir. 3 October 2003).   [353] 22 USC § 2371.

[354] 28 USC § 1605(a)(7)(A). To determine whether the State Department's later designation was a result of the act at issue in a case, a court will review the public record that existed at the time the designation was made. *Kerr v Islamic Republic of Iran*, 2003 WL 342108 at *4 (DDC 2003). *Cf. Roeder v Islamic Republic of Iran*, 195 F Supp 2d 140, 161 (DDC 2002), aff'd, 333 F 3d 228 (DC Cir 2003).

[355] This portion of the statute was added by the 2002 fiscal appropriations bill. Departments of Commerce, Justice, and State, the Judiciary, and Related Agencies Appropriations Act 2002, Pub L

(4) *Reasonable opportunity to arbitrate*

"[E]ven a foreign state listed as a sponsor of terrorism retains its immunity unless (a) it is afforded a reasonable opportunity to arbitrate any claim based on acts that occurred in that state[.]"[356]

This requirement has given rise to two issues: timeliness and reasonableness. The DC Circuit has held that an offer to arbitrate is not a condition precedent to filing a complaint under the state sponsored terrorism exception.[357] The offer to arbitrate need only allow the foreign state enough time to consider and respond to the proposal.[358] The offer to arbitrate must also be reasonable.[359]

(5) *US nationals only*

"[E]ven a foreign state listed as a sponsor of terrorism retains its immunity unless . . . either the victim or the claimant was a US national at the time that those acts took place."[360] This requirement has not been the subject of any litigation to date.[361]

28 U.S.C. § 1605(a)(7), note   3.055

Civil Liability for Acts of State Sponsored Terrorism

(a) An official, employee, or agent of a foreign state designated as a state sponsor of terrorism designated under section 6(j) of the Export Administration Act of 1979 [section 2405 (j) of the Appendix to Title 50, War and National Defense] while acting within the scope of his or her office, employment, or agency shall be liable to a United States national or the national's legal representative for personal injury or death caused by acts of that official, employee, or agent for which the courts of the United States may maintain jurisdiction under section 1605(a)(7) of title 28, United States Code [subsec. (a)(7) of this section] for money damages which may include economic damages, solatium,

---

No 107-77, 115 Stat. 748 (28 November 2001). The enumerated case, dealing with the 1979–1981 Iranian Hostage Crisis, is *Roeder*, 195 F Supp 2d at 140. This new exception to immunity, while seemingly giving new life to previously unsuccessful claims arising from the Iranian hostage crisis, appeared to question the Algiers Accords under which Iran was supposed to be immune from suits by hostages. See 195 F Supp 2d at 144. The *Roeder* court, however, found that the statute did not provide a clear expression of Congressional intent to abrogate the Algiers Accords. 195 F Supp 2d at 175–184.

[356] *Bettis*, 315 F 3d at 329–330 (citing *Price*, 294 F 3d at 88–89).

[357] See *Simpson*, 326 F 3d at 233.

[358] See *Simpson*, 326 F 3d at 233 (offer made two months prior to the filing of foreign state's motion to dismiss provided a reasonable opportunity to arbitrate).

[359] See *Price*, 294 F 3d at 84 (plaintiff's condition that she should not have to leave the United States found reasonable).

[360] *Bettis*, 315 F 3d at 329–330 (citing *Price*, 294 F 3d at 88–89).

[361] Note that prior to the 1997 amendment, some courts took the view that *both* the victim and the claimant were required to be United States nationals. H.R. 103–702, *Foreign Sovereign Immunities Amendments*, 3–4, 103d Congress 16 August 1994. See also *Alejandre v Republic of Cuba*, 996 F Supp 1239, 1248 (SD Fla 1997).

pain, and suffering, and punitive damages if the acts were among those described in section 1605(a)(7) [subsec. (a)(7) of this section].

(b) Provisions related to statute of limitations and limitations on discovery that would apply to an action brought under 28 U.S.C. 1605 (f) and (g) [subsecs. (f) and (g) of this section] shall also apply to actions brought under this section.

No action shall be maintained under this action [*sic*] if an official, employee, or agent of the United States, while acting within the scope of his or her office, employment, or agency would not be liable for such acts if carried out within the United States.

Commentary

3.056   Legislative history

The amendment, Civil Liability for Acts of State Sponsored Terrorism, was enacted on 30 September 1996 as part of the 1997 Omnibus Consolidated Appropriations Act.[362]

This provision of law is commonly referred to as the "Flatow Amendment":[363]

The Flatow Amendment is apparently an independent pronouncement of law, yet it has been published as a note to 28 U.S.C. § 1605, and requires several references to 28 U.S.C. § 1605(a)(7) *et seq.* to reach even a preliminary interpretation. As it also effects a substantial change to 28 U.S.C. § 1605(a)(7), it appears to be an implied amendment.[364]

3.057   Application

Both the Flatow Amendment and 28 USC § 1605(a)(7)[365] address the same subject matter, and were enacted during the same session of Congress, only five months apart. "Interpretation in *pari materia* is therefore the most appropriate approach to the construction of both provisions."[366]

It is unclear "whether the FSIA creates a federal cause of action for torture and hostage taking against foreign states, or only against their officials, employees, or

---

[362] Pub L 104–208, Div. A, Title I § 101(c) [Title V, § 589] (30 September 1996), 110 Stat 3009-3172 reprinted at 28 USC § 1605 note. See Omnibus Consolidated Appropriations Act, Omnibus Consolidated Appropriations Act, 1997 Pub L No 104-208, 110 Stat 3009, 3009-3172 (30 September 1996), codified at 28 USC 1605. See generally *Bettis v Islamic Republic of Iran*, 315 F 3d 325, 329–330 (DC Cir 2003). The Flatow Amendment "allows for non-economic and punitive damages against an official, employee, or agent of a foreign state designated as terrorist." 315 F 3d at 330. Although published as a note to s 1605, it has been held to be "an independent pronouncement of law" and interpreted in *pari materia* with other sections of the FSIA (see *Flatow v Islamic Republic of Iran*, 999 F Supp 1, 12–13 (DDC 1998)).

[363] *Bettis*, 315 F 3d at 330 ("This provision is known as the 'Flatow Amendment,' because its sponsor referred to the Flatow family—whose daughter, Alisa, was killed by a Palestinian suicide bomber while studying in Israel—when speaking in support of the statute").

[364] *Flatow*, 999 F Supp at 12.   [365] See 3.052–3.054 above.

[366] See *Kilburn v Republic of Iran*, 2003 WL 21982239, *12 (DDC 8 August 2003).

agents".[367] DC district judges have generally found that it does both,[368] with one notable exception.[369] The DC Court of Appeals has recognized but declined to answer this question.[370] The overwhelming majority of courts that have addressed this issue have held that the Flatow Amendment provides a cause of action against foreign states.[371]

> A cause of action under the Flatow Amendment requires proof of the following elements: 1) that personal injury or death resulted from an act of torture, extrajudicial killing, aircraft sabotage, or hostage taking; 2) the act was either perpetrated by the foreign state directly or by a non-state actor which receives material support or resources from the foreign state defendant; 3) the act or the provision of material support or resources is engaged in by an agent, official or employee of the foreign state while acting within the scope of his or her office, agency or employment; 4) the foreign state must be designated as a state sponsor of terrorism either at the time the incident complained of occurred or was later so designated as a result of such act; and 5) either the plaintiff or the victim was a United States national at the time of the incident.[372]

> Moreover, in order to establish a cause of action "plaintiffs must also show a proximate cause between the support and resources provided, and that the defendant knew and intended to further the criminal acts."[373]

> Courts have also held that s 1605 (a)(7) authorizes third party claims for contribution, indemnity, and restitution.[374]

28 U.S.C. § 1605   3.058

(b) A foreign state shall not be immune from the jurisdiction of the courts of the United States in any case in which a suit in admiralty is brought to enforce a maritime lien against a vessel or cargo of the foreign state, which maritime lien is based upon a commercial activity of the foreign state: *Provided*, That—

(1) notice of the suit is given by delivery of a copy of the summons and of the complaint to the person, or his agent, having possession of the vessel or cargo

[367] *Bettis*, 315 F 3d at 330; *Kilburn*, 2003 WL 21982239, *10).

[368] See *Cronin v Islamic Republic of Iran*, 238 F Supp 2d 222, 231 (DDC 2002).

[369] See *Roeder v Islamic Republic of Iran*, 195 F Supp 2d 140, 171–173 (DDC 2002), aff'd, 333 F 3d 228 (2003).

[370] See *Bettis*, 315 F 3d at 330; *Price v Socialist People's Libyan Arab Jamahiriya*, 294 F 3d 82, 87 (DC Cir 2002).

[371] *Kilburn*, 2003 WL 21982239, *10; *Smith v Islamic Emirate of Afghanistan*, 262 F Supp 2d 217, 226 (SDNY 2003). But see *Roeder*, 195 F Supp 2d at 171–173.

[372] *Smith*, 262 F Supp 2d at 226.

[373] *Smith*, 262 F Supp 2d at 226–227 (citing *Boim v Quranic Literacy Institute*, 291 F 3d 1000, 1011–1012, 1015, 1023 (7th Cir.2002)).

[374] See *Hartford Fire Ins. Co. v Socialist People's Libyan Arab Jamhiriya*, No CV98-3096 (TFH), 1999 WL 33589331 (DDC 24 September 1999) (holding that insurance companies had a third party cause of action to recover from foreign state for proceeds paid out to victims of airplane bombing).

against which the maritime lien is asserted; and if the vessel or cargo is arrested pursuant to process obtained on behalf of the party bringing the suit, the service of process of arrest shall be deemed to constitute valid delivery of such notice, but the party bringing the suit shall be liable for any damages sustained by the foreign state as a result of the arrest if the party bringing the suit had actual or constructive knowledge that the vessel or cargo of a foreign state was involved; and

(2) notice to the foreign state of the commencement of suit as provided in section 1608 of this title is initiated within ten days either of the delivery of notice as provided in paragraph (1) of this subsection or, in the case of a party who was unaware that the vessel or cargo of a foreign state was involved, of the date such party determined the existence of the foreign state's interest.

Commentary

3.059 Legislative history

Traditionally under maritime law, parties enforce a maritime lien by commencing an *in rem* action against a vessel, or in some instances, cargo. The FSIA eliminates this right with respect to vessels or cargo owed by foreign states. Section 1605(b) was intended to be a substitute for the maritime *in rem* action:[375]

> The purpose of [section 1605(b)] is to permit a plaintiff to bring suit in a U.S. district court arising out of a maritime lien involving a vessel or cargo of a foreign sovereign without arresting the vessel, by instituting an *in personam* action against the foreign state in a manner analogous to bringing such suit against the United States.[376]

Congress amended s 1605(b) in 1988.[377] Previous to the amendment, a party lost its entire claim if it improperly arrested a foreign state's vessel.[378] Currently, a plaintiff that improperly arrests a foreign state's vessel retains its claim but is liable for the damages caused by the arrest.[379]

---

[375] *To amend the Foreign Sovereign Immunities Act with respect to admiralty jurisdiction: Hearing on H.R. 1149 Before the Subcommittee on Administrative Law and Governmental Relations of House Comm. on the Judiciary*, 100th Cong. 147, 152 (28 May 1987) (statement of the Maritime Law Association of the United States).

[376] HR Rep No 94-1487, *Jurisdiction of United States Courts in Suits Against Foreign States*, 94th Cong. (9 September 1976) at 21 (reprinted in 1976 USCCAN 6604, 6620). See *Velidor v L/P/G Benghazi*, 653 F 2d 812, 816 (3d Cir. 1981) (section 1605(b) was drafted to "avoid the arrest of vessels owned by foreign sovereigns, since such seizures frequently touch sensitive diplomatic nerves"); *China Nat'l Chemical Import & Export Corp. v M/V Lago Hualaihue*, 504 F Supp 684, 688 (D Md 1981) ("The principal purpose of § 1605(b) . . . was and is to provide a forum where the rights and liabilities of the respective parties can be litigated in an admiralty proceeding in which a foreign government is protected from the sale of its vessel to satisfy an adverse judgment").

[377] Pub L 100-640, *An Act To Amend The Foreign Sovereign Immunities Act With Respect To Admiralty Jurisdiction*, 100th Cong 2d Sess (approved 9 November 1988).

[378] *Jet Line Services v M/V Marsa El Hariga*, 462 F Supp 1165 (D Md 1978).

[379] Pub L 100-640, *An Act To Amend The Foreign Sovereign Immunities Act With Respect To Admiralty Jurisdiction*, 100th Cong 2d Sess. (approved 9 November 1988).

Section 1605(b) does not "preclude a suit in accordance with other provisions of the [FSIA]—eg 1605(a)(2). Nor would it preclude a second action, otherwise permissible, to recover the amount by which the value of the maritime lien exceeds the recovery in the first action".[380]

Application   **3.060**

Sections 1605(b)–(d) provide a non-exclusive method for bringing suit against a foreign sovereign under a claim in admiralty. While an admiralty claim against a foreign state may also be brought under s 1605(a) if it meets the statutory requirements,[381] s 1605(b)–(d) were designed specifically for admiralty suits.[382]

Section 1605(b) denies foreign sovereigns immunity in actions brought to enforce a maritime lien against a vessel or cargo owned by the foreign state, if the maritime lien is based on the foreign state's commercial activity.[383] Unlike those suits brought under s 1605(a), suits in admiralty under s 1605(b) do not require that the commercial activity in question cause a direct effect in the United States, but only that the ship be present in the forum when service is effected.[384]

Section 1603 defines "commercial activity".[385] To assert jurisdiction under s 1605(b), the plaintiff need not have engaged in a commercial activity with the foreign state.[386]

Section 1605(b)(1)–(2) sets forth the method for serving process in an action to enforce a maritime lien under s 1605(b).[387] A plaintiff must serve process on

[380] HR Rep No 94-1487, *Jurisdiction of United States Courts in Suits Against Foreign States*, 94th Cong. (9 September 1976) at 22 (reprinted in 1976 USCCAN 6604, 6621)

[381] *Velidor*, 653 F 2d at 817–818. "Although § 1605(b) is specifically tailored to admiralty suits brought to enforce maritime liens, the legislative history reveals that § 1605(b) is not the exclusive vehicle for bringing cases concerning shipping."

[382] "The non-exclusive scope of § 1605(b) is consistent with well-settled admiralty procedures. Seamen wishing to assert claims for wages have always had the option of proceeding *in rem* against the vessel, or *in personam* against the owner or the ship's master." 653 F 2d at 818.

[383] See *Castillo v Shipping Corp. of India*, 606 F Supp 497, 502 (SDNY 1985).

[384] 606 F Supp at 503.

[385] See 3.020 above. See also *Virtual Countries, Inc. v Republic of South Africa*, 148 F Supp 2d 256, 265 fn. 9 (SDNY 2001), aff'd, 300 F 3d 230 (2d Cir. 2002) (quoting 28 USC § 1603(d), stating that "[t]he commercial character of any activity shall be determined by reference to the nature of the course of conduct or particular transaction or act, rather than by reference to its purpose").

[386] *China Nat'l Chemical Import & Export Corp.*, 504 F Supp at 689 (D Md 1981) (denying defendants' motion to dismiss for lack of subject matter jurisdiction and holding that Congress did not intend to limit the application of 1605(b) to cases where there is a commercial relationship between the injured party and the foreign state, rather it was "designed to provide a substitute for the usual *in rem* proceeding and to include collision claims").

[387] See *Castillo*, 606 F Supp at 502–503 (a "further prerequisite to the assertion of jurisdiction under section 1605 is that service be made upon 'the person, or his agent, having possession of the vessel,' 28 USC § 1605(b)(1) (1982) and upon the foreign state or instrumentality") In *Castillo*, the Southern District of New York dismissed the case because service had been made on the general agent of the corporate owner, rather than on the master of the ship or his second in command, as would have been proper. Service was also ineffective because it was improperly made when the vessel was absent from the forum. 609 F Supp at 503. See also *Cargill Int'l S.A. v M/T Pavel Dybenko*, No CIV.A. 903176, 1992 WL 42194, *6 (SDNY 27 February 1992), rev'd on other grounds, *Cargill Int'l S.A. v M/T Pavel Dybenko*, 991 F 2d 1012 (2d Cir. 1993) (no jurisdiction under § 1605(b) where service was

the person in possession of the ship (usually the ship's master or his second in command) and the foreign state.[388] "[A]lthough Congress has changed the procedures for obtaining jurisdiction, it has not altered the fundamental requirement that the ship be present in the forum when service is effected."[389] Once service of process has been made, the action is deemed an *in personam* claim limited to the value of the encumbered vessel or cargo.[390]

3.061   28 U.S.C. § 1605

(c) Whenever notice is delivered under subsection (b)(1), the suit to enforce a maritime lien shall thereafter proceed and shall be heard and determined according to the principles of law and rules of the practice of suits in rem whenever it appears that, had the vessel been privately owned and possessed, a suit in rem might have been maintained. A decree against the foreign state may include costs of the suit and, if the decree is for a money judgment, interest as ordered by the court, except that the court may not award judgment against the foreign state in an amount greater than the value of the vessel or cargo upon which the maritime lien arose. Such value shall be determined as of the time notice is served under subsection (b)(1). Decrees shall be subject to appeal and revision as provided in other cases of admiralty and maritime jurisdiction. Nothing shall preclude the plaintiff in any proper case from seeking relief in personam in the same action brought to enforce a maritime lien as provided in this section.

Commentary

3.062   Legislative history

Section 1605(c) was added as an amendment to the FSIA in 1988.[391] In passing the amendment, Congress sought to make plain that actions brought *in personam* to enforce a maritime lien against a foreign state were to be treated as *in rem* proceedings.[392]

---

improperly made on the general agent of the defendant rather than on the master of the vessel and service was made outside the forum).

[388] See *Castillo*, 606 F Supp at 502–503 (citing House Report at 21).

[389] *Castillo*, 606 F Supp at 503.

[390] See s 1605(c) and discussion at 3.061–3.063 below. See also *Castillo*, 606 F Supp at 503.

[391] Pub L 100-640, *An Act To Amend The Foreign Sovereign Immunities Act With Respect To Admiralty Jurisdiction*, 100th Cong. 2d Sess. (approved 9 November 1988).

[392] *To amend the Foreign Sovereign Immunities Act with respect to admiralty jurisdiction: Hearing on H.R. 1149 Before the Subcommittee on Administrative Law and Governmental Relations of House Comm. on the Judiciary*, 100th Cong., 147, 152 (28 May 1987) (statement of the Maritime Law Association of the United States) ("In light of the significant distinctions between in rem and in personam claims, it is important to make clear that Section 1605(b) cases are substitute *in rem* cases . . . [The present wording] may be confusing in light of the significant distinction between *in rem* and *in personam* cases").

Application   **3.063**

Claims asserted under the jurisdiction of s 1605(b) "are governed by the rules of law controlling *in rem* claims generally".[393] Just as in an *in rem* proceeding, a judgment under s 1605(b) is limited to the value of the encumbered vessel or cargo.[394]

This subsection codifies the congressional intent set forth in the House Report which states that s 1605(b) does not "preclude a suit in accordance with other provisions of the [FSIA]—eg 1605(a)(2). Nor would it preclude a second action, otherwise permissible, to recover the amount by which the value of the maritime lien exceeds the recovery in the first action".[395]

Further, although the FSIA provides a foreign sovereign immunity from seizure, the foreign sovereign is still liable at an action *in personam*.[396] The plaintiff's claim becomes one *in personam* against the foreign sovereign rather than *in rem*, but the principles of law and rules of practice applied by the court are still those of an *in rem* suit. "The exemption from seizure under the statute replaces one method of service for another, but it does not alter the liability."[397]

28 U.S.C. § 1605   **3.064**

(d) A foreign state shall not be immune from the jurisdiction of the courts of the United States in any action brought to foreclose a preferred mortgage, as defined in the Ship Mortgage Act, 1920 (46 U.S.C. 911 and following). Such action shall be brought, heard, and determined in accordance with the provisions of that Act and in accordance with the principles of law and rules of practice of suits in rem, whenever it appears that had the vessel been privately owned and possessed a suit in rem might have been maintained.

Commentary

Legislative history   **3.065**

Section 1605(d) was added as an amendment to the FSIA in 1988 as:[398]

---

[393] *J. Aron & Co. v M/V Tuzla*, Nos CIV.A. 920146, 920147, 920586, 920777, 1994 WL 202424, *3 (ED La 1994). See also *Maritrend, Inc. v M/V Sebes*, No CIV.A. 963140, 1997 WL 660614, *5 (ED La 23 October 1997); *Isbrandtsen Marine Services, Inc. v Shanghai Hai Xing Shipping Co., Ltd.*, No CIV.A. 901237, 1991 WL 211293 (D Or 1 April 1991).

[394] See *Borgships, Inc. v M/V Macarena*, Nos CIV.A. 923119, 93622, 1993 WL 278453, *2 (ED La 15 July 1993); *Kim Crest, S.A. v M/V Sverdlovsk*, 753 F Supp 642, 648 (SD Tex 1990); *Castillo v Shipping Corp. of India*, 606 F Supp 497, 503 (SDNY 1985).

[395] HR Rep No 94-1487, *Jurisdiction of United States Courts in Suits Against Foreign States*, 94th Cong. (9 September 1976) at 22 (reprinted in 1976 USCCAN 6604, 6621).

[396] *Kim Crest*, 753 F Supp at 648 (finding that the FSIA eliminated the "traditional maritime remedy of an *in rem* seizure of a vessel when it is owned by a foreign sovereign").

[397] 753 F Supp at 648. See also *Borgships, Inc.*, 1993 WL 278453 at *2 ("One of the basic principles of sovereign immunity under the Act is that the property of a foreign state is immune from attachment, arrest, or execution. . . . In lieu of an *in rem* action the FSIA provides that a foreign state will not be immune from the jurisdiction of American courts in any admiralty action brought to enforce a maritime lien").

[398] *An Act To Amend The Foreign Sovereign Immunities Act With Respect To Admiralty Jurisdiction*, Pub L 100-640, 100th Cong 2d Sess (approved 9 November 1988).

[t]he substitution of an *in personam* remedy for the traditional maritime *in rem* remedy by § 1605(b) of the FSIA, and the elimination of the arrest of a vessel . . . caused uncertainties with respect to the enforcement of the liens of preferred mortgages on vessels owned by foreign states.[399]

Section 1605(d), together with s 1610(e), makes clear that plaintiffs may foreclose preferred ship mortgages on vessels owned by foreign states, as they could under the Ship Mortgage Act 1920.

The Ship Mortgage Act 1920 was originally codified at 46 USC ss 911 *et seq*. The Act was repealed in 1988 by HR 3105, Public Law 100-710, Title I, s 106(b)(2), and re-enacted by s 102(c) thereof as chapters 301 and 313 of Title 46.

3.066   Application

The 1988 amendment provides that a foreign sovereign does not have immunity from an action to foreclose a preferred mortgage, as defined in the Ship Mortgage Act 1920.[400]

Under the Ship Mortgage Act 1920, the mortgagee has a lien on a mortgaged vessel in the amount of the outstanding mortgage indebtedness. The lien can be enforced by a suit *in rem*. This suit would be commenced by the arrest of the vessel. If the owner of the vessel does not appear promptly to defend the suit, the vessel is sold before final judgment, and the prompt sale both preserves the value of the vessel and gives good title against the world.[401]

3.067   28 U.S.C. § 1605

(e) For purposes of paragraph (7) of subsection (a)—

(1) the terms "torture" and "extrajudicial killing" have the meaning given those terms in section 3 of the Torture Victim Protection Act of 1991;
(2) the term "hostage taking" has the meaning given that term in Article 1 of the International Convention Against the Taking of Hostages; and
(3) the term "aircraft sabotage" has the meaning given that term in Article 1 of the Convention for the Suppression of Unlawful Acts Against the Safety of Civil Aviation.

---

[399] *To amend the Foreign Sovereign Immunities Act with respect to admiralty jurisdiction: Hearing on H.R. 1149 Before the Subcommittee on Administrative Law and Governmental Relations of House Comm. on the Judiciary*, 100th Cong. 147, 152 (28 May 1987) (statement of the Maritime Law Association of the United States).

[400] *Silver Star Enterprises v M/V Saramacca*, 19 F 3d 1008 (5th Cir. 1994), rev'd on other grounds, *Silver Star Enterprises v M/V Saramacca*, 82 F 3d 666 (5th Cir. 1996). See also *United States v Hendron*, 813 F Supp 973 (EDNY 1993) ("Section 1605(b) provides that a foreign state is not immune where the case is brought to enforce a maritime lien . . . Similar provisions appear in § 1605(d), where the action is to foreclose a ship mortgage").

[401] *To amend the Foreign Sovereign Immunities Act with respect to admiralty jurisdiction: Hearing on H.R. 1149 Before the Subcommittee on Administrative Law and Governmental Relations of House Comm. on the Judiciary*, 100th Cong. 147, 155–156 (28 May 1987).

Commentary

Legislative history   **3.068**

Section 1605(e) was added to the FSIA as part of the Anti-Terrorism Act 1996.[402] The stated purpose of the Anti-Terrorism Act is to deter terrorist acts against US nationals by foreign sovereigns or their agents and to provide for justice for victims of such terrorism.[403] Section 1605(e) defines by reference, certain terms used in the state-sponsored terrorism exception of s 1605(a)(7).[404]

Application   **3.069**

(1) *Torture*

Section 1605(e) defines "torture" by reference to the Torture Victim Protection Act of 1991. The Torture Victim Protection Act, s 3(b) defines torture as:

(1) Any act, directed against an individual in the offender's custody or physical control, by which severe pain or suffering (other than pain or suffering arising only from or inherent in, or incidental to, lawful sanctions), whether physical or mental, is intentionally inflicted on that individual for such purposes as obtaining from that individual or a third person information or a confession, punishing that individual for an act that individual or a third person has committed or is suspected of having committed, intimidating or coercing that individual or a third person, or for any reason based on discrimination of any kind; and (2) mental pain or suffering refers to prolonged mental harm caused by or resulting from

(A) the intentional infliction of severe physical pain or suffering;

(B) the administration or application, or threatened administration or application, of mind altering substances or other procedures calculated to disrupt profoundly the senses or the personality;

(C) the threat of imminent death; or

(D) the threat that another individual will imminently be subjected to death, severe physical pain or suffering, or the administration or application of mind altering substances or other procedures calculated to disrupt profoundly the senses or personality.[405]

The United States understands that, in order to constitute torture, an act must be a deliberate and calculated act of an extremely cruel and inhuman nature, specifically intended to inflict excruciating and agonizing physical or mental

---

[402] Antiterrorism and Effective Death Penalty Act of 1996, Pub L No 104-132, 110 Stat 1214, 1241 (24 April 1996).

[403] See HR 103–702, *Foreign Sovereign Immunities Amendments*, 103d Cong. 3–4 (16 August 1995)

[404] See 3.052–3.054 above.

[405] Torture Victim Protection Act 1991 § 3(b), Pub L No 102-256, 106 Stat 73 (12 March 1992), codified at 28 USC § 1350 (note). The TVPA's definition of torture is based upon the 1984 United Nations Convention Against Torture and Other Cruel, Inhuman or Degrading Treatment or Punishment, GA Res 39/46, UN GAOR, 39th Sess, Supp No 51 at 197, UN Doc A/39/51 (1984).

pain or suffering. This understanding thus makes clear that torture does not automatically result whenever individuals in official custody are subjected even to direct physical assault. Not all police brutality, not every instance of excessive force used against prisoners, is torture under the FSIA.[406]

The DC Circuit has adopted a strict pleading requirement with respect to torture. In the *Price* case, the court stated that "in light of the serious and far-reaching implications of the 1996 FSIA amendments, it is especially important for the courts to ensure that foreign states are not stripped of their sovereign immunity unless they have been charged with actual torture, and not mere police brutality".[407] The court found plaintiff's complaint insufficient where it did not describe the "details about the nature of the kicking, clubbing, and beatings that plaintiffs allegedly suffered . . . including their frequency, duration, the parts of the body at which they were aimed, and the weapons used to carry them out[.]"[408]

The same court has also stated that "torture can occur under the FSIA only when the production of pain is purposive, and not merely haphazard . . . [A] foreign state must impose suffering cruelly and deliberately, rather than as the unforeseen or unavoidable incident of some legitimate end".[409]

(2) *Extrajudicial killing*

Section 1605(e) defines "extrajudicial killing" by reference to the Torture Victim Protection Act 1991. The Torture Victim Protection Act, s 3(a) characterizes an extrajudicial killing as:

> A deliberated killing not authorized by a previous judgment pronounced by a regularly constituted court affording all the judicial guarantees which are recognized as indispensable by civilized peoples. Such term, however, does not include any such killing that, under international law, is lawfully carried out under the authority of a foreign nation.[410]

---

[406] *Price v Socialist People's Libyan Arab Jamahiriya*, 294 F 3d 82, 93 (DC Cir 2002).

[407] 294 F 3d at 93.

[408] 294 F 3d at 93. But see *Surette v Islamic Republic of Iran*, 231 F Supp 2d 260, 264 (DDC 2002) (torture found where victim was abducted and held for over 14 months in cruel and inhumane conditions, denied sufficient food and water, subjected to constant and deliberate demoralization, physically beaten, possibly subjected to gruesome physical torture and denied essential medical treatment); *Daliberti v Republic of Iraq*, 146 F Supp 2d 19, (DDC 2001) (holding a victim at gunpoint, threatening to injure him physically if he did not confess or provide information, incarcerating him in a room with no bed, window, light, electricity, water or toilet constituted torture). See also *Jenco v Islamic Republic of Iran*, 154 F Supp 2d 27, 32 (DDC 2001), aff'd, 315 F 3d 325 (DC Cir 2003); *Sutherland v Islamic Republic of Iran*, 151 F Supp 2d 27, 45 (DDC 2001).

[409] *Price*, 294 F 3d at 93.

[410] Torture Victim Protection Act 1991 § 3(a), Pub L No 102-256, 106 Stat 73 (12 March 1992), codified at 28 USC § 1350 (note). See *Stethem v Islamic Republic of Iran*, 201 F Supp 2d 78, 86 (DDC 2002) (finding defendants guilty of extrajudicial killing when they committed "a deliberate killing" in the course of a terrorist attack).

(3) *Hostage taking*

Section 1605(e) defines "hostage taking" by reference the International Convention Against the Taking of Hostages (the "Hostage Taking Convention"). President Reagan ratified the Hostage Taking Convention in 1981.

Article 1 of the International Convention Against the Taking of Hostages defines hostage taking as the act of:

> Any person who seizes or detains and threatens to kill, to injure or to continue to detain another person (hereinafter referred to as the "hostage") in order to compel a third party, namely, a State, an international intergovernmental organization, a natural or juridical person, or a group of persons, to do or abstain from doing any act as an explicit or implicit condition for the release of the hostage.[411]

(4) *Aircraft sabotage*

Section 1605(e) defines aircraft sabotage by reference the Convention for the Suppression of Unlawful Acts Against the Safety of Civil Aviation (the "Aviation Convention"). Article 1.1 of the Aviation Convention states that any person commits an offence if he unlawfully and intentionally:

> (a) performs an act of violence against a person on board an aircraft in flight if that act is likely to endanger the safety of that aircraft; or
>
> (b) destroys an aircraft in service or causes damage to such an aircraft which renders it incapable of flight of which is likely to endanger its safety in flight; or
>
> (c) places or causes to be placed on an aircraft in service, by any means whatsoever, a device or substance which is likely to destroy that aircraft, or to cause damage to it which renders it incapable of flight, or to cause damage to it which is likely to endanger its safety in flight; or
>
> (d) destroys or damages air navigation facilities or interferes with their operation, if any such act is likely to endanger the safety of aircraft in flight; or
>
> (e) communicates information which he knows to be false, thereby endangering the safety of an aircraft in flight.

Under Article 1.2 of the Aviation Convention, any person also commits an offence if he:

> (a) attempts to commit any of the offences mentioned in paragraph 1 of this Article, or
>
> (b) is an accomplice of a person who commits or attempts to commit any such offence.[412]

---

[411] TIAS No 1181, 1983 WL 144724 (Treaty), Article 1.

[412] Convention for the Suppression of Unlawful Acts Against the Safety of Civil Aviation, Article 1, 24 UST 565, TIAS 7570.

3.070 **28 U.S.C. § 1605**

(f) No action shall be maintained under subsection (a)(7) unless the action is commenced not later than 10 years after the date on which the cause of action arose. All principles of equitable tolling, including the period during which the foreign state was immune from suit, shall apply in calculating this limitation period.

Commentary

3.071 Legislative history

Section 1605(f) was added to the FSIA as part of the Anti-Terrorism Act 1996.[413] The 10-year statute of limitations was modeled on the limitations period set forth in the Torture Victim Protection Act.[414]

3.072 Application

This 10-year statute of limitations applies only in cases brought under the state-sponsored terrorism exception of s 1605(a)(7).[415] Congress indicated that the courts should apply all principles of equitable tolling when considering whether a case is barred by s 1605(f) In *Cicippio v Islamic Republic of Iran*,[416] the court refused to dismiss an action which was based on the abduction of several individuals more than a decade before the action was commenced.

3.073 **28 U.S.C. § 1605**

(g) Limitation on discovery—

(1) In general—(A) Subject to paragraph (2), if an action is filed that would otherwise be barred by section 1604, but for subsection (a)(7), the court, upon request of the Attorney General, shall stay any request, demand, or order for discovery on the United States that the Attorney General certifies would significantly interfere with a criminal investigation or prosecution, or a national security operation, related to the incident that gave rise to the cause of action, until such time as the Attorney General advises the court that such request, demand, or order will no longer so interfere.

---

[413] Antiterrorism and Effective Death Penalty Act of 1996, Pub L No 104-132, 110 Stat 1214, 1241 (24 April 1996).

[414] *A Bill to Amend Title 28 of the United States Code to Permit a Foreign State to be Subject to the Jurisdiction of Federal or State Courts in any Case Involving an Act of International Terrorism: Hearing on H.R. 1877 Before the Senate Subcomm. On Courts and Administrative Practice of the Comm. on the Judiciary,* 103rd Cong. 7 (21 June 1994). See Torture Victims Protection Act, 28 USC § 1350, note.

[415] See 3.052–3.054 above.

[416] 18 F Supp 2d 62, 68–69 (DDC 1998) ("the ten-year statute of limitations for actions under § 1605(a)(7) does not bar the claims in this case because, once again, Congress has provided that victims of terrorism be given benefit of all principles of equitable tolling, including the period during which the foreign state was immune from suit").

(B) A stay under this paragraph shall be in effect during the 12-month period beginning on the date on which the court issues the order to stay discovery. The court shall renew the order to stay discovery for additional 12-month periods upon motion by the United States if the Attorney General certifies that discovery would significantly interfere with a criminal investigation or prosecution, or a national security operation, related to the incident that gave rise to the cause of action.

(2) Sunset—(A) Subject to subparagraph (b), no stay shall be granted or continued in effect under paragraph (1) after the date that is 10 years after the date on which the incident that gave rise to the cause of action occurred.

(B) After the period referred to in subparagraph (A), the court, upon request of the Attorney General, may stay any request, demand, or order for discovery on the United States that the court finds a substantial likelihood would—

　(i) create a serious threat of death or serious bodily injury to any person;

　(ii) adversely affect the ability of the United States to work in cooperation with foreign and international law enforcement agencies in investigating violations of United States law; or

　(iii) obstruct the criminal case related to the incident that gave rise to the cause of action or undermine the potential for a conviction in such case.

(3) Evaluation of evidence.—The court's evaluation of any request for a stay under this subsection filed by the Attorney General shall be conducted ex parte and in camera.

(4) Bar on motions to dismiss.—A stay of discovery under this subsection shall constitute a bar to the granting of a motion to dismiss under rules 12(b)(6) and 56 of the Federal Rules of Civil Procedure.

(5) Construction.—Nothing in this subsection shall prevent the United States from seeking protective orders or asserting privileges ordinarily available to the United States.

Commentary

Legislative history   **3.074**

Section 1605(g) was added to the FSIA as part of the Anti-Terrorism and Effective Death Penalty Act 1996 ("Anti-Terrorism Act").[417] The stated purpose of

---

[417] Antiterrorism and Effective Death Penalty Act 1996, Pub L No 104-132, 110 Stat 1214, 1241 (24 April 1996).

the Anti-Terrorism Act is to deter terrorist acts against US nationals by foreign sovereigns or their agents and to provide for justice for victims of such terrorism.[418] This section reflects "the delicate legislative compromise out of which [state-sponsored terrorism exception] was born".[419]

3.075   Application

No published case has addressed this section.[420]

3.076   **28 U.S.C. § 1606**

Extent of liability

As to any claim for relief with respect to which a foreign state is not entitled to immunity under section 1605 or 1607 of this chapter, the foreign state shall be liable in the same manner and to the same extent as a private individual under like circumstances; but a foreign state except for an agency or instrumentality thereof shall not be liable for punitive damages; if, however, in any case wherein death was caused, the law of the place where the action or omission occurred provides, or has been construed to provide, for damages only punitive in nature, the foreign state shall be liable for actual or compensatory damages measured by the pecuniary injuries resulting from such death which were incurred by the persons for whose benefit the action was brought.

Commentary

3.077   Legislative history

Section 1606 was intended to make clear that if a foreign state, political subdivision, agency or instrumentality is not entitled to immunity from jurisdiction, liability exists as it would for a private party under like circumstances.[421] "However, the tort liability of a foreign state itself, and of its political subdivision (but not of an agency or instrumentality of a foreign state) does not extend to punitive damages."[422] This is because Congress concluded that "[u]nder current international practice, punitive damages are usually not assessed against foreign states".[423] However, "[i]nterest prior to judgment and costs may be assessed against a foreign state just as against a private party".[424]

---

[418] See *Foreign Sovereign Immunities Amendments*, HR 103–702, 103d Cong. 3–4 (16 August 1995).   [419] *Bettis v Islamic Republic of Iran*, 315 F 3d 325 at 329–330 (DC Cir 2003).
[420] For operation of other aspects of the 1996 legislation, see 3.052–3.057.
[421] See HR Rep No 94-1487, *Jurisdiction of United States Courts in Suits Against Foreign States*, 94th Cong. (9 September 1976) at 22 (reprinted in 1976 USCCAN 6604, 6621).
[422] HR Rep No 94-1487, *Jurisdiction of United States Courts in Suits Against Foreign States*, 94th Cong. (9 September 1976) at 22 (reprinted in 1976 USCCAN 6604, 6621).
[423] HR Rep No 94-1487, *Jurisdiction of United States Courts in Suits Against Foreign States*, 94th Cong. (9 September 1976) at 22 (reprinted in 1976 USCCAN 6604, 6621).
[424] HR Rep No 94-1487, *Jurisdiction of United States Courts in Suits Against Foreign States*, 94th Cong. (9 September 1976) at 22 (reprinted in 1976 USCCAN 6604, 6621) (citing 46 USC §§ 743, 745).

Consistent with s 1606, "a court could, when circumstances were clearly appropriate, order an injunction or specific performance".[425] But s 1606 "is not determinative of the power of the court to enforce such an order. For example, a foreign diplomat or official could not be imprisoned for contempt because of his government's violation of an injunction".[426]

Section 1606 and indeed the FSIA as a whole "does not attempt to deal with questions of discovery". This is because Congress felt that "[e]xisting laws appear[ed] to be adequate in this area".[427]

Application
3.078

In accordance with the intention expressed by Congress, courts have recognized that the FSIA in general, and s 1606 in particular, does not affect the substantive law of liability governing foreign states or their instrumentalities.[428] Rather, s 1606 was intended to "create rules governing liability of foreign governments for damages, and not to change the rules of primary conduct that apply to foreign governments".[429] In the context of the FSIA the term "liability" has been used as the functional equivalent of "damages".[430]

Where a foreign sovereign is not entitled to immunity under the FSIA, it will be subject to the substantive rules of liability as though it were a private individual.[431] That is to say that where the applicable law provides a rule of liability, the FSIA requires that a foreign state not entitled to immunity with respect to a particular claim be subject to that rule in the same manner as a private individual under like circumstances.[432] The only modification provided for is the standard of liability with respect to punitive damages and wrongful death actions.[433]

---

[425] HR Rep No 94-1487, *Jurisdiction of United States Courts in Suits Against Foreign States*, 94th Cong. (9 September 1976) at 22 (reprinted in 1976 USCCAN 6604, 6621).

[426] HR Rep No 94-1487, *Jurisdiction of United States Courts in Suits Against Foreign States*, 94th Cong. (9 September 1976) at 22 (reprinted in 1976 USCCAN 6604, 6621) (citing 22 USC § 252).

[427] HR Rep No 94-1487, *Jurisdiction of United States Courts in Suits Against Foreign States*, 94th Cong. (9 September 1976) at 22 (reprinted in 1976 USCCAN 6604, 6621).

[428] *First National City Bank v Banco Para El Comercio Exterior de Cuba*, 462 US 611, 620, 622 (1983), citing HR Rep No 94-1487, *Jurisdiction of United States Courts in Suits Against Foreign States*, 94th Cong. (9 September 1976) at 12 (reprinted in 1976 USCCAN 6604, 6610); see also *Verlinden B. V. v Central Bank of Nigeria*, 647 F 2d 320, 326 (2d Cir. 1981).

[429] *Walpex Trading Co. v Yacimentos Petroliferos Fiscales Bolivianos*, 789 F Supp 1268, 1277 (SDNY 1992).

[430] See *Bowers v Transportes Navieros Ecuadorianos (Transnave)*, 719 F Supp 166, 171 (SDNY 1989), cited in *Walpex*, 789 F Supp at 1277.

[431] See *Mukaddam v Permanent Mission of Saudi Arabia to the United Nations*, 111 F Supp 2d 457, 470 (SDNY 2000) (holding that the Saudi Arabian UN Mission was not immune from suit under Title VII in relation to its actions as an employer, and subject to the provisions thereof in the same manner as any employer).

[432] See *First National City Bank*, 462 US at 611. See also *Bettis v Islamic Republic of Iran*, 315 F 3d 325, 333 (DC Cir 2003) ("The fact that section 1606 requires courts to hold foreign sovereigns liable in the same manner as private individuals in 'like circumstances' reinforces the applicability of ordinary rules of liability by requiring judges to look to the common law of the states to determine the appropriate law applicable to a given set of facts").

[433] Providing that a foreign state shall not be liable for punitive damages, and in the case of a wrongful death action, if the applicable law provides for punitive damages only, actual or compensatory damages will be awarded. See *Verlinden B. V. v Central Bank of Nigeria*, 461 US 480 (1983).

The requirement that a foreign state be subject to the standard rules relating to liability also extends to ancillary aspects of a damage award, such as pre-judgment interest[434] and costs.[435]

Choice of law

Although the FSIA is the exclusive source of federal jurisdiction over foreign sovereigns and their agencies and instrumentalities,[436] the statute contains no express choice of law provision to guide federal courts in determining the substantive law applicable to cases brought thereunder.[437] This lack of legislative guidance has given rise to much judicial analysis and debate.[438]

Several district courts had previously relied on s 1606 as creating an implicit general choice of law rule. The district courts held that the substantive law of "the place where the action or omission occurred" which is the subject of the litigation should be applied in all cases brought under the FSIA.[439] The two circuit court decisions (the cases of *Harris* and *Barkanic*) that have addressed this issue rejected the analysis of the district courts reasoning that "the language of [this] provision[ ] relates only to the issue of punitive damages, not to the general question of choice of law".[440] However, these two circuit courts have reached very different conclusions with respect to the appropriate choice of law rules to be applied in FSIA cases.

In *Harris v Polskie Linie Lotnicze*[441] the Ninth Circuit held that the federal common law choice of law rules should apply in FSIA cases.[442] The court stated that "[i]n the absence of specific statutory guidance, we prefer to resort to the federal common law for a choice-of-law rule".[443] The court recognized that in

---

[434] See *Callen v Oulu O/Y and OY Finnlines Ltd.*, 711 F Supp 244, 250 (ED Pa 1989), aff'd, 897 F 2d 520 (3d Cir.), cert. denied, 498 US 816 (1990); *Felice Fedder Oriental Art Inc. v Scanlon*, 708 F Supp 551 (SDNY 1998), cert. denied, 498 US 816 (1990).

[435] See *McKesson Corporation, et al. v The Islamic Republic of Iran, et al.*, 116 F Supp 2d 13 (DDC 2000) (finding Iran liable for costs to the same extent as a private party would be).

[436] Where federal court jurisdiction is based on diversity of citizenship, there are clear rules regarding conflict of law principles (See *Klaxon Co. v Stentor Elec. Mfg. Co.*, 313 US 487, 496 (1941)). Diversity jurisdiction will still exist with respect to entities owned by a foreign sovereign where such entities are also citizens of a state of the United States (see 28 USC §§ 1603(a), (b)(2); 1332 (c), (d); *Harris v Polskie Linie Lotnicze*, 820 F 2d 1000, 1002 (9th Cir. 1987)).

[437] Where jurisdiction is established on the basis of federal legislation, the substantive law to be applied by the federal court will be based on choice-of-law rules provided, either implicitly or explicitly, by the statute, or on the federal common law choice-of-law rules. See *Barkanic v General Administration of Civil Aviation of the People's Republic of China*, 923 F 2d 957, 960 (2d Cir. 1991).

[438] See *Barkanic*, 923 F 2d at 957; *Harris*, 820 F 2d at 1000.

[439] In particular the district courts relied on the following language: "however, in any case wherein death was caused, *the law of the place where the action or omission occurred* provides, or has been construed to provide, for damages only punitive in nature, the foreign state shall be liable for actual or compensatory damages measured by the pecuniary injuries resulting from such death which were incurred by the persons for whose benefit the action was brought." 28 USC § 1606. See *Barkanic*, 923 F 2d, 959; *Harris*, 641 F Supp 94, 97 (ND Cal 1986), aff'd, 820 F 2d 1000 (9th Cir. 1987).

[440] *Barkanic*, 923 F 2d at 959. See *Harris*, 820 F 2d at 1003.   [441] *Harris*, 820 F 2d at 1000.

[442] The federal common law choice of law rule is the "most significant relationship test" drawn from the Restatement (Second) of Conflict of Laws ("Second Restatement").

[443] *Harris*, 820 F 2d at 1003. See also *Chuidian v Phillipine Nat'l Bank*, 976 F 2d 561, 564 (9th Cir. 1992) ("federal common law choice of law rules apply, not the choice of law rules of the

applying federal choice of law rules the court was treating the government instrumentality differently than it would a private individual in an identical case.[444] After applying the federal choice of law analysis the court determined that the law of the place of injury (Poland) should be applied to the case.

The Second Circuit has rejected the approach taken by the Ninth Circuit. In *Barkanic v General Administration of Civil Aviation of the People's Republic of China*[445] the court held that the application of the choice of law provision of the forum state best gave effect to Congress' intent that foreign states be liable "in the same manner and to the same extent" as private individuals in similar circumstances.[446]

In choosing a single federal choice of law provision, the Ninth Circuit prioritized certainty, predictability and uniformity of result for the body of federal case law,[447] whereas the Second Circuit prioritized the application of the same rules, starting with the forum's choice of law provision, to foreign sovereigns as would be applied to private individuals in given set of circumstances. In the context of a choice of law question, the Second Circuit held that it would be impossible to apply identical substantive laws to foreign states and private individuals without applying the same choice of law analysis.[448]

Claim based immunity

The opening language of s 1606 ("*As to any claim for relief*") has been interpreted as evidence that exceptions to immunity apply on a claim by claim basis, and jurisdiction under the FSIA over any given claim does not automatically confer jurisdiction over other claims for relief brought as part of the same case.[449]

28 U.S.C. § 1607   3.079

Counterclaims

In any action brought by a foreign state, or in which a foreign state intervenes, in a court of the United States or of a State, the foreign state shall not be

---

forum state" to FSIA actions); *Schoenberg v Exportadora de Sal, S.A. de C.V.*, 930 F 2d 777, 782 (9th Cir. 1991); *Liu v Republic of China*, 892 F 2d 1419, 1426 (9th Cir. 1989), cert. denied, 497 US 1058 (1990).

[444] *Harris*, 820 F 2d at 1004, n 5.   [445] *Barkanic*, 923 F 2d 957 (2d Cir 1991).

[446] 923 F 2d at 959 ("[R]ather than directing courts to apply the choice of law rules of the place of [the relevant events], the FSIA implicitly requires courts to apply the choice of law provisions of the forum state with respect to all issues governed by state substantive law") (citing *First National City Bank*, 462 US at 622 n 11) ("[W]here state law provides a rule of liability governing private individuals, the FSIA requires the application of that rule to foreign states in like circumstances"). See also *Karaha Bodas Co., L.L.C. v Perusahaan Pertambangan Minyak Dan Gas Bumi Negara*, 313 F 3d 70, 84 (2d Cir. 2002), cert. denied, 123 S Ct 2256 (2 June 2003); *Pescatore v Pan Am. World Airways, Inc.*, 97 F 3d 1, 12 (2d Cir. 1996); *Turkmani v Republic of Bolivia*, 193 F Supp 2d 165, 176 (DDC 28 March 2002); *Falcon Investments, Inc. v Republic of Venezuela*, No. 00–4123-DES, 2001 WL 584346 (D Kan 22 May 2001); *Virtual Defense and Development Intern., Inc. v Republic of Moldova*, 133 F Supp 2d 9 (DDC. 5 Febrauary 2001).   [447] *Harris*, 820 F 2d at 1004.

[448] *Barkanic*, 923 F 2d at 960.

[449] *Dar El-Bina Engineering & Contracting Company, Ltd. v The Republic of Iraq*, 79 F Supp 2d 374, 386 (SDNY 2000).

accorded immunity with respect to any counterclaim—

(a) for which a foreign state would not be entitled to immunity under section 1605 of this chapter had such claim been brought in a separate action against the foreign state; or

(b) arising out of the transaction or occurrence that is the subject matter of the claim of the foreign state; or

(c) to the extent that the counterclaim does not seek relief exceeding in amount or differing in kind from that sought by the foreign state.

Commentary

3.080   Legislative history

Section 1607 applies to counterclaims against a foreign state which brings an action or intervenes in an action in a federal or state court, denying the foreign state sovereign immunity.[450] Section 1607(a) is based upon Article 1 of the European Convention on State Immunity,[451] and denies immunity as to any counterclaim for which the foreign state would not be entitled to immunity under s 1605, if the counterclaim had been brought as a direct claim in a separate action against the foreign state. Section 1607(b) contains the same terminology used in the Federal Rules of Civil Procedure, r 13(a), is consistent with s 70(2)(b), Restatement of the Law, Second, Foreign Relations Law of the United States (1965),[452] and was enacted in order to ensure that a foreign state that brings an action in the United States cannot avoid legal liabilities arising from the same transaction or occurrence for which it seeks to obtain relief.[453] Section 1607(c) prevents foreign states from claiming immunity to setoffs, codifying the rule enunciated in *National Bank v Republic of China*.[454]

3.081   Application

Section 1607 is meant to reduce the scope of sovereign immunity, not enlarge it. "It withdraws immunity not only in a situation . . . where the foreign state would not be entitled to immunity under § 1605 if such a claim had been brought in a separate action against it, but in the two other situations described in § 1607(b) and (c)."[455] By enacting s 1607, Congress did not intend to limit the waiver of sovereign immunity to counterclaims exclusively, and thus cross-claims may also

---

[450] See HR Rep No 94-1487, *Jurisdiction of United States Courts in Suits Against Foreign States*, 94th Cong. (9 September 1976) at 23 (reprinted in 1976 USCCAN 6604, 6622).

[451] 11 Int'l Legal Materials 470 (1972).

[452] HR Rep No 94-1487, *Jurisdiction of United States Courts in Suits Against Foreign States*, 94th Cong. (9 September 1976) at 23 (reprinted in 1976 USCCAN 6604, 6622).

[453] See *Alfred Dunhill of London, Inc. v Cuba*, 425 US 682, cert. denied, 425 US 991 (1976).

[454] 348 US 356 (1955) (holding that defendant bank could bring a counterclaim seeking affirmative judgment for $1,634,432 on defaulted Treasury Notes as a setoff against plaintiff sovereign nation's suit to retrieve $200,000 deposited with bank).

[455] *Ministry of Supply, Cairo v Universe Tankships, Inc.* 708 F 2d 80, 86 (2d Cir. 1983).

be heard if the sovereign is not entitled to immunity under another section of the Act.[456]

Section 1607(a)

Section 1607(a) allows a defendant to assert counterclaims against a foreign state, if those claims qualify under the exceptions to immunity set forth in s 1605.[457]

Section 1607(b)

Section 1607(b) prevents the foreign sovereign from asserting immunity to cross-claims which arise out of the same transaction or occurrence that is the subject matter of the claim asserted by the foreign sovereign. By availing itself of the courts of the United States, the foreign sovereign is deemed to have waived its immunity with respect to such claims.

The test for claims arising out of the "same transaction or occurrence" under s 1607(b) corresponds to the test for compulsory counterclaims in the Federal Rules of Civil Procedure, r 13(a).[458] Courts have taken a liberal view of the "same transaction or occurrence" requirement, citing the pragmatism of joining all parties and claims in a single forum, the conservation of judicial resources, and the desire to unify the litigation of similar or related claims as justification.[459]

Courts have been willing to separate counterclaims by the same defendant into those that arise from the same transaction and those that do not. In *Cabiri v Gov't of the Republic of Ghana*,[460] a case which involved an eviction suit by Ghana against Bawol Cabiri, an employee of Ghana, Cabiri counterclaimed for claims regarding both the eviction and for injuries arising from his torture at the hands of the Republic of Ghana. The court determined that the event that gave rise to the eviction suit was Cabiri's employment contract and its termination. On that basis, the court allowed his breach of contract claim, but dismissed his claims regarding torture, holding that they did not concern whether the employment contract was lawfully terminated. The court held that it is not enough that the claims involved an employer–employee relationship; there needed to be a closer nexus between the foreign state's suit and the counterclaim.

---

[456] 708 F 2d, 86.   [457] See discussion at 3.030–3.075 below.

[458] See *In re Oil Spill By Amoco Cadiz*, 491 F Supp 161, 168 (ND Ill 1979); HR Rep 94-1487 *Jurisdiction of United States Courts in Suits Against Foreign States*, 94th Cong (9 September 1976) at 23 (reprinted in 1976 USCCAN 6604, 6622). "As a word of flexible meaning, 'transaction' may comprehend a series of many occurrences, depending not so much upon the immediateness of their connection as upon their logical relationship", *In re Oil Spill By Amoco Cadiz*, 491 F.Supp at 168, citing *Warshawsky & Co. v Arcata National Corp.*, 552 F 2d 1257, 1261 (7th Cir. 1977); see also *Cabiri v Gov't of the Republic of Ghana*, 165 F 3d 193, 610 (2d Cir 1999) (holding that the test for same transaction or occurrence does "not requir[e] an absolute identity of factual backgrounds . . . but only a logical relationship between them. This approach looks to the logical relationship between the claim and the counterclaim, and attempts to determine whether the essential facts of the various claims are so logically connected that considerations of judicial economy and fairness dictate that all the issues be resolved in one lawsuit").

[459] In *In re Oil Spill By Amoco Cadiz*, 491 F Supp at 161, the court held that the Republic of France had waived sovereign immunity as against counterclaims by Amoco because of France's efforts to litigate an oil spill off the coast of France in United States courts.   [460] 165 F 3d at 193.

The courts have also taken an expansive view of the type of claim to which a waiver under s 1607(b) applies; it does not necessarily apply to counterclaims exclusively, but also to analogous situations. For instance, the court has found a waiver of sovereign immunity against third party claims[461] and even waivers when the foreign states did not bring the action themselves but had intervened.[462]

This waiver of sovereign immunity only applies when the foreign state files an unconditional claim. When a state files a claim conditional on the court finding a waiver of sovereign immunity, s 1607(b) does not automatically allow the filing of counterclaims.[463]

The court in *Republic of the Philippines v Westinghouse Electric Corporation*[464] elaborated on the limitations of a waiver of sovereign immunity in this context. The court held that, although a sovereign subjects itself to jurisdiction over matters incident to a suit it brings in the United States, "it cannot be seriously suggested that the plaintiff sovereign gives up its essential attributes of sovereignty, including in particular its authority to administer in its sole discretion its own laws respecting its own citizens within its own territory".

Section 1607(c)

The rationale behind the s 1607(c) exception to sovereign immunity is the "desire to remove the basic unfairness of the situation in which '[w]e have a foreign government invoking our law but resisting a claim against it which fairly would curtail its recovery' ".[465]

There are not many cases dealing with s 1607(c). In *In Re Oil Spill By Amoco Cadiz*,[466] the court held that, although it found a waiver of sovereign immunity by France on the basis of s 1607(b), it was also possible to find a waiver under s 1607(c). The court concluded that:

> The Republic of France has undertaken an indemnification program, the result and full impact of which are as yet unclear. It is possible, however, that as these proceedings progress the claims of individuals, departments and communes will be subsumed under that of the Republic of France. If

---

[461] *In re Oil Spill By Amoco Cadiz*, 491 F Supp at 167–168 (finding that under s 1607(b) the Republic of France had waived sovereign immunity against third party claims).

[462] See *Lord Day & Lord v The Socialist Republic of Vietnam*, 134 F Supp 2d 549, 557 (SDNY 2001) (holding that, although Vietnam "neither brought the action nor intervened, but rather . . . pursue[d] its claim in interpleader", there still existed a waiver of sovereign immunity under 1607(b)); *Corporacion Mexicana De Servicios Maritimos, S.A. De C.V. v M/T Respect*, 89 F 3d 650 (9th Cir. 1996) (finding that the intervening party had waived part of its immunity by intervening and filing a claim against the defendants).

[463] *Rio Grande Transport, Inc. v Compagnie Nationale Algerienne De Navigation*, 516 F Supp 1155, 1159–1160 (SDNY 1981) (holding that Algeria had not waived sovereign immunity under s 1607(b) by filing an exoneration from or limitation of liability conditional on rejection of claim for sovereign immunity. The court distinguished this case from *In re Oil Spill By Amoco Cadiz*: "In that case, France had filed an unconditional affirmative action, whereas here CNAN has only filed a conditional claim and limitation proceeding").   [464] 43 F 3d 65, fn 18 (3d Cir 1995).

[465] *Alberti v Empresa Nicaraguense De La Carne*, 705 F 2d 250, 254 (7th Cir 1983), citing *National City Bank of New York v Republic of China*, 348 US 356 (1955) (the court here held that s 1607(c) did not apply because Nicaragua was forced into court by the plaintiff).   [466] 491 F Supp at 168.

this occurs, section 1607(c) comes into play. Amoco, then, would be counterclaiming for the same events and for the same relief as those of the claims of the Republic of France.[467]

28 U.S.C. § 1608   **3.082**

Service; time to answer; default

(a) Service in the courts of the United States and of the States shall be made upon a foreign state or political subdivision of a foreign state:

(1) by delivery of a copy of the summons and complaint in accordance with any special arrangement for service between the plaintiff and the foreign state or political subdivision; or

(2) if no special arrangement exists, by delivery of a copy of the summons and complaint in accordance with an applicable international convention on service of judicial documents; or

(3) if service cannot be made under paragraphs (1) or (2), by sending a copy of the summons and complaint and a notice of suit, together with a translation of each into the official language of the foreign state, by any form of mail requiring a signed receipt, to be addressed and dispatched by the clerk of the court to the head of the ministry of foreign affairs of the foreign state concerned; or

(4) if service cannot be made within 30 days under paragraph (3), by sending two copies of the summons and complaint and a notice of suit, together with a translation of each into the official language of the foreign state, by any form of mail requiring a signed receipt, to be addressed and dispatched by the clerk of the court to the Secretary of State in Washington, District of Columbia, to the attention of the Director of Special Consular Services—and the Secretary shall transmit one copy of the papers through diplomatic channels to the foreign state and shall send to the clerk of the court a certified copy of the diplomatic note indicating when the papers were transmitted.

As used in this subsection, a "notice of suit" shall mean a notice addressed to a foreign state and in a form prescribed by the Secretary of State by regulation.

(b) Service in the courts of the United States and of the States shall be made upon an agency or instrumentality of a foreign state:

(1) by delivery of a copy of the summons and complaint in accordance with any special arrangement for service between the plaintiff and the agency or instrumentality; or

---

[467] 491 F Supp at 168.

(2) if no special arrangement exists, by delivery of a copy of the summons and complaint either to an officer, a managing or general agent, or to any other agent authorized by appointment or by law to receive service of process in the United States; or in accordance with an applicable international convention on service of judicial documents; or

(3) if service cannot be made under paragraphs (1) or (2), and if reasonably calculated to give actual notice, by delivery of a copy of the summons and complaint, together with a translation of each into the official language of the foreign state—

   (A) as directed by an authority of the foreign state or political sub-division in response to a letter rogatory or request or

   (B) by any form of mail requiring a signed receipt, to be addressed and dispatched by the clerk of the court to the agency or instrumentality to be served, or

   (C) as directed by order of the court consistent with the law of the place where service is to be made.

(c) Service shall be deemed to have been made—

(1) in the case of service under subsection (a)(4), as of the date of trans-mittal indicated in the certified copy of the diplomatic note; and

(2) in any other case under this section, as of the date of receipt indicated in the certification, signed and returned postal receipt, or other proof of service applicable to the method of service employed.

(d) In any action brought in a court of the United States or of a State, a for-eign state, a political subdivision thereof, or an agency or instrumental-ity of a foreign state shall serve an answer or other responsive pleading to the complaint within sixty days after service has been made under this section.

(e) No judgment by default shall be entered by a court of the United States or of a State against a foreign state, a political subdivision thereof, or an agency or instrumentality of a foreign state, unless the claimant establishes his claim or right to relief by evidence satisfactory to the court. A copy of any such default judgment shall be sent to the foreign state or political sub-division in the manner prescribed for service in this section.

Commentary

3.083   Legislative history

"Section 1608 sets forth the exclusive procedures with respect to service on, the filing of an answer or other responsive pleading by, and obtaining a default

judgment against a foreign state or its political subdivisions, agencies or instrumentalities".[468] Section 1608 was "intended to fill a void in existing Federal and
State law, and to insure that private persons have adequate means for commencing a suit against a foreign state to seek redress in the courts".[469]

Section 1608 is inter-connected with other sections of the FSIA. "If notice
is served under section 1608 and if the jurisdictional contacts embodied in
sections 1605–1607 are satisfied, personal jurisdiction over a foreign state would
exist under section 1330(b)".[470]

Application   **3.084**

As appears from its legislative history, s 1608(a) "sets forth the exclusive procedures
for service on a foreign state, or political subdivision thereof, but not on an agency
or instrumentality of a foreign state which is covered in [s 1608(b)]".[471] There is a
specified preference for the order in which service of process should be made to a
foreign state or its political subdivision under s 1608(a). First, service should be
made in accordance with any special arrangement for service between the plaintiff
and the foreign state. Second, service should be made in accordance with an
applicable international convention on service of judicial documents. If these are
not available, s 1608(a)(3) allows service by mail pursuant to the requirements set
out in s 1608(a)(3). Last, s 1604(a)(4) authorizes the clerk of the court to mail
copies of the complaint and summons and a notice of suit, with translations, to the
Secretary of State in Washington, DC, whose office shall then transmit one copy
of the papers through diplomatic channels to the foreign state.[472]

Section 1608(b) provides the exclusive methods for the service of process of
an agency or instrumentality of a foreign state. Like the procedures for serving a
state or its political subdivision, there is a hierarchy of service methods. First,

> service must always be made in accordance with any special arrangement
> for service between a plaintiff and the agency or instrumentality. If no
> such arrangement exists, then service must be made under subsection (b)(2)
> which provides for service upon officers, or managing, general or appointed
> agents in the United States of the agency or instrumentality—or, in the alter
> native, in accordance with an applicable international convention such as

---

[468] HR Rep 94–1487 *Jurisdiction of United States Courts in Suits Against Foreign States*, 94th Cong.
(9 September 1976) at 23 (reprinted in 1976 USCCAN 6604, 6622).
[469] HR Rep 94–1487 *Jurisdiction of United States Courts in Suits Against Foreign States*, 94th Cong.
(9 September 1976) at 23 (reprinted in 1976 USCCAN 6604, 6622).
[470] HR Rep 94–1487 *Jurisdiction of United States Courts in Suits Against Foreign States*, 94th Cong.
(9 September 1976) at 23 (reprinted in 1976 USCCAN 6604, 6622); but see discussion of due
process at 3.004 above.
[471] HR Rep 94–1487 *Jurisdiction of United States Courts in Suits Against Foreign States*, 94th Cong.
(9 September 1976) at 24 (reprinted in 1976 USCCAN 6604, 6623).
[472] See, eg, *Flatow v Islamic Republic of Iran*, 999 F Supp, 1, 6, n 1 (DDC 1998) (entering default
judgment against Iran); *Daliberti v Republic of Iraq*, 97 F Supp, 2d 38, 42 (DDC 2000) (defendant
Iraq served via the US Interests Section of the Polish Embassy in Baghdad).

the Hague Convention on Service Abroad of Judicial and Extrajudicial Documents.[473]

Thereafter, if there is no special arrangement and if the agency or instrumentality has no representative in the United States,

> service may be made under one of the three methods provided in subsection (b)(3). The first two methods provide for service by letter rogatory or request or by mail. The third method, sub-paragraph (C), authorizes a court to fashion a method of service, for example under rule 83, F.R. Civ. P., provided the method is "consistent with the law of the place where service is to be made". This latter language takes into account the fact that the laws of foreign countries may prohibit the service in their country of judicial documents by process servers from the United States. It is contemplated that no court will direct service upon a foreign state by appointing someone to make a physical attempt at service abroad, unless it is clearly consistent with the law of the foreign jurisdiction where service is to be attempted. It is also contemplated that the courts will not direct service in the United States upon diplomatic representatives,[474] or upon consular representatives[475].[476]

Courts have interpreted the FSIA's service requirements differently, depending on whether a foreign state, agency or instrumentality is involved. A majority of circuit courts now hold that strict compliance is necessary for service of a foreign state[477] or political subdivision under s 1608(a), while substantial compliance is allowed under s 1608(b) for service of an agency or instrumentality of a foreign government. At least one circuit court has reasoned that this is because foreign agencies or instrumentalities are "typically international commercial enterprises, [and] often possess a sophisticated knowledge of the United States legal system that other organs of foreign governments may lack".[478]

While a majority of courts have found that "substantial compliance" with the FSIA's service rules is adequate with respect to agencies and instrumentalities,

---

[473] HR Rep 94–1487 *Jurisdiction of United States Courts in Suits Against Foreign States*, 94th Cong. (9 September 1976) at 25 (reprinted in 1976 USCCAN 6604, 6624).

[474] *Hellenic Lines Ltd. v Moore*, 345 F 2d 978 (DC Cir 1965).

[475] *Oster v Dominion of Canada*, 144 F Supp, 746 (NDNY), aff'd, 238 F. 2d 400 (2d Cir. 1956), cert. denied, 353 US 936 (1957).

[476] HR Rep 94–1487 *Jurisdiction of United States Courts in Suits Against Foreign States*, 94th Cong. (9 September 1976) at 25 (reprinted in 1976 USCCAN 6604, 6624).

[477] The definition of the term "foreign state" is different in s 1608 than in other sections of the FSIA. For example, s 1603(a) defines the term "foreign state" broadly to include a political subdivision of a foreign state and an "agency or instrumentality" of a foreign state. Section 1608 clearly delineates among these entities. See, eg *In re Air Crash Disaster near Roselawn, Inc. on Oct. 31, 1994*, 96 F 3d 932, 940 (7th Cir. 1996).

[478] See *Transaero, Inc. v La Fuerza Aerea Boliviana*, 30 F 3d 148 (DC Cir 1994), cert. denied, 513 US 1150 (1995) (holding that Bolivian Air Force should be considered a "foreign state" or its "instrumentality" under § 1608, and requiring strict compliance with section 1608(a) and substantial compliance with s 1608(b)).

particularly where the defendant has actual notice of the suit,[479] some courts have held that mere technical violations of the statute will excuse otherwise perfect service even if the defendant had notice of the lawsuit.[480] In all, courts have not been consistent in applying "substantial compliance" with respect to service of process under the FSIA. In *Gerritsen v Consulado General de Mexico*, for example, the Ninth Circuit held that a failure to provide a translation of the summons and complaint rendered service defective under the FSIA.[481] In contrast, the Sixth Circuit, in *Sherer v Construcciones Aeronatuitcas, S.A.*, held that a plaintiff had substantially complied with s 1608(b) even where it failed to provide a translation of the summons and complaint.[482]

Courts note that whether a defendant has actual notice of the lawsuit is an important fact to consider when deciding whether substantial compliance should be allowed. In the *Sherer* case, for example, when examining service of process cases under the FSIA, the Sixth Circuit noted that "[t]he common theme running through the vast majority of these cases, whether [resounding in] 'substantial compliance' or 'strict compliance,' is the importance of actual notice to the defendants."[483]

Examples from case law

In *Seetransport Wiking Trader Schiffarhtsgesellschaft MBH & Co. Kommanditgesellschaft v Navimpex Centrala Navala*, the plaintiff sought to effect service of process upon a state-owned Romanian shipbuilding contractor pursuant to s 1608(b)(2) and s 1608(b)(3)(B).[484] The shipbuilding company had been dissolved by official state decree, and by that same decree, all its assets and liabilities were taken over by a newly formed company.[485] On these facts, the Second Circuit determined that service on the previously dissolved company complied with the requirements of s 1608(b)(3)(B) with respect to service upon the newly formed company.

In *Richmark Corp. v Timber Falling Consultants, Inc.*, the Ninth Circuit evaluated the types of service to be made under s 1608(b).[486] There, a third-party defendant Chinese company served pursuant to s 1608(b)(3)(B) sought relief from a default judgment arguing that service of process on Chinese entities should be made pursuant to s 1608(b)(3)(A).[487] The Ninth Circuit found this

---

[479] See, eg *Magness v Russia*, 54 F Supp, 2d 700, 705 (SD Tex 1999), aff'd on other grounds, 247 F 3d 609 (5th Cir. 2001); *Daly v Castroal Llanes*, 30 F Supp, 2d 407, 416–417 (SDNY 1998).

[480] *Transaero*, 30 F 3d at 148.

[481] In *Straub v A P Green, Inc*, 38 F 3d 448 (9th Cir. 1994) the Ninth Circuit clarified its decision in *Gerritsen*, 989 F 2d 340, 345 (9th Cir. 1993), stating that failure to deliver a translation of the complaint in the correct language "is such a fundamental defect that it fails both a 'strict compliance' test and a 'substantial compliance' test". [482] 987 F 2d 1246 (6th Cir. 1993).

[483] *Sherer*, 987 F 2d at 1246 (allowing substantial compliance with s 1608 where defendant made a timely motion to dismiss the amended complaint and had not denied that it had actual notice and where defendant could not show any prejudice resulting from the lacking translation because it was represented by a US law firm and filed all responses and reports in English).

[484] 989 F 2d 572, 579 (2d Cir. 1993). [485] 989 F 2d at 580.

[486] 937 F 2d 1444 (9th Cir. 1991), cert. denied, 506 US 903 (1992). [487] 937 F 2d at 1447.

contention to be unconvincing, because it was based on information outside the record supposedly obtained from the US State Department, and "the express language of s 1608(b)(3) provides that [a party] may effect service under subsections (A) *or* (B) *or* (C)."[488] As s 1608(b)(3) only applies if service cannot be made under s 1608(b)(1) or (2), the court in the *Richmark* case also examined s 1608(b)(2), which the third-party defendant asserted could have been used to effect proper service.[489] Reviewing the FSIA's legislative history, the Ninth Circuit held that the Consular Convention Between the United States and the People's Republic of China was "not an 'applicable international convention *on service of judicial documents*' under s 1608(b)(2)".[490]

In *Velidor v L/P/G Benghazi*,[491] the Third Circuit addressed the issue of whether service of process on a ship's master was sufficient to fulfill the requirements of s 1608(b) for serving the instrumentality of a foreign sovereign so as to confer personal jurisdiction over the instrumentality under s 1605(a)(2).[492] The court noted that "[u]nder the analytic structure of the [FSIA], the existence of subject matter and personal jurisdiction, the requisites for service of process, and the availability of sovereign immunity as a defense are intricately coordinated inquiries".[493] The court's inquiry as to whether s 1608(b)(2) had been satisfied focused on whether a ship's master is an "agent" of the ship's owner for the purpose of receiving process. "Inasmuch as the master . . . is employed by the owner and is the owner's general agent for conducting the ship's business, he should be regarded as an 'agent' for accepting process within the meaning of s 1608(b)(2)".[494] Analyzing the congressional intent behind s 1608, the court explained that "[r]ather than making service on foreign instrumentalities a rigid, technical, or cumbersome procedure, Congress sought to facilitate the ability of private plaintiffs to serve foreign entities. In addition, Congress wished to insure that the sovereign owner would receive actual notice." Where officers of the instrumentality:

> immediately become aware of the suit, service on the master fully achieved the objective of actual notice . . . for us to hold that the master was not [the instrumentality's] agent within the meaning of § 1608(b) would be to impose on plaintiffs a procedural burden at odds with the avowed congressional desire to expand the means of serving process on the instrumentalities of foreign sovereigns.[495]

Service upon a foreign embassy by mail does suffice under s 1608(a)(3).[496] Where an entity is considered a "foreign state or political subdivision" under s 1608 of the FSIA, strict compliance with the requirements of service is required.[497]

---

[488] 937 F 2d at 1447-1448.   [489] 937 F 2d at 1448.

[490] 937 F 2d at 1444 (emphasis in original).   [491] 653 F 2d, 812 (3d Cir. 1981).

[492] 653 F 2d at 812.   [493] 653 F 2d at 817.   [494] 653 F 2d at 821.

[495] 653 F 2d at 821.

[496] See *Alberti v Empresa Nicaraguense De La Carne*, 705 F 2d 250, 252–253 (7th Cir. 1983) (rejecting the plaintiffs' argument that summons and complaint served by mail upon the Ambassador of Nicaragua in Washington, District of Columbia was sufficient under § 1608(a)(3)).

[497] *Transaero*, 149–153.

Time of service—section 1608(c)

Section 1608(c) "establishes the time when service shall be deemed to have been made under each of the methods provided in subsections (a) and (b)".[498]

Default judgments—section 1608(e)   **3.085**

Courts entering default judgments under s 1608(e) have applied varying standards for determining whether a plaintiff has established a "claim or right to relief by evidence [that is] satisfactory to the Court".[499] Some courts apply a "clear and convincing evidence" standard.[500] Others require evidence sufficient to support summary judgment, ie, a *prima facie* case.[501] Other courts have required a showing of "satisfactory evidence as to each element of [plaintiffs'] claims".[502] In *Ungar v Islamic Republic of Iran*,[503] the court stated that the correct standard is the standard for granting judgment as a matter of law under Federal Rules of Civil Procedure, r 50(a)—ie, a legally sufficient evidentiary basis for a reasonable jury to find for the plaintiff.

Even after a default judgment has been rendered against it, a foreign state does not forgo its right to claim sovereign immunity under the FSIA or challenge the default judgment entered against it on the same ground.[504] In *MCI Telecommunications Corp. v Alhadhood*, for example, the Fifth Circuit held that a waiver of sovereign immunity implied from a foreign state's failure to appear would be inconsistent with the FSIA, s 1608(e) requiring the court to satisfy itself that jurisdiction exists prior to entering a default judgment. By failing to appear, the foreign state merely loses its right to defend on the merits.[505]

Courts have set aside entry of the default judgment against an instrumentality of a foreign state under Federal Rules of Civil Procedure, r 60(b) analysis. In *Amernational Industries, Inc. v Action-Tungsram, Inc.*,[506] the Sixth Circuit court saw some merit in arguments that the (1) judgment cannot be entered against an instrumentality of a foreign state under s 1608(e) without a trial on the merits, but that (2) a default judgment may be entered against an instrumentality of a foreign state as a sanction for abuse of discovery.[507] Although s 1608(e) clearly "does not relieve foreign instrumentalities of the duty to defend cases or to obey court orders," the strong public policy stated in the FSIA "of encouraging

---

[498] HR Rep No 94-1487, *Jurisdiction of United States Courts in Suits Against Foreign States*, 94th Cong. (9 September 1976) at 25 (reprinted in 1976 USCCAN 6604, 6624).

[499] 28 USC 1608(e).

[500] See, eg, *Weinstein v Islamic Republic of Iran*, 184 F Supp, 2d 13, 16 (DDC 2002).

[501] See, eg, *Hill v Republic of Iraq*, 175 F Supp, 2d 36, 38 n 4 (DDC 2001).

[502] See *Compania Interamericana Export-Import, S.A. v Compania Dominicana de Aviacion*, 88 F 3d 948, 951 (11th Cir. 1996).   [503] 211 F Supp, 2d 91, 97 (DDC 2002).

[504] See *MCI Telecommunications Corp. v Alhadhood*, 82 F 3d 658, 661–662. (5th Cir. 1996).

[505] 82 F 3d at 662. See also *Commercial Bank of Kuwait v Rafidain Bank*, 15 F 3d 238 (2d Cir 1994) (holding that when a district court properly enters a default judgment against a foreign sovereign based on a determination that the plaintiff's allegations are supported by evidence; nothing out of the ordinary is required, noting that s 1608(e) does not require evidentiary hearings or explicit findings where the record shows that the plaintiff provided sufficient evidence in support of its claims).

[506] 925 F 2d 970 (6th Cir. 1991).   [507] See *Amernational Industries*, 925 F 2d at 975.

foreign states and their instrumentalities to appear before United States courts and allowing the merits of cases involving foreign sovereigns to be considered completely and carefully" should not be ignored.[508] Factors to be considered when a court exercises its discretion on this issue included "the policy expressed in the statute and the broad divergence of cultural, governmental, and political practices between the United States [and the foreign state]".

In *Straub v A.C. Green, Inc.*, the Ninth Circuit held that the plaintiff was not required to serve notice of a default judgment under s 1608(e) upon the defendant which was an instrumentality of a foreign state.[509] There, the court concluded that the second sentence of § 1608(e) which requires service of a copy of the default judgment only refers to a foreign state or political subdivision. Additionally, "when the term foreign state is used in section 1608, it does not encompass instrumentalities of foreign states".[510]

Under s 1608(e), "a default judgment must be treated differently than an ordinary default judgment . . . [as] the claimant must 'establish his claim or right to relief,' and must do so by 'evidence satisfactory to the court' ".[511] In *Compania Interamericana Export-Import, S.A. v Compania Dominicana De Aviacion*,[512] the Eleventh Circuit held that "Congress intended § 1608(e) to provide foreign states protection from unfounded default judgments rendered solely upon a procedural default."[513] "Although explicit findings may not always be required, the record must show that 'the plaintiff provided sufficient evidence in support of its claims' and that the evidence was considered by the court before the default judgment was entered".[514]

3.086   28 U.S.C. § 1609

Immunity from attachment and execution of property of a foreign state

Subject to existing international agreements to which the United States is a party at the time of enactment of this Act the property in the United States of a foreign state shall be immune from attachment arrest and execution except as provided in sections 1610 and 1611 of this chapter.

Commentary

3.087   Legislative history

One of the primary objectives of the FSIA was to "remedy, in part, the . . . predicament of a plaintiff who has obtained judgment against a foreign state".[515]

---

[508] 925 F 2d at 976 (citations omitted).   [509] See *Straub*, 38 F 3d at 454.   [510] 38 F 3d at 448.
[511] *Compania Interamericana Export-Import S.A. v Compania Dominica De Avicion*, 88 F 3d 948, 951 (11th Cir. 1996).   [512] 88 F 3d at 950.
[513] 88 F 3d at 950–951, citing HR Rep No 94-1487, *Jurisdiction of United States Courts in Suits Against Foreign States*, 94th Cong. (9 September 1976) at 26 (reprinted in 1976 USCCAN 6604, 6625).
[514] 88 F 3d at 951.
[515] HR Rep No 94-1487, *Jurisdiction of United States Courts in Suits Against Foreign States*, 94th Cong. (9 September 1976) at 8 (reprinted in 1976 USCCAN 6604, 6606).

Prior to the FSIA's enactment, a foreign state "enjoy[ed] absolute immunity from execution, even in ordinary commercial litigation where commercial assets [were] available for satisfaction of a judgment".[516] Section 1609, read together with the provisions of s 1610 and 1611, was intended to narrow such immunity and "to conform the execution immunity rules more closely to the jurisdiction immunity rules" provided in ss 1604 and 1605.[517]

Congress also intended the FSIA "to render unnecessary the practice of seizing and attaching the property of a foreign government for the purpose of obtaining jurisdiction".[518] Prior to the enactment of the FSIA, a plaintiff could attach a foreign state's property in the United States for jurisdictional purposes where the foreign state was not entitled, under international law, to immunity from suit, and where the property attached was "commercial in nature".[519] Such attachments of a foreign state's property had created problems within both the judicial and the executive branches. United States courts were forced to become involved "in litigation not involving any significant US interest or jurisdictional contacts, apart from the fortuitous presence of property in the jurisdiction".[520] In addition, they also "caused significant irritation to many foreign governments" which, in turn, led to "serious friction in United States' foreign relations".[521]

Congress sought to correct these problems through two mechanisms. First, the FSIA "makes attachment for jurisdictional purposes unnecessary in cases where there is a nexus between the claim and the United States".[522] Second, the FSIA precludes such attachments through the general prohibition found in s 1609 coupled with the lack of an exception in ss 1610 and 1611.[523]

Application   **3.088**

Section 1609 sets forth the general rule that "the property of a foreign state, as defined in section 1603(a), is immune from attachment and from execution," subject to the exceptions provided in ss 1610 and 1611.[524] As with a claim of

---

[516] HR Rep No 94-1487, *Jurisdiction of United States Courts in Suits Against Foreign States*, 94th Cong. (9 September 1976) at 8 (reprinted in 1976 USCCAN 6604, 6606).

[517] HR Rep No 94-1487, *Jurisdiction of United States Courts in Suits Against Foreign States*, 94th Cong. (9 September 1976) at 8 (reprinted in 1976 USCCAN 6604, 6606).

[518] HR Rep No 94-1487, *Jurisdiction of United States Courts in Suits Against Foreign States*, 94th Cong. (9 September 1976) at 8 (reprinted in 1976 USCCAN 6604, 6606).

[519] HR Rep No 94-1487, *Jurisdiction of United States Courts in Suits Against Foreign States*, 94th Cong. (9 September 1976) at 26 (reprinted in 1976 USCCAN 6604, 6625) (citing *Wellamann v Chase Manhattan Bank*, 21 Misc. 2d 1086, 192 NYS2d 469 (Sup Ct NY 1959)).

[520] HR Rep No 94-1487, *Jurisdiction of United States Courts in Suits Against Foreign States*, 94th Cong. (9 September 1976) at 26 (reprinted in 1976 USCCAN 6604, 6625) (noting additionally that "[s]uch cases frequently require the application of foreign law to events which occur entirely abroad").

[521] HR Rep No 94-1487, *Jurisdiction of United States Courts in Suits Against Foreign States*, 94th Cong. (9 September 1976) at 27 (reprinted in 1976 USCCAN 6604, 6626).

[522] HR Rep No 94-1487, *Jurisdiction of United States Courts in Suits Against Foreign States*, 94th Cong. (9 September 1976) at 27 (reprinted in 1976 USCCAN 6604, 6626).

[523] HR Rep No 94-1487, *Jurisdiction of United States Courts in Suits Against Foreign States*, 94th Cong. (9 September 1976) at 8, 26–27 (reprinted in 1976 USCCAN 6604, 6606, 6625–6626).

[524] HR Rep No 94-1487, *Jurisdiction of United States Courts in Suits Against Foreign States*, 94th Cong. (9 September 1976) at 26 (reprinted in 1976 USCCAN 6604, 6625).

immunity from jurisdiction under s 1604, it is the burden of the party claiming immunity to present a *prima facie* case that it is protected by the FSIA.[525] The burden then shifts to the plaintiff to establish that one of the exceptions to immunity, as provided in ss 1610 and 1611, applies.[526] A foreign state's failure "to invoke Section 1609 in its initial response to the opposing party's requests for an order of attachment," however, may bar "as untimely any later assertion of Section 1609's prohibitions."[527]

Courts generally apply s 1609's immunity from "attachment arrest" broadly.[528] While s 1609 provides a foreign state with immunity from "attachment arrest," courts have extended its protection to include other devices that have a similar effect on a foreign state's property.[529] Immunity from attachment, therefore, prohibits an injunction barring a foreign state beneficiary of a letter of credit from drawing on its proceeds.[530] Similarly, where no exception to immunity applies, s 1609 preempts a state statute requiring an immune defendant to post prejudgment security.[531]

Although the immunity of s 1609 generally applies only when a foreign state is a defendant in an action, courts have also held that its protection prohibits garnishment of a debt owed by a foreign state garnishee.[532] In a garnishment action the garnishee is a third-party creditor of the defendant-debtor, and not itself a defendant.[533] Garnishment is commonly used to obtain *quasi in rem* jurisdiction

---

[525] See *Caribbean Trading and Fidelity Corp. v Nigerian Nat'l Petroleum Corp.*, 948 F 2d 111, 115 (2d Cir. 1991), cert. denied, 504 US 910 (1992).

[526] *Cf. Stena Rederi AB v Comision de Contratos del Comite Ejecutivo General del Sindicato Revolucionario de Trabajadores Petroleros de la Republica Mexicana, S.C.*, 923 F 2d 380, 389–390 (5th Cir. 1991) ("After Pemex made a prima facie showing of FSIA protection, Stena assumed a burden of going forward with some facts to show that an exception to immunity existed" (citation and internal quotes omitted)).

[527] *Caribbean Trading and Fidelity Corp*, 948 F 2d at 115 (holding that local procedural rule "precluding arguments raised for the first time on a motion for reconsideration . . . does not infringe on the prerogatives of a foreign state under the FSIA").

[528] See, eg, *Stephens v National Distillers and Chem. Corp.*, 69 F 3d 1226, 1230 (2d Cir. 1995) ("[T]he principle behind the prohibition against attachments should apply broadly"); *S & S Machinery Co. v Masinexportimport*, 706 F 2d 411, 418 (2d Cir. 1983) ("The FSIA would become meaningless if courts could eviscerate its protections merely by denominating their restraints as injunctions against the negotiation or use of property rather than as attachments of that property").

[529] See *S & S Mach. Co.*, 706 F 2d at 418 ("Once the district court held . . . that [the defendants] were protected from prejudgment attachment by the FSIA, the court properly refused to sanction any other means to effect the same result").

[530] See *S & S Mach. Co.*, 706 F 2d at 418. But see *Sperry Int'l Trade, Inc. v Government of Israel*, 689 F 2d 301, 305 n 7 (2d Cir. 1982) (holding that arbitrators' award ordering payment of proceeds of letter of credit into escrow account "is an in personam order, not an attachment of the sort forbidden by § 1609").

[531] See *Stephens*, 69 F 3d at 1230 (holding that foreign sovereign reinsurer was exempt from state statute requiring unlicensed insurers to post prejudgment security). *Cf. International Ins. Co. v Caja Nacional de Ahorro y Seguro*, 293 F 3d 392, 399 n 13 (7th Cir. 2002) (noting that "the language of the FSIA . . . refers to attachment arrest, not to pre-judgment security, although it has been interpreted to extend to both," but expressing "no opinion on whether attachment arrest and pre-judgment security are identical for purposes of the FSIA"). [532] See *Stena Rederi AB*, 923 F 2d at 392 n 18.

[533] See *Stena Rederi AB*, 923 F 2d at 391.

over the credits of a defendant-debtor when *in personam* jurisdiction over the defendant is unavailable.[534] A court may exercise such *quasi in rem* jurisdiction, however, only "to the extent that it has jurisdiction 'over a person who is indebted to, or owes a duty to the defendant' ".[535] The FSIA, however, is the only means of obtaining jurisdiction over a "foreign state," as the term is defined in s 1603(a).[536] Therefore, absent an exception to immunity, a foreign state is "entitled to invoke the shield of sovereign immunity, whether against direct claims or an indirect writ of garnishment."[537]

The term "property," as used in s 1609, is not defined in the Act and the courts have provided minimal guidance.[538]

28 U.S.C. § 1610   3.089

Exceptions to the immunity from attachment or execution

(a) The property in the United States of a foreign state, as defined in section 1603(a) of this chapter, used for a commercial activity in the United States, shall not be immune from attachment in aid of execution, or from execution, upon a judgment entered by a court of the United States or of a State after the effective date of this Act, if—

  (1) the foreign state has waived its immunity from attachment in aid of execution or from execution either explicitly or by implication, notwithstanding any withdrawal of the waiver the foreign state may purport to effect except in accordance with the terms of the waiver, or

  (2) the property is or was used for the commercial activity upon which the claim is based, or

  (3) the execution relates to a judgment establishing rights in property which has been taken in violation of international law or which has been exchanged for property taken in violation of international law, or

  (4) the execution relates to a judgment establishing rights in property—

   (A) which is acquired by succession or gift, or

   (B) which is immovable and situated in the United States: Provided, that such property is not used for purposes of maintaining a

---

[534] See *Stena Rederi AB*, 923 F 2d at 391.

[535] *Stena Rederi AB*, 923 F 2d at 391 (quoting *Belcher Co. of Alabama, Inc. v M/V Maramatha Mariner*, 724 F 2d 1161, 1164 (5th Cir. 1984)). In addition to personal jurisdiction over the garnishee, constitutional due process requires some nexus between the garnished debt and the plaintiff's cause of action against the defendant-debtor. See *Shaffer v Heitner*, 433 US 186, 212 (1977).

[536] See HR Rep No 94-1487, *Jurisdiction of United States Courts in Suits Against Foreign States*, 94th Cong. (9 September 1976) at 12 (reprinted in 1976 USCCAN 6604, 6610) ("This bill . . . sets forth the sole and exclusive standards to be used in resolving questions of sovereign immunity raised by foreign states before Federal and State courts in the United States"). See also *Argentine Republic v Amerada Hess Shipping Corp.*, 488 US 428 (1989); *Verlinden B.V. v Central Bank of Nigeria*, 461 US 480, 491 n 16 (1983).   [537] *Stena Rederi AB v Comision de Contratos*, 923 F 2d at 392 (5th Cir. 1991).

[538] See, eg, *In re B-27 Aircraft Serial No. 21010*, 272 F 3d 264, 272 n 2 (5th Cir. 2001) ("Our research has revealed *no* cases defining 'property' as used in § 1609").

diplomatic or consular mission or the residence of the Chief of such mission, or

(5) the property consists of any contractual obligation or any proceeds from such a contractual obligation to indemnify or hold harmless the foreign state or its employees under a policy of automobile or other liability or casualty insurance covering the claim which merged into the judgment, or

(6) the judgment is based on an order confirming an arbitral award rendered against the foreign state, provided that attachment in aid of execution, or execution, would not be inconsistent with any provision in the arbitral agreement, or

(7) the judgment relates to a claim for which the foreign state is not immune under section 1605(a)(7), regardless of whether the property is or was involved with the act upon which the claim is based.

(b) In addition to subsection (a), any property in the United States of an agency or instrumentality of a foreign state engaged in commercial activity in the United States shall not be immune from attachment in aid of execution, or from execution, upon a judgment entered by a court of the United States or of a State after the effective date of this Act, if—

(1) the agency or instrumentality has waived its immunity from attachment in aid of execution or from execution either explicitly or implicitly, notwithstanding any withdrawal of the waiver the agency or instrumentality may purport to effect except in accordance with the terms of the waiver, or

(2) the judgment relates to a claim for which the agency or instrumentality is not immune by virtue of section 1605(a) (2), (3), (5), or (7), or 1605(b) of this chapter, regardless of whether the property is or was involved in the act upon which the claim is based.

(c) No attachment or execution referred to in subsections (a) and (b) of this section shall be permitted until the court has ordered such attachment and execution after having determined that a reasonable period of time has elapsed following the entry of judgment and the giving of any notice required under section 1608(e) of this chapter.

(d) The property of a foreign state, as defined in section 1603(a) of this chapter, used for a commercial activity in the United States, shall not be immune from attachment prior to the entry of judgment in any action brought in a court of the United States or of a State, or prior to the elapse of the period of time provided in subsection (c) of this section, if—

(1) the foreign state has explicitly waived its immunity from attachment prior to judgment, notwithstanding any withdrawal of the waiver the

foreign state may purport to effect except in accordance with the terms of the waiver, and

(2) the purpose of the attachment is to secure satisfaction of a judgment that has been or may ultimately be entered against the foreign state, and not to obtain jurisdiction.

(e) The vessels of a foreign state shall not be immune from arrest in rem, interlocutory sale, and execution in actions brought to foreclose a preferred mortgage as provided in section 1605(d).

(f) (1) (A) Notwithstanding any other provision of law, including but not limited to section 208(f) of the Foreign Missions Act (22 U.S.C. 4308(f)), and except as provided in subparagraph (B), any property with respect to which financial transactions are prohibited or regulated pursuant to section 5(b) of the Trading with the Enemy Act (50 U.S.C. App. 5(b)), section 620(a) of the Foreign Assistance Act of 1961 (22 U.S.C. 2370(a)), sections 202 and 203 of the International Emergency Economic Powers Act (50 U.S.C. 1701–1702), or any other proclamation, order, regulation, or license issued pursuant thereto, shall be subject to execution or attachment in aid of execution of any judgment relating to a claim for which a foreign state (including any agency or instrumentality or such state) claiming such property is not immune under section 1605(a)(7).

   (B) Subparagraph (A) shall not apply if, at the time the property is expropriated or seized by the foreign state, the property has been held in title by a natural person or, if held in trust, has been held for the benefit of a natural person or persons.

(2) (A) At the request of any party in whose favor a judgment has been issued with respect to a claim for which the foreign state is not immune under section 1605(a)(7), the Secretary of the Treasury and the Secretary of State should make every effort to fully, promptly, and effectively assist any judgment creditor or any court that has issued any such judgment in identifying, locating, and executing against the property of that foreign state or any agency or instrumentality of such state.

   (B) In providing such assistance, the Secretaries—
      (i) may provide such information to the court under seal; and
      (ii) should make every effort to provide the information in a manner sufficient to allow the court to direct the United States Marshall's office to promptly and effectively execute against that property.

(3) Waiver.—The President may waive any provision of paragraph (1) in the interest of national security.

Commentary

3.090   Legislative history

Section 1610 sets forth circumstances under which the property of a foreign state is not immune from attachment or execution to satisfy a judgment. At the time the FSIA was enacted "the enforcement for judgments against foreign state property [was] a somewhat controversial subject in international law". Congress however took note of "a marked trend toward limiting the immunity from execution" when adopting s 1610.

"[T]he traditional view in the United States concerning execution has been that the property of foreign states is absolutely immune from execution".[539] Even after the "Tate Letter" of 1952, this continued to be the position of the Department of State and of the courts.[540] Sections 1610(a) and (b) are intended to modify this rule by partially lowering the barrier of immunity from execution, so as to make this immunity conform more closely with the provisions on jurisdictional immunity in the bill.

(a) Execution Against Property of Foreign States.—Section 1610(a) relates to execution against property of a foreign state, including a political subdivision, agency, or instrumentality of a foreign state. The term "attachment in aid of execution" is intended to include attachments, garnishments, and supplemental proceedings available under applicable Federal or State law to obtain satisfaction of a judgment. See rule 69, F.R. Civ. P. The property in question must be used for a commercial activity in the United States. If so, attachment in aid of execution, and execution, upon judgments entered by Federal or State courts against the foreign state would be permitted in any of the circumstances set forth in paragraphs (1)-(5) of section 1610(a).

Paragraph (1) relates to explicit and implied waivers, and is governed by the same principles that apply to waivers of immunity from jurisdiction under section 1605(a)(1) of the bill. A foreign state may have waived its immunity from execution, *inter alia*, by the provisions of a treaty, a contract, an official statement, or certain steps taken by the foreign state in the proceedings leading to judgment or to execution. As in section 1605(a)(1), a waiver on behalf of an agency or instrumentality of a foreign state may be made either by the agency or instrumentality or by the foreign state itself.

Paragraph (2) of section 1610(a) denies immunity from execution against property used by a foreign state for a commercial activity in the United States, provided that the commercial activity gave rise to the claim upon

---

[539] *Dexter and Carpenter, Inc. v Kunglig Jarnvags-styrelsen*, 43 F 2d 705 (2d Cir. 1930).
[540] See *Weilamann v Chase Manhattan Bank*, 21 Misc. 2d 1086, 192 NYS 2d 469, 473 (Sup Ct NY 1959).

which the judgment is based. Included would be commercial activities encompassed by section 1605(a)(2). The provision also includes a commercial activity giving rise to a claim with respect to which the foreign state has waived immunity under section 1605(a)(1). In addition, it includes a commercial activity which gave rise to a maritime lien with respect to which an admiralty suit was brought under section 1605(b). One could, of course, execute against commercial property other than a vessel or cargo which is the subject of a suit under section 1605(b), provided that the property was used in the same commercial activity upon which the maritime lien was based.

The language "is or was used" in paragraph (2) contemplates a situation where property may be transferred from the commercial activity which is the subject of the suit in an effort to avoid the process of the court. This language, however, does not bear on the question of whether particular property is to be deemed property of the entity against which the judgment was obtained. The courts will have to determine whether property "in the custody of" an agency or instrumentality is property "of" the agency or instrumentality, whether property held by one agency should be deemed to be property of another, whether property held by an agency is property of the foreign state. See *Prelude Corp. v. Owners of F/V Atlantic*, 1971, A.M.C. 2651 (N.D. Calif.); *American Hawaiian Ventures v. M.V.J. Latuharhary*, 257 F Supp, 622, 626 (D. N.J. 1966).

Paragraph (3) would deny immunity from execution against property of a foreign state which is used for a commercial activity in the United States and which has been taken in violation of international law or has been exchanged for property taken in violation of international law. See the analysis to section 1605(a)(3).

Paragraph (4) would deny immunity from execution against property of a foreign state which is used for a commercial activity in the United States and is either acquired by succession or gift or is immovable. Specifically exempted are diplomatic and consular missions and the residences of the chiefs of such missions. This exemption applies to all of the situations encompassed by sections 1610(a) and (b); embassies and related buildings could not be deemed to be property used for a "commercial" activity as required by section 1610(a); also, since such buildings are those of the foreign state itself, they could not be property of an agency or instrumentality engaged in a commercial activity in the United States within the meaning of section 1610(b).

Paragraph (5) of section 1610(a) would deny immunity with respect to obligations owed to a foreign state under a policy of liability insurance. Such obligations would after judgment be treated as property of the foreign state subject to garnishment or related remedies in aid or in place of execution. The availability of such remedies would, of course, be governed by applicable State or Federal law. Paragraph (5) is intended to facilitate recovery by individuals who may be injured in accidents, including those involving vehicles operated by a foreign state or by its officials, or employees acting within the scope of their authority.[541]

Paragraph (6) of s 1610(a) was added as part of the Act to Implement the Inter-American Convention on International Commercial Arbitration.[542]

Paragraph (7) of s 1610(a) was added by the Antiterrorism Effective Death Penalty Act of 1996.[543]

Section 1610(b) provides for execution against the property of agencies or instrumentalities of a foreign state in circumstances additional to those provided in section 1610(a). However, the agency or instrumentality must be engaged in a commercial activity in the United States. If so, the plaintiff may obtain an attachment in aid of execution or execution against any property, commercial and noncommercial, of the agency or instrumentality, but only in the circumstances set forth in paragraphs (1) and (2).

Paragraph (1) denies immunity from execution against any property of an agency or instrumentality engaged in a commercial activity in the United States, where the agency or instrumentality has waived its immunity from execution. See the analysis to paragraph (1) of section 1610(a).

Paragraph (2) of section 1610(b) denies immunity from execution against any property of an agency or instrumentality engaged in a commercial activity in the United States in order to satisfy a judgment relating to a claim for which the agency or instrumentality is not immune by virtue of section 1605(a)(2), (3) or (5), or 1605(b). Property will be subject to execution irrespective of whether the property was used for the same commercial or other activity upon which the claim giving rise to the judgment was based.

Section 1610(b) will not permit execution against the property of one agency or instrumentality to satisfy a judgment against another, unrelated agency or instrumentality. See *Prelude Corp. v. Owners of F/V Atlantic*, 1971 A.M.C. 2651 (N.D. Calif.). There are compelling reasons for this. If the U.S. law did not respect the separate juridical identities of different agencies or instrumentalities, it might encourage foreign jurisdictions to disregard the judicial divisions between different U.S. corporations or between a U.S. corporation and its independent subsidiary. However, a court might find that property held by one agency is really the property of another. See the analysis to section 1610(a)(2).

(c) Necessity of court order following reasonable notice.—Section 1610(c) prohibits attachment or execution under sections 1610(a) and (b)

---

[541] H Rep No 94-1487, *Jurisdiction of United States Courts in Suits Against Foreign States*, 94th Cong. (9 September 1976) at 28–29 (reprinted in 1976 USCCAM 6604, 6627–6628).

[542] An Act to Implement the Inter-American Convention on International Commercial Arbitration, Pub L 100-669, 102 Stat 3969 (16 November 1988).

[543] Antiterrorism Effective Death Penalty Act of 1996, Pub L 104-132, 110 Stat 1214 (14 April 1996).

unless the court has issued an order for such attachment and execution. In some jurisdictions in the United States, attachment and execution to satisfy a judgment may be had simply by applying to a clerk or to a local sheriff. This would not afford sufficient protection to a foreign state. This subsection contemplates that the courts will exercise their discretion in permitting execution. Prior to ordering attachment and execution, the court must determine that a reasonable period of time has elapsed following the entry of judgment, or in cases of a default judgment, since notice of the judgment was given to the foreign state under section 1608(e). In determining whether the period has been reasonable, the courts should take into account procedures, including legislation, that may be necessary for payment of a judgment by a foreign state, which may take several months; representations by the foreign state of steps being taken to satisfy the judgment; or any steps being taken to satisfy the judgment; or evidence that the foreign state is about to remove assets from the jurisdiction to frustrate satisfaction of the judgment.

(d) Attachments upon explicit waiver to secure satisfaction of a judgment.—Section 1610(d) relates to attachment against the property of a foreign state, or of a political subdivision, agency or instrumentality of a foreign state, prior to the entry of judgment or prior to the lapse of the "reasonable period of time" required under section 1610(c). Immunity from attachment will be denied only if the foreign state, political subdivision, agency or instrumentality has explicitly waived its immunity from attachment prior to judgment, and only if the purpose of the attachment is to secure satisfaction of a judgment that has been or may ultimately be entered against the foreign state and not to secure jurisdiction. This subsection provides, in cases where there has been an explicit waiver, a provisional remedy, for example to prevent assets from being dissipated or removed from the jurisdiction in order to frustrate satisfaction of a judgment.[544]

Subsection 1610(e) was added by An Act to amend the Foreign Sovereign Immunities Act with respect to admiralty jurisdiction.[545]

Subsection 1610(f) was added by the Treasury Department Appropriations **3.091** Act, 1999[546] and amended by the Victims of Trafficking and Violence Protection Act 2000.[547] President William J Clinton signed Presidential Determination

---

[544] HR Rep No 94-1487, *Jurisdiction of United States Courts in Suits Against Foreign States*, 94th Cong. (9 September 1976) at 29–30 (reprinted in 1976 USCCAN 6604, 6628–6629)

[545] An Act to Amend the Foreign Sovereign Immunities Act with Respect to Admiralty Jurisdiction, Pub L 100-640, 1025 Stat 333 (9 November 1988).

[546] Omnibus Consolidated and Emergency Supplemental Appropriations Act, Pub L 105-277, 112 Stat 2681, Div A, § 101(h) [Title I § 117(a)] (21 October 1998) (part of the Omnibus Consolidated and Emergency Supplemental Appropriations Act 1999).

[547] Victims of Trafficking and Violence Protection Act 2000, Pub L 106-386, 114 Stat 1464, § 2002(g)(1)(B) (28 October 2000).

2001–03, waiving the attachment provisions of s 1610(f)(1) in the interest of national security. The language of the determination is set forth below:

> Determination To Waive Attachment Provisions Relating To Blocked Property Of Terrorist-List States
>
> Memorandum for the Secretary of State [and] the Secretary of the Treasury
>
> By the authority vested in me as President by the Constitution and laws of the United States of America, including section 2002(f) of H.R. 3244, "Victims of Trafficking and Violence Protection Act of 2000 [section 2002(f) of Pub.L. 106-386, Div. C, Oct. 28, 2000, 114 Stat. 1543, amending this section]," (approved October 28, 2000), I hereby determine that subsection (f)(1) of section 1610 of title 28, United States Code, which provides that any property with respect to which financial transactions are prohibited or regulated pursuant to section 5(b) of the Trading with the Enemy Act (50 U.S. App. 5(b), section 620(a) of the Foreign Assistance Act of 1961 (22 U.S.C. 2370(a)), sections 202 and 203 of the International Emergency Economic Powers Act (50 U.S.C. 1701–1702), and proclamations, orders, regulations, and licenses issued pursuant thereto, be subject to execution or attachment in aid of execution of any judgment relating to a claim for which a foreign state claiming such property is not immune from the jurisdiction of courts of the United States or of the States under section 1605(a)(7) of title 28, United States Code, would impede the ability of the President to conduct foreign policy in the interest of national security and would, in particular, impede the effectiveness of such prohibitions and regulations upon financial transactions. Therefore, pursuant to section 2002(f) of H.R. 3244, the "Victim's [*sic; probably should be 'Victims'*] of Trafficking and Violence Protection Act of 2000," I hereby waive subsection (f)(1) of section 1610 of title 28, United States Code, in the interest of national security. This waiver, together with the amendment of subsection (f)(2) of the Foreign Sovereign Immunities Act [*probably means subsec. (f)(2) of this section*] and the repeal of the subsection (b) of section 117 of the Treasury and General Government Appropriations Act, 1999 [Pub.L. 105-277, Div. A, § 101(h) [Title I, § 117(b)], Oct. 21, 1998, 112 Stat. 2681-491; see Tables for classification] [amending section 1606 of this title], supersedes my prior waiver of the requirements of subsections (a) [amending this section] and (b) of said section 117, executed on October 21, 1998 [Presidential Determination No. 99-1, Oct. 21, 1998, 63 F.R. 59201, formerly set out as a note under this section].
>
> The Secretary of State is authorized and directed to publish this determination in the Federal Register.

WILLIAM J. CLINTON[548]

---

[548] Presidential Determination No 2001–03, 65 FR 66483 (28 October 2000).

Application **3.092**

Section 1610 provides plaintiffs with a means to enforce judgments entered against foreign states, political subdivisions, and their agencies and instrumentalities.[549] The section sets forth the exceptions to immunity from execution and attachment conferred under s 1609. "Section 1610 provides different regimes for sovereign states on the one hand, and their agencies and instrumentalities on the other".[550] Subsection 1610(a) "governs the immunity from execution of property belonging to foreign states . . . [s] 1610(b) governs the immunity from execution of property belonging to an 'agency or instrumentality' of a foreign state engaged in commercial activity in the United States".[551] Section 1610 also distinguishes between prejudgment attachment and post-judgment attachment in aid of execution.

The exceptions to immunity from execution and attachment are similar to the exceptions to jurisdictional immunity.[552] But the exceptions to immunity from execution and attachment are nevertheless narrower than the exceptions to jurisdictional immunity.[553] There are instances under the FSIA where Congress provided plaintiffs with a right and no remedy for relief.[554]

If the assets of a foreign state, political subdivision, or agency or instrumentality are not immune from attachment, federal courts apply Federal Rule of Civil Procedure, r 69(a), which requires application of local state procedural rules.[555]

Property of a foreign state used for commercial activity

Subsection 1610(a), "regarding property belonging directly to a foreign state, permits execution only narrowly, when the property is 'in the United States' and 'used for a commercial purpose in the United States' ".[556] Moreover, the suit must satisfy one of seven other criteria outlined in ss 1610(a)(1)–(7).[557] Subsection 1610(a) addresses execution and attachment in aid of execution; it does not address pre-judgment attachment.

Subsection 1610(a) permits execution upon a foreign state's property only if such property is "used for a commercial activity".[558] "Commercial activity" is

---

[549] See *Frolova v Union of Soviet Socialist Republics*, 558 F Supp, 358, 361 (ND Ill 1983), *aff'd*, 761 F 2d 370 (7th Cir. 1985).

[550] *Karaha Bodas Co. v Pertamina*, 313 F 3d 70, 82 (2d Cir. 2002), *cert. denied*, 123 S Ct 2256 (2003).

[551] *Connecticut Bank of Commerce v Republic of Congo*, 309 F 3d 240, 252 (5th Cir. 2002); *Karaha Bodas*, 313 F 3d, 82 ("Section 1610 provides different regimes for sovereign states on the one hand, and their agencies and instrumentalities on the other").

[552] *City of Englewood v Socialist People's Libyan Arab Jamahiriya*, 773 F 2d 31, 36 (3d Cir. 1985).

[553] See *Connecticut Bank*, 309 F 3d, 252 (citing *De Letelier v Republic of Chile*, 748 F 2d 790. 798–799 (2d Cir. 1984).

[554] See *De Letelier v Republic of Chile*, 748 F 2d 790, 798 (2d Cir. 1984), cert. denied, 471 US 1125 (1985). [555] See *Karaha Bodas*, 313 F 3d at 83.

[556] *Connecticut Bank*, 309 F 3d at 252.

[557] See 28 USC § 1610(a)(1)–(7). See also *Socialist People's Libyan Arab Jamahiriya*, 773 F 3d at 36. This requirement is discussed more fully below in this section.

[558] 28 USC § 1610(a); *Socialist People's Libyan Arab Jamahiriya*, 773 F 2d at 36.

defined in s 1603(d).[559] The commercial character of the activity is determined by reference to the nature of the course of conduct or particular transaction or act, rather than by reference to its purpose.[560] Therefore courts look to the nature of the conduct and if it is private in nature, or is an activity that a private party could do, then it is a commercial act.[561]

Property is "used for a commercial activity" when it is put in the service of a commercial activity.[562] The appropriate question for the court is not whether the property was acquired by a commercial transaction or was a proceed of commercial activity.[563] Proceeds of a commercial joint venture are immune, unless those proceeds are shown to be used for a commercial activity.[564] In contrast, property that is acquired through a non-commercial, governmental source may be subject to execution if that property is used for a commercial purpose.[565]

An example helps clarify the point. Consider an airplane owned by a foreign government and used solely to shuttle a foreign head-of-state back and forth for official visits. If the plane lands in the United States, it would not be subject to attachment or execution. The plane is not "used for" any commercial activity, in the US or elsewhere. It plainly would not matter how the foreign government bought the plane, raised the purchase price or otherwise came into ownership. Even if the government received the plane as payment from a US company in an obvious commercial transaction, that would not somehow transform the "use" of the plane into a commercial use. Regardless of how the government came to own the plane, a US court could never under the terms of the FSIA confiscate a plane used solely to transport a foreign head-of-state on official business. Attaching the plane and selling it in execution of judgment would go too far in interrupting the public acts of a foreign state.[566]

A foreign state's property that is used for a commercial activity in the United States is subject to attachment or execution only if one of seven criteria outlined in ss 1610(a)(1)–(7) is satisfied.

---

[559] See discussion at 3.020 above. See also *DeLetelier*, 748 F 2d at 795–798.

[560] 28 USC § 1603(d).

[561] See discussion at 3.020 above. See also *Republic of Argentina v Weltover*, 504 US 607, 614, (1992); *Holden v Canadian Consulate*, 92 F 3d 918 (9th Cir. 1996), cert. denied, 519 US 1091 (1997) (an employee of the consulate who had no ministerial duties, but rather promoted business was commercial activity); *Rush-Presbyterian-St. Luke's Medical Center v Hellenic Republic*, 877 F 2d 574 (7th Cir. 1989), cert. denied, 493 US 937 (1982); *De Letelier*, 748 F 2d at 790; *Texas Trading & Miller Corp. v Federal Republic of Nigeria*, 647 F 2d 300 (2d. Cir. 1981), cert. denied, 454 US 1148 (purchasing of cement contracts and related letters of credit was commercial activity even if purchased for purposes of developing country's infrastructure); *LeDonne v Gulf Air, Inc.*, 700 F Supp, 1400 (ED Va 1988); *International Ass'n of Machinists and Aerospace Workers (IAM) v Organization of Petroleum Exporting Countries (OPEC)*, 477 F Supp, 553 (CD Cal 1979), aff'd, 649 F 2d 1354 (9th Cir. 1989), cert. denied, 454 US 1163 (1981).   [562] *Connecticut Bank*, 309 F 3d at 254.

[563] *Socialist People's Libyan Arab Jamahiriya*, 773 F 2d, 36; *Connecticut Bank*, 309 F 3d, 251.

[564] *Connecticut Bank*, 309 F 3d, 251. See also *Socialist People's Libyan Arab Jamahiriya*, 773 F 2d at 37; *US v County of Arlington*, 669 F 2d 925, 934 (4th Cir.), cert. denied, 459 US 801 (1982).

[565] *Connecticut Bank*, 309 F 3d, 251. See also *Atwood Turnkey Drilling v Petroleo Brasileiro*, 875 F 2d 1174 (5th Cir. 1989), cert. denied, 493 US 1075 (1990).

[566] *Connecticut Bank*, 309 F 3d, 253.

Waiver

Section 1610(a)(1) provides that property used for commercial activity in the United States will not be immune from post-judgment attachment or execution if the foreign state explicitly or implicitly waived its immunity from attachment or execution.[567] The means by which a foreign state may waive immunity is discussed in detail at 3.030–3.033 above.

In rem nexus with commercial property

Subsection 1610(a)(2) was meant to mirror the commercial activities exception to jurisdictional immunity.[568] Therefore, property will not be immune from attachment and execution if it is used for commercial activity in the United States and is the subject of a suit brought under the commercial activities exception of s 1605(a)(2).[569] If the property in question is predominantly used for sovereign activities, ancillary commercial use will not strip the entire property of its immunity from attachment.[570]

Property taken in violation of international law

Subsection 1610(a)(3) is limited to the illegal expropriation of property.[571] It states that illegally expropriated property located in the United States, or exchanged for property located within the United States, is not immune from attachment (if that property is also used for a commercial activity). Courts have applied s 1605(a)(3) jurisprudence in construing s 1610(a)(3).[572] The Second Circuit has held that the expropriation exception solely applies to tangible property.[573] The Ninth Circuit, on the other hand, has adopted a broader

---

[567] See *Connecticut Bank*, 309 F 3d at 247; *Liberian Eastern Timber Corp. v Government of Republic of Liberia*, 659 F Supp, 606, 610–611 (DDC 1987).

[568] See *De Letelier*, 748 F 2d, 797 citing *Arango v Guzman Travel Advisors Corp.*, 621 F 2d 1371 (5th Cir. 1980).   [569] See *De Letelier*, 748 F 2d, 797.

[570] See *Birch Shipping v Embassy of the United Republic of Tanzania*, 507 F Supp, 311 (DDC 1980); *Liberian Eastern Timber Corp. v Government of Republic of Liberia*, 659 F Supp, 606, 610–611 (DDC 1986).

[571] *Brewer v Socialist People's Republic of Iraq*, 890 F 2d 97, 100 (8th Cir. 1989) ("As will be seen below, a coherent reading of Section 1610(a)(3) indicates a plaintiff may only execute pursuant to that section if such property has been expropriated").

[572] See *Brewer*, 890 F 2d at 101–102. See also discussion at 3.040–3.042 below.

[573] See *Menendez v Saks & Co.*, 485 F 2d 1355, 1372 (2d Cir. 1973), rev'd in part on other grounds sub nom. *Alfred Dunhill of London, Inc. v Republic of Cuba*, 425 US 682 (1976); *Leutwyler v Office of Her Majesty Queen Rania Al-Abdullah*, 184 F Supp, 2d 277, 289 n 13 (SDNY 2001) (expropriation exception not applicable to taking of usage rights to intellectual property); *Lord Day & Lord v Socialist Republic of Vietnam*, 134 F Supp, 2d 549 (SDNY 2001) (noting in dicta that less than a majority stock interest does not constitute rights in property); *Braka v Bancomer, S.A.*, 589 F Supp, 1465, 1472–1473 (SDNY 1984), aff'd, 762 F 2d 222 (2nd Cir. 1985); *Canadian Overseas Ores Ltd. v Compania de Acero del Pacifico S.A.*, 528 F Supp, 1337, 1346 (SDNY 1982), aff'd, 727 F 2d 274 (2nd Cir. 1984) (holding that s 1605(a)(3) is not applicable to a contractual right to be paid). See also *Sampson v Federal Republic of Germany*, 975 F Supp, 1108, 1117 (ND Ill 1997), aff'd, 250 F 3d 1145 (7th Cir. 2001) (right to receive payments does not constitute property) (citing *Hirsh v State of Israel*, 962 F Supp, 377, 382–383 (SDNY 1997).

construction of "rights in property" which includes at least certain rights in intangible personal property.[574]

Rights in gift or immovable property

Subsection 1610(a)(4) relates to judgments establishing rights in property. Generally, judgments concerning property in the United States are enforceable against foreign sovereign defendants.[575] Specifically exempted from this general rule are diplomatic and consular missions and the residences of the chiefs of such missions.[576] In addition, living quarters for diplomatic mission staff other than the Chief of Mission may be considered non-commercial-use property and therefore immune from attachment and execution.[577]

Liability or casualty insurance

Subsection 1610(a)(5) is intended "to facilitate recovery by individuals who may be injured in accidents, including those involving vehicles operated by a foreign state or by its officials, or employees acting within the scope of their authority".[578] There are no published decisions addressing this section.

Arbitral awards

Subsection 1610(a)(6) provides that a party may attach the property of a foreign state, which is used for commercial purposes, in order to enforce an order confirming an arbitral award. There is no requirement of any nexus between the subject matter of the underlying arbitration and the property sought for attachment in aid of execution.[579]

Terrorism

Subsection 1610(a)(7) was added by the Antiterrorism Effective Death Penalty Act 1996. The subsection "created an exception to the sovereign immunity of those foreign states officially designated by the Department of State as terrorist states if the foreign state commits a terrorist act, or provides material support and resources to an individual or entity that commits such an act".[580] This subsection

---

[574] See *West v Multibanco Comermex, S.A.*, 807 F 2d 820, 826, 830–831 (9th Cir. 1987) (holding that at least some intangible property rights, including contractual rights involved in certificates of deposits, are rights in property for purposes of the expropriation exception). See also *Kalmazoo Spice Extraction Co. v Provisional Military Gov't of Socialist Ethiopia*, 616 F Supp, 660, 663 (WD Mich 1985) (holding that a majority interest in a company's stock does constitute rights in property).

[575] *2 Tudor City Place Associates v Libyan Arab Republic Mission to U.N.*, 121 Misc. 2d 945 (NY City Civ Ct 1983).

[576] *Socialist People's Libyan Arab Jamahiriya*, 773 F 2d at 37. See also *S & S Machinery Co. v Masinexportimport*, 802 F Supp, 1109, 1109 (SDNY 1992).

[577] *US v County of Arlington*, 702 F 2d at 488 (4th Cir. 1983).

[578] HR Rep No 94-1487, *Jurisdiction of United States Courts in Suits Against Foreign States*, 94th Cong. (9 September 1976) at 29 (reprinted in 1976 USCCAM 6604, 6628).

[579] See *Lloyd's Underwriters v AO Gazsnabtranzit*, 2000 WL 1719493, *1 (ND Ga Nov 2, 2000).

[580] *Flatow v Islamic Republic of Iran*, 308 F 3d 1065, 1067 (9th Cir. 2002), cert. denied, 123 S Ct 1632 (2003).

is of little practical use because foreign states designated as state sponsors of terrorism are unlikely to keep assets in the United States for commercial purposes. Indeed, at the time of writing, no plaintiff has employed subsection 1610(a)(7) with success.

Agencies and instrumentalities

3.093

Section 1610 treats agencies and instrumentalities of a foreign state differently from the foreign state itself.[581] Subsection 1610(b) is intended to be less restrictive than s 1610(a).[582] If an agency or instrumentality of a foreign state is engaged in commercial activity, property belonging to that agency or instrumentality may be subject to attachment regardless of whether the property is used for a commercial activity.[583]

Though the property of an instrumentality or agency may be subject to execution or attachment if there is a judgment against that instrumentality or agency, assets of an instrumentality or agency are *not* subject to attachment or execution under s 1610 *solely* because the *foreign state* itself is found liable. Rather, if the state is found liable, courts must determine whether property of an instrumentality or agency should be treated as property of the foreign state for the purposes of attachment or execution in aid of judgment.[584]

Court orders

Pursuant to s 1610(c), only a court, not a clerk of court or sheriff, may enter an order of attachment or execution against a foreign state's property.[585] The court may issue such an order only after "determining that a reasonable period of time has elapsed" following judgment, thus allowing a foreign state the time necessary to pass necessary legislation or make alternate payment arrangements.[586] Nothing in subsection 1610(c) refers to the court conferring judgment on the merits or makes any determination regarding the amenability of property to attachment or execution.[587]

Prejudgment attachment

3.094

Subsection 1610(d) addresses prejudgment attachment. Significantly, attachment *prior* to a judgment may occur only if the purpose of attachment is to satisfy a future judgment, and *not* to secure jurisdiction over a foreign state.[588] As long as the purpose is to obtain security, it is irrelevant that an effect of the

---

[581] *Banco Para El Commercio Exterior de Cuba v First National City Bank*, 658 F 2d 913, 919 (2d Cir. 1981); *Karaha Bodas*, 313 F 3d at 83.

[582] See *Connecticut Bank*, 309 F 3d, 252–253, citing *De Letelier*, 748 F 2d, 799; *Karaha Bodas*, 313 F 3d at 83.   [583] See *Connecticut Bank*, 309 F 3d at 252.

[584] See *First National City Bank v Banco Para El Commercio Exterior de Cuba (Bancec)*, 462 US 611, 621 n 8 (1983). Courts use the conceptual framework provided by the Supreme Court in the *Bancec* case to determine whether an agency or instrumentality is a separate juridical entity from the foreign state. See, eg, *DeLetelier*, 748 F 2d at 790.   [585] See *Connecticut Bank*, 309 F 3d at 247.

[586] See *Connecticut Bank*, 309 F 3d at 250.   [587] See *Connecticut Bank*, 309 F 3d at 250.

[588] See *Mangattu v M/V IBN Hayyan*, 35 F 3d 205, 209 (5th Cir. 1994).

attachment may be that it confers jurisdiction.[589] Subsection 1610(d) has been interpreted to include prejudgment security as well as attachment arrest.[590]

Waiver and prejudgment attachment

The FSIA exception which allows attachment prior to judgment, and prior to the time period designated by s 1610(c), is more narrow than that for post-judgment attachment and execution.

Waiver under s 1610(d), unlike waiver under ss 1610(a) and (b), must be explicit.[591] The waiver does not, however, have to explicitly state that it is a "pre-judgment attachment" waiver.[592] "Rather, a waiver of immunity from prejudgment attachment must be explicit in the common sense meaning of that word: the asserted waiver must demonstrate unambiguously the foreign state's intention to waive its immunity from prejudgment attachment".[593]

In *Libra Bank v Banco National de Costa Rica*, the Second Circuit held that the words "prejudgment attachment" are not required for a waiver to be explicit.[594] Rather, the requirement of an explicit waiver was intended to preclude an unintentional waiver. Thus, there was an explicit waiver under s 1610(d) on language that a party unconditionally waives "any right or immunity from legal proceedings including suit judgment or execution on grounds of sovereignty".[595] Likewise, in the Eleventh Circuit, explicit waiver was found where one party was entitled "to attach the cargo for the payment of the freight, dead freight, demurrages and losses due to detention," the reference to attachment encompassing both prejudgment and post-judgment attachment.[596]

However, the Second Circuit did not find an explicit waiver where a treaty provided that the sovereign could not claim immunity "from suit, execution of judgment, or from any other liability to which a privately owned and controlled enterprise is subject".[597] The Second Circuit also did not find explicit waiver where the sovereign, per a trade agreement, could not "claim or enjoy immunities from suit or execution of judgment or other liability . . . with respect to commercial or financial transactions . . ."[598] In both cases, the court found that "other liability" did not explicitly encompass prejudgment attachment, in particular stating in *S & S Machinery v Masinexport* that attachments are provisional remedies rather than liabilities.[599]

---

[589] See *Venus Lines Agency v CVG Industria Venezolana de Aluminio*, 210 F 3d 1309, 1312 (11th Cir. 2000).

[590] See *International Insurance Co. v Caja Nacional de Ahorro y Seguro*, 293 F 3d 392, 399 n 13 (7th Cir. 2002) (citing *Stephens v National Distillers*, 62 F 3d 1226, 1229–1230 (2d Cir. 1995)).

[591] *International Ins. Co*, 293 F 3d, 399; *Venus Lines Agency*, 210 F 3d at 1311.

[592] See *Banco de Seguros del Estado v Mutual Marine Office, Inc.*, 344 F 3d 255 (2d Cir. 2003); *S & S Machinery Co. v Masinexportimport*, 706 F 2d 411, 416 (2d Cir.), cert. denied, 464 US 850 (1983); *Libra Bank Ltd. v Banco Nacional de Costa Rica*, 676 F 2d 47, 49–50 (2d Cir.1982).

[593] *Banco de Seguros del Estado*, 344 F 3d at 255.   [594] *Libra Bank*, 676 F 2d at 49.

[595] *Libra Bank*, 676 F 2d at 50, 49.   [596] *Venus Lines Agency*, 210 F 3d at 1311–1312.

[597] *O'Connell Machinery Co v M.V. Americana*, 734 F 2d 115, 117 (2d Cir.), cert. denied, 469 US 1086 (1984).   [598] *S & S Mach. Co.*, 706 F 2d at 417.

[599] *S & S Mach. Co.*, 706 F 2d at 417, citing *Libra Bank*, 676 F 2d at 50.

Blocked assets **3.095**

Subsection 1610(f)(1)(A) provides that a foreign state's "property with respect to which financial transactions are prohibited or regulated" pursuant to, among other Acts, the International Emergency Economic Powers Act (50 USC 1701–1702) ("IEEPA"), are subject to attachment or execution of judgments relating to a claim for which the foreign state (or its agency or instrumentality) is not immune under s 1605(a)(7).[600] The Second Circuit has found that transactions authorized by a license from the Treasury Department's Office of Foreign Assets Control ("OFAC"), are, by the plain terms of the Office's regulatory programs, "regulated" under IEEPA.[601]

Subsection 1610(f)(1)(A) does not create liabilities for agencies and instrumentalities of foreign states, where judgments have been levied only against the foreign state and not the agencies or instrumentalities themselves.[602] As with s 1610(b), s 1610(f)(1)(A) does not allow a plaintiff to seek to satisfy a judgment against a foreign state by attachment or execution of assets of a foreign state's instrumentality or agency, unless the instrumentality or agency is found not to be a separate juridical entity from the state.[603]

The FSIA, s 1610(f)(1)(A) permits the attachment of a wide array of foreign property in satisfaction of judgments held against state sponsors of terrorism. Subsection 1610(f)(3), however, empowers the President to waive the broad attachment provisions of s 1610(f)(1)(A) in the interests of national security. The very day that s 1610(f)(1)(a) was signed into law, President Clinton issued Presidential Determination No 2001-03, which waived the plaintiffs' rights to attach blocked assets under the subsection.[604]

28 U.S.C. § 1610 note[605] **3.096**

Treatment of Terrorist Assets

(a) In general.—Notwithstanding any other provision of law, and except as provided in subsection (b) [of this note], in every case in which a person has obtained a judgment against a terrorist party on a claim based upon an act of terrorism, or for which a terrorist party is not immune under section 1605(a)(7) of title 28, United States Code, the blocked assets of that

---

[600] 28 USC § 1610(f)(1)(A).

[601] *Flatow v Islamic Republic of Iran*, 305 F 3d 1249, 1255 (DC Cir 2002).

[602] *Flatow*, 308 F 3d at 1069.

[603] *Flatow*, 308 F 3d at 1068. As is mentioned at 3.093 above, Courts use the *Bancec* case, *First National City Bank v Banco Para El Commercio Exterior de Cuba (Bancec)*, 462 US 611, 621 n 8 (1983), as a guide in determining separate juridical entity status.

[604] See Presidential Determination No 2001-03, 65 FR 66483 (28 October 2000), see 3.091 above. See also *Ministry of Defense and Support for Armed Forces of Islamic Republic of Iran v Cubic Defense Systems, Inc.*, 236 F Supp 2d 1140 (SD Cal 2002).

[605] Terrorism Risk Insurance Act 2002, Pub L 107-297, 116 Stat. 2322, Title II, § 201(a), (b), (d) (26 November 2002).

terrorist party (including the blocked assets of any agency or instrumentality of that terrorist party) shall be subject to execution or attachment in aid of execution in order to satisfy such judgment to the extent of any compensatory damages for which such terrorist party has been adjudged liable.

(b) Presidential waiver.—

    (1) In general.—Subject to paragraph (2), upon determining on an asset-by-asset basis that a waiver is necessary in the national security interest, the President may waive the requirements of subsection (a) [of this note] in connection with (and prior to the enforcement of) any judicial order directing attachment in aid of execution or execution against any property subject to the Vienna Convention on Diplomatic Relations or the Vienna Convention on Consular Relations.

    (2) Exception.—A waiver under this subsection shall not apply to—

        (A) property subject to the Vienna Convention on Diplomatic Relations or the Vienna Convention on Consular Relations that has been used by the United States for any nondiplomatic purpose (including use as rental property), or the proceeds of such use; or

        (B) the proceeds of any sale or transfer for value to a third party of any asset subject to the Vienna Convention on Diplomatic Relations or the Vienna Convention on Consular Relations.

(d) Definitions.—In this section [this note] the following definitions shall apply:

    (1) Act of terrorism.—The term "act of terrorism" means—

        (A) any act or event certified under section 102(1) [Pub.L. 107-297, Title I, § 102(1), Nov. 26, 2002, 116 Stat. 2323, which is set out in a note under 15 U.S.C.A. § 6701]; or

        (B) to the extent not covered by subparagraph (A), any terrorist activity (as defined in section 212(a)(3)(B)(iii) of the Immigration and Nationality Act (8 U.S.C. 1182(a)(3)(B)(iii))).

    (2) Blocked asset.—The term "blocked asset" means—

        (A) any asset seized or frozen by the United States under section 5(b) of the Trading With the Enemy Act (50 U.S.C. App. 5(b)) or under sections 202 and 203 of the International Emergency Economic Powers Act (50 U.S.C. 1701; 1702); and

        (B) Does not include property that—

            (i) is subject to a license issued by the United States Government for final payment, transfer, or disposition by or to a person subject to the jurisdiction of the United States in connection with a transaction for which the issuance of such license has been specifically required by statute other than the International

Emergency Economic Powers Act (50 U.S.C. 1701 et seq.) or the United Nations Participation Act of 1945 (22 U.S.C. 287 et seq.); or

(ii) in the case of property subject to the Vienna Convention on Diplomatic Relations or the Vienna Convention on Consular Relations, or that enjoys equivalent privileges and immunities under the law of the United States, is being used exclusively for diplomatic or consular purposes.

(3) Certain property.—The term "property subject to the Vienna Convention on Diplomatic Relations or the Vienna Convention on Consular Relations" and the term "asset subject to the Vienna Convention on Diplomatic Relations or the Vienna Convention on Consular Relations" mean any property or asset, respectively, the attachment in aid of execution or execution of which would result in a violation of an obligation of the United States under the Vienna Convention on Diplomatic Relations or the Vienna Convention on Consular Relations, as the case may be.

(4) Terrorist party.—The term "terrorist party" means a terrorist, a terrorist organization (as defined in section 212(a)(3)(B)(vi) of the Immigration and Nationality Act (8 U.S.C. 1182(a)(3)(B)(vi))), or a foreign state designated as a state sponsor of terrorism under section 6(j) of the Export Administration Act of 1979 (50 U.S.C. App. 2405(j)) or section 620A of the Foreign Assistance Act of 1961 (22 U.S.C. 2371)."

Commentary

Legislative history   **3.097**

Section 1610 was further revised by the Terrorism Risk Insurance Act 2002, approved on 26 November 2002 ("TRIA").[606] As stated by the conference report to the TRIA:

the purpose of [this note] is to deal comprehensively with the problem of enforcement of judgments rendered on behalf of victims of terrorism in any court of competent jurisdiction by enabling them to satisfy such judgments through the attachment of blocked assets of terrorist parties. It [was] the intent of the Conferees that [this note] establish that such judgments are to be enforced. [This note] builds upon and extends the principles in section 1610(f)(1) of the Foreign Sovereign Immunities Act (28 U.S.C. § 1610(f)(1)), authorizes the enforcement of judgments against terrorist organizations and eliminates the effect of any Presidential waiver issued

---

[606] Terrorism Risk Insurance Act of 2002, Pub L 107-297, Title II, § 201(a), (b), (d), 116 Stat 2322, 2337 (26 November 2002).

prior to the date of enactment purporting to bar or restrict enforcement of such judgments, thereby making clear that all such judgments are enforceable against any assets or property under any authorities referenced in Section 1610(f)(1).[607]

There is, however, Presidential authority to waive the provisions of this note in the interests of national security on an "asset-by-asset basis" with certain restrictions.[608]

3.098　　　Application

This subsection is not an appropriation by Congress of frozen assets to compensate the victims of terrorism.[609] The Second Circuit has held that:

> the plain meaning of [this note] is to give terrorist victims who actually receive favorable judgments a right to execute against assets that would otherwise be blocked. . . . [I]t confers no entitlement on victims who have not yet obtained judgments. Neither does it guarantee that any blocked assets will in fact be available when a particular victim seeks to execute on a judgment.[610] However, plaintiffs have succeeded in attaching assets under this note.[611]

Despite the narrow waiver provision of the TRIA, "nothing in the statutory language evinces Congressional intent to divest the President of authority to confiscate terrorist assets as provided in IEEPA § 1702(a)(1)(C)".[612] In cases where the blocked assets of a terrorist state are in the possession of the federal government the question of whether the federal government has waived its own sovereign immunity from suit is critical.[613] In *Weinstein v Islamic Republic of Iran*,[614] the court held that the TRIA did not amount to an explicit waiver of the US government's immunity from suit and therefore the plaintiffs could not attach two bank accounts deemed the property of the United States.

3.099　28 U.S.C. § 1611

Certain Types of Property Immune from Execution

(a) Notwithstanding the provisions of section 1610 of this chapter, the property of those organizations designated by the President as being entitled to enjoy the privileges, exemptions, and immunities provided by the International

---

[607] HR Rep No 107-779, *The Conference Report to Accompany HR. 3210—Terrorism Risk Protection Act*, Statement of the Managers, 4 (13 November 2002).

[608] 28 USC § 1610 (note)(b).

[609] See *Smith ex rel. Estate of Smith v Federal Reserve Bank of New York*,—F 3d—, 2003 WL 22272577 (2d Cir. 2003).　　　　　[610] *Smith*, 2003 WL 22272577 at *6.

[611] See *Weinstein v Islamic Republic of Iran*, 274 F Supp 2d 53 (DDC 2003); *Daliberti v J.P Morgan Chase & Co.*, 2003 WL 340734 (SDNY Feb. 5, 2003).

[612] *Smith*, 2003 WL 22272577 at *6.　　　　　[613] See *Weinstein*, 274 F Supp 2d at 53.

[614] 274 F Supp 2d at 53.

Organizations Immunities Act shall not be subject to attachment or any other judicial process impeding the disbursement of funds to, or on the order of, a foreign state as the result of an action brought in the courts of the United States or of the States.

(b) Notwithstanding the provisions of section 1610 of this chapter, the property of a foreign state shall be immune from attachment and from execution, if-

    (1) the property is that of a foreign central bank or monetary authority held for its own account, unless such bank or authority, or its parent foreign government, has explicitly waived its immunity from attachment in aid of execution, or from execution, notwithstanding any withdrawal of the waiver which the bank, authority or government may purport to effect except in accordance with the terms of the waiver; or

    (2) the property is, or is intended to be, used in connection with a military activity and

        (A) is of a military character, or

        (B) is under the control of a military authority or defense agency.

(c) Notwithstanding the provisions of section 1610 of this chapter, the property of a foreign state shall be immune from attachment and from execution in an action brought under section 302 of the Cuban Liberty and Democratic Solidarity (LIBERTAD) Act of 1996 to the extent that the property is a facility or installation used by an accredited diplomatic mission for official purposes.

Commentary

Legislative history   **3.100**

Due largely to foreign relations concerns, s 1611 preserves immunity from execution and attachment for certain types of property notwithstanding the provisions of s 1610. As stated by the House Report:

> Section 1611 exempts certain types of property from the immunity provisions of section 1610 relating to attachment and execution.
>
>   (a) Property held by international organizations.—Section 1611(a) precludes attachment and execution against funds and other property of certain international organizations. The purpose of this subsection is to permit international organizations designated by the President pursuant to the International Organizations Immunities Act, 22 U.S.C. 288, et seq., to carry out their functions from their offices located in the United States without hindrance by private claimants seeking to attach the payment of funds to a foreign state; such attachments would also violate the immunities accorded to such international institutions. See also article 9, section 3 of the Articles of Agreement of the International Monetary Fund, TIAS

1501, 60 Stat. 1401. International organizations covered by this provision would include, *inter alia*, the International Monetary Fund and the World Bank. The reference to "international organizations" in this subsection is not intended to restrict any immunity accorded to such international organizations under any other law or international agreement.

(b) Central bank funds and military property.—Section 1611(b)(1) provides for the immunity of central bank funds from attachment or execution. It applies to funds of a foreign central bank or monetary authority which are deposited in the United States and "held" for the bank's or authority's "own account"—i.e., funds used or held in connection with central banking activities, as distinguished from funds used solely to finance the commercial transactions of other entities or of foreign states. If execution could be levied on such funds without an explicit waiver, deposit of foreign funds in the United States might be discouraged. Moreover, execution against the reserves of foreign states could cause significant foreign relations problems.

Section 1611(b)(2) provides immunity from attachment and execution for property which is, or is intended to be, used in connection with a military activity and which fulfills either of two conditions: the property is either (A) of a military character or (B) under the control of a military authority or defense agency. Under the first condition, property is of a military character if it consists of equipment in the broad sense—such as weapons, ammunition, military transport, warships, tanks, communications equipment. Both the character and the function of the property must be military. The purpose of this condition is to avoid frustration of United States foreign policy in connection with purchases of military equipment and supplies in the United States by foreign governments.

The second condition is intended to protect other military property, such as food, clothing, fuel and office equipment which, although not of a military character, is essential to military operations. "Control" is intended to include authority over disposition and use in addition to physical control, and a "defense agency" is intended to include civilian defense organizations comparable to the Defense Supply Agency in the United States. Each condition is subject to the overall condition that property will be immune only if its present or future use is military (e.g., surplus military equipment withdrawn from military use would not be immune). Both conditions will avoid the possibility that a foreign state might permit execution on military property of the United States abroad under a reciprocal application of the act.[615]

Subsection 1611(c) was added to the FSIA as part of the Cuban Liberty and Democratic Solidarity (LIBERTAD) Act 1996.[616]

---

[615] HR Rep No 94-1487, *Jurisdiction of United States Courts in Suits Against Foreign States*, 94th Cong. (9 September 1976) at 31 (reprinted in 1976 USCCAM 6604, 6630).
[616] Cuban Liberty and Democratic Solidarity (LIBERTAD) Act 1996, Pub L 104-114, 110 Stat 785 (12 March 1996). One of the purposes of LIBERTAD is to "protect United States nationals

Application **3.101**

Property of designated international organizations

The International Organizations Immunities Act 1945 ("IOIA"),[617] grants to international organizations which are designated by the President "the same immunity from suit and every form of judicial process as is enjoyed by foreign governments, except to the extent that such organizations may expressly waive their immunity for the purpose of any proceedings or by the terms of any contract." Subsection 1611(a) makes clear that the grant of immunity under the IOIA survives the exceptions to immunity set forth in s 1610.

Under the IOIA, designated organizations enjoy absolute immunity from attachment and execution. Therefore, designated organizations enjoy a greater degree of immunity from attachment and execution than foreign states themselves.[618] Only specific reservations to immunity set forth by the President in an executive order[619] or an express waiver,[620] can defeat a designated organization's immunity from attachment and execution.

Property of foreign central banks or monetary authority

To enjoy the protection afforded by s 1611(b)(1), a defendant must establish that it is a foreign central bank or monetary authority. "Naked assertions"[621] of attorneys are insufficient.[622] Courts have indicated that accompanying documentary evidence, such as an affidavit from the country's ambassador, will be adequate.[623]

Pursuant to s 1611(b)(1), the property of a foreign central bank or monetary authority that is held for its own account is immune from attachment and execution. "Any funds in an account in the name of a foreign central bank are . . . funds 'of' that foreign central bank".[624]

Funds that are held by a foreign central bank "for its own account" are funds used to perform functions that are "normally understood to be [the functions] of a nation's central bank" rather than to finance the commercial transactions of

---

against confiscatory takings and the wrongful trafficking in property confiscated by the Castro regime." See Pub L 104-114, 3 (6).

[617] 22 USC § 288a(b).

[618] See *Atkinson v Inter-American Development Bank*, 156 F 3d 1335 (DC Cir 9 October 1998); *Broadbent v Organization of American States*, 628 F 2d 27, 31 (DDC 1980).

[619] 22 USC § 288.

[620] To establish express waiver, there must be a clear, complete, unambiguous and unmistakable manifestation of designated organization's intent to waive its immunity. See discussion at 3.032–3.033 above. See also *Aquinda v Texaco*, 175 FRD 50, 52 (SDNY 1997), vacated on other grounds sub. nom, *Jota v Texaco, Inc.*, 157 F 3d 153 (2d Cir. 1998); *Libra Bank Ltd. v Banco Nacional De Costa Rica, S.A.*, 676 F 2d 47, 49 (2d Cir. 1982).

[621] In *Sesostris, S.A.E. v Transportes Navales, S.A.*, 727 F Supp 737, 743–744 (D Mass 1989), one attorney's affidavit stating that the entity seeking immunity was a "state-owned and controlled bank" was by itself insufficient to establish that it was the "foreign central bank or central banking authority."

[622] See *International Insurance Co. v Caja Nacional de Ahorro y Seguro*, 293 F 3d 392 (7th Cir. 2002).

[623] See *Sesostris, S.A.E.*, 727 F Supp, at 737. See also *International Ins. Co.*, 293 F 3d at 398; *Weston Compagnie de Finance et d'Investissement, S.A. v La Republica del Ecuador*, 823 F Supp 1106, 1111 n 6 (SDNY 1993). [624] *Weston*, 823 F Supp, at 1112.

other entities or foreign states.[625] These functions include certain commercial activities.[626] "If the funds at issue are used for central bank functions as these are normally understood, then they are immune from attachment, even if used for commercial purposes."[627] However, the "mere placing of funds not used for a central banking function in an account of a foreign central bank will [not] immunize such funds from attachment."[628] With respect to accounts with mixed-uses, at least one court has distinguished between funds held for the central bank's own account and other funds.[629]

Waiver

Subsection 1611(b)(1) makes no mention of waiver with respect to prejudgment attachment. The courts that have considered this point have construed the subsection strictly. Those courts have held that a foreign central bank or monetary authority can waive immunity, with respect to funds held for their own account, only in cases of "attachment in aid of execution" or "execution," (ie post-judgment attachment) but not cases of prejudgment attachment.[630]

In connection with a "military activity"

Property is of a "military character" if it consists of equipment "in a broad sense," such as weapons, ammunition, communications equipment, warships, tanks, and military transport, and if its present or future use is military.[631] However, property that is considered "surplus equipment" or is withdrawn from military use is not immune under s 1611(b)(2).[632]

---

[625] H Rep No 94–1487, *Jurisdiction of United States Courts in Suits Against Foreign States*, 94th Cong. (9 September 1976) at 31 (reprinted in 1976 USCCAM 6604, 6630). *Weston*, 823 F Supp at 1113, citing Ernest T Patrikis, *Foreign Central Bank Property: Immunity from Attachment in the United States*, 1982 U Ill L Rev 265 (1982); see also *Olympic Chartering, S.A. v Ministry of Industry and Trade of Jordan*, 134 F Supp 2d 528, 534 (SDNY 2001); *Bank of Credit and Commerce International (Overseas) Limited v State Bank of Pakistan*, 46 F Supp 2d 231 (SDNY 15 April 1999); *Banco Central de Reserva del Peru v Riggs National Bank of Washington, D.C.*, 919 F Supp 13, 15 (DDC 1994); *Concord Reinsurance Co. v Caja Nacional de Ahorro y Seguro*, 1994 WL 86401, No 93 Civ 6606 (SDNY 16 March 1994).

[626] *Weston*, 823 F Supp at 1112 ("Property used for commercial activity and property of a central bank held for its own account are not mutually exclusive categories").

[627] *Olympic Chartering*, 134 F Supp 2d at 533.   [628] *Weston*, 823 F Supp at 1114.

[629] See *Weston*, 823 F Supp at 1114.

[630] See *Weston*, 823 F Supp at 1111; *Banque Compafina v Banco de Guatemala*, 583 F Supp 320 at 322 (SDNY 1984); see also *Concord Reins. Co.*, 1994 WL 86401, *4; accord *Sesostris, S.A.E.*, 727 F Supp at 743 (referring to § 1611(b)(1)'s grant of immunity of property of foreign central bank from prejudgment attachment as "unqualified").

[631] See *All American Trading Corp., v Cuartel General Fuerza Aerea Guardia Nacional de Nicaragua*, 818 F Supp 1552, 1555 (SD Fla 1993) (two aircraft, an MI-17 helicopter and a Cessna 404 airplane used to transport senior military officials was found to be of a military character despite being equipped with luxuries), quoting HR Rep No 94-1487, *Jurisdiction of United States Courts in Suits Against Foreign States*, 94th Cong. (9 September 1976) at 31 (reprinted in 1976 USCCAN 6604, 6630). See also *The Ministry of Defense and Support for the Armed Forces of the Islamic Republic of Iran v Cubic Defense Systems*, 236 F Supp 2d 1140, 1149 (SD Cal 2002).

[632] See *All American Trading Corp.*, 818 F Supp at 1555, quoting HR Rep No 94-1487, *Jurisdiction of United States Courts in Suits Against Foreign States*, 94th Cong. (9 September 1976) at 31 (reprinted in 1976 USCCAN 6604, 6630).

A judgment confirming an arbitration award in favor of Iran's Ministry of Defense was not deemed "property of a military character" in the *Ministry of Defense and Support for the Armed Forces of the Islamic Republic of Iran v Cubic Defense Systems*, despite the fact that the arbitration award arose out of a military's supplier's breach of contract regarding air combat maneuvering range.[633] In that case, the ministry of defense of Iran argued that "it was impossible to conceive of anything more military than an Air Combat Maneuvering Range." The court held, however, that the property at issue was the arbitration judgment, not the range.[634]

An entity seeking immunity under s 1611(b)(2) may face evidentiary hurdles in carrying its burden of showing immunity from attachment. The district court of New Jersey has denied immunity under s 1611(b)(2) based on the dearth of proof in the record that property sought to be attached was "of a military character".[635] The court held that the affidavit of an Iranian air force colonel stating that the materials were purchased for use in connection with the military activities of the Iranian air force was insufficient to establish that the property was "of a military character".[636]

LIBERTAD

No US decision has interpreted s 1611(c). Bills proposing to repeal LIBERTAD have been introduced in both the House of Representatives and the Senate.[637]

---

[633] *The Ministry of Defense and Support for the Armed Forces of the Islamic Republic of Iran*, 236 F Supp 2d at 1140 (SD Cal 2002).

[634] *The Ministry of Defense and Support for the Armed Forces of the Islamic Republic of Iran*, 236 F Supp 2d at 1140 (SD Cal 2002).

[635] *Behring International, Inc. v Imperial Iranian Air Force*, 475 F Supp 396, 407 (D NJ 1979).

[636] *Behring International, Inc.*, 475 F Supp at 407–408.

[637] *To Lift the Trade Embargo on Cuba, and for Other Purposes*, HR 188, 108th Cong. § 2(e); S. 403, 108th Cong. § 2(e) (7 January 2003).

PART 4
UNITED KINGDOM

State Immunity Act 1978[1]

4.001

An Act to make new provision with respect to proceedings in the United Kingdom by or against other States. To provide for the effect of judgments given against the United Kingdom in the courts of States parties to the European Convention on State Immunity; to make new provision with respect to the immunities and privileges of heads of State; and for connected purposes. [20th July 1978]

Commentary

Introduction

4.002

The State Immunity Act 1978 (UK) received the Royal Assent on 20 July 1978 and came into force on 22 November 1978.[2]

The primary purpose of the State Immunity Bill,[3] introduced in the House of Lords in early 1978,[4] was to enable the United Kingdom to ratify two international conventions, the European Convention on State Immunity,[5] signed by the UK on 16 May 1972, and the Convention for the Unification of Certain Rules concerning the Immunity of State-owned Ships signed at Brussels on 10 April 1926 (together with the Protocol to that Convention signed on 24 May 1934).[6] The provisions of the Bill, although applied to States other than contracting parties, were initially closely tailored to the provisions of these treaties, in particular to those of the European Convention.

---

[1] 1978, ch 33. Referred to in this commentary as the "1978 Act".

[2] State Immunity Act 1978 (Commencement) Order 1978 (SI 1978/1572). Note, however, the transitional provisions contained in s 23(3)–(4) (see 4.145 and 4.148 below).

[3] See 4.150–4.175 below.

[4] See Hansard, HL (5th series), vol 388, cols 51–78 (17 January 1978) (2nd reading); vol 389, cols 1480–1486, 1491–1540 (16 March 1978) (Committee); vol 389, cols. 1928–1941 (23 March 1978) (Report); vol 390, cols. 10–11 (4 April 1978) (3rd reading); vol 394, cols. 314–325 (28 June 1978) (Commons amendments); vol 395, cols. 1698–1700 (13 July 1978) (Commons amendments). Hansard, HC (5th series), vol 949, cols., 405–420 (3 May 1978) (Committee); vol 949, col. 937 (8 May 1978) (2nd reading); vol 951, cols. 841–845 (13 June 1978) (3rd reading); vol 953, cols. 616–620 (5 July 1978) (Lords amendments).

[5] Cmnd 5081; (1972) 11 ILM 470. See 1.025–1.067 above. Referred to below as the "European Convention".

[6] See 1.001–1.022 above. Referred to below as the "Brussels Convention". For further explanation of the United Kingdom's failure to ratify the Convention earlier, see Mann (1979) 50 BYIL 43.

At the same time, those promoting the Bill desired to place United Kingdom law more closely in line with established trends in the customary international law governing the immunities and privileges of states and state entities and, in particular, to move away from the practice of absolute immunity, which until recently had been observed by the English courts.[7] Although, at the time the Bill was introduced, the Privy Council and the English Court of Appeal had openly departed from that practice in two important decisions,[8] those developments (and the effect on English law of developments in the practice of other states) had yet to be considered judicially by the House of Lords.[9] Earlier decisions of the Court of Appeal[10] and judicial statements at the very highest level[11] continued to provide grist to the mill of those who asserted that change could come about only through legislation or, potentially, a decision of the House of Lords.[12] Until the opportunity arose for such examination (and in the absence of legislation), the English law of state immunity relating to immunity from suit in actions *in personam* stood in an uncomfortable state of flux. That relating to waiver of immunity and immunity from execution was in a no less unhappy state. As one commentator vividly notes:

> Judicial activism had sought to bend the tardy cripple-gaited common law back upon itself so that it should reflect the contemporary international scene, rather than the views of yesteryear, but the labour pains of the new doctrine were prolonged and disquieting to witness. Nor had they yet produced a healthy child whose survival was ensured.[13]

But those who had expected a radical restatement of the United Kingdom law on state immunity were to be disappointed by the provisions of the Bill introduced

---

[7] The development of the "rule" of absolute immunity in the English courts has been well chronicled elsewhere (see Fox, 101–117; Lewis, ch 3). For present purposes, it suffices to note that the position was never perhaps as clear as is commonly believed (see *Sultan of Johore v Abubakar Tunku Aris Bendahar* [1952] AC 318, at 343).

[8] *The Phillipine Admiral* [1977] AC 373; (1975) 64 ILR 90 (PC) (proceedings *in rem*); *Trendtex Trading Corporation v Central Bank of Nigeria* [1977] QB 529; (1977) 64 ILR 111 (CA) (proceedings *in personam*).

[9] An appeal was pursued to the House of Lords in the *Trendtex* case and was continuing at the time that the Bill was considered by a Committee of the House of Lords. The case was, however, settled and the opportunity for simultaneous clarification of the common law rules by the senior court was lost. Indeed, it was not until 1981 that the House of Lords was called upon to consider these issues again (see *The I° Congreso del Partido* [1983] 1 AC 244; (1981) 64 ILR 307 (HL)). The lost opportunity to influence not only the development of the common law but also the legislative process was lamented by, among others, Lord Wilberforce (who subsequently gave the leading judgment in *I° Congreso*) (see Lewis, 24).

[10] See, in particular, *Thai-Europe Tapioca Service v Government of Pakistan* [1975] 1 WLR 1485; (1975) 64 ILR 81 (CA).

[11] Most notably, that of Lord Atkin in *The Cristina* [1938] AC 485, 490–491 (HL) (also reported at (1938) 9 ILR 250).

[12] See the judgment of Donaldson J, after the coming into force of the 1978 Act, in *Uganda Co. (Holdings) v Government of Uganda* [1979] 1 Lloyd's Rep. 481; (1978) 64 ILR 209; cf. the comments of Lord Denning MR in *Hispano Americana Mercantil v Central Bank of Nigeria* [1979] 2 Lloyd's Rep. 277; (1979) 64 ILR 221 (CA).   [13] Lewis, 11.

into the House of Lords. In particular, the provisions concerning waiver,[14] commercial activities[15] and procedural privileges and immunities[16] attracted trenchant criticism on the Bill's Second Reading[17] from, among others, Lord Wilberforce and Lord Denning (in their legislative role).[18] As will be seen below, the criticisms of these and other individuals and interests, and the willingness of the Government to adapt the Bill to meet those criticisms, resulted in a substantially more radical restatement of the law than had originally been contemplated.

Finally, it should be noted that the passage of the 1978 Act was not driven purely by matters of international legal theory. Perhaps inevitably, financial and national interests had a part to play. The proposed clarification of United Kingdom law and the contraction of the immunities and privileges of foreign states were seen as wholly beneficial from the point of view of the London financial markets (and, indeed, the English courts) and as averting a wholesale transfer of the state loans market to New York (whose application of the doctrine of restrictive immunity had been confirmed by the passage of the Foreign Sovereign Immunities Act in 1976).[19] The demands for a "level playing field" in this particular respect were fuelled by recognition of the need for a response to a want of "reciprocity" on the part of other states. As matters stood (at least before the decision in the *Trendtex* case[20]), the UK had "the worst of both worlds"—it was often unable to assert immunity when sued abroad but appeared to have committed itself to grant immunity to foreign states when sued in the UK courts, often by UK nationals.[21]

The 1978 Act and the common law   **4.003**

Although the provisions of the 1978 Act, within their sphere of operation, provide a comprehensive code[22] and supersede the rules of the common law, the latter will continue to be relevant in the following circumstances:

(a) If the subject matter of the proceedings falls within any of the excluded matters set out in s 16(2)–(5).[23] In such cases, the provisions of Part I of the

---

[14] Clause 2 (see 4.153 and 4.017 below).

[15] Clauses 3 and 4 (see 4.154–4.155 and 4.027 below).

[16] Clause 14 (see 4.165 and 4.084 below).

[17] Hansard, HL (5th series), vol 388, cols. 51–78 (17 January 1978).

[18] Lord Denning MR expressed the "gravest misgivings" about the Bill and added: "The Bill, if it is passed into our statute law, will sterilise it and stabilise it, if you like, for the United Kingdom." (Hansard, HL (5th series), vol 388, cols. 70 and 73.)

[19] See, in particular, the comments of Lord O'Brien of Lothbury at the Committee Stage of the Bill-Hansard, HL (5th series), vol 389, cols 1506–1509 (16 March 1978).

[20] [1977] QB 529 (CA).

[21] See the Lord Chancellor (Lord Elwyn-Jones), Hansard, HL (5th series), vol 388, cols. 52–53 (17 January 1978).

[22] See *Al-Adsani v Government of Kuwait* (1996) The Times, 29 March; 107 ILR 536 at 542 (Stuart-Smith LJ) (CA); *R v Bow Street Metropolitan Stipendiary Magistrate, ex parte Pinochet Ugarte (No. 3)* [2000] 1 AC 147, at 209 (Lord Goff: "There can be no doubt, in my mind, that the Act is intended to provide the sole source of law on this topic.") (HL) (also reported at (1999) 119 ILR 367).

[23] See 4.112 and 4.118–4.123 below.

1978 Act do not apply. Significantly, that Part does not apply to criminal proceedings.[24]

(b) If the proceedings concern matters that occurred before 22 November 1978, including the particular matters set out in the transitional provisions in s 23(3).[25]

(c) In certain circumstances, common law authorities may be of assistance in construing, and giving substance to, the language of the 1978 Act. Most notably, the House of Lords has held, in *Kuwait Airways Corporation v Iraqi Airways Co.*,[26] that it is appropriate, in considering (for the purposes of s 14(2)) whether acts done by a separate entity are or are not acts done "in the exercise of sovereign authority"[27] to have regard to the English authorities[28] relating to the distinction between sovereign acts (*acta iure imperii*) and private acts (*acta iure gestionis*).

(d) Finally, one commentator has suggested that the parties to a transaction may agree that the 1978 Act shall not apply in the event of a dispute between them, with the consequence that the common law rules apply.[29] With respect, it is difficult to agree with that view. The provisions of the 1978 Act, it is submitted, are mandatory, in the sense that a court must give effect to them notwithstanding the intentions of parties to a transaction or parties to litigation. This view is supported by the language of s 1(2), requiring a court to give effect to a State's immunity under s 1(1) notwithstanding that State's non-appearance in the proceedings,[30] and by the provisions of ss 2(2), 3(2) and 8(2) of the 1978 Act, which provide specific sanction for the restriction or extension of the immunities conferred by the 1978 Act by written agreement.[31]

4.004   The 1978 Act and the European Convention on State Immunity

The 1978 Act having been passed for the purpose, *inter alia*, of enabling the United Kingdom to ratify the European Convention on State Immunity (and the Brussels Convention on the Immunity of State-owned Ships), the English courts may have regard to these international conventions and to the terms of

---

[24] s 16(4) (see 4.121 below).   [25] See 4.145 and 4.148 below.

[26] [1995] 1 WLR 1147, at 1159 (Lord Goff) (also reported at 103 ILR 340 with the earlier decisions of Evans J and the Court of Appeal on the immunity issue). For subsequent proceedings in relation to the immunity issue, see [2001] 1 WLR 429 (HL); [2003] EWHC 31 (Comm) (David Steel J). See also (1998) 116 ILR 534 (Mance J); [2002] 2 AC 883 (CA and HL) (act of state).

[27] As to which see s 14(2) (commentary at 4.103–4.104 below). See also s 3(3)(c) (commentary at 4.030 below).

[28] Most notably, the decision of the House of Lords in *The I° Congreso del Partido* [1983] 1 AC 244; (1981) 64 ILR 307.   [29] Lewis, 9.

[30] See 4.013 below.

[31] See 4.016, 4.026 and 4.065 below. In principle, it would be open to the parties to agree, pursuant to s 3(2), that the exception from immunity contained in s 3 (commercial transactions) should not apply to their agreement and also, pursuant to s 2(2), that the State party submits to the jurisdiction to the extent that it would not have enjoyed immunity under the rules of the common law. It is difficult, however, to envisage the commercial justification for such provision.

any relevant *travaux preparatoires*[32] in construing the provisions of the 1978 Act, at least where the statute is reasonably capable of more than one construction.[33] Nevertheless, in doing so, it is to be recalled that in certain respects the 1978 Act departs from the terms of the European Convention, most significantly in relation to commercial transactions.[34]

As a general rule, the 1978 Act treats States party to the European Convention and non-Convention States alike. In some circumstances, Convention States[35] may receive more favourable treatment, including in relation to certain procedural privileges and immunities,[36] recognition of judgments[37] and security for costs.[38]

The 1978 Act and customary international law   **4.005**

The rules of customary international law in this field are plainly also relevant in construing the provisions of the 1978 Act, in explaining its historical background, in explaining certain fundamental assumptions on which the statute is based[39] and in interpreting particular words and phrases. When Lord Goff referred in the *Kuwait Airways* case[40] to the necessity of referring to "English authorities" relating to the distinction between sovereign and private acts, he cannot, it is submitted, have intended to exclude from consideration the practice of other states from which the English courts have often drawn inspiration. As Lord Diplock observed in *Alcom v Republic of Columbia*,[41] the provisions of the 1978 Act "fall to be construed against the background of those principles of public international law as are recognised by the family of nations" and it is "highly unlikely that Parliament intended to require the United Kingdom courts to act contrary to international law unless the clear language of the statute compels such a conclusion".[42]

Conversely, the 1978 Act has a role to play in the development of customary international law. Although, in part, derived from an international agreement between European states, the 1978 Act has proved influential in a wider sphere, arguably more so than its American counterpart, forming the basis of legislation

---

[32] For the explanatory report on the European Convention, see 1.088–1.136 above.

[33] See *Salomon v Commissioners of Customs and Excise* [1967] 2 QB 116, esp at 141 (Lord Denning MR),143–144 (Diplock LJ) (also reported at (1966) 44 ILR 1) (CA). For reference to the European Convention in connection with the 1978 Act, see *Kuwait Airways Corporation v Iraqi Airways Co.* [1995] 1 WLR 1147 at 1159 (Lord Goff); *Government of the Kingdom of Saudi Arabia v Ahmed* (1993) 104 ILR 629 (EAT).

[34] In common with other contracting states, the United Kingdom made a declaration under Art 24 of the European Convention (see 1.049 and 1.069 above and 4.028 below).

[35] ie Austria, Belgium, Cyprus, Germany, Luxembourg, Switzerland and the Netherlands, apart from the United Kingdom (see 1.068 above). [36] See 4.091 below.

[37] See 4.127–4.130 below.   [38] See 4.092 below.

[39] For example, the distinction between immunity from jurisdiction and immunity from enforcement (see *Alcom v Republic of Columbia* [1984] AC 580 at 600 (HL), also reported, at (1981) 64 ILR 307).

[40] *Kuwait Airways Corporation v Iraqi Airways Co.* [1995] 1 WLR 1147, at 1159.

[41] [1984] AC 580.

[42] *Alcom*, at 597, 600. See also *Al-Adsani v Government of Kuwait* (1996) The Times, 29 March; 107 ILR 536, 541–542 (Stuart-Smith LJ), 547–549 (Ward LJ). In *Al Adsani*, the Court of Appeal has held that the general immunity conferred by s 1 of the 1978 Act[42] is not subject to any general qualification in relation to torture or other acts contrary to overriding principles of international law (see 4.053 below).

in South Africa,[43] Singapore[44] and Pakistan[45] and being influential in the framing of legislation in Australia[46] and Canada.[47]

Courts both in England and abroad have, however, been reluctant to accede to arguments to the effect that the 1978 Act (or indeed the US Foreign Sovereign Immunities Act 1976) accurately represents the state of international law and, by further extension, the common law.[48] Each case must depend on an examination of state practice, but it should be borne in mind that, in several respects,[49] the practice of the United Kingdom, of other parties to the European Convention and of Commonwealth states who have passed legislation in similar terms to the 1978 Act, departs from the practice of the majority of states, whether proponents of absolute immunity or of "restrictive immunity" (in the sense of immunity for sovereign, as opposed to private or commercial acts). The general and consistent practice necessary to establish a rule of customary international law[50] will often, therefore, be lacking. The 1978 Act cannot, of itself, develop international law.[51]

Customary international law also has a key role in the assessment of the compatibility of the 1978 Act with established human rights.[52]

4.006   The 1978 Act, the "act of state doctrine" and issues of justiciability

Before addressing the relationship between the 1978 Act and the "act of state doctrine", it is important to note the variety of uses to which this phrase has been put.[53] In the context of proceedings involving or relating to the actions of foreign states, two of those are of particular importance. First, to describe a rule which requires the English courts, save in limited circumstances, to accept without question the validity of the legislative and (probably) executive acts of a foreign state within its own territory.[54] Secondly, in describing a broader principle

---

[43]   Foreign States Immunities Act 1981 (S.Africa) (see 5.125–5.143 below).

[44]   State Immunity Act 1979 (Singapore) (see 5.105–5.124 below).

[45]   State Immunity Ordinance 1981 (Pakistan) (see 5.085–5.104 below).

[46]   Foreign States Immunities Act 1985 (Australia) (see 5.021–5.065 below).

[47]   State Immunity Act 1982 (Canada) (see 5.066–5.084 below).

[48]   *I° Congreso del Partido* [1983] 1 AC 244, at 260 (Lord Wilberforce: "to argue from the terms of a statute to establish what international law provides is to stand the accepted argument on its head") (HL). See also *Government of Canada v Employment Appeals Tribunal and Burke* [1992] ILRM 325; (1991) 95 ILR 468 (Sup. Ct. Ireland).

[49]   eg, by recognizing exceptions to immunity that apply whether or not the act(s) giving rise to proceedings was/were sovereign in character. Section 5 of the 1978 Act (personal injuries and damage to property) provides a notable example (see 4.049 below).

[50]   Brownlie, *Principles of Public International Law* (5th ed., 1998), 5–6.

[51]   And, in turn, the common law (see *Trendtex Trading Corporation v Central Bank of Nigeria* [1977] QB 529 (CA)).   [52]   See 4.007 below.

[53]   See the list of related doctrines identified by Mustill LJ in *Fayed v Al-Tajir* [1988] QB 712, at 723–724 (CA).

[54]   *Buttes Gas and Oil Co. v Hammer* [1982] AC 888, at 931 (Lord Wilberforce) (HL). For a meticulous analysis of the operation of this principle, see the judgment of Mance J in *Kuwait Airways Corporation v Iraqi Airways* (1998) 116 ILR 534, at 568–601 (also reported at [1999] CLC 631). See also the reasoning of the Court of Appeal and House of Lords in the same case [2002] 2 AC 883; [2002] UKHL 19, esp paras 265–338 of the judgment of the Court of Appeal.

of judicial restraint which inhibits the English courts from investigating the conduct of states, particularly in their relations with other states.[55] Both involve questions of justiciability but, whereas the former may provide a party to litigation with a conclusive answer to a claim or defence,[56] the latter may require an English court to decline to entertain proceedings or some part of them.[57]

The act of state doctrine and the doctrine of state immunity can undoubtedly be justified on similar grounds (respect for the independence and equality of foreign states) and may share a common heritage.[58] However that may be, it cannot be doubted that the two have now developed separate identities[59] and differ in important respects. Thus, state immunity is an objection to the jurisdiction and must be raised at an early stage in proceedings, at which stage it will be dealt with by reference to the matters alleged in the claim (and evidence adduced by the parties in support of or opposition to any exception to immunity that is relied on).[60] In contrast, the act of state doctrine, although it may be raised at an early stage, is more appropriately considered at a later stage, when the parties' contentions of fact and law have become clear.[61] There are other important points of distinction. State immunity will only be relevant if a State (or separate entity) is directly or indirectly impleaded before the English courts[62]; the act of state doctrine is of broader import.[63] State immunity can be waived,[64] but the matters that are capable of determination by the English courts cannot, it would seem, be extended by agreement between litigating parties.[65] The act of state

---

[55] *Buttes Gas and Oil Co. v Hammer* [1982] AC 888, at 931–938 (Lord Wilberforce) (HL). Lord Wilberforce preferred to refer to the principle described, not as a variety of "act of state" but one for judicial restraint or abstention. In *Maclaine Watson v International Tin Council* [1989] Ch. 253, Kerr LJ (at 284–285) described the principle as "act of state non-justiciability". See also *Kuwait Airways Corporation v Iraqi Airways Co.* (1998) 116 ILR 534, at 568–601 (Mance J) and, on appeal, *Kuwait Airways Corporation v Iraqi Airways Co. (Nos. 4 and 5)* [2002] 2 AC 883 (CA, HL); *Re Banco Nacional de Cuba* [2001] 1 WLR 2039, at 2054 (Lightman J). Unlike the first doctrine, the second may apply to the acts of a State outside its jurisdiction.   [56] eg *Luther v Sagor* [1921] 3 KB 532 (CA).
[57] As in *Buttes Gas and Oil v Hammer* [1982] AC 888 (HL). For discussion of the interaction of the two, see *Kuwait Airways Corporation v Iraqi Airways* (1998) 116 ILR 534, at 577–578 (Mance J).
[58] The decision of the House of Lords in *Duke of Brunswick v King of Hanover* (1844) 6 Beav 1; 2 HL Cas. 1 is prominent in discussions of both. See also *R v Bow Street Metropolitan Stipendiary Magistrate, exp. Pinochet Ugarte (No. 3)* [2000] 1 AC 147 at 267 (Lord Millett), 286–287 (Lord Phillips) (HL). In the light of the differences in their application referred to in the text and given that the 1978 Act may apply even if the State is only indirectly impleaded (see 4.012 below), the relationship between sovereign immunity "*ratione personae*", sovereign immunity "*ratione materiae*", the principle of judicial restraint or non-justiciability described in *Buttes Gas v Hammer* and the 1978 Act will require clarification in future decisions.
[59] See, eg, *Kuwait Airways Corporation v Iraqi Airways* [1995] 1 WLR 1147 (HL); *Re Banco Nacional de Cuba* [2001] 1 WLR 2039 (Lightman J).   [60] See 4.081 below.
[61] *Kuwait Airways Corporation v Iraqi Airways Co* [1995] 1 WLR 1147, at 1164–1168 (Lord Goff) (HL). See *Kuwait Airways Corporation v Iraqi Airways Co.* (1998) 116 ILR 534 (Mance J); *Kuwait Airways Corporation v Iraqi Airways Co. (Nos. 4 and 5)* [2002] 2 AC 883 (CA, HL).
[62] See 4.012 below.
[63] See, eg, *Buttes Gas v Hammer* [1982] AC 888 (HL) and *Fayed v Al-Tajir* [1988] QB 712 (CA) none of the parties to which was a State (or State entity).   [64] See 4.016–4.025.
[65] *Kuwait Airways Corporation v Iraqi Airways* [1995] 1 WLR 1147, at 1167, (Lord Goff) (HL). Cf. *The Playa Larga and Marble Islands* [1983] 2 Lloyd's Rep. 171, at 193–194 (CA).

doctrine may be limited by international law rules governing state conduct[66]; no similar limitation can be read into the 1978 Act.[67]

That said, it would seem that the development of the restrictive doctrine of immunity and the enactment of the 1978 Act have influenced the degree to which the English courts are prepared to subject the conduct of states (whether parties to the litigation before them or not) to judicial scrutiny. Thus, the Court of Appeal has expressed the view that the act of state doctrine does not apply in the context of commercial transactions.[68] More recently, the Court has drawn upon one of the exceptions to immunity in the 1978 Act in defining the scope of the the the principle of non-justiciability.[69] Given that the 1978 Act is not concerned directly with the act of state doctrine (in either of the senses described), perhaps the most that can be said is that it (together with developments in customary international law with regard to the immunity of States) will colour the attitude of the English courts towards pleas that the international or sovereign character of the subject matter precludes investigation, but that its content cannot be determinative of such pleas if the issues to be determined on the parties' respective cases go beyond those which must necessarily be determined to resolve the question whether a State is entitled to assert immunity under the 1978 Act.[70]

4.007   The 1978 Act and human rights issues[71]

It is possible to consider this issue on a number of levels. First, at the level of policy, the general immunity recognized by s 1 of the 1978 Act excludes litigants from access to English courts, with the potential consequence that in some cases wrongs will go unremedied. In some cases, "access to justice" objections are compounded by the fact that claims contain allegations of serious human rights violations, including torture[72] or extrajudicial killing. These objections must, however, be balanced against the desire to protect the independence and

---

[66] *Kuwait Airways Corporation v Iraqi Airways Co.* (1998) 116 ILR 534 (Mance J); *Kuwait Airways Corporation v Iraqi Airways Co. (Nos. 4 and 5)* [2002] 2 AC 883 (CA, HL).

[67] See 4.005 above. The New Zealand Court of Appeal has, however, suggested a similar "public policy" limitation to immunity at common law (see 4.123 below).

[68] *The Playa Larga and Marble Islands* [1983] 2 Lloyd's Rep. 171, at 194, drawing support from the decision of the United States Supreme Court in *Dunhill (Alfred) of London Inc. v The Republic of Cuba* (1976) 425 US 682. Cf. *Re Banco Nacional de Cuba* [2001] 1 WLR 2039, at 2054 (Lightman J).

[69] *A Ltd v B Bank (Bank of X intervening)* (1996) The Times, 15 August; [1997] FSR 165; 111 ILR 590 (CA), referring to the judgment of Kerr LJ in *Maclaine Watson v International Tin Council* [1989] Ch. 253, at 285 (CA) (cf. Ralph Gibson LJ, at 276).

[70] See *Australia and New Zealand Banking Group Limited v Commonwealth of Australia* (reported as *Amalgamated Metal Trading v Department of Trade and Industry* (1989) The Times, 21 March) Transcript, at 59–60 (Evans J); *Kuwait Airways Corporation v Iraqi Airways Co.* [1995] 1 WLR 1147, at 1164–1168 (Lord Goff) (HL); *Kuwait Airways Corporation v Iraqi Airways Co. (Nos. 4 and 5)* [2002] 2 AC 883, para 319 (CA); *Re Banco Nacional de Cuba* [2001] 1 WLR 2039, at 2054 (Lightman J).

[71] See, generally, the Report of the Human Rights Committee of the International Law Association (British Branch) on Civil Actions in the English Courts for Serious Human Rights Violations Abroad [2001] EHRLR 129; Jurgen Brohmer, *State Immunity and the Violation of Human Rights* (Dordrecht, 1997).

[72] *Al-Adsani v Government of Kuwait* (1996) The Times, 29 March; 105 ILR 536 (discussed at 4.053 below). See also the discussion of the decision in the *Pinochet* case (at 4.137 below).

integrity not only of foreign States acting in a sovereign capacity but also of the English courts. This balancing process is reflected in the terms of the 1978 Act, the European Convention and the ILC Draft Articles. It is a process that is continually undertaken as international standards and attitudes develop.

Secondly, it is necessary to have regard to the United Kingdom's international obligations, both under customary international law and under international instruments[73] (other than the European Convention on Human Rights, discussed in the following paragraph). Those obligations (as they stood in 1978) are part of the legislative background to the 1978 Act, but more importantly in their present form they may influence the construction of particular provisions[74] or require future amendment of the 1978 Act to ensure its compatibility with treaty obligations.

Thirdly, and most directly, the provisions of the 1978 Act must be scrutinised in the light of the Human Rights Act 1998 giving further effect to the rights and freedoms guaranteed under the European Convention on Human Rights, including (in particular) Article 6 which provides (so far as is relevant for present purposes):

> In the determinaion of his civil rights and obligations . . . everyone is entitled to a fair and public hearing within a reasonable time by an independent and impartial tribunal established by law.

The structure of the Human Rights Act 1998 is straightforward, although its effect may be unclear in individual cases.[75] Under s 3(1), so far as possible to do so, primary and subordinate legislation (whenever enacted) must be read and given effect to in a way which is compatible with the Convention rights.[76] Thus, a court or tribunal faced with a argument founded on Convention rights must strain to construe the 1978 Act in a manner consistent with the ECHR, even if that construction is inconsistent with an earlier decision of its own or of a higher court.[77] If that is not possible, however, no court has the power to strike down

---

[73] For example, the United Nations Convention against Torture and Other Cruel Inhuman and Degrading Treatment or Punishment, 10 December 1984 (Cm 1775) (ratified by the United Kingdom on 8 December 1988).

[74] A notable example being the approach by the majority of the House of Lords to the construction of the Diplomatic Privileges Act 1964, as applied by s 20 of the 1978 Act to Heads of State, in its application to criminal charges alleging torture against a former head of State: *R v Bow Street Metropolitan Stipendiary Magistrate, ex parte Pinochet Ugarte (No. 3)* [2000] 1 AC 147 (see 4.137 below).

[75] The Human Rights Act 1998 has only limited retrospective effect (see *Wainwright v Home Office* [2002] QB 1334; [2002] EWCA Civ 773, affirmed on other grounds [2003] 3 WLR 1137 (HL)) and should not, it is submitted, apply to proceedings commenced before 2 October 2000, the date on which it came substantially into force (see *Matthews v Ministry of Defence* (2002) The Times; [2002] EWHC 13 (QB), 30 January (Keith J), reversed on other grounds [2002] 1 WLR 2621; [2003] 1 AC 1163 (HL)).

[76] The "Convention Rights" are Arts 2–12 of the European Convention on Human Rights ("ECHR"), Arts 1–3 of the First Protocol and Arts 1–2 of the Second Protocol as read with Arts 16–18 of the Convention (Human Rights Act 1998, s 1(1)).

[77] See the views of Lord Lester [1998] EHRLR 665, at 669–670. During the House of Commons Committee stage of the Bill, the Home Secretary emphasized, however, that the courts should not

primary legislation,[78] but designated courts[79] have power to make a declaration of incompatibility.[80] Such a declaration is not binding on the parties in the proceedings in which it is made[81] but may lead to amendment of the legislation by statutory instrument, including amendment having retrospective effect.[82] Other courts and tribunals may not make a declaration of incompatibility having these effects, but may still find that legislation cannot be construed in a manner compatible with the ECHR.

Further, under s 6(1), it is unlawful for a public authority to act in a way which is incompatible with a Convention right. "Public authority" includes a court or tribunal,[83] but this prohibition does not apply if the public authority was acting so as to give effect to or enforce primary legislation which cannot be read or given effect in a way which is compatible with the ECHR.[84] Nevertheless, s 6(1) reinforces the duty of a court or tribunal to endeavour to find a construction consistent with the ECHR, and will also be potentially relevant in cases in which the right of a State to assert immunity is governed by common law rules.

In both *Fogarty v United Kingdom*[85] and (by a bare majority) in *Al-Adsani v United Kingdom*,[86] the European Court of Human Rights held the assertion of immunity under s 1 of the 1978 Act to be compatible with Article 6 and other provisions of the ECHR. Both cases concerned the scope of exceptions to the general immunity. In *Fogarty's* case the focus was upon a discrimination claim by a former embassy employee. In *Al-Adsani's* case, the focus was upon a civil claim by the victim of alleged torture committed outside the United Kingdom. These decisions are considered below in the commentary on ss 5 (*Al-Adsani*) and 16(1) (*Fogarty*).[87] In both cases, the Court held that (a) state immunity constituted a procedural bar which ought in principle to be examined for compatibility with the provisions of the ECHR,[88] and (b) the recognition by a legal system of state immunity barring civil actions, consistently with principles of customary international law, pursued a legitimate aim and was not disproportionate to

---

"contort the meaning of words to produce implausible or incredible meanings" (Hansard, HC (5th series), vol 313, col. 422 (3 June 1998)).

[78] Human Rights Act 1998, ss 3(2)(b) and 4(6)(a).

[79] Including the House of Lords, Court of Appeal (England and Northern Ireland), High Court (England and Northern Ireland), Court of Session (Scotland), High Court of Justiciary sitting otherwise than as a trial court (Scotland), Judicial Committee of the Privy Council (Human Rights Act 1998, s 4(5)).   [80] Human Rights Act 1998, s 4(1).

[81] Human Rights Act 1998, s 4(6)(b).   [82] Human Rights Act 1998, Sch 2, para (b).

[83] Human Rights Act 1998, s 6(3)(a).   [84] Human Rights Act 1998, s 6(2)(b).

[85] Application no 37112/97, Judgment of 21 November 2001; 12 BHRC 132; (2001) 123 ILR 53.

[86] Application no 35763/97, Judgment of 21 November 2001; 12 BHRC 89; (2001) 123 ILR 23. See also *McElhinney v Ireland*, Application no 31253/96; Judgment of 21 November 2001; 12 BHRC 114; (2001) 123 ILR 73. See Voyiakis (2003) 52 ICLQ 297.   [87] See 4.053 and 4.116 below.

[88] *Fogarty*, paras 24–28 (although the court left open, at para 28, the issue whether, because the claim related to Embassy recruitment, it did not concern a "civil right"); *Al-Adsani*, paras 46–49; Compare the approach of the House of Lords in *Holland v Lampen Wolfe* [2000] 1 WLR 1573, at 1577–1578 (Lord Hope), 1578 (Lord Cooke), 1581 (Lord Clyde), 1588–1589 (Lord Millett) (also reported at (2000) 119 ILR 367).

that aim. The Court reasoned in each case as follows:

> The Court must first examine whether the limitation pursued a legitimate aim. It notes in this connection that sovereign immunity is a concept of international law, developed out of the principle *par in parem non habet imperium*, by virtue of which one State shall not be subject to the jurisdiction of another State. The Court considers that the grant of sovereign immunity to a State in civil proceedings pursues the legitimate aim of complying with international law to promote comity and good relations between States through the respect of another State's sovereignty.
>
> The Court must next assess whether the restriction was proportionate to the aim pursued. It reiterates that the Convention has to be interpreted in the light of the rules set out in the Vienna Convention on the Law of Treaties of 23 May 1969, and that Article 31 § 3 (c) of that treaty indicates that account is to be taken of "any relevant rules of international law applicable in the relations between the parties". The Convention, including Article 6, cannot be interpreted in a vacuum. The Court must be mindful of the Convention's special character as a human rights treaty, and it must also take the relevant rules of international law into account (. . .). The Convention should so far as possible be interpreted in harmony with other rules of international law of which it forms part, including those relating to the grant of State immunity.
>
> It follows that measures taken by a High Contracting Party which reflect generally recognised rules of public international law on State immunity cannot in principle be regarded as imposing a disproportionate restriction on the right of access to a court as embodied in Article 6 § 1. Just as the right of access to a court is an inherent part of the fair trial guarantee in that Article, so some restrictions on access must likewise be regarded as inherent, an example being those limitations generally accepted by the community of nations as part of the doctrine of State immunity.[89]

Interestingly, in neither case did the Court appear to consider the absence of alternative means of recourse as a relevant factor. Indeed, in the *Al-Adsani* case the Court recorded the applicant's argument that even diplomatic assistance had been denied to him by the United Kingdom.[90] In this respect, the decisions may be contrasted with those in *Waite and Kennedy v Germany*[91] and *Beer and Regan v Germany*,[92] concerning the immunities of an international organization. There is, however, an obvious distinction between the immunities and privileges of a State and of an international organization, in that the latter being derived from treaty have struggled to establish themselves within the framework of

---

[89] *Al-Adsani*, paras 54–56. In the same terms, *Fogarty*, paras 34–36; *McElhinney*, paras 35–37.
[90] *Al-Adsani*, para 51.
[91] Application no 26083/94, Judgment of 18 February 1999; 6 BHRC 499; 30 EHRR 261; (1999) 118 ILR 121. See further Sands and Klein (ed.), *Bowett's Law of International Institutions* (5th edn, London, 2001), paras 15–035–15–085.
[92] Application no 28934/95, Judgment of 18 December 1999.

customary international law, largely due to the diversity of international organizations and the terms of the instruments establishing them.

4.008   Structure of the 1978 Act

The following paragraphs set out (and comment upon) the provisions of the 1978 Act in the order that they appear in the statute. From a structural point of view, however, the logical starting points are s 16, which contains limitations on the subject-matter scope of the 1978 Act, and s 23, which contains provisions governing the temporal application of the statute. Having established that the 1978 Act applies to the facts of a particular case, it will be necessary to consider separately ss 1–11, concerning immunity from the jurisdiction of the United Kingdom courts, and ss 12–13, concerning additional privileges and immunities accorded to States. Those provisions must be applied in the light of the definitions set out in ss 14, 17 and 22. Of the remaining provisions, s 15 permits restriction or extension by statutory instrument of the immunities and privileges conferred under the 1978 Act, ss 18–19 concern recognition of judgments given against the United Kingdom by courts in states party to the European Convention, s 20 contains provisions defining the immunities and privileges enjoyed by heads of state and s 21 provides for the certification of certain matters by the Secretary of State.

4.009   Index

PART I   PROCEEDINGS IN UNITED KINGDOM
BY OR AGAINST OTHER STATES

Supplementary provisions

14. States entitled to immunities and privileges
15. Restriction and extension of immunities and privileges
16. Excluded matters
17. Interpretation of Part I

PART II   JUDGMENTS AGAINST UNITED KINGDOM IN CONVENTION STATES

18. Recognition of judgments against United Kingdom
19. Exceptions to recognition

PART III   MISCELLANEOUS AND SUPPLEMENTARY

20. Heads of State
21. Evidence by certificate
22. General interpretation
23. Short title, repeals commencement and extent

BE IT ENACTED by the Queen's most Excellent Majesty, by and with the **4.010** advice and consent of the Lords Spiritual and Temporal, and Commons, in this present Parliament assembled, and by the authority of the same as follows:-

PART I

Proceedings in United Kingdom By or Against Other states

Immunity from jurisdiction

1 General immunity from jurisdiction

(1) A State is immune from the jurisdiction of the courts of the United Kingdom except as provided in the following provisions of this Part of this Act.
(2) A court shall give effect to the immunity conferred by this section even though the State does not appear in the proceedings in question.

Commentary

Legislative history   **4.011**

Section 1 reflects the terms of Article 15 of the European Convention on State Immunity.[93]

Application

Section 1 is the cornerstone of the 1978 Act. It applies to all situations which **4.012** involve the assertion of jurisdiction, directly or indirectly, by any court (or other

---

[93] See 1.040 above.

tribunal or body exercising judicial functions[94]) in the United Kingdom in respect of a State,[95] subject to the limitations on the material and temporal scope of the legislation.[96] Accordingly, its application is not limited to civil proceedings[97] brought directly against a foreign State but may impact, for example, on the following matters:[98]

(a) An action *in rem* against property in which the State has an interest.[99]

(b) Subject to the particular limitations contained in ss 6(3) and 6(4),[100] a claim relating to property in which the State claims an interest or which is in the possession or control of a State.[101]

(c) A claim against the servant or agent of the State in respect of official acts which give rise to a parallel obligation upon the State. In such cases, the State is impleaded by the claim as if the action had been brought against the State directly—the entitlement of a State to assert immunity cannot be avoided by pursuing its functionary instead.[102] Arguably, even if no such parallel obligation arises, the State may nevertheless be indirectly impleaded by such an action if its rights, interests or activities are otherwise affected by the subject matter of the action or the relief sought by the claimant,[103] including circumstances in which it is obliged ot indemnify its employee or agent against liability.[104]

(d) Procedures whose object is to oblige the State, or its representative, to give evidence or to produce documentation in proceedings to which it is not a party.[105]

---

[94] The term "court" is defined by s 22(1) (see 4.142 and 4.144 below).

[95] As defined by s 14 (see 4.094–4.108 below).

[96] See ss 15, 16 and 23(3)-(4) (see 4.109, 4.112 and 4.144 below).

[97] Part I of the 1978 Act does not apply to criminal proceedings: s 16(4) (see 4.121 below).

[98] See also the discussion of the "act of state doctrine" and issues of non-justiciability, at 4.06 above.

[99] See further s 10 (at 4.070–4.073 below). Many of the key decisions defining common law immunity concerned actions *in rem* against State-owned vessels (see, eg, *The Charkieh* (1873) LR 4 A and E 59 (Adm.); *The Parlement Belge* (1880) 5 PD 197 (CA); *The Phillipine Admiral* [1977] AC 373 (PC); *I° Congreso del Partido* [1983] 1 AC 244).   [100] See 4.059–4.060 below.

[101] See further ss 6(1) and 6(2) (at 4.055 and 4.057–4.058 below). For the common law position, see *Twycross v Dreyfus* (1877) 5 Ch.D. 605 (CA); *Re Russian Bank for Foreign Trade* [1933] Ch. 745 (Maugham J); *United States of America v Dolfus Mieg et Cie* [1952] AC 582; (1952) 19 ILR 163 (HL); *Rahimtoola v Nizam of Hyderabad* [1958] AC 379; (1957) 24 ILR 175 (HL).

[102] On this view, s 1 (read together with s 2(4)(a)) would apply even if the relevant official acts of the servant or agent were not "sovereign" in nature, although, in such a case, immunity would generally be removed by the provisions of ss 2–11. See, however, *Propend Finance v Sing* (1997) The Times, 2 May; 113 ILR 611 (CA) and the discussion at 4.105 below as to whether an agent is to be treated, in some circumstances, as part of the "State" for the purposes of the 1978 Act and the consequences of this characterization.

[103] See ILC Draft Articles 1991, Art 6.2(b) and commentary (at 2.012–2.013 above). See further *Rahimtoola v Nizam of Hyderabad* [1958] AC 379, esp at 402 (Lord Reid: "It was not disputed that, if the bank account had stood in the name of the State itself, the State could not have been made a party to this action against its will. It appears to me to follow that the State is entitled to object to its agent being made a party; the agent would merely be defending the action on behalf of his principal.") (HL).

[104] See further *R v Bow Street Metropolitan Stipendiary Magistrate, ex parte Pinochet Ugarte (No. 3)* [2000] 1 AC 147, at 254 (Lord Hutton) (HL) (discussed in further detail at 4.137 below).

[105] See the decision of the Irish Supreme Court in *Fusco v O'Dea* [1994] 2 ILRM 389; (1994) 103 ILR 318.

(e) Proceedings to enforce a foreign judgment against a State by registration of the judgment.[106]

A number of other matters concerning the application of this section may be noted. First, the immunity conferred by s 1 of the 1978 Act is an immunity from jurisdiction—it is procedural in nature.[107] It does not affect the existence of any cause of action that a claimant may possess against a foreign State and does not prevent a claimant from pursuing alternative means of recourse (whether by legal proceedings elsewhere[108] or otherwise).[109] By way of examples (a) a creditor may exercise contractual rights of set-off or combination against a State or enforce rights of security over property belonging to a state provided that he is not thereby required to have recourse to judicial process;[110] (b) a person guaranteeing or insuring the obligations of a State will be fully liable, notwithstanding that the 1978 Act may preclude proceedings against the State to enforce those obligations.[111] Nor, as a general rule, does s 1 (or any other provision of the 1978 Act) confer on a State any cause of action that it would not otherwise have.

Secondly, "jurisdiction" in s 1 means *authority to determine the substance of a claim.* The 1978 Act does not remove all of the powers of courts or tribunals in the United Kingdom vis-à-vis a State. In particular, they retain the authority to determine whether "jurisdiction" (in the sense described above) exists[112] and to make any order necessary for the fair determination of that issue, including, for example an order requiring disclosure of information.[113]

Thirdly, the entitlement of a foreign State to assert the immunity conferred by s 1 is expressly subject to "the following provisions" of Part I of the 1978 Act.

4.013

---

[106] *AIC Ltd v Federal Government of Nigeria* [2003] EWHC 1357 (QB) (Stanley Burnton QC). See further 4.130 below.

[107] See *Intpro Properties v Sauvel* [1983] QB 1019, at 1033 (May LJ) (CA) (also reported at (1983) 64 ILR 384) citing *Empson v Smith* [1966] 1 QB 426, at 438; (Diplock LJ, CA); *Central Bank of Yemen v Cardinal Finance Investments Corp.* [2001] 1 Lloyd's Rep. Bank. 1 (CA); *Al-Adsani v UK*, Application no. 35753/97, Judgment of 21 November 2001; 12 BHRC 88, para 48; 12 BHRC 89 (ECtHR). As a matter of statutory construction, legislation may not apply to foreign sovereign States (see, eg, 4.123 below concerning the liability of foreign States to taxation).

[108] Subject to any immunity in the relevant jurisdiction.

[109] *Dickinson v Del Solar* [1930] 1 KB 376; (1929) 5 ILR 299 (Lord Hewart CJ) (a case concerning diplomatic immunity). But see *The Tervaete* [1922] P 259 (CA) in which the Court of Appeal held that no maritime lien was imposed following a collision for which a State-owned ship was responsible.

[110] Legal set-off may fall to be treated differently given that it requires claim and counterclaim to be before the court (see s 2(6) at 4.016 and 4.022 below). Query how equitable set-off should be treated given that its historical origin lies in the grant by the courts of equity of an injunction (see Derham, *The Law of Set-Off* (3rd edn; 2003, paras 4.02 and 4.31; also s 13(2)(a) at 4.083 and 4.087 below).

[111] eg, because the underlying transaction is one between States. Cf. *Cardinal Financial Investment Corp. v Central Bank of Yemen* [2001] 1 Lloyd's Rep Bank 1.

[112] See *Canada Trust v Stolzenberg* [1997] 1 WLR 1582, at 1588–1589 (Millett LJ) (CA). Indeed, s 1(2) of the 1978 Act requires a court to consider this issue.

[113] See *J H Rayner (Mincing Lane) Ltd v Department of Trade and Industry* [1989] 1 Ch. 72, at 194 (Kerr LJ), 252 (Ralph Gibson LJ) (CA) (also reported at (1988) 80 ILR 47). Such orders should be sparingly made—cf. *Rome v Punjab National Bank* [1989] 2 All ER 136, at 141 (Hirst J requiring the "clearest possible demonstration" of necessity). See also s 13(1) (at 4.083 and 4.086 below).

These words refer to ss 2–11, which set out (exhaustively[114]) the limitations on that entitlement.[115] The English courts have yet to give detailed consideration to the interaction between these various exceptions. It would appear, however, that they should be construed, so far as possible, so as to avoid overlap with each other.[116]

Fourthly, although ss 2–11 contain exceptions to the general immunity from suit contained in s 1, they do not, of themselves, confer jurisdiction on United Kingdom courts to determine proceedings falling within their scope.[117] The claimant must therefore establish that jurisdiction exists in the normal manner including, where necessary, by applying for permission to serve process out of the jurisdiction.[118]

Fifthly, although, in the normal course, the State, in relying on the immunity conferred by s 1, will usually be in the position of defendant, that will not always be the case. In certain circumstances, s 1 will apply to a state in the position of claimant[119] or third party.[120]

4.014   *Standard and burden of proof*

The structure of ss 1–11 of the 1978 Act, in providing for immunity generally subject to specific exceptions, confirms that, in any particular case, the onus will lie on the non-State party (usually the claimant) to show that the circumstances are such that the general rule is displaced.[121] That conclusion is reinforced by the terms of s 1(2), requiring United Kingdom courts and tribunals to give effect to the immunity conferred under s 1(1) even if the State does not appear before it.[122] This overriding duty has also been held to provide sufficient justification for extending time limits so as to enable a State to assert immunity.[123] It would also

---

[114] See *Al-Adsani v Government of Kuwait* (1996) The Times, 29 March; 107 ILR 536 at 542 (Stuart-Smith LJ) (CA).

[115] Many of the sections are, in turn, subject to detailed and sometimes "convoluted" reservations (see *Alcom v Republic of Columbia* [1984] AC 580, at 600 (Lord Diplock) (HL)).

[116] For support, see *Alcom v Republic of Columbia* [1984] AC 580, at 603–604 (Lord Diplock) (HL). See also *Intpro Properties v Sauvel* [1983] QB 1019, at 1031 (CA) where the point was left open.

[117] See Dicey and Morris, para 10–007. Compare the United States Foreign Sovereign Immunities Act 1976 (see 3.004 above).

[118] As to which, see s 12(7) (at 4.077 and 4.080). In some instances, however, the facts necessary to establish an exception to the general rule of immunity will also suffice to establish a ground for service out of the jurisdiction. For example, s 5 of the 1978 Act is similarly worded to Civil Procedure Rules, r 6.20(8).   [119] See 4.022 (submission by institution of proceedings)

[120] See, eg, *Bank of Credit and Commerce International (Overseas) v Price Waterhouse (Abu Dhabi and others, third parties)* [1997] 4 All ER 108; (1996) 111 ILR 604.

[121] *J H Rayner (Mincing Lane) Ltd v Department of Trade and Industry* [1989] 1 Ch. 72, at 193–195 (Kerr LJ) (CA); *Al-Adsani v Government of Kuwait* (1996) The Times, 29 March; 107 ILR 536, at 545 (Stuart-Smith LJ), 550 (Ward LJ) (CA). Cf. Mann (1979) 50 BYIL 43, 62.

[122] See *Intpro Properties v Sauvel* [1983] QB 1019, 1022 (Bristow J), at 1029–1030 (May LJ) (CA).

[123] *United Arab Emirates v Abdelghafar* [1995] ICR 65; (1994) 104 ILR 647 (EAT), affirmed (1995) 107 ILR 627 (CA). That case concerned the time for appealing from the decision of an employment tribunal. The same considerations, it is submitted, would apply on an application to extend time for acknowledging service. See also *Arab Republic of Egypt v Gamal-Eldin* [1996] 2 All ER 237, at 242–243 (Mummery J) (EAT) (departure from normal rules of evidence on appeals) (also

support a cautious approach in determining whether a State has, by its conduct in litigation, submitted to the jurisdiction and thereby waived its immunity.[124]

The standard of proof required of a claimant will depend on the stage at which the issue of immunity is raised. Where a claimant seeks permission to serve a claim form upon a State defendant out of the jurisdiction, he must, *inter alia*, adduce sufficient evidence to satisfy the court that there is a *good arguable case* that defendant is not entitled to immunity under s 1(1).[125] Where, however, a State appears to assert its immunity (or the claimant seeks to enter judgment in default of appearance[126]), before the claimant may proceed with his claim, he must establish on the *balance of probabilities* the facts necessary to defeat the claim to immunity.[127] If necessary, the court must give directions for the final determination of any disputed fact relevant to the immunity issue.[128]

Approach to construction   **4.015**

It is also arguable that ss 2–11, being exceptions to a general rule, should be construed narrowly. It is to be noted, however, that the European Convention on State Immunity adopts a different structure, setting out circumstances in which no immunity exists before providing for a residual immunity.[129] An unquestioning, restrictive interpretation of the exceptions to the general rule of immunity would seem, therefore, to be at odds with the spirit of the European Convention as indeed would an expansive approach which sought to deny immunity wherever possible.[130] The ordinary meaning of the words must be sought, having regard in cases of ambiguity to the provisions of the European Convention and to customary international law.

---

reported at [1996] ICR 13; (1995) 104 ILR 673); *Military Affairs Office of the Embassy of the State of Kuwait v Caramba-Coker* (2003) unreported, 10 April (EAT).

[124] See 4.023 below.

[125] *Al-Adsani v Government of Kuwait* (1994) (CA, 21 January); *Al-Adsani v Government of Kuwait* (1996) The Times, 29 March; 107 ILR 536, at 545 (Stuart-Smith LJ), 551 (Ward LJ) (CA). See also Fox, 178 querying whether the "good arguable case" standard can be reconciled with s 1(2) of the 1978 Act.

[126] As to which, see Civil Procedure Rules, Part 13, Practice Direction, para 4.4(2) (see further 4.081 below).

[127] *J H Rayner (Mincing Lane) Ltd v Department of Trade and Industry* [1989] 1 Ch. 72, at 193–195 (Kerr LJ), 252 (Ralph Gibson LJ) (CA); *Al-Adsani v Government of Kuwait* (1996) The Times, 29 March; 107 ILR 536, at 545 (Stuart-Smith LJ), 551 (Ward LJ) (CA). Staughton J at first instance in *J H Rayner* raised the question whether a different standard should apply in the case of s 7 by reason of the use of the words "alleged infringement" (see [1987] BCLC 667, at 677).

[128] See *J H Rayner (Mincing Lane) Ltd v Department of Trade and Industry* [1989] 1 Ch. 72, at 194 (Kerr LJ), 252 (Ralph Gibson LJ) (CA).

[129] European Convention, Arts 1–15 (see 1.026–1.040 above).

[130] See Mann (1979) 50 BYIL 43, at 50. Compare the approach of Lord Edmund-Davies in *Iº Congreso del Partido* [1983] AC 244, at 276, applying a dictum of the United States Court of Appeals (2nd Circuit) in *Victory Transport v Comisaria General de Abastecimientos y Transportes* (1964) 336 F 2d 354, at 360 (also reported at 35 ILR 110), that sovereign immunity "should be accorded only in clear cases". See also *Larson v Domestic and Foreign Corporation* (1949) 337 US 682, at 703, describing sovereign immunity as "an archaic hangover" that should "be limited whenever possible" (US Supreme Court).

4.016 *Exceptions from immunity*

2 Submission to jurisdiction

(1) A State is not immune as respects proceedings in respect of which it has submitted to the jurisdiction of the courts of the United Kingdom.

(2) A State may submit after the dispute giving rise to the proceedings has arisen or by a prior written agreement; but a provision in any agreement that it is to be governed by the law of the United Kingdom is not to be regarded as a submission.

(3) A State is deemed to have submitted—

    (a) if it has instituted the proceedings; or

    (b) subject to subsections (4) and (5) below, if it has intervened or taken any step in the proceedings.

(4) Subsection (3)(b) above does not apply to intervention or any step taken for the purpose only of—

    (a) claiming immunity; or

    (b) asserting an interest in property in circumstances such that the State would have been entitled to immunity if the proceedings had been brought against it.

(5) Subsection (3)(b) above does not apply to any step taken by the State in ignorance of facts entitling it to immunity if those facts could not reasonably have been ascertained and immunity is claimed as soon as reasonably practicable.

(6) A submission in respect of any proceedings extends to any appeal but not to any counterclaim unless it arises out of the same legal relationship or facts as the claim.

(7) The head of a State's diplomatic mission in the United Kingdom, or the person for the time being performing his functions, shall be deemed to have authority to submit on behalf of the State in respect of any proceedings; and any person who has entered into a contract on behalf of and with the authority of a State shall be deemed to have authority to submit on its behalf in respect of proceedings arising out of the contract.

Commentary

4.017 Legislative history

At common law, a State could waive its entitlement to assert immunity by submitting to the jurisdiction of the English courts.[131] For such to be effective,

---

[131] For discussion of the common law position and of waiver of immunity generally, see *Halsbury's Laws of England* (4th edn), vol 18, para 1555; *Lewis*, ch. 8; Oppenheim, vol 1, 352–355. See also

however, the State (or its duly authorized representative) was required to conduct itself following the commencement of proceedings, and in the face of the court, in a manner inconsistent with its continued objection to the exercise of jurisdiction and in the full knowledge of the right being waived.[132] An agreement to submit to the jurisdiction in the event of a dispute was not sufficient for this purpose, and a State was fully entitled to disregard such agreement.[133] This rule was much criticized,[134] as was the proposition that a State was required to submit separately to the execution of any judgment arising out of civil proceedings which it had contested.[135] By proposing a relaxation of the former, but not the latter,[136] restriction, the State Immunity Bill attracted substantial criticism for not going far enough.[137] Despite this criticism, only one amendment was made to clause 2 in the course of the Bill's passage, namely to remove from clause 2(1) both the requirement that a written agreement by a State to submit to the jurisdiction be "between the parties to the dispute"[138] and the separate reference to submission by international agreement.[139]

Application   **4.018**

In considering the application of s 2 of the 1978 Act, it is helpful to consider the following situations separately:

(1) submission by prior written agreement;
(2) submission by treaty, convention or other international agreement;
(3) submission by agreement after the dispute giving rise to the proceedings has arisen;
(4) submission by institution of proceedings (including submission to counterclaims);
(5) submission by appearance.

One general matter worth noting concerns the terminology of s 2, insofar as it refers not to *waiver of immunity* but to *submission to jurisdiction*. This arguably[140] confuses the recognition of consent as a basis for the jurisdiction of the English

European Convention, Arts 1–3, 13 (at 1.026 to 1.028 and 1.038 above); ILA Draft Articles 1991, Arts 7–9 (at 2.014–2.019 above).

[132] *Baccus v Servicio Nacional del Trigo* [1957] QB 438; (1956) 23 ILR 160 (CA).

[133] *Kahan v Pakistan Federation* [1951] 2 KB 1003; (1951) 18 ILR 210 (CA).

[134] See, eg, Cohn (1958) 34 BYIL 260.

[135] See *Duff Development Corporation v Kelantan Government* [1923] 1 Ch 385; (1924) 2 ILR 124 (arbitration award).

[136] Indeed, s 13(3) expressly preserves this distinction (see 4.090 below).

[137] See the amendments proposed at the Committee Stage in the House of Lords: Hansard, HL (5th series), vol 389, col. 1480–1486, 1492–1500 (16 March 1978). See also 4.084 below.

[138] See 4.018 below.

[139] Section 17(2) (introduced by amendment) makes clear that references to an agreement include references to "a treaty, convention or other international agreement".

[140] See, however, the analysis of this issue by Laws J in *Propend Finance v Sing* (1996) 111 ILR 611, at 642 ("So it is at the State's choice whether, for its own ends, to accept in any proceedings the legal power of a foreign court: hence the question as regards the State will be whether it has submitted to the

courts generally[141] with its recognition as a basis for their jurisdiction over foreign sovereign states.[142] Subject to one matter raised below,[143] this observation appears to be of theoretical consequence only—the agreed submission by a State of disputes to a national court so as to vest that court with jurisdiction implies (as a necessary consequence or in order to give business efficacy to the term containing the submission) the surrender of the State's jurisdictional immunities. Moreover, conduct falling short of agreement but nevertheless evidencing an intention not to assert such immunities may be described, without too much artifice, as involving "submission".[144]

Two other introductory points may be more briefly mentioned. First, the importance of s 2 should not be overestimated. In view of the scope of the incursion into the general rule of immunity by the exceptions contained in ss 3–11 of the 1978 Act, it is unlikely to be of significance in many cases. In particular, proceedings to enforce a written agreement containing a submission to the jurisdiction of the English courts will usually fall within s 3 (commercial transactions etc.) or s 4 (contracts of employment). To date, the section has been relied on principally in the context of disputes concerning employees of foreign diplomatic missions[145] or in circumstances where a State otherwise entitled to immunity is alleged, by its conduct, to have taken a step in the proceedings.[146] Secondly, s 2 concerns only a State's immunity from jurisdiction and does not address waiver of the other immunities and privileges conferred on a State by Part I of the 1978 Act. As appears below, many of those privileges may also be disapplied by agreement of the State.[147]

4.019   (1) *Submission by written agreement*

A State may, in accordance with section 2(2) of the 1978 Act, submit to the jurisdiction of the English Courts by a written agreement made before the dispute giving rise to proceedings arose. As noted above,[148] this provision represented a departure from the established common law position. A party relying on this provision must nevertheless satisfy the relevant court or tribunal of four matters:

(a) That there is an agreement (ie a consensus) between the State and another person. Generally,[149] such agreement will take the form of a binding contract

---

jurisdiction. But the diplomat cannot by submitting himself to the jurisdiction be stripped of his immunity . . . unless his sending State says otherwise: unless it waives his immunity").

[141] Dicey and Morris, para 11R–106 and following.

[142] Properly characterized as waiver of immunity. See Lord Wilberforce at the Committee Stage of the State Immunity Bill in the House of Lords: Hansard, HL (5th series), vol 389, col. 1484–1485 (16 March 1978).   [143] See 4.019.

[144] Section 2(3) of the 1978 Act employs the technique of deeming such conduct to constitute a submission.   [145] See 4.116 below.

[146] See 4.023 below.   [147] See s 12(6) (at 4.077 and 4.080) and s 13(3) (at 4.090) below.

[148] See 4.017.

[149] Arguably, the term, "agreement" is broader than this and would encompass, for example, a mutual understanding unsupported by consideration. This construction is also supported by the use of the term "contract" elsewhere in the 1978 Act (see s 3(3)(a) (at 4.026) and s 4(1) (at 4.036). Nevertheless, Art 2 of the European Convention (see 1.027 above) refers only to a "contract in writing" and

between the State and the claimant. It is clear, however, that the agreement need not be between the parties to the dispute.[150]

(b) That the agreement was entered into on or after 22 November 1978.[151]

(c) That the whole of the agreement itself is in writing. It is not sufficient that the agreement is partly in writing[152] (eg a written acceptance) or is merely recorded in writing. In this context, writing includes typing, printing and other modes of representing or reproducing words in a visible form[153] but some doubt remains as to whether it is capable of encompassing contracts concluded electronically.[154]

(d) That the agreement is for the submission by the State to the jurisdiction of a court or courts in the United Kingdom. The words of submission must be express,[155] not implied, although it is not necessary for those words to take the (usual) form of "[Foreign State] agrees to submit all disputes arising out of this agreement to the courts of [England]". Thus, for example, an agreement to appoint an agent for service of process within the jurisdiction would almost certainly be sufficient for this purpose.[156]

Some difficulty may arise, however, in the event that an agreement contains, not a provision submitting disputes to the English courts (or other courts in the United Kingdom), but a provision merely setting out the State's agreement to waive any immunity that it may possess in any jurisdiction in which the counterparty should choose to bring proceedings. Such an agreement does not fit comfortably within the framework of s 2. The English courts may have jurisdiction in respect of the subject-matter of proceedings brought against a State in

---

this led the Employment Appeals Tribunal in *Government of the Kingdom of Saudi Arabia v Ahmed* (1993) 104 ILR 629, at 635–636 (Knox J) to conclude that s 2(2) required "a prior written contractual agreement, or *a prior written agreement in the nature of a contract*" (emphasis added); see also [1996] ICR 25 at 32–34; (1993) 104 ILR 629 at 645–646 (Peter Gibson LJ) (CA)). For the possibility that a proclamation to the world may constitute an "agreement" for this purpose (in the context of s 12(6)) see *ABCI v Banque Franco-Tunisienne* [2003] EWCA Civ. 205, para 29 (CA)).

[150] See 4.017 above. Thus, an assignee or successor-in-title could rely on the submission to jurisdiction.

[151] The date on which the 1978 Act came into force: s 23(3)(a) (see 4.148 below).

[152] *Ahmed v Government of the Kingdom of Saudi Arabia* [1996] ICR 25, at 34 (Peter Gibson LJ) (CA) (also reported at (1995) 104 ILR 629).   [153] Interpretation Act 1978, Sch 1.

[154] See the DTI's "Building Confidence in Electronic Commerce—A Consultation Document" (5 March 1999), para 16 but compare the Law Commission's advice (published at [2002] LMCLQ 468, at 471–473). Section 8 of the Electronic Communications Act 2000 delegates the power to extend references to writing to include electronic communications. To date, the 1978 Act is not one of the pieces of legislation in respect of which a change has been proposed.

[155] See the dictum of Lord Goff in *R v Bow Street Metropolitan Stipendiary Magistrate, ex p. Pinochet Ugarte (No. 3)* [2000] 1 AC 147, at 216–217 (HL), applied by the Employment Appeals Tribunal in *United States of America v Mills* (2000) 120 ILR 612, permission to appeal refused (CA, 20 May 2000). See also *Pinochet (No. 3)* at 267 (Lord Saville), 289–290 (Lord Phillips); *Friedland v United States of America* (1999) 120 ILR 417 (CA Ont), para 15 of judgment. For the position in relation to submission to the jurisdiction generally see *New Hampshire Insurance Co. v Strabag Bau* [1992] 1 Lloyd's Rep 361, at 371–372 (Lloyd LJ) (CA); Dicey and Morris, para 14–072. Ordinary principles of commercial construction apply (see the cases cited at fn 526 below).

[156] cf. Dicey and Morris, para 14–070.

these circumstances,[157] but that would not be because the State had submitted to the jurisdiction in the normal sense.[158] To fall within s 2(1), the waiver of immunity provision would have to be characterized as a submission by the State to the jurisdiction of the English courts *to the extent that such courts may have jurisdiction under their own rules in the absence of consent*. It is submitted, that such characterization, whilst not free from artifice, would accord with the spirit of this section.

Section 2(2) expressly confirms that a provision in an agreement that it is to be governed by "the law of the United Kingdom" is not to be regarded as a submission. Aside from the obvious incongruence of the reference to "United Kingdom" law (as opposed to the law of a part of the United Kingdom), this language does no more than reflect the prevailing view expressed in cases dealing with submission to the jurisdiction generally.[159] Nevertheless, it attracted strong criticism during the passage of the State Immunity Bill.[160]

A fortiori, a provision in an agreement whereby a State agrees to give effect to the provisions of a particular statute or substantive area of law (eg "United Kingdom employment law"), although not a choice of law provision, ought not to be treated as a submission.[161]

The State may dispute the validity of the contract in which the submission to jurisdiction is contained. As a matter of principle, however, the agreement on jurisdiction ought to be treated as independent and capable of surviving a challenge to the contract itself.[162] Any question as to whether the ground of objection to the contract (eg fraud) also undermines the agreement on jurisdiction must be resolved at the outset.[163]

4.020   (2) *Submission by treaty, convention or other international agreement*

The definition of agreement for the purposes of s 2(2) includes "a treaty, convention or other international agreement".[164] There would appear to be no decision of the English courts in which a waiver by treaty has been pleaded under this section.[165] Again, however, any waiver must be express and not implied.[166] Moreover, the treaty etc. must have been entered into[167] on or after 22 November 1978.

---

[157] For example, because the agreement was made within the jurisdiction: Civil Procedure Rules, r 6.20(5)(a).

[158] See *New Hampshire Insurance Co. v Strabag Bau* [1992] 1 Lloyd's Rep. 361, at 372 (Lloyd LJ) (CA).

[159] Ibid. See also *Dunbee v Gilman & Co.* [1968] 2 Lloyd's Rep. 394 (Sup.Ct. NSW).

[160] See Hansard, HL (5th series), vol 389, cols. 1492–1496 (16 March 1978).

[161] *United States of America v Mills* (2000) 120 ILR 612 (EAT); permission to appeal refused (CA, 9 May 2000).   [162] See Nygh, *Autonomy in International Contracts* (Oxford, 1999), 79–84.

[163] See 4.014 above.

[164] s 17(2). Cl 2(2) of the State Immunity Bill referred only to "international agreement". This phrase was criticized by Lord Wilberforce (Hansard, HL (5th series), vol 389, col. 1492 (16 March 1978)) as "puzzling", but would encompass, for example, agreements between one or more States and an international organization (or another subject of international law) (see the definition of "treaty" in Art 2(1)(a) of the Vienna Convention on the Law of Treaties 1980).

[165] cf. Lewis, 71–72, discussing case law of the United States' courts.

[166] See *R v Bow Street Metropolitan Stipendiary Magistrate, ex p. Pinochet Ugarte (No. 3)* [2000] 1 AC 147, at 215–217 (Lord Goff), 267 (Lord Saville), 289–290 (Lord Phillips) (HL) (see 4.137 below).

[167] In most cases, this will involve ratification or accession to the treaty etc by the State (see Brownlie, *Principles of Public International Law* (5th edn, 1998), 611–612).

(3) *Submission by agreement after the dispute giving rise to the* **4.021**
    proceedings has arisen

A State may submit, without formality, after the dispute giving rise to the proceedings has arisen.[168] It is not necessary for proceedings to have been issued, or even threatened, but it is submitted that the issue between the parties must have crystallized—the latent existence of facts in respect of which the claim ultimately arises is insufficient.

(4) *Submission by institution of proceedings/submission to counterclaims* **4.022**

A State is deemed to have submitted if it has instituted the proceedings.[169] This is straightforward and reflects the common law position and the European Convention.[170] The submission extends to any counterclaim arising out of the same legal relationship or facts as the claim, as well as any appeal.[171] Subject to relevant procedural rules,[172] a counterclaim may also be brought if it falls within one of the other exceptions set out in ss 3–11 of the 1978 Act.

(5) *Submission by appearance* **4.023**

A State is deemed to have submitted if it has taken any step in the proceedings[173] unless such step was taken *either*:

(a) for the purpose only of (i) claiming immunity or (ii) asserting an interest in property in circumstances such that a State would have been entitled to immunity if the proceedings had been brought against it[174]; *or*

(b) at a time when the State was ignorant of the facts entitling it to claim immunity (provided that those facts could not reasonably have been ascertained and the immunity is claimed as soon as reasonably practicable after ascertaining those facts).[175]

The term "step" in this connection bears the technical sense of "step in the proceedings"[176] (ie an act that impliedly affirms the correctness of the proceedings

---

[168] s 2(2).

[169] s 2(3)(a). See *Propend Finance v Sing* (1996–1997) 111 ILR 611, at 640–641, 651–652 (Laws J) at 658–659, 664–665 (CA) (proceedings brought by third party).

[170] European Convention, Art 1.1; *Sultan of Johore v Abubakar Tunku Aris Bendahar* [1952] AC 318 (HL).

[171] s 2(6). See Hansard, HL (5th series), vol 389, col. 1498–1500 (16 March 1978) for discussion as to the effect of this provision. Similar language is used in Limitation Act 1980, s 35(5). For the (more restrictive) common law position, see *Duke of Brunswick v King of Hanover* (1844) 6 Beav. 1, at 38 (Lord Langdale, HL); *South African Republic v La Compagnie Franco-Belge* [1898] 1 Ch. 190 (cf. [1897] 2 Ch 487); *High Commissioner for India v Ghosh* [1960] 1 QB 134; (1959) 28 ILR 150 (CA). See also *Propend Finance v Sing* (1996) 111 ILR 611, at 638–639 (Laws J) (diplomatic immunity); *Friedland v United States of America* (2000) 120 ILR 417 (CA Ont).

[172] See Civil Procedure Rules, Part 20.   [173] s 2(3)(b).

[174] s 2(4). As for the assertion by a State of an interest in property, see s 6 (at 4.054–4.060 below).

[175] s 2(5).

[176] *Kuwait Airways Corporation v Iraqi Airways* [1995] 1 Lloyd's Rep. 25, at 31–32 (Nourse LJ), 34 (Leggatt LJ), 37–38 (Simon Brown LJ) (CA).

and the willingness of the State to go along with them[177]; an act serving a useful purpose only if the State has waived its entitlement to dispute the jurisdiction[178]). Thus, for example, a State will not be considered to have submitted merely by applying to set aside a default judgment[179] or for the execution of a default judgment to be stayed,[180] by disputing the court's jurisdiction on other grounds,[181] by merely acknowledging service[182] or by applying to transfer the hearing of its jurisdiction application to another courts. On the other hand, a State clearly takes a step in the proceedings if it files a defence or applies for summary judgment.[183] In these and similar cases, the State will be deemed to have submitted for the purposes of the 1978 Act unless it is able to establish that either of the relieving provisions summarized above applies. Thus, for example, a defence whose only content is an assertion of immunity will not amount to a submission.[184] It is, however, difficult to envisage circumstances in which the relieving provision contained in s 2(5) will apply—a State will usually be fully aware of, or reasonably capable of discovering, the facts entitling it to immunity (usually its statehood or interest in property alone).[185] Ignorance of the legal entitlement to assert immunity is not sufficient.[186]

Inevitably, this aspect of s 2 requires greater caution on the part of States and their legal advisers than any other. In one case, a State was held to have submitted to the jurisdiction of the English courts by applying for a stay of proceedings on *forum conveniens* grounds, thereby implicitly accepting the jurisdiction of the English courts.[187] Whilst the result in that case might have been different had the State expressly qualified the stay application as being without prejudice to its assertion of immunity[188] or obtained the claimant's agreement not to raise the

---

[177] See *Eagle Star Insurance Co. v Yuval Insurance Co.* [1978] 1 Lloyd's Rep. 357, at 361 (Lord Denning MR) (CA).   [178] See *Rein v Stein* (1892) 66 LT 469 (CA).

[179] *Paprocki v German State* (1995) 104 ILR 684 (CA).

[180] *Kuwait Airways Corporation v Iraqi Airways* [1995] 1 Lloyd's Rep 25 (CA).

[181] *Kuwait Airways Corporation v Iraqi Airways Corporation* [1995] 1 Lloyd's Rep 25 (CA) (reliance on act of state doctrine). In *Crescent Oil and Shipping Services Ltd v Banco Nacional de Angola* (Comm, 28 May 1999) (Cresswell J), the immunity of the defendants pursuant to the 1978 Act was one of many factors taken into account on application to set aside service out of the jurisdiction.

[182] Provided that it subsequently makes an application disputing the court's jurisdiction within the relevant time limit: Civil Procedure Rules, r 11(5) (see 4.081 below). See also *London Branch of the Nigerian Universities Commission v Bastians* [1995] ICR 358 (transmission of blank appearance form to tribunal via Foreign and Commonwealth Office not a submission) (EAT); *Arab Republic of Egypt v Gamal-Eldin* [1996] 2 All ER 237, at 243–245 (Mummery J) (EAT).

[183] Unless, it would appear, the application for summary judgment is expressly conditional on rejection of the assertion of immunity (*Kuwait Airways Corporation v Iraqi Airways* [1995] 1 Lloyd's Rep. 25, at 38 (Simon Brown LJ) (CA)). See, in a different context, *Capital Trust Investments v Radio Design TJ* [2002] 2 All ER 159 (CA).

[184] *Kuwait Airways Corporation v Iraqi Airways* [1995] 1 Lloyd's Rep. 25, at 31–32 (Nourse LJ) (CA).

[185] See Hansard, HL (5th series), vol 389, cols. 1496–1497 (16 March 1978).

[186] *Malaysian Industrial Development Authority v Jeyasingham* (EAT, 5 December 1997). In this respect, the 1978 Act is more restrictive than the common law (see *Baccus v Servicio Nacional del Trigo* [1957] 1 QB 438; (1956) 23 ILR 160 (CA)). The apparent suggestions to the contrary in *Propend Finance v Sing* (1996–1997) 111 ILR 611, 653 (Laws J), at 671 (CA) are, it is submitted, incorrect.

[187] *A Company v B Company* (Comm, 3 April 1993) (Saville J).

[188] See *Kuwait Airways Corporation v Iraqi Airways* [1995] 1 Lloyd's LR 25, at 38 (Simon Brown LJ) (CA).

question of waiver, the safer course is to take no action that might be viewed by a court as affecting the merits of the claim. Procedural acts falling within this uncertain sphere include applications for discovery,[189] for security for costs[190] or for the transfer of the whole proceedings to another court and the giving of consent to the amendment of the claim documents.

In the High Court, the form for acknowledgment of service allows a defendant to indicate that it wishes to contest the jurisdiction.[191] Equivalent forms in other tribunals may need to be adapted or replaced by a letter setting out the State's position.

A State is also deemed to have submitted if it intervenes in proceedings otherwise than for the purpose of (i) claiming immunity, or (ii) asserting an interest in property in circumstances such that the State would have been entitled to immunity if the proceedings had been brought against it.[192] This would include, for example, circumstances where a State applies to be joined as a party to,[193] or otherwise seeks to be heard in, proceedings involving third parties.[194] Whether a State merely funding litigation by a third party would be deemed to have submitted to jurisdiction, thereby allowing the court to make an order for costs against it is debatable.[195]

Authority to submit **4.024**

The step(s) alleged to constitute a submission must have been authorized by the State concerned, although such steps will inevitably be taken by its servants or agents (often solicitors or counsel). In this connection, both (a) the head of the State's diplomatic mission in the United Kingdom or the person for the time being performing the functions of head of mission, and (b) any person who has entered into a contract on behalf of and with the authority of the State, are deemed to have authority to submit (the former in respect of any proceedings, the latter in respect of proceedings arising out of the contract).[196] This deeming provision appears to have been intended to resolve doubt as to whether the persons listed have authority to submit.[197] In other cases, the authority of the State's representatives must be established by evidence, if challenged.[198] In such cases, there can be no question of ostensible authority, this being a species of estoppel and incapable therefore of extending the court's jurisdiction.[199]

---

[189] cf. *Kurz v Stella Musical* [1990] Ch 196 (Hoffmann J).

[190] cf. *Lhoneux Limon v HSBC* (1886) 33 Ch D 446; *Baccus v Servicio Nacional del Trigo* [1957] 1 QB 438; (1956) 23 ILR 160. A suitably qualified application for security might not amount to a step in the proceedings (see *Hewden Stuart v Leo Gottwald* (CA, 13 May 1992).

[191] See 4.081 below.   [192] s 2(4).   [193] Civil Procedure Rules, rr 19.2 and 19.4.

[194] See 4.105 below concerning proceedings brought against its servants or agents.

[195] Supreme Court Act 1981, s 51. See *The Ikarian Reefer (No. 2)* [2000] 1 WLR 603 (CA).

[196] s 2(7).

[197] cf. *Baccus v Servicio Nacional del Trigo* [1957] AC 438; (1956) 23 ILR 160 (HL).

[198] See *Malaysian Industrial Development Authority v Jeyasingham* (EAT, 3 December 1997); *Propend Finance v Sing* (1996–1997) 111 ILR 611, at 652–653 (Laws J), at 671 (CA).

[199] *Ahmed v Government of the Kingdom of Saudi Arabia* [1995] ICR 25, at 33 (Peter Gibson LJ) (CA) citing *Secretary of State for Employment v Globe Elastic Thread* [1979] ICR 706. See also *Al-Kadhimi v Government of the Kingdom of Saudi Arabia* (EAT, 8 July 2003).

4.025   *Effect of submission*

A State submitting to (or otherwise held to be subject to[200]) the jurisdiction of a court or tribunal in the United Kingdom is generally treated like an ordinary litigant[201] and must, therefore, comply with all applicable procedural rules (including those concerning disclosure and the provision of evidence) unless (a) those rules are according to their terms incapable of applying to a foreign State,[202] or (b) particular provision is made by the 1978 Act or otherwise for proceedings involving a foreign State.[203]

In principle, a State having submitted will also be amenable to the court's powers to permit amendments to the nature of the claim or the relief sought. The submission, once made, cannot be withdrawn.[204] Nevertheless, where a State has submitted (whether in advance of proceedings, immediately following service of proceedings or following an unsuccessful attempt to assert immunity), the court must, it is submitted, proceed with extreme caution before allowing any application by the claimant to amend so as to ensure that the State is not prejudiced by its decision to submit (taken on the basis of the originally pleaded case). If, submission aside, the State would have been entitled to assert immunity if the new claim had been brought in its own right then permission should not be given unless the terms of the submission expressly and unequivocally contemplate that possibility.[205]

4.026   **3 Commercial transactions and contracts to be performed in the United Kingdom**

(1) A State is not immune as respects proceedings relating to—

    (a) a commercial transaction entered into by the State; or

    (b) an obligation of the State which by virtue of a contract (whether a commercial transaction or not) falls to be performed wholly or partly in the United Kingdom.

(2) This section does not apply if the parties to the dispute are States or have otherwise agreed in writing; and subsection (1)(b) above does not apply if the contract (not being a commercial transaction) was made in the territory of the State concerned and the obligation in question is governed by its administrative law.

---

[200] eg, on an application to enter judgment in default (see 4.081 below).

[201] See Lewis, 77; *Halsbury's Laws of England* (4th edn), vol 18, para 1559.

[202] In this connection, it is to be noted that, although a state has legal personality, it is not a company or, arguably, a body corporate for the purposes of rules of procedure (see Marston, (1997) 56 CLJ 374).

[203] See ss 12 and 13 (at 4.077–4.093 below).

[204] At least without permission of the court (see Civil Procedure Rules, r 3.10; *Yendall v Commonwealth of Australia* (1984) 107 ILR 590 (EAT)).

[205] See *J H Rayner (Mincing Lane) Ltd v Department of Trade and Industry* (CA, 7 May 1987); *Australia and New Zealand Banking Group Limited v Commonwealth of Australia* (reported as *Amalgamated Metal Trading v Department of Trade and Industry* (1989) The Times, 16 May) Transcript, 64–68 (Evans J); *Yendall v Commonwealth of Australia* (1984) 107 ILR 591 at 599 (EAT). See also *Grupo Torras v Al-Sabah* [1995] 1 Lloyd's Rep. 374, at 392 (Mance J) (service out of the jurisdiction).

(3) In this section "commercial transaction" means—
   (a) any contract for the supply of goods or services;
   (b) any loan or other transaction for the provision of finance and any guarantee or indemnity in respect of any such transaction or of any other financial obligation; and
   (c) any other transaction or activity (whether of a commercial, industrial, financial, professional or other similar character) into which a State enters or in which it engages otherwise than in the exercise of sovereign authority;

but neither paragraph of subsection (1) above applies to a contract of employment between a State and an individual.

Commentary

Legislative history   **4.027**

The exception for "commercial transactions" contained in s 3(1)(a) of the 1978 Act is undoubtedly the most significant qualification to the immunity conferred by s 1. Yet, as originally formulated, clause 3 of the State Immunity Bill[206] was more limited in its ambition, being restricted to the conduct of certain types of activity through a place of business in the United Kingdom. The exception for obligations to be performed in the United Kingdom, now contained in s 3(1)(b) of the 1978 Act, was set out separately in clause 4.[207]

The limited scope of these two clauses, which reflected the terms of Articles 4 and 7 of the European Convention[208] rather than the state of English law as declared by the Court of Appeal in the *Trendtex* case,[209] was the subject of damning criticism by eminent members of the House of Lords. Lord Denning MR, who had given the leading judgment in the *Trendtex* case, was the most strident of these critics expressing "the gravest misgivings about the contents of this Bill".[210] The Lord Chancellor expressed "dismay" at the reception given to the Bill and promised that the Government would re-examine matters.[211] These deliberations resulted in the introduction by amendment of a single clause combining a substantially broader "commercial transactions" exception with a modified version of the former clause 4.[212] Although the form of s 3, as enacted, remained substantially similar to this proposal, subsequent amendments resulted in important modifications to the definition of "commercial transaction".[213]

---

[206] See 4.154 below.   [207] See 4.155 below.   [208] See 1.029 and 1.032 above.

[209] *Trendtex Trading Corporation v Central Bank of Nigeria* [1977] QB 529 (CA) (drawing a distinction between sovereign and commercial acts without regard to their connection with the United Kingdom).

[210] Hansard, HL (5th series), vol 388, col. 70 (17 January 1978). See also Lord Wilberforce, at cols 66–67.   [211] Hansard, HL (5th series), vol 388, col. 78.

[212] Hansard, HL (5th series), vol 389, cols. 1501–1505 (16 March 1978) (Lord Elwyn-Jones).

[213] See Hansard, HL (5th series), vol 389, col. 1930 (23 March 1978) (addition of words "professional" and "enters or in which it" in what became s 3(3)(c)—for explanation, see vol 389,

4.028   Application

The result of these amendments is a provision whose scope is broader than the
well established (if not entirely straightforward) international law distinction
between sovereign acts (*acta iure imperii*) and commercial or private acts (*acta
iure gestionis*) in at least two respects, as follows:[214]

(a) The words "otherwise in the exercise of sovereign authority" which, in the
     context of s 14(2),[215] have been accepted as coming close to the sovereign/
     private act dichotomy[216] are contained only in s 3(3)(c) and do not qualify
     either sub-section (a) (supply of goods or services) or sub-section (b)
     (loans etc.).[217] Whilst, having regard to the criteria applied by the English
     courts in classifying an act as sovereign or private,[218] most transactions falling
     within either of these sub-sections would probably have been characterized as
     private, there are clearly examples whose status is not so straightforward.[219]

(b) Section 3(1)(b) removes immunity in the case of proceedings relating to any
     obligation of a State which, by virtue of a contract falls to be performed
     in the United Kingdom, whether that contract (or that obligation) is itself
     a "commercial transaction".[220]

Whilst the importance of these departures should not be underestimated, it
is notable that both Article 24 of the European Convention, which entitles the
Convention States to derogate from the provisions of Chapter I of the Convention
concerning immunity from jurisdiction,[221] and the United Kingdom's declaration
under this provision, are expressly stated to be "without prejudice to the immunity
from jurisdiction which foreign States enjoy in respect of acts performed in the
exercise of sovereign immunity". In construing s 3, therefore, due regard should
be had to principles of customary international law, for to ignore these may effect

cols. 1509–1510 (16 March 1978) (Baroness Elles)); Hansard, HC (5th series), vol 951, cols. 841–843
(13 June 1978) (addition of words "or other transaction" and deletion of words "raised by a State" in
what became s 3(3)(b)); Hansard, HL (5th series), vol 394, cols. 314–316 (28 June 1978) (approval
of Commons amendment at Committee Stage substituting final definition of "commercial transaction" in clause 3(3)).

   [214] See *Kuwait Airways Corporation v Iraqi Airways* [1995] 1 WLR 1147, at 1159 (Lord Goff) (HL).
   [215] See 4.103 below.
   [216] *Alcom v Republic of Columbia* [1984] AC 580, at 600 (Lord Diplock) (H.L); *Kuwait Airways
Corporation* [1995] 1 WLR 1147, at 1159 (Lord Goff) (HL); *Australia and New Zealand Banking
Group Limited v Commonwealth of Australia* (reported as *Amalgamated Metal Trading v Department of
Trade and Industry* (1989) The Times, 21 March) (Evans J).
   [217] See *Alcom*, at 603 (Lord Diplock, HL).   [218] As to which, see 4.103 below.
   [219] eg, the construction and operation of a military base (*Francischiello v USA* (1959) 28 ILR 158
(Tribunal of Naples, Italy), *Re Canada Labour Code* (1992) 92 ILR 264 (Sup. Ct. Canada)); the
printing of banknotes (cf. *A Ltd v B Bank (Bank of X intervening)* [1997] FSR 165; (1996) 111 ILR
590 (CA)).
   [220] In its application to non-contractual claims, however, s 3 may be narrower in scope than the
common law exception for *acta iure gestionis* (see 4.032 below).
   [221] In particular, Arts 4, 7 and 15 (see 1.029, 1.032 and 1.040 above).

a more radical departure from the United Kingdom's international obligations than Parliament intended.[222]

Meaning of the words "proceedings relating to . . ." **4.029**

The exception in s 3(1), in common with other exceptions to the general rule of immunity, is introduced by the words:

A State is not immune as respects proceedings relating to . . .[223]

The words "relating to" have been argued to have a wide import, requiring only that the claiming party establish a factual connection of any degree between the matter to which the exception relates (in the case of s 3, a commercial transaction or obligation to be performed in the United Kingdom) and the subject matter of the proceedings.[224] The better view, however, is that the proceedings must be "about" or "arise out of" the excepted matter.[225]

In complex cases, the enquiry that a court or tribunal must make will comprise three stages. The first will be to identify each separate claim[226] advanced against the State.[227] The second will be to elicit from the particulars of claim, and the evidence before the court on any application in which the issue of jurisdiction is addressed, the alleged acts or omissions of the State on which each claim is based (ie the constituent elements of the pleaded claim and not merely the factual background[228]). It is to these acts or omissions that, on the approach favoured above, the proceedings "relate" for the purposes of the 1978 Act. The third step will be to assess whether the claim is based (a) only on acts or omissions covered by the relevant exception, (b) on such acts or omissions as well as acts or omissions falling outside the exception (or any other exception), or (c) only on

---

[222] As noted above (see 4.004), the 1978 Act did not distinguish between the immunities from jurisdiction of States party to the European Convention and those enjoyed by other States. See also 4.015 above.

[223] ss 4, 6(1), 6(2), 7, 8, 11. Section 5 refers to "proceedings in respect of . . ." (see 4.047 below). Section 9 refers to "proceedings which relate to . . ." (see 4.064 below). See also s 16(2) (see 4.112 and 4.118 below).

[224] See *Holland v Lampen-Wolfe* [1999] 1 WLR 188, 193–194 (CA). The Court of Appeal was prepared to assume (without deciding) that this view was correct, but held that the connection had not been proven in that case. See also [2000] 1 WLR 1573, at 1579 (Lord Clyde) (HL).

[225] [2000] 1 WLR 1573, at 1587 (Lord Millett). See also, in a different context, *Gatoil v Arkwright-Boston Manufacturers Mutual Assurance Company* [1985] 1 AC 255, at 270–271 (Lord Keith, HL) (requirement of "direct connection").

[226] Support for this view of the meaning of term "proceedings" is derived from the references in s 10(1)(b) and s 10(2) to "claim" and "cause of action" (see 4.070 below); cf. ss 10(1)(a) and 12 (see 4.070 and 4.077) which arguably support the opposite conclusion. The point was left open by Evans J in *Australia and New Zealand Banking Group Limited v Commonwealth of Australia* (reported as *Amalgamated Metal Trading v Department of Trade and Industry* (1989) The Times, 16 May) Transcript, 5–6 (Evans J).

[227] If a course of conduct by the State is relied on, it may be necessary for this purpose to divide that conduct into separate elements, each constituting a legally separate claim (as in *Kuwait Airways Corporation v Iraqi Airways* [1995] 1 WLR 1147 (HL)).

[228] In *Holland v Lampen-Wolfe*, the commercial transaction on which the claimant relied was simply part of the factual background to the claim (see [2000] 1 WLR 1573, at 1587 (Lord Millett) (HL)).

acts or omissions falling outside the exception (or any other exception). In a category (a) or category (c) case, the conclusion from the enquiry will be clear—the State will either be immune (category (c)) or not (category (a)).

The difficult cases, needless to say, will be those falling within category (b). In such cases, the correct approach (it is suggested) requires the court to analyse carefully whether the acts or omissions that fall outside the exception can be described as being *de minimis* or subordinate to the acts or omissions falling within the exception.[229] If not, there appears to be a reasonable argument (as yet untested) that the general immunity should prevail on the ground that the proceedings do not solely or principally "arise out of" non-immune acts or omissions. Although it is thought that a court or tribunal, faced with this difficulty, might well be minded to adopt a broad construction of the words "relating to", this approach cannot (at least in relation to s 3) easily be reconciled with the UK's international obligations under the European Convention[230] or, indeed, with the "restrictive theory" of immunity.[231] The argument for a narrow construction may also be supported by the fact that Parliament considered it necessary to include express provision in s 4 to encompass proceedings in respect of statutory rights and duties arising from the employer-employee relationship.[232]

These matters have yet to be addressed directly by the English courts. One possible area of contention concerns claims for breach of contract. Commentators have generally assumed that a claim for breach of an obligation arising from a "commercial transaction" will fall within the scope of s 3 even if the act alleged to constitute the breach is a sovereign act (and not itself a "commercial transaction").[233] That this conclusion, however, does not necessarily follow from the language of the section appears to have been acknowledged by Lord Goff in *Kuwait Airways Corporation v Iraqi Airways*.[234] In some cases, what will be alleged is the simple non-performance of an obligation and the circumstances surrounding the non-performance will usually be either irrelevant or subordinate to the obligations assumed by the State under the commercial transaction.[235] In others, the allegedly "sovereign act" may be properly characterized as performance of the commercial transaction.[236] But in cases that cannot be so explained, the position is (unsatisfactorily) less clear.

---

[229] For an application of the *de minimis* rule of construction in this context, see *Alcom v Republic of Columbia* [1984] AC 580, at 604 (Lord Diplock) (HL).   [230] See 4.028 above.
[231] *I° Congreso del Partido* [1983] AC 244, at 263 (Lord Wilberforce: "If a trader is always a trader, a state remains a state and is capable at any time of acts of sovereignty . . . . The 'restrictive' theory does not and could not deny capability of a state to resort to sovereign action: it merely asserts that acts done within the trading or commercial activity are not immune.") (HL).
[232] s 4(6) (see 4.036 and 4.039).
[233] See, eg, Lewis, 43; Mann (1979) 50 BYIL 43, at 52. This, of course, is similar the question addressed at common law in *I° Congreso del Partido* which divided their Lordships (see [1983] AC 244 (HL)).   [234] [1995] 1 WLR 1147 at 1159 (HL).
[235] The explanation for non-performance may, in due course, raise issues of justiciability (see *The Playa Larga and Marble Islands* [1983] 2 Lloyd's Rep 171).
[236] See the conclusion reached by the majority in *I° Congreso del Partido* [1983] AC 244 (HL).

A "commercial transaction" entered into by the State **4.030**

The transaction in question must be entered into by the State. Thus, the fact that a State acts in relation to a contract between other persons will not suffice. The question whether a State has entered into a transaction will fall to be determined by its governing law, bearing in mind that the burden lies on the claiming party to establish the existence of the relevant transaction (on the balance of probabilities).[237] It is doubtful whether the exception extends to claims that a State has, for whatever reason, not enterered into a transaction[238] or for a declaration that no binding transaction has been concluded. The claiming party, however, need not be a party to the transaction, nor indeed a successor-in-title.

The meaning of "commercial transaction" is set out in s 3(1)(c) and has three elements:

(a) *"any contract for the supply of goods and services"*: the range of contracts encompassed by this language is broad, including any contract for the sale, hire or exchange of goods of any description (from microchips to battleships) and/or for the provision of services[239] (including services having an apparently sovereign element, for example repairs to embassy premises[240] or the storage of currency reserves[241]). The State may act as supplier, recipient or in another capacity.

Particular difficulties may arise in applying the "supply of goods" element of the definition, as follows:

- *Choses in action*: The meaning of term "goods" is not addressed by the 1978 Act but is defined by the Sale of Goods Act 1979, s 61 as including "all personal chattels other than things in action and money".[242] In *Ford & Sheldon's case*,[243] however, the view was expressed that choses in action could constitute "goods" for the purposes of an enactment and the cases appear to be divided on this point.[244] In the absence of authority in the present context, it is uncertain whether s 3(3)(a) applies to the transfer of shares, debts or other choses in action.[245]

- *Natural resources*: Resources (such as oil, gas or water) may well constitute "goods" for this purpose—the subject matter of the contract, however, must be the extracted product and not merely the right to extract it from the ground.[246]

---

[237] See 4.014 above.
[238] cf. *Banai v Canadian High Commission* (1990) 107 ILR 600 (EAT).
[239] Contracts of employment are expressly excluded from the scope of s 3(1).
[240] cf. *Planmount v Republic of Zaire* [1980] 2 Lloyd's Rep 393 (Lloyd J).
[241] cf. *A Limited v B Bank (Bank of X intervening)* [1997] FSR 165; (1996) 111 ILR 590 (CA).
[242] For discussion, see Guest (ed.), *Benjamin's Sale of Goods* (6th edn, 2002), para 1-078 and following.   [243] (1606) 12 Co Rep 1.
[244] *The Noordam* [1920] AC 904. See also the references collected at Stroud's Judicial Dictionary of Words and Phrases (6th edn, 2000), 1085–1091.
[245] s 3(3)(c) (discussed below) would apply, provided that the State entered into or engaged in the transaction otherwise than in the exercise of sovereign authority.
[246] See Guest (ed.), *Benjamin's Sale of Goods* (6th edn, 2002), para 1-087.

- *Other*: The proper characterization of computer software (particularly when transferred in a dematerialized form) is also unclear.[247]

(b) "*any loan or other transaction for the provision of finance and any guarantee or indemnity in respect of any such transaction or of any other financial obligation*": two aspects of this element of the definition are of note. The first is that the provision of finance may be either by or to the State. Secondly, there would appear to be a distinction drawn between a "transaction for the provision of finance" and "any other financial obligation" (a mere financial obligation does not fall within the definition of "commercial transaction" in its own right), but the nature of this distinction is elusive. The former phrase would certainly encompass any bond or other bearer debt instrument, derivative transaction, letter of credit, bill of exchange or promissory note as well as the provision of security for indebtedness. Bank overdrafts would also seem to be covered. The intention behind the latter phrase is less clear, but it may well cover other monetary obligations of third parties, such as the price under a sale of goods contract, rental payments or maintenance obligations.[248]

(c) "*any other transaction or activity (whether of a commercial, industrial, financial, professional or other similar character) into which a State enters or in which it engages otherwise than in the exercise of sovereign authority*": s 3(3)(c) is rather more complex than its bedfellows. If the act or acts of the State on which the claim is based do not fall within the other parts of the sub-section, the "commercial transaction" exception will only be capable of applying apply if the court or tribunal is satisfied of the following:

- The relevant acts (or at least some of them[249]) consist of one or more "transactions" or "activities". The former term arguably encompasses not only contracts but also gifts and non-binding statements such as letters of comfort. As to the meaning of the term "activity", although one English judge has construed this term broadly as consisting of "the act or series of acts (or omissions) upon which the allegation of [. . .] liability is founded",[250] Lord Millett has recently argued that "[t]he context suggests a commercial relationship akin to but falling short of contract (perhaps because gratuitous) rather than a unilateral tortious act".[251] If this narrower (albeit *obiter*) view is correct, the scope for applying the "commercial transaction" exception to tortious claims will be extremely limited.[252]

---

[247] See Guest (ed.), *Benjamin's Sale of Goods* (6th edn, 2002), para 1-086.

[248] Rental payments of the State in respect of immovable property in the United Kingdom fall within the scope of s 6(1)(b)—see 4.054 and 4.057 below.   [249] See 4.029 above.

[250] *Australia and New Zealand Banking Group Limited v Commonwealth of Australia* (reported as *Amalgamated Metal Trading v Department of Trade and Industry* (1989) The Times, 21 March) Transcript, at 56 (Evans J) ("I cannot see that any degree of repetition or continuity is a necessary part of any relevant activity, because otherwise a tortious act, committed once, could never be an activity, and would presumably always be immune, so far as sub-section (3)(c) is concerned").

[251] *Holland v Lampen-Wolfe* [2000] 1 WLR 1573, at 1587. See also the comments of Lord Mustill in his (dissenting) speech in *Kuwait Airways Corporation v Iraqi Airways Co.* [1995] 1 WLR 1147, at 1171 (HL).

[252] See 4.032 below.

- Each transaction or activity is of a commercial, industrial, financial, professional or other similar character. This test is intentionally broad and is unlikely to be decisive in many cases but would appear to exclude, for example, cultural or domestic arrangements.

- Any transaction or activity must have been entered into or engaged in by the State otherwise than *in the exercise of sovereign authority*. This latter phrase has been held to invoke the common law distinction between sovereign and private acts, a distinction considered further in the discussion of s 14(2) below.[253]

Contracts of employment are expressly excluded from the scope of s 3(1) as arguably, by implication, are other transactions covered expressly by other exceptions within Part I of the 1978 Act, including those creating interests in land (such as leases[254]), the contract between a company and its members[255] and agreements to arbitrate[256] It is to be noted that the concluding words of s 3(3) do not state that contracts of employment cannot constitute "commercial transactions", but that was the effect given to them by Lord Diplock in *Alcom v Republic of Columbia*.[257]

An obligation of the State which falls to be performed   **4.031**
in the United Kingdom

Section 3(1)(b) is in terms, far more limited and has been relied on successfully (so far as the authors are aware) only in the litigation relating to the collapse of the International Tin Council.[258] The following points are of note:

(a) The obligation in question need not be contractual but may arise in tort or otherwise.[259]

(b) The place of performance of the obligation should, it is submitted, be determined under its governing law. Under that law, the place of performance must, by virtue of a contract, lie within the territorial limits of the United Kingdom, as extended by ss 17(3) and (4).[260]

(c) The relevant contract (which cannot be a contract of employment[261]) need not be a commercial transaction or a contract under which the obligation arises, nor need the State be a contracting party.[262] That said, s 3(1)(b) is

---

[253] See 4.103. The suggestion by the late F A Mann that this phrase qualifies only the term "activities" (see (1979) 50 BYIL 43, at 53) appears incorrect.

[254] s 6(1): *Intpro Properties v Sauvel* [1983] QB 1019, at 1033 (May LJ) (CA).   [255] s 8.

[256] s 9.

[257] [1984] AC 580, at 603 (HL). For implications of this analysis, see 4.044 and 4.091 below.

[258] *J H Rayner (Mincing Lane) Ltd v Department of Trade and Industry* [1989] Ch 72 (CA); *Amalgamated Metal Trading v Department of Trade and Industry* (1989) The Times, 21 March (Evans J).

[259] *Australia and New Zealand Banking Group Limited v Commonwealth of Australia* (reported as *Amalgamated Metal Trading v Department of Trade and Industry* (1989) The Times, 21 March) Transcript, at 58 (Evans J).   [260] See 4.124 below.

[261] s 3(3).

[262] *J H Rayner (Mincing Lane) Ltd v Department of Trade and Industry y* [1989] Ch 72, at 195 (Kerr LJ), 222 (Nourse LJ), 252 (Ralph Gibson LJ) (CA).

unlikely to be decisive in many cases. For almost all purposes, s 3(1)(a) will provide a more attractive alternative for claiming parties.

4.032   *Application of s 3 to non-contractual claims*

Although the focus of those drafting s 3 was upon claims to enforce commercial transactions, it appears to have been accepted that the exception is equally capable of applying to non-contractual claims, including claims in tort.[263] Nonetheless, given the requirement that the proceedings relate to a commercial transaction entered into by the State[264] and the restricted interpretation recently given to the term "activity" in s 3(3)(c),[265] the potential for such application is likely to be limited. Other provisions of the 1978 Act are more suited to claims in tort.[266]

4.033   *Dispute between States*

The exception in s 3(1) does not apply where the parties to the *dispute* are States.[267] It is to be noted that the focus is on neither the parties to the relevant *transaction*,[268] nor on the parties to the *proceedings*, but on the parties to the *dispute*. This suggests that a State may be unable successfully to assert immunity in response to a claim brought by an assignee of rights under a State-to-State contract,[269] but may be able to assert immunity in response to a claim brought by a person acting as agent or nominee for another State.[270]

4.034   *Agreement in writing to confer immunity*

Section 3(2) permits the parties to a dispute to agree in writing that the "commercial transaction" exception should not apply. The conclusion of an agreement in such express terms appears improbable, although an arbitration clause or choice of a foreign court may well be sufficient.[271]

4.035   *Contracts governed by "administrative law" of State concerned*

The exception in s 3(1)(b) (obligations to be performed in the UK) does not apply if the contract (not being a commercial transaction) was made in the

---

[263] *Australia and New Zealand Banking Group Limited v Commonwealth of Australia* (reported as *Amalgamated Metal Trading v Department of Trade and Industry* (1989) The Times, 21 March) Transcript, at 53 (Evans J) (mis-statement); *Crescent Oil and Shipping Services Ltd v Banco Nacional de Angola* (Comm, 28 May 1999) (Cresswell J) (interference with contractual relations); *Re Banco Nacional de Cuba* [2001] 1 WLR 2039 (Lightman J) (transaction defrauding creditors under Insolvency Act 1986, s 423).

[264] See 4.029–4.030 above.   [265] See para 4.030 above.

[266] See s 5 (at 4.047–4.053), s 6(1)(b) (at 4.054 and 4.057), s 7(b) (4.061–4.063) and 10 (4.070–4.073) below.   [267] s 3(2).

[268] For recognition of the distinction between parties to the transaction and parties to the dispute in a related context, see Hansard, HL (5th series), vol 389, col. 1491 (16 March 1978). S 4(2)(a) of the 1978 Act, in contrast to s 2(2), refers to "the parties to the contract". Compare also Art 4.2(a) of the European Convention ("a contract concluded between States") with Art 7 ("parties to the dispute are States").   [269] Assuming that assignment is possible under the terms of the contract.

[270] See *Cardinal Financial Investments Corp. v Central Bank of Yemen* [2001] 1 Lloyd's Rep Bank 1 (CA) (reliance on s 3(2) flawed because counter-party to transaction not a State but a State-owned entity); *Kuwait Airways Corporation v Iraqi Airways* [1995] 1 Lloyd's Rep 25, at 30 (Nourse LJ) (CA).

[271] See para 29 of the Explanatory Report on the European Convention (at 1.095 above).

territory of the relevant State and is governed by its "administrative law".[272] Again, this exclusion[273] appears unlikely to trouble the English courts on a regular basis.

4 Contracts of employment

(1) A State is not immune as respects proceedings relating to a contract of employment between the State and an individual where the contract was made in the United Kingdom or the work is to be wholly or partly performed there.

(2) Subject to subsections (3) and (4) below, this section does not apply if—

  (a) at the time when the proceedings are brought the individual is a national of the State concerned; or

  (b) at the time when the contract was made the individual was neither a national of the United Kingdom nor habitually resident there; or

  (c) the parties to the contract have otherwise agreed in writing.

(3) Where the work is for an office, agency or establishment maintained by the State in the United Kingdom for commercial purposes, subsection[274] (2)(a) and (b) above do not exclude the application of this section unless the individual was, at the time when the contract was made, habitually resident in that State.

(4) Subsection (2)(c) above does not exclude the application of this section where the law of the United Kingdom requires the proceedings to be brought before a court of the United Kingdom.

(5) *In subsection (2)(b) above "national of the United Kingdom" means—*

  (a) a British citizen, a British Dependent Territories Citizen, a British National (Overseas) or a British Overseas citizen; or

  (b) a person who under the British Nationality Act 1981 is a British subject, or

  (c) a British protected person (within the meaning of that Act).[275]

(6) In this section "proceedings relating to a contract of employment" includes proceedings between the parties to such a contract in respect of any statutory rights or duties to which they are entitled or subject as employer or employee.

---

[272] See Lewis, 47.
[273] Reflecting the terms of Art 4.2(c) of the European Convention. Para 29 of the Explanatory Report to the Convention cites, by way of example, contracts relating to scholarships or subsidies (see 1.095 above). [274] *Sic.*
[275] As amended by British Nationality Act 1981, s 52(6) and Sch 7 and by Hong Kong (British Nationality) Order 1986 (SI 1986/948), para 8 and Schedule.

Commentary

4.037   Legislative history

In comparison to the provisions described above, the passage of clause 5 of the State Immunity Bill (based on Article 5 of the European Convention) was relatively untroubled. The only substantial amendment resulted in the addition of the reference in sub-section (1) to contracts made in the United Kingdom.[276]

4.038   Application[277]

Section 4 has quite often been relied on by claimants in cases brought before employment tribunals (formerly industrial tribunals)[278] and this body of claims has led to a number of decisions of the Employment Appeals Tribunal and the Court of Appeal.[279] Many of these decisions have concerned the position of employees of foreign diplomatic missions and consular posts and this aspect of the operation of s 4 is analysed in the commentary to s 16 below.[280]

4.039   *"Proceedings relating to a contract of employment"*[281]

Section 4(6) extends the scope of this exception to include proceedings between the parties to a contract of employment in respect of any statutory rights or duties to which they are entitled or subject as employer or employee. It encompasses, therefore, claims for unfair dismissal,[282] or alleging discrimination on grounds of sex[283] or race[284] in employment, although these are in the nature of statutory torts. It would also apply to claims to recover a redundancy payment[285] or to obtain compensation under equal pay legislation.[286] The requirement that the rights or duties arise out of an existing employer–employee relationship means, however, that s 4 does not extend to claims of discrimination or other unlawful treatment in the selection of employees.[287]

4.040   *Contract made or work to be performed in the United Kingdom*

The s 4 exception requires that *either* the contract be made *or* the work is to be wholly or partly performed in the United Kingdom.[288] These matters must, it is

---

[276] Following an intervention by Baroness Elles (see Hansard, HL (5th series), vol 389, cols. 1511–1512 (16 March 1978); Hansard, HL (5th series), vol 389, cols. 1931–1933 (23 March 1978)). A further suggested extension to persons recruited in the United Kingdom to work overseas was withdrawn. Other amendments were necessary to take into account the demise of clauses 3 and 4 in their initial form (see Hansard, HL (5th series), vol 389, col. 1514 (16 March 1978)).

[277] See Fox (1996) 66 BYIL 97; Garnett (1997) 46 ICLQ 81; Fox, 303–309. For the position of members of visiting forces and their civilian component, see Visiting Forces Act 1952, s 6 (see 4.118 below).

[278] An employment tribunal constitutes a "court" for the purposes of the 1978 Act in accordance with the definition in s 22(1) (see 4.143).

[279] See the cases cited in the commentary to this section and at 4.116 below.

[280] See 4.116 below.

[281] For discussion of the meaning of the words "proceedings relating to", see 4.029 above.

[282] Employment Rights Act 1996, Part X.   [283] Sex Discrimination Act 1975.

[284] Race Relations Act 1976.   [285] Employment Rights Act 1996, Part XI.

[286] Equal Pay Act 1970.

[287] *Banai v Canadian High Commission* (1990) 107 ILR 600 (EAT).

[288] For the meaning of "United Kingdom" in s 4(1), see ss 17(3) and (4) (at 4.124 and 4.126 below).

submitted, be determined by reference to the law governing the employment contract. The former requirement is similar to the basis in the Civil Procedure Rules 1998 r 6.20(5)(a) for obtaining permission to serve a claim form out of the jurisdiction.[289] The latter requirement requires an assessment of where, in accordance with the terms of the contract, the parties intended that the work was to be performed and not where, in fact, the employee has carried out his duties. It should, however, be borne in mind that the place of employment may be capable of being altered, either by mutual consent or by unilateral designation in accordance with the terms of the contract. The courts will also ignore any term of the contract that is a "sham" and does not reflect the parties' true agreement. The exception will apply if the parties intended that the employee was to carry out his work wholly or partly in the United Kingdom, although a *de minimis* connection (for example, an obligation to fly annually to the UK for appraisal) is likely to be ignored for this purpose.[290]

Application to particular categories of employee   **4.041**

Sub-sections (2) and (3) apply the exception to differing degrees in the case of certain categories of employees, and dis-apply it in the case of others, as follows:

(a) *Nationals of the employing State*: the exception applies to such individuals only if (i) the work is for an office, agency or establishment maintained by the employing State in the United Kingdom[291] for commercial purposes,[292] and (ii) the individual was not resident in that State at the time the contract was made.[293] The exception does not apply if the parties to the contract have otherwise agreed in writing and that agreement is effective.[294]

(b) *UK nationals*[295]: the exception applies to such individuals unless the parties to the contract have otherwise agreed in writing and that agreement is effective.[296]

(c) *Others*: the exception applies to such individuals only if *either* (i) they were habitually resident in the UK at the time when the contract was made,[297] *or* (ii) they were not habitually resident in the employing State at the time the contract was made[298] and the work is for an office, agency or establishment maintained by that State in the UK for commercial purposes.[299] The exception does not apply if the parties to the contract have otherwise agreed in writing and that agreement is effective.[300]

The difference in treatment between United Kingdom and other European Community nationals would appear *prima facie* to infringe the prohibition on

---

[289] Formerly RSC Ord. 1(1)(d)(i). See Dicey and Morris, para 11-155.
[290] See *Alcom v Republic of Columbia* [1984] AC 580, at 604 (Lord Diplock) (HL) (a case concerning s 13).
[291] For the meaning of "United Kingdom" in s 4, see s 17(3) (at 4.124 and 4.126 below).
[292] See 4.044 below; *Arab Republic of Egypt v Gamal-Eldin* [1996] 2 All ER 237, at 246–247 (Mummery J) (EAT).   [293] s 4(3).
[294] See 4.045 below.   [295] See 4.043 below.   [296] See 4.045 below.
[297] s 4(2)(b).   [298] s 4(3).   [299] See 4.044 below.   [300] See 4.045 below.

discrimination on the ground of nationality in Articles 12 (formerly 6) and 39 (formerly 48) of the EC Treaty, as well as Article 7(2) of Regulation 1612/68.[301] If so, United Kingdom courts and tribunals would very arguably be required to apply s 4 so as to give the same treatment to all EC nationals.[302]

4.042   *Meaning of "habitual residence"*

The concept of "habitual residence" is not defined in the 1978 Act, nor it would seem in other statutory contexts in which it is employed. The expression is not to be treated as a term of art, but according to the natural and ordinary meaning of the two words.[303] It seems that duration of residence, past or prospective, is only one of a number of relevant factors.[304] Habitual residence may continue during temporary absences, but will be lost if a person leaves a country with a settled intention not to return.[305]

4.043   *Meaning of "national of the United Kingdom"*

Defined by s 4(5), the concept of a "national of the United Kingdom" is far from straightforward, and detailed examination of its meaning is beyond the scope of this commentary. It includes the following categories of individual:

— British citizens;
— British Dependent Territories Citizens;
— British Nationals (Overseas);
— British Overseas citizens;
— persons who under the British Nationality Act 1981 are British subject; and
— British protected person (within the meaning of the British Nationality Act 1981).[306]

4.044   *"Office, agency or establishment maintained . . . for commercial purposes"*

As noted above,[307] the scope of the s 4 exception broadens significantly if the employee's work is for an office, agency or establishment maintained by the State in the United Kingdom for commercial purposes.[308] This phrase has two elements:

(1) *Office, agency or establishment*: whether a State has an office, agency or other establishment in the UK will be a question of fact in each case. The words used suggest that some degree of permanence is required.[309]

---

[301] See also Fox, 162 querying compatibility with Art 6 (and Art 14) of the European Convention on Human Rights.   [302] See *Factortame v Secretary of State for Transport* [1990] 2 AC 85 (HL).
[303] *Re J (A Minor) (Abduction)* [1990] 2 AC 562 (in the context of the Hague Convention on the Civil Aspects of Child Abduction). Cf. Dicey and Morris, paras 6-123 and 6-126.
[304] Dicey and Morris, para 6-124.   [305] Dicey and Morris, para 6-124.
[306] See *Halsbury's Laws of England* (4th edn), vol 4(2), paras 5 and following.   [307] See 4.041.
[308] s 4(3).
[309] See the case law on Art 5.5 of the 1968 EC Convention on jurisdiction and the enforcement of judgments in civil and commercial matters ("branch, agency or other establishment") (Dicey and Morris, paras 11R-269 and following).

(2) *Maintained for "commercial purposes"*: the office, agency or establishment must be maintained for the purposes of commercial transactions (as defined by s 3(3) of the 1978 Act).[310] It is submitted that this requires the court to focus on the external activities of the unit, for otherwise the application of s 4(3) would arguably be precluded in every case by the existence, for example, of contracts of employment between the unit's employees and the State.[311] If, however, the unit's external activities include material non-commercial transactions or activities,[312] then it cannot be said that the unit is maintained for commercial purposes.[313]

Agreement in writing to exclude exception   **4.045**

The s 4 exception may be excluded by agreement in writing between the parties, including (probably) a provision for arbitration or resolution of disputes in a foreign court. An agreement to this effect will be ignored, however, to the extent that United Kingdom law requires that proceedings be brought before a court (or tribunal) in the United Kingdom.[314] This limitation (based on Article 5.2(c) of the European Convention) would appear to address legislation preventing ouster of the jurisdiction of employment tribunals.[315]

Employees of foreign diplomatic missions and consular posts   **4.046**

By section 16(1)(a) of the 1978 Act, s 4 does not apply to proceedings concerning the employment of the members of a mission within the meaning of the 1961 Vienna Convention on diplomatic relations or the members of a consular post within the meaning of the 1963 Vienna Convention on consular relations. The effect of this sub-section upon the operation of s 4 is considered in the commentary on s 16 below.[316]

5 Personal injuries and damage to property   **4.047**

A State is not immune as respects proceedings in respect of—

(a) death or personal injury; or
(b) damage to or loss of tangible property,

caused by an act or omission in the United Kingdom.

---

[310] s 17(1). For commentary on s 3(3) see 4.030 above.

[311] See the closing words of s 3(3) and the final paragraph of 4.030 above.

[312] A *de minimis* exception applies (as to which see *Alcom v Republic of Columbia* [1984] AC 580, at 604 (Lord Diplock) (HL)).

[313] The conclusion reached by the EAT in *Arab Republic of Egypt v Gamal Eldin* [1996] 2 All ER 237, at 246–247 can be explained on this basis—although the State's medical office clearly entered into commercial transactions, by procuring medical services, it was principally engaged in providing gratuitous medical and related services to Egyptian nationals. The Tribunal concluded that these activities were entered into in the exercise of sovereign authority.   [314] s 4(4).

[315] See, eg, Employment Rights Act 1996, s 203.   [316] See 4.116 below.

Commentary

4.048   Legislative history

Clause 6 of the State Immunity Bill enjoyed an untroubled passage to become s 5 of the 1978 Act.

4.049   Application

Section 5 corresponds broadly to Article 11 of the European Convention.[317] Article 11 and s 5 are notable in representing, respectively, the Convention's and the 1978 Act's clearest departures from the traditional distinction between sovereign and private acts.[318] Conduct in the United Kingdom attributable to a foreign State causing death, personal injury or damage to property anywhere in the world may be the subject of proceedings in a United Kingdom court, however sovereign its character—for example, the actions of a foreign secret service[319] or presidential bodyguard.

The structure of s 5 is relatively straightforward.[320] It applies only insofar as the proceedings are in respect of death, personal injury or damage to or loss of tangible property (including pecuniary losses, such as lost earnings, suffered directly as a result of such injury), but not otherwise. The courts will regard with some scepticism attempts to evade the operation of the general immunity by alleging, for example, personal injury,[321] although even the successful introduction of such a claim will not affect the treatment of claims to recover damages for unrelated heads of loss (even those based on the same or similar facts). In any case, clear evidence will be required, the burden in this regard lying (as always) on the claiming party.[322] It is to be noted, however, that there is no restriction on the cause of action that may be relied on. Thus, although claims in respect of which s 5 is relied on will usually be pleaded in tort (including statutory torts[323] or claims for breach of statutory duty), the claimant may rely instead on, for example, a breach of contract or of the duties of a bailee.

---

[317] See 1.036 above.

[318] For discussion of the international law position, see *McElhinney v Ireland* (Application no. 31253/96), Judgment of 21 November 2001; 12 BHRC 114; 123 ILR 73 (European Court of Human Rights).

[319] See the discussion at 3.000 above of *Letelier v Republic of Chile* (1980) 488 F Supp 665; 63 ILR 378 (US District Court, DC) and *Liu v Republic of China* (1989) 892 F 2d. 1419, 101 ILR 519 (US Court of Appeals, 9th Circuit).

[320] F A Mann commented, perhaps too optimistically, that "[t]he provision and its application are fairly obvious and will only in the most exceptional cases give rise to any problem of construction" (see (1979) 50 BYIL 43, at 54).

[321] *Al-Adsani v Government of Kuwait* (1995) 103 ILR 420, at 432 (Mantell J); see also (1995) 105 ILR 536, at 544 (Stuart-Smith LJ) (CA).

[322] See 4.014 above. The *Al-Adsani* decision (discussed at 4.053 below) provides the clearest example of this.

[323] eg, unfair dismissal or unlawful discrimination (see *Government of the State of Kuwait v Fevzi* (EAT, 18 January 1999), permission to appeal refused (CA, 27 May 1999). *Military Affairs Office of the Embassy of the State of Kuwait v Caramba-Coker* (EAT, 10 April 2003).

"Death or personal injury" **4.050**

A claim in respect of "death" includes not only a claim by the deceased's estate in accordance with the Law Reform (Miscellaneous Provisions) Act 1934, but also a claim on behalf of the deceased's dependents under the Fatal Accidents Act 1976, s 1.[324]

"Personal injury" is not defined in the 1978 Act (nor the comparable phrase "injury to the person" in the European Convention), but "personal injuries" has been defined in other statutory contexts to include "any disease and any impairment of a person's physical or mental condition".[325] In this connection, the phrase would seem to encompass recognizable psychiatric illnesses[326] and also, perhaps, physical inconvenience or discomfort, but not injury to feelings, stigma or mental distress falling short of a recognizable illness and not arising from or linked to a physical injury.[327]

"Damage to or loss of tangible property" **4.051**

The requirement that the damage be to tangible property excludes claims for "pure economic loss", including interference with choses in action and intellectual property rights.[328] Cheques and negotiable instruments and other similar documents may well, however, constitute tangible property for this purpose (although their value lies in the intangible rights that they represent).[329]

"Caused by an act or omission in the United Kingdom" **4.052**

In the (typical) case of a motor accident resulting from negligent driving, no difficulty will arise in applying the causal test in s 5. Unfortunately, not every case will be so straightforward.[330] The following analysis is suggested:

(a) The act or omission referred to in s 5 could be construed as being either (i) the wrongful act of (or on behalf of) the State on which the claimant's action is based, or (ii) the immediate cause of the injury in respect of which the claimant sues.[331] On balance, the former view is to be preferred,

---

[324] See generally Dugdale (ed.), *Clerk & Lindsell on Torts* (18th edn, 2000), paras 29-64–29-107.

[325] See Limitation Act 1980, s 38(1); Supreme Court Act 1981, s 35(5).

[326] See Dugdale (ed.), *Clerk & Lindsell on Torts* (18th edn, 2000), para 7-63.

[327] *Military Affairs Office of the Embassy of the State of Kuwait v Caramba-Coker* (EAT, 10 April 2003). See also *Friedland v United States of America* (1999) 120 ILR 417, para 25 (CA, Ontario).

[328] Certain intellectual property rights are provided for separately in s 7 of the 1978 Act (see 4.061–4.063 below).

[329] See Dugdale (ed.), *Clerk & Lindsell on Torts* (18th edn, 2000), para 14-41. In *Propend Finance Pty Ltd v Sing* (1996/1997) 111 ILR 611, Laws J (with whom the Court of Appeal agreed on this point) rejected an argument that s 5(b) applied to a claim arising from the seizure of documents pursuant to a court order. Laws J suggested (at 652) that s 5 is concerned with "ordinary private law claims". In any event, the loss of the documents had been due to an act outside the jurisdiction, rendering s 5 inapplicable in any event.

[330] During the passage of the 1978 Act, Lord Wilberforce described the mechanism of s 5 in relation to composite acts as "unscientific" (Hansard, HL (5th series), vol 389, col. 1515 (16 March 1978)).

[331] Art 11 of the European Convention (see 1.036 above) requires that (a) the "facts which occasioned the damage" must occur in the forum State, and (b) the "author of the injury or damage"

on the basis that it focuses on the State's conduct within the territory in question.[332]

(b) In the case of continuing wrongs (such as false imprisonment) or multiple acts of wrongdoing, it may be necessary to separate acts or omissions that occurred while the actor was outside the United Kingdom from those occurring within the United Kingdom.[333]

(c) If the claimant alleges a single legal wrong comprising more than one act or omission[334] must have occurred while the actor was in the United Kingdom.[335]

4.053   *Conduct contrary to international law—Al-Adsani v Government of Kuwait*[336]

As s 5 encompasses only claims arising from acts or omissions in the United Kingdom, it provides no general basis for the removal of immunity in proceedings by individuals to obtain recompense for injury suffered in consequence of a foreign State's disregard of fundamental principles of international law (so-called "*jus cogens* principles",[337] including but not limited to the prohibitions on torture and genocide). No other provision of the 1978 Act fills what some would see as a lacuna, and an attempt to limit the general immunity conferred in such cases has been forcefully rejected by the Court of Appeal in *Al-Adsani v Government of Kuwait*.[338] The court treated the 1978 Act as providing a comprehensive code with

must be present in the State of the forum at the time the relevant facts occurred. Lewis (para 6.17) treats this language as supporting the second possibility set out above, but his reasoning is unconvincing. It is submitted that the "author" is the person (or persons) on whose (wrongful) conduct the claim is based.

[332] See *Propend Finance Pty v Sing* (1996–1997) 113 ILR 611, at 652 (Laws J), at 664–665 (CA). This view is consistent with the insistence of the Court of Appeal in *Al-Adsani v Government of Kuwait* (1996) The Times, 29 March; 105 ILR 536 that the claimant prove, on the balance of probabilities, that acts in the United Kingdom were attributable to the State defendant. Cf. Lewis, para 6.15.

[333] See *Al-Adsani v Government of Kuwait* (1995) 103 ILR 420, at 424 (Mantell J).

[334] Subject to a *de minimis* exception.

[335] Compare the approach to multi-jurisdictional torts under the former RSC Ord 11 (see *Metall & Rohstoff AG v Donaldson Lufkin & Jenrette* [1990] 1 QB 391 (CA)).

[336] See, generally, the Report of the Human Rights Committee of the International Law Association (British Branch) on Civil Actions in the English Courts for Serious Human Rights Violations Abroad ([2001] EHRLR 129); Jurgen Brohmer, *State Immunity and the Violation of Human Rights* (Dordrecht, 1997); Report of the ILC Working Group on Jurisdictional Immunities of States and their Property (6 July 1999), 56–58; Fox, ch 13. See also *Bouzari v Islamic Republic of Iran* (2002) judgment, 1 May (Superior Court of Justice, Ontario).

[337] The use of this term in this context is controversial and is used only for convenience to describe fundamental, non-derogable rules of customary international law binding on all States and concerned with the protection of basic individual rights. See also Brownlie, *Principles of Public International Law* (5th edn, 1998), 514–517.

[338] (1996) The Times, 29 March; 105 ILR 536. Al-Adsani, a dual British/Kuwaiti national, alleged that he had been tortured (in Kuwait) and received death threats (in Kuwait and London) from agents of the Government of Kuwait resulting in physical and psychological injury. For the earlier decision of the Court of Appeal, allowing service on the Government of Kuwait outside the jurisdiction, see (1994) 100 ILR 465. For procedural aspects of the decisions in *Al-Adsani*, see 4.014 above. See also *Jones v Ministry of the Interior, Kingdom of Saudi Arabia* (QB, 30 July 2003) (Master Whitaker) (noted *Scorer* (2003) 153 NLJ 1708).

regard to the entitlement of a State to assert immunity[339] and expressed concern at the practical consequences of allowing claims of this nature to be brought before the English courts.[340] The denial of Al-Adsani's rights of access to a remedy in the English courts has since been held by the European Court of Human Rights[341] to be compatible with Articles 3, 6.1 and 13 of the European Convention on Human Rights.[342] The leading majority judgment in the European Court reasoned as follows:

> While the Court accepts, on the basis of these authorities, that the prohibition of torture has achieved the status of a peremptory norm in international law, it observes that the present case concerns not, as in *Furundzija* and *Pinochet*, the criminal liability of an individual for alleged acts of torture, but the immunity of a State in a civil suit for damages in respect of acts of torture within the territory of that State. Notwithstanding the special character of the prohibition of torture in international law, the Court is unable to discern in the international instruments, judicial authorities or other materials before it any firm basis for concluding that, as a matter of international law, a State no longer enjoys immunity from civil suit in the courts of another State where acts of torture are alleged. In particular, the Court observes that none of the primary international instruments referred to (Article 5 of the Universal Declaration of Human Rights, Article 7 of the International Covenant on Civil and Political Rights and Articles 2 and 4 of the UN Convention) relates to civil proceedings or to State immunity.
>
> . . .
>
> The Court, while noting the growing recognition of the overriding importance of the prohibition of torture, does not accordingly find it established that there is yet acceptance in international law of the proposition that States are not entitled to immunity in respect of civil claims for damages for alleged torture committed outside the forum State. The 1978 Act, which grants immunity to States in respect of personal injury claims unless the damage was caused within the United Kingdom, is not inconsistent with those limitations generally accepted by the community of nations as part of the doctrine of State immunity.

In these circumstances, the application by the English courts of the provisions of the 1978 Act to uphold Kuwait's claim to immunity cannot

---

[339] *Al-Adsani* (1996) 105 ILR 536, at 540 (Stuart-Smith LJ) (CA). His Lordship drew support (at 542–543) for his conclusion from the decision of the United States Supreme Court in *Argentine Republic v Amerada Hess Shipping Corporation* (1989) 488 US 428; 81 ILR 658 and the decision of the US Court of Appeals (9th Circuit) in *Siderman de Blake v Republic of Argentina* (1992) 965 F 2d 699; 103 ILR 454.

[340] At 544 (Stuart-Smith LJ). See also the concurring opinion of Judges Pellonpää and Bratza in *Al-Adsani v UK* (Application no 35763/97), Judgment of 21 November 2001 (European Court of Human Rights).

[341] Albeit (in the case of Art 6.1) by the narrowest of majorities: *Al-Adsani v United Kingdom* (Application no 35763/97), Judgment of 21 November 2001; 12 BHRC 89; 123 ILR 24.

[342] See further 4.007 above.

be said to have amounted to an unjustified restriction on the applicant's access to a court.[343]

As matters stand, it appears that international law continues to recognize a State's right to immunity from civil proceedings in these circumstances,[344] although the possibility of further development cannot be excluded.[345]

4.054 **6 Ownership, possession and use of property**

(1) A State is not immune as respects proceedings relating to—

    (a) any interest of the State in, or its possession or use of, immovable property in the United Kingdom; or

    (b) any obligation of the State arising out of its interest in, or its possession or use of, any such property.

(2) A State is not immune as respects proceedings relating to any interest of the State in movable or immovable property, being an interest arising by way of succession, gift or bona vacantia.

(3) The fact that a State has or claims an interest in any property shall not preclude any court from exercising in respect of it any jurisdiction relating to the estates of deceased persons or persons of unsound mind or to insolvency, the winding up of companies or the administration of trusts.

(4) A court may entertain proceedings against a person other than a State notwithstanding that the proceedings relate to property—

    (a) which is in the possession or control of a State; or

    (b) in which a State claims an interest,

if the State would not have been immune had the proceedings been brought against it or, in a case within paragraph (b) above, if the claim is neither admitted nor supported by prima facie evidence.

Commentary

4.055   Legislative history

Section 6 (clause 7) of the 1978 Act collects together certain provisions relating to the ownership, possession and use of property.[346] Its parliamentary passage was relatively untroubled, only one amendment being made to remove from

---

[343] *Al-Adsani v United Kingdom* (2001) 12 BHRC 89; 123 ILR 24, paras 61 and 66–67. Compare the dissenting judgments of the minority.

[344] See *R v Bow Street Metropolitan Stipendiary Magistrate, ex parte Pinochet Ugarte (No. 3)* [2000] 1 AC 147, at 264–265 (Lord Hutton), 278 (Lord Millett), 281, 286–287 (Lord Phillips) (HL).

[345] It is understood that the claimant is appealing against the decision to uphold immunity in the case of *Jones* (referred to in fn. 338 above).

[346] Derived from Arts 9, 10, 13 and 14 of the European Convention (see 1.034–1.035, and 1.038–1.039 above).

clause 7(3) qualifying words excluding its operation in cases where the State is a trustee.[347] During debate, Lord Wilberforce expressed his regret at the formulation of clause 7(4) (s 6(4)) on the ground that, in his view, it was a statutory recognition of the decision of the House of Lords in *Dolfus Mieg v Bank of England*.[348]

Application **4.056**

The provisions of s 6, which have rarely troubled the English courts, must be considered separately. In particular, it is important to draw a clear distinction between sub-sections (1) and (2), which contain exceptions to the general immunity conferred by s 1 of the 1978 Act, and sub-sections (3) and (4) which merely limit the circumstances in which a State will be considered to have been impleaded in proceedings to which it is not a party (and therefore entitled to assert the general immunity, unless excluded).[349] In other words, sub-sections (3) and (4), unlike sub-sections (1) and (2), provide no basis for removing the general immunity where the State itself is a party to proceedings.

Proceedings involving immovable property **4.057**

Section 6(1) reflects closely the terms of Article 9 of the European Convention.[350] As the commentary upon Article 9 in the Explanatory Report recognizes,[351] the expressions "rights", "use" and "possession" must be interpreted broadly. Thus s 6(1) would seem to encompass not only disputes as to the ownership or possession of land (the paradigm example of a case falling within the exception), but also, for example, proceedings relating to mortgages of land, actions for nuisance and trespass to land, landlord and tenant disputes,[352] occupier's liability actions (although such claims are likely to fall also within s 5[353]) and civil liability imposed on a landowner under legislation concerned with protection of the environment.[354]

The proceedings must, however, be proceedings "relating to"[355] a State's interest in, or possession or use of, immovable property or an obligation "arising out" of such interest, possession or use. Thus, for example, a claim by a contractor to recover the price of a swimming pool built on land belonging to a State would not fall within s 6(1) as the proceedings would relate to and arise out of the building contract, rather than the State's possession or use of land.[356] That said, the point here is of theoretical interest only as proceedings would fall clearly within the s 3 exception for commercial transactions.

---

[347] Hansard, HL (5th series), vol 389, cols. 1515–1516 (16 March 1978).
[348] Reported as *United States of America v Dolfus Mieg et Cie* [1952] AC 582. See also *Juan Ysmael & Co. Inc. v Government of the Republic of Indonesia* [1955] AC 72; (1954) 21 ILR 95 (PC).
[349] See 4.012 above.   [350] See 1.034 above.
[351] See paragraphs 43–44, at 1.100 above.
[352] See, eg, *Intpro v Sauvel* [1983] 1 QB 1019 (CA).   [353] See 4.047–4.053 above.
[354] See, eg, Part IIA of the Environmental Protection Act 1990.
[355] For discussion of the meaning of the words "relating to", see 4.029 above.
[356] Compare Lewis, 54.

The term "immovable property" is not co-extensive with the term "real property" familiar to common lawyers, but is recognized in English private international law.[357] It encompasses the following types of interest in land: leaseholds, rentcharges, mortgages, interests under a trust for sale and (probably) the interest of an unpaid vendor.

Section 16(1)(b) of the 1978 Act provides that s 6(1) does not apply to proceedings concerning a State's title to or its possession of property used for the purposes of a diplomatic mission. The effect of this sub-section upon the operation of s 6(1) is considered in the commentary on section 16 below.[358]

4.058   *Proceedings involving interests arising by way of succession,*
            gift or bona vacantia

Section 6(2) reflects closely the terms of Article 10 of the European Convention.[359] That provision is unusual among the exceptions to immunity contained in the Convention in that it lacks any connecting factor with the forum.[360] For this reason, special provision has been made for the enforcement of judgments between convention states where jurisdiction has been founded on Article 10.[361] Section 6(2) applies equally to movable and immovable property, including (it would seem) intangible property.[362] It applies only if the proceedings in question are proceedings "relating to" the State's interest. [363]

It has been suggested that s 6(2) allows proceedings to be brought against a State to enforce any liability acquired by the State by reason of its universal succession to the assets and liabilities of a corporation.[364] It is said that the phrase "interest of the State in movable or immovable property" is broad enough to encompass such liabilities. With respect, it is submitted that this stretches language and the jurisdiction of the English courts too far.[365]

4.059   *Administration of estates and trusts, insolvency proceedings*

Section 6(3) is derived from Article 14 of the European Convention (which refers generally to the administration of property, citing as examples trust property or the estate of a bankrupt).[366] As noted above, the sub-section is not phrased in terms of a general exception to the general immunity conferred on a State by s 1. Indeed, the words "immune" and "immunity" do not appear. Rather, it prevents a State from asserting that it has been impleaded in proceedings to

---

[357] Dicey and Morris, paras 22-004–22-019.   [358] See 4.117.   [359] See 1.035 above.
[360] See paragraph 45 of the Explanatory Memorandum to the Convention, at 1.101 above.
[361] See s 19(3) of the 1978 Act (at 4.127 below).   [362] Dicey and Morris, para 22-010.
[363] For discussion of the meaning of the words "relating to", see 4.029 above.
[364] Mann (1979) 50 BYIL 43, at 55.
[365] Suppose, for example, that a foreign central bank (having separate status) intervenes in currency markets in the exercise of its economic functions. Subsequently, the foreign State dissolves its bank, thereby acquiring its assets and liabilities by universal succession. On the suggested interpretation of s 6(2), an action could now be brought against the State by aggrieved investors even though the bank would itself have been immune (see *Crescent Oil and Shipping Services Ltd v Banco Nacional de Angola* (Comm, 28 May 1999) (Cresswell J)).   [366] See 1.039 above.

which it is not a party solely on account that it claims an interest in the property being administered.[367] Section 6(3) provides no basis for removing the general immunity in proceedings against a State, for example proceedings to set aside a preference or in respect of an alleged transaction at an undervalue.[368] Nor would it permit a winding-up petition against an insolvent State (although the Insolvency Act 1986 would provides no obvious basis for this in any event and it is virtually inconceivable that an English court would be willing to make such an order[369]). Nor would it prevent a State from contending that it is impleaded in an action by reason of factors other than its interest in property.[370]

State interests in property   **4.060**

Section 6(4), derived from Article 13 of the European Convention,[371] must be read together with s 6(3).[372] It performs a similar function (ie precluding a State from intervening successfully in proceedings on the ground that it is indirectly impleaded by virtue of its interest), but unlike s 6(3) is conditional. Typically, its provisions will be invoked where proceedings concern property held by an agent, trustee or bailee on behalf of the State.[373] The first alternative condition, that the State would not have been immune had the proceedings been brought against it, emphasizes the obligation of a court or tribunal to give effect to the general immunity (unless removed) even if a State does not appear in the proceedings.[374] The second condition, that the interest in property of a State is neither admitted nor supported by *prima facie* evidence reflects the decision of the Privy Council in *Juan Ysmael v Government of the Republic of Indonesia*.[375]

It would seem to follow that, if neither of these conditions is satisfied then (unless s 6(3) applies) a State is to be treated as being impleaded and, therefore, immune if the proceedings relate to property of the character specified. In this connection, it is observed that there is no limitation as to the form which the property must take; indeed, the word "control" in sub-paragraph (a) may have been inserted with a mind to intangible property such as debts and other choses in action.[376]

---

[367] See 4.012 above.

[368] This point was, however, left open by Browne-Wilkinson V-C in *Re Rafidain* [1992] BCLC 301, at 304. In that case, the State (Iraq) sought, rather optimistically, to argue that its general immunity from suit under s 1 prevented a winding-up petition from proceeding against a bank of which it was a creditor. The court held that the winding-up of a company does not directly implead a foreign state which is simply a creditor. Cf. *Re Banco Nacional de Cuba* [2001] 1 WLR 2039 (discussed at 4.104 below). See Fox, 165.

[369] See *Banco Nacional de Cuba v Cosmos Trading Corp.* [2000] 1 BCLC 813, at 820 (Scott V-C) (CA) (foreign central bank) (see further 4.107 below). Cf. *Republic of Zaire v Duclaux* (1989) 20 Neth.YBIL 296 (Netherlands).

[370] For example, the fact that a claim is made against its agent (see 4.012 above).

[371] See 1.038 above.   [372] See 4.059 above.

[373] See *United States of America v Dolfus Mieg et Cie* [1952] AC 52 (HL); *Rahimtoola v Nizam of Hyderabad* [1958] AC 379 (HL).   [374] s 1(2) (see 4.014 above).

[375] [1955] AC 72 (PC).

[376] See *Rahimtoola v Nizam of Hyderabad* [1958] AC 379, at 395–396 (Visc. Simonds) (HL).

4.061   **7 Patents, trade-marks etc.**

A State is not immune as respects proceedings relating to—

(a) any patent, trade-mark, design or plant breeders' rights belonging to the State and registered or protected in the United Kingdom or for which the State has applied in the United Kingdom;

(b) an alleged infringement by the State in the United Kingdom of any patent, trade-mark, design, plant breeders' rights or copyright; or

(c) the right to use a trade or business name in the United Kingdom.

Commentary

4.062   Legislative history

Section 7 (clause 8) of the 1978 Act was approved without amendment.[377]

4.063   Application

Section 7 is broadly worded and its application seems unlikely to cause difficulties. It has yet to be relied on directly before an English court.[378] Sub-paragraphs (b) and (c) provide examples of the 1978 Act allowing claims in tort to be brought against a State.[379] It is not clear whether the use of the words "alleged infringement" in sub-paragraph (b) affect the standard of proof ordinarily required to overcome the immunity in s 1.[380]

4.064   **8 Membership of bodies corporate etc.**

(1) A State is not immune as respects proceedings relating to its membership of a body corporate, an unincorporated body or a partnership which—

(a) has members other than States; and

(b) is incorporated or constituted under the law of the United Kingdom or is controlled from or has its principal place of business in the United Kingdom, being proceedings arising between the State and the body or its other members or, as the case may be, between the State and the other partners.

(2) This section does not apply if provision to the contrary has been made by an agreement in writing between the parties to the dispute or by the constitution or other instrument establishing or regulating the body or partnership in question.

---

[377] s 7 is derived from Art 8 of the European Convention.
[378] cf. *A Ltd v B Bank (Bank of X intervening)* [1997] FSR 165; (1996) 111 ILR 590 (CA); *Gerber Products Co. v Gerber Foods International Ltd* [2002] EWHC (Ch) 428. Contrast *Vavasseur v Krupp* (1878) 9 Ch.D. 351 (CA). For the meaning of "United Kingdom" in s 7, see ss 17(3) and (4) (at 4.126 below).
[379] Paragraph (c) may be broad enough to encompass an action for passing off.
[380] See *J H Rayner (Mincing Lane) Ltd v Department of Trade and Industry* [1987] BCLC 667, at 677 (Staughton J).

Commentary

Legislative history **4.065**

Section 8 (clause 9) of the 1978 Act was approved without amendment.[381]

Application **4.066**

Section 8 has a limited scope. For the general immunity to be disapplied, the following requirements must be satisfied:

(a) The proceedings must relate to the State's membership of a body corporate, an unincorporated body or a partnership.

(b) The body or partnership in question must have members other than States.

(c) The body or partnership in question must be incorporated or constituted under United Kingdom law or be controlled from or have its principal place of business in the United Kingdom.[382] (Accordingly, the section may extend to proceedings involving a foreign entity, even one incorporated in the relevant foreign State.)

(d) The proceedings must be between the State and the body or between the State and the other members of the body or the other partners.

(e) The parties to the dispute must not have agreed otherwise in writing and there must be no contrary provision in the constitution or instrument establishing or regulating the body or partnership.[383]

One potentially "surprising" consequence of s 8 was noted by the Court of Appeal in *Maclaine Watson v International Tin Council*.[384] Whereas Article 6 of the European Convention refers to participation with "one or more private persons", s 8(1) requires only one or more non-State members. Might this encompass a joint venture between one or more States and an international organization or, more problematically, an international organization one of whose members was another such organization?[385] The Court of Appeal, while not deciding the point, thought that there were difficulties in justifying any other construction. In the light, however, of the wording of Article 6 and the fact that (in the case of an international organization) any claim between members would be unlikely to be justiciable in the English courts,[386] a more limited construction may be justified.[387]

---

[381] This section is derived from Article 6 of the European Convention (see 1.031 above), although there is at least one difference in language (see 4.066 below).

[382] For the meaning of "United Kingdom" in s 8, see s 17(3) (at 4.124 and 4.126 above).

[383] s 8(2).   [384] [1989] Ch 253, at 282–283 (Ralph Gibson LJ) (CA).

[385] Such as the International Tin Council.

[386] *J H Rayner (Mincing Lane) Ltd v Department of Trade and Industry* [1990] 2 AC 418; (1989) 81 ILR 670 (HL). As to the relationship between the 1978 Act and the question of justiciability, see 4.006 above.

[387] For a similar approach to legislative construction, see *Re International Tin Council* [1989] Ch 309; (1988) 80 ILR 181 (CA) (winding-up of an international organization as an "unregistered company" under the Companies Act 1985 not contemplated by Parliament).

4.067 9 Arbitrations

(l) Where a State has agreed in writing to submit a dispute which has arisen, or may arise, to arbitration, the State is not immune as respects proceedings in the courts of the United Kingdom which relate to the arbitration.

(2) This section has effect subject to any contrary provision in the arbitration agreement and does not apply to any arbitration agreement between States.

Commentary

4.068   Legislative history

Two important amendments were made to the text of clause 10 of the Bill in its passage through Parliament. First, clause 10(2) excluding the operation of the exception in "proceedings for the enforcement of an award" was omitted.[388] Secondly, words limiting the operation of the exception to an arbitration "in or according to the law of the United Kingdom" were excluded, thereby permitting proceedings relating to foreign arbitrations (including proceedings to register a foreign award for enforcement).[389]

4.069   Application

Section 9 reverses the position under the common law, whereby an agreement to arbitrate did not constitute a submission to the jursidiction of the English courts in respect of that arbitration.[390] The requirement of a written agreement conforms with the Arbitration Act 1996, s 5.[391] Where such an agreement has been concluded by a State, it will enjoy no immunity in proceedings, for example, (a) to appoint an arbitral tribunal,[392] (b) for removal of an arbitrator,[393] (c) for the determination of a preliminary point of jurisdiction,[394] (d) seeking exercise of the court's powers associated with the conduct of an arbitration,[395] (e) to enter judgment on an award (English or foreign) or register an award for enforcement,[396] or (f) to set aside or appeal any award.[397]

As one commentator has noted,[398] s 9 appears in three respects to be broader than the corresponding provision in Article 12 of the European

---

[388] Hansard, HL (5th series), vol 389, cols. 1516–1517 (16 March 1978).

[389] Hansard, HL (5th series), vol 394, col. 316 (16 June 1978) (approving a Commons amendment).

[390] *Duff Development Company v Government of Kelantan* [1924] AC 797 (HL). See, generally, Oppenheim, vol 1, p. 352, fn 37; Fox (1988) 37 ICLQ 1, esp 10–18; Fox (1996) 12 Arbitration Int. 89; Vibhute [1998] JBL 550–563.

[391] See further 4.019 as to the requirement of a written agreement.

[392] Arbitration Act 1996, s 18.   [393] Arbitration Act 1996, s 24.

[394] Arbitration Act 1996, s 32.   [395] Arbitration Act 1996, ss 42–45.

[396] Arbitration Act 1996, s 66; Part III (New York Convention); Arbitration Act 1950, Part II (Geneva Convention); Administration of Justice Act 1920, Part II. See generally Dicey and Morris, paras 16R-058 and following. The available procedures for execution of a registered arbitral award, or a judgment entered on an arbitral award, are limited by the provisions of s 13 of the 1978 Act (see 4.083–4.093 below, especially 4.088). So much is clear from the wording of s 13(2)(b).

[397] Arbitration Act 1996, ss 67–71.   [398] Fox (1988) 37 ICLQ 1, 11–18.

Convention.[399] First, the dispute need not be of a civil or commercial nature. Secondly, the arbitration need not take place in the United Kingdom or according to the law of a part of the United Kingdom. Finally, the category of proceedings to which s 9 applies is limited only by the words "which relate to the arbitration"[400] and not to the more limited types of application referred to in Article 12. As noted above, s 9 applies to proceedings to enter judgment on an award or register an award for enforcement, although proceedings for execution of the award are subject to the limitations imposed by s 13.[401]

By s 9(2), this exception from immunity is subject to any contrary provision in the arbitration agreement and does not apply to an arbitration agreement between States. In this latter respect, s 9(2) can be contrasted with s 3(2) which excludes the commercial transaction exception in cases where the parties *to the dispute* are States.[402]

The procedural requirements in s 12[403] apply equally to arbitration claims before the English courts, including proceedings to enter judgment on an award or register an award for enforcement.[404]

10 Ships used for commercial purposes   **4.070**

(1) This section applies to—

(a) Admiralty proceedings; and

(b) proceedings on any claim which could be made the subject of Admiralty proceedings.

(2) A State is not immune as respects—

(a) an action in rem against a ship belonging to that State; or

(b) an action in personam for enforcing a claim in connection with such a ship, if, at the time when the cause of action arose, the ship was in use or intended for use for commercial purposes.

(3) Where an action in rem is brought against a ship belonging to a State for enforcing a claim in connection with another ship belonging to that State, subsection (2)(a) above does not apply as respects the first-mentioned ship unless, at the time when the cause of action relating to the other ship arose, both ships were in use or intended for use for commercial purposes.

---

[399] Compare also Foreign Sovereign Immunities Act, 28 USC §1605(a)(6) (see 3.040–3.051 above); Foreign States Immunities Act 1985, s 17 (Aus.) (see 5.038 below); ILC Draft Articles, Art 17 (see 2.036–2.037 above).

[400] See the discussion at 4.029 above as to the meaning of the words "relating to" in other sections of the 1978 Act.   [401] As to which, see 4.083–4.093 below.

[402] See 4.033 above.   [403] See 4.077–4.082 below.

[404] *Norsk Hydro ASA v State Property Fund of Ukraine* [2002] EWHC 2120 (Comm) (Gross J).

(4) A State is not immune as respects—

 (a) an action in rem against a cargo belonging to that State if both the cargo and the ship carrying it were, at the time when the cause of action arose, in use or intended for use for commercial purposes; or

 (b) an action in personam for enforcing a claim in connection with such a cargo if the ship carrying it was then in use or intended for use as aforesaid.

(5) In the foregoing provisions references to a ship or cargo belonging to a State include references to a ship or cargo in its possession or control or in which it claims an interest; and, subject to subsection (4) above, subsection (2) above applies to property other than a ship as it applies to a ship.

(6) Sections 3 to 5 above do not apply to proceedings of the kind described in subsection (1) above if the State in question is a party to the Brussels Convention and the claim relates to the operation of a ship owned or operated by that State, the carriage of cargo or passengers on any such ship or the carriage of cargo owned by that State on any other ship.

Commentary

4.071 Legislative history

It will be recalled that one of the objectives of the 1978 Act was to give effect to the Convention for the Unification of Certain Rules concerning the Immunity of State-owned Ships signed at Brussels on 10 April 1926 (together with the Protocol to that Convention signed on 26 May 1934).[405] Clause 11 of the Bill was drafted for this purpose. In proposing several amendments, Lord McCluskey stated:[406]

> The drafting of Clause 11 has been particularly difficult because of the desire to achieve a number of objectives, which objectives are not always easy to reconcile and I will list them. First, that ships used for commercial purposes should not be immune; secondly that the provisions should be such as would enable the United Kingdom to ratify the Brussels Convention for the unification of certain rules concerning the immunity of State-owned ships, a Convention which is of unusual complexity and involved language; thirdly, that immunity should not be accorded even to State-owned ships used for non-commercial purposes where immunity could be denied in accordance with both the Brussels Convention and the European Convention; fourthly, to ensure that the wording is wide enough to cover not only ships owned by

---

[405] Convention: Cmd 5672; 176 LNTS 199. Protocol: Cmd 5673; 176 LNTS 215. See 1.001 to 1.022 above. For further explanation of the United Kingdom's failure to ratify the Convention earlier, see Mann (1979) 50 BYIL 43.

[406] Hansard, HL (5th series), vol 389, cols. 1517–1518 (16 March 1978). See also Hansard, HL (5th series), vol 389, cols. 1934–1935 (23 March 1978).

States but also any interests which States might have in ships; and, fifthly, to apply these principles to actions *in rem* and actions *in personam* alike, and to apply them to cargoes in the complex circumstances stipulated in the Brussels Convention.

The language of Clause 11 was considered to be imprecise, and a number of changes were made for the purpose of clarification. The question whether s 10, as amended, achieves successfully the objective of implementing the provisions of the Brussels Convention and the European Convention[407] is considered in the following paragraphs.

Scope of s 10   **4.072**

Section 10 applies to Admiralty proceedings[408] and to any claim which could be made the subject of Admiralty proceedings, irrespective of the manner in which that claim is actually brought before an English court or tribunal.

Application[409]   **4.073**

Section 10 should be read together with s 13(2), conferring a privilege (qualified by the following provisions of s 13) in an action *in rem* from the arrest, detention or sale of property belonging to a State.[410]

   Sub-sections (2) and (4) contain exceptions to the general immunity in s 1. Their provisions should be relatively straightforward to apply in most cases, provided that the following points are borne in mind:

(a) The exceptions apply to property other than a ship[411] (eg an aircraft[412]) insofar as it may be subject to Admiralty proceedings.[413]

(b) The exceptions apply to both actions *in rem* and actions *in personam*, provided that in the case of an action *in personam* the action is to enforce a claim in connection with the ship or, as the case may be, the cargo belonging to a State.[414]

(c) A ship, cargo or other property is treated as belonging to a State for the purposes of this section if it is in the possession or control of the State or if the State claims an interest in it.[415]

(d) The exceptions contained in the two sub-sections generally require that the ship(s), cargo or other property involved should, at the time when the

---

[407] See Art 30 of the European Convention (at 1.055 above) excluding from its scope matters covered by the Brussels Convention.

[408] See Supreme Court Act 1981, ss 20–24; County Courts Act 1984, ss 26–31; Civil Procedure Rules, Part 61.

[409] For discussion of the development of the common law, see Lewis, 60–66; Fox, 103–117.

[410] See 4.089 below.

[411] References to a ship include a hovercraft (see s 17(1) at 4.124 below). See also Hovercraft Act 1968, s 1.   [412] See Civil Aviation Act 1982, s 91.

[413] s 10(5).   [414] ss 10(2)(b) and 10(4)(b).

[415] s 10(5). See s 6(4) (discussed at 4.060 above).

cause of action arose, have been in use or intended for use for commercial purposes. Accordingly, a subsequent change of use (actual or intended) from a non-commercial to a commercial purpose will not be relevant.

(e) The expression "commercial purposes" would seem to require that claimant prove that the ship etc was, at the relevant time, in use or intended for use exclusively for the purposes of commercial transactions, subject to a *de minimis* exception.[416] This construction cannot, however, be easily reconciled with the language of the Brussels Convention.[417]

(f) During parliamentary debate, doubts were raised as to whether the words "or intended for use" could be reconciled with the Brussels Convention and would cause difficulty if, for example, a commercial vessel had been used at the relevant time to carry troops.[418] No amendment was considered necessary. It is submitted that there is no difficulty if the expressions "use" and "intended for use" are construed strictly in the alternative.[419] Either a ship etc is being used (in which case its current use must be examined rather than any intended future use) or it is not being used (in which case its next intended use must be examined). Difficult cases may arise if the non-commercial use of a ship is temporary or if the act giving rise to a cause of action is the conversion of the ship or cargo from a commercial to a non-commercial use.[420]

(g) In the case of an action *in personam* (but not an action *in rem*) involving cargo, only the ship need be in use or intended for use for commercial purposes.[421] This marks an attempt, albeit imperfect, to reflect the provisions of Article 3(3) of the Brussels Convention.[422]

(h) If the ship etc belongs to a State which is not a party to the Brussels Convention, the general immunity may also be removed by the exceptions contained in ss 3–5.[423] Those sections do not apply to ships owned or operated by a State party to the Brussels Convention if the proceedings fall within the scope of section 10.[424]

(i) Part I of the 1978 Act (including s 10) does not apply to proceedings relating to anything done by or in relation to the armed forces of a State while present in the United Kingdom (including its territorial waters and any area designated under the Continental Shelf Act 1964, s 1(7)).[425]

---

[416] s 17(1), as construed and applied in *Alcom v Republic of Columbia* [1984] AC 580, at 604 (Lord Diplock) (HL).

[417] See the reference to "vessels owned or operated by a State and employed *exclusively* . . . on Government and non-commercial service" in Art 3(1) of the Brussels Convention (at 1.004 above).

[418] Hansard, HL (5th series), vol 389, col. 1519 (16 March 1978). Brussels Convention, Art 3(1) (see 1.004 above).

[419] The purpose of the latter being, it is submitted, to apply s 10 to ships while they are out of service (eg in dry dock for repair).   [420] Cf. *I° Congreso del Partido* [1983] AC 244 (HL).

[421] s 10(4)(b).   [422] See 1.004 above.   [423] See 4.026–4.053 above.   [424] s 10(6).

[425] s 16(2) read together with s 17(4) (see 4.112, 4.117 and 4.124 below). For discussion of the position of warships and other military vessels, see the materials cited at 1.001 above, fn 1.

11 Value added tax, customs duties etc.

A State is not immune as respects proceedings relating to its liability for—

(a) value added tax, any duty of customs or excise or any agricultural levy; or
(b) rates in respect of premises occupied by it for commercial purposes.

Commentary

Legislative history

The shortest provision of the 1978 Act, s 11 (clause 12 of the Bill) was even shorter in its original form. The provision removing immunity in relation to rates on premises occupied for commercial purposes was introduced by amendment to avoid any possible misunderstanding as to the obligations of States in this regard.[426]

Application

The exception contained in s 11 is extremely limited in scope. As s 16(5) makes clear, the 1978 Act does not apply to proceedings relating to taxation other than those mentioned in s 11.[427] Nor does it apply to criminal proceedings.[428] Nor docs it affcct the exemptions from taxation granted under the Diplomatic Privileges Act 1964 or the Consular Relations Act 1968.[429]

The requirement that premises be occupied "for commercial purposes" would seem to require that the premises be occupied exclusively for the purposes of commercial transactions (as defined in s 3), subject to a *de minimis* exception.[430]

Procedure

12 Service of process and judgments in default of appearance

(1) Any writ or other document required to be served for instituting proceedings against a State shall be served by being transmitted through the Foreign and Commonwealth Office to the Ministry of Foreign Affairs of the State and service shall be deemed to have been effected when the writ or document is received at the Ministry.

(2) Any time for entering an appearance (whether prescribed by rules of court or otherwise) shall begin to run two months after the date on which the writ or document is received as aforesaid.

(3) A State which appears in proceedings cannot thereafter object that subsection (1) above has not been complied with in the case of those proceedings.

---

[426] Hansard, HL (5th series), vol 394, cols. 316–317 (16 March 1978).
[427] See 4.123 for discussion of immunity in relation to taxation.
[428] s 16(4) (see 4.121 below).
[429] See, in particular, Sch. 1, Art 23 to the 1964 Act and Sch. 1, Art 32 to the 1968 Act.
[430] See 4.091 below.

(4) No judgment in default of appearance shall be given against a State except on proof that subsection (1) above has been complied with and that the time for entering an appearance as extended by subsection (2) above has expired.

(5) A copy of any judgment given against a State in default of appearance shall be transmitted through the Foreign and Commonwealth Office to the Ministry of Foreign Affairs of that State and any time for applying to have the judgment set aside (whether prescribed by rules of court or otherwise) shall begin to run two months after the date on which the copy of the judgment is received at the Ministry.

(6) Subsection (1) above does not prevent the service of a writ or other document in any manner to which the State has agreed and subsections (2) and (4) above do not apply where service is effected in any such manner.

(7) This section shall not be construed as applying to proceedings against a State by way of counter-claim or to an action in rem; and subsection (1) above shall not be construed as affecting any rules of court whereby leave is required for the service of process outside the jurisdiction.

Commentary

4.078 Legislative history

Only one amendment was made to clause 13 of the State Immunity Bill[431] during its Parliamentary passage, by the introduction of what became s 12(6) of the 1978 Act allowing a State to agree to an alternative method of service. Lord Wilberforce described this amendment as "very beneficial" and added:[432]

> It is undoubtedly greatly desired by those who work in this field, by solicitors, and by the City. In fact, they provide always for their own method of service, and that gets rid of all the complicated rules which apply only if they have not agreed.

4.079 Application

Section 12 is the first of two provisions of the 1978 Act conferring upon States certain procedural immunities and privileges in proceedings before English courts and tribunals. The first point to be made is that this section applies only to proceedings in personam[433] in which a State (or a constituent territory of a federated State[434]) is the defendant and not, for example, to proceedings against a separate entity[435] or (probably) against a State employee,[436] although the State

---

[431] See European Convention, Art 16 (at 1.041 above).
[432] Hansard, HL (5th series), vol 389, cols. 1519–1520 (16 March 1978).   [433] s 12(7).
[434] See s 14(5) (at 4.094 and 4.108 below).
[435] See s 14(2) (at 4.094 and 4.103–4.104 below).
[436] See, however, the discussion at 4.105 below.

may be indirectly impleaded by such proceedings.[437] In these cases, however, there may well be a good case for a court to exercise by its procedural powers (for example, to extend time or require a hearing before entering default judgment) by analogy with s 12, particularly if the court has reason to believe that the defendant has been chosen with a view to evading the restrictions that the section imposes.

Service of originating process **4.080**

Section 12(1) concerns the service of originating process. Unless the parties have agreed an alternative mechanism for service,[438] a claim form or other document to be served in order to institute proceedings[439] *must* be served by transmission through the Foreign and Commonwealth Office (FCO) to the Ministry of Foreign Affairs of the defendant State.[440] In practice, service is effected by the FCO through diplomatic channels[441] by transmission to the British Embassy or High Commission in the State concerned for delivery to the Ministry of Foreign Affairs under cover of a diplomatic note. This sub-section does not permit service to be effected by any other (non-agreed) means,[442] even if the absence of diplomatic relations between the United Kingdom and the relevant State means that service cannot be effected.[443]

Service under s 12(1) is deemed to have been effected when the claim form or other originating document is "received at" the Ministry of Foreign Affairs. Under s 21(d),[444] the Secretary of State may certify (with conclusive effect) the date upon which process has been served on or received at the Foreign Ministry of a State. It is, therefore, sensible in practice to enquire of the Protocol Department of the FCO[445] as to the recorded date for service, rather than relying solely on information received from the foreign State. The formulation of this deeming provision, however, begs the question as to whether a State may refuse to receive a diplomatic communication and thereby prevent service from being effected upon it.[446] Although diplomatic communications can be rejected, thereby conferring on them an uncertain status,[447] the FCO might be expected to take a robust approach and to be prepared to certify that process has been received at the Ministry if it has been delivered there, even if it has been subsequently returned. On the other hand, the return of a claim form through diplomatic

---

[437] And entitled to intervene to assert its immunity (see 4.105 below).　　　[438] s 12(6).

[439] Including an arbitration claim form seeking permission to enforce an arbitration award (*Norsk Hydro ASA v State Property Fund of Ukraine* [2002] EWHC 2120 (Comm) (Gross J)).

[440] *Paprocki v German State* (1995) 104 ILR 684 (CA).

[441] See *Kuwait Airways Corporation v Iraqi Airways Co.* [1995] 1 WLR 1147, at 1155–1156 (Lord Goff) (HL).　　　[442] Such as delivery to an embassy or consular mission.

[443] *Westminster City Council v Islamic Republic of Iran* [1986] 1 WLR 979 (1986) 108 ILR 557 (Gibson J); *Kuwait Airways Corporation v Iraqi Airways* [1995] 1 WLR 1147, at 1155–1156 (Lord Goff) (HL).　　　[444] See 4.139–4.141.

[445] The current telephone number for the Protocol Department is 020 7008 0185.

[446] Compare the formulation of the corresponding provision in the Australian immunities legislation (see 5.045 below).

[447] See Lord Gore-Booth, *Satow's Guide to Diplomatic Practice* (5th edn, London, 1979), 51–53.

channels should remind the court or tribunal of its duty to consider of its own motion whether the State is immune.[448]

In proceedings before the High Court or the county courts, s 12(1) must be read together with the more detailed procedural rules in Part 6 of the Civil Procedure Rules 1998.[449] The claimant must file in the Central Office of the Royal Courts of Justice (a) a request for service to be arranged by the FCO, (b) a copy of the claim form, and (c) a translation if required.[450] The Senior Master will send those documents to the FCO with a request for service.

As noted, it is possible for the parties to agree to service being effected by other means, most obviously through the appointment of an independent process agent.[451] In practice, however, states are often reluctant to accede to such a request, and may suggest that service be effected at its Embassy or consular premises in the United Kingdom, or upon its ambassador or other holder of a diplomatic or consular post. This arrangement is, however, problematic insofar as those persons or premises may themselves be entitled to immunities and privileges, which the state may be unable to waive in writing.[452] It should be avoided if possible.

Neither s 12(1) nor the remaining provisions of the 1978 Act themselves confer personal jurisdiction upon the English courts in respect of claims against a state. Section 12(1) requires that service be effected outside the jurisdiction and, accordingly, the claimant must either apply for permission to serve his claim form abroad or, if appropriate, certify that permission is not required.[453]

4.081   *Steps following service/ entry of judgment in default*

By virtue of s 12(2), if service has taken place under s 12(1) a State defendant is given an additional two months from service to respond to the service of the document instituting proceedings.[454] This extension of time, based on Article 26.4 of the European Convention,[455] is similar to the 60-day period prescribed by the US Foreign Sovereign Immunities Act.[456] It is a recognition of

---

[448] s 1(2) (see 4.014 above). See also *U Kyaw Din v British Government* (1948) 23 ILR 215 (High Court of Rangoon).

[449] Civil Procedure Rules, r 6.27. These rules may also be applied in other tribunals.

[450] As to the requirement for a translation, see Civil Procedure Rules, r 6.28.

[451] *AN International Bank v Republic of Zambia* (1997) 118 ILR 602 (Moore-Bick J). As s 12(6) does not depend for its efficacy upon the creation of an agent-principal relationship, service may be effective even though the process agent's mandate has expired or been terminated (see the judgment of Moore-Bick J in *AN International Bank*, at 609, 613). For the possibility that a proclamation to the world may constitute an "agreement" for this purpose, see *ABCI v Banque Franco-Tunisienne* [2003] EWCA Civ. 205, para 29 (CA)).

[452] See *A Co. v Republic of X* [1990] 2 Lloyd's Rep. 520, at 524 (Saville J). Compare, however, *R v Bow Street Metropolitan Stipendiary Magistrate, ex p. Pinochet (No. 3)* [2000] 1 AC 147, at 217 (Lord Goff), 267 (Lord Saville), 290 (Lord Phillips) (HL). For further detail, see Denza, 127–129.

[453] s 12(7); Civil Procedure Rules, rr 6.19 and 6.20.

[454] The precise time allowed for responding is prescribed by rules of court and will vary according to the State in question (see Civil Procedure Rules, rr 6.22–6.2 and PD6 (Service out of the jurisdiction), para 7). If permission is required to serve the claim form out of the jurisdiction under Civil Procedure Rules, r 6.20, the order giving permission must specify the periods within which the defendant may file an acknowledgment of service, admission or defence (Civil Procedure Rules, r 6.21(4)).

[455] See 1.051 above.   [456] See 3.082 above.

the bureaucratic processes that States may have to follow in directing judicial documents to the correct authorities and in obtaining authorization to instruct legal advisers and to respond in a particular manner. Section 12(2) does not apply if a State has agreed to some other form of service, although the practical difficulties already described may make it appropriate for the court to exercise its discretion to extend time[457] to allow the State to prepare its response.

If there is no dispute as to whether s 12(1) or any agreement on service has been complied with, a State against whom High Court proceedings are brought may respond in a number of ways, as follows:

(a) *If the State has been properly served but objects to the jurisdiction of the High Court:*[458] The State must, within the prescribed time (having regard to the two-month extension)[459] file an acknowledgment of service in the prescribed form indicating that the State wishes to challenge the jurisdiction of the High Court to entertain the claim.[460] Within 14 days (or in the Commercial Court, within 28 days[461]) after filing an acknowledgment of service,[462] the State must make an application under Part 11 of the Civil Procedure Rules disputing the Court's jurisdiction, supported by evidence.[463] The application must set out all of the grounds on which the State objects to the exercise of jurisdiction over it.[464] If the State fails to make this application within the prescribed time, it will be treated as having submitted to the jurisdiction.[465]

If the State's application succeeds in its entirety, the court will declare that it has no jurisdiction and will ordinarily set aside the claim form and service of the claim form.[466] Subject to an appeal, the proceedings are at an end. If the State's application fails in its entirety, the court will ordinarily make no order (except as to costs), but the State's acknowledgment of service will automatically cease to have effect and the State may file a further acknowledgment of service within 14 days (or such period as the court may direct) indicating an intention to defend the proceedings.[467] If the State's application

---

[457] Civil Procedure Rules, r 3.2(a).

[458] As to the position where the state wishes to contest service of the claim form, see paragraph (d) below.   [459] See Civil Procedure Rules, r 6.22 and PD6, para 7.3.

[460] Civil Procedure Rules, Part 10 and r 11(2).   [461] Civil Procedure Rules, r 58.7(2).

[462] Or within such further period as the court may allow (Civil Procedure Rules, r 3.2(a)). As Civil Procedure Rules, r 11(5) arguably prescribes a sanction for a party failing to make the application within the 14-day period, it may not be open to the parties to extend time by agreement (Civil Procedure Rules, r 3.8(3)). Any application (or request) for an extension must refer specifically to the application disputing the court's jurisdiction (see *Montrose Investments Ltd v Orion Nominees* [2001] CP Rep 109).   [463] Civil Procedure Rules, r 11(4).

[464] The assertion of immunity is foremost among these. It will, however, be proper at the same time for the State to raise any other jurisdictional objection, including (for example) a challenge to the basis upon which permission to serve out of the jurisdiction has been granted (see, eg, *Crescent Oil and Shipping Services v Banco Nacional de Angola* (Comm, 28 May 1999) (Cresswell J)). See also 4.023 above.

[465] Civil Procedure Rules, r 11(5). The acknowledgment of service would arguably be treated (in view of the State's failure to contest jurisdiction) for the purposes of s 2 of the 1978 Act as being a step taken otherwise that for the purpose of claiming immunity.   [466] Civil Procedure Rules, r 11(6).

[467] Civil Procedure Rules, r 11(7). If the defendant files a further acknowledgment of service, he is treated as having accepted that the court has jurisdiction to try the claim (Civil Procedure Rules, r 11(8)).

succeeds only in part (ie the court rules that it has jurisdiction with respect to some but not all of the claims), the court should make a limited declaration as to the claims in respect of which it has no jurisdiction and strike those claims from the claim form. Its order should expressly provide also that the State's acknowledgment of service shall cease to have effect and give the State a further period within which to decide whether to acknowledge service and defend the remaining claims.[468]

(b) *If the State wishes to defend the proceedings*: The State must take the procedural steps necessary to file a defence to the claim. The applicable procedures will vary according to the division of the court in which proceedings have been brought.[469] The filing of a defence (or of an unconditional acknowledgment that the State intends to contest jurisdiction) will, of course, constitute a submission to the jurisdiction.[470] The procedural position of a State that submits in this manner is discussed elsewhere.[471]

(c) *If the State does not (or cannot) object to the jurisdiction of the High Court and does not wish to defend the proceedings*: The State may admit the claim or may take no step in response to the claim form. Either way, judgment may be entered against it, although no default judgment will be entered against a State without proof that s 12(1) has been complied with and that the period for entering an appearance has expired.[472] The court must also consider of its own motion whether the State is entitled to immunity.[473]

The claimant must follow the prescribed procedures to obtain a default judgment against a State.[474] A formal application is required, and the court may direct that a copy of the application notice is served on the State. On an application without notice to the defendant State, the claimant must (in addition to the matters specified by the relevant practice direction[475]) make full disclosure of all material facts.[476] The evidence must be in the form of an affidavit.[477]

(d) *If the State asserts that the requirements of s 12 have not been complied with*: In this scenario, the State finds itself in a difficult position. It cannot file an acknowledgment of service (even to dispute the jurisdiction) for this would constitute an "appearance"[478] so as to preclude it from alleging non-compliance with s 12(1).[479] It is suggested that the solution to this conundrum lies in s 12(4), by

---

[468] The rules of court do not provide expressly for this eventuality, but the suggested solution was endorsed by Evans J in *Australia and New Zealand Banking Group Limited v Commonwealth of Australia* (reported as *Amalgamated Metal Trading Ltd v Department of Trade and Industry* (1989) The Times, 16 May).

[469] For example, in the Commercial Court an acknowledgment of service must be filed before the defence.   [470] See 4.023 above.

[471] See 4.025 above and 4.085 below.   [472] s 12(5).   [473] s 1(2) (see 4.014 above).

[474] See Civil Procedure Rules, rr 12.10(b)(iii) and 12.11(5) and PD12, para 4.4.

[475] Civil Procedure Rules, PD12, para 4.4.

[476] See *AN International Bank v Republic of Zambia* (1997) 118 ILR 602 (Moore-Bick J).

[477] Civil Procedure Rules, PD12, para 4.5.   [478] s 22(2) (see 4.142 below).

[479] s 12(3). Contrast the formulation of the corresponding provision in the Australian legislation (see 5.047 below; *Robinson v Kuwait Liaison Office* (1997) 145 ALR 68 (Moore J, Industrial Relations Court of Australia)).

which no default judgment may be entered against a state without proof that s 12(1) has been complied with. An application to enter default judgment[480] will be heard by the court, which may direct that a copy of the application notice be served on the state.[481] The state (through its legal advisers) may then intervene to protect its interests. In the meantime, the state's legal advisers should write to the claimant's legal advisers putting them on notice of the objection to the mode of service and asking them to draw this matter to the court's attention on any future application to enter judgment in default.[482]

Service of default judgment   **4.082**

A copy of any judgment obtained against a State in default of appearance must be served on the State by transmitting it through the FCO to the Ministry of Foreign Affairs of the State.[483] A further court order is not required to serve the judgment out of the jurisdiction.[484] Unlike the identical requirement for service of originating process,[485] this requirement may not be departed from by agreement of the state.[486] The time within which a State may apply to set the default judgment aside[487] will begin to run two months after a copy of the judgment is received at the Ministry.[488]

13 Other procedural privileges   **4.083**

(1) No penalty by way of committal or fine shall be imposed in respect of any failure or refusal by or on behalf of a State to disclose or produce any document or other information for the purposes of proceedings to which it is a party.

(2) Subject to subsections (3) and (4) below—

    (a) relief shall not be given against a State by way of injunction or order for specific performance or for the recovery of land or other property; and

    (b) the property of a State shall not be subject to any process for the enforcement of a judgment or arbitration award or, in an action in rem, for its arrest, detention or sale.

(3) Subsection (2) above does not prevent the giving of any relief or the issue of any process with the written consent of the State concerned; and any

---

[480] For further discussion of the procedural requirements, see paragraph (c) above.

[481] Civil Procedure Rules, r 12.11(5)(a). The application notice may be served on the State without further order in accordance with the procedure set out in Civil Procedure Rules, r 6.27.

[482] As they will be obliged to do in compliance with the obligation to give "full and frank disclosure" (see *Brinks Mat v Elcombe* [1988] 1 WLR 1350 (CA); *AN International Bank v Republic of Zambia* (1997) 118 ILR 602 (Moore-Bick J)).

[483] s 12(4). Civil Procedure Rules, r 12(5)(c) applying the procedure set out in r 6.27.

[484] Civil Procedure Rules, r 12.11(5)(b).   [485] See 4.079 above.

[486] *AN International Bank v Republic of Zambia* (1997) 118 ILR 602, at 615–618 (Moore-Bick J); *Crescent Oil and Shipping Services Ltd v Importang UEE* [1998] 1 WLR 919 (Thomas J).

[487] See, eg, *Paprocki v German State* (1995) 104 ILR 684 (CA). For the procedural rules governing an application to set aside any default judgment, see Civil Procedure Rules, Part 13.

[488] As certified by the Secretary of State in accordance with s 20(5) (see 4.139–4.141 below).

such consent (which may be contained in a prior agreement) may be expressed so as to apply to a limited extent or generally; but a provision merely submitting to the jurisdiction of the courts is not to be regarded as a consent for the purposes of this subsection.

(4) Subsection (2)(b) above does not prevent the issue of any process in respect of property which is for the time being in use or intended for use for commercial purposes; but, in a case not falling within section 10 above, this subsection applies to property of a State party to the European Convention on State Immunity only if—

  (a) the process is for enforcing a judgment which is final within the meaning of section 18(1)(b) below and the State has made a declaration under Article 24 of the Convention; or
  (b) the process is for enforcing an arbitration award.

(5) The head of a State's diplomatic mission in the United Kingdom, or the person for the time being performing his functions, shall be deemed to have authority to give on behalf of the State any such consent as is mentioned in subsection (3) above and, for the purposes of subsection (4) above, his certificate to the effect that any property is not in use or intended for use by or on behalf of the State for commercial purposes shall be accepted as sufficient evidence of that fact unless the contrary is proved.

(6) In the application of this section to Scotland—

  (a) the reference to "injunction" shall be construed as a reference to "interdict";
  (b) for paragraph (b) of subsection (2) above there shall be substituted the following paragraph—

    "(b) the property of a State shall not be subject to any diligence for enforcing a judgment or order of a court or a decree arbitral or, in an action in rem, to arrestment or sale"; and

  (c) any reference to "process" shall be construed as a reference to "diligence", any reference to "the issue of any process" as a reference to "the doing of diligence" and the reference in subsection (4)(b) above to "an arbitration award" as a reference to "a decree arbitral".

Commentary

4.084 Legislative history

The procedural privileges initially contemplated by clause 14 of the State Immunity Bill were more extensive than those ultimately conferred by s 13 as enacted. With the exception of proceedings to which clause 11 (s 10) would apply

("Ships used for commercial purposes"[489]), clause 14 in its original form provided that no process could be issued for enforcing a judgment against a State except with the State's permission in writing and that relief could in no circumstances be granted against a State by way of injunction or order for specific performance or for the recovery of land or other property. Perhaps unsurprisingly, clause 14 attracted trenchant criticism on the second reading of the Bill,[490] with the result that substantial amendments were made at the Committee Stage in the House of Lords and subsequently.[491] The combined effect of these amendments was as follows:

(a) To delete the prohibition in clause 14(1) upon an award of security for costs against a State.[492]

(b) To allow a State to agree in writing (including by a prior agreement) to the grant of relief by way of injunction etc or to the issue of process for the enforcement of a judgment against property of a State or (in an action *in rem*) its arrest, detention or sale.[493]

(c) To permit the issue of process for the enforcement of a judgment against property of a State in use for commercial purposes (such permission being qualified in the case of States party to the European Convention).[494]

(d) To deem the head of a State's diplomatic mission in the United Kingdom to have the authority to consent to the issue of process against property of the State.

Despite the changes, some believed that the amended clause 14 did not go far enough. They argued that injunctive relief should be available in relation to commercially used assets and that, by depriving the courts of the procedural means for pre-judgment freezing of assets,[495] the 1978 Act threatened the prospects of ultimate enforcement of judgments against States.[496] In this respect, however, no further amendment was forthcoming.[497]

Application   **4.085**

Section 13, as enacted, confers certain additional procedural privileges upon foreign States. Although a foreign State that has submitted to the jurisdiction

---

[489] See 4.070–4.073 above.

[490] See Hansard, HL (5th series), vol 388, cols. 61–62 (Baroness Elles) (17 January 1978), col. 67 (Lord Wilberforce).

[491] See Hansard, HL (5th series), vol 389, cols. 1519–1529 (16 March 1978); Hansard, HL (5th series), vol 389, cols. 1935–1938 (23 March 1978); Hansard, HL (5th series), vol 394, cols. 319–320 (28 June 1978).

[492] See Hansard, HL (5th series), vol 388, col. 62 (17 January 1978), vol 389, col. 1520 (16 March 1978). See further 4.092 below.   [493] See 4.092 below.

[494] See 4.091 below.

[495] The English courts had, at the time, recently developed the *Mareva* injunction (now termed a "freezing injunction"). See, generally, Civil Procedure Rules, Part 25.

[496] Compare *Hispano Americana v Central Bank of Nigeria* [1979] 2 Lloyd's Rep 277 (CA) (decided before the coming into force of the 1978 Act).

[497] See Hansard, HL (5th series), vol 389, cols. 1526–1528 (16 March 1978); Hansard, HL (5th series), vol. 389, cols. 1935–1938 (23 March 1978) (two amendments proposed by Lord Wilberforce, but withdrawn).

of an English court or tribunal (whether as claimant or as defendant) must in general comply with the rules of the relevant court or tribunal (including, for example, those relating to disclosure[498]), it may be in a more favourable position in two respects. First, the rule or statutory basis for a rule may be framed in such a way as not to apply to a foreign State.[499] Secondly, if the court has a discretion in applying a rule, considerations of comity may favour the exercise of that discretion in favour of the State.[500]

4.086   *Failure to disclose documents or information*

Under s 13(1) a court or tribunal may not impose a fine or commit any person to prison as a result of the failure by a State to disclose or produce any document or other information for the purposes of proceedings to which it is a party. Section 13(1) does not, however, prevent a court or tribunal from taking other procedural action, including (for example) striking out a statement of case,[501] preventing a State from relying on a document at trial[502] or even (in an extreme case) requiring a State to make a payment into court.[503]

In principle, a State may be joined as a party to proceedings or an application made against a State for the purposes of obtaining disclosure, but the State will generally enjoy immunity under s 1.[504]

4.087   *Injunctions, specific performance, recovery of land or other property*

Unless a State consents in writing,[505] no injunction[506] or order for specific performance or for the recovery of land or other property may be given against a State.[507] For these purposes a simple order for the payment of money from no specified source is not an injunction.[508] Nevertheless, the effect of this provision is, in most cases, to prevent the control of a State's assets before or after judgment by means of a freezing injunction. This may clearly impact on the ability of a claimant ultimately to enforce a judgment in his favour (at least against assets in the United Kingdom[509]), but the view appears to have been taken that the enforcement of such orders by contempt proceedings would be inimical to the relationship between the United Kingdom Government and the governments of foreign States.[510]

---

[498] See *Halsbury's Laws of England* (4th edn), vol 18, para 1559; Lewis, 77.
[499] See, eg, the discussion at 4.092 as to orders to provide security for costs.
[500] See, eg, *Camdex International v Central Bank of Zambia* [1997] 1 All ER 728 (CA).
[501] Civil Procedure Rules, r 3.4.   [502] Civil Procedure Rules, r 31.21.
[503] Civil Procedure Rules, r 3.1(5).
[504] Cf. the decision of the Irish Supreme Court in *Fusco v O'Dea* (1994) 103 ILR 318.
[505] s 13(3).   [506] In Scotland, for "injunction" read "interdict" (s 13(6)(a)).
[507] s 13(2)(a). For the common law position, see *Hispano Americana Mercantil v Central Bank of Nigeria* [1979] 2 Lloyd's Rep 277 (CA).
[508] *Saleh Boneh v Uganda Government* [1993] 2 Lloyd's Rep 209 (CA).
[509] Other jurisdictions may take a more favourable view.
[510] See Hansard, HL (5th series), vol 389, cols. 1526–1528 (16 March 1978); Hansard, HL (5th series), vol 389, cols. 1935–1938 (23 March 1978).

Process for the enforcement of judgment or arbitral award   **4.088**

Subject to the exceptions contained in sub-sections (3) and (4),[511] the property of a State may not be subject to any process[512] for the enforcement of a judgment or arbitral award.[513] It would seem, however, that a bankruptcy or winding-up petition does not constitute a *process for the enforcement of a judgment or arbitral award*, as it relates to all of the insolvent party's assets and liablities.[514] Petitions of this type constitute proceedings, from which a State will be immune unless (which seems almost inconceivable) one of the exceptions explained above can be shown to apply.[515] The expression "property" is broad enough to encompass, for example, a debt owed to a State by its bankers.[516]

Additional procedural protections apply where execution of a judgment against a State is sought by means of a writ of *fieri facias*, charging order or third party debt (formerly garnishee) order.[517] Before the writ of *fieri facias* is issued, the procedural judge (Master) must be informed in writing and his direction sought. The evidence in support of an application to a Master for a charging or third party debt order must include a statement that the execution sought is against a foreign State.[518] On being so informed, the Master will as soon as practicable inform the Foreign and Commonwealth Office of the application and will not permit the making of an order in the meantime.[519] Further, the Master may postpone a decision as to whether to make an order for so long as he considers reasonable for the purposes of enabling the FCO to furnish further information relevant to his decision, but not for longer than three days from the time of his contacting the FCO.[520]

Arrest, detention or sale of ship or other property of State   **4.089**

Subject to ss 13(3) and (4), a ship or other property of a State may not, in an action *in rem*,[521] be subject to arrest, detention or sale.[522] In the case of ships or cargoes owned or operated by a State party to the Brussels Convention,[523] the reference in sub-section (4) to property which is for the time being "in use or intended for use for commercial purposes" may be difficult to reconcile with the terms of Article 3 of the Convention and Article III of the additional Protocol.[524]

---

[511] See 4.090–4.091 below.

[512] eg, a third party debt order (Civil Procedure Rules, Part 72), charging order (Civil Procedure Rules, Part 73) or writ of *fieri facias* (Civil Procedure Rules, Sch 1, Ord 47). In Scotland, for "process" read "diligence" (s 13(6)(c)).

[513] s 13(2)(b). In Scotland, for "arbitral award" read "decree arbitral" (s 13(6)(c)).

[514] *Banco Nacional de Cuba v Cosmos Trading Corp.* [2000] 1 BCLC 813, at 820 (Scott V-C, CA). See also *Re A Company* [1915] 1 Ch 520, at 525–526 (Phillimore LJ) (CA); *Re Parker Davis and Hughes* [1953] 1 WLR 1349 (Roxburgh J); *Re International Tin Council* [1988] 1 Ch 409, at 454–456 (Millett J); [1989] 1 Ch 309, at 331–334 (CA).   [515] See, in particular, 4.059 above.

[516] *Alcom v Republic of Columbia* [1984] AC 580, at 602 (Lord Diplock) (HL).

[517] Queen's Bench Guide (2000), para 11.9.

[518] Queen's Bench Guide (2000), para 11.9.1(1).

[519] Queen's Bench Guide (2000), para 11.9.1(2).

[520] Queen's Bench Guide (2000), para 11.9.1(3).

[521] In Scotland, only in relation to admiralty proceedings (s 17(5)).   [522] s 13(2)(b).

[523] See 1.023 above.   [524] See the discussion in relation to s10 (at 4.073 above).

4.090   *Written consent to relief or process*

An injunction, order for specific performance, order for the recovery of land or other property may be granted against a State and the property of a State may be subjected to any process for the enforcement of a judgment or arbitral award or (in an action *in rem*) for its arrest, detention or sale if the State gives written consent,[525] either to a limited extent or generally.[526] The consent may, but need not be, contained in a prior agreement,[527] but a submission (by appearance or agreement) to the jurisdiction of the courts will not be sufficient.[528] The head of a State's diplomatic mission in the United Kingdom, or the person for the time being performing his functions, is deemed to have authority to give this consent.[529]

4.091   *Property in use for commercial purposes*

As against a State not party to the European Convention,[530] the property of a State may be subject to any process for the enforcement of a judgment or arbitral award or (in an action *in rem*) for its arrest, detention or sale if, at the time of issue of that process, it is in use or intended for use for commercial purposes.[531] The following points are noted:

(a) It is submitted that the expressions "use" and "intended for use" are to be construed strictly in the alternative. If property is actively in use, it does not matter that it might in the future be applied for commercial purposes. On this basis, the credit balance of a bank account would fall within the category of property not in use, requiring its intended use to be considered.[532]

(b) The expression "commercial purposes" means for the purposes of commercial transactions, as defined in s 3(3).[533] It is necessary, subject to

---

[525] For the meaning of "written", see 4.019 above.

[526] s 13(3). In a commercial context, ordinary principles of construction apply: *A Company v Republic of X* [1990] 2 Lloyd's Rep 520, in which Saville J refused to give a restrictive construction to a waiver in the following terms, "The Ministry of Finance hereby waives whatever defence it may have of sovereign immunity for itself or its property (present or subsequently acquired)"; *Sabah Shipyard (Pakistan) Ltd v Islamic Republic of Pakistan* [2002] EWCA Civ. 1643, para 25; [2003] 2 Lloyd's Rep 571, 577–578 (Waller LJ) (CA) (consent to interim anti-suit injunction by the words "The Guarantor . . . waives any right of immunity which it . . . now has . . . in connection with any such proceedings"). See European Convention, Art 23 (at 1.048 above).

[527] Including a treaty (see s 17(2)—see 4.124 and 4.126 below). For the possibility that a proclamation to the world may constitute an "agreement" for this purpose (in the context of s 12(6)) see *ABCI v Banque Franco-Tunisienne* [2003] EWCA Civ. 205, para 29 (CA)).

[528] cf. *Duff Development Company v Government of Kelantan* [1924] AC 797 (HL). The term "court" is defined in s 22(1) (see 4.142 and 4.144 below). It appears to be an open question whether it is capable of encompassing a private arbitral tribunal. Note that the term "courts" is used in s 13(3) without the qualifying words "of the United Kingdom" which are used, for example, in ss 1 and 9.

[529] See the commentary on the similar provision in s 2(6) (at 4.024 above).

[530] See 1.068 above for a list of parties to the European Convention.   [531] s 13(4).

[532] *Alcom v Republic of Columbia* [1984] AC 580, at 603–605 (Lord Diplock) (HL).

[533] See 4.030 above.

a *de minimis* exception, that the property be in use (or intended for use) exclusively for such purposes. If, for example, the credit balance of a bank account is intended for use partly for transactions or activities falling outside the scope of s 3(3) (eg payments to employees), it will fall outside the scope of the exception.[534]

(c) The burden of proving that property is in use for commercial purposes lies on the judgment creditor. By s13(5), the head of a State's diplomatic mission in the UK, or the person for the time being performing his functions, may certify that property is not in use or intended for use for commercial purposes. That certificate shall be accepted as sufficient evidence of the fact unless the contrary is proved.[535]

(d) States party to the European Convention are in a special position by virtue of the terms of Article 23 of the Convention.[536] As against these States, the "commercial property" exception applies only (i) to a case falling within s 10;[537] or (ii) if the State has made a declaration under Article 24 of the Convention[538] and the judgment to be enforced is final;[539] or (iii) if the process is to enforce an arbitral award.

The first qualification seeks to give effect to Articles 1–3 of the Brussels Convention and Article I of the additional Protocol.[540] The second is an attempt to reflect the terms of Article 26 of the European Convention,[541] but s 13 in its application to these Convention States is both too broad and too narrow. On the one hand, Article 26 is expressed to apply only "in proceedings relating to an industrial or commercial activity, in which the State is engaged in the same manner as a private person", but s 13 is not so limited. On the other, those drafting the Convention contemplated that preventative measures might be taken against a State to which Article 26 applied,[542] but the procedural means for achieving this in England (the freezing injunction) is excluded by s 13(2)(a) unless the State consents in writing. Finally, the third qualification is consistent with Article 23 of the European Convention, as that Article does not apply to arbitration awards.[543]

(e) Part I of the 1978 Act (including s 13) does not apply to proceedings relating to anything done by or in relation to the armed forces of a State while present

---

[534] *Alcom v Republic of Columbia* [1984] AC 580, at 601–605 (Lord Diplock) (HL).

[535] *Alcom,* at 604–605; *AIC Ltd v Federal Government of Nigeria* [2003] EWHC 1357 (QB), paras 53, 55–59 (Stanley Burnton QC). But see Art 5 of the Brussels Convention (at 1.006 above).

[536] See 1.048 above.   [537] See 4.080 to 4.073 above.

[538] Declarations under Art 24 have been made by Belgium, Germany, Luxembourg, Netherlands, Switzerland and the UK (see 1.069 above).   [539] See s 18(1)(b) (at 4.127 below).

[540] See 1.005 and 1.017 above. See also European Convention, Art 30 (at 1.055 above). For doubts as to whether the language of the 1978 Act can be reconciled with the Brussels Convention, see 4.073 above.   [541] See 1.051 above.

[542] See para 106 of the Explanatory Report (at 1.117 above).

[543] See paras 51 and 95 of the Explanatory Report (at 1.103 and 1.114 above).

in the United Kingdom (including its territorial waters and any area designated under the Continental Shelf Act 1964 s 1(7)).[544]

4.092   *Security for costs*

The 1978 Act does not prevent the English courts from ordering that a State provide security for costs,[545] whether as a claimant in proceedings,[546] as an appellant or otherwise.[547] No such bar existed at common law, and in some cases an order of this kind may be essential for the protection of the defendant or respondent (as the case may be).[548] Nevertheless, a court may well have regard to considerations of comity and to the executive's responsibility for the conduct of foreign relations and be reluctant to order a State to provide security for costs in the absence of clear and satisfactory evidence that the State had taken steps to put assets out of the reach of a successful opponent. Further, it is to be noted that several of the statutory grounds for ordering security for costs[549] would not apply to a State, which is neither an individual nor a company nor (arguably) an incorporated body of any other kind.[550] Finally, Article 17 of the European Convention precludes any requirement that a contracting State provide any security, bond or other deposit to guarantee the payment of judicial costs or expenses which could not have been required in the forum state of a national of that state or person domiciled or resident there.[551]

4.093   *Foreign central banks and monetary authorities*

By s 14(4), ss 13(1)–(3)[552] apply to a foreign central bank or monetary authority even if the bank or authority is a separate entity (and not, therefore, part of the State) under s 14(1). Under the same provision, property of a State's central bank or monetary authority is to be conclusively regarded as not being in use or intended for use for commercial purposes, and may, therefore, only be subject to a process for the enforcement of a judgment or arbitral award with the written consent of the bank or authority.[553] This presumption would arguably not extend, for example, to a credit balance in the name of a State or other governmental

---

[544] s 16(2) read together with s 17(4) (see 4.118 and 4.124 below). As to the position of warships and other military vessels, see the materials cited at 1.001 above, fn 1.

[545] Compare clause 14(1) of the State Immunity Bill (para 4.165 below).

[546] Civil Procedure Rules, r 25.12.

[547] Civil Procedure Rules, r 25.15. See also CPR, r 59.2(1)(b).

[548] See Dicey and Morris, para 10–026, citing *Republic of Costa Rica v Erlanger* (1876) LR 2 Ch App 582; *The Newbattle* (1885) 10 PD 33; *Ministère de la Culture v Lieb* (1981) The Times, 24 December; *Halsbury's Laws of England* (4th edn), vol 18, para 1559, citing *Republic of Costa Rica v Erlanger* as well as *King of Greece v Wright* (1837) 6 Dowl 12 and *Emperor of Brazil v Robinson* (1837) 5 Dowl 522.   [549] See Civil Procedure Rules, r 25.13.

[550] See Marston (1997) 56 CLJ 374.   [551] See 1.042 above.

[552] See 4.090–4.091 above.

[553] *Crescent Oil and Shipping Services Ltd v Banco Nacional de Angola* (Comm, 28 May, 1999) (Cresswell J); *Camdex International Ltd v Bank of Zambia* [1997] 1 All ER 728 (CA); *AIC Ltd v Federal Government of Nigeria* [2003] EWHC 1357 (QB) (Stanley Burnton QC). See also Blair [1998] CLJ 374; Proctor [2000] JIBFL 70.

entity with the central bank or gold reserves held by the central bank as bailee, being property of the State or other entity rather than the central bank.[554]

Supplementary provisions

14 States entitled to immunities and privileges

4.094

(1) The immunities and privileges conferred by this Part of this Act apply to any foreign or commonwealth State other than the United Kingdom, and references to a State include references to—

(a) the sovereign or other head of that State in his public capacity;

(b) the government of that State; and

(c) any department of that government,

but not to any entity (hereafter referred to as a "separate entity") which is distinct from the executive organs of the government of the State and capable of suing or being sued.

(2) A separate entity is immune from the jurisdiction of the courts of the United Kingdom if, and only if—

(a) the proceedings relate to anything done by it in the exercise of sovereign authority; and

(b) the circumstances are such that a State (or, in the case of proceedings to which section 10 above applies, a State which is not a party to the Brussels Convention) would have been so immune.

(3) If a separate entity (not being a State's central bank or other monetary authority) submits to the jurisdiction in respect of proceedings in the case of which it is entitled to immunity by virtue of subsection (2) above, subsections (1) to (4) of section 13 above shall apply to it in respect of those proceedings as if references to a State were references to that entity.

(4) Property of a State's central bank or other monetary authority shall not be regarded for the purposes of subsection (4) of section 13 above as in use or intended for use for commercial purposes; and where any such bank or authority is a separate entity subsections (1) to (3) of that section shall apply to it as if references to a State were references to the bank or authority.

(5) Section 12 above applies to proceedings against the constituent territories of a federal State; and Her Majesty may by Order in Council provide for the other provisions of this Part of this Act to apply to any such constituent territory specified in the Order as they apply to a State.

---

[554] There is no provision in s 14 equivalent to s 10(5) (as to which, see 4.070 above). See, however, *AIC Ltd v Federal Government of Nigeria* [2003] EWHC 1357 (QB) (Stanley Burnton QC) (no enquiry into beneficial ownership of chose in action in name of Nigerian central bank).

(6) Where the provisions of this Part of this Act do not apply to a constituent territory by virtue of any such Order subsections (2) and (3) above shall apply to it as if it were a separate entity

Commentary

4.095   Legislative history

Sub-sections (3) (procedural privileges of separate entities) and (4) (foreign central bank or monetary authority) of what is now s 14[555] were inserted during the passage of the State Immunity Bill through Parliament.[556] In addition, two changes were made to the definition of "separate entity" in s 14(1), by inserting the reference to the "executive organs of the government" (to affirm that separate legal personality is not the sole criterion[557]) and by removing reference to the law of the foreign State (leaving open the question of applicable law).[558]

4.096   Application

Section 14(1) contains the key definition for the purposes of the 1978 Act, that of "State". Sub-sections 14(2)–(5) extend, to a limited extent, the immunities and privileges conferred on States by ss 1–13 to other persons against which proceedings might be brought.

4.097   *Meaning of "State"*

Section 14(1) must be analysed together with s 21(a),[559] whereby a certificate by or on behalf of the Secretary of State is to be treated as conclusive evidence on any question whether any country is a "State" for the purposes of Part I of the 1978 Act, whether any territory is a constituent territory of a federal State for those purposes or as to the person or persons to be regarded for those purposes as the head or government of a State. The current practice of the UK Government, however, is to recognize states rather than governments[560] and, in light of this practice, the FCO may decline to certify whether a defendant is to be regarded as the "government" of a State. In such a case, the court or tribunal will be required to consider the matter itself by reference to well-established criteria.[561]

---

[555] Clause 15 of the State Immunity Bill (see 4.166 below).
[556] See Hansard, HC (5th series), vol 951, col. 845 (13 June 1978); Hansard, HL (5th series), vol 394, cols. 320–321 (28 June 1978).
[557] See para 108 of the Explanatory Report to the European Convention (at 1.118 above) and the discussion at 4.102 below.
[558] See Hansard, HL (5th series), vol 389, cols. 1529–1630 (16 March 1978). See further 4.102.
[559] See 4.139–4.141 below.
[560] Hansard, HC (5th series), vol 983, cols. 277–279 (23 May 1980).
[561] See, eg, *Propend Finance Pty Limited v Sing* (1996–1997) 111 ILR 611. For the modern approach of the English courts to the recognition of governments, see *Republic of Somalia v Woodhouse Drake & Carey (Suisse) SA* [1993] QB 54; *Sierra Leone Telecommunications Co. Ltd v Barclays Bank plc* [1998] 2 All ER 821; *Kuwait Airways Corporation v Iraqi Airways Co. (Nos. 4 and 5)* [2002] 2 AC 883, paras 339–360 (CA).

The immunities and privileges conferred by the 1978 Act apply to any foreign or Commonwealth State, but only if it is recognized as such by the United Kingdom.[562] Entities not recognized as States may nevertheless possess legal personality[563] and may even be entitled to certain immunities and privileges as a "separate entity"[564] for acts in the exercise of sovereign authority *of the State of which they form part.*[565] Special provision is made for the constituent territories of federal States.[566]

Head of State in public capacity

4.098

The concept of a State as a legal person capable of suing and being sued is now well established.[567] Formerly, however, the legal identity of a State was equated with its sovereign ruler and even now doubts are occasionally raised as to whether the State or its ruler is the correct defendant.[568] Sub-paragraph (a) of section 14(1) equates a State for the purposes of the 1978 Act with its sovereign or other head of State *acting in his public capacity.* The correct demarcation, it is submitted, is between cases in which the sovereign is impleaded in respect of his own actions (or those of a servant or agent employed by him personally) giving rise to a personal liability[569] and cases in which the sovereign is impleaded for acts (whether his own or of others) carried out in the name of the State.[570] In the latter case, but not the former, the head of state is acting in a public capacity. Even if a head of State is acting in a personal capacity, certain immunities and privileges may be conferred on him by s 20[571] and a head of State acting in a public capacity would seem to be entitled also to these immunities and privileges.[572]

Government of a foreign State

4.099

Litigants, lawyers and judges have often treated the "government" of a foreign State as the appropriate party to suits addressed to the State. But, as one author notes, the "inherent uncertainty of their membership and duration makes governments unlikely legal persons".[573] Moreover, the former practice of the United Kingdom in according formal recognition to governments (both *de jure* and *de facto*) ended in April 1980 and it is a matter of speculation whether s 14(1) of the 1978 Act would have been differently formulated had this change of practice occurred earlier.

In its treatment of references to a State as including references to the "government" of that State, s 14(1)(b) of the 1978 Act is open to more than one

---

[562] For the characteristics of statehood, see Brownlie, *Principles of Public International Law* (5th edn, 1998), ch IV. [563] *Gur Corp v Trust Bank of Africa* [1987] QB 599 (CA).
[564] See 4.103. [565] *BCCI v Price Waterhouse (No. 4)* [1997] 4 All ER 108, at 113 (Laddie J).
[566] See 4.108 below.
[567] cf. Marston, *The Personality of the Foreign State in English Law* (1997) 56 CLJ 374.
[568] See *BCCI v Price Waterhouse (No. 4)* [1997] 4 All ER 108 (Laddie J).
[569] eg, *Mighell v Sultan of Johore* [1894] 1 QB 149 (CA).
[570] See *BCCI v Price Waterhouse (No. 4)* [1997] 4 All ER 108 (Laddie J).
[571] See 4.131–4.138.
[572] See s 20(5) (at 4.131 below). The point was left open in *BCCI v Price Waterhouse (No.4)* [1997] 4 All ER 108, at 113–114 (Laddie J). [573] See Marston (1997) 56 CLJ 374, 408–409.

interpretation. At two extremes, the Parliamentary draftsman's intention could have been simply to take account of the practice, described above, of identifying the "government" of a foreign State as defendant, or he could have intended to treat on an equal footing to a State each and every individual and entity forming part of a foreign government. Used in the former sense, "government" is no more than the name for the body of persons (natural and legal) carrying on the process of governing. This narrow construction has a logical attraction. It is one thing to consider the collective, ever changing in its constitution, as having sufficient identity with the State; it is quite another to extend that treatment to each of its constituent parts for the time being. The argument in favour of this construction appears to be supported by the existence of separate references in s 14(1) to "department" and "executive organs" as subordinate parts of a "government". Admittedly, however, the alternative construction (ie treating "government" as including a reference to each of its constituent members) is itself supported by the reference in s 21(a) to the "person or persons to be regarded for these purposes as the . . . government of a state".[574] Nevertheless, the logical and practical consequences in terms of the operation of the 1978 Act of the broader construction are more difficult to justify. If references to "State" in the 1978 Act are to be treated as including each and every member of a foreign government or person carrying out government functions in a foreign State, then not only would those persons be entitled to claim immunity on the same terms as a State even when sued in their personal capacities,[575] but by parallel reasoning they would also take the benefit of the procedural privileges and immunities described above[576] and would be capable of binding the State by a submission to jurisdiction. The broader construction also raises complex issues as to who or what is part of a foreign government. Does it, for example, include members of the legislature, the civil service and the police force as well as ministers?[577]

To advocate the narrower construction outlined above is not to argue, however, that a State may never assert immunity in the event that proceedings are instituted in the United Kingdom against a member of its government or person carrying out government functions. In these circumstances, provided that the proceedings relate to acts carried out under the authority of the State, the State will be indirectly impleaded and entitled to intervene to assert immunity.[578]

4.100   Significantly, however, the Foreign and Commonwealth Office and the English courts appear to have construed the term "government" in the broader sense outlined above. In *Ex parte Trawnik*,[579] proceedings were issued in the English High Court against the British military commandant in Berlin.[580] Subsequently,

---

[574] See 4.141 below.

[575] Unless a functional analysis is applied (for which there is no support in the language of s 14), this would appear to go substantially further than international law requires (see 4.138).

[576] Would the junior tourism minister of a foreign state be entitled to assert the procedural privileges in ss 12 and 13 in an action to recover debts incurred by him during a private visit to London?

[577] See the discussion of the *Propend* case below.   [578] See 4.012 above.

[579] *R v Secretary of State for Foreign and Commonwealth Affairs, ex p. Trawnik* (1986) The Times, 21 February.   [580] See *Trawnik v Ministry of Defence* [1985] 1 WLR 532.

the Foreign Secretary issued a certificate under s 21(a) of the 1978 Act to the effect that Germany was a State and that the *persons* to be regarded as its government included the defendant, as a member of the Kommandatura of Berlin. The Court of Appeal refused leave to review the certificate judicially. In *Propend Finance v Sing*,[581] proceedings were issued in the High Court against both Superintendent Sing, an officer of the Australian Federal Police (AFP), and the Commissioner of the AFP (sued in a representative capacity).[582] Immunity was asserted in these proceedings under the 1978 Act.[583] Laws J held that the reference in s 14(1) was to the executive branch of government and that the Commissioner fulfilled a role independent of the executive, so as not to constitute part of the government of Australia.[584] The Court of Appeal, in reversing that decision, took a broader view:[585]

> In our view, the word "government" in Section 14 must be given a broader meaning than that contemplated by the judge. Far from leading to bizarre or absurd conclusions, a broad reading corresponds with the requirement of comity and with a body of law from many countries on the scope of sovereign immunity as a concept which covers *acta iure imperii*. In our judgment, Parliament had that jurisprudence in mind when enacting Section 14 and intended a broad interpretation of the word "government" in Section 14(1). The expression "sovereign authority" or a similar expression appears frequently in the authorities. While in Section 14 it appears only in Section 14(2) dealing with "separate entities" and not in section 14(1) dealing with "government", it would be curious if separate entities were immune from the jurisdiction in proceedings relating to acts done by them in the exercise of sovereign authority if the government of the State were not also immune. The word government should be construed in the light of the concept of sovereign authority.

With respect, it is difficult to follow this reasoning. A more straightforward explanation for the omission of the expression "sovereign authority" from s 14(1) is that it was not required to delimit the circumstances in which the "government" of a State, in the narrow sense described above, was entitled to assert immunity.

Having considered authorities on the meaning of the expression "sovereign authority",[586] the court continued:[587]

> The word 'government' should not be confined to what in other contexts would in English law mean the government of the United Kingdom. Once

---

[581] *Propend Finance Pty Limited v Sing* (1996–1997) 111 ILR 611 (Laws J and CA). For criticism, see Barker (1998) ICLQ 950; Byers (1997) 67 BYIL 312–318.

[582] See the judgment of the Court of Appeal (1997) 111 ILR 611, at 661–664.

[583] The individual officer, who had diplomatic accreditation, successfully claimed diplomatic immunity (see (1997) 111 ILR, at 635–645 (Laws J), 656–661 (CA)).

[584] *Propend* (1997) 111 ILR 611, at 646–653.   [585] *Propend,* at 667.

[586] Including *I° Congreso del Partido* [1983] AC 244 (HL) and *Kuwait Airways Corp. v Iraqi Airways Co.* [1995] 1 WLR 1147 (HL).   [587] *Propend,* (1997) 111 ILR 611, at 669.

the broad scope of government or sovereign authority is, for this purpose, accepted, the performance of police functions is essentially a part of governmental activity . . .

The Court of Appeal concluded that the individual officer and (if vicarious liability were to be established) the Commissioner were "covered by State immunity" and that the Superintendent was "part of the Government of Australia within the meaning of that term in Section 14(1) of the Act".[588] The finding of immunity seems right, and the court was probably correct to describe the role of police (and judges) as "governmental" even though they are not part of the executive from an English perspective. Moreover, it is true that the policy underlying the 1978 Act would undoubtedly be undermined if State agents or employees could be sued whenever the State was immune. It is submitted, however, that s 14(1) protects those agents or employees not because in their performance of sovereign acts they are indistinguishable from the "government" of the foreign State under whose authority they operate, but because the State itself is indirectly impleaded and can intervene if necessary to assert immunity. The State can also waive its immunity. This issue is returned to below, in considering the position of agents and employees.[589]

The entitlement of serving heads of government and foreign ministers to immunities and privileges at common law is addressed in the commentary on s 20 below.[590]

4.101   *Department of government*

The 1978 Act provides no guidance as to the test to be applied to determine whether a party to proceedings is a department of the government of a foreign State for the purposes of s 14(1)(c).[591] Some assistance, however, can be derived from case law pre-dating the 1978 Act.[592] In *Trendtex Trading Corporation v Central Bank of Nigeria*, Shaw LJ stated:[593]

> Whether a particular organisation is to be accorded the status of a department of government or not must be dependent on its constitution, its powers and duties and its activities. These are the basic factors to be considered. The view of the Government concerned must be taken into account but it is not of itself decisive . . . ; it does not relieve a court before which the issue of sovereign immunity arises of the responsibility of examining all the relevant circumstances . . .

---

[588] *Propend*, at 671.   [589] See 4.105 below.   [590] See 4.131–4.138 below.
[591] This is not one of the matters in respect of which a certificate can be given under s 21(a) (see 4.139 below).
[592] See *Krajina v Tass Agency* [1949] 2 All ER 274 (CA); *Baccus v Servicio Nacional de Trigo* [1957] 1 QB 438 (CA); *Mellenger v New Brunswick Development Corporation* [1971] 1 WLR 604 (CA); *Trendtex v Central Bank of Nigeria* [1977] 1 QB 529, esp. at 559–561 (Lord Denning MR), at 567 (Stephenson LJ), at 573–575 (Shaw LJ) (CA).   [593] [1977] 1 QB 529, at 573.

It is suggested that the following principles can be derived from these cases:

(a) The characterization of a party to proceedings as a department of the government of a foreign sovereign State depends not on any single factor, but on a consideration of all relevant circumstances.

(b) The status of the party under the law of its home state is one relevant factor, but is not decisive. Nor is the presence of separate legal personality itself decisive against characterizing a party as a department of government.

(c) A detailed analysis of the constitution, function, powers and activities of the party and of its relationship with the state is likely to be essential. The existence of State control is not, however, a sufficient criterion.

(d) The courts are likely to exercise caution before treating a party having separate legal personality as a department of government.

(e) The range of functions performed by and degree of independence usually granted to (and, indeed, required of[594]) a foreign central bank make it unlikely that a separate legal entity performing such a role will be characterized as a department of government.

The principles to be applied in determining whether an entity is a "department of government" for this purpose are closely related to and mirror those for determining whether an entity is a "separate entity".[595] Indeed, it is submitted that there should be no scope for a finding that a governmental entity falls between the two categories, into a judicial no-man's land.

"Separate entity" **4.102**

An entity is a "separate entity" if it is "distinct from the executive organs of the government" and "capable of suing or being sued". Although the 1978 Act does not specify the system of law to be applied in determining whether these conditions are satisfied (except insofar as the legislative history supports the view that the law of the foreign State should not be applied exclusively[596]), ordinary rules of English private international law suggest that the ability to sue and be sued should be tested primarily by reference to the law of the place of incorporation of the entity.[597] As for the requirement that the entity be distinct from the executive organs of government, this would appear to require a careful examination of the entity's constitution, functions, powers and activities and its relationship with the State in order to determine whether the required degree of separation exists. As for the reference to "executive organs", the decision of the Court of Appeal in the *Propend* case (discussed above[598]) supports a broad interpretation to include entities performing criminal investigation and, perhaps, judicial functions, although the court was content to leave the point open.[599]

---

[594] EC Treaty, Arts 108, 109 and 121. See Proctor (2001) 1 JIBFL 23.   [595] See 4.102 below.
[596] See 4.095 above.   [597] Dicey and Morris, para 30R-099 and following.
[598] See 4.100 above.   [599] (1997) 111 ILR 611, at 670–671.

Further guidance is provided by Article 27 of the European Convention, from which the final sentence of s 14(1) and s 14(2) are derived, and the explanatory notes thereto.[600] The notes suggest that the entities referred to in Article 27 may be, *inter alia*, political subdivisions (subject to the provisions regarding constituent territories of federal states[601]) or State agencies, such as national banks or railway administrations.[602] Article 27 itself refers expressly to legal entities "of" a contracting State, a connecting factor which Lord Goff in *Kuwait Airways Corporation v Iraqi Airways Co.* thought should be read into the final sentence of s 14(1).[603]

4.103   *The immunities and privileges of a "separate entity"*

The "separate entity" occupies a curious position under the 1978 Act, for which there is no clear precedent in customary international law.[604] Although not equated with the State,[605] it enjoys its own (limited) immunity from jurisdiction, can waive that immunity by submitting to the jurisdiction and enjoys certain procedural privileges if it submits to the jurisdiction in proceedings in which it would otherwise have enjoyed immunity.

For a separate entity to enjoy immunity from the jurisdiction of a court or tribunal in the United Kingdom under s 14(2) of the 1978 Act, two conditions must be satisfied and, in this regard, the burden of satisfying those conditions lies upon the entity.[606]

The first condition is that the proceedings must relate to[607] a thing done by it *in the exercise of sovereign authority*. It is now clearly established that the closing words require the court or tribunal to consider whether the acts that are the subject matter of proceedings are sovereign acts (*acta jure imperii*) or private acts (*acta iure gestionis*) according to well-established principles of customary international law.[608] The former category only is to be equated with things done "in the exercise of sovereign authority". In summary, the following principles can be derived from the speech of Lord Wilberforce in the leading decision of

---

[600] See 1.052 and 1.118 above; *Kuwait Airways Corporation v Iraqi Airways Co.* [1995] 1 WLR 1147, at 1158 (Lord Goff) (HL).   [601] See 4.108 below.
[602] Explanatory Report, para 109 (see 1.118 above).
[603] [1995] 1 WLR 1147, at 1158 (HL), where the point was left open. In *Propend Finance v Sing* (1997) 111 ILR 611, the Court of Appeal (at 670) construed "of" as meaning "created by". On this basis, if an entity incorporated otherwise than in the relevant foreign State acts as agent of that State, it may not assert immunity under section 14(2) as a separate entity, although the State may be able to intervene to assert its own immunity (see 4.105 below). Query whether an entity incorporated under the laws of a State is "created by" the State if it is promoted by private persons? Fox (1996) 112 LQR 186, at 188 takes Lord Goff to be suggesting the exclusion of all private law corporations (see also Fox, *The Law of State Immunity* (Oxford, 2002), 140).
[604] See, however, Article 27 of the European Convention (at 1.052 above).   [605] s 14(1).
[606] *Kuwait Airways Corporation v Iraqi Airways Co.* [1995] 1 WLR 1147, at 1161 (Lord Goff) (HL).
[607] See the discussion at 4.029 above as to the meaning of the words "relating to" in other sections of the 1978 Act.
[608] *Kuwait Airways Corporation v Iraqi Airways* [1995] 1 WLR 1147, at 1159–1160 (Lord Goff) (HL). See also *Crescent Oil and Shipping Services Ltd v Banco Nacional de Angola* (1999) unreported, 28 May (Cresswell J); *Re Banco Nacional de Cuba* [2001] 1 WLR 2039 (Lightman J).

the House of Lords in *I° Congreso del Partido*[609] and that of Lord Goff in *Kuwait Airways Corporation v Iraqi Airways Co.*:[610]

(a) The activities of States cannot always be compartmentalized into trading or governmental activities. A State may have displayed both a commercial and a sovereign or governmental interest. The court or tribunal must ask, "To which is the critical action to be attributed?"[611]

(b) The mere existence of a governmental purpose or motive will not convert what would otherwise be a private, non-sovereign act into a sovereign act.[612]

(c) In characterizing the acts upon which the claim is based, *the court must consider the whole context in which the claim against the State is made*, with a view to deciding whether those acts should, *in that context*, be considered as fairly within an area of activity, trading or commercial, or otherwise of a private law character, in which the state has chosen to engage, or whether the relevant acts should be considered as having been done outside that area, and within the sphere of governmental or sovereign activity.[613]

(d) The ultimate test of what constitutes an act *jure imperii* is whether the act in question is of its own character a governmental act, as opposed to an act which any private citizen can perform.[614]

(e) It is not enough that the entity should have acted on the directions of the State (ie literally with the authority of the sovereign), because such an act need not possess the character of a sovereign act.[615]

If the proceedings do relate to sovereign acts then, even if they also relate to private acts, the first condition will be satisfied.[616]

The second condition is that the circumstances must be such that a State (or, in a case to which s 10 applies, a State not party to the Brussels Convention) would have been immune if proceedings had been brought against it. The application of this condition has been little considered by the English courts[617] but requires that ss 1–11 of the 1978 Act be applied as if the acts, omissions or interests of the separate entity were acts, omissions or interests of a State.[618]

---

[609] [1983] 1 AC 244.   [610] [1995] 1 WLR 1147 (HL).

[611] *I° Congreso*, at 264 (Lord Wilberforce).

[612] *I° Congreso*, at 267 (Lord Wilberforce); *Kuwait Airways*, at 1160 (Lord Goff).

[613] *I° Congreso*, at 267 (Lord Wilberforce).   [614] *Kuwait Airways*, at 1160 (Lord Goff).

[615] *Kuwait Airways*, at 1160 (Lord Goff). Cf. the dissenting speeches of Lords Mustill, at 1171–1172, and Slynn, at 1174–1175.

[616] The claiming party may, of course, be able to modify its claim so as to exclude reference to sovereign acts.

[617] As Lord Goff noted in *Kuwait Airways Corporation v Iraqi Airways Co.* [1995] 1 WLR 1147, at 1159, the exclusion of *acta iure gestionis* by the first requirement leaves little scope for the operation under s 14(2)(b) of the commercial transactions exception in s 3 (see 4.026 to 4.035 above). Indeed, in *Re Banco Nacional de Cuba* [2001] 1 WLR 2039, Lightman J (at 2051) appeared to elide the two. Nevertheless, the second requirement will take on a greater importance in cases where the proceedings are founded on acts of a sovereign character and an exception to immunity other than that contained in s 3 (commercial transactions) is relied on.

[618] See, for example, the approach of the Court of Appeal (whose decision was later reversed) in *Kuwait Airways Corporation v Iraqi Airways Co.* [1995] 1 Lloyd's Rep 25.

Thus, for example, if proceedings were brought by a UK company against a separate entity in respect of its membership of the company, the separate entity would not be immune if any other member of the company was not a State but might enjoy immunity if all other members were States (ie s 8(1) would be applied as if the separate entity sued were a State, but the same treatment would not extend to other separate entities who happened to be members[619]). By identical reasoning, a separate entity would be capable of submitting to the jurisdiction (and thereby waiving its immunity) through the application by s 14(2)(b) of s 2 of the 1978 Act.[620] On this approach, the State that created the separate entity would also probably retain the right to waive the immunity of that entity by submitting to the jurisdiction.[621]

4.104   Applying this dual requirement, the English courts have applied s 14(2), as follows:

(a) In denying immunity:

—to a state controlled airline in respect of its use of unlawfully seized aircraft after a State decree which purported to vest ownership of the aircraft in the airline; although immunity was recognized in respect of prior acts of assistance in the seizure of the aircraft;[622]

—to a foreign central bank in respect of a claim that it had benefited from the voluntary transfer by another entity (the former central bank) of assets at an undervalue, notwithstanding that the transfer had taken place against the background of a reorganization of the State's central bank structures.[623]

(b) In according immunity:

—to a foreign central bank in respect of a claim that it had interfered with contractual relations between two commercial entities through its control of foreign currency reserves.[624]

---

[619] For the application of s 8, see 4.064–4.066 above.

[620] See *Kuwait Airways Corporation v Iraqi Airways Co.* [1995] 1 Lloyd's Rep 25, at 31 (Nourse LJ), 37 (Simon Brown LJ) (CA).

[621] Note that s 14(2)(b) does not require one to read ss 1–11 as if references to a State were references to a separate entity, but simply to assume that the defendant entity is a State for the purpose of assessing its immunity. Compare s 14(3) (discussed below).

[622] *Kuwait Airways Corporation v Iraqi Airways Co.* [1995] 1 WLR 1147 (HL), reversing the Court of Appeal ([1995] 1 Lloyd's Rep. 25), in turn reversing Evans J ((1992) 103 ILR 340. Criticized by Fox (1996) 112 LQR 186. See also *Kuwait Airways Corporation v Iraqi Airways Co. (No. 2)* [2001] 1 WLR 429 (HL) (unsuccessful attempt to re-open their Lordships' decision); *Kuwait Airways Corporation v Iraqi Airways Corporation* [2003] EWHC 31 (Comm) (David Steel J) (setting aside the decision of the House of Lords in part in respect of a period before the decree during which the airline had taken steps to incorporate the aircraft in its fleet).

[623] *Re Banco Nacional de Cuba* [2001] 1 WLR 2039 (Lightman J).

[624] *Crescent Oil and Shipping Services Ltd v Banco Nacional de Angola* (Comm, 28 May 1999) (Cresswell J) drawing support from United States case law, notably *De Sanchez v Nicaragua* (1985) 770 F 2d. 1385 (US Court of Appeals, 5th Circuit). See also *Banco Nacional de Cuba v Cosmos Trading Corp* [2000] 1 BCLC 813 (discussed at 4.107 below).

Under s 14(3) of the 1978 Act, a separate entity (other than a central bank or other monetary authority)[625] which submits to the jurisdiction in respect of proceedings for which it would otherwise have been entitled to assert immunity under s 14(2), shall be entitled to the same immunities and privileges enjoyed by a State under ss 13(1)–(4).[626]

Agent or employee of foreign state or separate entity   **4.105**

In *Propend Finance v Sing*,[627] the Court of Appeal recognized that the concept of an "entity . . . distinct from the executive organs of the government of the State and capable of suing or being sued" is not one which would normally be identified with a natural person and had no application to a claim against the Commissioner of the Australian Federal Police (in his representative capacity) and an individual police officer, Superintendent Sing.[628] The court continued:[629]

> The protection afforded by the Act of 1978 to States would be undermined if employees, officers (or as one authority puts it, "functionaries") could be sued as individuals for matters of State conduct in respect of which the State they were serving had immunity. Section 14(1) must be read as affording to individual employees or officers of a foreign State protection under the same cloak as protects the State itself.

This reasoning in the first sentence is, in itself, unexceptionable.[630] The Court of Appeal, however, based its decision (that the 1978 Act barred proceedings against Superintendent Sing) on the finding that "[t]he Superintendent is a part of the Government of Australia within the meaning of that term in Section 14(1) of that Act" by reason of the fact that he had acted in the exercise of sovereign authority.[631] Although the result appears correct, it is submitted that this reasoning is less than satisfactory. The 1978 Act should apply to proceedings brought against an employee or agent of a foreign State not because that employee or agent is to be identified in certain cases with the State for the purposes of s 14(1), but because the proceedings against the employee/agent indirectly implead the State as employer/principal. The general immunity in s 1 protects the State (in the *Propend* case , the Commonwealth of Australia) whether it is directly or indirectly impleaded, but (if not already a party) the State must intervene in proceedings to assert its own immunity, if available. At the very least, this requires that evidence

---

[625] See 4.106 below.   [626] See 4.083–4.091 above.
[627] (1996–1997) 113 ILR 611. See 4.100 above.   [628] At 669.
[629] At 669. In support of this proposition, the court cited the *Church of Scientology* case (1978) 65 ILR 193 (German Supreme Court); *Jaffe v Miller* (1993) 95 ILR 446 (Ontario Court of Appeals); *Herbage v Meese* (1990) 98 ILR 101 (US District Court, DC). For the position at common law, see *Rahimtoola v Nizam of Hyderabad* [1958] AC 379, esp at 397 (Viscount Simonds), 402 (Lord Reid), 407 (Lord Cohen) (HL). See also *Twycross v Dreyfus* (1877) 5 Ch.D. 605 (CA); *Grunfeld v United States of America* [1968] 3 NSWR 36 (Sup. Ct. NSW); *Schmidt v Home Secretary* [1995] 1 ILRM 301; 103 ILR 322 (Irish High Court); *McElhinney v Williams* [1996] 1 ILRM 276; (1995) 104 ILR 691 (Irish Supreme Court); Eagleton, *The Responsibility of States in International Law* (New York, 1928), ch III; cf. *Saorstat and Continental Steamship Company v De Las Morenas* [1945] IR 291 (Irish Supreme Court).
[630] See also *Re P (No. 2)* (1998) 114 ILR 486; [1998] 1 FLR 1027.   [631] See 4.103 above.

be placed before the court by an authorized representative of the State as to the State's intention to assert immunity and the facts supporting that assertion of immunity.[632]

A literal application of the reasoning of the Court of Appeal in the *Propend* case, identifying an employee or agent with the State raises the following difficulties:

(a) It would seem to follow that the employee or agent *qua State* would enjoy the procedural privileges in ss 12 and 13, at least when sued in respect of governmental acts.[633] A claimant unsure or unaware of the capacity in which the potential defendant had performed the acts giving rise to the dispute, or unable to characterize them as sovereign or private, may be placed in an invidious position. While it is true that the protection afforded to a State by ss 12 and 13 may equally be undermined if proceedings are brought instead against the State's agent or employee, it is submitted that any prejudice to the State can be avoided through the exercise of the court's discretion in relation to such matters as the extension of time periods and measures of execution.[634]

(b) The employee or agent *qua State* would also arguably be able to waive his own immunity by submitting to the jurisdiction in accordance with s 2 of the 1978 Act (including by defending proceedings). But the *Propend* case itself conflicts with this analysis, as the court emphasized that the relevant question on the issue of waiver was whether the Commonwealth of Australia (or anyone duly authorized by it) had waived immunity.[635]

(c) The requirement that the employee or agent has acted in the exercise of sovereign authority places an unwarranted gloss on the State's immunity, which should be judged according to the principles contained in ss 1–11 of the 1978 Act and not according to customary international law.

These issues were not addressed in the *Propend* case and it is submitted that neither that case, nor any other decision of the English courts, should be taken as authority that the immunity belongs to the employee or agent, rather than the State. Employees and agents enjoy protection under the 1978 Act only through the intervention of the sovereign power on whose behalf they act.

Similarly, it would seem that a separate entity may intervene to assert its own limited immunity under s 14(2)[636] in the event that its employees or agents are sued in circumstances in which the entity would have been entitled to immunity if it had been named as a defendant instead.[637]

---

[632] The court may require that the State be joined as a party for the purposes of asserting its immunity (see Civil Procedure Rules, r 19.2; *Re P (No. 2)* (1998) 114 ILR 488; [1998] 1 FLR 1027, where the United States of America intervened to assert State and diplomatic immunity).

[633] ie according to the court, acts performed in the exercise of sovereign authority (see 4.107 above).   [634] See 4.085 above.

[635] *Propend* (1997) 113 ILR 611, at 671 (CA).   [636] See 4.103.

[637] *Propend* (1997) 113 ILR 611, at 670 (CA).

As already noted, central banks and other monetary authorities are favourably treated under s 13 of the 1978 Act.[639] They do not occupy any special position in relation to immunity from jurisdiction, the approach to which will depend on whether the bank or authority is a separate entity.[640] If the bank is a separate entity, it will be entitled to immunity only if the two conditions in s 14(2) are satisfied.[641]

The terms "foreign central bank" and "monetary authority" are not defined in the 1978 Act, nor does the Act provide for certification as to whether a foreign entity falls within either of these categories. It seems probable, therefore, that in borderline cases a court will have to carry out a structural and functional analysis. As one commentator has noted:[642]

> The term "central bank" is descriptive of a bank's functions, rather than its legal status. The functions include note-issue, monetary policy, the efficient operation of the national financial system, including payment systems, banking regulation and supervision, the provision of banking services for the government, the management of gold and foreign exchange reserves, debt management, exchange controls and development and promotional tasks. Not all central banks conduct all of these functions. . . . Whatever the precise scope of any particular central bank's functions, it may be said that the essence of central banking lies in its responsibilities. A central bank may be organised on commercial lines, but as a bank its imperatives are not solely commercial.

The fact that an entity may perform commercial, as well as sovereign functions (for example, the issue of letters of credit or performance bonds) should not, of itself, prevent it from being characterized as a "central bank" or "monetary authority".

One issue which may trouble the courts in the future is the status of central banks performing functions not solely on behalf of its own sovereign, but within the framework of an international financial system. In particular, the central banks of certain Member States of the European Union are part of the European System of Central Banks (ESCB) established pursuant to Article 8 of the EC Treaty.[643] As part of the ESCB, the national central banks contribute capital to and act as shareholders of the European Central Bank and perform certain other functions (including in relation to the foreign reserve assets of the ECB). In performing these functions, the national central banks are required to act independently of their member states. It may be questioned whether, in so acting, the banks are acting "in the exercise of sovereign authority" so as to satisfy the first limb of s 14(2).[644]

---

[638] See Blair (1998) 57 CLQ 374; Proctor (2000) 15 JIBFL 70; (2001) 1 JIBFL 23.
[639] s 14(4) (see 4.093 above).   [640] See 4.101–4.102 above.   [641] See 4.103 above.
[642] Blair (1998) 54 CLJ 374, at 375.
[643] For a more detailed commentary, see Proctor (2001) 16 JIBFL 23.
[644] Whether the national central banks are entitled to protection under the EC Treaty, and associated instruments, is a separate question not addressed here.

At the same time, other functions formerly performed by the national central banks (including the issue of currency) have been transferred to the ECB. One commentator has raised (but rejected[645]) the argument that this loss of function deprives these banks of their status as "central banks" for the purposes of the 1978 Act. That argument has yet to be tested before an English court.[646]

4.107   *Winding up proceedings in respect of a "separate entity"*
           (including a central bank)

In *Banco National de Cuba v Cosmos Trading Corp*, Sir Richard Scott V-C suggested[647] that s 14(2) of the 1978 Act would operate to bar a winding-up petition against the central bank of a foreign state. He left this point open, however, noting that even if the language of s 14(2) were thought not quite to cover a petition for a winding-up order against a central bank (or, conceivably, any separate entity exercising sovereign functions), it was inconceivable that a court would as a matter of discretion be willing to make such an order.[648] It is submitted that s 14(2) would apply to a winding-up petition against a separate entity and that if any of the functions and activities of the entity were of a sovereign character (subject to a *de minimis* threshold) the section would operate to confer a jurisdictional immunity (subject to waiver).[649] In the case of a central bank, enforcement of a winding up order against the assets of the bank within the jurisdiction would (in the absence of waiver) also seem to be precluded by the bank's s 13 privileges.[650] Indeed, the statutory trust imposed on the making of a winding up order may, of itself, run counter to s 13(2)(b).

4.108   *Constituent territory of a federal State*

The constituent territories of federal States do not form part of a "State" under s 14(1) of the 1978 Act. Under ss 14(5) and 14(6), however, certain immunities and privileges are conferred on those territories. In this regard, constituent territories may fall into one of two categories, as follows:

—Those designated by Order in Council under s 14(5) of the 1978 Act ("designated territories"). This facility was intended to enable the United Kingdom to comply with its obligations in respect of a notification under Article 28, paragraph 2 of the European Convention. Germany and Austria have given notifications under this paragraph and Orders in Council have been made designating their constituent territories for this purpose.[651]

---

[645] In the authors' view, correctly.   [646] See Proctor (2001) 16 JIBFL 23.
[647] [2000] 1 BCLC 813, at 820 (CA).
[648] [2001] 1 BCLC 813, at 820 (CA). See also *Re Rafidain* [1992] BCLC 1.
[649] A winding-up order is in respect not only of the obligation(s) owed to the petitioning creditor, but the rights, obligations, functions and activities of the relevant entity as a whole (see 4.088 above). See also 4.059 above.   [650] See 4.093 above.
[651] State Immunity (Federal States) Order 1979 (SI 1979/457) (Austria: Burgenland, Carinthia, Lower Austria, Upper Austria, Salzburg, Styria, Tyrol, Vorarlberg and Vienna); State Immunity (Federal States) Order 1993 (SI 1993/2809) (Germany: Baden-Württemberg, Bavaria, Berlin, Brandenberg, Bremen, Hamburg, Hesse, Mecklenberg-Western Pomerania, Lower Saxony, North-Rhine/Westphalia,

—Those not so designated ("non-designated territories"). It is understood that HM Government has no plans to make further Orders in Council under s 14(5) designating for this purpose the constituent territories of other federal States with whom it enjoys friendly relations.

The position of constituent territories under the 1978 Act can be summarized as follows:

(a) *Service of process and judgments in default of appearance*: Section 12 applies to proceedings against both designated and non-designated territories, so that the document initiating proceedings and any default judgment must ordinarily (and in the absence of contrary agreement) be served by being transmitted through the Foreign and Commonwealth Office to the Ministry of Foreign Affairs of the federal State.[652] Curiously, however, the rules of court implementing s 12[653] apply in terms only to States (as defined in s 14 of the 1978 Act). It is submitted that, in order to give effect to the intent of s 14(5), these provisions should be construed broadly as applying to constituent territories of federal States (whether designated or not). Alternatively, the court should seek to exercise its powers (for example, to set aside a default judgment of its own motion) in order to give the same protection to the constituent territory.

(b) *Immunities and privileges of designated territories*: Otherwise the provisions of Part I of the 1978 Act (including the general rule of immunity, the exceptions to immunity and the procedural privileges) apply to designated territories as they apply to a State. The protection extends, therefore, to the head of the territory in his public capacity, the government of the territory and any department of that government, but not any entity distinct from the executive organs of the government of the territory and capable of suing or being sued.[654] A designated territory may waive its immunity.[655]

(c) *Immunities and privileges of non-designated territories*: Otherwise non-designated territories are equated to separate entities of the 1978 Act for the purpose of determining their immunities and privileges under the 1978 Act.[656] In particular, a designated territory[657] will be entitled to assert immunity if (i) the proceedings relate to anything done by it in the exercise

Rhineland-Palatinate, Saarland, Saxony, Saxony-Anhalt, Schleswig-Holstein and Thuringia). On 4 September 2003, Belgium also made a declaration under this paragraph (see 1.069) designating the French Community, the Flemish Community and the German-speaking Community as well as the Walloon Region, the Flemish Region and the Brussels-Capital Region but, at the time of writing, no designating Order in Council had been made.
  [652] s 14(5). See 4.080 above.
  [653] Civil Procedure Rules, rr 6.27, 12.10(a)(iii) and 12.11(5); PD12, para 4.4.
  [654] See 4.097–4.102.
  [655] It is not clear whether the federal State may waive the immunity of designated territories.
  [656] s 14(6). See 4.103.
  [657] Or, it is suggested, its government, a department of its government or the head of the territory acting in his public capacity (assuming that the ruler of the designated territory is not also the head of the federal State—see (d) below).

of sovereign authority, and (ii) the circumstances are such that the federal State would have been immune.

    (d) *Head of constituent territory.* The head of a constituent territory may also be head of the federal State. If so, he is entitled to the immunities conferred on a head of state by virtue of s 14(1) (but only when acting in his public capacity as head of the federal State) and s 20.[658] Otherwise, as noted, the head of a designated territory in his public capacity is treated in the same way as the head of a State and the head of a non-designated territory sued in a public capacity may be treated as a separate entity. The heads of constituent territories who are not also heads of State have no immunities and privileges under the 1978 Act when acting in a private capacity, as s 20 applies only to heads of State. The question remains whether they have any residual immunities or privileges at common law. The purposes of the 1978 Act are stated to include "new provision with respect to the immunities and privileges of heads of State" and "connected purposes" but that would not seem sufficient to exclude common law rules in the case of persons other than heads of State.[659] The English courts have in the past recognized that rulers of a constituent part of a State may enjoy certain immunities and privileges, although those cases are not recent and may need to be reconsidered against the background of development in customary international law.[660]

4.109 ## 15 Restriction and extension of immunities and privileges

    (1) If it appears to Her Majesty that the immunities and privileges conferred by this Part of this Act in relation to any State—

        (a) exceed those accorded by the law of that State in relation to the United Kingdom; or

        (b) are less than those required by any treaty, convention or other international agreement to which that State and the United Kingdom are parties.

    Her Majesty may by Order in Council provide for restricting or, as the case may be, extending those immunities and privileges to such extent as appears to Her Majesty to be appropriate.

    (2) Any statutory instrument containing an Order under this section shall be subject to annulment in pursuance of a resolution of either House of Parliament.

---

[658] *BCCI v Price Waterhouse* [1997] 4 All ER 108 (Laddie J). See 4.098 above and paras 4.131–4.137 below. [659] See also 4.138 below (heads of government and senior ministers).
[660] See *Statham v Statham* [1912] P 92; *Mighell v Sultan of Johore* [1894] 1 QB 149; *Sayce v Ameer Ruler of Bahawalpur State* [1952] 2 QB 390; *Antoun v Harrison and Sons Ltd* (1965) The Times, 24 September (Waller J). See also *Kubacz v Shah* (1983) 118 ILR 293 (Sup. Ct., Western Australia); *First American Corporation v Al-Nahyan* (1996) 948 F Supp. 1107; 121 ILR 577 (US District Court, DC). The point did not arise for consideration in *BCCI v Price Waterhouse*, as the defendant was also head of State (United Arab Emirates) and entitled, at least when acting in a private capacity, to the immunities and privileges recognized by s 20 of the 1978 Act (see 4.098).

Commentary

Legislative history **4.110**

Sub-section (2) of what is now s 15 (clause 16 of the State Immunity Bill) was inserted by amendment. In debate, Lord Denning has described the provisions of the section as "shutting the door after the horse has bolted".[661]

The State Immunity (Merchant Shipping) (Union of Soviet Socialist Republics) Order[662] was enacted to give effect to the provisions of an international agreement between the UK and the USSR.[663] In *The Guiseppe di Vittorio*[664] the Commercial Court and the Court of Appeal ruled that, following the break-up of the USSR, the treaty should not be interpreted as including property owned by Ukraine, one of the former constituent territories. The State Immunity (Merchant Shipping) Order[665] was issued in response to this judgment. It was in essentially the same terms as its predecessor, except that it was expressed to apply to Georgia, the Russian Federation and the Republic of Ukraine rather than the USSR. In *The Guiseppe di Vittorio (No. 2)*,[666] Clarke J refused to give the 1997 Order retrospective effect. The 1997 Order was repealed by the State Immunity (Merchant Shipping) (Revocation) Order[667] with effect from the UK's termination of the relevant international agreement on 29 April 1999.

Application **4.111**

No order is currently in force under s 15.[668] There may be a case for using an order under s 15 to remedy infelicities between the 1978 Act and the European Convention, but only insofar as the latter is more favourable to Convention States.[669] Section 15 does not allow the restriction of immunities on the basis of a treaty, convention or other international agreement.

16 Excluded matters **4.112**

(1) This Part of this Act does not affect any immunity or privilege conferred by the Diplomatic Privileges Act 1964 or the Consular Relations Act 1968; and—

(a) section 4 above does not apply to proceedings concerning the employment of the members of a mission within the meaning of the Convention scheduled to the said Act of 1964 or of the members of

---

[661] Hansard, HL (5th series), vol 388, col. 74 (17 January 1978).   [662] SI 1978/1524.

[663] Art 2 of the protocol to the 1968 Treaty of Merchant Navigation between the UK and the USSR provided: ". . . Vessels and cargoes owned by one High Contracting Party shall not be liable to seizure in connection with the execution of any judgment of . . . the Court of the other High Contracting Party in proceedings to which Article 1 . . . applies".

[664] [1998] 1 Lloyd's Rep 136. See also *Coreck Maritime GmbH v Sevrybokholodflot* [1994] SLT 893 (Ct Sess (OH), Scot).   [665] SI 1997/2591.

[666] [1998] 1 Lloyd's Rep 661.   [667] SI 1999/668.

[668] As already noted, the State Immunity (Merchant Shipping) Order (SI 1997/2591) was revoked by the State Immunity (Merchant Shipping) (Revocation) Order (SI 1999/668).

[669] See, eg, 4.028 above.

a consular post within the meaning of the Convention scheduled to the said Act of 1968;

(b) section 6(1) above does not apply to proceedings concerning a State's title to or its possession of property used for the purposes of a diplomatic mission.

(2) This Part of this Act does not apply to proceedings relating to anything done by or in relation to the armed forces of a State while present in the United Kingdom and, in particular, has effect subject to the Visiting Forces Act 1952.

(3) This Part of this Act does not apply to proceedings to which section 17(6) of the Nuclear Installations Act 1965 applies.

(4) This Part of this Act does not apply to criminal proceedings.

(5) This Part of this Act does not apply to any proceedings relating to taxation other than those mentioned in section 11 above.

Commentary

4.113   Legislative history

The European Convention was essentially concerned with private law disputes between individuals and States and excluded from its scope certain areas of a "public law" nature.[670] Further, the Convention was expressed not to apply to or to affect existing immunities and privileges in areas that were understood to be addressed in multilateral treaties or special agreements between States.[671] Section 16 of the 1978 Act (Clause 17 of the State Immunity Bill) has its foundation in these provisions, without reproducing them word for word. Clause 17 was only amended in minor respects during the passage of the Bill through Parliament.[672]

4.114   Application

Section 16 contains a list of "excluded matters". These exclusions, and the reasons for them, are considered in the following paragraphs. By way of introduction:

(a) Sub-section (1) operates differently to sub-sections (2)–(5). Whereas the former preserves certain statutory immunities and privileges and qualifies the scope of two of the exceptions to the general rule of immunity in s 1 (leaving that immunity intact), the latter exclude the provisions of Part I of the 1978 Act (including the s 1 immunity) in relation to the matters set out.

(b) Sub-sections (2) to (5) do not, of themselves, confer any immunity or privilege on the State, or debar the State from asserting any immunity or privilege

---

[670] Art 29 (see 1.054 above).   [671] Arts 30–33 (see 1.055–1.058 above).
[672] See Hansard, HL (5th series), vol 389, cols. 1532–1533 (amendments to clause 17(1) (s 16(1)) consequential on proposed amendments to clause 21); col. 1533 (amendment to limit scope of armed forces exclusion in clause 17(2) (s 16(2)) to things done in the United Kingdom).

in relation to the matters set out. Nor do they exclude the operation of the whole of the 1978 Act.[673] Instead, the courts have held that the effect of these sub-sections is to leave any question as to the existence of a privilege or immunity within the excluded matters to other rules of English law, including the common law (and, therefore, rules of customary international law).[674]

Diplomatic and consular immunities and privileges   **4.115**

The effect of the opening words of s 16(1) is to preserve the immunities and privileges conferred on diplomatic missions, consular posts and their respective staff by the Vienna Conventions on diplomatic[675] and consular[676] relations, so far as those immunities had been given effect in the United Kingdom by legislation.[677] Thus, for example, the rules in s 13 governing consent to measures of execution do not apply to the premises of the mission, the inviolability of which[678] cannot it seems (at least on existing authority) be waived by prior agreement.[679]

Sections 16(1)(a) and 16(1)(b) qualify two of the statutory exceptions to the general rule of immunity in s 1. If either of those provisions applies, s 1 will operate to confer immunity on the State in the proceedings unless another exception to the general rule is capable of applying on the facts of the case.

*Section 16(1)(a): Claims by employees of diplomatic
missions and consular posts*   **4.116**

Sub-section (1)(a) has been applied on several occasions by the Employment Appeals Tribunal and on at least one occasion by the Court of Appeal[680] in relation

---

[673] Thus, eg, the provisions of s 20 apply to criminal proceedings as shown in *Pinochet(No. 3)* (see 4.137 below).

[674] *Littrell v United States of America (No. 2)* [1995] 1 WLR 82 (CA); *Holland v Lampen-Wolfe* [2000] 1 WLR 1573 (HL). See 4.005 above.

[675] Vienna Convention on Diplomatic Relations 1961 (Cmnd 1368) (referred to in the following paragraphs as the "1961 Vienna Convention").

[676] Vienna Convention on Consular Relations 1963 (Cmnd 2113) (referred to in the following paragraphs as the "1963 Vienna Convention").

[677] Diplomatic Privileges Act 1964; Consular Relations Act 1968. See, generally, Denza, *Diplomatic Law* (2nd edn, 1998); Lee, *Consular Law and Practice* (2nd edn, 1991).

[678] 1961 Vienna Convention, Art 22.3. Cf. Art 31 of the 1963 Vienna Convention; Lee, 397.

[679] *A Company Ltd. v Republic of X* [1990] 2 Lloyd's Rep 520, at 524 (Saville J) citing *Kahan v Pakistan Federation* [1951] 2 KB 1003 (CA). Compare, however, *R v Bow Street Metropolitan Stipendiary Magistrate, ex p Pinochet Ugarte* [2000] 1 AC 147, at 217 (Lord Goff), 267 (Lord Saville), 290 (Lord Phillips) (HL).

[680] See, eg, *Jayetilleke v High Commissioner of the Commonwealth of the Bahamas* (1994) 107 ILR 622 (EAT); *United Arab Emirates v Abdelghafar* (1995) 105 ILR 627 (EAT); *Egypt v Gamal-Eldin* [1996] 2 All ER 237 (EAT); *Ramsay v Arab Republic of Egypt* (EAT, 10 November 1997); *Richards v High Commissioner for Zambia* (1996) unreported, 29 July; *Ahmed v Government of the Kingdom of Saudi Arabia* [1996] ICR 25 (CA); *Glinoer v Greek School of London* (EAT, 20 April 1998); *Government of the State of Kuwait v Fevzi* (EAT, 18 January 1999), permission to appeal refused (CA, 27 May 1999); *Mills v United States of America* (2000) 120 ILR 612 (EAT), permission to appeal refused (CA, 9 May 2000); *Government of the Kingdom of Saudi Arabia v Nasser* [2000] All ER (D) 1390 (EAT), permission to appeal refused (CA, 14 November 2000); *Military Affairs Office of the Embassy of the State of Kuwait v Caramba-Coker* (EAT, 10 April 2003). See also Pigott (2000) NLJ (28 January), 80–82. For the position at common law, see *Sengupta v Republic of India* [1983] ICR 221; (1982) 64 ILR 352.

to claims by embassy staff. These authorities confirm that (a) the exclusion covers not only proceedings brought by high level mission employees, including diplomatic personnel, but also lower grade administrative, technical and domestic staff, including, for example, drivers, and (b) that the effect of the sub-section is to disable the exception in s 4, leaving the general immunity from suit in s 1 intact.

Article 1(a) of the 1961 Vienna Convention defines "members of the mission" as including the head of the mission and the members of the staff of the mission. Article 1(c) defines the "members of staff of the mission" as the members of the diplomatic staff, of the administrative and technical staff and of the service staff of the mission. The "members of the diplomatic staff" are the members of the staff of the mission having diplomatic rank.[681] There should be little scope for dispute as to whether an individual falls within this category. The "members of the administrative and technical staff" are the members of the staff of the mission employed in the administrative and technical service of the mission.[682] The "members of the service staff" are the members of the staff of the mission in the domestic service of the mission.[683] As one commentator points out, these two categories are objective definitions based on function.[684] Their combined scope is clearly wide.[685] However, "private servants", persons in the domestic service of a member of the mission and not employees of the sending State, are not "members of the mission".[686]

Similarly, Article 1(g) of the 1963 Vienna Convention defines "members of the consular staff" as including consular officers, consular employees and members of the service staff. "Consular officers" are persons, including the head of the consular post, entrusted with the exercise of consular functions.[687] "Consular employees" are persons employed in the administrative and technical service of the consular post.[688] "Members of the service staff" are persons employed in the domestic service of a consular post.[689] "Members of the private staff", persons employed exclusively in the private service of a member of the consular post, are not themselves members of the consular post. Again, these are objective categories based on function and distinctions between the categories may be difficult.[690]

The exclusion of the s 4 exception applies if the employee is employed by the mission or consular post and falls within one of the prescribed categories, irrespective of the nationality of the employee[691] and his/her position within the Embassy.[692] Nor is notification to the United Kingdom authorities in accordance

---

[681] 1961 Vienna Convention, Art 1(d).   [682] Art 1(f).   [683] Art 1(g).
[684] Denza, 15.
[685] Denza, 15: "Although there are borderline categories of staff such as doorkeepers and messengers, it is generally possible to distinguish administrative and technical service such as interpretation, secretarial, clerical, social, financial, security, and communications services from domestic services such as driving, cooking, gardening, and cleaning."   [686] Art 1(h).
[687] 1963 Vienna Convention, Art 1(d).   [688] Art 1(e).   [689] Art 1(f).
[690] Lee, 40–41.
[691] The appointment of nationals of the receiving state as "members of the diplomatic staff" or "consular officers" requires the consent of the receiving State (1961 Vienna Convention, Art 8(2); 1963 Vienna Convention, Art 22(2)).   [692] *Ahmed* [1996] ICR 25, at 30–31 (Peter Gibson LJ), (CA).

with Article 10 of the 1961 Convention (or Article 19 of the 1963 Convention) a pre-requisite to recognition by the court of the status of an employee as a "member of a mission" (or a "member of a consular post").[693]

Although it is self-evident that proceedings (or the threat of proceedings) challenging decisions of senior mission personnel on employment matters may jeopardize the efficient conduct of the mission's day-to-day business, the connection with the immunities and privileges conferred under the Diplomatic Privileges Act 1964 and the Consular Relations Act 1968 is not immediately apparent.[694] It is, however, perhaps noteworthy that one of the provisions of the Vienna Convention on diplomatic relations which it was not considered necessary to transpose into United Kingdom law in 1964 was Article 7 which provides:

> Subject to the provisions of Articles 5, 8, 9 and 11, *the sending State may freely appoint the members of the staff of the mission* . . .[695]

That enactment was, however, passed at a time when foreign States were considered to enjoy absolute immunity before English courts and tribunals and there was no possibility of a challenge to employment decisions (absent waiver). If, as seems logical,[696] the freedom to recruit mission employees encompasses the freedom to dismiss and to determine the terms of employment, s 16(1)(a) can be seen as redressing the loss of immunity which would otherwise have resulted from the adoption of s 4.[697] Although it is clear that some legal systems take a narrower view of the qualification required in the case of diplomatic and consular personnel,[698] the European Court of Human Rights observed in the *Fogarty* case that:[699]

> [T]here appears to be a trend in international and comparative law towards limiting state immunity in respect of employment-related disputes. However, where the proceedings relate to employment in a foreign mission or embassy, international practice is divided on the question whether state immunity continues to apply and, if it does so apply, whether it covers disputes relating to the contracts of all staff or only more senior members of the mission. Certainly, it cannot be said that the United Kingdom is alone in holding that immunity attaches to suits by employees at diplomatic missions or that, in affording such immunity, the United Kingdom falls outside any currently accepted international standards.
>
> The court further observes that the proceedings which the applicant wished to bring did not concern the contractual rights of a current embassy employee, but instead related to alleged discrimination in the recruitment

---

[693] *R v Secretary of State for the Home Department, ex p Bagga* [1991] 1 QB 485 (CA).

[694] cf. Art 32 of the European Convention (see 1.057 above).

[695] See also Art 19(1) of the 1963 Vienna Convention which provides "Subject to the provisions of Articles 20, 22 and 23, the sending state may freely appoint the members of the consular staff".

[696] See Denza, 52–55.   [697] See 4.036–4.046 above.

[698] See Fox (1995) 66 BYIL 97; Fox, *The Law of State Immunity* (Oxford, 2002), 306–308.

[699] *Fogarty v United Kingdom* (Application no. 37112/97), Judgment of 21 November 2001; 12 BHRC 132, paras 37–38.

process. Questions relating to the recruitment of staff to missions and embassies may by their very nature involve sensitive and confidential issues, related, *inter alia*, to the diplomatic and organisational policy of a foreign state. The court is not aware of any trend in international law towards a relaxation of the rule of state immunity as regards issues of recruitment to foreign missions . . .[700]

4.117   *Section 16(1)(b): Premises used for the purposes of diplomatic mission*

The exclusion in s 16(1)(b) operates to disable the exception to immunity set out in s 6(1) of the 1978 Act (proceedings relating to immovable property).[701] Its application was considered by the Court of Appeal in *Intpro v Sauvel*.[702] The court held:

(a) That the phrase "used for the purposes of a diplomatic mission" contemplates that the premises should be used for the professional diplomatic purposes of the mission. It is not enough that the premises are used as a private residence by a diplomatic agent, even though incidentally the diplomatic agent has certain social obligations which he carries out at the premises.[703]

(b) That premises could not be said to be used "for the purposes of the mission" if they were not part of the "premises of the mission" for the purposes of the Diplomatic Relations Act 1964.[704] The Diplomatic and Consular Premises Act 1987 has been enacted since the decision of the Court of Appeal in *Intpro v Sauvel*. Section 1 of the 1987 Act requires the consent of the Secretary of State before any land may be regarded as diplomatic premises for this purpose and, if a State ceases to use land for the purposes of its mission, that land immediately ceases to be diplomatic premises.

(c) That the phrase "proceedings concerning a State's title to or its possession of property" does not, in contrast to the language of s 6(1)[705] extend to proceedings relating to a State's *use* of property, including proceedings for breaches of leasehold covenants.[706]

Section 16(1)(b) does not extend to consular premises, presumably because those premises do not enjoy comparable inviolability under the 1963 Vienna Convention to that of diplomatic premises under the 1961 Vienna Convention.[707]

---

[700] In the *Fogarty* case, the application of the s 16(1)(a) exclusion was unnecessary as there was no "contract of employment" between the applicant and the State which would trigger application of the exception to immunity in s 4(1) (see 4.039 above).   [701] See 4.054 and 4.057 above.
[702] [1983] QB 1019.   [703] *Intpro*, at 1031–1032 (May LJ).
[704] *Intpro*, at 1032–1033 (May LJ). Art 1 of the 1961 Vienna Convention, scheduled to the 1964 Act defines "premises of the mission" as "the buildings or parts of buildings and the land ancillary thereto, irrespective of ownership, used for the purposes of the mission including the residence of the head of the mission".   [705] See 4.054 above.
[706] *Intpro*, at 1033 (May LJ).
[707] Art 31 of the 1963 Vienna Convention; Art 22 of the 1963 Vienna Convention.

Armed forces are organs of the state which maintains them, being created to maintain the independence, authority, and safety of the state. They have that status even when on foreign territory, provided that they are in the service of their state, and not for some private purpose.[708]

Article 31 of the European Convention provides that its provisions are not to affect "any immunities or privileges enjoyed by a contracting state in respect of anything done or omitted to be done by, or in relation to, its armed forces when on the territory of another contracting state"[709] and this reservation was translated to the 1978 Act as an exclusion of Part I of the Act in the case of visiting forces, with particular reference to the Visiting Forces Act 1952. As noted above, the effect of s 16(2) is not to confer any immunity or privilege on members of a visiting force, but to leave the question of any immunity or privilege to the residual body of law, including (so far as relevant) the 1952 Act and the common law.[710]

The exclusion applies only to proceedings relating to anything done by or in relation to the armed forces of a State while present in the United Kingdom. Accordingly, Part I of the 1978 Act applies to proceedings which do relate only to acts outside the jurisdiction.[711]

The Visiting Forces Act 1952[712] applies to the armed forces of the Commonwealth countries listed in s 1(a) and other territories designated by statutory instrument.[713] The provisions of Part I of the 1952 Act were primarily intended to enable the UK Government to ratify the NATO Status of Forces Agreement 1951 ("SOFA").[714] Sections 2 to 5 concern criminal jurisdiction. Section 6 bars proceedings before UK courts with regard to the pay of members of a visiting force or its civilian component, their terms of service or their discharge from service. Section 7 makes provision for inquests and related matters. Section 8 provides for the modification of UK law in its application to visiting forces.[715]

---

[708] Oppenheim, vol 1, para 556. For discussion of the status of armed forces on foreign territory, see Oppenheim, vol 1, paras 556–564; Fox, 461–467. See also Fleck (ed.), *The Handbook of the Law of Visiting Forces* (Oxford, 2001), esp ch IV. [709] See 1.056 above.

[710] *Littrell v United States of America* [1995] 1 WLR 82; (1993) 100 ILR 452 (CA); *Holland v Lampen-Wolfe* [2000] 1 WLR 1573 (HL). Lord Millett in *Holland* (at 1584–1585) described section 16(2) as a "somewhat curious provision" and suggested that the draftsman's intention had been simply to exclude the exceptions to immunity in Part I leaving the general immunity intact.

[711] For discussion as to the meaning of the words "relating to", see 4.029 above.

[712] See also the International Headquarters and Defence Organisations Act 1964.

[713] See Visiting Forces Act (Application to Colonies) Order 1954 (SI 1954/636, as amended); Visiting Forces (Designation) (Colonies) Order 1954 (SI 1954/637, as amended); Visiting Forces (Designation) Order 1956 (SI 1956/2041); Visiting Forces (Designation) Order 1961 (SI 1961/1511); Visiting Forces Act (Application to the Isle of Man) Order 1962 (SI 1962/170); Visiting Forces (Designation) (Sovereign Base Areas of Akrotiri and Dhekelia) Order 1962 (SI 1962/1639); Visiting Forces (Designation) Order 1989 (SI 1989/1329); Visiting Forces (Designation) Order 1997 (SI 1997/1779); Visiting Forces (Designation) Order 1998 (SI 1998/1268); Visiting Forces Act (Application to Bermuda) Order 2001 (SI 2001/3922).

[714] London, 19 June 1951 (Cmd 9363). See *Littrell v United States of America* [1995] 1 WLR 82, at 85–87 (Rose LJ) (CA).

[715] See Visiting Forces and International Headquarters (Application of Law) Order (SI 1999/1736).

In particular, it allows provision to be made to confer on a visiting force, its members, service courts and property any privilege or immunity "being a privilege or immunity which would be enjoyed by, or would be capable of being conferred on, the force, members, courts, persons or property if the force were a part of any of the home forces".[716] Section 9 concerns civil claims against visiting forces and is discussed in the following paragraph. Section 10 defines membership of the civilian component of a visiting force.[717] Section 11 deals with matters of evidence by certificate. Section 12, the final section of Part I of the 1952 Act, addresses the interpretation of that Part and s 17 addresses interpretation generally.

Section 9 enables the Secretary of State for Defence to make arrangements for satisfying claims in respect of acts or omission of members of visiting forces, or connected persons, by payments made by the Secretary of State of such amounts as may be adjudged by any UK court or as may be agreed between the claimant and the Secretary of State or otherwise as provided in the arrangements. This provision was intended to give effect to the claims procedure contained in Article VIII of SOFA but, although the procedures for satisfying claims have been set out in greater detail in a Legal Notice issued by the Secretary of State,[718] Article VIII has not been incorporated into English law and its provisions cannot be relied on to establish rights before the English courts.[719] Nor does the Legal Notice address the question of the immunities and privileges of foreign States or individual members of their armed forces.

4.119   Accordingly, in civil proceedings, the immunity of a State in respect of the activities of its armed forces when in the United Kingdom or individual members of its armed forces falls to be determined as a matter of common law, and in turn by reference to rules of customary international law and the distinction between acts *jure imperii* (immune) and acts *iure gestionis* (non-immune).[720] In *Littrell v United States of America (No. 2)*,[721] a serving member of the United States armed forces in the United Kingdom brought proceedings against the United States of America claiming that he had been treated negligently at a US military hospital. Hoffmann LJ, having referred to the House of Lords decision in *I° Congreso del Partido*,[722] stated:[723]

> The context in which the act took place was the maintenance by the United States of a unit of the United States Air Force in the United Kingdom. This looks about as imperial an activity as could be imagined. But it would be facile to regard this context as determinative of the question. Acts done within the context could range from arrangements concerning the flights

---

[716] s 8(1)(b).

[717] Note, however, that compliance with the requirements of this section is not necessary for a State to assert immunity in proceedings brought against a civilian member of the visiting force (see *Holland v Lampen-Wolfe* [2000] 1 WLR 1573, esp at 1585 (Lord Millett), (HL)).

[718] Legal Notice (revised 22 July 1965)—Visiting Forces Act, 1952, and International Headquarters and Defence Organisations Act, 1964.

[719] *Littrell v United States of America (No. 2)* [1995] 1 WLR 82 (CA).   [720] See 4.103 above.

[721] [1995] 1 WLR 82 (CA).   [722] [1983] 1 AC 244.

[723] *Littrell (No. 2)*, at 94–95 (Hoffmann LJ). See also Rose LJ, at 91; Nourse LJ, at 95–96.

of bombers—plainly *jure imperii*—to ordering milk for the base from a local dairy or careless driving by off-duty airmen on the roads of Suffolk. Both of the latter would seem to me to be *jure gestionis*, fairly within an area of private law activity. I do not think that there is a single test or 'bright line' by which cases on either side can be distinguished. Rather, there are a number of factors which may characterise the act as nearer to or further from the central military activity.

In the present case I think that the most important factors are the answers to the following questions. First, where did it happen? In cases in which foreign troops are occupying a defined and self-contained area, the authorities on customary international law attach importance to whether or not the act was done within the 'lines' or 'the rayon [radius] of the [fortress]'. . . Secondly, whom did it involve? Acts involving only members of the visiting force are less likely to be within the jurisdiction of local municipal courts than acts involving its own citizens as well. Thirdly, what kind of act was it? Some acts are wholly military in character, some almost entirely private or commercial and some in between.

The court held that the United States was entitled to assert immunity.

In *Holland v Lampen-Wolfe*[724] a visiting professor who taught courses in the United Kingdom to US armed forces and their families brought libel proceedings against the UK-based Department of Defense official responsible for implementation of those courses. The proceedings related to a report by the defendant criticizing the claimant's performance. Again, the United States' assertion of immunity was upheld on the ground that the preparation of the report was a sovereign act in connection with the maintenance by the United States of its armed forces in the United Kingdom.[725]

Nuclear installations   **4.120**

Sections 10 and 12 of the Nuclear Installations Act 1965 impose (subject to limited exceptions) strict liability to pay compensation in prescribed circumstances on a person who, for the purposes of an international agreement with respect to third party liability in the field of nuclear energy to which the United Kingdom is party,[726] is the operator of a nuclear installation to which that international agreement applies. Compensation is payable to any person who suffers injury or damage to property arising out of or resulting from the radioactive (or radioactive and other) properties of nuclear matter.

---

[724] [2000] 1 WLR 1573 (HL). Noted Fox (2001) 117 LQR 10; Yang [2001] CLJ 17. The application of the European Convention on Human Rights is discussed at 4.007 above.

[725] At 1577 (Lord Hope), 1578 (Lord Cooke), 1580–1581 (Lord Clyde), 1581 (Lord Hobhouse), 1586–1587 (Lord Millett). See also *Hicks v United States of America* (1995) 120 ILR 606 (EAT); *Gerber Products Co v Gerber Foods International Ltd* [2002] EWHC 428 (Ch) (Morritt V-C).

[726] Other than an agreement relating to liability in respect of nuclear reactors comprised in means of transport (see s 26 of the 1965 Act). See *Halsbury's Laws of England* (4th edn), vol 19(2), paras 1107–1109, 1128.

The detail of these provisions is beyond the scope of this work.[727] Section 17(6) of the 1965 Act, however, provides:

> Where, in the case of any claim by virtue of section 10 of this Act, the relevant foreign operator is the government of a relevant territory, then, for the purposes of any proceedings brought in a court in the United Kingdom to enforce that claim, that government shall be deemed to have submitted to the jurisdiction of that court, and accordingly rules of court may provide for the manner in which any such action is to be commenced and carried on; but nothing in this subsection shall authorise the issue of execution, or in Scotland the execution of diligence, against the property of that government.

Section 17(6) of the 1965 Act effectively operates, therefore, as a deemed waiver of any immunity from jurisdiction available at common law, but without prejudice to any immunity or privilege relating to execution of a judgment. Section 16(3) of the 1978 Act preserves its operation.

4.121   *Criminal proceedings*

The common law has provided only limited guidance as to the position of foreign States and their representatives in criminal matters. As a starting point, it seems doubtful whether there exists a procedural mechanism for bringing a foreign State before a criminal court in England and Wales to answer charges. Further, heads of State are protected from criminal proceedings by s 20 of the 1978 Act,[728] other senior government ministers may enjoy protection at common law during, and after, their tenure of office[729] and the State itself enjoys absolute immunity (absent waiver).[730]

The position of officials, employees and other representatives of the State is even more controversial. At one end of the spectrum, spies and other clandestine agents are regularly prosecuted following capture,[731] although the issue of immunity does not appear to have been addressed directly in such cases.[732] As regards other representatives of foreign States,[733] the reasoning of the House of Lords in the *Pinochet* case (although not without its difficulties[734]) suggests that the State may assert immunity in proceedings relating to official acts, subject to an exception in the case of certain international crimes recognized by treaty.[735] As yet, no general exception for international crimes has been recognized as a matter of

---

[727] See *Halsbury's Laws of England* (4th edn), vol 19(2), paras 1272 and following.
[728] See 4.131–4.137 below.   [729] See 4.138 below.
[730] See, generally, *R v Bow Street Metropolitan Stipendiary Magistrate, ex p. Pinochet Ugarte (No. 3)* [2000] 1 AC 147; *Case concerning the Arrest Warrant of 11 April 2000 (Democratic Republic of Congo v Belgium)*, Judgment of 14 February 2002 (ICJ); Fox, 503–504; Lewis, 90.   [731] See Fox, 512.
[732] As the authors of Oppenheim note (vol 1, para 568), spies are commonly publicly disowned by their sponsor State.
[733] Other than those entitled to diplomatic or consular privileges (see 1961 Vienna Convention, Art 31; 1963 Vienna Convention, Art 34).
[734] For further analysis of the *Pinochet* case, see 4.137 below.   [735] See Fox, 509–512.

customary international law,[736] although a vigorous debate continues.[737] The use in that debate, without precise definition, of concepts such as "*jus cogens* rules", "*erga omnes* obligations" and "universal jurisdiction" is, it is submitted, unhelpful. If observation of the practice of States reveals that prohibition of certain conduct is so fundamental that it necessitates the prosecution of the offender *in local courts* irrespective of the character of the act and the actor then a rule of customary international law qualifying immunity can be established without recourse to these concepts. On the other hand, the fact that the international community may condemn such conduct, enter into treaties prohibiting it and establish international tribunals to prosecute offenders is not necessarily incompatible with the assertion of immunity by a State to protect its representatives, leaving to one side the possibility that treaty provision may constitute a waiver or preclude a foreign State from asserting that conduct had official sanction.

The exclusion from Part I of the 1978 Act of criminal proceedings extends **4.122** to extradition proceedings.[738] Particular mention is required, however, of the position regarding extradition of persons to stand trial before the International Criminal Court.[739] In this connection, s 23 of the International Criminal Court Act 2001[740] provides:

Provisions as to state or diplomatic immunity

(1) Any state or diplomatic immunity attaching to a person by reason of a connection with a state party to the ICC Statute does not prevent proceedings under this Part in relation to that person.

(2) Where—

(a) state or diplomatic immunity attaches to a person by reason of a connection with a state other than a state party to the ICC Statute, and
(b) waiver of that immunity is obtained by the ICC in relation to a request for that person's surrender,

the waiver shall be treated as extending to proceedings under this Part in connection with that request.

(3) A certificate by the Secretary of State—

(a) that a state is or is not a party to the ICC Statute, or
(b) that there has been such a waiver as is mentioned in subsection (2),

is conclusive evidence of that fact for the purposes of this Part.

(4) The Secretary of State may in any particular case, after consultation with the ICC and the state concerned, direct that proceedings (or further proceedings) under this Part which, but for subsection (1) or (2), would be prevented by state or diplomatic immunity attaching to a person shall not be taken against that person.

---

[736] See, however, the views of Lords Millett and Phillips in *Pinochet* summarized at 4.137 below.
[737] See, generally, Fox, ch 12 and 13.
[738] *R v Bow Street Metropolitan Stipendiary Magistrate, ex p. Pinochet (Nos. 1 and 3)* [2000] 1 AC 61, 147.　　　　　[739] See the articles of the ICC Stature reproduced at 1.137–1.148 above.
[740] See also International Criminal Court (Scotland) Act 2001.

(5) The power conferred by section 1 of the United Nations Act 1946 (c 45) (power to give effect by Order in Council to measures not involving the use of armed force) includes power to make in relation to any proceedings such provision corresponding to the provision made by this section in relation to the proceedings, but with the omission—

(a) in subsection (1), of the words "by reason of a connection with a state party to the ICC Statute", and
(b) of subsections (2) and (3),

as appears to Her Majesty to be necessary or expedient in consequence of such a referral as is mentioned in article 13(b) (referral by the United Nations Security Council).

(6) In this section "state or diplomatic immunity" means any privilege or immunity attaching to a person, by reason of the status of that person or another as head of state, or as representative, official or agent of a state, under—

(a) the Diplomatic Privileges Act 1964 (c 81), the Consular Relations Act 1968 (c 18), the International Organisations Act 1968 (c 48) or the State Immunity Act 1978 (c 33),
(b) any other legislative provision made for the purpose of implementing an international obligation, or
(c) any rule of law derived from customary international law.

4.123   *Proceedings relating to taxation*

Section 11 contains an exception to the general immunity in the case of proceedings relating to VAT, customs and excise duties, agricultural levies and rates in respect of premises occupied for commercial purposes. Section 16(5) otherwise excludes proceedings relating to taxation from the scope of Part I of the 1978 Act.[741] Accordingly, the existence of any immunity from suit in taxation matters is a matter for the common law, drawing upon principles of customary international law.

In this context, however, a broader issue arises, namely whether a State or any related person is immune from taxation, on the basis that taxation is as much an exercise of sovereign power as the assertion of jurisdiction, or whether any exemption is simply a matter of courtesy.[742] The current practice of the United Kingdom tax authorities would appear to be to recognize a broader immunity from direct taxation in relation to all income and gains beneficially owned by the head of state and government of a recognized foreign State,[743] but in *R v Inland Revenue Commissioners, ex p Camacq Corporation*[744] the UK government

---

[741] See Art 29 of the European Convention (at 1.054 above).

[742] See the authorities cited by Oppenheim, vol 1, para 111, fn 7 including *Municipality of the City and County of Saint John, Logan and Clayton v Fraser-Brace Overseas Corporation* (1958) 13 DLR 177; 26 ILR 165. Immunity of a foreign State from taxation can arguably be viewed as a complement to the rule of private international law whereby the English courts will not enforce the revenue laws of a foreign State (see Dicey and Morris, rule 3 and commentary).

[743] Inland Revenue Manuals, *Double Taxation Relief Manual*, para 325 (March 2003).

[744] [1990] 1 WLR 191 (CA) (noted Venables (1995) 5 Offshore Planning Tax Review 73). See also *Caglar v Billingham* [1996] STC (SCD) 150.

advanced the argument that sovereign immunity meant no more than an immunity from suit in the United Kingdom courts rather than immunity from income tax. Although it was not necessary for the Court of Appeal to decide the point, Dillon LJ expressed the view (*obiter*) that this would constitute "a revolutionary reversal of previous practice"[745] and that the argument was "misconceived".[746] He added:[747] "The point is important and it is very desirable that it should be clarified by legislation if the Crown intend to maintain the new position."

A further issue concerns the scope of any immunity from taxation or any immunity from suit in taxation matters. By analogy with the rules on immunity from suit generally, it would seem stongly arguable that, at the very least, any immunity should not extend to income or gains from commercial activities actively carried on by the State within the United Kingdom.[748] Further, the New Zealand Court of Appeal, in *Controller and Auditor-General v Davison*,[749] appeared to recognize an exception from sovereign immunity on policy grounds in the case of tax evasion,[750] although one leading commentator has contended that the decision's impact is diminished by the circumstances of the case.[751]

In any event, under Article 23 of the 1961 Vienna Convention on Diplomatic Relations,[752] a State and the head of its mission in the United Kingdom are exempt from all national, regional or municipal dues and taxes in respect of the premises of the mission, other than those representing payment for specific services.[753]

17 Interpretation of Part I   **4.124**

(1) In this Part of this Act—

"the Brussels Convention" means the International Convention for the Unification of Certain Rules Concerning the Immunity of State-owned Ships signed in Brussels on 10th April 1926;
"commercial purposes" means purposes of such transactions or activities as are mentioned in section 3(3) above;
"ship" includes hovercraft.

(2) In sections 2(2) and 13(3) above references to an agreement include references to a treaty, convention or other international agreement.

---

[745] At 200.

[746] At 201, referring to *Municipality of the City and County of Saint John, Logan and Clayton v Fraser-Brace Overseas Corporation* (1958) 13 DLR 177; 26 ILR 165.   [747] At 201.

[748] See American Law Institute, *Restatement of the Law (3d), Foreign Relations Law of the United States*, §462; (1989) 60 BYIL 631 quoting from Hansard, HC Standing Committee A, Finance Bill (No. 2) cols. 577–578; *Controller and Auditor-General v Davison* [1996] 2 NZLR 279, at 288–289 (Cooke P), 308 309 (Henry J), 303 (Richardson J), 310–313 (Thomas J) (CA New Zealand).

[749] [1996] 2 NZLR 279.

[750] [1996] 2 NZLR 279, at 287 (Cooke P), 304–307 (Richardson J), 313–319 (Thomas J).

[751] Fox, 291–292, 519–520.

[752] Given force of law under the Diplomatic Privileges Act 1964.

[753] See also Art 34 governing the exemption from taxation of diplomatic agents and Arts 32 and 49 of the 1963 Vienna Convention.

(3) For the purposes of sections 3 to 8 above the territory of the United Kingdom shall be deemed to include any dependent territory in respect of which the United Kingdom is a party to the European Convention on State Immunity.

(4) In sections 3(l), 4(1), 5 and 16(2) above references to the United Kingdom include references to its territorial waters and any area designated under section 1(7) of the Continental Shelf Act 1964.

(5) In relation to Scotland in this Part of this Act "action in rem" means such an action only in relation to Admiralty proceedings.

Commentary

4.125   Legislative history

The definition of "commercial purposes" in sub-section (1) and sub-sections (2) and (5) were introduced by amendment in the course of the Bill's Parliamentary passage.[754]

4.126   Application

Section 17 deals with matters of interpretation particular to Part I of the 1978 Act.[755] The following matters are to be noted:

(a) The defined term "commercial purposes", which cross refers to the transactions and activities described in s 3(3)[756] appears in ss 4(3), 10, 11(b), 13(4) and 14(4). Its operation is discussed in the commentary on those sections.[757]

(b) The words "treaty, convention or other international agreement" in sub-section (2) encompass, it would appear, all consensual instruments which are binding in international law.[758]

(c) The United Kingdom is a party to the European Convention in respect of the following dependent territories:

Belize, British Antarctic Territory, British Virgin Islands, Cayman Islands, Falkland Islands and dependencies, Gilbert Islands, Montserrat, Pitcairn, Henderson, Ducie and Oeno Islands, St Helena and dependencies, Turks and Caicas Islands, UK Sovereign base areas of Akratiri and Dhekelia in the Island of Cyprus, Guernsey, Jersey and the Isle of Man.

Although the expansive definition of the territory of the United Kingdom for the purposes of ss 3–8 may give rise to curiosities, in most cases its impact will be mitigated by the separate requirement to establish jurisdiction by serving the claim form on the defendant (if necessary, by obtaining permission from the court).[759]

---

[754] See Hansard, HL (5th series), vol 389, cols. 1533–1535; vol 389, cols. 1939–1940.
[755] See also the general interpretation provisions in s 22 (at 4.142–4.144 below).
[756] See 4.030 above.   [757] See 4.044, 4.073, 4.076, 4.091 and 4.093 above.
[758] Hansard, HL (5th series), vol 389, col. 1939 (Lord Elwyn-Jones LC).
[759] See 4.013 above.

PART II

Judgments Against United Kingdom in Convention States

18 Recognition of judgments against United Kingdom   **4.127**

(1) This section applies to any judgment given against the United Kingdom by a court in another State party to the European Convention on State immunity, being a judgment—

 (a) given in proceedings in which the United Kingdom was not entitled to immunity by virtue of provisions corresponding to those of sections 2 to 11 above; and

 (b) which is final, that is. to say, which is not or is no longer subject to appeal or, if given in default of appearance, liable to be set aside.

(2) Subject to section 19 below, a judgment to which this section applies shall be recognised in any court in the United Kingdom as conclusive between the parties thereto in all proceedings founded on the same cause of action and may be relied on by way of defence or counter-claim in such proceedings.

(3) Subsection (2) above (but not section 19 below) shall have effect also in relation to any settlement entered into by the United Kingdom before a court in another State party to the Convention which under the law of that State is treated as equivalent to a judgment.

(4) In this section references to a court in a State party to the Convention include references to a court in any territory in respect of which it is a party.

19 Exceptions to recognition   **4.128**

(1) A court need not give effect to section 18 above in the case of a judgment—

 (a) if to do so would be manifestly contrary to public policy or if any party to the proceedings in which the judgment was given had no adequate opportunity to present his case; or

 (b) if the judgment was given without provisions corresponding to those of section 12 above having been complied with and the United Kingdom has not entered an appearance or applied to have the judgment set aside.

(2) A court need not give effect to section 18 above in the case of a judgment—

 (a) if proceedings between the same parties based on the same facts and having the same purpose—

  (i) are pending before a court in the United Kingdom and were the first to be instituted; or

  (ii) are pending before a court in another State party to the Convention, were the first to be instituted and may result in a judgment to which that section will apply; or

    (b) if the result of the judgment is inconsistent with the result of another judgment given in proceedings between the same parties and—

        (i) the other judgment is by a court in the United Kingdom and either those proceedings were the first to be instituted or the judgment of that court was given before the first-mentioned judgment became final within the meaning of subsection (1)(b) of section 18 above; or

       (ii) the other judgment is by a court in another State party to the Convention and that section has already become applicable to it.

(3) Where the judgment was given against the United Kingdom in proceedings in respect of which the United Kingdom was not entitled to immunity by virtue of a provision corresponding to section 6(2) above, a court need not give effect to section 18 above in respect of the judgment if the court that gave the judgment—

    (a) would not have had jurisdiction in the matter if it had applied rules of jurisdiction corresponding to those applicable to such matters in the United Kingdom; or

    (b) applied a law other than that indicated by the United Kingdom rules of private international law and would have reached a different conclusion if it had applied the law so indicated.

(4) In subsection (2) above references to a court in the United Kingdom include references to a court in any dependent territory in respect of which the United Kingdom is a party to the Convention, and references to a court in another State party to the Convention include references to a court in any territory in respect of which it is a party.

Commentary

4.129a   Legislative history

Clauses 19 and 20 of the State Immunity Bill (ss 18 and 19 of the 1978 Act) were agreed to without amendment.

4.129b   Application

Sections 18 and 19 have yet to trouble the English courts. They concern the preclusive effect of judgments given against the United Kingdom by courts in other States party to the European Convention. Under Article 20 of the European Convention,[760] the United Kingdom is required to satisfy any such judgment against it, and provision for enforcement is, accordingly, unnecessary.

---

[760] See 1.045 above.

Enforcement and recognition of foreign judgments against states **4.130**

In this connection, mention is also required to be made of s 31 of the Civil Jurisdiction and Judgments Act 1982, which concerns the enforcement in the United Kingdom of judgments against one foreign State issued by the courts of another State. In material part, s 31 of the 1982 Act provides:

(1) A judgment given by a court of an overseas country against a state other than the United Kingdom or the state to which that court belongs shall be recognised and enforced in the United Kingdom if, and only, if—

(a) it would be so recognised and enforced if it had not been given against a state; and

(b) that court would have had jurisdiction in the matter if it had applied rules corresponding to those applicable to such matters in the United Kingdom in accordance with sections 2 to 11 of the State Immunity Act 1978.[761]

(2) References in subsection (1) to a judgment given against a state include references to judgments of any of the following descriptions given in relation to a state—

(a) judgments against the government of, or a department of the government, of the state but not (except as mentioned in paragraph (c)) judgments against an entity which is distinct from the executive organs of government;

(b) judgments against the sovereign or head of state in his public capacity;

(c) judgments against any such separate entity as is mentioned in paragraph (a) given in proceedings relating to anything done by it in the exercise of the sovereign authority of the state.[762]

. . .[763]

(4) Sections 12, 13 and 14(3) and (4) of the State Immunity Act 1978 (service of process and procedural privileges) shall apply to proceedings for the recognition or enforcement in the United Kingdom of a judgment given by a court of an overseas country (whether or not that judgment is within subsection (1) of this section) as they apply to other proceedings.[764]

(5) In this section state, in the case of a federal state, includes any of its constituent territories.[765]

Section 31 is broadly worded and, on its face, applies not only to the recognition or enforcement of a judgment at common law but also to the recognition and/or

---

[761] For commentary on ss 2–11 of the 1978 Act, see 4.096–4.076 above.

[762] This wording reflects ss 14(1) and 14(2) of the 1978 Act, see 4.094 and 4.097–4.102.

[763] Sub-section (3) which excludes from the scope of s 31 certain statutory provisions applying the enforcement provisions of Part I of the Foreign Judgments (Reciprocal Enforcement) Act 1933 to judgments under international conventions (mainly in the field of transport) is omitted here (but remains in force). [764] See 4.077–4.093, 4.094 and 4.103–4.104 above.

[765] See 4.108 above.

enforcement of a judgment under the statutory provisions in Part II of the Administration of Justice Act 1920, the Foreign Judgments (Reciprocal Enforcement) Act 1933, the Civil Jurisdiction and Judgments Act 1982 or even Regulation (EC) 44/2001 on jurisdiction and the recognition and enforcement of judgments in civil and commercial matters.

Under Regulation 44/2001 (and its predecessor conventions) a judgment to be enforced in one member State must be "enforceable" in the member State of its origin. The term "enforceable" has, however, been given a restricted meaning by the European Court of Justice, so that immunities and privileges available to a State in the country of origin would appear to be irrelevant to enforcement of the judgment in the United Kingdom.[766]

Section 4(3) of the 1933 Act provides that:

> Notwithstanding anything in subsection (2) of this section, the courts of the country of the original court shall not be deemed to have had jurisdiction— . . . (c) if the judgment debtor, being a defendant in the original proceedings, was a person who under the rules of public international law was entitled to immunity from the jurisdiction of the courts of the country of the original court and did not submit to the jurisdiction of that court.

This provision has been superseded by s 31 of the 1981 Act in its application to judgments falling within the scope of that section, but continues to apply to judgments against other persons entitled to immunity under rules of public international law (eg diplomats, international organizations and, arguably, heads of government and foreign ministers[767]).

Neither s 31 of the 1982 Act nor s 4(3) of the 1933 Act applies to the enforcement of judgments against a foreign State given by the courts of that State. Nevertheless, Part I of the State Immunity Act 1978 applies and, in principle, the State would appear to be entitled to assert immunity (there being no applicable exception).[768]

PART III
Miscellaneous and Supplementary

4.131　**20　Heads of State**

(1) Subject to the provisions of this section and to any necessary modifications, the Diplomatic Privileges Act 1964 shall apply to—

(a) a sovereign or other head of State;

(b) members of his family forming part of his household; and

(c) his private servants,

---

[766] *Coursier v Fortis Bank SA* [1999] ECR I-2543.　　[767] See 4.138.

[768] *AIC Ltd v Federal Government of Nigeria* [2003] EWHC 1357 (QB) (Stanley Burnton J).

as it applies to the head of a diplomatic mission, to members of his family forming part of his household and to his private servants.

(2) The immunities and privileges conferred by virtue of subsection (1)(a) and (b) above shall not be subject to the restrictions by reference to nationality or residence mentioned in Article 37(1) or 38 in Schedule 1 to the said Act of 1964.

(3) Subject to any direction to the contrary by the Secretary of State, a person on whom immunities and privileges are conferred by virtue of subsection (1) above shall be entitled to the exemption conferred by section 8(3) of the Immigration Act 1971.

(4) Except as respects value added tax and duties of customs or excise, this section does not affect any question whether a person is exempt from, or immune as respects proceedings relating to, taxation.

(5) This section applies to the sovereign or other head of any State on which immunities and privileges are conferred by Part I of this Act and is without prejudice to the application of that Part to any such sovereign or head of State in his public capacity.

Commentary

Legislative history
4.132

In the *Pinochet* case, Lord Browne-Wilkinson traced the legislative history of s 20 of the 1978 Act (clause 21 of the Bill) in the following terms:[769]

> [T]he original section 20(1)(a) read "a sovereign or other head of state who is in the United Kingdom at the invitation or with the consent of the Government of the United Kingdom". On that basis, the section would have been intelligible. However it was changed by a government amendment the mover of which said that the clause as introduced "leaves an unsatisfactory doubt about the position of heads of state who are not in the United Kingdom;" he said that the amendment was to ensure that heads of state would be treated like heads of diplomatic missions "irrespective of presence in the United Kingdom".[770]

Application
4.133

Under s 21(a) of the 1978 Act, a certificate by or on behalf of the Secretary of State shall be conclusive evidence of the status of a person as the head of a State.[771]

Lord Browne-Wilkinson in the *Pinochet* case expressed the view that the operation of s 20(1) was "baffling". Its application appears to require a three-stage

---

[769] *R v Bow Street Metropolitan Stipendiary Magistrate, ex p Pinochet Ugarte (No. 3)* [2000] 1 AC 147 at 203. See also Lord Phillips, at 291–292.
[770] See Hansard, HL (5th series), vol 389, cols. 1536–1538.   [771] See 4.139–4.141 below.

process. First, to identify (having regard to the nature of the proceedings) the manner in which the Diplomatic Privileges Act 1964 applies to the head of a diplomatic mission (or to members of his family forming part of his household or his private servants). Secondly, to consider the effect of sub-sections (2)–(5).[772] Finally, to consider whether any modifications are necessary to the immunities enjoyed by a head of State (or to members of his family forming part of his household or to his private servants). The following paragraphs, consider the first and last of these stages in greater detail.

4.134   *Position under the Diplomatic Privileges Act 1964—*
Immunities and privileges of a head of mission

Section 2(1) of the 1964 Act gives the force of law in the United Kingdom to the Articles of the 1961 Vienna Convention on Diplomatic Relations set out in Sch 1 to that Act. The principal provisions of Sch 1 of the 1964 Act relating to heads of mission are as follows:[773]

(a) "Diplomatic agent" includes the head of the mission.[774]

(b) The "premises of the mission" include the residence of the head of the mission.[775]

(c) The premises of the mission shall be inviolable. Together with their furnishings and other property thereon they shall be immune from search, requisition, attachment or execution.[776]

(d) The head of the mission shall be exempt from all national, regional or municipal dues and taxes in respect of the premises of the mission, other than such as represent payment for specific services rendered.[777]

(e) The person of the diplomatic agent shall be inviolable. He shall not be liable to any form of arrest or detention. The receiving State shall treat him with due respect and shall take all appropriate steps to prevent any attack on his person, freedom or dignity.[778]

(f) The papers, correspondence and (subject to permitted measures of execution) property of a diplomatic agent shall be inviolable.[779]

(g) A diplomatic agent shall enjoy immunity from the criminal jurisdiction of the receiving State.[780]

(h) A diplomatic agent shall also enjoy immunity from the civil and administrative jurisdiction of the receiving State except in the case of:

    (i) a real action relating to private immovable property situated in the territory of the receiving State, unless he holds it on behalf of the sending State for the purposes of the mission;

---

[772] For discussion of taxation issues, see 4.123. For discussion of the application to heads of State of Part I of the 1978 Act, see 4.098 above.

[773] For commentary on the 1961 Vienna Convention, see generally Denza, *Diplomatic Law* (2nd edn, Oxford, 1998).   [774] Art 1(e).

[775] Art 1(i).   [776] Art 22. See also Art 30.

[777] Art 23.1. Note, however, the provisions of s 20(4) of the 1978 Act.   [778] Art 29.

[779] Art 30.   [780] Art 31.1.

    (ii) an action relating to succession in which the diplomatic agent is involved as executor, administrator, heir or legatee as a private person and not on behalf of the sending State;

    (iii) an action relating to any professional or commercial activity exercised by the diplomatic agent in the receiving State outside his official functions.[781]

(i) A diplomatic agent is not obliged to give evidence as a witness.[782]

(j) No measures of execution may be taken in respect of a diplomatic agent except in cases falling within sub-paragraphs (i) to (iii) of paragraph (h) above and provided that such measures can be taken without infringing the inviolability of the diplomatic agent or his residence (see paragraphs (c) and (e) above).[783]

(k) A diplomatic agent shall be exempt from all dues and taxes, personal or real, national, regional or municipal, except those falling within certain categories.[784]

(l) The members of the family of a diplomatic agent forming part of his household shall enjoy the privileges and imunitities described in paragraphs (e)–(k) above.[785]

(m) Every person entitled to privileges and immunities shall enjoy them from the moment he enters the territory of the receiving State on proceeding to take his post or, if already in the territory, from the moment when his appointment is notified to the Ministry of Foreign Affairs.[786]

(n) When the functions of a person enjoying privileges and immunities have come to an end, such privileges and immunities shall normally cease at the moment when he leaves the country, or on expiry of a reasonable period in which to do so, but shall subsist until that time.[787] With respect, however, to acts performed by such a person in the exercise of his functions as a member of the mission, immunity shall continue to subsist.[788]

Immunity from jurisdiction—Necessary modifications   **4.135**
to language of 1964 Act

Substituting references to "head of State" for the references in the 1964 Act to a head of mission, at least four questions present themselves for consideration in determining what modifications under s 20(1) are necessary to the language of the 1964 Act in considering the immunity from jurisdiction, and associated privileges, in the United Kingdom of a head of State. The first is temporal: do the immunities and privileges apply only when the head of State is present in the United Kingdom? The second is geographical: does the immunity apply to conduct of the head of State outside the United Kingdom, or are such cases left to be decided by reference to the rules of the common law? The third relates to the immunities of a former head of State: how widely are the "functions of a head

---

[781] Art 31.1.   [782] Art 31.2.   [783] Art 31.3.
[784] Art 34. Note, however, the provisions of s 20(4) of the 1978 Act.   [785] Art 37.
[786] Art 39.1.   [787] Art 39.2.   [788] Art 39.2.

of State" (in respect of which immunity continues) to be construed? The fourth relates to the scope of the exceptions to the immunity from the civil and administrative jurisdiction of United Kingdom courts.[789]

The first three questions were touched on in the *Pinochet* case. The majority of their Lordships took the view that s 20(1) should be applied so as to give effect to the immunities of a head of State[790] under customary international law.[791] On this basis, the s 20(1) immunities supplant those applicable under the common law and this is consistent with the stated purpose of the 1978 Act "to make new provision with respect to the immunities and privileges of heads of State".[792] Consistently with that approach, the questions posed above receive the following answers:

(a) The immunity from jurisdiction of a serving head of State pursuant to s 20(1) continues while in office whether he is present in the United Kingdom or not when proceedings are commenced.

(b) The immunity from jurisdiction of a head of State or former head of State pursuant to s 20(1) extends to proceedings relating to conduct outside the United Kingdom.

(c) The exceptions to immunity from civil and administrative jurisdiction contained in the 1964 Act should apply, consistently with the position of States.[793] Arguably and consistently with the approach in (b) above, the professional or commercial activity exception should not be subject to any territorial limitation.[794]

(d) The immunity from jurisdiction of a former head of State pursuant to s 20(1) should extend to acts done as part of his official functions as head of State, the critical question being "whether the conduct was engaged in under colour of or in ostensible exercise of the head of state's public authority".[795]

---

[789] See Sch. 1, Art 31.1 to the 1964 Act.   [790] Or, as in *Pinochet*, a former head of State.

[791] *R v Bow Street Metropolitan Stipendiary Magistrate, ex p. Pinochet Ugarte (No. 3)* [2000] 1 AC 147, at 202–203 (Lord Browne-Wilkinson), 210 (Lord Goff), 240–241 (Lord Hope), 250–251 (Lord Hutton), 265 (Lord Saville) (HL).

[792] See especially Lord Goff, [2000] 1 AC 147, at 209. Compare the views of Lord Millett, at 268–270 (strong argument for limiting immunity of former head of State under s 20(1) to functions distinctive of head of State) and Lord Phillips, at 291–292 (s 20(1) does not apply to conduct outside the United Kingdom). Their Lordships did not seem to consider that they were bound to consider the position under customary international law in 1978. Compare Lord Denning's concerns during the passage of the State Immunity Bill (see 4.002, fn 18 above).

[793] An exception to the immunity of serving heads of State in the case of "commercial activities" would seem to be less firmly established under customary international law in the case of heads of State than in the case of States (see Watts, *The Legal Position in International Law of Heads of States, Heads of Government and Foreign Ministers* (Recueil des cours, volume 247, 1994-III), 37; *Mighell v Sultan of Johore* [1894] 1 QB 149; *Antoun v Harrison and Sons Ltd* (1965) The Times, 24 September (Waller J); *First American Corporation v Al-Nahyan* (1996) 948 F Supp. 1107; 121 ILR 577 (US District Court, DC)).

[794] See, however, *BCCI v Price Waterhouse* [1997] 4 All ER 108, at 111 (Laddie J), although the conclusion on this point does not appear to have been questioned and the decision preceded the more detailed analysis of s 20 in *Pinochet (No. 3)*.

[795] Watts, *The Legal Position in International Law of Heads of States, Heads of Government and Foreign Ministers* (Recueil des cours, volume 247, 1994-III), 56 cited with apparent approval by Lord

That authority is not limited to those functions which are distinctive of a head of State, but include functions performed by a head of State in other official capacities (eg head of government or armed forces).[796] As a general proposition, it is irrelevant that the conduct in question was unlawful under United Kingdom law, the law of the State in question or even international law.[797] This latter proposition, however, must now be qualified in the case of certain international crimes in light of the decision in the *Pinochet* case.[798]

Taking into account these "necessary modifications", Articles 31.1 and 39.2 would read as follows:

Article 31.1

A [head of State] shall enjoy immunity from the criminal jurisdiction of the [United Kingdom]. He shall also enjoy immunity from its civil and administrative jurisdiction except in the case of:

(a) a real action relating to private immovable property situated in the [United Kingdom], unless he holds it on behalf of the [. . .] State [. . .];

(b) an action relating to succession in which the [head of State] is involved as executor, administrator, heir or legatee as a private person and not on behalf of the [. . .] State;

(c) an action relating to any professional or commercial activity exercised by the [head of State] [. . .] outside his official functions.

Article 39.2

When the functions of a [head of State] have come to an end, [his] privileges and immunities shall normally cease at the moment when he leaves [his office]. However, with respect to acts performed by [a former head of State] in the exercise of his functions [as a head of State], immunity shall continue to subsist.

Waiver of immunity   **4.136**

Although it is convenient to speak of the immunities and privileges "of" a head of State, those immunities and privileges belong to the State and can be waived by it accordingly.[799] Under the 1964 Act, any waiver must be express, the traditional view being that the waiver must be by appearance in the face of the court, rather than by prior agreement.[800]

Goff (at 210) and Lord Hope (at 242) in *Pinochet (No. 3)*. See also *Pinochet (No. 3)*, at 203 (Lord Browne-Wilkinson), 250–251 (Lord Hutton), 265 (Lord Saville).

[796] *Pinochet (No. 3)*, at 241–242 (Lord Hope). Compare Lord Millett, at 270. See also *R v Bow Street Metropolitan Stipendiary Magistrate, ex p. Pinochet Ugarte (No. 1)* [2000] 1 AC 61, at 73–74 (Lord Slynn), 108–109 (Lord Nicholls), 114–116 (Lord Steyn) (HL).

[797] *Pinochet (No. 3)*, at 203 (Lord Browne-Wilkinson), 210 (Lord Goff), 242 (Lord Hope), 251 (Lord Hutton), 270 (Lord Millett), 287 (Lord Phillips).   [798] See 4.0137 below.

[799] *Pinochet (No. 3)*, at 205 (Lord Browne-Wilkinson), 215 (Lord Goff), 243 (Lord Hope), 263 (Lord Hutton), 265 (Lord Saville), 268 (Lord Millett).

[800] *A Company Ltd. v Republic of X* [1990] 2 Lloyd's Rep 520, at 524 (Saville J) citing *Kahan v Pakistan Federation* [1951] 2 KB 1003 (CA). Compare, however *Pinochet (No. 3)*, at 217 (Lord Goff), 267 (Lord Saville), 290 (Lord Phillips).

4.137   *Pinochet (No. 3)*

In the *Pinochet* case,[801] the seven-member House of Lords decided (by a majority of six : one[802]) to reject Chile's assertion of immunity in respect of alleged offences of torture and conspiracy to torture against Senator Pinochet, Chile's former head of State, occurring after 8 December 1988.[803] Chile's assertion of immunity in respect of alleged offences of murder and conspiracy to murder was, however, upheld (by a majority of five : two[804]). It is, however, extremely difficult to extract from the speeches of the panel members a single basis for their decision. Indeed, each of the judges appears to have adopted distinct reasoning. In summary:[805]

— For Lord Browne-Wilkinson, torture could no longer be counted as an official function of the head of State once Chile and the United Kingdom had ratified the Torture Convention, thereby agreeing that all signatory states should have jurisdiction to try official torture.[806] No reason had been advanced why the ordinary rule of immunity should not apply to the murder/conspiracy to murder charges.

— For Lord Hope, it was strongly arguable that the Torture Convention did not remove immunity from a former head of State for every act of torture, although it did so where the torture involved a systematic attack upon the civilian population. This was not a question of waiver or of implication of a term into the Torture Convention, but of customary international law at the date on which Chile ratified the Torture Convention overriding the immunity *ratione materiae* of a former head of State.[807]

— For Lord Hutton, Chile could not claim that acts of torture after the date on which the UK legislation giving effect to the Torture Convention came into force were functions of the head of State. Again, this was not a question of waiver.[808]

— For Lord Saville, the immunity of a former head of State could not exist consistently with the terms of the Torture Convention. This was simply a question of applying the express terms of the Torture Convention, the parties to which had clearly and unambiguously agreed that official torture

---

[801] The case, and its predecessors, attracted a great deal of academic comment and criticism. For comment on *Pinochet (No. 3)*, see, eg, Barker (1999) 48 ICLQ 937; Byers (1999) 70 BYIL 277–295; [2000] Duke J of Comp and Int'l L 415; Chinkin (1999) 93 AJIL 703; Denza (1999) 48 ICLQ 958; Fox (1999) 48 ICLQ 687; Hopkins (1999) 58 CLJ 461; Woodhouse (ed.), *The Pinochet Case: A Legal and Constitutional Analysis* (Oxford, 2000).   [802] Lord Goff dissenting.

[803] This being the date on which the United Kingdom ratified the 1984 United Nations Convention against Torture and Other Cruel, Inhuman or Degrading Treatment or Punishment (referred to in the following paragraphs as the "Torture Convention"). Implementing legislation (the Criminal Justice Act 1988, s 134) had come into force on 29 September 1988. Chile ratified the Convention on 30 October 1988.   [804] Lords Millett and Phillips dissenting.

[805] See also the speeches in *Pinochet* (No. 1) [2000] 1 AC 161.

[806] *Pinochet (No. 3)*, at 205. See Torture Convention, Art 7.   [807] *Pinochet (No. 3)*, at 246–248.

[808] *Pinochet (No. 3)*, at 262–263.

should be dealt with in a way which would otherwise amount to an interference with their sovereignty.[809]

— For Lord Goff (dissenting on the torture/conspiracy to torture charges) removal of the immunity of a former head of State required express waiver.[810] Those framing the Torture Convention did not address issues of immunity and there were good reasons for preserving the right of State parties to assert immunity.[811]

— For Lord Millett (dissenting on the murder/conspiracy to murder charges) crimes prohibited by international law attract universal jurisdiction if two criteria are satisfied.[812] First, they must be contrary to a peremptory norm of international law so as to infringe a *jus cogens*. Secondly, they must be so serious and on such a scale that they can justly be regarded as an attack on the international legal order. English courts have always had extraterritorial criminal jurisdiction in respect of crimes of universal jurisdiction under customary international law.[813] The use of torture on a large scale and as an instrument of state policy had joined piracy, war crimes and crimes against peace as an international crime of universal jurisdiction by as early as 1973.[814] The plea of immunity *ratione materiae* is not available in respect of an offence committed in the forum State, whether England or Spain.[815] The definition of torture in the Torture Convention and the implementing UK legislation is entirely inconsistent with the existence of a plea of immunity *ratione materiae*, as the official or governmental nature of the act is an essential ingredient of the offence.[816] This was not a question of waiver, as there was no immunity to waive.[817]

— For Lord Phillips (dissenting on the murder/conspiracy to murder charges) the immunity asserted by Senator Pinochet was not established in international law. Immunity *ratione materiae* cannot co-exist with international crimes and extra-territorial jurisdiction. The exercise of extra-territorial jurisdiction overrides the principle that one State will not intervene in the internal affairs of another.[818] The entirety of Senator Pinochet's alleged conduct was a violation of the norms of international law.[819] The State parties to the Torture Convention proceeded on the premise that no immunity could exist *ratione materiae* in respect of torture.[820]

It remains to be seen which of these approaches will be adopted by the English courts as the basis for decision in the *Pinochet* case in subsequent criminal proceedings involving former heads of State (or other State officials) and offences other than torture. The (*obiter*) views of their Lordships on two other aspects of

---

[809] *Pinochet (No. 3)*, at 266–267.
[810] *Pinochet (No. 3)*, at 215–217. Lord Goff expressly rejected the functions based argument and the possibility of an implied term in the Torture Convention removing immunity.
[811] *Pinochet (No. 3)*, at 218–220.   [812] *Pinochet (No. 3)*, at 275.
[813] *Pinochet (No. 3)*, at 276.   [814] *Pinochet (No. 3)*, at 276.   [815] *Pinochet (No. 3)*, at 277.
[816] *Pinochet (No. 3)*, at 277.   [817] *Pinochet (No. 3)*, at 277–278.
[818] *Pinochet (No. 3)*, at 289.   [819] *Pinochet (No. 3)*, at 290.   [820] *Pinochet (No. 3)*, at 290.

immunity for conduct contrary to international law are, however, clearer. First, it appears to have been accepted that immunity *ratione personae* could have been asserted in criminal proceedings involving a serving head of State.[821] Indeed, in the view of Lord Millett (whose approach noted above was more restrictive of the immunities of a former head of State than those of his colleagues), it would have been an "intolerable affront" to Chile to arrest or detain its serving head of State.[822] Secondly, Lords Hutton, Millett and Phillips did not think it inconsistent to deny immunity to Senator Pinochet while allowing the assertion of immunity in civil proceedings against the State or its representatives based on the same conduct.[823]

4.138   *Heads of government, senior ministers and rulers of*
              constituent territories

Section 20 of the 1978 Act applies only to a sovereign or other head of a recognized State and does not apply to heads of government or to rulers of constituent territories of federal States who do not hold the position of head of State.[824] Nor does it apply to senior ministers (including, for example, a serving foreign minister). The position of rulers of constituent territories has already been considered in the commentary on s 14(6) above.[825] As for serving heads of government and senior ministers, one possibility, discussed and rejected above,[826] is that each of them is to be equated with the State as part of the "government" of the State for the purposes of s 14(1). If that approach is rejected, heads of government and foreign ministers, at least, may continue to enjoy certain immunities and privileges at common law, through the application of customary international law,[827] on the basis that their position is not addressed by the 1978 Act. In its decision in the *Arrest Warrant* case, the International Court of Justice held that the Democratic Republic of Congo was entitled to assert immunity in respect of criminal proceedings brought in Belgium against its serving foreign minister, although the charges alleged war crimes and crimes against humanity.[828] The mere issue by Belgium of an international arrest warrant constituted a violation of international law. In addition, proceedings against a serving or former head of State or government may indirectly implead the State, so entitling it to assert its own immunity.[829]

---

[821] *Pinochet (No. 3)*, at 201–202 (Lord Browne-Wilkinson), 210 (Lord Goff), 244 (Lord Hope), 261 (Lord Hutton), 265 (Lord Saville), 269 (Lord Millett), 280 (Lord Phillips). See also *Case concerning the Arrest Warrant of 11 April 2000 (Democratic Republic of Congo v Belgium)*, Judgment of 14 February 2002 (ICJ), concerning the immunities of a serving foreign minister (see 4.138 below).

[822] *Pinochet (No. 3)*, at 269.

[823] *Pinochet (No. 3)*, at 252–254, 264–265 (Lord Hutton), 278 (Lord Millett), 284–285, 285–288 (Lord Phillips). See 4.053 above.

[824] See *BCCI v Price Waterhouse* [1997] 4 All ER 108, in which the ruler of Abu Dhabi was also the head of State of the United Arab Emirates.   [825] See 4.108.

[826] See 4.099.

[827] See Watts, *The Legal Position in International Law of Heads of States, Heads of Government and Foreign Ministers* (Recueil des cours, vol 247, 1994-III), 102–110. Cf. *The New Chile Gold Mining Company v Blanco* (1888) 4 TLR 346 (Q.B.D.).

[828] *Case concerning the Arrest Warrant of 11 April 2000 (Democratic Republic of Congo v Belgium)*, Judgment of 14 February 2002 (ICJ).   [829] See 4.012 above.

21 Evidence by certificate

4.139

A certificate by or on behalf of the Secretary of State shall be conclusive evidence on any question—

(a) whether any country is a State for the purposes of Part I of this Act, whether any territory is a constituent territory of a federal State for those purposes or as to the person or persons to be regarded for those purposes as the head or government of a State;

(b) whether a State is a party to the Brussels Convention mentioned in Part I of this Act;

(c) whether a State is a party to the European Convention on State Immunity, whether it has made a declaration under Article 24 of that Convention or as to the territories in respect of which the United Kingdom or any other State is a party;

(d) whether, and if so when, a document has been served or received as mentioned in Section 12(1) or (5) above.

Commentary

Legislative history

4.140

Clause 22(c) of the State Immunity Bill (s 21(c) of the 1978 Act) was amended to allow certification by the Secretary of State (for the purposes of s 13(4) of the 1978 Act) as to whether a State party to the European Convention has made a declaration under Article 24 of the Convention.[830]

Application

4.141

In the ordinary course, a certificate under s 21 as to one of the prescribed matters will be given by the Foreign and Commonwealth Office in response to a request by the court or tribunal, rather than the parties.[831] The conclusive nature of the certificate is consistent with the earlier practice of the English courts,[832] but might arguably be inconsistent with Article 6.1 of the European Convention on Human Rights by excluding even the possibility of judicial review.[833]

---

[830] For the text of Art 24, see 1.049 above.

[831] See (1995) 66 BYIL 647–648. For examples of certificates given in proceedings before the English courts, see (1997) 68 BYIL 519 (*Kuwait Airways v Iraqi Airways*); (1996) 67 BYIL 709 (*BCCI v Price Waterhouse*). See also *R v Secretary of State for Foreign and Commonwealth Affairs, exp. Trawnik* (1986) The Times, 21 February (CA) (discussed at 4.100 above); *Caglar v Billingham* [1996] STC (SCD) 150 (Special Commissioners for Taxation).

[832] *The Arantzazu Mendi* [1939] AC 256 (HL).

[833] *R v Secretary of State for Foreign and Commonwealth Affairs, ex p. Trawnik* (1986) The Times, 21 February (CA); Mann (1979) 50 BYIL 43, at 47–48. For the approach of the English courts under the Human Rights Act 1998 in a different context, the decision of the House of Lords in *R (Alconbury Ltd) v Secretary of State for the Environment Transport and the Regions* [2001] 2 WLR 1389.

4.142 **22 General interpretation**

(1) In this Act "court" includes any tribunal or body exercising judicial functions; and references to the courts or law of the United Kingdom include references to the courts or law of any part of the United Kingdom.

(2) In this Act references to entry of appearance and judgments in default of appearance include references to any corresponding procedures.

(3) In this Act "the European Convention on State Immunity" means the Convention of that name signed in Basle on 16th May 1972.

(4) In this Act "dependent territory" means—

    (a) any of the Channel Islands;

    (b) the Isle of Man;

    (c) any colony other than one for whose external relations a country other than the United Kingdom is responsible; or

    (d) any country or territory outside Her Majesty's dominions in which Her Majesty has jurisdiction in right of the government of the United Kingdom.

(5) Any power conferred by this Act to make an Order in Council includes power to vary or revoke a previous Order.

Commentary

4.143   Legislative history

Clause 23 of the State Immunity Bill (s 22 of the 1978 Act) was agreed to without amendment.

4.144   Application

The following matters are noted:

(a) In considering whether any body exercises judicial functions and so constitutes a "court" for the purposes of the 1978 Act, it may be helpful to refer to case law in other contexts, particularly in the fields of defamation and contempt of court.[834] Although an arbitral tribunal may arguably constitute a "court" within this definition, it is submitted that it would not constitute a court "of the United Kingdom", an analysis supported by the language of s 9 which speaks only of "proceedings in the courts of the United Kingdom *which relate to the arbitration*".

(b) In the English High Court and county courts, the corresponding procedures to the former procedure of entry of an appearance are those referred to in Part 9

---

[834] See *Trapp v Mackie* [1979] 1 WLR 377 (HL); *General Medical Council v BBC* [1998] 3 All ER 426 (CA).

of the Civil Procedure Rules (ie defence, admission or acknowledgment of service). If the defendant wishes to dispute the court's jurisdiction, he must first file an acknowledgment of service.[835]

4.145

23 Short title, repeals, commencement and extent

(1) This Act may be cited as the State Immunity Act 1978.

(2) Section 13 of the Administration of Justice (Miscellaneous Provisions) Act 1938 and section 7 of the Law Reform (Miscellaneous Provisions) (Scotland) Act 1940 (which become unnecessary in consequence of Part I of this Act) are hereby repealed.

(3) Subject to subsection (4) below, Parts I and II of this Act do not apply to proceedings in respect of matters that occurred before the date of the coming into force of this Act and, in particular—

  (a) sections 2(2) and 13(3) do not apply to any prior agreement, and

  (b) sections 3, 4 and 9 do not apply to any transaction, contract or arbitration agreement, entered into before that date.

(4) Section 12 above applies to any proceedings instituted after the coming into force of this Act.

(5) This Act shall come into force on such date as may be specified by an order made by the Lord Chancellor by statutory instrument.

(6) This Act extends to Northern Ireland.

(7) Her Majesty may by Order in Council extend any of the provisions of this Act, with or without modification, to any dependent territory.

Commentary

Legislative history

4.146

Under clause 24(3) of the State Immunity Bill, it was proposed that the legislation should not apply to (a) proceedings instituted before its coming into force, or (b) to proceedings in respect of matters occurring before 16 May 1972 (being the date of the European Convention). Strong exception was taken to that formulation at the committee stage[836] and by a series of amendments, clause 24(3) (now s 23(3)) was moulded to its present form and what is now s 23(4) was added.[837] The purpose of those amendments was to ensure "that the United Kingdom should not be seen to be acting in a way that would alter retrospectively the terms and conditions of existing agreements, or upset the basis on which foreign States might have taken decisions".[838]

---

[835] Civil Procedure Rules, r 11(2).   [836] Hansard, HL (5th series), vol 389, col. 1539.
[837] See Hansard, HL (5th series), vol 389, cols. 1940–1941; vol 394, cols. 321–323; vol 395, cols. 1699–1700; Hansard, HC (5th series), vol 953, cols. 617–620.
[838] Hansard, HL (5th series), vol 389, col. 1940 (Lord Elwyn-Jones LC).

4.147   Application

The 1978 Act came into force on 22 November 1978.[839]

4.148   *Transitional provisions*

The effect of the transitional provisions in s 23(3) and (4) is that (with the exception of s 12 which applies to any proceedings to which Part I applies brought after 22 November 1978) ss 1–19 of the 1978 Act have no application to proceedings in respect of matters occurring prior to 22 November 1978. In such cases, the rules of the common law (applying customary international law) will apply to determine whether a State is entitled to assert any immunity or other privilege.[840] In particular:

(a) the effect of any submission to jurisdiction under s 2(2) or consent to enforcement under s 13(3) prior to 22 November 1978 will fall to be determined by reference to common law rules;[841]

(b) the scope of any exception to immunity in proceedings arising out of a commercial transaction or contract of employment entered into prior to 22 November 1978 will also fall to be determined by reference to common law rules, irrespective of the date of the breach or other event giving rise to proceedings.

4.149   *Application to dependent territories*

The United Kingdom has, by delegated legislation, extended the provisions of the 1978 Act (with appropriate modifications) to Belize, British Antarctic Territory, British Virgin Islands, Cayman Islands, Falkland Islands and Dependencies, Gilbert Islands, Montserrat, Pitcairn, Henderson, Ducie and Oeno Islands, Sovereign Base Areas of Akrotiri and Dhekelia, Turks and Caicos Islands,[842] Guernsey,[843] Isle of Man[844] and Jersey.[845]

---

[839] State Immunity Act 1978 (Commencement) Order 1978 (SI 1978/1572).

[840] See *Uganda Co (Holdings) Ltd v Government of Uganda* [1979] 1 Lloyd's Rep 481 (Donaldson J); *Hispano Americana Mercantil SA v Central Bank of Nigeria* [1979] 2 Lloyd's Rep 277 (CA); *Planmount Ltd v Republic of Zaire* [1980] 2 Lloyd's Rep 393 (Lloyd J); *Sengupta v Republic of India* [1983] ICR 221; Lewis, 11.

[841] See 4.017 above. See also, in this connection, the comments of the Solicitor General, Peter Archer, Hansard, HC (5th series), vol 953, col. 619.

[842] State Immunity (Overseas Territories) Order 1979 (SI 1979/458).

[843] State Immunity (Guernsey) Order 1980 (SI 1980/871).

[844] State Immunity (Isle of Man) Order 1981 (SI 1981/1112).

[845] State Immunity (Jersey) Order 1985 (SI 1985/1642). It appears that St Helena has enacted its own legislation by the State Immunity (Application) Order 1979 (see Fox, 134).

State Immunity Bill (H.L.)[846]

4.150

Explanatory Memorandum

The Bill restricts the immunity which Sovereign States can claim from the jurisdiction of civil courts and tribunals in the United Kingdom. The common law which until recently accorded immunity from virtually all judicial proceedings is to be replaced by a statutory and residual immunity (*Clause* 1). Activities which could equally be performed by trading corporations or private individuals will generally no longer enjoy immunity (*Clauses* 2–12). The Bill enacts provisions which accord with the European Convention on State Immunity (Cmnd. 5081) signed by the United Kingdom on 16th May 1972. Its enactment will also enable the United Kingdom to ratify the Convention for the Unification of Certain rules concerning the Immunity of State-owned Ships signed at Brussels on April 10th 1926 (Cmd. 5672) and the Protocol to that Convention signed at Brussels on May 24th 1934 (Cmd. 5673). In addition the Bill regulates the personal immunities of Heads of State, visiting the United Kingdom at the invitation or with the consent of Her Majesty's Government, by equating them to those conferred on an Ambassador (*Clause* 21).

Clause 1 provides that a State is immune from the jurisdiction of the courts in the United Kingdom except as provided in the Bill. A court is required to give effect to this immunity even thought the State does not appear in the proceedings.

Clause 2 provides that a State is *not* immune if it has submitted to the jurisdiction of the court. Submission may take place after the cause of action arose or by prior written agreement, and a State is deemed to have submitted if it has instituted the proceedings or when it takes a step in the proceedings. However, a State does not submit by appearing solely in order to assert its immunity or an interest in property.

Clause 3 provides that a State is *not* immune as respects proceedings relating to any commercial, industrial or financial activity carried on through an office, agency or establishment in the United Kingdom in the same manner as a private person.

Clause 4 provides that a State is *not* immune as respects proceedings relating to a contractual obligation of the State which falls to be performed by the State wholly or partly in the United Kingdom: there is an exception where the contract is made in the territory of the State concerned and the obligation is governed by its administrative law.

---

[846] For legislative history, see commentary on the 1978 Act (see 4.001–4.149 above).

Clauses 3 and 4 do not apply if the parties to the dispute are States or have otherwise agreed in writing.

Clause 5 makes special provisions for contracts of employment: a State is *not* to be immune in proceedings relating to work which is to be performed wholly or partly in the United Kingdom, under a contract made between the State and an individual. But the Clause does not apply in certain circumstances where the individual is not a national of the United Kingdom, or if the parties to the contract have otherwise agreed in writing.

Clause 6 provides that a State is *not* immune as respects proceedings in respect of death, personal injuries or damage to tangible property caused by an act or omission in the United Kingdom

Clause 7 provides that a State is *not* immune from certain proceedings relating to immovable property in the United Kingdom: or relating to an interest of the State in movable or immovable property which has arisen by way of succession, gift or bona vacantia. The Clause also provides that the fact that a State has or claims an interest in property shall not prevent the exercise of jurisdiction over estates of deceased persons and persons of unsound mind, bankruptcies, the winding up of companies or the administration of trusts. Finally, the clause provides that the court may entertain proceedings against a perinea who is not a State and relating to property in which a State claims an interest, unless the State would itself have been immune if the proceedings had been brought against it.

Clause 8 provides that a State is *not* immune as respects certain proceedings relating to patents, trade marks and similar rights.

Clause 9 provides that a State is *not* immune as respects certain proceedings relating to its membership of a body corporate, unincorporated body or partnership.

Clause 10 provides that where a State has agreed in writing to submit a dispute to arbitration in or according to the law of the United Kingdom the State is *not* immune as respects proceedings which relate to the arbitration. The Clause does not apply to the enforcement of the award or if there is a contrary provision in the arbitration agreement or if the parties to the agreement are States.

Clause 11 provides that a State is not immune as regards proceedings involving ships or cargo used for commercial purposes. As regards ships or cargo used for non-commercial purposes a State is not immune if *Clauses* 2 to 6 are applicable. There are, however, certain exceptions if the State is a party to the Brussels Convention of 1926.

Clause 12 provides that a State is *not* immune in respect of proceedings relating to value added tax, customs and excise duties or agricultural levies.

Clauses 13 and 14 regulate the service of process and transmission of judgments against the State, extend the time limits for taking various steps in the proceedings and provide for other procedural privileges which must be extended to a State. No security for costs can be required of and no order for penalties, injunctions or specific performance can be issued against a State.

There is to be no execution against State property except against commercial ships or cargoes: ships or cargoes used for non-commercial purposes may not be arrested.

Clause 15 identifies the bodies and organisations which qualify for the immunities and privileges of States under the bill. A "separate entity", owned by a State but distinct from it in law, has immunity only if it is acting in the exercise of sovereign authority ("*jure imperii*") and if the State itself would be entitled to immunity. A constituent part of a Federal State will be treated like a "separate entity" in the absence of an Order in Council which requires it to be treated as a Sovereign State.

Clause 16 enables an Order in Council to be made on a basis of reciprocity restricting or extending the immunities and privileges set out in the Bill.

Clause 17 excludes certain classes of proceedings from this Part of the Bill. These include matters covered by diplomatic or consular immunity, proceedings relating to the armed forces of another State, and all criminal proceedings.

Clause 18 defines certain terms used in the bill.

Clauses 19 and 20 require final judgments given against the United Kingdom by a court in another State party to the European Convention to be recognised in the United Kingdom whenever, broadly speaking, United Kingdom courts would, in corresponding circumstances, have entertained proceedings against that State. But there are exceptions, for instance, where the judgments conflict with other earlier judgments or with the public policy of the United Kingdom.

Clause 21 provides that with the necessary modifications the diplomatic Privileges Act 1964 shall apply to a Sovereign or other head of a State while he is in the United Kingdom at the invitation or with the consent of the Government as it applies to the head of a diplomatic mission. Members of a visiting Sovereign's immediate family and his private servants are accorded privileges corresponding to those of the family and private servants of the head of the mission.

Clauses 22 to 24 provide that certain certificates of the Secretary of State shall be conclusive evidence, define terms used in the Bill and deal with the commencement and territorial extent of the Bill.

Financial effects of the Bill and effects on public service manpower

The Bill could have a slightly favourable effect on public funds as a result of the removal of immunity from jurisdiction, particularly in relation to value added tax and customs duties, but the amount is too speculative to be quantifiable. No significant public expenditure will result from the Bill nor is it likely to have any significant effect on public service manpower.

4.151   State Immunity Bill (H.L.)

Arrangement of Clauses

PART I

Proceedings in United Kingdom By or Against Other States

Immunity from jurisdiction

Clause

1. General immunity from jurisdiction.

Exceptions from immunity

2. Submission to jurisdiction.
3. Commercial, industrial and financial activities.
4. Contracts to be performed in United Kingdom.
5. Contracts of employment.
6. Personal injuries and damage to property.
7. Ownership, possession and use of property.
8. Patents, trade-marks etc.
9. Membership of bodies corporate etc.
10. Arbitrations.
11. Ships used for commercial purposes.
12. Value added tax, customs duties etc.

Procedure

13. Service of process and judgments in default of appearance.
14. Other procedural privileges.

Supplementary provisions

15. States entitled to immunities and privileges.
16. Restriction and extension of immunities and privilege.
17. Excluded matters.
18. Interpretation of Part. 1.

PART II

Judgments Against United Kingdom in Convention States

19. Recognition of judgments against United Kingdom.
20. Exceptions to recognition.

PART III

Miscellaneous and Supplementary

21. Visiting heads of State.
22. Evidence by certificate.
23. General interpretation.
24. Short title, repeals, commencement and extent.

A Bill Intituled

An Act to make new provision with respect to proceedings in the United Kingdom by or against other State; to provide for the effect of judgments given against the United Kingdom in the courts of States parties to the European Convention on State Immunity; to make new provision with respect to the immunities and privileges of visiting heads of State; and for connected purposes.

BE IT ENACTED by the Queen's most Excellent Majesty, by and with the advice and consent of the Lords Spiritual and Temporal, and Commons, in this present Parliament assembled, and by the authority of the same, as follows:—

PART I

Proceedings in United Kingdom By or Against Other States

Immunity from jurisdiction

1. General immunity from jurisdiction   4.152

(1) A State is immune from the jurisdiction of the courts of the United Kingdom except as provided in the following provisions of this Part of this Act.

(2) A court shall give effect to the immunity conferred by this section even though the State does not appear in the proceedings in question.

Exceptions from immunity

2. Submission to jurisdiction   4.153

(1) A State is not immune as respects proceedings in respect of which it has submitted to the jurisdiction of the courts of the United Kingdom.

(2) A State may submit after the dispute giving rise to the proceedings has arisen or by a prior written agreement between the parties to the dispute or by an international agreement; but a provision in an agreement that it is to be governed by the law of the United Kingdom is not to be regarded as a submission.

(3) A State is deemed to have submitted—

    (a) if it has instituted the proceedings; or

    (b) subject to subsections (4) and (5) below, if it has intervened or taken any step in the proceedings.

(4) Subsection (3)(b) above does not apply to intervention or any step taken for the purpose only of—

    (a) claiming immunity; or

    (b) asserting an interest in property in circumstances such that the State would have been entitled to immunity if the proceedings had been brought against it.

(5) Subsection (3)(b) above does not apply to any step taken by the State in ignorance of facts entitling it to immunity if those facts could not reasonably have been ascertained and immunity is claimed as soon as reasonably practicable.

(6) A submission in respect of any proceedings extends to any appeal but not to any counter-claim unless it arises out of the same legal relationship or facts as the claim.

(7) The head of a State's diplomatic mission in the United Kingdom, or the person for the time being performing his functions, shall be deemed to have authority to submit on behalf of the State in respect of any proceedings; and any person who has entered into a contract on behalf of and with the authority of a State shall be deemed to have authority to submit on its behalf in respect of proceedings arising out of the contract.

4.154 **3. Commercial, industrial and financial activities**

(1) A State is not immune as respects proceedings relating to any commercial, industrial or financial activity in which it has engaged in the same manner as a private person through an office, agency or establishment maintained by it for that purpose in the United Kingdom.

(2) This section does not apply if the parties to the dispute are States or have otherwise agreed in writing.

4.155 **4. Contracts to be performed in United Kingdom**

(1) A State is not immune as respects proceedings relating to an obligation of the State which falls to be performed wholly or partly in the United Kingdom by virtue of a contract other than a contract of employment.

(2) This section does not apply if—

    (a) the parties to the contract are States or have otherwise agreed in writing; or

    (b) the contract was made in the territory of the State concerned and the obligation in question is governed by its administrative law.

5. Contracts of employment 4.156

(1) A State is not immune as respects proceedings relating to a contract of employment between the State and an individual where the work is to be performed wholly or partly in the United Kingdom.

(2) Subject to subsections (3) and (4) below, this section does not apply if—

   (a) at the time when the proceedings are brought the individual is a national of the State concerned; or

   (b) at the time when the contract was made the individual was neither a national of the United Kingdom nor habitually resident there; or

   (c) the parties to the contract have otherwise agreed in writing.

(3) Where the work is for any such office, agency or establishment of the State as is mentioned in section 3 above, subsection (2)(a) and (b) above do not exclude the application of this section unless the individual was, at the time when the contract was made, habitually resident in that State.

(4) Subsection (2)(c) above does not exclude the application of this section where the law of the United Kingdom requires the proceedings to be brought before a court of the United Kingdom.

(5) In subsection (2)(b) above "national of the United Kingdom" means a citizen of the United Kingdom and Colonies, a person who is a British subject by virtue of section 2, 13 or 16 or the British Nationality Act 1948 or by virtue of the British Nationality Act 1965, a British protected person within the meaning of the said Act of 1948 or a citizen of Southern Rhodesia.

(6) In this section "proceedings relating to a contract of employment" includes proceedings between the parties to such a contract in respect of any statutory rights or duties to which they are entitled or subject as employer or employee.

6. Personal injuries and damage to property 4.157

A State is not immune as respects proceedings in respect of—

(a) death or personal injury; or

(b) damage to tangible property,

caused by an act or omission in the United Kingdom.

7. Ownership, possession and use of property 4.158

(1) A State is not immune as respects proceedings relating to—

   (a) any interest of the State in, or its possession or use of, immovable property in the United Kingdom; or

   (b) any obligation of the State arising out of its interest in, or its possession or use of, any such property.

(2) A State is not immune as respects proceedings relating to any interest of the State in movable or immovable property, being an interest arising by way of succession, gift or bona vacantia.

(3) The fact that a State has or claims an interest in any property shall not preclude any court form exercising in respect of it any jurisdiction relating to the estates of deceased persons or persons of unsound mind or to insolvency, the winding up of companies or, except in a case where the State is trustee, the administration of trusts.

(4) A court may entertain proceedings against a person other than a State notwithstanding that the proceedings relate to property

(a) which is in the possession or control of a State; or
(b) in which a State claims an interest,

if the State would not have been immune had the proceedings been brought against it or, in a case within paragraph (b) above, if the claim if neither admitted nor supported by prima facie evidence.

4.159 **8. Patents, trade-marks etc.**

A State is not immune as respects proceedings relating to—
(a) any patent, trade-mark, design or plant breeders' rights belonging to the State and registered or protected in the United Kingdom or for which the State has applied in the United Kingdom
(b) an alleged infringement by the State in the United Kingdom of any patent, trade-mark, design, plant breeders' rights or copyright; or
(c) the right to use a trade or business name in the United Kingdom.

4.160 **9. Membership of bodies corporate etc.**

(1) A State is not immune as respects proceedings relating to its membership of a body corporate, an unincorporated body or a partnership which—

(a) has members other than State; and
(b) is incorporated or constituted under the law of the United Kingdom or is controlled from or has its principal place of business in the United Kingdom, being proceedings arising between the State and the body or its other members or, as the case may be, between the State and the other partners.

(2) This section does not apply if provision to the contrary has been made by an agreement in writing between the parties to the dispute or by the constitution or other instrument establishing or regulating the body or partnership in question.

10. Arbitrations

(1) Where a State has agreed in writing to submit a dispute which has arisen, or may arise, to arbitration in or according to the law of the United Kingdom, the State is not immune as respects proceedings in the courts of the United Kingdom which relate to the arbitration.

(2) This section does not apply to proceedings for the enforcement of an award.

(3) This section has effect subject to any contrary provision in the arbitration agreement and does not apply to any arbitration agreement between States.

11. Ships used for commercial purposes

(1) This section applies to—

    (a) Admiralty proceedings; and

    (b) Proceedings on any claim which could be made the subject of Admiralty proceedings.

(2) A State is not immune as respects any ship against or in connection with which the proceedings are brought if, at the time when the cause of action arose, it was in use or intended for use for commercial purposes.

(3) Where an action in rem is brought against a ship for enforcing a claim based on a cause of action concerning another ship, a State is not immune as respects the first-mentioned ship if, at the time when the cause of action arose, both ships were in use or intended for use for commercial purposes.

(4) A State is not immune as respects any cargo against or in connection with which the proceedings are brought if—

    (a) both the cargo and the ship carrying it were at the time when the cause of action arose, in use or intended for use for commercial purposes; or

    (b) the ship was then in use or intended for use as aforesaid and the proceedings are not an action in rem against the cargo.

(5) Subject to subsection (4) above, subsection (2) above applies to property other than a ship as it applies to a ship.

(6) Sections 3 to 6 above do not apply to proceedings of the kind described in subsection (1) above if the State in question is a party to the Brussels Convention and the claim relates to the operation of a ship owned or operated by that State, the carriage of cargo or passengers on any such ship or the carriage of cargo owned by that State on any other ship.

4.163   **12. Value added tax, customs duties etc.**

A State is not immune as respects proceedings relating to its liability for value added tax, any duty of customs or excise or any agricultural levy.

Procedure

4.164   **13. Service of process and judgments in default of appearance**

(1) Any writ or other document required to be served for instituting proceedings against a State shall be served by being transmitted through the foreign and Commonwealth Office to the Ministry of Foreign Affairs of the State and service shall be deemed to have been effected when the writ or document is received at the Ministry.

(2) Any time for entering an appearance (whether prescribed by rules of court or otherwise) shall begin to run two months after the date on which the writ or document is received as aforesaid.

(3) A State which appears in proceedings cannot thereafter object that subsection (1) above has not been complied with in the case of those proceedings.

(4) No judgment in default of appearance shall be given against a State except on proof that subsection (1) above has been complied with and that the time for entering an appearance as extended by subsection (2) above has expired.

(5) A copy of any judgment given against a State in default of appearance shall be transmitted through the Foreign and Commonwealth Office to the Ministry of Foreign Affairs of that State and any time for applying to have the judgment set aside (whether prescribed by rules of court or otherwise) shall begin to run two months after the date on which the copy of the judgment is received at the Ministry.

(6) This section shall not be construed as applying to proceedings against a State by way of counter-claim or to an action in rem; and subsection (1) above shall not be construed as affecting any rules of court whereby leave is required for the service of process outside the jurisdiction.

4.165   **14. Other procedural privileges**

(1) A State shall not be required to give security for costs.

(2) No penalty by way of committal or fine shall be imposed in respect of any failure or refusal by or on behalf of a State to disclose or produce any document or other information for the purposes of proceedings to which it is a party.

(3) Relief shall not be given against a State by way of injunction or order for specific performance or for the recovery of land or other property.

(4) No process shall be issued for enforcing a judgment against a State except—

    (a) where and to the extent that the State has given its consent in writing; or

    (b) subject to subsection (5) below, where the judgment is in proceedings to which section 11 above applies and the process is in respect of the ship or other property to which the claim relates.

(5) A ship or other property which is for the time being in use or intended for use by or on behalf of a State for non-commercial purposes shall not be subject to any process by virtue of subsection (4)(b) above or, in an action in rem, to any process for its arrest, detention or sale.

(6) For the purposes of subsection (5) above a certificate by the head of a State's diplomatic mission in the United Kingdom or the person for the time being performing his functions, to the effect that a ship or other property is in use or intended for use by or on behalf of the State for non-commercial purposes shall be accepted as sufficient evidence of that fact unless the contrary is proved.

(7) In the application of this section to Scotland, references to costs and injunction shall be construed respectively as references to expenses and interdict; and, except as provided in subsection (4) above, no judgment or order in Scotland shall warrant any diligence or execution against a State.

Supplementary provisions

15. States entitled to immunities and privileges   **4.166**

(1) The immunities and privileges conferred by the Part of this Act apply to any foreign or commonwealth State other than the United Kingdom; and references to a State include references to—

    (a) the sovereign or other head of that State in his public capacity;

    (b) the government of that State; and

    (c) any department of that government,

but not to any entity thereafter referred to as a "separate entity" which under the law of that State is distinct from the State and capable of suing or being sued.

(2) A separate entity is immune from the jurisdiction of the courts of the United Kingdom if, and only if—

    (a) the proceedings relate to anything done by it in the exercise of sovereign authority; and

    (b) the circumstances are such that a State (or, in the case of proceedings to which section 11 above applies, a State which is not a party to the Brussels Convention) would have been so immune;

and if such an entity submits to the jurisdiction in respect of any such proceedings section 14 above shall apply to it with the necessary modifications.

(3) Section 13 above applies to proceedings against the constituent[847] territories of a federal State; and Her Majesty may by Order in Council provide for the other provisions of the Part of this Act to apply to any such constituent[848] territory specified in the Order as they apply to a State.

(4) Where the provisions of this Part of this Act do not apply to a constituent territory by virtue of any such Order subsection (2) above shall apply to it as if it were a separate entity.

4.167   **16. Restriction and extension of immunities and privileges**

If it appears to Her Majesty that the immunities and privileges conferred by this Part of this Act in relation to any State—

(a) exceed those accorded by the law of that State in relation in the United Kingdom; or

(b) are less than those required by any international agreement to which that State and the United Kingdom are parties.

(c) Her Majesty may by Order in Council provide for restricting or, as the case may be, extending those immunities and privileges to such extent as appears to Her Majesty to be appropriate.

4.168   **17. Excluded matters**

(1) This Part of this Act does not affect any immunity or privilege conferred by the Diplomatic Privileges Act 1964 or the Consular Relations Act 1968, and

  (a) section 5 above does not apply to proceedings concerning the employment of the members of a mission within the meaning of the Convention scheduled to the said Act of 1964 or of the members of a consular post within the meaning of the Convention scheduled to the said Act of 1968;

  (b) section 7(1) above does not apply to proceedings concerning a State's title to or its possession of property used for the purposes of a diplomatic mission or premises falling within section 21(3) below.

(2) This Part of this Act does not apply to proceedings relating to the armed forces of a State and, in particular, has effect subject to the Visiting Forces Act 1952.

(3) This Part of this Act does not apply to proceedings to which section 17 (6) of the Nuclear Installations Act 1965 applies.

---

[847] *Sic*   [848] *Sic*

(4) This Part of this Act does not apply to criminal proceedings.

(5) This Part of this Act does not apply to any proceedings relating to taxation other than those mentioned in section 12 above.

18. Interpretation of Part I 4.169

(1) In this Part of this Act—

"the Brussels Convention" means the International Convention for the Unification of Certain Rules Concerning the Immunity of State-owned Ships signed in Brussels on 10th April 1926;

"ship" includes hovercraft.

(2) For the purposes of sections 3 to 9 above the territory of the United Kingdom shall be deemed to include any dependent territory in respect of which the United Kingdom is a party to the European Convention on State Immunity.

(3) In sections 4(1), 5(1) and 6 above references to the United Kingdom include references to its territorial waters and any area designated under section 1(7) of the Continental Shelf Act 1964.

PART II

Judgments Against United Kingdom in Convention States

19. Recognition of judgments against United Kingdom 4.170

(1) This section applies to any judgment given against the United Kingdom by a court in another State party to the European Convention on State Immunity, being a judgment—

(a) given in proceedings in which the United Kingdom was not entitled to immunity by virtue of provisions corresponding to those of sections 2 to 12 above; and

(b) which is final, that is to say, which is not or is no longer subject to appeal or, if given in default of appearance, liable to be set aside.

(2) Subject to section 20 below, a judgment to which this section applies shall be recognised in any court in the United Kingdom as conclusive between the parties thereto in all proceedings founded on the same cause of action and may be relied on by way of defence or counter-claim in such proceedings.

(3) Subsection (2) above (but not section 20 below) shall have effect also in relation to any settlement entered into by the United Kingdom before a court in another State party to the Convention which under the law of that State is treated as equivalent to a judgment.

(4) In this section references to a court in a State party to the Convention include references to a court in any territory in respect of which it is a party.

4.171 **20. Exceptions to recognition**

(1) A court need not give effect to section 19 above in the case of a judgment—

    (a) if to do so would be manifestly contrary to public policy or if any party to the proceedings in which the judgment was given had no adequate opportunity to present his case; or

    (b) if the judgment was given without provisions corresponding to those of section 13 above having been complied with and the United Kingdom has not entered an appearance or applied to have the judgment set aside.

(2) A court need not give effect to section 19 above in the case of a judgment—

    (a) if proceedings between the same parties, based on the same facts and having the same purpose—

      (i) are pending before a court in the United Kingdom and were the first to be instituted; or

      (ii) are pending before a court in another State party to the Convention, were the first to be instituted and may result in a judgment to which that section will apply; or

    (b) if the result of the judgment is inconsistent with the result of another judgment given in proceedings between the same parties and—

      (i) the other judgment is by a court in the United Kingdom and either those proceedings were the first to be instituted or the judgment of that court was given before the first-mentioned judgment became final within the meaning of subsection (1)(b) of section 19 above; or

      (ii) the other judgment is by a court in another State party to the Convention and that section has already become applicable to it.

(3) Where the judgment was given against the United Kingdom in proceedings in respect of which the United Kingdom was not entitled to immunity by virtue of a provision corresponding to section 7(2) above, a court need not give effect to section 19 above in respect of the judgment if the court that gave the judgment—

    (a) would not have had jurisdiction in the matter if it had applied rules of jurisdiction corresponding to those applicable to such matters in the United Kingdom; or

    (b) applied a law other than that indicated by the United Kingdom rules of private international law and would have reached a different conclusion if it had applied the law so indicated.

(4) In subsection (2) above references to a court in the United Kingdom include references to a court in any dependent territory in respect of which the United Kingdom is a party to the Convention, and references to a court in another State party to the Convention include references to a court in any territory in respect of which it is a party.

PART III

Miscellaneous and Supplementary

21. Visiting heads of State

4.172

(1) Subject to the provisions of this section and to any necessary modifications, the Diplomatic Privileges Act 1964 shall apply to—

    (a) a sovereign or other head of State who is in the United Kingdom at the invitation or with the consent of the government of the United Kingdom;

    (b) members of his family forming part of his household who are in the United Kingdom as aforesaid; and

    (c) his private servants,

as it applies to the head of a diplomatic mission, to members of his family forming part of his household and to his private servants.

(2) The immunities and privileges conferred by virtue of subsection (1)(a) and (b) above shall not be subject to the restrictions by reference to nationality or residence mentioned in Article 37(1) or 38 in Schedule 1 to the said Act of 1964.

(3) Premises used as the principal residence in the United Kingdom of a person within subsection (1)(a) above shall be treated for the purposes of—

    (a) Article 23 in the said Schedule (fiscal privileges of premises of diplomatic mission); and

    (b) Articles 31(1)(a) and 34(b) in that Schedule (immunity from suit and fiscal privileges of private immovable property),

as if they were premises of a diplomatic mission and not private immovable property; and in their application by virtue of this section to other premises the provisions mentioned in paragraph (b) above shall have effect as if references to property held on behalf of the sending State for the purposes of the mission were references to property used wholly or mainly for the official purposes of the State in question.

(4) This section applies to the sovereign or other head of any State on which immunities and privileges are conferred by Part 1 of this Act and is without prejudice to the application of that Part to any such sovereign or head of State in his public capacity.

4.173 **22. Evidence by certificate**

A certificate by or on behalf of the Secretary of State shall be conclusive evidence on any question—

    (a) whether any country is a State for the purposes of Part 1 of this Act, whether any territory is a constituent territory of a federal State for those purposes or as to the person or persons to be regarded for those purposes as the head or government of a State;

    (b) whether a State is a party to the Brussels Convention mentioned in Part 1 of this Act;

    (c) whether a State is a party to the European Convention on State Immunity or as to the territories in respect of which the United Kingdom or any other State is a party;

    (d) whether, and if so when, a document has been served or received as mentioned in section 13 above.

4.174 **23. General interpretation**

    (1) In this Act "court" includes any tribunal or body exercising judicial functions; and references to the courts or law of the United Kingdom include references to the courts or law of any part of the United Kingdom.

    (2) In this Act references to entry of appearance and judgments in default of appearance include references to any corresponding procedures.

    (3) In this act "the European Convention on State Immunity" means the Convention of that name signed in Basle on 16th May 1972.

    (4) In this Act "dependent territory" means—

        (a) any of the Channel Islands;

        (b) the Isle of Man;

        (c) any colony other than one for whose external relations a country other than the United Kingdom is responsible; or

        (d) any country or territory outside Her Majesty's dominions in which Her Majesty has jurisdiction in right of the government of the United Kingdom.

    (5) Any power conferred by this Act to make an Order in Council includes power to vary or revoke a previous Order.

24. Short title, repeals, commencement and extent

    (1) This Act may be cited as the State Immunity Act 1977.

    (2) Section 13 of the Administration of Justice (Miscellaneous Provisions) Act 1938 and section 7 of the Law Reform (Miscellaneous Provisions)(Scotland)

Act 1940 (which become unnecessary in consequence of Part 1 of this Act) are hereby repealed.

(3) This Act does not apply to proceedings instituted before the coming into force of this Act or to proceedings in respect of matters that occurred before 16th May 1972; and section 10 above applies only where the arbitration agreement is made after the coming into force of this Act.

(4) This Act shall come into force on such date as may be specified by an order made by the Lord Chancellor by statutory instrument.

(5) This Act extends to Northern Ireland.

(6) Her Majesty may by Order in Council extend any of the provisions of this Act, with or without modification, to any dependent territory.

PART 5
OTHER NATIONAL
LEGISLATION

Argentina: Inmunidad Jurisdiccional de los Estados Extranjeros ante los Tribunales Argentinos

Ley N° 24.488

Sancionada: Mayo 31 de 1995.

Promulgada Parcialmente: Junio 22 de 1995.

El Senado y Cámara de Diputados de la Nación Argentina reunidos en Congreso, etc., sancionan con fuerza de Ley:

INMUNIDAD DE JURISDICCION DE LOS ESTADOS EXTRANJEROS ANTE LOS TRIBUNALES ARGENTINOS

002   **ARTICULO 1°**—Los Estados extranjeros son inmunes a la jurisdicción de los tribunales argentinos, en los términos y condiciones establecidos en esta ley.

003   **ARTICULO 2°**—Los Estados extranjeros no podrán invocar inmunidad de jurisdicción en los siguientes casos:

a)   Cuando consientan expresamente a través de un tratado internacional, de un contrato escrito o de una declaración en un caso determinado, que los tribunales argentinos ejerzan jurisdicción sobre ellos;

b)   Cuando fuere objeto de una reconvención directamente ligada a la demanda principal que el Estado extranjero hubiere iniciado;

c)   Cuando la demanda versare sobre una actividad comercial o industrial llevada a cabo por el Estado extranjero y la jurisdicción de los tribunales argentinos surgiere del contrato invocado o del derecho internacional;

d)   Cuando fueren demandados por cuestiones laborales, por nacionales argentinos o residentes en el país, derivadas de contratos celebrados en la República Argentina o en el exterior y que causaren efectos en el territorio nacional;

e)   Cuando fueren demandados por daños y perjuicios derivados de delitos o cuasidelitos cometidos en el territorio;

f) Cuando se tratare de acciones sobre bienes inmuebles que se encuentren en territorio nacional;

g) Cuando se tratare de acciones basadas en la calidad del Estado extranjero como heredero o legatario de bienes que se encuentren en el territorio nacional;

h) Cuando, habiendo acordado por escrito someter a arbitraje todo litigio relacionado con una transacción mercantil, pretendiere invocar la inmunidad de jurisdicción de los tribunales argentinos en un procedimiento relativo a la validez o la interpretación del convenio arbitral, del procedimiento arbitral o referida a la anulación del laudo, a menos que el convenio arbitral disponga lo contrario.

5.004 *[ARTICULO 3°—Si se presentaren demandas ante los tribunales argentinos contra un Estado extranjero invocando una violación al Derecho Internacional de los Derechos Humanos, el tribunal interviniente se limitará a indicar al actor el órgano de protección internacional en el ámbito regional o universal ante el que podrá formular su reclamo, si correspondiere. Asimismo, remitirá copia de la demanda al Ministerio de Relaciones Exteriores, Comercio Internacional y Culto, a fin de que tome conocimiento del reclamo y adopte las medidas que correspondan en el orden Internacional.]*[1]

5.005 ARTICULO 4°—La presentación de los Estados extranjeros ante los tribunales argentinos para invocar la inmunidad de jurisdicción no debe interpretarse como aceptación de competencia. La interposición de la defensa de inmunidad jurisdiccional suspenderá el término procesal del traslado o citación hasta tanto dicho planteamiento sea resuelto.

5.006 ARTICULO 5°—Los jueces, a pedido del Estado extranjero, podrán ampliar prudencialmente los plazos para contestar la demanda y oponer excepciones.

5.007 ARTICULO 6°—Las previsiones de esta ley no afectarán ninguna inmunidad o privilegio conferido por las Convenciones de Viena de 1961 sobre Relaciones Diplomáticas, o de 1963 sobre Relaciones Consulares.

5.008 ARTICULO 7°—En el caso de una demanda contra un Estado extranjero, el Ministerio de Relaciones Exteriores, Comercio Internacional y Culto podrá expresar su opinión sobre algún aspecto de hecho o de derecho ante el tribunal interviniente, en su carácter "amigo del tribunal".

---

[1] Art 3 is not in force (see Decree 849/95 at 5.010 and 5.020 below).

ARTICULO 8°—Comuníquese al Poder Ejecutivo.

5.009

—ALBERTO R. PIERRI.—EDUARDO MENEM.—Esther H. Pereyra Arandía de Pérez Pardo.—Edgardo Piuzzi.

DADA EN SALA DE SESIONES DEL CONGRESO ARGENTINO, EN BUENOS AIRES, A LOS TREINTA Y UN DIAS DEL MES MAYO DEL AÑO MIL NOVECIENTOS NOVENTA Y CINCO

Decreto 849/95

5.010

Bs. As., 22/6/95

VISTO el Proyecto de Ley N° 24.488, sancionado con fecha 31 de mayo de 1995, y comunicado por el HONORABLE CONGRESO DE; LA NACION a los fines del artículo 78 de la Constitución Nacional, y CONSIDERANDO:

Que el artículo 3° del Proyecto de Ley citado en el Visto establece que si se presentaren demandas ante los tribunales argentinos contra un Estado extranjero Invocando una violación al Derecho Internacional de los Derechos Humanos, el tribunal interviniente se limitará a Indicar al actor el órgano de protección Internacional en el ámbito regional o universal ante el que podrá formular su reclamo, si correspondiere.

Que tal norma es contraria a lo dispuesto por el artículo 46, Inciso 1, apartado a) de la CONVENCION AMERICANA SOBRE DERECHOS HUMANOS, aprobada por la Ley N° 23.054, e Incorporada con rango constitucional a nuestra Ley Fundamental por el artículo 75 Inciso 22), que para la admisión por parte de la comisión de una petición o comunicación exige que previamente se hayan interpuesto y agotado los recursos de jurisdicción Interna, conforme a los principios del Derecho Internacional generalmente reconocidos.

Que la COMISION INTERAMERICANA DE DERECHOS HUMANOS, organismo del cual la REPUBLICA ARGENTINA es ESTADO parte, reiteradamente ha sostenido que es preciso antes de acudir a un organismo o tribunal Internacional, utilizar los recursos disponibles en el derecho interno que sean de tal naturaleza a suministrar un medio eficaz y suficiente de reparar la queja que constituye el objeto de la acción internacional, que según resulta de la letra y del espíritu del proyecto de ley sancionado se distingue entre actos de imperio de los Estados y actos de gestión administrativa, constituyendo las violaciones a los derechos humanos, por lo general, actos de imperio.

Que asimismo tienen rango constitucional la CONVENCION SOBRE LA PREVENCION Y LA SANCION DEL DELITO DE GENOCIDIO y la CONVENCION CONTRA LA TORTURA Y OTROS TRATOS O PENAS

CRUELES, INHUMANOS O DEGRADANTES, delitos que pueden dar lugar a responsabilidad civil, por lo que parece impropio denegar el acceso a la justicia para demandar respecto de tales supuestos.

Que el presente Decreto se dicta en Acuerdo General de Ministros del PODER EJECUI'IVO NACIONAL, y no altera el espíritu ni la unidad del proyecto sancionado por el HONORABLE CONGRESO DE LA NACION.

Que las facultades para el dictado del presente surgen de los dispuesto en el artículo 80 de la CONSTITUCION NACIONAL.

Por ello.

EL PRESIDENTE DE LA NACION ARGENTINA EN ACUERDO GENERAL DE MINISTROS

DECRETA:

Artículo 1°—Obsérvase el artículo 3° del proyecto de ley registrado bajo el N° 24.488.

Art. 2°—Con la salvedad establecida en el artículo precedente, cúmplase, promúlguese y téngase por Ley de la Nación, el proyecto de Ley registrado bajo el N° 24.488.

Art. 3°—Dése cuenta al HONORABLE CONGRESO DE LA NACION a los efectos previstos en el artículo 99 inciso 3) de la CONSTITUCION NACIONAL.

Art. 4°—Comuníquese, publíquese, dése a la Dirección Nacional del Registro Oficial y archívese.

—MENEM.—Rodolfo C. Barra.—José A. Caro Figueroa.—Jorge A. Rodríguez.—Alberto J. Mazza.—Carlos V. Corach.—Domingo F. Cavallo.— Guido Di Tella.

[Note: Unofficial translation of Law no. 24,488 and Decree 849/95 follows at 5.011 and 5.020][2]

[2] Prepared by Tomas Cerdan and Edu Prim of Clifford Chance, Madrid.

Immunity of Foreign States from the Jurisdiction of Argentinean Courts

Law no. 24,488
Approved: 31 May 1995
Partially Enacted: 22 June 1995

The Senate and the House of Representatives of Argentina, gathered in Congress, etc., approve with the force of Law:

Immunity of foreign States from the jurisdiction of Argentinean Courts

Article 1

Foreign States are immune from the jurisdiction of Argentinean Courts in accordance with the following provisions of this law.

Article 2

Foreign States may not invoke jurisdictional immunity in the following cases:

(a) where they have consented expressly to the jurisdiction of Argentinean Courts by virtue of an international treaty, written agreement or declaration in any particular case;

(b) where the foreign State is subject to a counterclaim directly linked to a main claim which it initiated;

(c) where the claim affects a commercial or industrial activity carried out by the foreign State and the jurisdiction of Argentinean Courts is applicable under the corresponding contract or under international law;

(d) where the foreign State is subject to a claim by Argentineans or residents of Argentina, relating to a contract of employment executed in Argentina or abroad with effects in Argentina;

(e) where the foreign State is subject to a claim for losses or damages derived from crimes or offences committed in Argentina;

(f) in the event of actions over real estate located in Argentina;

(g) in the event of actions based on the foreign State's position as an heir or beneficiary of assets located in Argentina;

(h) where the foreign State, after agreeing in writing to submit a dispute arising from a commercial transaction to arbitration, wishes to invoke jurisdictional immunity from Argentinean Courts in proceedings involving the validity or interpretation of the arbitration agreement or the arbitration proceedings or the cancellation of the arbitration award, unless the arbitration agreement provides otherwise.

5.014 *[Article 3*

If claims were brought before the Argentinean Courts against a foreign State based on a violation of human rights under international law, the intervening court shall restrict itself to indicating to the claimant the international body before which it may bring its claim, if applicable, under local or universal jurisdiction. Likewise, it shall forward a copy of the claim to the Ministry of Foreign Affairs, International Commerce and Culture, so that it may examine the claim and adopt the corresponding measures under international jurisdiction.][3]

5.015 Article 4

The appearance of foreign States before Argentinean Courts in order to invoke jurisdictional immunity shall not be interpreted as an acceptance of the competence of the Argentinean Courts. The filing of a defence based on jurisdictional immunity shall suspend the procedural deadlines for the transfer or summons until the issue is resolved.

5.016 Article 5

The judges, at the foreign State's request, may prudently extend the deadlines in which to reply to the claim and present exceptions.

5.017 Article 6

The provisions of this Law shall not affect any immunity or privilege conferred by virtue of the Vienna Convention of 1961 on diplomatic relations or the 1963 Convention on consular relations.

5.018 Article 7

If a claim is brought against a foreign State, the Ministry of Foreign Affairs, International Commerce and Culture may express its opinion on any factual or legal issue before the intervening court, in its role as "friend to the court".

5.019 Article 8

To be notified to the Executive—Alberto R Pierri—Eduardo Menem—Esther H Pereyra Arandía de Pérez Pardo—Edgardo Piuzzi.

Given in the Hall of Sessions of the Argentinean Congress, in Buenos Aires, on 31 May 1995.

5.020 **Partial Veto of Law 24,488**

Decree 849/95

Buenos Aires, 22 June 1995

---

[3] Art 3 is not in force (see Decree 849/95 at 5.010 above and 5.020 below).

WHEREAS:

Article 3 of Bill 24,488, approved on 31 May 1995 and notified by the Honourable Congress of State for the purposes of Article 78 of the Constitution establishes that if claims are brought before the Argentinean Courts against a foreign State based on a violation of human rights under International Law, the intervening court shall restrict itself to indicating to the claimant the international body before which it may bring its claim, if applicable, under regional or universal jurisdiction.

Article 3 of Bill 24,488 is contrary to Article 46.1.a) of the American Convention on Human Rights, approved by Law 23,054 and incorporated into our Constitution by virtue of Article 75.22, under which, in order for a petition or communication to be accepted by the Commission, all procedures under local law must have been filed and exhausted pursuant to generally accepted principles of International Law.

The Inter-American Commission of Human Rights, of which the Republic of Argentina is a Member State, has repeatedly held that, before resorting to an international body or court, any procedures available under local law, which are capable of providing an effective and sufficient means of remedying the complaint that is the subject of the international claim, should first be exhausted. Pursuant to the letter and spirit of the Bill approved, a distinction is made between acts of State control and administrative management acts; in general, violations of human rights are acts of State control.

The Convention on the Prevention and Punishment of Genocide Crimes and the Convention against Torture and other Cruel, Inhuman or Degrading Treatment or Punishment both have constitutional status. Given that these crimes may give rise to civil liability, it would be improper to refuse access to the Courts in the event of such claims.

The present decree is issued pursuant to a general resolution adopted by the Ministers of the Executive, and does not modify the spirit or the unity of the Bill approved by the Honourable Congress of State.

The powers on which this decree is based derive from Article 80 of the Constitution.

The President of Argentina, pursuant to a general ministerial resolution, hereby DECREES:

Article 1

Note the exception of Article 3 of the Bill recorded under number 24,488.

Article 2

Subject to the exception mentioned in Article 1, the Bill recorded under number 24,488 is executed, enacted and raised to legal status.

Article 3

To be notified to the Honourable Congress of State for the purposes of Article 99.3 of the Constitution.

Article 4

To be notified, published and archived by the National Official Registry.

Menem—Rodolfo C Barra—José A Caro Figueroa—Jorge A Rodríguez—Alberto J Mazza—Carlos V Corach—Domingo F Cavallo—Guido Di Tella.

Australia: Foreign States Immunities Act 1985[4]   **5.021**

No. 196 of 1985

An Act relating to foreign State immunity

(Assented to 16 December 1985)

BE IT ENACTED by the Queen, and the Senate and the House of Representatives of the Commonwealth of Australia, as follows:

PART 1—PRELIMINARY

Short title   **5.022**

1. This Act may be cited as the Foreign States Immunities Act 1985.

Commencement   **5.023**

2. The provisions of this Act shall come into operation on such day as is, or such respective days as are, fixed by Proclamation.

Interpretation   **5.024**

3. (1) In this Act, unless the contrary intention appears—"agreement" means an agreement in writing and includes—

(a) a treaty or other international agreement in writing; and
(b) a contract or other agreement in writing;

"Australia", when used in a geographical sense, includes each of the external Territories;

"bill of exchange" includes a promissory note;

"court" includes a tribunal or other body (by whatever name called) that has functions, or exercises powers, that are judicial functions or powers or are of a kind similar to judicial functions or powers;

"diplomatic property" means property that, at the relevant time, is in use predominantly for the purpose of establishing or maintaining a diplomatic or consular mission, or a visiting mission, of a foreign State to Australia;

---

[4] As amended. The legislation is based on the proposal contained in the Australian Law Reform Commission's Report No 24 "Foreign State Immunities" (1984) (see http://www.alrc.gov.au/publications/finalreps.htm). With the exception of s 18(2) (which came into force on 1 January 1989), the Act came into force on 1 April 1986.

"foreign State" means a country the territory of which is outside Australia, being a country that is—

(a) an independent sovereign State; or
(b) a separate territory (whether or not it is self-governing) that is not part of an independent sovereign State;

"initiating process" means an instrument (including a statement of claim, application, summons, writ, order or third party notice) by reference to which a person becomes a party to a proceeding;

"law of Australia" means—

(a) a law in force throughout Australia; or
(b) a law of or in force in a part of Australia,

and includes the principles and rules of the common law and of equity as so in force;

"military property" means—

(a) a ship of war, a Government yacht, a patrol vessel, a police or customs vessel, a hospital ship, a defence force supply ship or an auxiliary vessel, being a ship or vessel that, at the relevant time, is operated by the foreign State concerned (whether pursuant to requisition or under a charter by demise or otherwise); or
(b) property (not being a ship or vessel) that is—
    (i) being used in connection with a military activity; or
    (ii) under the control of a military authority or defence agency for military or defence purposes;

"proceeding" means a proceeding in a court but does not include a prosecution for an offence or an appeal or other proceeding in the nature of an appeal in relation to such a prosecution;

"property" includes a chose in action;

"separate entity", in relation to a foreign State, means a natural person (other than an Australian citizen), or a body corporate or corporation sole (other than a body corporate or corporation sole that has been established by or under a law of Australia), who or that—

(a) is an agency or instrumentality of the foreign State; and
(b) is not a department or organ of the executive government of the foreign State.

(2) For the purposes of the definition of "separate entity" in sub-section (1) a natural person who is, or a body corporate or a corporation sole that is, an agency of more than one foreign State shall be taken to be a separate entity of each of the foreign States.

(3) Unless the contrary intention appears, a reference in this Act to a foreign State includes a reference to—

(a) a province, state, self-governing territory or other political subdivision (by whatever name known) of a foreign State;

(b) the head of a foreign State, or of a political subdivision of a foreign State, in his or her public capacity; and

(c) the executive government or part of the executive government of a foreign State or of a political subdivision of a foreign State, including a department or organ of the executive government of a foreign State or subdivision,

but does not include a reference to a separate entity of a foreign State.

(4) A reference in this Act to a court of Australia includes a reference to a court that has jurisdiction in or for any part of Australia.

(5) A reference in this Act to a commercial purpose includes a reference to a trading, business, a professional and an industrial purpose.

(6) A reference in this Act to the entering of appearance or to the entry of judgment in default of appearance includes a reference to any like procedure.

External Territories   5.025

4. This Act extends to each external Territory.

Act to bind Crown   5.026

5. This Act binds the Crown in all its capacities.

Saving of Other Laws   5.027

6. This Act does not affect an immunity or privilege that is conferred by or under the Consular Privileges and immunities Act 1972, the Defence (Visiting Forces) Act 1963, the Diplomatic Privileges and immunities Act 1967 or any other Act.

Application   5.028

7. (1) Part II (other than section 10) does not apply in relation to a proceeding concerning—

(a) a contract or other agreement or a bill of exchange that was made or given;

(b) a transaction or event that occurred;

(c) an act done or omitted to have been done; or

(d) a right, liability or obligation that came into existence,

before the commencement of this Act.

(2) Section 10 does not apply in relation to a submission mentioned in that section that was made before the commencement of this Act.

(3) Part III and section 36 do not apply in relation to a proceeding instituted before the commencement of this Act.

(4) Part IV only applies where, by virtue of a provision of Part II, the foreign State is not immune from the jurisdiction of the courts of Australia in the proceeding concerned.

5.029 Application to courts

8. In the application of this Act to a court, this Act has effect only in relation to the exercise or performance by the court of a judicial power or function or a power or function that is of a like kind.

PART II—IMMUNITY FROM JURISDICTION

5.030 General immunity from jurisdiction

9. Except as provided by or under this Act, a foreign State is immune from the jurisdiction of the courts of Australia in a proceeding.

5.031 Submission to jurisdiction

10. (1) A foreign State is not immune in a proceeding in which it has submitted to the jurisdiction in accordance with this section.

(2) a foreign State may submit to the jurisdiction at any time, whether by agreement or otherwise, but a foreign State shall not be taken to have so submitted by reason only that it is a party to an agreement the proper law of which is the law of Australia.

(3) A submission under sub-section (2) may be subject to a specified limitation, condition or exclusion (whether in respect of remedies or otherwise).

(4) Without limiting any other power of a court to dismiss, stay or otherwise decline to hear and determine a proceeding, the court may dismiss, stay or otherwise decline to hear and determine a proceeding it if is satisfied that, by reason of the nature of a limitation, condition or exclusion to which a submission is subject (not being a limitation, condition or exclusion in respect of remedies), it is appropriate to do so.

(5) An agreement by a foreign State to waive its immunity under this Part has effect to waive that immunity and the waiver may not be withdrawn except in accordance with the terms of the agreement.

(6) Subject to sub-section (7), (8) and (9), a foreign State may submit to the jurisdiction in a proceeding by—

(a) instituting the proceeding; or

(b) intervening in, or taking a step as a party to, the proceeding.

(7) a foreign State shall not be taken to have submitted to the jurisdiction in a proceeding by reason only that—

(a) it has made an application for costs; or
(b) it has intervened, or has taken a step, in the proceeding for the purpose or in the course of asserting immunity.

(8) Where the foreign State is not a party to a proceeding, it shall not be taken to have submitted to the jurisdiction by reason only that it has intervened in the proceeding for the purpose or in the course of asserting an interest in property involved in or affected by the proceeding.

(9) Where—

(a) the intervention or step was taken by a person who did not know and could not reasonably have been expected to know of the immunity; and
(b) the immunity is asserted without unreasonable delay,

the foreign State shall not be taken to have submitted to the jurisdiction in the proceeding by reason only of that intervention or step.

(10) Where a foreign State has submitted to the jurisdiction in a proceeding, them, subject to the operation of sub-section (3), it is not immune in relation to a claim made in the proceeding by some other party against it (whether by way of set-off, counter-claim or otherwise), being a claim that arises out of and relates to the transactions or events to which the proceeding relates.

(11) In addition to any other person who has authority to submit, on behalf of a foreign State, to the jurisdiction—

(a) the person for the time being performing the functions of the head of the State's diplomatic mission in Australia has that authority; and
(b) a person who has entered into a contract on behalf of and with the authority of the State has authority to submit in that contract, on behalf of the State, to the jurisdiction in respect of a proceeding arising out of the contract.

Commercial transactions 5.032

11. (1) A foreign State is not immune in a proceeding in so far as the proceeding concerns a commercial transaction.

(2) Sub-section (1) does not apply—

(a) if all the parties to the proceeding—
   (i) are foreign States or are the Commonwealth and one or more foreign States; or
   (ii) have otherwise agreed in writing; or

(b) in so far as the proceeding concerns a payment in respect of a grant, a scholar-ship, a pension or a payment of a like kind.

(3) In this section, "commercial transaction" means a commercial, trading, business, professional or industrial or like transaction into which the foreign State has entered or a like activity in which the State has engaged and, without limiting the generality of the foregoing, includes—

(a) a contract for the supply of goods or services;
(b) an agreement for a loan or some other transaction for or in respect of the provision of finance; and
(c) a guarantee or indemnity in respect of a financial obligation, but does not include a contract of employment or a bill of exchange.

5.033   Contracts of employment

12. (1) A foreign State, as employer, is not immune in a proceeding in so far as the proceeding concerns the employment of a person under a contract of employment that was made in Australia or was to be performed wholly or partly in Australia.

(2) A reference in sub-section (1) to a proceeding includes a reference to a proceeding concerning—

(a) a right or obligation conferred or imposed by a law of Australia on a person as employer or employee; or
(b) a payment the entitlement to which arises under a contract of employment.

(3) Where, at the time when the contract of employment was made, the person employed was—

(a) a national of the foreign State but not a permanent resident of Australia; or
(b) an habitual resident of the foreign State,

sub-section (1) does not apply.

(4) Sub-section (1) does not apply where—

(a) an inconsistent provision is included in the contract of employment; and
(b) a law of Australia does not avoid the operation of, or prohibit or render unlawful the inclusion of, the provision.

(5) Sub-section (1) does not apply in relation to the employment of—

(a) a member of the diplomatic staff of a mission as defined by the Vienna Convention on Diplomatic Relations, being the Convention the English text of which is set out in the Schedule to the Diplomatic Privileges and Immunities Act 1967; or

(b) a consular officer as defined by the Vienna Convention on consular Relations, being the Convention the English text of which is set out in the Schedule to the Consular Privileges and Immunities Act 1972.

(6) Sub-section (1) does not apply in relation to the employment of—

(a) a member of the administrative and technical staff of a mission as defined by the Convention referred to in paragraph (5)(a); or
(b) a consular employee as defined by the Convention referred to in paragraph (5)(b),

unless the member or employee was, at the time when the contract of employment was made, a permanent resident of Australia.

(7) In this section, "permanent resident of Australia" means—

(a) an Australian citizen; or
(b) a person resident in Australia whose continued presence in Australia is not subject to a limitation as to time imposed by or under a law of Australia.

Personal injury and damage to property   5.034

13. A foreign State is not immune in a proceeding in so far as the proceeding concerns—

(a) the death of, or personal injury to, a person; or
(b) loss of or damage to tangible property,

caused by an act or omission done or omitted to be done in Australia.

Ownership, possession and use of property, &c.   5.035

14. (1) A foreign State is not immune in a proceeding in so far as the proceeding concerns—

(a) an interest of the State in, or the possession or use by the State of, immovable property in Australia; or
(b) an obligation of the State that arises out of its interest in, or its possession or use of, property of that kind.

(2) A foreign State is not immune in a proceeding in so far as the proceeding concerns an interest of the State in property that arose by way of gift made in Australia or by succession.

(3) A foreign State is not immune in a proceeding in so far as the proceeding concerns—

(a) bankruptcy, insolvency or the winding up of a body corporate; or
(b) the administration of a trust, of the estate of a deceased person or of the estate of a person of unsound mind.

5.036 **Copyright, patents, trade marks, &c.**

15. (1) A foreign State is not immune in a proceeding in so far as the proceeding concerns—

(a) the ownership of a copyright or the ownership, or the registration or protection in Australia, of an invention, a design or a trade mark;
(b) an alleged infringement by the foreign State in Australia of copyright, a patent for an invention, a registered trade mark or a registered design; or
(c) the use in Australia of a trade name or a business name.

(2) Sub-section (1) does not apply in relation to the importation into Australia, or the use in Australia, of property otherwise than in the course of or for the purposes of a commercial transaction as defined by sub-section 11 (3).

5.037 **Membership of bodies corporate, &c.**

16. (1) A foreign State is not immune in a proceeding in so far as the proceeding concerns its membership, or a right or obligation that relates to its membership, of a body corporate, an unincorporated body or a partnership that—

(a) has a member that is not a foreign State or the Commonwealth; and
(b) is incorporated or has been established under the law of Australia or is controlled from, or has its principal place of business in, Australia,

being a proceeding arising between the foreign State and the body or other members of the body or between the foreign State and one or more of the other partners.

(2) Where a provision included in—

(a) the constitution or other instrument establishing or regulating the body or partnership; or
(b) an agreement between the parties to the proceeding,

is inconsistent with sub-section (1), that sub-section has effect subject to that provision.

5.038 **Arbitrations**

17. (1) Where a foreign State is a party to an agreement to submit a dispute to arbitration, then, subject to any inconsistent provision in the agreement, the foreign State is not immune in a proceeding for the exercise of the supervisory jurisdiction of a court in respect of the arbitration, including a proceeding—

(a) by way of a case stated for the opinion of a court;
(b) to determine a question as to the validity or operation of the agreement or as to the arbitration procedure; or
(c) to set aside the award.

(2) Where—

(a) apart from the operation of sub-paragraph 11(2)(a)(ii), sub-section 12(4) or sub-section 16(2), a foreign State would not be immune in a proceeding concerning a transaction or event; and

(b) the foreign State is a party to an agreement to submit to arbitration a dispute about the transaction or event,

then, subject to any inconsistent provision in the agreement, the foreign State is not immune in a proceeding concerning the recognition as binding for any purpose, or for the enforcement, of an award made pursuant to the arbitration, wherever the award was made.

(3) Sub-section (1) does not apply where the only parties to the agreement are any 2 or more of the following:

(a) A foreign State;
(b) The Commonwealth;
(c) An organisation the members of which are only foreign State or the Commonwealth and one or more foreign State.

Actions *in rem*

5.039

18. (1) A foreign State is not immune in a proceeding commenced as an action *in rem* against a ship concerning a claim in connection with the ship if, at the time when the cause of action arose, the ship was in use for commercial purposes.

(2) A foreign State is not immune in a proceeding commenced as an action *in rem* against a ship concerning a claim against another ship if—

(a) at the time when the proceeding was instituted, the ship that is the subject of the action *in rem* was in use for commercial purposes; and

(b) at the time when the cause of action arose, the other ship was in use for commercial purposes.

(3) A foreign State is not immune in a proceeding commenced as an action *in rem* against cargo that was, at the time when the cause of action arose, a commercial cargo.

(4) The preceding provisions of this section do not apply in relation to the arrest, detention or sale of a ship or cargo.

(5) A reference in this section to a ship in use for commercial purposes or to a commercial cargo is a reference to a ship or a cargo that is commercial property as defined by sub-section 32(3).

5.040 **Bills of exchange**

19. Where—

(a) a bill of exchange has been drawn, made, issued or indorsed by a foreign State in connection with a transaction or event; and

(b) the foreign State would not be immune in a proceeding in so far as the proceeding concerns the transaction or event,

the foreign State is not immune in a proceeding in so far as the proceeding concerns the bill of exchange.

5.041 **Taxes**

20. A foreign State is not immune in a proceeding in so far as the proceeding concerns an obligation imposed on it by or under a provision of a law of Australia with respect to taxation, being a provision that is prescribed, or is included in a class of provisions that is prescribed, for the purposes of this section.[5]

5.042 **Related proceedings**

21. Where, by virtue of the operation of the preceding provisions of this Part, a foreign State is not immune in a proceeding in so far as the proceeding concerns a matter, it is not immune in any other proceeding (including an appeal) that arises out of and relates to the first-mentioned proceeding in so far as that other proceeding concerns that matter.

5.043 **Application of Part to separate entities**

22. *The preceding provisions of this Part (other than sub-paragraph 11(2)(a)(I), sub-section 16(1) and sub-section 17(3) apply in relation to a separate entity of a foreign State as they apply in relation to the foreign State.*[6]

PART III—SERVICE AND JUDGMENTS

5.044 **Service of initiating process by agreement**

23. Service of initiating process on a foreign State or on a separate entity of a foreign State may be effected in accordance with an agreement (wherever made and whether made before or after the commencement of this Act) to which the State or entity is a party.

---

[5] See the Foreign States Immunities Regulations 1987 (SI 1987 No 77, as amended).
[6] As amended by the Statute Law (Miscellaneous Provisions) Act 1987.

Service through the diplomatic channel

24. (1) Initiating process that is to be served on a foreign State may be delivered to the Attorney-General for transmission by the Department of Foreign Affairs to the department or organ of the foreign State that is equivalent to that Department.

(2) The initiating process shall be accompanied by—

(a) a request in accordance with Form 1 in the schedule;

(b) a statutory declaration of the plaintiff or applicant in the proceeding stating that the rules of court or other laws (if any) in respect of service outside the jurisdiction of the court concerned have been complied with; and

(c) if English is not an official language of the foreign State—

(i) a translation of the initiating process into an official language of the foreign State; and

(ii) a certificate in that language, signed by the translator, setting out particulars of his or her qualifications as a translator and stating that the translation is an accurate translation of the initiating process.

(3) Where the process and documents are delivered to the equivalent department or organ of the foreign State in the foreign State, service shall be taken to have been effected when they are so delivered.

(4) Where the process and documents are delivered to some other person on behalf of and with the authority of the foreign State, service shall be taken to have been effected when they are so delivered.

(5) Sub-sections (1) to (4) (inclusive) do not exclude the operation of any rule of court or other law under which the leave of a court is required in relation to service of the initiating process outside the jurisdiction.

(6) Service of initiating process under this section shall be taken to have been effected outside the jurisdiction and in the foreign State concerned, wherever the service is actually effected.

(7) The time for entering an appearance begins to run at the expiration of 2 months after the date on which service of the initiating process was effected.

(8) This section does not apply to service of initiating process in a proceeding commenced as an action *in rem*.

Other service ineffective

25. Purported service of an initiating process upon a foreign State in Australia otherwise than as allowed or provided by section 23 or 24 is ineffective.

5.047 **Waiver of objection to service**

26. Where a foreign State enters an appearance in a proceeding without making an objection in relation to the service of the initiating process, the provisions of this Act in relation to that service shall be taken to have been complied with.

5.048 **Judgment in default of appearance**

27. (1) A judgment in default of appearance shall not be entered against a foreign State unless—

(a) it is proved that service of the initiating process was effected in accordance with this Act and that the time for appearance has expired; and

(b) the court is satisfied that, in the proceeding, the foreign State is not immune.

(2) A judgment in default of appearance shall not be entered against a separate entity of a foreign State unless the court is satisfied that, in the proceeding, the separate entity is not immune.

5.049 **Enforcement of default judgments**

28. (1) Subject to sub-section (6), a judgment in default of appearance is not capable of being enforced against a foreign State until the expiration of 2 months after the date on which service of—

(a) a copy of the judgment, sealed with the seal of the court or, if there is no seal, certified by an officer of the court to be a true copy of the judgment; and

(b) if English is not an official language of the foreign State—

(i) a translation of the judgment into an official language of the foreign State; and

(ii) a certificate in that language, signed by the translator, setting out particulars of his or her qualifications as a translator and stating that the translation is an accurate translation of the judgment,

has been effected in accordance with this section on the department or organ of the foreign State that is equivalent to the Department of Foreign Affairs.

(2) Where a document is to be served as mentioned in sub-section (1), the person in whose favour the judgments was given shall give it, together with a request in accordance with Form 2 in the Schedule, to the Attorney-General for transmission by the Department of Foreign Affairs to the department or organ of the foreign State that is equivalent to that Department.

(3) Where the document is delivered to the equivalent department or organ of the foreign State in the foreign State, service shall be taken to have been effected when it is so delivered.

(4) Where the document is delivered to some other person on behalf of and with the authority of the foreign State, service shall be taken to have been effected when it is so delivered.

(5) The time, if any, for applying to have the judgment set aside shall be at least 2 months after the date on which the document is delivered to or received on behalf of that department or organ of the foreign State.

(6) Where a judgment in default of appearance has been given by a court against a foreign State, the court may, on the application of the person in whose favour the judgment was given, permit, on such terms and conditions as it thinks fit, the judgment to be enforced in accordance with this Act against the foreign State before the expiration of the period mentioned in sub-section (1).

Power to grant relief 5.050

29. (1) Subject to sub-section (2), a court may make any order (including an order for interim or final relief) against a foreign State that it may otherwise lawfully make unless the order would be inconsistent with an immunity under this Act.

(2) A court may not make an order that a foreign State employ a person or re-instate a person in employment.

PART IV—ENFORCEMENT

Immunity from execution 5.051

30. Except as provided by this Part, the property of a foreign State is not subject to any process or order (whether interim or final) of the courts of Australia for the satisfaction or enforcement of a judgment, order or arbitration award or, in Admiralty proceedings, for the arrest, detention or sale of the property.

Waiver of immunity from execution 5.052

31. (1) A foreign State may at any time by agreement waive the application of section 30 in relation to property, but it shall not be taken to have done so by reason only that it has submitted to the jurisdiction.

(2) The waiver may be subject to specified limitations.

(3) An agreement by a foreign State to waive its immunity under section 30 has effect to waive that immunity and the waiver may not be withdrawn except in accordance with the terms of the agreement.

(4) A waiver does not apply in relation to property that is diplomatic property or military property unless a provision in the agreement expressly designates the property as property to which the waiver applies.

(5) In addition to any other person who has authority to waive the application of section 30 on behalf of a foreign State or a separate entity of the foreign State, the person for the time being performing the functions of the head of the State's diplomatic mission in Australia has that authority.

5.053 **Execution against commercial property**

32. (1) Subject to the operation of any submission that is effective by reason of section 10, section 30 does not apply in relation to commercial property.

(2) Where a foreign State is not immune in a proceeding against or in connection with a ship or cargo, section 30 does not prevent the arrest, detention or sale of the ship or cargo if, at the time of the arrest or detention—

(a) the ship or cargo was commercial property; and

(b) in the case of a cargo that was then being carried by a ship belonging to the same or to some other foreign State—the ship was commercial property.

(3) For the purposes of this section—

(a) commercial property is property, other than diplomatic property or military property, that is in use by the foreign State concerned substantially for commercial purposes; and

(b) property that is apparently vacant or apparently not in use shall be taken to be being used for commercial purposes unless the court is satisfied that it has been set aside otherwise than for commercial purposes.

5.054 **Execution against immovable property, &c.**

33. Where—

(a) property—
   (i) has been acquired by succession or gift; or
   (ii) is immovable property; and

(b) a right in respect of the property has been established as against a foreign State by a judgment or order in a proceeding as mentioned in section 14,

then, for the purpose of enforcing that judgment or order, section 30 does not apply to the property.

5.055 **Restrictions on certain other relief**

34. A penalty by way of fine or committal shall not be imposed in relation to a failure by a foreign State or by a person on behalf of a foreign State to comply with an order made against the foreign State by a court.

Application of Part to separate entities 5.056

35. (1) This Part applies in relation to a separate entity of a foreign State that is the central bank or monetary authority of the foreign State as it applies in relation to the foreign State.

(2) Subject to sub-section (1), this Part applies in relation to a separate entity of the foreign State as it applies in relation to the State if, in the proceeding concerned—

(a) the separate entity would, apart from the operation of section 10, have been immune from the jurisdiction; and

(b) it has submitted to the jurisdiction.

PART V—MISCELLANEOUS

Heads of foreign States 5.057

36. (1) Subject to the succeeding provisions of this section, the Diplomatic Privileges and Immunities Act 1967 extends, with such modifications as are necessary, in relation to the person who is for the time being—

(a) the head of a foreign State; or

(b) a spouse of the head of a foreign State.

As that Act applies in relation to a person at a time when he or she is the head of a diplomatic mission.

(2) This section does not affect the application of any law of Australia with respect to taxation.

(3) This section does not affect the application of any other provision of this Act in relation to a head of a foreign State in his or her public capacity.

(4) Part III extends in relation to the head of a foreign State in his or her private capacity as it applies in relation to the foreign State and, for the purpose of the application of Part III as it so extends, a reference in that Part to a foreign State shall be read as a reference to the head of the foreign State in his or her private capacity.

Effect of agreements on separate entities 5.058

37. An agreement made by a foreign State and applicable to a separate entity of that State has effect, for the purposes of this Act, as though the separate entity were a party to the agreement.

Power to set aside process, &c. 5.059

38. Where, on the application of a foreign State or a separate entity of a foreign State, a court is satisfied that a judgment, order or process of the court made or

issued in a proceeding with respect to the foreign State or entity is inconsistent with an immunity conferred by or under this Act, the court shall set aside the judgment, order or process so far as it is so inconsistent.

5.060 Discovery

39. (1) A penalty by way of fine or committal shall not be imposed in relation to a failure or refusal by a foreign State or by a person on behalf of a foreign State to disclose or produce a document or to furnish information for the purposes of a proceeding.

(2) Such a failure or refusal is not of itself sufficient ground to strike out a pleading or part of a pleading.

5.061 Certificate as to foreign State, &c.

40. (1) The Minister for Foreign Affairs may certify in writing that, for the purposes of this Act—

(a) a specified country is, or was on a specified day, a foreign State;

(b) a specified territory is or is not, or was or was not on a specified day, part of a foreign State;

(c) a specified person is, or was at a specified time, the head of, or the government or part of the government of, a foreign State or a former foreign State; or

(d) service of a specified document as mentioned in section 24 or 28 was effected on a specified day.

(2) The Minister for Foreign Affairs may, either generally or as otherwise provided by the instrument of delegation, delegate by instrument in writing to a person his or her powers under sub-section (1) in relation to the service of documents.

(3) A power so delegated, when exercised by the delegate, shall, for the purposes of this Act, be deemed to have been exercised by the Minister.

(4) A delegation under sub-section (2) does not prevent the exercise of the power by the Minister.

(5) A certificate under this section is admissible as evidence of the facts and matters stated in it and is conclusive as to those facts and matters.

5.062 Certificate as to use

41. For the purposes of this Act, a certificate in writing given by the person for the time being performing the functions of the head of a foreign State's

diplomatic mission in Australia to the effect that property specified in the certificate, being property—

(a) in which the foreign State or a separate entity of the foreign State has an interest; or

(b) that is in the possession or under the control of the foreign State or of a separate entity of the foreign State,

is or was at a specified time in use for purposes specified in the certificate is admissible as evidence of the facts stated in the certificate.

Restrictions and extensions of immunities and privileges   5.063

42. (1) Where the Governor-General is satisfied that an immunity or privilege conferred by this Act in relation to a foreign State is not accorded by the law of the foreign State in relation to Australia, the Governor-General may make regulations modifying the operation of this Act with respect to those immunities and privileges in relation to the foreign State.

(2) Where the Governor-General is satisfied that the immunities and privileges conferred by this Act in relation to a foreign State differ from those required by a treaty, convention or other agreement to which the foreign State and Australia are parties, the Governor-General may make regulations modifying the operation of this Act with respect to those immunities and privileges in relation to the foreign State so that this Act as so modified conforms with the treaty, convention or agreement.

(3) Regulations made under sub-section (1) or (2) that are expressed to extend or restrict an immunity from the jurisdiction may be expressed to extend to a proceeding that was instituted before the commencement of the regulations and has not been finally disposed of.

(4) Regulations made under sub-section (1) or (2) that are expressed to extend or restrict an immunity from execution or other relief may be expressed to extend to a proceeding that was instituted before the commencement of the regulations and in which procedures to give effect to orders for execution or other relief have not been completed.

(5) Regulations in relation to which sub-section (3) or (4) applies may make provision with respect to the keeping of property, or for the keeping of the proceeds of the sale of property, with which a proceeding specified in the regulations is concerned, including provision authorising an officer of a court to manage, control or preserve the property or, if, by reason of the condition of the property, it is necessary to do so, to sell or otherwise dispose of the property.

(6) Regulations under this section have effect notwithstanding that they are inconsistent with an Act (other than this Act) as in force at the time when the regulations came into operation.

(7) Jurisdiction is conferred on the Federal Court of Australia and, to the extent that the Constitution permits, on the courts of the Territories, and the courts of the States are invested with federal jurisdiction, in respect of matters arising under the regulations but a court of a Territory shall not exercise any jurisdiction so conferred in respect of property that is not within that Territory or a Territory in which the court may exercise jurisdiction and a court of a State shall not exercise any jurisdiction so invested in respect of property that is not within that State.

5.064   Regulations

43. The Governor-General may make regulations, not inconsistent with this Act, prescribing matters—

(a) required or permitted by this Act to be prescribed; or
(b) necessary or convenient to be prescribed for carrying out or giving effect to this Act.

5.065   Schedule

FORM 1

Request For Service of Originating Process On A Foreign State

TO: The Attorney-General of the Commonwealth

A proceeding has been commenced in (name of court, tribunal, etc.) against (here insert name of foreign State).

The proceeding concerns (short particulars of the claim against the foreign State).

In accordance with section 24 of the Foreign States Immunities Act 1985, enclosed are:

(a) the initiating process in the proceeding;
(b) a statutory declaration;
(c) *a translation of the initiating process into (name of language), an official language of the foreign State; and
(d) *a certificate signed by the translator,

and it is requested that the initiating process, *the translation and the certificate be transmitted by the Department of Foreign Affairs to the department or organ of the foreign State that is equivalent to that Department.

It is further requested that, when service of the initiating process and other documents has been effected on the foreign State in accordance with that Act, the Minister for foreign Affairs certify accordingly under section 40 of that Act, and forward the certificate to (name and address of person to whom certificate of service should be forwarded).

DATED this day of 19

(signature of plaintiff or applicant)

*delete if not applicable.

FORM 2

Request For Service Of Default Judgment On A Foreign State

TO: The Attorney-General of the Commonwealth

In a proceeding in (name of court, tribunal, etc.), a judgment in default of appearance has been given against (name of foreign State).

The proceeding concerns (short particulars of the claim against the foreign State).

In accordance with section 28 of the Foreign States Immunities Act 1985, enclose are:

(a) a copy of the judgment, authenticated as required by that Act;
(b) *a translation of the judgment into (name of language), an official language of the foreign State; and
(c) *a certificate signed by the translator,

and it is requested that the judgment, *the translation and the certificate be transmitted by the Department of Foreign Affairs to the department or organ of the foreign State that is equivalent to that Department.

It is further requested that, when service of the judgment and other documents has been effected on the foreign State in accordance with that Act, the Minister for Foreign Affairs certify accordingly under section 40 of that Act, and forward the certificate to (name and address of person to whom certificate of service should be forwarded).

DATED this day of 19

(signature of judgment creditor)

5.067   **Canada: State Immunity Act[7]**

CHAPTER S-18

An Act to provide for state immunity in Canadian courts

SHORT TITLE

5.067 *Short title*

1. This Act may be cited as the *State Immunity Act*.
1980-81-82-83, c. 95, s. 1

INTERPRETATION

5.068 *Definitions*

2. In this Act,

"agency of a foreign state" *«organisme d'un État étranger»*

"agency of a foreign state" means any legal entity that is an organ of the foreign state but that is separate from the foreign state;

"commercial activity" *«activité commerciale»*

"commercial activity" means any particular transaction, act or conduct or any regular course of conduct that by reason of its nature is of a commercial character;

"foreign state" *«État étranger»*

"foreign state" includes

(*a*) any sovereign or other head of the foreign state or of any political subdivision of the foreign state while acting as such in a public capacity,

(*b*) any government of the foreign state or of any political subdivision of the foreign state, including any of its departments, and any agency of the foreign state, and

(*c*) any political subdivision of the foreign state;

"political subdivision" *«subdivision politique»*

"political subdivision" means a province, state or other like political subdivision of a foreign state that is a federal state.

1980-81-82-83, c. 95, s. 2

---

[7] R.S.,1985, c S-18, as amended. Originally codified in 1980 (1980–81–82–83), c 95. Source: http://laws.justice.gc.ca/en/S-18/93811.html (Consolidated Statutes and Regulations, maintained by the Department of Justice). See http://www.canliiorg/ca/sta/s-18/whole.html

STATE IMMUNITY

State immunity

3. (1) Except as provided by this Act, a foreign state is immune from the jurisdiction of any court in Canada.

Court to give effect to immunity

(2) In any proceedings before a court, the court shall give effect to the immunity conferred on a foreign state by subsection (1) notwithstanding that the state has failed to take any step in the proceedings.

Immunity waived

4. (1) A foreign state is not immune from the jurisdiction of a court if the state waives the immunity conferred by subsection 3(1) by submitting to the jurisdiction of the court in accordance with subsection (2) or (4).

State submits to jurisdiction

(2) In any proceedings before a court, a foreign state submits to the jurisdiction of the court where it

(*a*) explicitly submits to the jurisdiction of the court by written agreement or otherwise either before or after the proceedings commence;

(*b*) initiates the proceedings in the court; or

(*c*) intervenes or takes any step in the proceedings before the court.

Exception

(3) Paragraph (2)(*c*) does not apply to

(*a*) any intervention or step taken by a foreign state in proceedings before a court for the purpose of claiming immunity from the jurisdiction of the court; or

(*b*) any step taken by a foreign state in ignorance of facts entitling it to immunity if those facts could not reasonably have been ascertained before the step was taken and immunity is claimed as soon as reasonably practicable after they are ascertained.

Third party proceedings and counter-claims

(4) A foreign state that initiates proceedings in a court or that intervenes or takes any step in proceedings before a court, other than an intervention or step to which paragraph (2)(*c*) does not apply, submits to the jurisdiction of the court in respect of any third party proceedings that arise, or counter-claim that

arises, out of the subject-matter of the proceedings initiated by the state or in which the state has so intervened or taken a step.

Appeal and review

(5) Where, in any proceedings before a court, a foreign state submits to the jurisdiction of the court in accordance with subsection (2) or (4), that submission is deemed to be a submission by the state to the jurisdiction of such one or more courts by which those proceedings may, in whole or in part, subsequently be considered on appeal or in the exercise of supervisory jurisdiction.

1980-81-82-83, c. 95, s. 4.

5.071 ### Commercial activity

5. A foreign state is not immune from the jurisdiction of a court in any proceedings that relate to any commercial activity of the foreign state.

1980-81-82-83, c. 95, s. 5.

5.072 ### Death and property damage

6. A foreign state is not immune from the jurisdiction of a court in any proceedings that relate to

(*a*) any death or personal or bodily injury, or
(*b*) any damage to or loss of property

that occurs in Canada.

R.S., 1985, c. S-18, s. 6, as amended by Federal Law—Civil Law Harmonization Act, No. 1 2001, c. 4, s. 121.

5.073 ### Maritime law

7. (1) A foreign state is not immune from the jurisdiction of a court in any proceedings that relate to

(*a*) an action *in rem* against a ship owned or operated by the state, or
(*b*) an action *in personam* for enforcing a claim in connection with a ship owned or operated by the state,

if, at the time the claim arose or the proceedings were commenced, the ship was being used or was intended for use in a commercial activity.

5.074 ### Cargo

(2) A foreign state is not immune from the jurisdiction of a court in any proceedings that relate to

(*a*) an action *in rem* against any cargo owned by the state if, at the time the claim arose or the proceedings were commenced, the cargo and the ship carrying the cargo were being used or were intended for use in a commercial activity; or

(*b*) an action *in personam* for enforcing a claim in connection with any cargo owned by the state if, at the time the claim arose or the proceedings were commenced, the ship carrying the cargo was being used or was intended for use in a commercial activity.

Idem

(3) For the purposes of subsections (1) and (2), a ship or cargo owned by a foreign state includes any ship or cargo in the possession or control of the state and any ship or cargo in which the state claims an interest.

1980-81-82-83, c. 95, s. 7.

Property in Canada

5.074

8. A foreign state is not immune from the jurisdiction of a court in any proceedings that relate to an interest of the state in property that arises by way of succession, gift or *bona vacantia*.

1980-81-82-83, c. 95, s. 8.

PROCEDURE AND RELIEF

Service on a foreign state

5.075

9. (1) Service of an originating document on a foreign state, other than on an agency of the foreign state, may be made

(*a*) in any manner agreed on by the state;
(*b*) in accordance with any international Convention to which the state is a party; or
(*c*) in the manner provided in subsection (2).

Idem

(2) For the purposes of paragraph (1)(*c*), anyone wishing to serve an originating document on a foreign state may deliver a copy of the document, in person or by registered mail, to the Deputy Minister of Foreign Affairs or a person designated by him for the purpose, who shall transmit it to the foreign state.

Service on an agency of a foreign state

(3) Service of an originating document on an agency of a foreign state may be made

(*a*) in any manner agreed on by the agency;
(*b*) in accordance with any international Convention applicable to the agency; or
(*c*) in accordance with any applicable rules of court.

Idem

(4) Where service on an agency of a foreign state cannot be made under subsection (3), a court may, by order, direct how service is to be made.

Date of service

(5) Where service of an originating document is made in the manner provided in subsection (2), service of the document shall be deemed to have been made on the day that the Deputy Minister of Foreign Affairs or a person designated by him pursuant to subsection (2) certifies to the relevant court that the copy of the document has been transmitted to the foreign state.

R.S., 1985, c. S-18, s. 9, as amended by Department of Foreign Affairs and International Trade Act 1995, c. 5, s. 27.

5.076 *Default judgment*

10. (1) Where, in any proceedings in a court, service of an originating document has been made on a foreign state in accordance with subsection 9(1), (3) or (4) and the state has failed to take, within the time limited therefor by the rules of the court or otherwise by law, the initial step required of a defendant or respondent in those proceedings in that court, no further step toward judgment may be taken in the proceedings except after the expiration of at least sixty days following the date of service of the originating document.

Idem

(2) Where judgment is signed against a foreign state in any proceedings in which the state has failed to take the initial step referred to in subsection (1), a certified copy of the judgment shall be served on the foreign state

(*a*) where service of the document that originated the proceedings was made on an agency of the foreign state, in such manner as is ordered by the court; or

(*b*) in any other case, in the manner specified in paragraph 9(1)(*c*) as though the judgment were an originating document.

Idem

(3) Where, by reason of subsection (2), a certified copy of a judgment is required to be served in the manner specified in paragraph 9(1)(*c*), subsections 9(2) and (5) apply with such modifications as the circumstances require.

Application to set aside default judgment

(4) A foreign state may, within sixty days after service on it of a certified copy of a judgment pursuant to subsection (2), apply to have the judgment set aside.

1980-81-82-83, c. 95, s. 9.

5.077

No injunction, specific performance, etc., without consent

11. (1) Subject to subsection (3), no relief by way of an injunction, specific performance or the recovery of land or other property may be granted against a foreign state unless the state consents in writing to that relief and, where the state so consents, the relief granted shall not be greater than that consented to by the state.

Submission not consent

(2) Submission by a foreign state to the jurisdiction of a court is not consent for the purposes of subsection (1).

Agency of a foreign state

(3) This section does not apply to an agency of a foreign state.

1980-81-82-83, c. 95, s. 10.

5.078

Execution

12. (1) Subject to subsections (2) and (3), property of a foreign state that is located in Canada is immune from attachment and execution and, in the case of an action *in rem*, from arrest, detention, seizure and forfeiture except where

(*a*) the state has, either explicitly or by implication, waived its immunity from attachment, execution, arrest, detention, seizure or forfeiture, unless the foreign state has withdrawn the waiver of immunity in accordance with any term thereof that permits such withdrawal;

(*b*) the property is used or is intended for a commercial activity; or

(*c*) the execution relates to a judgment establishing rights in property that has been acquired by succession or gift or in immovable property located in Canada.

Property of an agency of a foreign state is not immune

(2) Subject to subsection (3), property of an agency of a foreign state is not immune from attachment and execution and, in the case of an action *in rem*, from arrest, detention, seizure and forfeiture, for the purpose of satisfying a judgment of a court in any proceedings in respect of which the agency is not immune from the jurisdiction of the court by reason of any provision of this Act.

Military property

(3) Property of a foreign state

(*a*) that is used or is intended to be used in connection with a military activity, and

(*b*) that is military in nature or is under the control of a military authority or defence agency is immune from attachment and execution and, in the case of an action *in rem*, from arrest, detention, seizure and forfeiture.

Property of a foreign central bank immune

(4) Subject to subsection (5), property of a foreign central bank or monetary authority that is held for its own account and is not used or intended for a commercial activity is immune from attachment and execution.

Waiver of immunity

(5) The immunity conferred on property of a foreign central bank or monetary authority by subsection (4) does not apply where the bank, authority or its parent foreign government has explicitly waived the immunity, unless the bank, authority or government has withdrawn the waiver of immunity in accordance with any term thereof that permits such withdrawal.

1980-81-82-83, c. 95, s. 11.

5.079 ### No fine for failure to produce

13. (1) No penalty or fine may be imposed by a court against a foreign state for any failure or refusal by the state to produce any document or other information in the course of proceedings before the court.

Agency of a foreign state

(2) Subsection (1) does not apply to an agency of a foreign state.

1980-81-82-83, c. 95, s. 12.

GENERAL

5.080 ### Certificate is conclusive evidence

14. (1) A certificate issued by the Minister of Foreign Affairs, or on his behalf by a person authorized by him, with respect to any of the following questions, namely,

(*a*) whether a country is a foreign state for the purposes of this Act,

(*b*) whether a particular area or territory of a foreign state is a political subdivision of that state, or

(*c*) whether a person or persons are to be regarded as the head or government of a foreign state or of a political subdivision of the foreign state,

is admissible in evidence as conclusive proof of any matter stated in the certificate with respect to that question, without proof of the signature of the Minister of Foreign Affairs or other person or of that other person's authorization by the Minister of Foreign Affairs.

Idem

(2) A certificate issued by the Deputy Minister of Foreign Affairs, or on his behalf by a person designated by him pursuant to subsection 9(2), with respect to service of an originating or other document on a foreign state in accordance with that subsection is admissible in evidence as conclusive proof of any matter stated in the certificate with respect to that service, without proof of the signature of the Deputy Minister of Foreign Affairs or other person or of that other person's authorization by the Deputy Minister of Foreign Affairs.

R.S., 1985, c. S-18, s. 14, as amended by Department of Foreign Affairs and International Trade Act 1995, c. 5, ss. 25, 27.

Governor in Council may restrict immunity by order

5.081

15. The Governor in Council may, on the recommendation of the Minister of Foreign Affairs, by order restrict any immunity or privileges under this Act in relation to a foreign state where, in the opinion of the Governor in Council, the immunity or privileges exceed those accorded by the law of that state.[8]

R.S., 1985, c. S-18, s. 15, as amended by Department of Foreign Affairs and International Trade Act 1995, c. 5, s. 25.

Inconsistency

5.082

16. If, in any proceeding or other matter to which a provision of this Act and a provision of the *Extradition Act*, the *Visiting Forces Act* or the *Foreign Missions and International Organizations Act* apply, there is a conflict between those provisions, the provision of this Act does not apply in the proceeding or other matter to the extent of the conflict.

R.S., 1985, c. S-18, s. 16, as inserted by Crimes Against Humanity and War Crimes Act 2000, c. 24, s. 70.

Rules of court not affected

5.083

17. Except to the extent required to give effect to this Act, nothing in this Act shall be construed or applied so as to negate or affect any rules of a court, including rules of a court relating to service of a document out of the jurisdiction of the court.

1980-81-82-83, c. 95, s. 16.

Application

5.084

18. This Act does not apply to criminal proceedings or proceedings in the nature of criminal proceedings.

1980-81-82-83, c. 95, s. 17.

---

[8] See Order Restricting Certain Immunity in Relation to the United States (PC 1997-242, 18 February 1997).

5.085 ## Pakistan: The State Immunity Ordinance

Ordinance No. VI of 1981

AN ORDINANCE

To amend and consolidate the law relating to the immunity of States from the jurisdiction of courts

Whereas it is expedient to amend and consolidate the law relating to the immunity of States from the jurisdiction of courts;

And whereas the President is satisfied that circumstances exist which render it necessary to take immediate action;

Now, therefore, in pursuance of the Proclamation of the fifth day of July, 1977, read with the Laws (Continuance in Force) Order, 1977 (C.M.L.A. Order No. 1 of 1977), and in exercise of all powers enabling him in that behalf, the President is pleased to make and promulgate the following Ordinance:

5.086   1. *Short title, extend*[9] *and commencement.* (1) This Ordinance may be called the State Immunity Ordinance, 1981.

(2) It extends to the whole of Pakistan.

(3) It shall come into force at once.

5.087   2. *Interpretation.* In this Ordinance, "court" includes any tribunal or body exercising judicial functions.

Immunity from jurisdiction

5.088   3. *General immunity from jurisdiction.* (1) A State is immune from the jurisdiction of the courts of Pakistan except as hereinafter provided.

(2) A court shall give effect to the immunity conferred by subsection (1) even if the State does not appear in the proceedings in question.

Exceptions from Immunity

5.089   4. *Submission to jurisdiction.* (1) A State is not immune as respects proceedings in respect of which it has submitted to jurisdiction.

(2) A State may submit to jurisdiction after the dispute giving rise to the proceedings has arisen or by a prior agreement; but a provision in any agreement that it is to be governed by the law of Pakistan shall not be deemed to be a submission.

Explanation In this subsection and in subsection (3) of section 14, "agreement" includes a treaty, convention or other international agreement.

---

[9] *Sic*

(2) A State shall be deemed to have submitted:

(a) if it has instituted the proceedings; or

(b) subject to subsection (4) it has intervened or taken any step in the proceedings.

(3) Clause (b) of subsection (3) does not apply:

(a) to intervention or any step taken for the purpose only of:

(i) claiming immunity; or

(ii) asserting an interest in property in circumstances such that the State would have been entitled to immunity if the proceedings had been brought against it; or

(b) to any step taken by the State in ignorance of the facts entitling it to immunity if those facts could not reasonable have been ascertained and immunity is claimed as soon as reasonable practicable.

(4) A submission in respect of any proceedings extends to any appeal but not to any counter claim unless it arises out of the same legal relationship or facts as the claim.

(5) The head of a State's diplomatic mission in Pakistan, or the person for the time being performing his functions, shall be deemed to have authority to submit on behalf of the State in respect of any proceedings; and any person who has entered into a contract on behalf of and with the authority of a State shall be deemed to have authority to submit on its behalf in respect of proceedings arising out of the contract.

5. *Commercial transactions and contracts to be performed in Pakistan.* (1) A State is not immune as respects proceedings relating to: **5.090**

(a) a commercial transaction entered into by the State; or

(b) an obligation of the State which by virtue of a contract, which may or may not be a commercial transaction, falls to be performed wholly or partly in Pakistan.

(2) Subsection (1) does not apply to a contract of employment between a State and an individual or if the parties to the dispute are States or have otherwise agreed in writing; and clause (b) of that subsection does not apply if the contract, not being a commercial transaction, was made in the territory of the State concerned and the obligation in question is governed by its administrative law.

(3) In this section "commercial transaction" means:

(a) any contract for the supply of goods or services;

(b) any loan or other transaction for the provision of finance and any guarantee or indemnity in respect of any such transaction or of any other financial obligation; and

(c) any other transaction or activity, whether of a commercial, industrial, financial, professional or other similar character, into which a State enters or in which it engages otherwise than in the exercise of its sovereign authority.

5.091 6. *Contracts of employment.* (1) A State is not immune as respects proceedings relating to a contract of employment between a State and an individual where the contract was made, or the work is to be wholly or partly performed, in Pakistan.

Explanation. In this subsection, "proceedings relating to a contract of employment" includes proceedings between the parties to such a contract in respect of any statutory rights or duties to which they are entitled or subject as employer or employee.

(2) Subject to subsections (3) and (4), subsection (1) does not apply if:

(a) at the time when the proceedings are brought the individual is a national of the State concerned; or

(b) at the time when the contract was made the individual was neither a citizen of Pakistan nor habitually resident in Pakistan; or

(c) the parties to the contract have otherwise agreed in writing.

(3) Where the work is for an office, agency or establishment maintained by the State in Pakistan for commercial purposes, clauses (a) and (b) of subsection (2) do not exclude the application of subsection (1) unless the individual was, at the time when the contract was made, habitually resident in that State.

(4) Clause (c) of subsection (2) does not exclude the application of subsection (1) where the law of Pakistan requires the proceedings to be brought before a court in Pakistan.

5.092 7. *Ownership, possession and use of property.* (1) A State is not immune as respects proceedings relating to:

(a) any interest of the State in, or its possession or use of, immovable property in Pakistan; or

(b) any obligation of the State arising out of its interest in, or its possession or use of, any such property.

(2) A State is not immune as respects proceedings, relating to any interest of the State in movable or immovable property, being an interest arising by way of succession, gift or *bona vacantia*.

(3) The fact that a State has or claims an interest in any property shall not preclude any court from exercising in respect of such property any jurisdiction relating to the estates of deceased persons or persons of unsound mind or to insolvency, the winding up of companies or the administration of trusts.

(4) A court may entertain proceedings against a person other than a State notwithstanding that the proceedings relate to property:

(a) which is in the possession of a State; or

(b) in which a State claims an interest,

if the State would not have been immune had the proceedings been brought against it or, in a case referred to in clause (b), if the claim is neither admitted nor supported by prima facie evidence.

8. *Patents, trade marks, etc.* A State is not immune as respects proceedings relating to: **5.093**

(a) any patent, trade mark, design or plant breeders' rights belonging to the State which are registered or protected in Pakistan or for which the State has applied in Pakistan;

(b) an alleged infringement by the State in Pakistan of any patent, trade mark, design, plant breeders' rights or copyright; or

(c) the right to use a trade or business name in Pakistan.

9. *Membership of bodies corporate, etc.* (1) A State is not immune as respects proceedings relating to its membership of a body corporate, an unincorporated body or a partnership which: **5.094**

(a) has members other than States; and

(b) is incorporated or constituted under the law of Pakistan or is controlled from, or has its principal place of business in, Pakistan,

being proceedings arising between the State and the body or its other members or, as the case may be, between the State and the other partners.

(2) Subsection (1) does not apply if provision to the contrary has been made by an agreement in writing between the parties to the dispute or by the constitution or other instrument establishing or regulating the body or partnership in question.

10. *Arbitrations.* (1) Where a State has agreed in writing to submit a dispute which has arisen, or may arise, to arbitration, the State is not immune as respects proceedings in the courts of Pakistan which relate to the arbitration. **5.095**

(2) Subsection (1) has effect subject to the provisions of the arbitration agreement and does not apply to an arbitration agreement between States.

11. *Ships used for commercial purposes.* (1) The succeeding provisions of this section apply to: **5.096**

(a) Admiralty proceedings; and

(b) Proceedings on any claim which could be made the subject of Admiralty proceedings.

(2) A State is not immune as respects:

(a) an action in rem against a ship belonging to it; or

(b) an action in personam for enforcing a claim in connection with such a ship;

if, at the time when the cause of action arose, the ship was in use or intended for use for commercial purposes.

(3) Where an action in rem is brought against a ship belonging to a State for enforcing a claim in connection with another ship belonging to that State clause (a) of subsection (2) does not apply as respects the first-mentioned ship unless, at the time when the cause of action relating to the other ship arose, both ships were in use or intended for use for commercial purposes.

(4) A State is not immune as respects:

(a) an action in rem against a cargo belonging to that State if both the cargo and the ship carrying it were, at the time when the cause of action arose, in use or intended for use for commercial purposes; or

(b) an action in personam for enforcing a claim in connection with such a cargo if the ship carrying it was then in use or intended for use as aforesaid.

(5) In the foregoing provisions references to a ship or cargo belonging to a State include references to a ship or cargo in its possession or control or in which it claims an interest; and, subject to subsection (4), subsection (2) applies to property other than a ship as it applies to a ship.

(6) Section 5 and 6 do not apply to proceedings of the nature mentioned in subsection (1) if the State in question is a party to the Brussels Convention and the claim relates to the operation of a ship owned or operated by that State, the carriage of cargo or passengers on any such ship or the carriage of cargo owned by that State on any other ship.

Explanation. In this section, "Brussels Convention" means the International Convention for the Unification of Certain Rules Concerning the Immunity of State-owned Ships signed in Brussels on the tenth day of April, 1926, and "ship" includes hovercraft.

5.097 12. *Value added tax, customs-duties, etc.* A State is not immune as respects proceedings relating to its liability for;

(a) value added tax, any duty of customs or excise or any agricultural levy; or

(b) rates in respect of premises occupied by it for commercial purposes.

Procedure

5.098 13. *Services*[10] *of process and judgment in default of appearance.* (1) Any notice or other document required to be served for instituting proceedings against

---

[10] *Sic*

a State shall be served by being transmitted through the Ministry of Foreign Affairs of Pakistan to the Ministry of Foreign Affairs of the State and service shall be deemed to have been effected when the notice or document is received at the latter Ministry.

(2) Any proceedings in court shall not commence earlier than two months after the date on which the notice or document is received as aforesaid.

(3) A State which appears in proceedings cannot thereafter object that subsection (1) has not been complied with as respects those proceedings.

(4) No judgment in default of appearance shall be given against a State except on proof that subsection (1) has been complied with and that the time for the commencement of proceedings specified in subsection (2) has elapsed.

(5) A copy of any judgment given against a State in default of appearance shall be transmitted through the Ministry of Foreign Affairs of Pakistan to the Ministry of Foreign Affairs of the State and the time for applying to have the judgment set aside shall begin to run two months after the date on which the copy of the judgment is received at the latter Ministry.

(6) Subsection (1) does not prevent the service of a notice or other document in any manner to which the State has agreed and subsections (2) and (4) do not apply where service is effected in any manner.

(7) The preceding provisions of this section shall not be construed as applying to proceedings against a State by way of a counter-claim or to an action in rem.

14. *Other procedural privileges.* (1) No penalty by way of committal to prison or fine shall be imposed in respect of any failure or refusal by or on behalf of a State to disclose or produce any document or information for the purposes of proceedings to which it is a party. **5.099**

(2) Subject to subsections (3) and (4).

(a) relief shall not be given against a State by way of injunction or order for specific performance or for the recovery of land or other property; and

(b) the property of a State, not being property which is for the time being in use or intended for use for commercial purposes, shall not be subject to any process for the enforcement of a judgment or arbitration award or, in an action in rem, for its arrest, detention or sale.

(3) Subsection (2) does not prevent the giving of any relief or the issue of any process with the written consent of the State concerned; and any such consent, which may be contained in a prior agreement, may be expressed so as to apply to a limited extent or generally:

Provided that a provision merely submitting to the jurisdiction of the courts shall not be deemed to be a consent for the purposes of this subsection.

(4) The head of a State's diplomatic mission in Pakistan, or the person for the time being performing his functions, shall be deemed to have authority to give on behalf of the State any such consent as is mentioned in subsection (3) and, for the purposes of clause (b) of subsection (2), his certificate that any property is not in use or intended for use by or on behalf of the State for commercial purposes shall be accepted as sufficient evidence of that fact unless the contrary is proved.

Supplementary provisions

5.100   15. *States entitled to immunities and privileges.* (1) The immunities and privileges conferred by this Act apply to any foreign State; and references to State include references to:

(a) the sovereign or other head of that State in his public capacity;
(b) the government of that State; and
(c) any department of that government,

but not to any entity, hereinafter referred to as a "separate entity", which is distinct from the executive organs of the government of the State and capable of suing or being sued.

(2) A separate entity is immune from the jurisdiction of the courts of Pakistan if, and only if:

(a) the proceedings relate to anything done by it in the exercise of sovereign authority; and
(b) the circumstances are such that a State would have been so immune.

(3) If a separate entity, not being a State's central bank or other monetary authority, submits to the jurisdiction in respect of proceedings in the case of which it is entitled to immunity by virtue of subsection (2) of this section, the provisions of subsections (1) to (3) of section 14 shall apply to it in respect of those proceedings as if references to a State were references to that entity.

(4) Property of a State's central bank or other monetary authority shall not be regarded for the purposes of subsection (3) of section 14 as in use or intended for use for commercial purposes; and where any such bank or authority is a separate entity subsections (1) and (2) of that section shall apply to it as if references to a State were references to the bank or authority.

(5) Section 13 applies to proceedings against the constituent territories of a federal State; and the Federal Government may, by notification in the official Gazette, provide for the other provisions of this Ordinance to apply to any such constituent territory specified in the notification as they apply to a State.

(6) Where the provisions of this Ordinance do not apply to a constituent territory by virtue of a notification under subsection (5), the provisions of subsections (2) and (3) shall apply to it as if it were a separate entity.

16. *Restriction and extension of immunities and privileges.* (1) If it appears to the **5.101**
Federal Government that the immunities and privileges conferred by this
Ordinance in relation to any State:

(a) exceed those accorded by the law of that State in relation to Pakistan; or
(b) are less than those required by a treaty, convention or other international
agreement to which that State and Pakistan are parties,

the Federal Government may, by notification in the official Gazette, provide
for restricting or, as the case may be, extending those immunities and privileges
to such extent as it may deem fit.

17. *Savings, etc.* (1) This Ordinance does not affect any immunity or privi- **5.102**
lege conferred by the Diplomatic and Consular Privileges Act, 1972 (IX of
1972); and

(a) section 6 does not apply to proceedings concerning the employment of the
members of a mission within the meaning of the Convention set out in the
First Schedule to the said Act of 1972 or of the members of a consular post
within the meaning of the Convention set out in the Second Schedule to
that Act;
(b) subsection (1) of section 7 does not apply to proceedings concerning a
State's title to, or its possession of, property used for the purposes of a
diplomatic mission.

 (2) This Ordinance does not apply to:

(a) proceedings relating to anything done by or in relation to the armed forces
of a State while present in Pakistan;
(b) criminal proceedings; or
(c) proceedings relating to taxation other than those mentioned in section 12.

18. *Proof as to certain matters.* A certificate under the hand of a Secretary to the **5.103**
Government of Pakistan shall be conclusive evidence on any question.

(a) whether any country is a State for the purposes of this Ordinance, whether
any territory is a constituent territory of a federal State for those purposes
or as to the person or persons to be regarded for those purposes as the head
or government of a State; or
(b) whether, and if so when, a document has been served or received as mentioned in subsection (1) or subsection (5) of section 13.

19. *Repeal.* Sections 86 and 87 of the Code of Civil Procedure, 1908 (Act V of **5.104**
1908), are hereby repealed.

5.105 **Singapore: State Immunity Act**[11]

PART I

Preliminary

5.106 Short title and application.

1.—(1) This Act may be cited as the State Immunity Act.

(2) Subject to subsection (3), Part II does not apply to proceedings in respect of matters that occurred before the commencement of this Act and, in particular—

(a) sections 4 (2) and 15 (3) do not apply to any prior agreement; and

(b) sections 5, 6 and 11 do not apply to any transaction, contract or arbitration agreement,

entered into before that date.

(3) Section 14 applies to any proceedings instituted after the commencement of this Act.

5.107 Interpretation.

2.—(1) In this Act—

"commercial purposes" means purposes of such transactions or activities as are mentioned in section 5 (3);

"court" includes any tribunal or body exercising judicial functions;

"ship" includes hovercraft.

(2) In this Act—

(a) references to an agreement in sections 4 (2) and 15 (3) include references to a treaty, convention or other international agreement;

(b) references to entry of appearance and judgments in default of appearance include references to any corresponding procedures.

---

[11] Ch 313. Revised version, 1985. First adopted in 1979 (No. 19 of 1979), as amended by Act 25/196. Source: http://statutes.agc.gov.sg/ (Singapore Statutes Online, maintained by the Attorney General's Chambers and the Managing for Excellence Office, MOF).

PART II

Proceedings in Singapore By or Against Other States

Immunity from Jurisdiction

General immunity from jurisdiction. 5.108

3.—(1) A State is immune from the jurisdiction of the courts of Singapore except as provided in the following provisions of this Part.

(2) A court shall give effect to the immunity conferred by this section even though the State does not appear in the proceedings in question.

Exceptions from Immunity

Submission to jurisdiction. 5.109

4.—(1) A State is not immune as respects proceedings in respect of which it has submitted to the jurisdiction of the courts of Singapore.

(2) A State may submit after the dispute giving rise to the proceedings has arisen or by a prior written agreement; but a provision in any agreement that it is to be governed by the law of Singapore is not to be regarded as a submission.

(3) A State is deemed to have submitted—

(a) if it has instituted the proceedings; or
(b) subject to subsections (4) and (5), if it has intervened or taken any step in the proceedings.

(4) Subsection (3) (*b*) does not apply to intervention or any step taken for the purpose only of—

(a) claiming immunity; or
(b) asserting an interest in property in circumstances such that the State would have been entitled to immunity if the proceedings had been brought against it.

(5) Subsection (3) (*b*) does not apply to any step taken by the State in ignorance of facts entitling it to immunity if those facts could not reasonably have been ascertained and immunity is claimed as soon as reasonably practicable.

(6) A submission in respect of any proceedings extends to any appeal but not to any counter-claim unless it arises out of the same legal relationship or facts as the claim.

(7) The head of a State's diplomatic mission in Singapore, or the person for the time being performing his functions, shall be deemed to have authority to submit on behalf of the State in respect of any proceedings; and any person who has entered into a contract on behalf of and with the authority of a State shall

be deemed to have authority to submit on its behalf in respect of proceedings arising out of the contract.

5.110 Commercial transactions and contracts to be performed in Singapore.

5.—(1) A State is not immune as respects proceedings relating to—

(a) a commercial transaction entered into by the State; or

(b) an obligation of the State which by virtue of a contract (whether a commercial transaction or not) falls to be performed wholly or partly in Singapore,

but this subsection does not apply to a contract of employment between a State and an individual.

(2) This section does not apply if the parties to the dispute are States or have otherwise agreed in writing; and subsection (1) (*b*) does not apply if the contract (not being a commercial transaction) was made in the territory of the State concerned and the obligation in question is governed by its administrative law.

(3) In this section "commercial transaction" means—

(a) any contract for the supply of goods or services;

(b) any loan or other transaction for the provision of finance and any guarantee or indemnity in respect of any such transaction or of any other financial obligation; and

(c) any other transaction or activity (whether of a commercial, industrial, financial, professional or other similar character) into which a State enters or in which it engages otherwise than in the exercise of sovereign authority.

5.111 Contracts of employment.

6.—(1) A State is not immune as respects proceedings relating to a contract of employment between the State and an individual where the contract was made in Singapore or the work is to be wholly or partly performed in Singapore.

(2) Subject to subsections (3) and (4), this section does not apply if—

(a) at the time when the proceedings are brought the individual is a national of the State concerned;

(b) at the time when the contract was made the individual was neither a citizen of Singapore nor habitually resident in Singapore; or

(c) the parties to the contract have otherwise agreed in writing.

(3) Where the work is for an office, agency or establishment maintained by the State in Singapore for commercial purposes, subsection (2) (*a*) and (*b*) does not exclude the application of this section unless the individual was, at the time when the contract was made, habitually resident in that State.

(4) Subsection (2) (*c*) does not exclude the application of this section where the law of Singapore requires the proceedings to be brought before a court in Singapore.

(5) In this section, "proceedings relating to a contract of employment" includes proceedings between the parties to such a contract in respect of any statutory rights or duties to which they are entitled or subject as employer or employee.

Personal injuries and damage to property.   5.112

7. A State is not immune as respects proceedings in respect of—

(a) death or personal injury; or
(b) damage to or loss of tangible property,

caused by an act or omission in Singapore.

Ownership, possession and use of property.   5.113

8.—(1) A State is not immune as respects proceedings relating to—

(a) any interest of the State in, or its possession or use of, immovable property in Singapore; or
(b) any obligation of the State arising out of its interest in, or its possession or use of, any such property.

(2) A State is not immune as respects proceedings relating to any interest of the State in movable or immovable property, being an interest arising by way of succession, gift or *bona vacantia*.

(3) The fact that a State has or claims an interest in any property shall not preclude any court from exercising in respect of it any jurisdiction relating to the estates of deceased persons or persons of unsound mind or to insolvency, the winding up of companies or the administration of trusts.

(4) A court may entertain proceedings against a person other than a State notwithstanding that the proceedings relate to property—

(a) which is in the possession or control of a State; or
(b) in which a State claims an interest,

if the State would not have been immune had the proceedings been brought against it or, in a case within paragraph (*b*), if the claim is neither admitted nor supported by prima facie evidence.

Patents, trademarks, etc.   5.114

9. A State is not immune as respects proceedings relating to—

(a) any patent, trademark or design belonging to the State and registered or protected in Singapore or for which the State has applied in Singapore;

(b) an alleged infringement by the State in Singapore of any patent, trademark, design or copyright; or

(c) the right to use a trade or business name in Singapore.

5.115 **Membership of bodies corporate, etc.**

10.—(1) A State is not immune as respects proceedings relating to its membership of a body corporate, an unincorporated body or a partnership which—

(a) has members other than States; and

(b) is incorporated or constituted under the law of Singapore or is controlled from or has its principal place of business in Singapore,

being proceedings arising between the State and the body or its other members or, as the case may be, between the State and the other partners.

(2) This section does not apply if provision to the contrary has been made by an agreement in writing between the parties to the dispute or by the constitution or other instrument establishing or regulating the body or partnership in question.

5.116 **Arbitrations.**

11.—(1) Where a State has agreed in writing to submit a dispute which has arisen, or may arise, to arbitration, the State is not immune as respects proceedings in the courts in Singapore which relate to the arbitration.

(2) This section has effect subject to any contrary provision in the arbitration agreement and does not apply to any arbitration agreement between States.

5.117 **Ships used for commercial purposes.**

12.—(1) This section applies to—

(a) Admiralty proceedings; and

(b) proceedings on any claim which could be made the subject of Admiralty proceedings.

(2) A State is not immune as respects—

(a) an action *in rem* against a ship belonging to that State; or

(b) an action *in personam* for enforcing a claim in connection with such a ship,

if, at the time when the cause of action arose, the ship was in use or intended for use for commercial purposes.

(3) Where an action *in rem* is brought against a ship belonging to a State for enforcing a claim in connection with another ship belonging to that State, subsection (2) (*a*) does not apply as respects the first-mentioned ship unless, at the

time when the cause of action relating to the other ship arose, both ships were in use or intended for use for commercial purposes.

(4) A State is not immune as respects—

(a) an action *in rem* against a cargo belonging to that State if both the cargo and the ship carrying it were, at the time when the cause of action arose, in use or intended for use for commercial purposes; or

(b) an action *in personam* for enforcing a claim in connection with such a cargo if the ship carrying it was then in use or intended for use as aforesaid.

(5) In subsections (2) to (4) references to a ship or cargo belonging to a State include references to a ship or cargo in its possession or control or in which it claims an interest; and, subject to subsection (4), subsection (2) applies to property other than a ship as it applies to a ship.

Customs duties, etc.

5.118

13. A State is not immune as respects proceedings relating to its liability for—

(a) any customs duty or excise duty;
(aa) any goods and services tax; or
(b) any tax in respect of premises occupied by it for commercial purposes.[12]

Procedure

Service of process and judgments in default of appearance.

5.119

14.—(1) Any writ or other document required to be served for instituting proceedings against a State shall be served by being transmitted through the Ministry of Foreign Affairs, Singapore, to the ministry of foreign affairs of the State and service shall be deemed to have been effected when the writ or document is received at that ministry.

(2) Any time for entering an appearance (whether prescribed by Rules of Court or otherwise) shall begin to run two months after the date on which the writ or document is received as aforesaid.

(3) A State which appears in proceedings cannot thereafter object that subsection (1) has not been complied with in the case of those proceedings.

(4) No judgment in default of appearance shall be given against a State except on proof that subsection (1) has been complied with and that the time for entering an appearance as extended by subsection (2) has expired.

---

[12] As amended by Act 25/96 with effect from 16 August 1996.

(5) A copy of any judgment given against a State in default of appearance shall be transmitted through the Ministry of Foreign Affairs, Singapore, to the ministry of foreign affairs of that State and any time for applying to have the judgment set aside (whether prescribed by Rules of Court or otherwise) shall begin to run two months after the date on which the copy of the judgment is received at that ministry.

(6) Subsection (1) does not prevent the service of a writ or other document in any manner to which the State has agreed and subsections (2) and (4) do not apply where service is effected in any such manner.

(7) This section shall not be construed as applying to proceedings against a State by way of counter-claim or to an action *in rem*; and subsection (1) shall not be construed as affecting any Rules of Court whereby leave is required for the service of process outside the jurisdiction.

5.120 Other procedural privileges.

15.—(1) No penalty by way of committal or fine shall be imposed in respect of any failure or refusal by or on behalf of a State to disclose or produce any document or other information for the purposes of proceedings to which it is a party.

(2) Subject to subsections (3) and (4)—

(a) relief shall not be given against a State by way of injunction or order for specific performance or for the recovery of land or other property; and

(b) the property of a State shall not be subject to any process for the enforcement of a judgment or arbitration award or, in an action *in rem*, for its arrest, detention or sale.

(3) Subsection (2) does not prevent the giving of any relief or the issue of any process with the written consent of the State concerned; and any such consent (which may be contained in a prior agreement) may be expressed so as to apply to a limited extent or generally; but a provision merely submitting to the jurisdiction of the courts is not to be regarded as a consent for the purposes of this subsection.

(4) Subsection (2) (*b*) does not prevent the issue of any process in respect of property which is for the time being in use or intended for use for commercial purposes.

(5) The head of a State's diplomatic mission in Singapore, or the person for the time being performing his functions, shall be deemed to have authority to give on behalf of the State any such consent as is mentioned in subsection (3)

and, for the purposes of subsection (4), his certificate to the effect that any property is not in use or intended for use by or on behalf of the State for commercial purposes shall be accepted as sufficient evidence of that fact unless the contrary is proved.

PART III

Supplementary Provisions

States entitled to immunities and privileges. 5.121

16.—(1) The immunities and privileges conferred by Part II apply to any foreign or Commonwealth State other than Singapore; and references to a State include references to—

(a) the sovereign or other head of that State in his public capacity;
(b) the government of that State; and
(c) any department of that government,

but not to any entity (referred to in this section as a separate entity) which is distinct from the executive organs of the government of the State and capable of suing or being sued.

(2) A separate entity is immune from the jurisdiction of the courts in Singapore if, and only if—

(a) the proceedings relate to anything done by it in the exercise of sovereign authority; and
(b) the circumstances are such that a State would have been so immune.

(3) If a separate entity (not being a State's central bank or other monetary authority) submits to the jurisdiction in respect of proceedings in the case of which it is entitled to immunity by virtue of subsection (2), section 15 (1) to (4) shall apply to it in respect of those proceedings as if references to a State were references to that entity.

(4) Property of a State's central bank or other monetary authority shall not be regarded for the purposes of section 15 (4) as in use or intended for use for commercial purposes; and where any such bank or authority is a separate entity section 15 (1) to (3) shall apply to it as if references to a State were references to the bank or authority.

(5) Section 14 applies to proceedings against the constituent territories of a federal State; and the President may by order provide for the other provisions of this Part to apply to any such constituent territory specified in the order as they apply to a State.

(6) Where the provisions of Part II do not apply to a constituent territory by virtue of any such order subsections (2) and (3) shall apply to it as if it were a separate entity.

5.122   Restriction and extension of immunities and privileges.

17. If it appears to the President that the immunities and privileges conferred by Part II in relation to any State—

(a) exceed those accorded by the law of that State in relation to Singapore; or

(b) are less than those required by any treaty, convention or other international agreement to which that State and Singapore are parties,

the President may, by order, provide for restricting or, as the case may be, extending those immunities and privileges to such extent as appears to the President to be appropriate.

5.123   Evidence by certificate.

18. A certificate by or on behalf of the Minister for Foreign Affairs shall be conclusive evidence on any question—

(a) whether any country is a State for the purposes of Part II, whether any territory is a constituent territory of a federal State for those purposes or as to the person or persons to be regarded for those purposes as the head or government of a State;

(b) whether, and if so when, a document has been served or received as mentioned in section 14 (1) or (5).

5.124   Excluded matters.

19.—(1) Part II does not affect any immunity or privilege applicable in Singapore to diplomatic and consular agents, and section 8 (1) does not apply to proceedings concerning a State's title to or its possession of property used for the purposes of a diplomatic mission.

(2) Part II does not apply to—

(a) proceedings relating to anything done by or in relation to the armed forces of a State while present in Singapore and, in particular, has effect subject to the Visiting Forces Act;

Cap. 344.

(b) criminal proceedings; and

(c) proceedings relating to taxation other than those mentioned in section 13.

South Africa: Foreign States Immunities Act[13]   **5.125**

NO 87 OF 1981

as amended by Foreign States Immunities Amendment Act, No. 48 of 1985[14]

ACT

To determine the extent of the immunity of foreign states from the jurisdiction of the courts of the Republic; and to provide for matters connected therewith.

1. *Definitions.*—(1) In this Act, unless the context otherwise indicates—   **5.126**

"commercial purposes" means purposes of any commercial transaction as defined in section 4(3);

"consular post" means a consulate-general, consulate, consular agency, trade office or labour office;

"Republic" includes the territorial waters of the Republic, as defined in section 2 of the Territorial Waters Act, 1963 (Act No. 87 or 1963);

"separate entity" means an entity referred to in subsection (2)(I).

(2) Any reference in this Act to a foreign state shall in relation to any particular foreign state be construed as including a reference to—

(a) the head of state of that foreign state, in his capacity as such head of state;
(b) the government of that foreign state; and
(c) any department of that government,

but not as including a reference to—

(i)   any entity which is distinct from the executive organs of the government of that foreign state and capable of suing or being sued; or
(ii) any territory forming a constituent part of a federal foreign state.

2. *General immunity from jurisdiction.*—(1) A foreign state shall be immune   **5.127** from the jurisdiction of the courts of the Republic except as provided in this Act or in any proclamation issued thereunder.

(2) A court shall give effect to the immunity conferred by this section even though the foreign state does not appear in the proceedings in question.

(3) The provisions of this Act shall not be construed as subjecting any foreign state to the criminal jurisdiction of the courts of the Republic.

---

[13] Assented to: 6 October 1981. Date of commencement: 20 November 1981. English translation of Afrikaans text signed by the State president.
[14] See 5.144 below. See the further amendments contained in the Foreign States Immunities Amendment Act No. 5 of 1988 (at 5.145 below), but not yet in operation.

5.128 3. *Waiver of immunity.*—(1) A foreign state shall not be immune from the jurisdiction of the courts of the Republic in proceedings in respect of which the foreign state has expressly waived its immunity or is in terms of subsection (3) deemed to have waived its immunity.

(2) Waiver of immunity may be effected after the dispute which gave rise to the proceedings has arisen or by prior written agreement, but a provision in an agreement that it is to be governed by the law of the Republic shall not be regarded as a waiver.

(3) A foreign state shall be deemed to have waived its immunity—

(a) if it has instituted the proceedings; or
(b) subject to the provisions of subsection (4), if it has intervened or taken any step in the proceedings.

(4) Subsection (3)(b) shall not apply to intervention or any step taken for the purpose only of—

(a) claiming immunity; or
(b) asserting an interest in property in circumstances such that the foreign state would have been entitled to immunity if the proceedings had been brought against it.

(5) A waiver in respect of any proceedings shall apply to any appeal and to any counter-claim arising out of the same legal relationship or facts as the claim.

(6) The head of a foreign state's diplomatic mission in the Republic, or the person for the time being performing his functions, shall be deemed to have authority to waive on behalf of the foreign state its immunity in respect of any proceedings, and any person who has entered into a contract on behalf of and with the authority of a foreign state shall be deemed to have authority to waive on behalf of the foreign state its immunity in respect of proceedings arising out of the contract.

5.129 4. *Commercial transactions.*—(1) A foreign state shall not be immune from the jurisdiction of the courts of the Republic in proceedings relating to—

(a) a commercial transaction entered into by the foreign state; or
(b) an obligation of the State which by virtue of a contract (whether a commercial transaction or not) falls to be performed wholly or partly in the Republic.

(2) Subsection (1) shall not apply if the parties to the dispute are foreign states or have agreed in writing that the dispute shall be justiciable by the courts of a foreign state.

(3) In subsection (1) "commercial transaction" means—

(a) any contract for the supply of services or goods;

(b) any loan or other transaction for the provision of finance and any guarantee or indemnity in respect of any such loan or other transaction or of any other financial obligation; and

(c) any other transaction or activity or a commercial, industrial, financial, professional or other similar character into which a foreign state enters or in which it engages otherwise than in the exercise of sovereign authority,

but does not include a contract of employment between a foreign state and an individual.

5. *Contracts of employment.*—(1) a foreign state shall not be immune from the jurisdiction of the courts of the Republic in proceedings relating to a contract of employment between the foreign state and an individual if— **5.130**

(a) the contract was entered into in the Republic or the work is to be performed wholly or partly in the Republic; and

(b) at the time when the contract was entered into the individual was a South African citizen or was ordinarily resident in the Republic; and

(c) at the time when the proceedings are brought the individual is not a citizen of the foreign state.

   (2) Subsection (1) shall not apply if—

(a) the parties to the contract have agreed in writing that the dispute or any dispute relating to the contract shall be justiciable by the courts of a foreign state; or

(b) the proceedings relate to the employment of the head of a diplomatic mission or any member of the diplomatic mission or any member of the diplomatic, administrative, technical or service staff of the mission or to the employment of the head of a consular post or any member of the consular, labour, trade, administrative, technical or service staff of the post.

6. *Personal injuries and damage to property.*—A foreign state shall not be immune from the jurisdiction of the courts of the Republic in proceedings relating to— **5.131**

(a) the death or injury of any person; or

(b) damage to or loss of tangible property,

caused by an act or omission in the Republic.

7 *Ownership, possession and use of property.*—(1) A foreign state shall not be immune from the jurisdiction of the courts of the Republic in proceedings relating to— **5.132**

(a) any interest of the foreign state in, or its possession or use of, immovable property in the Republic;

(b) any obligation of the foreign state arising out of its interest in, or its possession or use of, such property; or

(c) any interest of the foreign state in movable or immovable property, being an interest arising by way of succession, gift or bona vacantia.

(2) Subsection (1) shall not apply to proceedings relating to a foreign state's title to, or its use or possession of, property used for a diplomatic mission or a consular post.

5.133 8. *Patents, trade-marks, etc.*—A foreign state shall not be immune from the jurisdiction of the courts of the Republic in proceedings relating to—

(a) any patent, trade-mark, design or plant breeder's right belonging to the foreign state and registered or protected in the Republic or for which the foreign state has applied in the Republic; or
(b) an alleged infringement by the foreign state in the Republic of any patent, trade-mark, design, plant breeder's right or copyright; or
(c) the right to use a trade or business name in the Republic.

5.134 9. *Membership of associations and other bodies.*—(1) A foreign state which is a member of an association or other body (whether a juristic person or not), or a partnership, which—

(a) has members that are not foreign states; and
(b) is incorporated or constituted under the law of the Republic or is controlled from the Republic or has its principal place of business in the Republic,

shall not be immune from the jurisdiction of the courts of the Republic in proceedings which—

(i)   relate to the foreign state's membership of the association, other body or partnership; and

(ii) arise between the foreign state and the association or other body or its other members, or as the case may be, between the foreign state and the other partners.

(2) Subsection (1) shall not apply if—

(a) in terms of an agreement in writing between the parties to the dispute; or
(b) in terms of the constitution or other instrument establishing or governing the association, other body or partnership in question,

the dispute is justiciable by the courts of a foreign state.

5.135 10. *Arbitration.*—(1) A foreign state which has agreed in writing to submit a dispute which has arisen, or may arise, to arbitration, shall not be immune from the jurisdiction of the courts of the Republic in any proceedings which relate to the arbitration.

(2) Subsection (1) shall not apply if—

(a) the arbitration agreement provides that the proceedings shall be brought in the courts of a foreign state; or

(b) the parties to the arbitration agreement are foreign states.

11. *Admiralty proceedings.*—(1) A foreign state shall not be immune from the admiralty jurisdiction of any court of the Republic in—   **5.136**

(a) an action *in rem* against a ship belonging to the foreign state; or

(b) an action *in personam* for enforcing a claim in connection with such a ship,

(c) if, at the time when the cause of action arose, the ship was in use or intended for use for commercial purposes.

(2) A foreign state shall not be immune from the admiralty jurisdiction of any court of the Republic in—

(a) an action *in rem* against any cargo belonging to the foreign state if both the cargo and the ship carrying it were, at the time when the cause of action arose, in use or intended for use for commercial purposes; or

(b) an action *in personam* for enforcing a claim in connection with any such cargo if the ship carrying it was, at the time when the cause of action arose, in use or intended for use for commercial purposes.

(3) Any reference in this section to a ship or cargo belonging to a foreign state shall be construed as including a reference to a ship or cargo in the possession or control of a foreign state or in which a foreign state claims an interest, and, subject to the provisions of subsection (2), subsection (1) shall apply to property other than a ship as it applies to a ship.

12. *Taxes and duties.*—A foreign state shall not be immune from the jurisdic-tion of the courts of the Republic in proceedings relating to the foreign state's liability for—   **5.137**

(a) sales tax or any customs or excise duty; or

(b) rates in respect of premises used by it for commercial purposes.

13. *Service of process and default judgments.*—(1) any process or other doc-ument required to be served for instituting proceedings against a foreign state shall be served by being transmitted through the Department of Foreign Affairs and Information of the Republic to the ministry of foreign affairs of the foreign state, and service shall be deemed to have been effected when the process or other document is received at that ministry.   **5.138**

(2) Any time prescribed by rules of court or otherwise for notice of intention to defend or oppose or entering an appearance shall begin to run two months after the date on which the process or document is received as aforesaid.

(3) A foreign state which appears in proceedings cannot thereafter object that subsection (1) has not been complied with in the case of those proceedings.

(4) No judgment in default of appearance shall be given against a foreign state except on proof that subsection (1) has been complied with and that the time for notice of intention to defend or oppose or entering an appearance as extended by subsection (2) has expired.

(5) A copy of any default judgment against a foreign state shall be transmitted through the Department of Foreign Affairs and Information of the Republic to the ministry of foreign affairs of the foreign state, and any time prescribed by rules of court or otherwise for applying to have the judgment set aside shall begin to run two months after the date on which the copy of the judgment is received at that ministry.

(6) Subsection (1) shall not prevent the service of any process or other document in any manner to which the foreign state has agreed, and subsections (2) and (4) shall not apply where service is effected in any such manner.

(7) The preceding provisions of this section shall not be construed as applying to proceedings against a foreign state by way of counter-claim or to an action *in rem*, and subsection (1) shall not be construed as affecting any rules of court whereby leave is required for the service of process outside the jurisdiction of the court.

5.139 14. *Other procedural privileges.*—(1) Subject to the provisions of subsections (2) and (3)—

(a) relief shall not be given against a foreign state by way of interdict or order for specific performance or for the recovery of any movable or immovable property; and

(b) the property of a foreign state shall not be subject to any process—
  (i) for its attachment in order to found jurisdiction;
  (ii) for the enforcement of a judgment or an arbitration award; or
  (iii) in an action *in rem*, for its attachment or sale.

[*Para. (b) substituted by s. 1 of Act No. 48 of 1985*]

(2) Subsection (1) shall not prevent the giving of any relief or the issue of any process with the written consent of the foreign state concerned, and any such consent, which may be contained in a prior agreement, may be expressed so as to apply to a limited extent or generally, but a mere waiver of a foreign state's immunity from the jurisdiction of the courts of the Republic shall not be regarded as a consent for the purposes of this subsection.

(3) Subsection (1)(b) shall not prevent the issue of any process in respect of property which is for the time being in use or intended for use for commercial purposes.

15. *Immunity of separate entities.*—(1) A separate entity shall be immune from the jurisdiction of the courts of the Republic only if— **5.140**

(a) the proceedings relate to anything done by the separate entity in the exercise of sovereign authority; and

(b) the circumstances are such that a foreign state would have been so immune.

(2) If a separate entity, not being the central bank or other monetary authority of a foreign state, waives the immunity to which it is entitled by virtue of subsection (1) in respect of any proceedings, the provisions of section 14 shall apply to those proceedings as if references in those provisions to a foreign state were references to that separate entity.

(3) Property of the central bank or other monetary authority of a foreign state shall not be regarded for the purposes of subsection (3) of section 14 as in use or intended for use for commercial purposes, and where any such bank or authority is a separate entity the provisions of subsections (1) and (2) of that section shall apply to it as if references in those provisions to a foreign state were references to that bank or authority.

16. *Restriction and extension of immunities and privileges.*—If it appears to the State President that the immunities and privileges conferred by this Act in relation to a particular foreign state— **5.141**

(a) exceed or are less than those accorded by the law of that foreign state in relation to the Republic; or

(b) are less than those required by any treaty, convention or other international agreement to which that foreign state and the Republic are parties,

he may by proclamation in the Gazette restrict or, as the case may be, extend those immunities and privileges to such extent as appears to him to be appropriate.

17. *Evidence by certificate.*—A certificate by or on behalf of the Minister of Foreign Affairs and Information shall be conclusive evidence on any question— **5.142**

(a) whether any foreign country is a state for the purposes of this Act;

(b) whether any territory is a constituent part of a federal foreign state for the said purposes;

(c) as to the person or persons to be regarded for the said purposes as the head of state or government of a foreign state;

(d) whether, and if so when, any document has been served or received as contemplated in section 13(1) or (5).

18. *Short title and commencement.*—This Act shall be called the Foreign States Immunities Act 1981, and shall come into operation on a date to be fixed by the State President by proclamation in the Gazette. **5.143**

5.144   Foreign State Immunities Amendment Act[15]

NO 48 OF 1985

ACT

To amend the Foreign States Immunities Act, 1981, so as to make it clear that the property of foreign state shall not be subject to attachment in order to found jurisdiction; and to provide for matters connected therewith.

1. Amends section 14(1) of the Foreign States Immunities Act, No. 87 of 1981, by substituting paragraph (b).

2. Short title.—This Act shall be called the Foreign States Immunities Amendment Act, 1985.

5.145   Foreign State Immunities Amendment Act[16]

NO 5 OF 1988

ACT

To amend the Foreign States Immunities Act, 1981, so as to confirm the Immunity of foreign states from the jurisdiction of the courts of the Republic,; and to remove certain ambiguities; and to provide for matters connected therewith.

1. Amendment of section 2 of Act 87 of 1981.

Section 2 of the Foreign States Immunities Act, 1981 (hereinafter referred to as the principal Act), is hereby amended by the addition of the following subsection:

"(4) The exceptions to the immunity of foreign states from the jurisdiction of the courts of the Republic provided for in this Act shall not apply in disputes in which all the parties are sovereign states.".

2. Amendment of section 9 of Act 87 of 1981.

Section 9 of the principal Act is hereby amended by the substitution for paragraph (a) of subsection (1) of the following paragraph:

"(a) has members that are not states; and".

3. Amendment of section 10 of Act 87 of 1981.

---

[15] Assented to: 12 April 1985. Date of commencement: 24 April 1985. English text signed by the State president.
[16] Assented to 3 March 1988. Not yet in operation. English translation of Afrikaans text signed by the State president.

Section 10 of the principal Act is hereby amended by the substitution for paragraph (b) of subsection (2) of the following paragraph:

"(b) the parties to the arbitration agreement are states".

4. Amendment of section 13 of Act 87 of 1981.

Section 13 of the principal Act is hereby amended—

(a) by the substitution for subsection (1) of the following subsection:

"(1) any process or other document required to be served for instituting proceedings against a foreign state shall be served by delivering it through the Department of Foreign Affairs of the Republic to the ministry of foreign affairs of the foreign state, or by making it available in any other manner to the foreign state in accordance with an agreement to which the Republic and that foreign state are parties, and service shall be deemed to have been effected when the process or other document is delivered to that ministry or made available to the foreign state, as the case may be.",

(b) by the substitution for subsection (2) of the following subsection:

"(2) Any time prescribed by rules of court or otherwise for notice of intention to defend or oppose or entering an appearance shall begin to run two months after the date on which the process or document is served as aforesaid"; and

(c) by the substitution for subsection (5) of the following subsection:

"(5) A copy of any default judgment against a foreign state shall be delivered through the Department of Foreign Affairs of the Republic to the ministry of foreign affairs of the foreign state, or made available to the foreign state in accordance with an agreement to which the Republic and the foreign state are parties, and any time prescribed by rules of court or otherwise for applying to have the judgment set aside shall begin to run two months after the date on which the copy of the judgment is delivered to that ministry or made available to the foreign state, as the case may be.".

5. Amendment of section 14 of Act 87 of 1981.

Section 14 of the principal Act is hereby amended by the substitution for paragraph (b) of subsection (1) of the following paragraph:

"(b) the property or any right or interest of a foreign state shall not be subject to any process—
(i) for its attachment in order to found or to confirm jurisdiction;
(ii) for the enforcement of a judgment or an arbitration award; or
(iii) in an action *in rem*, for its attachment or sale.".

6. Amendment of section 17 of Act 87 of 1981.

Section 17 of the principal Act is hereby amended—

  (a) by the substitution for the words preceding paragraph (a) of the
      following words:

"17. A certificate by or on behalf of the Minister of Foreign Affairs shall be
conclusive evidence on any question-"; and

  (b) by the substitution for paragraph (d) of the following paragraph;

"(d) whether, and if so when, any document has been delivered or made
available as contemplated in section 13(1) or (5).".

7. Short title and commencement.

  This Act shall be called the Foreign States Immunities Act, 1988, and shall
come into operation on a date to be fixed by the State President by proclamation
in the Gazette.[17]

---

[17] This amending Act has not yet come into operation.

Index

All indexing is to section number.